Feeding the World

Feeding the World chronicles the rise of Brazil as a world agricultural powerhouse during the second half of the twentieth century. Tracing the history of Brazilian agricultural development, Herbert S. Klein and Francisco Vidal Luna focus specifically on how Brazil came to be the largest net food exporter in the world. Brazil was always an agricultural export country, but it was traditionally an exporter of a single crop. However, the country's agriculture underwent significant changes after 1960. Since then, Brazil has become one of the top five world producers of some 36 agricultural products and is now the world's primary exporter of such agricultural goods as orange juice, sugar, meat, corn and soybeans. Drawing heavily on historical and economic social science research, this book not only details how Brazil became an international leader in commercial agriculture, but offers careful insight into one of the most important developments in modern world history.

Herbert S. Klein is Gouverneur Morris Professor Emeritus of History at Columbia University and Research Fellow and Latin American Curator at the Hoover Institution at Stanford University.

Francisco Vidal Luna is Professor of Economics in the Faculty of Economics and Administration (FEA) at the University of São Paulo.

Feeding the World

Brazil's Transformation into a Modern Agricultural Economy

HERBERT S. KLEIN

Columbia University and Stanford University

FRANCISCO VIDAL LUNA

Universidade de São Paulo

CAMBRIDGE
UNIVERSITY PRESS

CAMBRIDGE
UNIVERSITY PRESS

University Printing House, Cambridge CB2 8BS, United Kingdom

One Liberty Plaza, 20th Floor, New York, NY 10006, USA

477 Williamstown Road, Port Melbourne, VIC 3207, Australia

314–321, 3rd Floor, Plot 3, Splendor Forum, Jasola District Centre, New Delhi – 110025, India

79 Anson Road, #06–04/06, Singapore 079906

Cambridge University Press is part of the University of Cambridge.

It furthers the University's mission by disseminating knowledge in the pursuit of education, learning, and research at the highest international levels of excellence.

www.cambridge.org
Information on this title: www.cambridge.org/9781108473095
DOI: 10.1017/9781108569101

First published 2019

Printed in the United States of America by Sheridan Books, Inc.

A catalogue record for this publication is available from the British Library.

Library of Congress Cataloging-in-Publication Data
NAMES: Klein, Herbert S., author. | Luna, Francisco Vidal, author.
TITLE: Feeding the world : Brazil's transformation into a modern agricultural economy / Herbert S. Klein, Columbia University and Stanford University, Francisco Vidal Luna, Universidade de Sao Paulo.
DESCRIPTION: New York : Cambridge University Press, [2019] | Includes bibliographical references.
IDENTIFIERS: LCCN 2018036622 | ISBN 9781108473095
SUBJECTS: LCSH: Agriculture – Economic aspects – Brazil.
CLASSIFICATION: LCC HD1872 .K54 2019 | DDC 338.10981–dc23
LC record available at https://lccn.loc.gov/2018036622

ISBN 978-1-108-47309-5 Hardback
ISBN 978-1-108-46097-2 Paperback

Dedicated to
Stanley L. Engerman
João Sayad
Henri Philippe Reichstul

Contents

List of Maps		*page* viii
List of Graphs		ix
List of Tables		xii
	Introduction	1
1	Antecedents	5
2	The New Agricultural Economy post 1960	48
3	Causes for the Modernization of Brazilian Agriculture	91
4	Inputs, Technology, Productivity and Sustainability	139
5	Regional Pattern of Agriculture	190
6	The Case of Mato Grosso	232
7	Rio Grande do Sul	273
8	São Paulo	313
9	The Agrarian Question	355
	Conclusion	405
Bibliography		414
Index		445

Maps

2.1   Brazilian soybean production 2015 by *município*   *page* 61
2.2   Brazilian corn production 2015 by *município*   69
5.1   Regions and states of Brazil   192
6.1   The Cerrado region of Brazil   236
6.2   The five mesoregions of Mato Grosso   257
6.3   Mato Grosso soybean production by *município*, 2015   258
6.4   Mato Grosso corn production by *município*, 2015   260
6.5   Mato Grosso cotton production by *município*, 2015   262
6.6   Mato Grosso cattle breeding by *município*, 2015   264
7.1   Seven mesoregions of Rio Grande do Sul   300
7.2   Rio Grande do Sul soybean production (tons) by *município* in 2015   301
7.3   Rio Grande do Sul rice production (tons) by *município* in 2015   303
7.4   Rio Grande do Sul tobacco production (tons) by *município* in 2015   304
7.5   Rio Grande do Sul grape production (tons) by *município* in 2015   306
7.6   Rio Grande do Sul cattle production (head) by *município* in 2015   307
8.1   São Paulo orange production in 2015 by *município*   326
8.2   The mesoregions of São Paulo   344
8.3   São Paulo sugarcane production in 2015 by *município*   349
8.4   São Paulo soybean production in 2015 by *município*   351
8.5   São Paulo cattle production in 2015 by *município*   352
8.6   São Paulo egg production in 2015 by *município*   353

Graphs

1.1 Change in GDP of industry and agriculture,
1926–1960   *page* 20
1.2 Population employed by sector, 1920–1960   22
1.3 Coffee: world production, consumption and price,
1940–1960   31
2.1 Balance of international agricultural trade of Brazil,
1980–2016   59
2.2 Growth of soybean production in Brazil, 1976/
77–2015/16   60
2.3 Volume of soybean exports by Argentina, Brazil and the USA,
1961–2014   62
2.4 Brazilian exports of orange juice, 1961–2015   66
2.5 Total output of first and second harvest corn, 1976/
77– 2015/16   67
2.6 Growth of stock of animals, 1920–2015   74
2.7 Value of frozen beef exports by major importing countries,
2016   76
2.8 Value of exports of chicken fresh & frozen by major
importing countries, 2016   78
2.9 Value of Brazilian exports to the four leading importing
countries, 1999–2017   84
3.1 Real interest rates of rural credit, 1970–2003   106
3.2 Rural credit in relation to GDP agriculture, 1960–2004   110
3.3 Relation between prices received and paid by producers,
1986–2005   110
3.4 Composition of formal and informal credit in the regions
South and Center-West (harvest, 2011)   113
3.5 Area (ha), production and yield (kg/ha, 1976–2018)   115

3.6 Productivity by regions (tons/ha), 1976–2018   116

3.7 Productivity of wheat, corn and soybeans, 1976/2018 (tons/ha)   117

3.8 Productivity of cotton, rice and beans (tons/ha), 1976–2018   118

3.9 Index of product, inputs and TFP   120

3.10 FAO price index, nominal, 1961–2017   130

3.11 Primary interest rates and real interest rates, 2000–2016   134

3.12 Effective rate of exchange in relation to change of salary, 1994–2016   135

3.13 Industrial participation in the GDP and participation of manufactures in exports, 1964–2015   136

3.14 Total factor productivity of the Brazilian economy, 1982–2013   137

4.1 Area cultivated and use of fertilizers, 1950–2016   143

4.2 Relation of exchange between product per ton of fertilizer, 2000–2017   145

4.3 Average area of cultivation per tractor (ha), 1920–2006   149

4.4 Number of cultivars registered by Embrapa   167

4.5 Cultivated fields using no-till planting in Brazil, 1985–2015   169

4.6 Annual deforestation of the legal Amazon, 1977–2016   182

4.7 Greenhouse gas emissions from the biomes and Amazon deforestation, 1988–2010   183

5.1 Share of total harvest by region, 1976–2016   208

5.2 Three-year moving average of the comparative yield per hectare of soybeans by region, 1990–2016   211

5.3 Comparative yields of corn per hectare of the major regions, 1990–2016   212

5.4 Production of sugarcane by region and nation, 1990–2016   213

5.5 Share of bean production by region, 1990–2016   215

5.6 Comparative productivity of bean production per hectare by region, 1990–2016   216

5.7 Percentage of agricultural exports within total regional exports, 1997–2016   220

5.8 Participation of regions in the value of all soybean exports, 1999–2017   220

5.9 Participation of regions in the value of all cereals, flour and prepared products exported by region, 1997–2016   221

5.10 Share of gross value of agricultural production by state, 2016   231

6.1 Age pyramid of Mato Grosso population, percentage in each age cohort by sex, 1960   238

6.2 Age pyramid of Mato Grosso population, percentage in each age cohort by sex, 2010   240

6.3 Share of soybean production by mesoregion, 1990–2016   259

6.4 Share of corn production by mesoregion, 1990–2016   261

6.5 Relative participation of mesoregions in cotton production, 1995–2016   263

6.6 Percentage distribution of heads of cattle by mesoregion, 1990–2016   265

6.7 Percentage distribution of number of all poultry by mesoregions, 1990–2016   265

6.8 Commercial balance of the value of imports and exports of Mato Grosso, 1997–2017   272

7.1 Distribution of type of worker by size of farm or ranch, 2006   282

7.2 Ratio of soybean production by mesoregions, Rio Grande do Sul, 1990–2016   300

7.3 Ratio of rice production by mesoregions of Rio Grande do Sul, 1990–2016   302

7.4 Ratio of tobacco production by mesoregions of Rio Grande do Sul, 1990–2016   302

7.5 Distribution of poultry by mesoregions, Rio Grande do Sul 1990–2016   305

7.6 Ratio of milk production by mesoregion, Rio Grande do Sul, 1990–2016   308

8.1 Growth of lands dedicated to permanent and temporary crops, São Paulo, 1970–2016   328

8.2 Distribution of sugarcane production by mesoregion of São Paulo, 1990–2016   349

8.3 Distribution of soybean production by mesoregion of São Paulo, 1990–2016   350

8.4 Distribution of corn production in the mesoregions of São Paulo, 1990–2016   351

8.5 Distribution of egg production by mesoregions of São Paulo, 1990–2016   352

Tables

1.1 Participation of principal crops in total exports,
1821–1939   *page* 13
1.2 Crops as percentage of total value of agricultural
production, 1920 and 1930   17
1.3 Participation of the principal crops in agricultural exports,
1940–1960   23
1.4 Index of production of principal agricultural products,
1920–1960   24
1.5 Yield per hectare of the principal agricultural crops,
1931–1962   25
1.6 Farms by size and utilization, 1920–1960   26
1.7 Area cultivated, workers, tractors and plows used by region
and selected states, 1950–1960   30
1.8 Composition of foreign commerce, 1947–1960   32
1.9 Farms by size by units and area, census 1960   33
1.10 Size of farms by area, census 1920, 1940, 1950 and 1960   34
1.11 Workers, sharecroppers and number of people employed
by farm, 1960   36
2.1 Type of farm tenancy in Brazil, 1970–2006   55
2.2 Index of productivity change of major crops, 1970–2015   56
2.3 Value of all agricultural production by crop and product in
2015   58
2.4 Area planted in coffee and total production, 1961–2018   71
3.1 Estimates of the government subsidies to agriculture,
1986–1990   95
3.2 AGF and EGF programs, 1975–1992   97
3.3 Source of rural credit, 2003–2013   108

3.4 Rural financing – programs and application of resources – harvests 2012/2013 and 2013/2014   113
3.5 Sources for growth of Brazilian agriculture, 1975–2011   119
3.6 Total factor productivity by state, 1970–2006   123
3.7 Agricultural production by countries and groups of countries and value of production, and total factor productivity, 1961–2009   124
3.8 Agricultural GDP and composition and participation in the Brazilian GDP, 1996–2017   127
3.9 Gross value of production – farming and pastoral, 2015   129
3.10 Value of total exports and of agricultural exports from Brazil, 1977–2016   131
3.11 Differences in the "Brazil Cost" in relation to other world regions   134
4.1 Apparent consumption of fertilizers (NPK), 1950–2016   142
4.2 Sales, production, importation and exportation of wheeled tractors and grain harvesters, 1961–2017   147
4.3 Budget and expenditures of Embrapa, 1975–2015   162
4.4 Expenditures on agricultural research as a % of agricultural GDP, Brazil and selected countries, 1981–2013   164
4.5 Emissions of CO_2eq by sector, for the years 1990–2014   187
5.1 Population resident in the regions of Brazil, 1960–2010   193
5.2 Changing population per square kilometer by region, 1960–2010   195
5.3 Percentage of native-born who resided in the region of their birth, by region of residence, 1991–2010   195
5.4 Percentage of rural population by region, 1970–2010   195
5.5 Life expectancy at birth by regions of Brazil, 1960–2010   196
5.6 Total fertility rate by region for total and rural population, 1970–2010   197
5.7 Percentage of population 0–14 in total population by region, 1970–2010   198
5.8 Rate of literacy of persons over 10 or 15 years of age by region, 1970–2010   198
5.9 Color of the Brazilian population by region, 1960–2010   199
5.10 Distribution of farmlands by region in 1960 and 2006   201
5.11 Distribution of the farms by farm size by region in 1970 and 2006   203
5.12 Changing volume of lands devoted to seasonal and permanent crops by region, 1970–2006   204
5.13 Share of value of crops by region, 2016/2017   206

5.14 Share of value of major pastoral products by region, 2016/
2017   206

5.15 Share of the value of crops and livestock and total gross
value of production by region, 2016   207

5.16 Distribution of principal animal groups by region,
1970–2006   210

5.17 Percentage of farms and ranches with tractors and hectares
per tractor by region, 1970–2006   217

5.18 Ratio of farms and of lands that use fertilizers by region
by type of cropland, 2006   218

5.19 Ratio of farms and of lands that use insecticides by region
by type of cropland, 2006   219

5.20 Percentage importance of principal states/regions in the
value of soybean production, 2007–2016   223

5.21 Percentage importance of principal states/regions in the
value of cattle production, 2007–2016   224

5.22 Percentage importance of principal states/regions in the
value of chicken production, 2007–2016   226

5.23 Percentage importance of principal states/regions in the
value of sugarcane production, 2007–2016   227

5.24 Percentage importance of principal states/regions in the
value of corn production, 2007–2016   229

5.25 Human Development Index of Brazilian states,
1991–2010   230

6.1 Size and share of rural population and sex ratio of Mato
Grosso population by residence, 1970–2010   239

6.2 Growth of major agricultural products in Mato Grosso,
1970–2015   242

6.3 Relative distribution of farmlands by farm size in selected
states, 1970–2006   244

6.4 Ratio of gross production value of principal agriculture
products in Mato Grosso, 2007–2017   246

6.5 Quantity of soybeans, cotton, corn and sugarcane produced
and state's share of total Brazilian production,
1990–2016   249

6.6 Number of meatpackers, animals and tonnage of cattle
slaughtered of principal meat-producing states, all four
periods of 2015   252

6.7 Quantity of cattle and chickens produced by Mato Grosso
and share of total Brazilian stock, 1980–2016   253

6.8 Land distribution all farming units by land area in the
mesoregions of Mato Grosso in 2006   266

6.9 Distribution of farms growing seasonal crops by size of farm, macroregions, 2006   267

6.10 Distribution of ranches by size of unit, macroregions, 2006   268

6.11 Distribution of farms in Mato Grosso by agricultural practices, 2006   270

7.1 Size and share of rural population and sex ratio of Rio Grande do Sul population by residence, 1970–2010   278

7.2 Distribution of farms by size of land holding in Rio Grande do Sul, 1960 and 2006   280

7.3 Distribution of farm labor by family membership and type of crop, Rio Grande do Sul, 2006   281

7.4 Total gross value of major crops produced in Rio Grande do Sul, 2007–2016   281

7.5 Value of principal agricultural products exported from Mato Grosso and Rio Grande do Sul in 2016   283

7.6 Quantity of soybeans, rice, poultry, tobacco and grapes produced in Rio Grande do Sul and state's share of total Brazilian production, 1990–2016   285

7.7 Number of meatpackers, animals and tonnage of chickens slaughtered of principal meat-producing states, 2016   290

7.8 Number of meatpackers, animals and tonnage of pigs slaughtered of principal meat-producing states, 2016   292

7.9 Growth of major agricultural products in Rio Grande do Sul, 1970–2016   294

7.10 Units processing milk and quantity of milk produced by major producing states, 2016   299

7.11 Land distribution all farming units by land area in the macroregions of Rio Grande do Sul in 2006   309

7.12 Land distribution all seasonal crop farms by land area in the macroregions of Rio Grande do Sul in 2006   310

7.13 Land distribution all ranches by land area in the macroregions of Rio Grande do Sul in 2006   311

8.1 São Paulo: size and share of rural population and sex ratio of population by residence, 1970–2010   315

8.2 Value of principal agricultural Products Exported from São Paulo and Mato Grosso in 2016   319

8.3 Distribution of farms by size of land holding in São Paulo, 1960–2006   321

8.4 Growth of major agricultural products in São Paulo, 1970–2016   322

8.5 Distribution of orange producers in São Paulo by number of trees, 2009   325

8.6   Total gross value of major crops produced in São Paulo,
      2007–2016   339
8.7   Distribution of lands in mesoregions of São Paulo in
      2006   346
9.1   Agrarian reform – number of projects, families settled and
      area in hectares granted by region, from inception
      to July 2016   363
9.2   Rural conflicts, violence and confrontations in Brazil,
      2007–2016   365
9.3   Number of properties and by size of holdings in hectares,
      census 1920–2006   368
9.4   Number of properties and by size of holdings in hectares by
      region, census 1920–2006   371
9.5   Value of production and number of farms by size and region,
      agrarian census of 2006   372
9.6   Production of principal agricultural products by size of
      property, agricultural census 2006   374
9.7   Farmers by level of education and size of farms by region,
      agricultural census of 2006   377
9.8   Type of agriculture practiced by size of farm and region,
      agricultural census of 2006   379
9.9   Farms which receive technical training by type of training
      and size of farm, agricultural census 2006   381
9.10 Value of rural credit by family and commercial farms, 2003/
      04–2014/15   388
9.11 Family and non-family farms by value of production,
      agricultural census of 2006   389
9.12 Family and non-family farms by size and region, agrarian
      census of 2006   391
9.13 Family and non-family farms by numbers of persons
      employed by region, agricultural census of 2006   392
9.14 Farm families and non-family farms with outside work by
      household and region, agricultural census 2006   393
9.15 Family and non-family farmers who obtained credit for
      investments, operating costs and marketing of products,
      agricultural census of 2006   395
9.16 Family farms by origin of the value of production and region,
      agricultural census of 2006   396
9.17 Distribution of the annual gross value of production, by
      classes of minimum monthly salaries, agricultural census of
      2006   399

9.18 Annual gross value of production of poor farms of less than
      two monthly minimum salaries, 2006   400
9.19 Distribution of gross value of production by value of monthly
      minimum salary, by region, agricultural census 2006   401
9.20 Net and gross income of farms in terms of minimum
      monthly salary, agricultural census of 2006   403

Introduction

The rise of Brazil as a world agricultural powerhouse is one of the most important developments in modern world history. Since 1960 Brazil has gone from being a food importer to becoming the largest net food exporter in the world. It is now among the top five world producers of some thirty-six agricultural products and has become the world's primary exporter of dozens of agricultural products, from orange juice to sugar, from meats to soybeans. Brazil now is one of the world's most important granaries and the most important tropical one on the planet. Without Brazilian production the world's food supplies would be greatly reduced. Yet this growth to world power status has only occurred in recent times. Though Brazil was always an agricultural export country, it was essentially an exporter of a single product first with sugar in the colonial period and then with coffee in the nineteenth and twentieth centuries. From time to time it also exported cotton, rubber and cacao. But all this was produced with the simplest non-machine technology and with the constant use of virgin soils to which little or no fertilizer or insecticides were ever applied. Labor was unskilled, farm credit minimal and a moving frontier into virgin lands was the primary input into agriculture.

All this changed in the second half of the twentieth century and above all after 1960. Today commercial agriculture in Brazil is highly mechanized, with access to abundant public and private credit, and is a major world consumer of fertilizers and insecticides. It also has one of the most advanced agricultural research programs in the world and a large class of highly trained agronomists. Despite difficulties in transport and government regulation, since the 1990s this agriculture has been able to successfully compete in the world market even against the United States.

The modernization of Brazilian agriculture is here defined as the transformation of commercial agriculture with the introduction of new products, the occupation of new spaces and the utilization of the most modern technology available in the market, part of which technology was developed by Brazilian researchers, particularly focused on the technology of tropical agricultural production. It is also defined by new complex relations between producers, and processors and by a sophisticated system of public and private finance. This modernization was a carried out by government policies designed to support the creation of a major industrial park in Brazil and in which agriculture's role was to provide cheap food to the growing industrial workforce and exports to pay for capital goods imports.

Brazil at mid-twentieth century had a traditional low productivity agricultural economy based on a highly unequal land tenure system with quite extensive latifundia throughout the nation. While other Latin American countries in this period were turning toward land reform as a way to open up traditional agriculture to modern technology, the Brazilian governments of the era decided instead to provide incentives for traditional landowners to become modern farmers. The result was a process of modernization based on a traditional land tenure system, what many have called a conservative agricultural revolution. Given the abundance of underutilized lands the government could repress the demand for land reform by promoting massive colonization of poor farmers, leaving the highly stratified land tenure system intact in the settled areas.

It is the aim of this study to explain how and why this agricultural revolution occurred and how Brazil has evolved in the past half century from a monoproduction exporter of coffee into becoming such a world agricultural producer, completely open to the international market. We have defined a crucial turning point beginning with a major change in government policies in the 1960s which led to a massive infusion of capital into the rural world and to direct government intervention in the marketing of agricultural products. We next examine the impact of the government's partial withdrawal from this market in the crises of the 1980s and the subsequent impact of the adoption of free trade in the 1990s. This two-decade crisis seriously affected the agricultural sector and forced it to reorganize its systems of credit, marketing and integration with a host of new credit sources, from supermarkets and major cooperatives to producers of agricultural inputs and international trading companies. Paradoxically, national industry, the primary concern of earlier governments, would suffer from this opening to world markets, while agriculture would experience an extraordinary growth.

Throughout the book we are concerned with the causes of this agricultural "revolution." This involves everything from detailed analysis of the massive mobilization of capital which began under the military regimes of the 1964–1985 period to the systemic creation of a modern research program which was led by Embrapa, one of the world's largest agricultural research institutes. It also involved the creation of a national agricultural machinery program as well as a modern chemical industry to supply the basic inputs needed to modernize national agriculture. Finally we look at the human capital which has emerged in the rural area and how it has affected this modernization process.

What is impressive is that the process was not constant. After a promising start, the impact of the depressions of the 1980s followed by the opening up of the Brazilian economy to the world market in the 1990s had a tremendous shock on agriculture and forced it to make significant changes. Brazilian industry was also forced to go through this difficult period of adjustment to an open economy, but in contrast to what occurred in industry, agriculture was able to recover its footing and to compete in the international market in the following decades, evolving to become one of the world's largest agricultural producers and one of its dominant agricultural exporters. Why agriculture succeeds and industry, except in a few instances, fails is one of the issues we also examine.

We then analyze how the farm sector responded to these changes at the regional and state level. For this analysis we have provided a broad regional analysis of where and how this modernization evolved. We also examine three case studies which are most representative of this change: Rio Grande do Sul, the model of small commercial farming; São Paulo, home to large-scale farms producing a large number of different crops, and the leading agricultural state in the nation; and Mato Grosso, the classic example of the new grain-producing centers, which in turn has become the second largest agricultural producer in Brazil.

Given our interest in explaining this agricultural revolution, most of this study concentrates on the part of the rural world that would become modern. But we also examine in detail the parts which were left behind and still practice subsistence agriculture and how and why this has occurred. We also examine the debates about agrarian reform, and the alternative colonization models offered by both the military and civilian governments in the post-1985 period. We also try to explain why a significant sector of the rural world was unable to respond to the new market incentives.

Our survey is based on annual or monthly data and the agricultural censuses. This work went to press as the preliminary results of the latest agricultural census of 2017 are being published. From these partial data it is evident that no major structural changes have occurred since the census of 2006. There was a reduction of 2% in the number of farms, an increase of 5% in area cultivated and a modest increase in the average size estate from 68 to 69 hectares. Farms under 100 hectares increased from 86% to 89% of all farms with little change in their share of lands, while those over 1,000 hectares remained at 1% of all farms and only increased their share by 4% to 48% of all land. Earlier secular trends continued in 2017, with agricultural workers declining by some 1.5 million from 2006, with farm mechanization increasing and farm owners and managers having more years of education.

Finally we should note that what this book does not do is to try to study the social conflicts over land that have become the norm in the more traditional regions of the North and Northeast, or the major question of the dismantling of the Amazon. As we intend to demonstrate, this agricultural revolution has occurred and continues to evolve without the need for more land expansion or for the continued dismantling of the rainforest. The illegal mining and cutting of timber in the Amazon, though a major problem for Brazil and the world, is not fundamental to the modern commercial sector of the national economy.

We should stress that we do not treat all crops and all regions equally, but have used only selected crops and selected states which we feel define the basic problems we are dealing with. Given the complexities of this subject, we do not consider this a complete history of modern Brazilian agriculture, which would need several volumes to fully describe just the period since 1960. But it is hoped that this broad survey will provide a basic analysis of how and why Brazil has emerged as a world agricultural producer on a par with the United States, Canada, Australia, China and the European Union.

The authors would like to thank Sonia Rocha, William Summerhill, Renato Augusto Rosa Vidal and Matiko Kume Vidal for their thoughtful comments and help in producing the manuscript.

I

Antecedents

Like all the European colonizers of the New World who followed the
Spanish, the Portuguese had to obtain a product that was exportable to
Europe to sustain their American colonial enterprise. Without precious
metals, the Portuguese only had access to Indian slave labor and had to
develop new products acceptable to the European market. The solution
was the establishment of a slave-based plantation economy producing
cane sugar, a product which the Portuguese had already developed in
their Atlantic islands in the fifteenth century. First using captured Indian
slave labor, the plantations of Brazil by 1600 were already being manned
by African slave labor brought by Portuguese slavers from West Africa.
By the middle of the sixteenth century Brazil had become the world's
largest producer of cane sugar, and the industry provided the funds
necessary for the Portuguese to maintain their continental possession in
the New World.

The settlement of Brazil occurred in distinct phases. In the first phase
the economy and population were concentrated on the northeastern coast.
It was here that the sugar plantation economy was first developed on
a major scale, and this region continued to dominate the colonial economy
and the world sugar market for more than a century. A second center of
settlement quickly developed in the southeastern region around the port of
Rio de Janeiro and its hinterland and at the coastal ports to the south and
in the interior zone around what would become the current city of São
Paulo. Here a frontier culture developed with whites, mestizos (*caboclos*)
and Indians and this population carried out raiding and exploration
expeditions in the western and southern frontiers of the country. It was
these raiders, known as *bandeirantes*, who discovered both gold and

diamonds in this hinterland in the late seventeenth and early eighteenth century. Brazil then entered an intensive mining phase in areas now belonging to the states of Goiás, Mato Grosso and Minas Gerais. In the latter region the wealth of the alluvial gold deposits drew Africans and Portuguese in large numbers and there rapidly evolved a mosaic of major interior urban centers. The mining activity peaked in the mid-eighteenth century, which led to a long-term decline in what had now become the most populous region of the colony.

But the growth of sugar in the hinterland of Rio de Janeiro and in the highlands near São Paulo counterbalanced the decline of mining and also helped to shift the center of both population and economic activity to the southeastern region. The growth of the French and English Caribbean sugar plantation economies in the eighteenth century led to a decline in the relative importance of Brazilian sugar on the international market. Nevertheless Brazil was still a major exporter to southern Europe, and the sugar economy sustained the growth of the southeastern as well as northeastern regions until the early nineteenth century.

The arrival of coffee as a new slave plantation crop began in earnest in the late colonial and early imperial period. Moreover it was in the southeastern region that this slave plantation economy would be centered and it was to this region that several million African slaves arrived in the period up to 1850. The continued dynamism of Brazil, from sugar and gold cycles through the coffee boom, led to the massive introduction of African slaves over the three centuries of colonial settlement. It had already absorbed more African slaves, currently an estimated 3 million Africans, than any other single region in the Americas to 1850,[1] and with the end of slavery in 1888 it was able to attract an even greater number of free European immigrants. It was one of the few Latin American states able to compete with the North American countries in taking a share of the great European transatlantic migration of the late nineteenth and early twentieth century.

Despite the never-ending expansion into the western and southern frontiers, the population of Brazil was still highly concentrated near the coast even into the nineteenth century. Most of the interior space was lightly populated and consisted primarily of forest and grasslands. But much of this would change in the last quarter of the nineteenth century as the railroads and the coffee plantations moved westward to open the

---

[1] This is the latest estimate of Africans disembarked in Brazil generated from The Trans-Atlantic Slave Trade Database, accessed May 29, 2017, at www.slavevoyages.org/voyage/search#.

interior to settlement. The expansion of coffee production in the second quarter of the nineteenth century provided Brazil with an international export whose demand systematically grew through increasing adoption of coffee drinking by a growing and ever more urban and richer population in the advanced countries of the world. Given Brazil's exceptional physical conditions for coffee cultivation, the country quickly assumed the position of world leader in the supply of this product, and was easily capable of increasing production adequately to respond to expanding world demand. For more than sixty years, coffee was produced with slave labor, but at end of the nineteenth century slaves were replaced by free wage labor based on the participation of European and Asian immigrants. The concentration of coffee production in the axis formed by the states of Rio de Janeiro, São Paulo and Minas Gerais gave this region an economic and political supremacy within the nation which was maintained until 1930.

Along with the substitution of slaves by free wage workers in 1888, the monarchy was replaced by a republic a year later. The emergence of the republic led to a fundamental reorganization of the locus of national power, which shifted from a centralized state to a more federal one, and their appeared new regional political actors who would consolidate their position throughout the period of the so-called Old Republic to 1930. São Paulo state emerged as the leading economic center of the country as coffee production moved west to the interior of the state of São Paulo, and this allowed São Paulo to become the leading state within the national economy.[2]

The initial expansion of coffee occurred in the Paraíba Valley, first in the part pertaining to Rio de Janeiro in the region of Vassouras. Coffee plantations then moved north and west into the region called the *zona da mata* in the southwestern part of the province of Minas Gerais and the areas around the counties (or *municípios*) of Areias and Bananal in the northeastern part of the province of São Paulo. Until the middle decades of the century the Paraíba Valley was the world's single largest producer of coffee. By 1850 Brazil accounted for half of world production, and coffee in turn accounted for half the value of national exports. As world demand increased, Brazilian coffee production expanded at an even faster pace,

---

[2] On the evolution of coffee see the two-volume survey by Francisco Vidal Luna and Herbert S. Klein, *Slavery and the Economy of São Paulo, 1750–1850* (Stanford, Calif.: Stanford University Press, 2003); and *The Economic and Demographic History of São Paulo 1850–1950* (Stanford, Calif.: Stanford University Press, 2018).

and in the last five years of the century Brazil accounted for 70% of world production. Land was abundant and cheap, and thus labor was the principal factor limiting the expansion of coffee. Initially the end of the slave trade in 1850 put at risk the expansion of coffee, but this was resolved by importing slaves from the non-coffee-producing regions. The result was that the coffee areas steadily increased their share of slaves after 1850.

Although planters as early as the 1850s began to experiment with using salaried European workers in the coffee fields, these initial attempts failed as free workers did not accept the conditions offered nor were they willing to work alongside slaves. Eventually government subsidization was needed to attract free laborers. In 1884, under pressure from the coffee growers, the government of the state of São Paulo assumed the entire cost of the travel of all immigrants from Europe to the farms of São Paulo.[3] It was this law which definitely established the basis for a massive introduction of European immigrants to São Paulo. The formal abolition of slavery in 1888 removed the last obstacle. There now occurred a major flow of immigration to the state of São Paulo. Between 1827 and 1884, only 37,000 foreign immigrants had arrived to São Paulo, but in the decade after 1884 half a million immigrants reached the state. Of the 2.3 million immigrants who came to São Paulo between 1887 and 1928, half were subsidized by the government. Other states also received immigrants in this same period, and in total some 4 million foreign-born immigrants arrived in Brazil between 1884 and 1940.[4] Thus despite the progressive dismantling and final abolition of slavery in the decade of the 1880s, there was no discontinuity in the production of coffee.

In this new free labor era, the west of São Paulo became the hegemonic producer of coffee within Brazil. The movement of coffee toward the west paulista plains was initiated in the 1870s following the introduction of railroads. The paulista western zone and other newly evolving areas of the state were developed on virgin lands with high soil productivity, and local planters were more open to experimenting with new labor regimes. In contrast, the lower-productivity coffee plantations of the Paraiba Valley went into decline and were no longer competitive without slave labor.

---

[3] Law 28 of 29 March 1884. www.al.sp.gov.br/portal/site/Internet/
[4] For São Paulo see *Anuário Estatístico do Brasil* (hereafter cited as *AEB*),1939–1940, 1307, and for all Brazil *AEB*, 1950, 55.

Along with labor, the other obstacle to the expansion of coffee production was transport. From the middle of the nineteenth century the necessity of creating an efficient rail transportation system to ship coffee to the coast was recognized as a fundamental necessity. The traditional system of transporting the crop by mules created high costs and limited the potential expansion of the system. The solution came in 1853 when the government guaranteed interest on the funds invested in railroad construction.[5] The *Estrada de Ferro D. Pedro II*, which went from the port of Rio de Janeiro to Cachoeira in the state of São Paulo, was the first railroad to be successfully built. It served the coffee region of the Paraiba Valley, permitting the export of coffee to the port of Rio de Janeiro.

The newer São Paulo coffee zones continued to rely on mule transport to reach their natural export port of Santos, located some 60 km from the city of São Paulo. But in 1867 the São Paulo Railway was inaugurated which connected Santos to the city of Jundiaí, which was the traditional entrance to the western paulista region. Using local planter capital, a complex railroad network was created which spread through the interior of the province and reached into the unexplored backlands. The railroads permitted the exploitation of lands of exceptional quality, particularly apt for coffee cultivation. Thus by the second half of the century Brazilian coffee planters resolved the two crucial blockages that limited the expansion of coffee: the insufficiency of labor and the lack of a cheap transport system. These railroads also moved other types of goods between ports and between different regions, creating a more integrated regional market, both for domestic production as well as for imports and exports.

Given its extensive agricultural frontier and virgin lands, São Paulo could now meet the increasing world demand for coffee. Between 1852 and 1900 the rate of growth of world coffee consumption was 2.5% per annum. In this period world consumption went from 4.6 million sacks of coffee to 18.1 million sacks, of which 73% was produced by Brazil.[6] There were also important changes in the regional base of coffee production in this period. The state of São Paulo surpassed Rio de Janeiro as the dominant coffee region in the 1890s. This growth continued into the next

[5] Subsidies were essential since private financiers feared that their profits would prove insufficient. William R. Summerhill, *Order against Progress: Government, Foreign Investment, and Railroads in Brazil, 1854–1913* (Stanford, Calif., Stanford University Press, 2003), 40.

[6] Edmar L. Bacha and Robert Greenhill, *150 Anos de Café* (2nd edn. rev.; Rio de Janeiro: Marcellino Martins & E. Johnston Exportadores, 1993), tables 1.1 and 1.2.

century, and by the 1910s São Paulo alone accounted for 70% of total Brazilian production.

But the special characteristics of supply and demand for coffee created an unstable market with great fluctuations in price. World demand grew steadily due to the growth of population, urbanization and income in the consuming countries, but at the same time was seriously affected by periodic crises in the economies of Europe and the United States.[7] Although plantings were influenced by prices, other exogenous factors sometimes delayed this price influence for several years. Coffee trees, for example, only began to produce at four years of age and continued to produce for some twenty to thirty years, and sometimes even as much as fifty years. Finally, a factor of major importance was the exchange rate. Prices were quoted in English pounds but the relevant price for the producer was in national currency. Thus, beyond the internal costs in national money, fluctuations in the exchange rate influenced the decisions of producers as much as changing international prices. All of these factors led to delayed responses to changes in demand in the coffee market.[8]

Until the 1890s there was a stability between demand and supply. In 1892, however, the international price of coffee began a long secular decline. But given the strong devaluation of local currency these falling international prices did not lead to a decline in national production or new plantings, which created a structural excess of supply. This paradox of continued expansion and falling prices and profitability was the result of earlier coffee plantings gradually entering into production, thus leading to overproduction.[9]

Given the growing coffee overproduction crisis characterized by low coffee prices and the accumulation of stocks of coffee, there was increasing pressure on the government to intervene. By 1902 the state of São Paulo was forced to prohibit the planting of new trees for a five-year period. Even after this state intervention, there was another major harvest in 1906/1907.[10] By now Brazil alone in one year produced more than the

---

[7] On this theme see the seminal work of Antonio Delfim Netto, *O Problema do Café no Brasil* (São Paulo: IPE-USP, 1981), chap. I a IV. In various parts of this section devoted to interventions in the coffee market, we have used the work of Delfim Netto.

[8] Ibid., chap. I a IV.   [9] Ibid., chap. II.

[10] The stockpile of coffee bags was 11 million bags for a consumption of 16 million. And the initial estimate of the 1906/1907 harvest was 16 million, but production reached 20 million bags. There was no place to offer a crop of this magnitude. As previously noted, coffee trees began to produce only at 4 years of age and continued to produce for some 20 to 30 years, and sometimes even as much as 50 years. Thus, although the crisis was evident, the production did not depend on current decisions, but plantings made at

world consumed in that year. At a meeting of the Brazilian producers in 1906, the Taubaté Agreement was signed in which the government agreed to buy the excess coffee production at a minimum pre-established price. It was also decided to restrict the production of low-quality coffee, and stimulate internal consumption and promote the product abroad.[11]

But these programs were only partially successful and could not be maintained by the individual states. At the end of the 1906/1907 harvest the world stocks of coffee were 16.4 million tons, half of which pertained to the state of São Paulo. At this point the federal government decided to support the government of the state of São Paulo and took out international loans which it then passed on to the state government for its coffee control (valorization) program. This first valorization scheme was a success, prices recuperated on the international market and the state was able to gradually sell stockpiled coffee in the market. This first intervention in the coffee market was followed by two more successful programs, one in 1914 and another in the early 1920s.[12]

These three interventions were quite temporary, relating to short market crises and an annual overproduction. Part of the inventory was taken off the market. There were also temporary controls of planting and natural fluctuations in coffee production which led to a rebalance in the coffee market. The success of these intervention schemes promoted the idea of establishing a permanent defense of coffee. When stocks of the third recovery operation were sold, the federal government transferred operation of the defense of coffee to the state of São Paulo, which created the Institute for the Permanent Defense of Coffee which subsequently became the Coffee Institute of São Paulo.

The crisis of 1929 hit the coffee market at a moment of local overproduction, a natural result of the policies of long-term protection which had been adopted. Maintaining the policy of regulating total shipments of coffee to the ports, the exceptional harvests of the late 1920s created ever-increasing stocks in the warehouses, and also increased demand for credit both to purchase the stocks and to finance the time they remained warehoused. Given the system of convertibility then in place, the increase in credit would depend on the reserves of gold in the financial system. But as soon as signs of an international crisis appeared, there was an immediate

---

least five years earlier. Delfim Netto affirms that the regime of exploitation in São Paulo, based on the *colonato* regime, made the crisis more acute in São Paulo, in relation to other producing states. Ibid., 44–45.

[11] Ibid., chaps. II and III.   [12] Luna and Klein, *Slavery and the Economy*, chap.1.

restriction of credit in the international market. As in all such crises, there was also a flight of capital to the more developed countries. This crisis of confidence thus stimulated the demand for foreign currency and simultaneously reduced the gold reserves and dramatically decreased the money supply. In this situation it was practically impossible to expand credit and to maintain convertibility of the national currency.

The government of Getúlio Vargas, installed after a 1930 revolution, faced the same crisis of coffee overproduction and was obliged to support the coffee sector in order to avoid a more profound crisis. It created a mechanism which pardoned part of the debts of the coffee growers, and then it restricted production. The extraordinarily large harvest of 1929 was repeated in the two following years, reaching maximum levels in 1933. To maintain prices at a profitable level for producers, the government began destroying the stocks of reserve that existed which could not be sold. In 1933 the debts of the coffee growers were reduced by half and the remaining debt financed over a ten-year period. It prohibited not only new plantings, but re-plantings of old trees, and created a program which divided all the coffee being sent to the ports in three parts: 30% would be exported, 30% placed in stocks and 40% would be destroyed. With periodic adaptations, this system would be maintained until 1944, resulting in the burning of 78.2 million sacks of coffee, the equivalent of three times annual world consumption. This program of control succeeded in gradually diminishing national production. World prices remained low until the end of the 1930s, only recuperating after the beginning of World War II. This control scheme also helped Brazil's competitors who continued to export at even very low prices, and Brazil by the end of the decade lost 10% of its world market share.[13]

In spite of the importance of coffee production to the national economy, other agricultural crops were produced throughout Brazil, some of which entered both the international and internal markets. In the export market, sugar was the leading crop after coffee. As late as the 1820s, sugar accounted for a third of the value of Brazilian exports, as compared to a fourth of the value obtained by cotton and just a fifth for coffee exports But coffee soon dominated and progressively led mid and late nineteenth-century imperial exports, and throughout the period of the Old Republic it accounted for an average of some 65% of the value of exports (see Table 1.1).

[13] Ibid., 142–157.

TABLE 1.1: *Participation of principal crops in total exports, 1821–1939*

	Coffee	Sugar	Cocoa	Yerba mate	Tobacco	Cotton	Rubber	Leather & skins
1821–30	21%	34%	1%	0%	3%	25%	0%	16%
1831–40	49%	27%	1%	1%	2%	12%	0%	9%
1941–50	47%	30%	1%	1%	2%	9%	0%	10%
1851–60	54%	23%	1%	2%	3%	7%	2%	8%
1861–70	50%	14%	1%	1%	3%	20%	3%	7%
1871–80	59%	12%	1%	2%	4%	10%	6%	6%
1881–90	67%	11%	2%	1%	3%	5%	9%	4%
1891–1900	67%	6%	2%	1%	2%	3%	16%	3%
1901–10	54%	1%	3%	3%	3%	2%	30%	5%
1911–20	62%	3%	4%	4%	3%	2%	14%	7%
1921–30	79%	2%	4%	3%	2%	3%	3%	5%
1931–39	69%	1%	5%	2%	2%	15%	1%	5%

Source: IBGE, *Anuário* (1939–1940)

Although sugar lost its supremacy in the 1830s, it maintained its importance as the second most import export crop until the 1890s, only being temporarily displaced by cotton during the period of the US Civil War. Brazilian sugar had been produced in traditional mills until the 1870s. As other competitors introduced new milling technology with the so-called central mills, Brazilian influence in the world market declined, even though local production increased to meet the growing needs of the internal market. From the 1880s Brazil's sugar exports declined systematically, with only a temporary short recovery in the 1920s. But in general, Brazilian sugar was of little importance in the international market until after World War II.[14] The key factor here was the late development of a modern sugar milling industry in Brazil, compared to the earlier adoption of such technology by its competitors.[15] It was not until the first years

[14] Noel Deerr, *The History of Sugar* (London: Chapman and Hall Ltd., 1949).

[15] Eisenberg examined the technological backwardness of production in Pernambuco. Peter Eisenberg, *The Sugar Industry in Pernambuco: Modernization without Change, 1840–1910* (Berkeley: University of California Press, 1974), 42–43. On the evolution of the sugar-producing process see also Gileno de Carli, *O Açúcar na Formação Econômica do Brasil* (Rio de Janeiro: Annuário Açucareiro, 1937); Eisenberg, *The Sugar Industry in Pernambuco*; and Alice P. Canabrava, "A grande Lavoura," in Sérgio Buarque de

of the twentieth century that, with government support, the first *Usinas* (or sugar factories) were established. These were modern milling operations with their own vast fields of cane production, which only partially depended on the cane production of others.[16] Once transformation of the industry began, change was rapid. In 1917 there already existed 215 *usinas* and they now produced half of the national sugar output.[17] In that year Pernambuco accounted for 40% of national production, Rio de Janeiro for 20% and Alagoas for 10%. São Paulo, with just 8% of national output could only supply 40% of its own sugar needs and had to import the rest from other parts of Brazil.[18] As of 1939 there were 345 *usinas* and 18,000 *engenhos*, with the *usinas* now producing 70% of the sugar. The survival of the old mills despite the rapid growth of the modern mills shows how delayed was the transition to the new technology, especially compared with Cuba and other international producers who had all made a complete transition to the new system by this time. But the rise of the *usinas* did have an impact on national production as older zones declined in importance and new zones which were using the new mills rose in importance. By the end of the Old Republic, the Northeastern share of output had declined significantly and the Southeastern states had increased their importance.[19]

Cotton had two periods of major importance in the history of Brazilian exports. The first occurred at the beginning of the nineteenth century when European wars favored exports, and the second during the "cotton famine" of the US Civil War period when US cotton exports were drastically reduced, giving a new space for Brazilian production. But once this war was resolved, international sales were reduced and during the Old Republic period cotton was a relatively minor Brazilian export.[20] But cotton production continued to evolve in the twentieth century when Brazilian industrialization created a growing internal market for its

---

Holanda, ed., *História da Civilização Brasileira* (São Paulo: Difusão Europeia do Livro, 1971), II, no. 4, 85–140.

[16] Eisenberg, *The Sugar Industry in Pernambuco*, chap. 5.

[17] Carli, *O Açúcar na Formação Econômica do Brasil*, 32–33.

[18] Ministério da Agricultura, Indústria e Comércio, *Indústria Assucareira no Brazil* (Rio de Janeiro: Directoria Geral de Estatística, 1919), 44 and 68.

[19] *Anuário Estatístico do Brasil*, 1939–40, 198–203. This activity employed 134,000 persons, being 98,000 in agriculture, 25,000 in factories, 3,000 specialized work and 8,000 in the railroads.

[20] On this theme see Alice P. Canabrava, *O Algodão no Brasil, 1861–1875* (São Paulo: T. A. Queiróz Editor, 1984).

consumption, and it only became a significant export again in the twenty-first century.[21]

Natural rubber, especially in the period just before and during the Old Republic, became an important product. Native to the Amazonian region, rubber gained major importance in the world economy in the second half of the nineteenth century as methods were developed to process rubber and use it in industrial activities. But the major growth came with the use of rubber for tires in the new automobile industry at the end of the nineteenth century. With the expansion of auto production, the demand for rubber grew exponentially. The problem was that rubber trees grew naturally and so the production was artisanal. As it developed in Brazil, rubber collecting required a large quantity of workers given the dispersed nature of the rubber trees in the forest. These rubber collectors worked in terrible environmental and working conditions and their productivity was quite low. Moreover these workers had to be imported from other regions. It is estimated that the Amazon rubber zones received around 260,000 laborers from the Northeastern states. These workers arrived already in debt and were subject to a brutal labor system.[22] The government stimulated production in the Amazon, and for a short period Brazil held a monopoly on world production, including rubber shipped from other Amazonian regions such as Bolivia. But the development of new rubber tree varieties in the 1910s allowed Asian producers to develop major plantations of the rubber trees and compete successfully with Brazilian production.[23] By the late 1910s the East Asian producers were beginning to export and quickly surpassed Brazilian production. As prices fell on the international market, the higher-cost non-plantation-produced rubber of Brazil lost market share to its rubber plantation producing rivals in East Asia. In the 1920s Henry Ford, wishing to free himself from what was now the British colonial Asian

[21] Brazil in 2017 was ranked as the world's fifth largest producer of cotton and the fourth largest exporter of this crop. USDA, FSA, *Cotton: World Markets and Trade, June 2017*, table 1.

[22] Celso Furtado, *Formação Econômica do Brasil* (São Paulo: Cia Editora Nacional, 1968), chap. 23. In that chapter the author offers a magisterial analysis of what he called the Transumância Amazônica. On this theme also see Barbara Weinstein, *The Amazon Rubber Boom, 1850–1920* (Stanford, Calif.: Stanford University Press, 1983); Maria Lígia Prado and Maria Helena Rolim Capelato, "A borracha na economia brasileira na primeira república," in Boris Fausto, ed., *História Geral da Civilização Brasileira*, III, no. 1: 285–307; Zephyr Frank and Aldo Musacchio, Overview of the Rubber Market, 1870–1930, at http://eh.net/encyclopedia/article/frank.international.rubber.market.

[23] Although synthetic rubber was developed outside of Brazil, it was initially not an adequate substitute for the natural product.

monopoly of rubber production, tried to establish rubber plantations in the Amazon.[24] But the project was a failure despite the enormous amounts spent, since Brazilian rubber trees were destroyed by parasites as soon as they were planted close together. The result was that by the end of the twentieth century Brazil was an importer of natural rubber, although in recent years Brazil has finally succeeded in producing a modern rubber plantation regime outside the Amazon.

Another product of importance in this period was also native to Brazil and that was cacao, which was also an Amazonian product. Like rubber it was initially gathered naturally and with low productivity due to the forest environment in which it was produced. Brought from the Amazon to southern Bahia in the second half of the nineteenth century, it was then more systematically planted and harvested, allowing Brazil to become a major participant in the world market. This development of the cacao industry in southern Bahia produced both a major social transformation in the region as well as major conflicts over land between local landlords (the so-called coronels *coronéis*) and peasants as was depicted in the novels of Jorge Amado. During the period from 1890 to 1930 cacao production grew at an annual rate of over 6%. In turn, prices remained stable until 1929 when they began to fall, declining by 75% by 1939, thus creating a profound crisis in this sector.[25]

There were also other primary products which were significant in the local, regional and national markets. In both 1920 and 1930 corn was the second most important agricultural product in terms of value, only surpassed by coffee. Given its importance in human and animal consumption, it is no surprise that in the census of 1920 some 2.4 million hectares were planted in corn, which was greater than the 2.2 million hectares planted in coffee. Other products with significant internal markets included rice, beans, manioc and sugar (see Table 1.2). Moreover the cattle industry now accounted for 47% of agricultural output. Most of these major products destined for the internal market were produced on family farms based on family labor and sometimes a few hired hands, in contrast to the large production units with salaried workers in coffee and

---

[24] See Greg Grandin, *Fordlandia: The Rise and Fall of Henry Ford's Forgotten Jungle City* (New York: Metropolitan Books, 2009).

[25] To create instruments of market intervention in 1931 the Cacao Institute of Bahia was created. Later, in 1957, the Executive Commission for Rural Economic-Recovery of Cocoa Farming (CEPLAC) was established. The emergence of a plant plague in the 1980s devastated production in the south of Bahia and the country went from being an exporter to an importer of cacao.

TABLE 1.2: *Crops as percentage of total value of agricultural production, 1920 and 1930*

Crop	% in 1920	% in 1930
Coffee	26%	48%
Corn	25%	13%
Manioc	11%	6%
Sugarcane	9%	5%
Beans	6%	4%
Rice	4%	4%
Cotton (lint)	3%	3%
Tobacco	3%	3%
Oranges	2%	2%
Potatoes	2%	2%
Grapes	2%	1%
Bananas	1%	1%
Others	6%	8%
	100%	100%

Source: IBGE, *Recenseamento Geral*, 1920 & 1930

sugar. Moreover this production had less of a multiplying effect on the economy, in contrast to coffee.[26]

By 1920 Brazil was still a minor player in the world agricultural market except for coffee. It was the leader in coffee production, accounting for 75% of world output, and was second in the production of cacao – but accounted for only 16% of world production. It produced only 6% of world corn output, 7% of its tobacco and just 3% of the world's cotton. In all other products such as rice, potatoes and wheat it was a distinctly modest producer. This low output by world standards was due to the still poor application of even minimum technology to Brazilian agriculture in this period. In 1920, of the 224,000 rural establishments which were listed in the census, only 1,652 even possessed plows.[27] Machines and

[26] In a study which we made of the agricultural census of São Paulo state in 1905, we found a large part of the cereal production occurred on coffee fazendas, showing that these coffee estates were not mono-production units. See Francisco Vidal Luna, Herbert S. Klein and William Summerhill, "Paulista agriculture in 1905," *Agricultural History*, 90, no.1 (Winter 2016): 22–50.

[27] Instituto Brasileiro de Geografia e Estatística (IBGE), *Recenseamento Geral do Brasil, 1920*, v. 3, parte 3, vii and xiv, and the *Censo Agrícola de 1905*, available in digital format from the Núcleo de Estudos de População (NEPO) of the Universidade de Campinas.

agricultural equipment accounted for only 3% of the total value of these rural establishments in 1920. Even in São Paulo, the value of machines was only 4%, while lands represented 79% and other improvements another 18%.[28]

Whatever the weakness of the Brazilian agricultural sector in international terms, there is little question that the expansion of agriculture in the nineteenth century had a major impact on the internal economy and was crucial in modernizing ample sectors of the economy. The intensification of the agro-exporting sector required investments in machines and equipment beyond the farm gate, as well as the expansion and modernization of the transport system from railroads to ports. The last quarter of the nineteenth and beginning of the twentieth century saw the full elaboration of an extensive railroad system and the construction of deep water ports and modern docks with national and foreign capital.

But agriculture was not the only economic sector to expand in this period. There would also be the beginnings of an industrial economy in Brazil. Given the revolution in transport, there was a reduction in the costs of moving goods throughout the country, and the transition to a salaried rural workforce was another factor which promoted the growth of an internal market.[29] The expansion of wage labor increased dramatically with the abolition of slavery and the introduction of millions of immigrants, and it had multiple effects. It increased the size and diversified the consumer market, it encouraged an increase in monetary circulation, and finally created a modern labor market. It was this growth of a wage labor force which set the stage for the industrial transformation of Brazil which was started with the earnings generated by the coffee export sector. The agro-exporting sector, though not as modernized as other late nineteenth- and early twentieth-century agricultural societies, nevertheless generated the resources needed to invest in infrastructure, and extend and modernize the internal productive structure.[30] During the 1930s, despite the severity of the international crisis

---

[28] IBGE, *Recenseamento Geral do Brasil, 1920*, v. 3, parte 3, LX.
[29] As Celso Furtado argued in his classic work of economic history, the factor of major importance which occurred in the Brazilian economy in the last quarter of the nineteenth century was the increase in importance of the wage labor sector. Furtado, *Formação Econômica do Brasil*: chap. XXVI.
[30] There is an interesting insight developed by Nicol, who sought to analyze the relationship between the agricultural revolution and the process of industrialization in developed countries, believing that the path of industrialization is the technological revolution in agriculture. When he studies Brazil, he also identifies agriculture in the nineteenth century as the dynamic factor in industry. But although there was a large agricultural growth in

and the critical coffee situation which lasted through the decade, gross domestic product (GDP) declined moderately in the first two years of the crisis and maintained consistent growth in the following years. This reflected the fact that the agro-exporting economy was being replaced by the domestic market. Given the external restrictions on trade and credit, the government was able to maintain support for industrialization throughout the first Vargas period of government (1930–1945). In addition, the federal government made profound changes in the structure of the state, and created major agencies to promote specific agricultural products, from sugar and cacao to mate and salt. The financing of agriculture was supported by the creation of the Carteira de Crédito Agrícola e Industrial (CREAI) of the Banco do Brasil, which became the principal source of agricultural credit.

Until the beginning of World War II, the international crisis necessitated strict import control. As the economy recovered relatively quickly, domestic demand, once supplied by imports, could not be sustained because of balance of payments constraints. The government deliberately promoted a policy of import substitution, manipulating a complex tariff system to favor the import of essential commodities, raw materials and capital goods, and applying heavy taxes on finished products. These tariffs and the expensive and controlled access to foreign currency created sufficient protection for capitalists to invest in national production.[31]

The Second World War made this situation more complex, as there was strong external demand for some specific Brazilian products, with an increase in prices and quantities exported that resulted in an increase in the capacity to import. But the world war also meant that there was a shortage of goods to import, which further stimulated domestic industrial production.[32] By acting to address specific infrastructure blockades and providing basic raw materials, the government greatly aided the industrial sector.[33] With the creation of manufacturing and infrastructure companies, the federal government implemented a new form of direct

that century, there was no agricultural revolution by European or Japanese standards. Technologically, Brazilian agriculture had not evolved very far. That conditioned the pattern of development of Brazilian industry. Robert N. V. C. Nicol, "A agricultura e a Industrialização no Brasil (1850/1930)" (PhD thesis, Universidade de São Paulo, FFLCH-USP, 1974).

[31] A. Fishlow, "Origens e consequências da substituição de importações no Brasil," in F. R. Versiani and J. R. M. de Barros, eds., *Formação Econômica do Brasil: A Experiência Brasileira* (São Paulo: Saraiva, 1977): 7–41.

[32] Tavares "Auge e declínio do processo de substituição de importações no Brasil": 60.

[33] Lourdes Sola, ed., *O Estado da transição: política e economia na Nova República* (São Paulo: Vértice, 1988), p, 275.

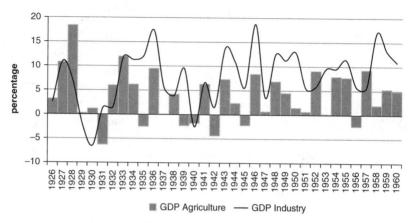

GRAPH 1.1: Change in GDP of industry and agriculture, 1926–1960
Source: Ipeadata

intervention in the productive sphere in areas where private enterprise was
not interested in applying the necessary capital, either because of the risk,
the low profitability or the amount of resources needed. All of these efforts
by the government succeeded in stimulating the economy. Despite the
slow recovery of the international economy, Brazilian GDP grew at 4%
per year in the period from 1930 to 1945. While agriculture grew at 2.1%
per year and services at 3.9%, industry grew at an impressive 6.2% per
annum, increasing its position in the national economy from 20.3% in
1929 to 28.6% in 1945. The share of agriculture fell from 36.9% to
28.0% in the same period (See Graph 1.1).[34]

    This extraordinary industrial growth can be seen in the changes that
occurred between the industrial census of 1920 and 1950: the number of
industrial establishments multiplied by seven, workers by four, and
energy, measured by the force of the motors employed, by eight.
Agriculture, as well as industry, expanded in this period of international
crisis. This sector was responsible for supplying foodstuffs to the domestic
market, for generating exportable surpluses, such as coffee, and producing raw materials necessary for the fast-growing and diversified industry,
especially for the textile and food industries. Thus, an increasing share of
agricultural production was directed to the market. Agriculture accounted
for the generation of exportable surpluses and the supply of the domestic

---

[34] Raymond W. Goldsmith, *Brasil 1850–1984. Desenvolvimento Financeiro Sob um Século
de Inflação* (São Paulo: Editora Harper & Row do Brasil Ltda, 1986), 148.

market for food and raw materials that replaced imports. For this reason, the government of Getúlio Vargas finally provided sustained and substantial credit for agriculture with the Banco do Brazil's CREAI,[35] and growth was the norm in agriculture the period between 1930 and 1950.[36]

This growth did not lead to any change in the traditional productive structure of agriculture, nor to the high concentration of land ownership or traditional rural labor contracts. Despite the extensive labor legislation promulgated by Vargas, there were no benefits for rural workers, who remained trapped in archaic labor relations in the countryside. Until the end of the 1940s, traditional "colonel" landowners were still predominant in some areas.[37]

Although agriculture still absorbed 60% of the national workforce by the end of 1950, after 1920 there was a gradual fall in this percentage in favor of industry and services. This liberation of the labor force from traditional agriculture was essential to consolidate the urban industrial sector, and although the rural population continued to grow, its rate of growth was smaller than that of the urban population. Between 1920 and 1940 the economically active population increased rapidly in the area of services (see Graph 1.2).[38] The increasing relative importance of industry significantly influenced the overall productivity of the economy, because industry had greater productivity than agriculture. In 1948, agriculture accounted for 28% of the national GDP, but its importance varied widely among states. In São Paulo, it accounted for approximately one-third of domestic income, but in most states it was approximately 50%.

In 1945, agricultural and livestock products accounted for 90% of Brazilian exports, with coffee alone accounting for just over two-thirds

---

[35] Iliane Jesuina da Sillva, "Estado e agricultura no primeiro governo Vargas (1930–1945)" (PhD thesis, Universidade Estadual de Campinas, 2010), chap. 4.

[36] Between 1920 and 1950, the percentage of the economically active population employed in manufacturing increased from 5% to 8%. Over the same period, the share in agriculture remained stable at 37%. Thomas Merrick and Douglas Graham, "População e desenvolvimento no Brasil: Uma perspectiva histórica," in Paulo Nauhaus, ed., *Economia Brasileira: Uma Visão Histórica* (Rio de Janeiro: Editora Campus, 1980), 45–88. Thomas Merrick and Douglas H. Graham, *Population and Economic Development in Brazil, 1800 to the Present* (Baltimore: Johns Hopkins University Press, 1979).

[37] Given his reliance on the traditional rural elite, who supported his government and allowed him to advance in urban areas, Vargas had no interest in promoting social transformations in the countryside. Maria Isaura Pereira de Queiroz, *O mandonismo local na vida política brasileira* (São Paulo: Alfa-Omega, 1976), parts 1 and 2.

[38] In the services sector, the percentage was 134%; in industry 86% and in agriculture 61%. Merrick and Graham, "População e desenvolvimento no Brasil," 45–88.

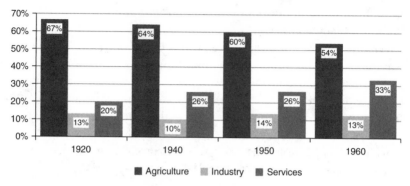

GRAPH 1.2: Population employed by sector, 1920–1960
Source: Merrick & Graham

of the value of all exports. Approximately 22% of the value of exports consisted of raw cotton or cotton textiles.[39] Clearly, textiles were the most important exported manufactured goods in this period.[40] Cotton traditionally was concentrated in the Northeast Region and was primarily arboreal and still produced by traditional methods. However, in the 1940s, São Paulo became the largest producer using planted cotton and soon supplied two-thirds of production. Other traditional agricultural exports, such as sugar, rubber, cocoa, mate and tobacco, played only a modest role and accounted for only 8% of exports in 1945, the same level as in 1920 (see Table 1.3).

Although agriculture's relative share of GDP declined from 1930 to 1945, production expanded substantially. Rice and manioc, essential food consumption for the national population, grew at an impressive rate of 6% per year, and sugar and bean production at 2.4% per year. On the other hand, corn, a staple food for animals and humans, only maintained a stable production throughout the period, while coffee,

[39] *AEB, 1946*, 296–299.
[40] As we noted, historically, cotton was produced for the overseas market and, for this reason, when international demand grew, as during the Civil War period in the United States, there was an increase in Brazilian production to serve the international market. Since Brazilian cotton was of low quality and high cost, as soon as international markets returned to normal, domestic production and exports declined. This situation changed in the early twentieth century due to the establishment of a national textile industry, which created a new and growing market for cotton. Alice P. Canabrava, *O algodão no Brasil, 1861–1875* (São Paulo: T.A. Queiróz Editor, 1984); Alexandre Bragança Coelho "A cultura do Algodão e a questão da integração entre preços internos e externos" (MA thesis, Universidade de São Paulo, 2002).

TABLE 1.3: *Participation of the principal crops in agricultural exports,*
1940–1960

Year	Sugar	Cotton	Rubber	Cacao	Coffee	Mate	Tobacco
1940	1%	29%	3%	7%	56%	2%	2%
1941	0%	28%	3%	9%	57%	2%	1%
1942	2%	20%	5%	7%	62%	2%	2%
1943	0%	11%	5%	9%	72%	2%	2%
1944	2%	12%	7%	6%	70%	2%	3%
1945	1%	17%	5%	4%	68%	2%	4%
1946	1%	27%	2%	6%	59%	1%	4%
1947	2%	24%	2%	8%	60%	1%	3%
1948	5%	23%	0%	7%	62%	1%	2%
1949	1%	13%	0%	6%	77%	1%	2%
1950	0%	10%	0%	7%	80%	1%	2%
1953	2%	8%	0%	6%	82%	1%	1%
1954	1%	16%	0%	10%	69%	1%	1%
1955	4%	11%	0%	8%	73%	1%	2%
1956	0%	7%	0%	5%	83%	1%	2%
1957	4%	4%	0%	7%	80%	1%	2%
1958	6%	3%	0%	10%	75%	2%	2%
1959	5%	4%	0%	6%	79%	1%	2%
1960	6%	5%	0%	7%	76%	1%	2%

Source: Séries Históricas, IBGE

which had gone through a serious crisis in the 1930s and 1940s, seemed to be growing again, especially in the 1950s (see Table 1.4).

Of all the harvests (*safras*) in this period, seven products predominated – coffee, cotton, corn, rice, beans, manioc and sugar – which accounted for 85% of the value of agricultural production between 1938 and 1947. In terms of planted area, coffee, cotton, corn and rice occupied more than 90% of the area under cultivation in that period. Corn was the crop that occupied the largest area of land, about a third of the total area planted, followed by coffee and cotton. In the period from 1920 to 1950 cotton went through the greatest expansion of cultivated area and of output, with national production growing from 330 thousand to 1.1 million tons in the period from 1920 to 1950.

Even coffee-growing regions changed during this period. The production of Paraná increased significantly and was rapidly approaching the level of

TABLE 1.4: *Index of production of principal agricultural products,*
1920–1960 (1931=100)

	Crops typically exported				Crops typically for internal market			
	Cotton	Cacao	Coffee	Sugar	Beans	Manioc	Corn	Rice
1920	89	87	61	86	106		105	77
1925	126	78	68	77	81		94	66
1930	85	90	126	109	101		106	85
1931	100	100	100	100	100	100	100	100
1935	264	166	87	103	119	87	125	127
1940	416	167	77	137	112	141	103	122
1945	299	156	64	155	146	219	102	199
1950	311	199	82	201	182	241	127	298
1955	331	206	105	252	215	285	141	347
1960	429	213	320	350	252	338	183	445

Source: IBGE, Séries Históricas Retrospectivas

São Paulo production. There was still coffee produced in Minas Gerais, Espírito Santo and Rio de Janeiro. In 1950, São Paulo had 137 million newly planted coffee trees and a stock of 956 million trees in production. At the same time, Paraná had 118 million new coffee trees and a total of 160 million coffee trees in production. In the five-year period 1956–1960, coffee production in Paraná had already surpassed that of São Paulo. In the following five years, Paraná's production was 85% higher than that of the State of São Paulo.

Despite increased crop output there was only a modest increase in productivity in this period. Coffee changed little, and, there was a decline in cotton and cacao productivity in the late 1940s. Only rice, of the most important agricultural products, showed a clearly upward trend in yield per hectare (see Table 1.5).

This stability or even decline in productivity was due to the use of traditional agricultural techniques in most crops. Even plows were rarely used. In 1950 there was only one plow for 400 hectares of rural property, and the ratio was a plow for every 28 hectares in cultivated lands. Tractors were still little used, and as of 1940, only a quarter of the farms used some sort of agricultural machinery and these farms were highly concentrated in a few regions. The Northeast and Central-West regions used virtually no machinery, while in Rio Grande do Sul 81% of the farms had machines and 48% of the farms in São Paulo. Fertilizer use only became widely

TABLE I.5: *Yield per hectare of the principal agricultural crops, 1931–1962 (tons/hectares)*

Year	Cotton	Rice	Cacao	Coffee	Sugar	Beans	Manioc	Corn	Wheat	Soybeans
1931	0.51	1.50	0.50	0.36	46.63	1.32	22.94	1.50		
1940	0.65	1.51	0.56	0.40	39.44	0.79	12.55	1.25		
1950	0.43	1.64	0.55	0.40	39.45	0.69	13.09	1.29		
1960	0.55	1.62	0.35	0.94	42.48	0.68	13.12	1.30	0.63	1.20
1961	0.57	1.70	0.33	1.02	36.35	0.68	13.07	1.31	0.53	1.13
1962	0.56	1.66	0.85	0.98	42.64	0.63	13.44	1.30	0.92	1.10

Source: IBGE, Séries Históricas Retrospectivas

distributed in Brazilian agriculture after 1960, and local production of tractors, which would increase greatly after the 1960s, was still incipient. But by the end of the decade, total tractor production reached 75,000 vehicles per annum.[41] As of 1940, only 5% of the arable land used fertilizer, regardless of the size of the property.

Growth between 1920 and 1960 was primarily due to an increase in the number of farms and in the cultivated area. Temporary or seasonal crops grew from 6.6 million hectares in 1920 to 12.9 in 1940 and 20.9 million hectares in 1960. Permanent crops, however, declined from 6 million hectares in 1940 to just 4.4 million hectares in 1950 but recovered to 7.8 million hectares in 1960 (there is no data in the 1920 census). In 1950, only 8% of the total areas in the listed properties were cultivated for both seasonal and permanent crops; this increased to 11% in 1960 (Table 2.3). The more intensively cultivated farms were concentrated in few states, such as São Paulo, Minas Gerais, Rio Grande do Sul and Rio de Janeiro, while other regions, such as the Cerrado,[42] for example, which today is a large grain-producing region, were still largely unoccupied or underutilized (see Table 1.6).

[41] Anfavea – Associação Nacional dos Fabricantes de Veículos Automotores, accessed May 17, 2017, at www.anfavea.com.br/estatisticas.html

[42] With an area of 2,036,448 square kilometers, the Cerrado covers 22% of the Brazilian territory and includes the Federal District, Goiás, Tocantins, much of Maranhão, Mato Grosso do Sul and Minas Gerais, as well as smaller parts of than six other states. The Cerrado is the source of three important river systems in South America (Amazonia / Tocantins, San Francisco and La Plata), which results in high aquifer potential and great biodiversity.

TABLE 1.6: *Farms by size and utilization, 1920–1960 (areas in hectares)*

	1920	1940	1950	1960
Total farms	648,153	1,904,589	2,064,642	3,337,569
Total area in hectares	175,104,675	197,720,247	232,211,106	249,862,142
Crops				
Permanent		5,961,770	4,402,426	7,797,488
Seasonal	6,642,057	12,873,660	14,692,631	20,914,721
Pastures				
Natural		83,068,814	92,659,363	102,272,053
Planted		5,072,319	14,973,060	20,068,333
Woods and forests				
Natural	48,916,653	49,085,464	54,870,087	55,875,299
Planted			1,128,994	2,069,806
Productive lands not used		29,296,497	34,310,721	
Inappropriate		12,361,127	15,173,204	
Uncultivatable				28,174,779
Equipment				
Tractors	1,706	3,380	8,372	61,345
Plows	141,196	447,556	714,259	977,101

Source: IBGE, Séries Históricas Retrospectivas e Censos Agrícolas

But land ownership changed little. The Gini inequality indexes of farm-land ownership remained at the same level from 0.83 to 0.84 in the period from 1920 to the census of 1960. The most productive states in agriculture showed the lowest inequality indexes in the nation.

In the immediately post-war period, there were two major changes in Brazil's trade flows: the reduction in exports of raw materials and manu-factured goods in general, particularly in the case of cotton; and the increase in imports of items that had suffered the greatest shortages during the war, such as machinery and equipment. Moreover, accumulated reserves, which could have been used to balance the external accounts, were not composed of convertible reserves, but rather of funds formed mainly by British pound rights, the usefulness of which was then very limited. The exchange rates were kept fixed, despite the strong inflation that occurred in that period. The control of inflation and the fear of a reduction in the international price of coffee were the main causes of exchange rate rigidity, which led to the strong appreciation of the national currency in the second half of the 1940s. Coffee prices increased slowly in the early postwar years, and rose sharply in the period 1949–1950. The shortage of products during the war disappeared with the end of the war and the return of the traditional producers to the international market prejudiced Brazil's traditional exports. It also led to the return of traditional international suppliers of the Brazilian market, which in turn had a negative impact on local producers.

But coffee and continued government support for industry softened the negative impact of the immediate postwar period. In the early 1950s, coffee recovered its former importance and accounted for two-thirds of the value of Brazilian exports. Continued exchange control and import licenses were a great stimulus for the industrial sector. This mechanism of control of the exchange market constituted an effective protection to the local producers. As usual, the permanent external bottleneck made exchange control the main instrument of economic policy and was used to avoid the deterioration of the price of coffee in the international market and to aid in inflation control.[43]

In October 1953, during the second period of the Vargas government, a change occurred in this policy. The government started to buy the foreign exchange from the exporters, paying the official rate plus a bonus differentiated by product, which represented an important stimulus for exports in general, which had lost competitiveness due to the overvaluation of the local currency.[44] Imports, in turn, began to be divided into categories and participated in specific auctions, with limited supply of foreign currency for each category and setting a minimum premium on the official rate at each auction, which led to the bureaucratic process of granting licenses to be replaced by market rules. The difference between the values of the purchase and sale of foreign currency was appropriated by the government and, from then on, became a significant portion of the tax revenue. This change was of enormous importance for industrialization, because it consolidated a market reserve for the production of the goods that replaced the imported ones, as it increased the effective cost of imports. Industrialists began to have access to privileged

---

[43] Antonio Claudio Sochaczewski, *O desenvolvimento econômico e financeiro do Brasil, 1952–1968* (São Paulo: Trajetória Cultural, 1993), chap. 3.

[44] Although Instruction no. 70 of Sumoc benefited the exporters in general, who received a bonus beyond the official rate, there was opposition from the coffee growers, who received a smaller bonus. On this theme see Sérgio Besserman Vianna, "Duas Tentativas de Estabilização: 1951–1954," in Marcelo de Paiva Abreu, ed., *A ordem do Progresso* (Rio de Janeiro: Editora Campus, 1992).

exchange rates and there was an implicit subsidy for imports of capital goods and inputs needed for the industrialization process.[45] This system, with some modifications, lasted until 1957.

Under the government of Juscelino Kubitschek (1956–1961) an ambitious investment plan was adopted. It gave absolute priority to building the more sophisticated industries needed to supplement traditional ones and provided for government funding to create these new sectors.[46]

This period of basic infrastructure construction with state financing was crucial for the Brazilian economy. Apart from investments in the construction of Brasília, electricity, transportation and heavy industry received almost all the government investments. But only 3% of the government's development plan was related to agriculture. Although not directly related to the so-called food sector, several actions directly or indirectly benefited agriculture, such as expanding electricity supply, refurbishing and building new railways, paving and expanding the road network, expanding ports and the merchant navy and promoting the chemical industry. Also the successful implantation of the automobile industry in Brazil included the production of trucks and tractors, and the construction of Brasília would have great influence in the later process of expansion of the agricultural frontier, particularly with the opening-up to the nearby Cerrado region.

Although agriculture was not, in fact, a government priority, little change occurred in the sector in this period. Nevertheless this sector did not represent an obstacle to the development of the industry, since it was able to meet the needs of basic food for an expanding population, increasing production by traditional means of incorporation of new areas and more workers. The demographic explosion that occurred in this period due to falling mortality rates allowed the rural sector to release labor to the urban area without putting pressure on the salaries in force in the countryside. On the other hand, the large supply of land suitable for agriculture also did not stimulate the

---

[45] Carlos Lessa, *Quinze Anos de Política Econômica* (São Paulo, Brasiliense/ Unicamp, 1975), 11.
[46] Maria da Conceição Tavares, "Auge e declínio do processo de substituição de importações no Brasil," in Maria da Conceição Tavares, *Da Substituição de Importações ao Capitalismo Financeiro* (Rio de Janeiro: Zahar, 1973): 27–115; and Lessa, *Quinze Anos de Política Econômica*, 14.

intensive use of capital in the form of plows, tractors, fertilizers and agricultural pesticides.

Agricultural production in the 1960s was extremely concentrated in only ten crops, which accounted for three-quarters of the value of production. In 1960, these ten crops occupied an area of 25 million hectares, with maize cultivation occupying the largest area (7.3 million hectares), followed by coffee, cotton and rice. By then plows and tractors were now more present on Brazilian farms (Table 2.4). During the 1950s, approximately 10.6 million hectares of new land went into production, and the number of agricultural workers increased by 4.5 million, considered modest compared to previous years. However, in that decade, machines began to appear in significant numbers on Brazilian farms and, as expected, most of these tractors and plows were concentrated in the South and Southeast regions. At that time, the Northeast had only one plow for each 310 hectares, while in the South the proportion was one plow for every 5 hectares, and in the Southeast, one for every 11 hectares. As for tractors, there was one for each 3,144 hectares in the Northeast, and one for each 292 hectares in the Southeast, with São Paulo leading among the states, with a proportion of one tractor per 177 hectares (see Table 1.7).

During this period coffee began to show new signs of overproduction. In 1959, Brazilian coffee production reached 44 million bags and total world production reached 79 million bags but world consumption was only 42 million bags. By 1963 the world had accumulated a stock of 81 million bags, of which 63 million belonged to Brazil, causing a sharp drop in prices in the international market and a decline in the value of coffee exports.

This time instead of burning stocks, international quotas became the prime instrument of control. In 1959 an agreement was signed between Latin American and African producers, defining quotas of coffee exports. In 1962, a new agreement was signed, with the participation of practically all producing countries and the United States. That year the International Coffee Organization (ICO) was established and in 1963 an international agreement led to eradication of coffee trees around the world. Between 1962 and 1967 almost half of the coffee trees in the world were eradicated. It was in this period of expansion and contraction that the coffee industry in Brazil suffered its greatest geographical movement. The state of Paraná went from 5% of national production in the 1940s to more than half of national production in the final years of the 1950s (Graph 1.3).

TABLE 1.7: *Area cultivated, workers, tractors and plows used by region and selected states, 1950–1960*

Region/state	Area of crops (ha)		Persons occupied		Tractors		Plows	
Year	1950	1960	1950	1960	1950	1960	1950	1960
North	234,512	458,490	326,502	536,619	61	266	381	306
Northeast	5,283,804	9,306,681	4,334,936	6,566,035	451	2,989	14,489	21,171
Southeast	8,447,903	10,297,939	3,999,860	4,465,344	5,155	35,215	318,863	394,696
Minas Gerais	2,937,126	3,673,466	1,868,657	2,076,829	763	5,024	79,968	93,040
São Paulo	4,257,633	4,973,300	1,531,664	1,683,038	3,819	28,101	244,947	286,580
South	4,530,566	8,279,870	1,949,923	3,174,233	2,566	22,720	383,435	604,050
Paraná	1,358,222	3,471,131	507,607	1,276,854	280	4,996	30,405	82,324
Rio Grande do Sul	2,502,691	3,795,840	1,071,404	1,277,390	2,245	16,675	312,001	440,467
Center-West	608,272	1,416,805	385,613	678,623	139	2,303	3,091	11,797
Total	19,095,057	29,759,785	10,996,834	15,521,701	8,372	63,493	714,259	1,031,930

Source: IBGE: Séries Históricas Retrospectivas

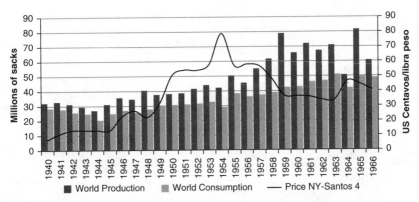

GRAPH 1.3: Coffee: World production, consumption and price, 1940–1960
Source: Bacha and Greenhill, *150 anos de café*, pp. 288–340

The structure of Brazilian imports and exports also underwent significant transformations between 1947 and 1960. There was a relative decline of raw materials and relative increase of foodstuffs in exports. Wood (mainly pine) and metallic ores (mainly iron ore) increased and cotton declined. Sugar and cocoa increased and coffee increased. Imports, in turn, remained stable, with raw materials, food products and manufactures among the main items. However, it was not long before the latter category started to change, due to the growth of national industries. Thus, car imports, for example, which accounted for 9% of Brazilian imports in 1947, practically disappeared in 1960. In addition, in the case of food products, about 80% of these imports were wheat and cod. At that time, Brazil was already basically self-sufficient in the production of most agricultural products (see Table 1.8).

The agricultural census of 1960 shows that modest growth was occurring with still little change in basic structure. In that year there were 3.4 million farms and ranches with a total of almost 250 million hectares, an increase of 1.3 million properties and 17.7 million hectares from the 1950 census. The vast majority of land used consisted of natural pastures (41%) and natural forests (22%). Temporary or seasonal crops occupied 20.9 million hectares (8% of the area) and permanent crops 7.8 million hectares (3% of the area). Reforestation was still insignificant, and even smaller was the proportion of irrigated land, only 461 thousand hectares.

The 1960 census still showed the usual high concentration of land ownership. Although all regions had high concentration indices, large farms were more representative in the North and Central West, while in

TABLE 1.8: *Composition of foreign commerce, 1947–1960*

	1947	1960
Exports		
Primary material	39%	23%
Cotton	16%	4%
Food	53%	74%
Sugar	1%	5%
Cacao	5%	8%
Coffee	37%	56%
Manufactures	8%	3%
Imports		
Primary materials	22%	24%
Food	18%	14%
Manufactures	60%	63%

Source: Anuários Estatísticos do Brasil, 1948 and 1962

the Northeast the farms of 5 hectares or less represented over half the farms. Farms of up to 100 hectares represented over 90% of all farms in all regions (see Table 1.9).

Thus Brazilian agriculture differed little in basic indicators from the censuses of 1920, 1940 and 1950. There was a relative increase of establishments with less than 100 hectares, starting from 72% in 1920 and reaching 89% in 1960. There was also a proportional increase in the share of land related to this size of property, which increased from 9% in 1920 to around 20% in the three subsequent censuses. However, the largest settlements, with more than 1,000 hectares, which accounted for between 1% and 2% of rural establishments, still owned between 44% and 51% of the agricultural lands in the 1940 and the 1960 censuses. Farms with more than 10,000 hectares included only some 1,700 properties, but controlled a proportion of between 15% and 20% of the land surveyed. These properties undoubtedly represented latifundia, probably with extremely low productivity (see Table 1.10).

Despite the population exodus from the rural area which occurred in these years, the agrarian population continued to grow in absolute terms because of the high rate of population growth in this period. Although the percentage of the population employed in agriculture dropped sharply from 67% in 1920 to 54% in 1960, the population occupied in agriculture reached 15.6 million persons in the 1960 census, of whom 71% were men.

TABLE 1.9: *Farms by size by units and area, census 1960*

	Proportion			
	Farms	Area (ha)	% Farms	% Area
Less than 1 hectare	133,477	103,792	4.0%	0.0%
More than 1 hectare & less than 2	276,740	381,556	8.3%	0.2%
More than 2 hectares & less than 5	619,119	2,051,455	18.6%	0.8%
More than 5 hectares & less than 10	465,634	3,415,578	14.0%	1.4%
More than 10 hectares & less than 20	546,079	7,684,200	16.4%	3.1%
More than 20 hectares & less than 50	672,675	20,818,118	20.2%	8.4%
More than 50 hectares & less than 100	272,661	19,062,972	8.2%	7.7%
More than 100 hectares & less than 200	157,422	21,764,444	4.7%	8.8%
More than 200 hectares & less than 500	116,645	35,851,678	3.5%	14.5%
More than 500 hectares & less than 1,000	40,764	26,413,333	1.2%	10.7%
More than 1000 hectares & less than 2,000	18,392	25,172,435	0.6%	10.2%
More than 2,000 hectares & less than 5,000	10,138	30,187,634	0.3%	12.2%
More than 5,000 hectares & less than 10,000	2,353	16,060,835	0.1%	6.5%
More than 10,000 hectares & less than 100,000	1,569	33,226,159	0.0%	13.4%
More than 100,000 hectares	28	5,666,953	0.0%	2.3%
Total	3,333,696	247,861,142	100%	100.0%

Source: IBGE, *Censo Agrícola 1960 – VII Recenseamento Geral do Brasil*, vol. II, 1a. Parte, 17–31

Unpaid family members accounted for 9.8 million people, almost two-thirds of whom were men. A significant proportion of unpaid family members (2.2 million) were younger than fifteen years of age. Only

TABLE 1.10: Size of farms by area, census 1920, 1940, 1950 and 1960

Area in hectares	Farms				Area (ha)			
	1920	1940	1950	1960	1920	1940	1950	1960
Total	648,153	1,904,589	2,064,642	3,337,769	175,104,575	197,720,247	232,111,106	249,862,142
<10		654,557	710,934	1,495,020		—	2,893,439	5,952,381
10–50		770,735	833,229	1,218,754		18,856,067	20,185,868	28,503,318
50–100		204,705	219,326	272,661		14,256,093	15,376,879	19,062,972
100–500		212,340	231,061	274,067		44,609,197	49,371,043	57,616,122
500–1,000		31,478	37,098	49,764		21,575,802	26,149,674	28,413,333
1,000–10,000		26,539	31,017	30,863		62,024,817	73,093,482	71,420,904
>10,000		1,273	1,611	1,597		33,504,832	45,008,788	38,893,112
Less than 100	463,879				15,708,314			
100–1,000	157,959				48,415,737			
1,000–10,000	24,647				65,487,928			
>10,000	1,668				45,492,696			

Source: IBGE, Censo Agrícola 1960 – VII Recenseamento Geral do Brasil, vol. II, 1a. Parte 17–31

Notes: The data for 1920 are distributed differently; there is a difference between the total and the sum of the farms with no information.

812,000 farms had employees, totaling 4.4 million workers, of whom 1.4 million were permanent and 3.0 million temporary. The census shows the existence of 186,939 establishments with sharecroppers (*com parcerias*), which contained 916,039 people. The existence of these sharecroppers supports the belief that Brazilian agriculture still retained feudal features in this period.

Farm workers averaged 3 workers per unit. In establishments with employees, the average was 5.4 employees per unit and for establishments with sharecroppers there was an average of 4.9 partners. Some 68% of the establishments which employed workers had less than 5 employees and these units contained 36% of these employed workers; 30% had between 5 and 20 employees and they accounted for 48% of the employed workforce. Finally, only 2% of establishments occupied more than 20 people and these employed 16% of the employed workforce. Given the traditional agricultural methods then employed, with little use of equipment and tractors, it would not have been possible to exploit large productive units with such a small labor force per unit (see Table 1.11).

Regionally, coffee was concentrated in the Southeast and South; rice had a significant position in the Northeast and in the South, with Rio Grande do Sul being the major producer. The average unit of rice production in the South was 46 hectares, which was twice the size of the average production unit in the Northeast (19 hectares). Cocoa was concentrated in the Northeastern region, primarily in Bahia. There were 20,000 producers of cacao, using 1.4 million hectares for cocoa, with an average area of 70 hectares. Corn was concentrated in the South, with both 57% of establishments and cultivated area. In the case of livestock, although the Center-West represented only 9% of the registered establishments, these controlled 38% of the area nationally. The Southeast and the South also appeared with a large proportion of establishments and area, but in smaller units in terms of occupied area. In the Center-West, for example, there were 49 thousand establishments, with a total area of 44 million hectares, representing an average of 905 hectares per establishment. The Center-West was still essentially a region of large-scale livestock production.

Although agriculture did not present a significant evolution in technical terms in this period of rapid industrialization, reflected by the relative stagnation of productivity, the sector was able steadily to increase its production with a proportional increase of factors of production, above all land and labor. Thus the performance evaluation of agriculture cannot be measured solely by its relative growth against industry and the service

TABLE 1.11: *Workers, sharecroppers and number of people employed by farm, 1960*

	Brazil total
Total farms	3,337,769
Total persons	15,633,985
Total men	11,111,551
Total women	4,522,434
Non paid family members – Total	9,848,727
Non paid family Members – Men	6,444,198
Non paid family members – Women	3,404,529
Farms with employees	812,158
Employees – Total	4,412,674
Employees – Men	3,613,449
Employees – Women	799,225
Permanent employees – Total	1,429,350
Permanent employees – Men	1,162,702
Permanent employees – Women	266,648
Temporary employees – Total	2,983,324
Temporary employees – Men	2,450,747
Temporary employees – Women	532,577
Farms with sharecroppers	186,939
Sharecroppers – Total	916,039
Sharecroppers – Men	708,962
Sharecroppers – Women	207,077
Number of persons in previous censuses	
1920 census	6,312,323
1940 census	11,343,415
1950 census	10,996,834

Source: IBGE, Censo Agrícola 1960 – vol. II, 1a. Parte, 17–31

sector. Its performance must be considered in the general process of growth and development that occurred in Brazil. The large growth of industry, strongly stimulated by the state, and the service sector, grew naturally by rural exodus and rapid urbanization. This did not occur in agriculture, which logically lost relative share in terms of participation in GDP and in the economically active population. But this did not signify that agriculture did not successfully participate in terms of its expected activities in this period.[47] There was growth but lower than what occurred in the service sector and industry, which explained the reduction in its relative participation.

Although the integration of industry and agriculture was particularly evident by the 1970s, in the whole process of Brazilian industrialization, agriculture played a fundamental role. There was such an abundant supply of labor that agriculture could produce the positive balance of payments and supply the economy with basic inputs, without changing the levels of rural worker remuneration. So abundant was that labor that it could also support the great rural exodus – an army of reserve labor sufficient to enable the process of urban growth, as well as the expansion of the labor in industry and services. The rural population actually increased, although the portion of the population employed in agriculture was significantly reduced. Because of expansion into the western frontiers the area explored was expanded and thus it was possible to systematically increase agricultural production.

It was in the period of military governments from 1964–1985 that agricultural policy finally became a priority of the government. The new government saw in agriculture an important source of inflationary pressure because of its shortcomings in the supply of the domestic market, and improving supply and reducing food costs was essential to contain wage pressures. In an underdeveloped country like Brazil, with low wages and a perverse distribution of income, food was a basic component of the cost of living and therefore had a strong impact on the formation of real wages.

This modernization of agriculture was to occur without any transformation in the agrarian structure, characterized as we have seen by a high concentration of land ownership.[48] Compared with most Latin American countries, Brazil never underwent a genuine process of land reform or engaged in free land distribution. In the countryside, land traditionally represented power and the reserve of value. In general, ownership and economic exploitation were not associated. Until the mid-twentieth century, unproductive latifundia and archaic labor relations prevailed in many regions of the country. In the 1950s and 1960s, the deficient structure of

---

[47] An interesting discussion on the interdependence of the agricultural with the other sectors of the economy can be obtained in Tamáz Szmrecsányi, "O desenvolvimento da produção agropecuária (1930–1970)," in Boris Fausto, ed., *História da Civilização Brasileira*, III. O Brasil Republicano, vol. 4, "*Economia e Cultura (1930–1964)*" (Rio de Janeiro: Beltrand Brasil, 1995): 107–207.

[48] Ruy Cirne Lima. *Pequena História Territorial do Brasil. Sesmarias e Terras Devolutas* (São Paulo: Secretaria do Estado da Cultura, 1990).

agriculture was identified as the main impediment to the country's development, by restricting the expansion of productive forces and allowing the survival of a backward and conservative power structure. Concentration of land, in addition to being politically conservative and socially damaging, it was argued, would impede the modernization of agriculture, and the proposed solution to the problem was agrarian reform.[49] However, the military governments put an end to the agrarian reform debate. Instead, with the goal of having plenty of cheap food, they began to encourage the modernization of agriculture and, thus, the transfer of the rural worker to urban industry, opening up agricultural production to international markets and using it to generate the foreign exchange necessary for growth. But despite all the proposed modernization, the government did not act against the concentration of land ownership and did not challenge the power of conservative rural elites.

Military support for agricultural modernization involved several areas. First, and fundamentally, there was the supply of abundant and subsidized credit. In 1965, the National Rural Credit System (SNCR) was created to provide substantial funds for agricultural producers and represented the main government instrument in promoting agriculture. In addition to the credit system, the guarantee of minimum prices and the formation of regulatory stocks were used to avoid large price variations for producers and consumers. Prior to planting, the government fixed minimum prices for the main products, especially those destined for the domestic market. It financed production and marketing through the Federal Government Acquisitions (AGF) and the Federal Government Loans (EGF). AGF was the instrument of direct purchase of products; the EGF represented loans to producers, who had the right to sell the product to the federal government, when market prices remained below minimum prices. Until the

---

[49] On the debates concerning the factors that influenced the evolution of Brazilian agriculture, see Affonso Celso Pastore, Guilherme L. Silva Dias and Manoel C. Castro, "Condicionantes da produtividade da pesquisa agrícola no Brasil," *Estudos Econômicos*, 6, no. 3 (1976): 147–81; Charles Mueller and George Martine, "Modernização agropecuária, emprego agrícola e êxodo rural no Brasil – a década de 1980," *Revista de Economia Política*, 17, no. 3 (Jul.–Sept. 1997), 85–104; Rodolfo Hoffmann, "Evolução da distribuição da posse de terra no Brasil no período 1960–80," *Reforma Agrária*, 12, no. 6 (Nov.–Dec. 1982):17–34; Carlos Nayro Coelho, "70 anos de política agrícola no Brasil, 1931–2001," *Revista de Política Agrícola*, 10, no.3 (Jul.–Sept. 2001): 3–58; Affonso Celso Pastore, *A Resposta da Produção Agrícola aos Preços no Brasil* (São Paulo: APEC, 1973); Alberto Passos Guimarães, *Quatro Séculos de Latifúndio* (Rio de Janeiro: Paz e Terra, 1977); Ruy Muller Paiva, "Reflexões sobre as tendências da produção, da produtividade e dos preços do setor agrícola no Brasil," in F. Sá, ed., *Agricultura Subdesenvolvida* (Petrópolis: Vozes, 1968).

1980s, much of the cotton, rice and soybean crops were financed by the EGF. In addition, the government created other special programs for regional development. Polocentro and Prodocer were the most important. The first, which began in 1975 and ended in 1982, aimed to stimulate the development and modernization of the Center-West in the Cerrado region, and was also based on the granting of subsidized credit. The second was the Japan–Brazil Cooperation Program for the Development of Cerrados (Prodocer), created through the Japanese Agency for International Cooperation (JCA), also to promote the agricultural development of the Cerrados. This program, besides foreseeing the participation of large companies, dedicated part of the land to family agriculture, through settlements. The program gave a great stimulus to the agricultural production of the savannahs of northwestern Minas Gerais, Bahia, parts of the Center-West and Maranhão.[50] Another important institution created by the government was the Brazilian Agricultural Research Corporation (Embrapa). Founded in 1973, it would play a fundamental role in the modernization of Brazilian agriculture.[51]

The rural credit system was based on public funds, via Banco do Brasil's "Conta Movimento" or on loans of the Central Bank of Brazil, and the "Exigibilities," which corresponded to a portion of commercial banks' demand deposits, compulsorily applied to credit operations for agriculture. The operation of the "Movement Account," which represented an automatic rediscounting of the Banco do Brasil, gave this bank a power of issue, and represented an effective increase in the money supply. The subsidy on credit came from the setting of interest rates in nominal terms, usually below inflation.

---

[50] Coelho, "70 anos de política agrícola no Brasil," *Revista de Política Agrícola*, X (Número Especial) (Jul./Aug./Sept. 2001): 29–31.

[51] "At the same time, it became clear that the opportunities for agricultural expansion in traditional areas were becoming limited. Increasing productivity in already opened areas, and incorporating the 'unproductive' Cerrado – the savannah-type biome in Brazil – was perceived as a means to guarantee the increase in agricultural production and to ensure food to the growing urban population at affordable prices. Thus, it was necessary to improve agricultural land and labor productivity significantly. The government's response to the challenge of creating a new era in agriculture resulted in the creation in 1973 of the Brazilian Agricultural Research Corporation, Embrapa, a 'research arm' of the Ministry of Agriculture, Livestock and Food Supply. This institution was given the mission of coordinating the Brazilian Agricultural Research System, composed of state agricultural research organizations, universities (agricultural colleges) and Embrapa itself." Geraldo B. Martha Jr., Elisio Contini and Eliseu Alves, "Embrapa: its origins and changes," in Werner Baer, ed. *The Regional Impact of National Policies. The Case of Brazil* (Cheltenham and Northampton, Mass.: Edward Elgar, 2012): 204–226.

During the 1970s, the volume of agricultural credit increased fourfold, having its best year in 1979. The abundance and negative cost of government credit to the producer financed the modernization of agriculture in terms of equipment and inputs. In the 1970s, an industrial complex was established in Brazil that supplied machinery, implements, fertilizers and pesticides; and the demand generated by agricultural modernization was an important factor in the rapid industrial development of that period. Between 1960 and 1980, the cultivated area almost doubled, from 25 million to 47 million hectares, and this was accompanied by increasing mechanization. In the same period, the number of hectares per tractor decreased from 410 to only 99, a proportion that remains stable to this day. Average fertilizer consumption per hectare increased from 8.3 kg in 1964 to 27.8 kg in 1970 and to 88 kg in 1980.[52]

Thus, the government provided three key pro-agricultural policies: subsidized credit, minimum prices, and purchase of regulatory stocks. The market for agricultural products was totally regulated. Domestic production was protected by customs tariffs and prior import authorizations, which made the market virtually immune to external competition. In this way, the government managed to guarantee both producer income and consumer price stability. It also helped the producer by controlling the price of inputs. Even products destined for foreign markets were heavily government-controlled. In addition to control over the exchange rate (essential variable for exportable items) and subsidized credit, regulations were established to guide exports, in many cases through the action of important public agencies such as the Sugar and Alcohol Institute (IAA) and the Brazilian Coffee Institute (IBC).[53]

In the case of sugar and alcohol, the government operated a complex system that controlled production per refinery (Usina), provided subsidies to compensate for regional differences in productivity and determined export quotas. Wheat was under another complex control system of the federal government, which was responsible for internal and external purchases of the product and regulated the supply to the mills of the country, also through a quota system. As the domestic producer was not competitive, the government controlled imports, bought wheat at prices

---

[52] There is an excellent series of statistics on agriculture on the sites of the Ministério da Agriculture: www.agricultura.gov.br; IBGE. *Estatísticas do século XX*, available at www,ibge.gov.br; Banco Central, www.bcb.gov.br/?RELRURAL; and in Ipeadata, under Temas: produção, available at: http://ipeadata.gov.br/epeaweb.dll/epeadata? 52305371.

[53] The two institutes were closed at the beginning of the 1990s.

reflecting the high costs of domestic production, and sold the final product to the consumer with subsidies to avoid the impact that such an important item would have on consumer price indices.[54] These support policies stimulated the modernization of agriculture in terms of machines, implements, fertilizers and pesticides, but created distortions in resource allocation and discouraged productivity growth.

In addition to credit incentives and the minimum price policy, the federal government, under the leadership of Embrapa, implemented a major research program crucial to Brazilian agriculture's ability to modernize. With a focus on agribusiness, the goal was to provide solutions for the development of agriculture through the generation, adaptation and transfer of scientific and technological knowledge. Embrapa's sophisticated research work best explains agricultural productivity gains over the past twenty years. In retrospect, the performance of Brazilian agriculture from 1960 to 1980 can be considered reasonably favorable, since it represented the first leap into modernity, with an increase in cultivated area and productivity per hectare. Considering seven of the major grains, production rose from 18 million tons in 1960 to 52 million in 1980, made possible by an increase in the cultivated area from 17 million hectares to 38 million hectares and a relative increase in productivity, from 1,083 kilos per hectare to 1,363 kilos per hectare. Productivity was still very small but showing signs of growth, which would mark Brazilian agriculture in the next thirty years, particularly since the 1990s.

Soybeans stood out among the new grains that were part of agricultural modernization. Introduced in the late 1950s, they reached a production level of 15 million tons in 1980, a level of output only surpassed by corn. Among other items that began to be exported on a large scale in this period was orange juice. Sugarcane also had a strong expansion, especially after the implementation of the Proálcool program in 1975, which replaced

---

[54] On the transformations which then occurred see Guilherme Leite da Silva Dias and Cicely Moutinho Amaral, "Mudanças estruturais na agricultura brasileira, 1980–1998," in Renato Baumann, ed., *Década de Transição* (Rio de Janeiro: Campus/Cepal, 2000); Guilherme Delgado, "Expansão e modernização do setor agropecuário no pós-guerra: um estudo da reflexão agrária," *Estudos Avançados USP*, 15 no. 43 (Sept.–Dec. 2001): 157–172; Eliseu Alves, *Dilema da Política Agrícola Brasileira: Produtividade ou Expansão da Área Agricultável* (Brasília: Embrapa, 1983); Fernando B. Homem de Melo, "Agricultura de exportação e o problema da produção de alimentos" (São Paulo: FEA-USP, Texto para Discussão 30, 1979); and Fernando B. Homem de Melo, "Composição da produção no processo de expansão da fronteira agrícola brasileira," *Revista de Economia Política*, 5, no. 1 (Jan.–Mar. 1985): 86–111.

gasoline with ethanol. Even a traditional crop like wheat was transformed by strong government incentives. Generally complemented by imports, the Brazilian crop, thanks to government support, increased greatly in volume and productivity. In the mid-1980s, for the first time in modern times, domestic production finally managed to supply most of domestic consumption. However, other commodities did not perform as well. Corn and rice almost doubled in the period, but with little increase in productivity. Beans and manioc, essential items in the national diet, also did not experience any change in productivity and their harvests did not increase as well.

Traditionally, most of the Brazilian population had been rural. But an intense migratory movement toward the cities began in the middle of the twentieth century causing an average annual increase of 4.7% in the urban population between 1960 and 1980. During the same period, the rural population grew at the modest rate of less than 1% per year. By the early 1980s, two-thirds of Brazilians lived in urban areas, mostly concentrated in large cities. This exodus from rural workers to often marginal urban activities represented a serious social problem, although it was important for the productivity of the rural labor force.

Like all other sectors of the economy, agriculture was affected by the crisis of the 1980s, which began with the surge in oil prices in the previous decade and intensified with the Mexican debt crisis in 1982. This led to the deterioration of the accounts, inflation and a dramatic balance of payments crisis, which resulted in a moratorium on external debt and a sharp decline in economic activity. The need for internal and external adjustments led to the adoption of recessive policies reinforced by agreements with the IMF – which, in turn, led to adjustments lasting more than a decade. The supply of rural credit, based on large government subsidies and the use of funds derived from demand deposits, was greatly reduced. Inflation made demand deposits scarce, and these accounts were the basis of rural credit requirements, and the need to control public accounts restricted agricultural subsidies. In 1984, credit available to agriculture accounted for only 37% of the 1979 volume; in 1990, it fell to 23% of that figure. At the same rate, the share of credit in agricultural GDP fell. In the second half of the 1970s total credit represented around 70% of agricultural GDP; in the 1990s it remained slightly above 20%.[55]

---

[55] Banco Central do Brasil – Departamento de Regulação, Supervisão e Controle das Operações do Crédito Rural e do Proagro-DEROP. Registro Comum de Operações Rurais – RECOR.

In addition, from the mid-1980s, rural lending was adjusted for monetary correction: thus the cost of credit became positive and gradually rose as much as other market rates. Finally, the need to control inflation induced the government to permanently manipulate the price of products in the domestic market, especially food, which was sometimes costly for the producer. The policy of minimum prices, the purchase of agricultural products by the government, and the price control policy were reduced or eliminated due to the need to reduce public spending and to control inflation. Most of these measures had a negative impact on the producer and had little positive impact on inflation. Similarly, the succession of recessive policies and heterodox plans were generally ineffective in containing rising inflation, which created considerable uncertainty and negatively affected agriculture, which operates with long cycles of production.

When we compare the evolution of credit granted with the quantity produced, we see that there was a systematic fall in the value of credit granted while the quantity produced increased continuously. This generated an expressive drop in the average credit per ton (US$ per ton). According to a study by the Brazilian Development Bank (BNDES), in the early 1980s, financing per ton surpassed all international prices of grains, creating an overabundance of financial resources, which were often misapplied. Already in the 1990s, credit per ton was scarce. As the average annual production in the period 1999–2001 was 70% higher than in the early 1980s, disbursement per ton fell by 80% over the same period.[56]

However, the adjustment of the 1980s, although dramatically affecting agriculture, like the other sectors of the economy, provided opportunities. The international oil crisis and its consequences for the external accounts which would culminate in the 1987 moratorium gave agriculture a new role, as the government promoted the replacement of oil with alcohol. In addition, in the face of external bottlenecks, the government began to stimulate agricultural exports. Differentiated policies were established for products destined for the foreign market (such as coffee, sugar, soybeans, orange juice, cocoa, cotton and tobacco) and those destined for the domestic market (such as rice, potatoes, beans, maize, cassava, onion). The latter were protected from foreign competition by tariffs and import quotas.

---

[56] Paulo Favaret Filho, "Evolução do Crédito Rural e Tributação sobre alimentos na década de 1990: implicações sobre as cadeias de aves, suínos e leite" (Rio de Janeiro, BNDES Setorial, no. 16), 34.

In the case of domestic products, the greatest concern was the impact of prices on explosive inflationary levels. In order to control prices, the government, as we have seen, regulated the supply in numerous ways. However, these costly controls on the domestic market soon became threatened by the growing public deficit. The maintenance of low prices to control the cost of living also served to stimulate consumption. However, the cost of the consumer subsidy policy and the income protection of the producer burdened the public accounts. With the deterioration of public funds, there was increasing pressure for abolishing these subsidies, pressure that came in particular from international institutions such as the World Bank and the International Monetary Fund (IMF). The importance of wheat in the basic diet and the potential political impact of adopting real prices postponed the decision to end subsidies. But in 1987 they were finally eliminated; and in 1990 the free market was established for all stages of wheat production and marketing. Although in the protectionist period the productivity of Brazilian wheat increased, with the end of the subsidies to the product, the local crops could not compete with the imports. In 1987, domestic production reached 6.2 million tons, meeting 90% of domestic demand. In 1995, wheat production had fallen to 1.4 million tons, accounting for only 17% of the market. In addition to the impact on production, by eliminating the producer incentive, the withdrawal of subsidies to consumption affected domestic consumption, which remained practically stable at around 6 million tons per year throughout the 1980s.[57]

With the oil crisis, the ambitious Proálcool was implemented to promote the domestic production of ethyl alcohol for use as an automotive fuel. Launched in 1975, the program expanded in 1979, following the second oil shock. Apart from adding alcohol to all gasoline sold in the country, the government gave incentives to manufacture cars that would run exclusively on hydrated alcohol. Fuel production targets had been set at 3 billion liters per year for the first phase and rose to 7.7 billion liters for the second, starting in 1979. In order to promote the program, numerous tax incentives were made available, along with government funding. Gasoline sold in Brazil already contained 20% alcohol, and

[57] Célio Alberto Cole, "A cadeia produtiva do trigo no Brasil: contribuição para geração de emprego e renda" (MA thesis, Porto Alegre: Iepe/UFRGS, 1998); J. F. Fernandes filho, "A política brasileira de fomento à produção de trigo, 1930–1990," *Anais do XXXIII Congresso Brasileiro de Economia Rural* (Brasília: Sober, 1995), 1: 443–74; Roque Silvestre Annes Tomasini and Ivo Ambrosi, "Aspectos econômicos da cultura do trigo," *Cadernos de Ciência e Tecnologia*, 15 no. 2 (May–Aug. 1998): 59–84.

this percentage rose to 22% in 1980. The first ethanol-fueled cars on the market were just adapted gasoline vehicles, but from the early 1980s onwards completely new and very efficient engines emerged that had been designed for the use of fuel alcohol. This enforced a policy that efficiently remunerated the alcohol producer and, at the same time, made that fuel competitive. Although the program was expensive for the government, Proálcool proved effective, since the market adopted almost exclusively alcohol-based vehicles: by 1984, 95% of cars manufactured in Brazil had an alcohol engine.

During that decade, the program was criticized for the costs and prioritization of sugarcane at the expense of other crops, especially those directed at domestic consumption. Cane for ethanol production was planted in the best soils of the country, with extremely efficient and mechanized cultivation. A national sugarcane processing technology was developed, which compared to the best in the world. However, with the subsequent decline in international oil prices, the program became too costly for the government, and alcohol could no longer compete with gasoline prices. In 1985, the Proálcool began to face a crisis, with the progressive decrease of the sales of alcohol motor cars, and by the mid-1990s such sales had almost ceased. The government, however, still required alcohol to be mixed with the common fuel. But continued oil shocks and an increase in government funding brought a new revitalized program into existence in the twenty-first century.[58]

As a result, the 1980s were turbulent for agriculture due to the country's long economic crisis. In the decade, the sector had average annual growth of 3%, which was above the average increase of GDP in that period. However, it was an erratic performance, alternating positive years with zero or negative growth phases and exhibiting better results in export products than in staples of domestic consumption. If we consider the instability and recessionary policies of the country plus the reduction in fiscal incentives for the sector and especially the loss of cheap and abundant subsidized credit, agricultural performance was better than could have been expected. The emergence of financing alternatives for the

---

[58] In Brazil, three types of gasoline were marketed: common, common additive and premium. By law, all three must contain alcohol in a proportion of 20% to 25%, depending on the availability of that fuel in the market. About such a program, see Fernando B. Homem de Melo and Eduardo Giannetti, *Proálcool, Energia e Transportes* (São Paulo: Fipe/Pioneira,1981); Fernando B. Homem de Melo, *O Problema Alimentar no Brasil* (Rio de Janeiro: Paz e Terra, 1983); José Cláudio Bittencourt Lopes, "O Proálcool: uma avaliação" (MA thesis, Universidade Federal de Viçosa, 1992).

sector, involving other segments of agribusiness, was fundamental to explain that reasonable performance. Suppliers of inputs and equipment started to directly finance rural producers and there was greater financial and operational integration with the other end of the productive process, such as processing industries, wholesale and retail distribution channels (including supermarket chains) and trading companies. These new sources were used to finance the productive process in agriculture. The integration between producer, supplier and client, which began in the 1980s due to the sudden withdrawal of government credit, would become in the next decade the primary source of rural credit and still constitutes the financing system of Brazilian agribusiness.

Along with this important shift in credit sources, government-sponsored agricultural research was crucial in fostering the subsequent agricultural revolution. The activities of Embrapa and other research centers, such as the Agronomic Institute of Campinas, which accumulated an historical archive of the main products of Brazilian agriculture, and their regional characteristics, were among the main factors explaining the relative dynamism of agriculture, even during the crisis that devastated Brazil for more than fifteen years. Over the past two decades, there has been a steady increase in productivity across all crops and the progressive expansion of the agricultural frontier through the introduction of new seed varieties, which are compatible with local soil and climatic conditions. In the 1980s, the Cerrado began to be exploited, where several crops (especially soybeans) adapted very well to previously unproductive lands. The expansion of the agricultural frontier to the virgin soils of the Center-West region also had a positive impact, as it allowed the use of new and (now) extremely productive areas. But on the other hand, it imposed a burden on the state in terms of the need to invest in infrastructure if these new zones were to be exploited efficiently, which in turn denied these resources to traditional production zones. Given the progressive expansion of the agricultural frontier in the last twenty-five years, the itinerant character of Brazilian agriculture continues. Largely because of the public investments that accompany the opening of new agricultural regions, areas that were previously unprofitable are gaining value.

What we can consider the second phase of Brazilian agricultural modernization occurred in the 1980s, when the loss of government subsidies forced agriculture to become integrated into the market. In those years, the Brazilian farmer reached a level of modernization and efficiency that allowed him to survive and thrive in the market economy. To do so, the sector would need to make major adjustments. Thus on the eve of its greatest expansion in the twenty first century, Brazil had passed through several stages of growth and crisis. Most of the period since 1900 had involved some aspect of government intervention to keep agriculture viable. But there was little modernization in the period to 1960. It was only with the governments of the military era that a systematic approach was taken to advance agriculture. Though the final organization of agribusiness as a free market enterprise would be far different from what these military governments anticipated, the massive support they gave agriculture would be fundamental to its transformation and ultimate success.

2

The New Agricultural Economy post 1960

In 1960, Brazil was still a country with high levels of hunger and malnutrition despite significant food imports.[1] Today malnutrition and hunger no longer affect the Brazilian population,[2] and Brazil no longer imports a significant amount of food.[3] There has been a major increase in agricultural production per inhabitant, particularly since 1990. In 1960 the production of grains per inhabitant was 376 kg, the production of meat 26 kg and milk 70 liters; in 1990 this per capita production had increased only modestly to 384 kg, 35 kg and 100 liters respectively. By 2015 these indicators per inhabitant were more than two and a half times the 1960

---

[1] On the crisis in malnutrition prior to the 1970s, see Josué de Castro, *Geografia da Fome: o Dilema Brasileiro – Pão ou Aço* (10th edn. rev.; Rio de Janeiro: Edições Antares, 1984).

[2] For the recent decline in malnutrition as measured by heights and weights of children see Malaquias Batista Filho and Anete Rissin, "A transição nutricional no Brasil: tendências regionais e temporais," *Cadernos de Saúde Pública*, 19, Supl .1 (2003): 181–91; and Carlos Augusto Monteiro and Wolney Lisboa Conde, "Tendência secular da desnutrição e da obesidade na infância na cidade de São Paulo (1974–1996)," *Revista de Saúde Pública*, 34, no.6 (2000): 52–61. Although both studies stress public health initiatives – inoculation and pre-natal care – as important in improving child heights, there is little question that cheap and abundant supplies of food were also crucial. This is clearly recognized in a second study by Monteiro. See Carlos Augusto Monteiro, Lenise Mondini and Renata BL Costa, "Mudanças na composição e adequação nutricional da dieta familiar nas áreas metropolitanas do Brasil (1988–1996)," *Revista de Saúde Pública*, 34, no. 3 (Jun. 2000): 251–258.

[3] The value of agricultural imports was less than 2% of the total imports, of which wheat was the most important (0.7%) followed by malt (0.2%) and fish (0.2%). MDIC, SECEX, "Importação Brasileira, Principais Produtos – Ordem Decrescente Janeiro/Dezembro – 2015," found at http://www.desenvolvimento.gov.br/sitio/interna/interna.php?area=5&menu=5266&refr=1161.

indices, and were now at 1,004 kg of grains per inhabitant, 118 kg of meat and 171 liters of milk.[4]

Coffee in 1960 accounted for over half the value of all exports as it had since the 1840s, but in 2016 it accounted for just 3% of the value of all exports.[5] Soybeans, only introduced as a commercial crop in the late 1950s, now account for 30% of all agricultural exports. In 1961 the value of Brazil's agricultural exports was less than a tenth of the United States and it ranked 19th among exporting nations. It then produced 15 million tons of cereals and was ranked ninth largest producer in the world behind such countries as France, Germany and Japan, and with just 2% of world production. By 2014 it produced 101.4 million metric tons of cereals and ranked as the world's fifth largest producer behind China, the US, India and the Russian Federation. In 1961 it produced only 9% of US cereals output, by 2014 it was at 23% of US output.[6] By 2016 it ranked fourth in the world in total value of agricultural exports behind the United States, the Netherlands and Germany, but because it was a minimal importer of foods, it ranked first in the world in the net value of its agricultural world trade, more than double Canada and the Netherlands, its nearest competitors. Whereas the United States, the world's largest agricultural exporter, shipped double the value of Brazilian agricultural exports in that year, its positive balance of agricultural trade was just US$1.9 billion, compared to Brazil's agricultural net surplus of US$69 billion.[7]

This transformation has occurred within the space of the past half century and is still an ongoing process as Brazil has dramatically increased its share of world production and exports in numerous new and older crops in the past two decades. Today it is the world's largest exporter of processed beef and chicken, oranges, sugar and soybeans, and second in the export of corn. It has expanded and became a competitive world producer at the same time as national industry has declined and lost its ability to compete in international markets. How this agricultural

---

[4] Ipeadata data. Grains here are defined as cotton, rice, beans, soy, corn, wheat and peanuts. For meat we compute the production of beef, pig and poultry carcasses.

[5] For agricultural and total exports in 2016 see MAPA, "Balança comercial do agronegócio – síntese … " accessed May 30, 2017, at www.agricultura.gov.br/internacional/indicadores-e-estatisticas/balanca-comercial. For 1960 see *AEB 1962*, table I.6, 164–169.

[6] World Bank, World Development Indicators, World Cereal Production, found at http://data.worldbank.org/indicator/AG.PRD.CREL.MT.

[7] World Trade Organization (WTO), Time Series on International Trade, accessed February 10, 2018, at http://stat.wto.org/StatisticalProgram/WsdbExport.aspx?Language=E.

revolution occurred and in what areas the changes took place are the themes of this chapter.

There were several distinct cycles of growth of Brazilian agriculture even in the modern period. Throughout most of the twentieth century this growth followed a traditional pattern. The increasing output of all crops was fueled by expanding the amount of land in production rather than by any increase in productivity. From 1920 when comparable data are available on croplands and farms, the country experienced a major growth of land dedicated to crops as well as the number of farms in production, a pattern of growth which continued into the mid-1980s. But the number of farms, their size and their productivity began to change after that date. Growth of production is now less dependent on land expansion and increasing the number of farms, and more on increasing output on land already in production. Thus the number of farms which had been increasing steadily peaked in 1985, slowly declining ever since. Equally, average farm size has declined steadily since the 1970s. The large and low-productivity latifundia are slowly being replaced by medium size farms which have a much higher percentage of their lands in crops, and are systematically using machines, insecticides and fertilizers, all of which had been little used before the middle of the twentieth century.

Lands devoted to crops went from 6.6 million hectares in 1920 to a peak of 62.8 million hectares in 1985, then dropped to 59.8 million hectares in the agricultural census of 2006, and have since dropped further to an estimated 58.3 million hectares in the harvest of 2016.[8] The number of farms peaked in the 1980s at 5.9 million units, and declined to 5.2 million by the agricultural census of 2006 and presently is estimated to be about 5 million and will probably remain at that number for the foreseeable future.[9]

The number of farm workers also followed this pattern. It rose from 17.6 million workers in 1970 to 23.4 million in 1985, its historic peak, and then has consistently dropped through the next two agricultural censuses reaching just 16.6 million in 2006.[10] By 2016 the total dropped further to 13.6

---

[8] Instituto Brasileiro de Geografia e Estatística (IBGE), *Indicadores IBGE: Estatística da Produção Agrícola* (Sept. 2016), p. 18, table 3.

[9] DIEESE, "O mercado de trabalho assalariado rural brasileiro," *Estudos e Pesquisas*, no. 74 (Oct. 2014): 6.

[10] IBGE, *Censo Agropecuário 2006, Resultados preliminares* (Rio de Janeiro, 2006), table 1.1.

million,[11] and is expected to decline to 8.2 million workers by 2050.[12] This has resulted in a decline in the average number of workers per farm, which went from 9.7 workers in 1930 to just 3.2 in 2006, and this was accompanied by a decline in average farm size which went from a national average of 270 hectares to just 64 hectares by the census of 2006.[13]

A combination of technical modernization of farming and a decline of virgin lands explains these trends. In the post-1960 period there has been a systematic increase in the application of better seeds, insecticides, fertilizers and machines by Brazilian farms. Along with the decline in available virgin lands, there has been the entrance into major production of older and previously neglected lands in traditional areas. By the last two decades of the twentieth century most of the remaining frontier lands had been settled, while regions such as the Cerrado, which encompassed large sections of older regions, were better exploited with new seeds and new treatment of the soil. Thus fertilizer consumption increased steadily from 1960 to 2015, with Brazilian farm consumption of phosphorus, nitrogen and potassium going from 243,000 tons in the former year to 13.7 million tons in 2015.[14] In 2015 Brazil produced 9 million tons of processed fertilizers and imported 21 million tons.[15] Despite being a tropical country and one with uneven qualities of soil, its consumption of fertilizers per hectare of arable land (176 kg per hectare in 2013) ranked it 52nd in such usage in the world and well below other Latin American countries.[16]

---

[11] This is the estimate for persons fifteen years of age and older. Pesquisa Nacional por Amostra de Domicílios (PNAD), *Síntese de Indicadores 2014*, table 4.1.8, found at www.ibge.gov.br/home/estatistica/populacao/trabalhoerendimento/pnad2014/sinte se_defaultxls.shtm.

[12] DIEESE, "O mercado de trabalho assalariado rural," p. 6, gráfico 3.

[13] José Garcia Gasques, Eliana Teles Bastos, Miriam Rumenos Piedade Bacchi and Constanza Valdes, "Produtividade Total dos Fatores e Transformações da Agricultura Brasileira: análise dos dados dos Censos Agropecuários," *48th Congresso, SOBER Sociedade Brasileira de Economia, Administração e Sociologia Rural*, Campo Grande MS, 2010, table 1, p. 4.

[14] International Plant Nutrition Institute, "Evolução do consumo aparente de N, P, K e Total de NPK no Brasil," found at http://brasil.ipni.net/article/BRS-3132#evolucao.

[15] ANDA, Associação Nacional para Difusão de Adubos, data found at http://anda.org.br/index.php?mpg=03.00.00.

[16] This figure was well below that of many EU countries and was low by South American standards. Colombia used 649 kg per hectare, Chile 428, Ecuador 229. Argentina was the dramatic exception, using only 36 kg, well below the world standard of 125 kg. World Bank, World Development Indicators, Fertilizer consumption (kilograms per hectare of arable land), found at http://data.worldbank.org/indicator/AG.CON.FERT.ZS?view=chart.

Equally the use of machinery of all kinds has gone from being a rare farm item to being a normal part of farm resources. By 2013 Brazilian industry produced 98% of the 77,000 farm machinery sold in the country.[17] In that year 65,000 tractors were sold, or 3% of all tractors sold in the world. This was double the volume of tractors sold in Canada in that year and was greater than sales in the Russian Federation, Turkey or any European country.[18] In 2014, for example, Brazilian farmers purchased 68,000 machines of which 82% were wheel tractors, 9% were combines, 6% loaders and back hoes, 2% tillers and 1% crawler tractors.[19] These numbers were roughly 40% of US machinery production in the same year, though nothing compared to India and China, the two leading farm machinery producers in the world.[20] Most of the major world agricultural equipment makers were operating in Brazil by this time, and in fact US exporters reported that more than half of the agricultural equipment shipped to Brazil in the second decade of the twenty-first century was parts, compared to only a third being parts for its total world exports.[21] This was due to the large local manufacturing facilities established in Brazil. The biggest of these multinational manufacturers in 2015 were the US company AGCO which accounted for 21% of production, followed by John Deere (18% of production); Valtra, a subdivision of AGCO which produced 17% from a single plant in São Paulo; and the Italian company CNH-Industrial's New Holland division (with 15% of production). Other manufactures of tractors, combine harvesters and sprayers include Agrale (the only national producer), Caterpillar and Komatsu. The biggest center of agricultural machine production was in Rio Grande do Sul (which produced 47% of the machines) followed by São Paulo (26%) and Paraná (23%) and Minas Gerais (5%). All of these

---

[17] EMIS, *Machinery and Equipment Sector Brazil*, January 2014, p. 18, found at www.emis.com/sites/default/files/EMIS%20Insight%20-%20Brazil%20Machinery%20and%20Equipment%20Sector.pdf.

[18] CEMA, *Economic Committee Tractor Market Report Calendar year 2014*, found at cema-agri.org/sites/default/files/publications/2015-02%20Agrievolution%20Tractor%20Market%20Report.pdf.

[19] *Anuário da Indústria Automobilística Brasileira 2016*, p. 128, table 3.3.

[20] VDMA Agricultural Machinery Report 2015, p. 30, found at http://lt.vdma.org/documents/105903/8575467/VDMA%20Economic%20Report%202015%20public%20version.pdf/a25a564f-614e-4e67-95f2-6f16b7604f9b.

[21] US Department of Commerce, International Trade Administration, Industry & Analysis, *2015 Top Markets Report: Agricultural Equipment – A Market Assessment Tool for U.S. Exporters July 2015*, p. 26.

companies produced only agricultural machines, except for Agrale which also produced trucks and buses. By 2016 some 80% of the inputs used to produce these machines were made in Brazil. Although Brazil exports on average 18% of the machines it manufactures, these exports are usually inter-company trading activity, and only 2% of the machines sold in the country in that year were imports.[22]

There are also significant changes in the amount of land devoted to specific crops. The area planted in grains, for example, has steadily expanded from 49.8 million hectares in the harvest of 2010/11 to an estimated 58.3 million hectares in the 2015/16 harvest. In examining croplands along with pasture lands in more detail, it is evident that growth in land usage was influenced by the introduction of both new crops and the application of modern farming technologies to traditional crops. This was most evident in seasonal crops, which progressively increased their share of agricultural lands at the expense of the more traditional permanent crops. Thus lands devoted to such permanent crops as coffee, bananas and citrus fruits remained relatively stable in the period from 1970 (when comparable data becomes available) to the present day. They used between 8 and 10 million hectares until 2006 and have since dropped to 5.7 million hectares in 2015.[23] In contrast there was an explosion of lands in seasonal crops involving everything from sugarcane, rice, corn, beans and wheat, to cotton, soybeans and sunflowers which went from 26 million hectares to 48 million hectares by 2006 and to 71 million hectares in 2015.[24] Equally there was a basic change in pasture lands due to the growth and modernization of animal herds, with planted pastures becoming more important than natural ones by the census of 1995 and continuing to increase thereafter as natural pastures continued to decline.

These changes in land use had a great deal to do with both the changing importance of different crops, especially with the relative decline of permanent crop coffee and the rise of new seasonal crops such as soybeans as well as the explosive growth of traditional crops such as corn. In the

---

[22] Bradesco/Depec (Departamento de Pesquisas e Estudos Econômicos), "Tratores e Máquinas Agrícolas, Janeiro de 2017," in "Setor e Regional/Informações Setoriais," found at www.economiaemdia.com.br.

[23] IBGE, SIDRA, *Produção Agrícola Municipal* (hereafter *PAM*), "Tabela 1613 – Área destinada à colheita, área colhida, quantidade produzida, rendimento médio e valor da produção das lavouras permanentes," found at https://sidra.ibge.gov.br/tabela/1613.

[24] All data for 2006 have been updated to the latest revised numbers found in *Censo Agropecuário 2006, Brasil, Grandes Regiões e Unidades da Federação Segunda apuração* (Rio de Janeiro, 2012) and will appear in all tables as "revised" with table number.

harvest of 1975/1976, for example, Brazil produced 47 million tons of grains on seasonal crop lands; by 1990 it produced 58 million tons, it passed 100 million tons by 2000/2001 and reached 225 million tons in the harvest of 2016/2017, from these seasonal cropping lands.[25]

Although median farm size changed over time, there was little change in the distribution of land ownership. From 1920 to 2006 the GINI index of distribution of land remained virtually unchanged between .832 and .872.[26] While this is very high by world standards, it is close to the norm for most countries in Latin America, the region with the highest inequality in land distribution.[27] But there was variation by crop, with the GINI index for basic food crops being much lower than the average, whereas it was the highest in soybean and above all in sugar (.88).[28]

Despite this great inequality in land ownership, actual production of commercial agricultural products is not confined to the largest estates. There is a significant participation of small and medium sized farms in commercial agricultural production despite the increasing importance of large farms of 1,000 hectares or more. Most wealth-producing farms of Brazil in 2006, some 20% of all farms, were in the 5–20 hectare range, 37% in the 20–100 hectare size group and 22% in the 100–500 hectare range. In total 79% of the wealthiest farms were under 500 hectares.[29]

In this respect Brazil is not that different from the USA in terms of the dominance of a small ratio of farms in accounting for most of agricultural production. In the United States, only some 600,000 farms out of 2 million, or about 30%, have any significant commercial output, and of

[25] Conab (Companhia Nacional de Abastecimento), Séries históricas, "Brasil-Safras 1976/77 a 2016/17 Em mil toneladas," found at www.conab.gov.br/conteudos.php?a=1252&; and Conab, *Acompanhamiento da safra brasileira, grãos, v. 5 Safra 2017/18 – Quinto levantamento* (Brasília, Feb. 2018): 8, found at: www.conab.gov.br/OlalaCMS/uploads/arquivos/18_02_08_17_09_36_fevereiro_2018.pdf.

[26] See Bastiaan Philip Reydon, "Governança de terras e a questão agrária no Brasil," in Antônio Márcio Buainain, et al., eds., *O Mundo Rural no Brasil do Século 21: A Formação de um Novo Padrão Agrário e Agrícola* (Brasília: Embrapa, 2014): 736, table 3.

[27] Dietrich Vollrath, "Land distribution and international agricultural productivity," *American Journal of Agricultural Economics*, 89, no.1 (Feb. 2007): 204, table 1.

[28] Luiz A. Martinelli, Rosamond Naylor, Peter M. Vitousek and Paulo Moutinho, "Agriculture in Brazil: impacts, costs, and opportunities for a sustainable future," *Current Opinion in Environmental Sustainability*, 2, nos. 4–5 (2010): 433, table 1.

[29] Steven M. Helfand, Vanessa da Fonseca Pereira and Wagner Lopes Soares, "Pequenos e médios produtores na agricultura brasileira: situação atual e perspectivas,"in Buainain et al., *O Mundo Rural no Brasil*: 543, table 1.

TABLE 2.1: *Type of farm tenancy in Brazil, 1970–2006*

Farmer tenancy	1970	1975	1980	1985	1995	2006[*]
Owner	62.9%	64.1%	65.7%	64.6%	74.2%	76.2%
Renter	12.9%	11.4%	11.4%	9.9%	5.5%	4.7%
Sharecropper	7.7%	6.0%	6.2%	7.7%	5.7%	2.9%
Occupant	16.5%	18.5%	16.8%	17.8%	14.6%	8.4%
Sum	100.0%	100.0%	100.0%	100.0%	100.0%	92.2%
Total Farms	4,919,089	4,993,251	5,159,850	5,802,206	4,859,865	5,175,489

Notes: * In 2006 the category of farms without lands was included and comprised 4.9% of all farms listed.
Source: Mapa, Sec. de Política Agrícola, based on IBGE, Censo Agropecuário 1995/96, and table 1.3 of IBGE, Censo Agropecuário, Brasil, Grandes Regiões e Unidades da Federação, segunda apuração

these only some 120,000 farms, or 6% of all farms, produce three-quarters of all US commercial production. Farms selling more than US$1 million in output per annum by 2007 accounted for 59% of all agricultural sales.[30]

Another major change that could be expected with the modernization of large numbers of farms is the increasing legalization of title and decline of squatters, renters and sharecroppers. From 1970 onward there is an increasing percentage of farms directly owned and with full title to the land (see Table 2.1). By the agricultural census of 2006 over three-quarters of the farms were owned by the farmer producer.

The modernization of Brazilian agriculture can also be seen in the increasing productivity of all crops as well as the introduction of major new commercial crops. What is impressive is that even crops primarily directed to the national market have experienced increasing productivity as well as primarily export crops. Only cacao declined in yield in the period 1950–2015, and only oranges grew at less than double the 1950 level of productivity due to local plagues. There were also crops that were wiped out in a local region due to a particular plague. This occurred in the Northeast where the boll weevil wiped out long fiber production in the 1980s and 1990s, and cocoa suffered an equal plague crisis in the same

---

[30] Daniel A. Sumner, "American farms keep growing: size, productivity, and policy," *Journal of Economic Perspectives*, 28, no. 1 (Winter 2014): 147–149.

TABLE 2.2: *Index of productivity change of major crops, 1970–2015* (1970=100)

	Initial year kg/ha	1970	1975	1980	1985	1995	2006	2015
Coffee	523	100	158	124	201	225	304	290
Cacao	484	100	135	153	126	73	79	83
Oranges	15,323	100	122	116	126	111	132	169
Grapes	5,674	100	123	109	148	138	156	229
Rice	1,287	100	109	116	142	222	321	471
Beans	525	100	110	107	101	136	193	290
Corn	1,254	100	112	127	123	204	301	463
Wheat	706	100	73	99	164	184	188	241
Soybeans	862	100	179	190	206	271	302	351
Sugarcane	26,861	100	108	134	151	155	172	186
Cotton	878	100	109	132	125	157	352	457

Source: Gasques et al., "Produtividade Total," table 1, p. 4, for 1950 to 2006; and IBGE, SIDRA, *Pesquisa Pecuária Municipal*, tables 1612 & 1613.

period.[31] All the other crops increased by two to four times their kilogram per hectare output in this sixty-five-year period (see Table 2.2). It is also worth noting that many of the traditional crops such as rice, beans and corn increased their yields quite recently, with no secular trends of growth until the 1980s. Even wheat, a crop difficult to produce in Brazil which had needed subsidies by the government to prosper for most of the twentieth century, increased yield per hectare and went from 926 kg per hectare in 1970 to 2,672 kg by 2016/2017. Despite national production reaching an average of 5–6 million tons by the mid-2010s Brazilian farmers accounted for only half of national needs. Thus wheat remains the single most significant agricultural import of Brazil to the present day, but even here wheat imports have declined from supplying 85% of

[31] On the cacao plague of 1989, see Antônio Carlos de Araújo, Lúcia Maria Ramos Silva and Rosalina Ramos Midlej, "Valor da produção de cacau e análise dos fatores responsáveis pela sua variação no estado da Bahia," *43 Congresso da Sociedade Brasileira de Economia, Administração e Sociologia Rural – SOBER*, 2005. For the impact of the boll weevil on the traditional northeast production see Eliana M. G. Fontes et al., "The cotton agricultural context in Brazil," in Angelika Hilbeck, David A. Andow and Eliana M. G. Fontes, eds., *Environmental Risk Assessment of Genetically Modified Organisms: Methodologies for Assessing Bt Cotton in Brazil* (Wallingford: CABI. 2006): 21–66.

consumption in the 1990s to 50% in the 2010s.[32] Almost all of this imported wheat still comes from neighboring Argentina, which has always been Brazil's primary source for this imported product since the nineteenth century.[33]

There was also a significant change in recent years in the value of crops and animal products produced. The once dominant coffee economy is no longer the major force in Brazilian agriculture. As can be seen from the value of crops produced in 2015, coffee has been replaced by soybeans, sugar and corn among crops and is less valuable a product than milk. Seasonal and permanent crops make up 75% of the value of agricultural production, and pastoral products make up 35% of the total gross value by 2015 (see Table 2.3).

All these changes have meant that Brazil was able not only to satisfy internal demand, which resulted in a very significant drop in malnutrition in the country from the 1970s onward, but was also able to export significant quantities of agricultural products to the world market. Even some crops traditionally directed primarily to the local market have recently become significant international exports. The extraordinary growth of productivity in Brazilian agriculture meant that Brazil not only became self-sufficient in almost all food crops and many commercial ones, but that it could become a world powerhouse in the exportation and sale of a wide variety of agricultural products. This despite the fact that infrastructural and tax costs are high by developed-world standards.[34]

Already by the 1970s Brazil was producing an ever rising amount of non-traditional agricultural exports. In 1980, for example, Brazil exported just US$7.4 billion worth of agricultural products, and already had achieved a surplus in its agricultural world trade. In turn this surplus has been growing at a rate of 6.6% per annum

---

[32] Conab, table "Brasil: Oferta e demanda de produtos selecionados" found at www.agricultura.gov.br/vegetal/estatisticas.

[33] Argentina is the principal country supplying agricultural imports to Brazil and accounts for approximately a quarter of all agricultural imports, though this ratio has been slowly declining as local wheat crops increase. In turn cereals – above all wheat flour – are the leading agricultural import to Brazil and accounted for c. 20–25% of the value of all agricultural imports in the second decade of the twenty-first century. Data from MAPA, Agrostat, Estatisticas de Comercio Exterior do Agronegócio Brasileiro, found at http://indicadores.agricultura.gov.br/agrostat/index.htm.

[34] José Roberto Mendonça de Barros, "Prolegômenos. O passado no presente: a visão do economista," in Buainain et al., *O mundo rural no Brasil do século 21*: 15–22.

TABLE 2.3: *Value of all agricultural production by crop and product in 2015 (in billions of R$)*

Product	Gross value	%
Soybeans	113.84	21.5%
Cows	76.94	14.6%
Chickens	53.13	10.1%
Sugarcane	52.71	10.0%
Corn	43.68	8.3%
Milk	29.17	5.5%
Coffee	20.56	3.9%
Pigs	15.55	2.9%
Tomatoes	15.07	2.9%
Cotton	13.87	2.6%
Eggs	12.60	2.4%
Oranges	11.60	2.2%
Rice	10.96	2.1%
Bananas	10.17	1.9%
Beans	8.79	1.7%
Tobacco	7.97	1.5%
Manioc	7.50	1.4%
Potatoes	5.77	1.1%
Others	18.47	3.5%
TOTAL	528.36	100%

Source: MAPA, "Valor Bruto da Produção – Principais Produtos Agropecuários – julho/2016," found at: www.agricultura.gov.br/min isterio/gestao-estrategica/valor-bruto-da-producao

since that date (see Graph 2.1). By 2016 Brazilian agricultural exports reached US$76.9 billion which now represented 42% of the value of all Brazilian exports.[35] In 2015, as in all subsequent

---

[35] The data on Brazilian agricultural trade comes from MAPA, table "Balança Comercial Brasileira e Balança Comercial do Agronegócio: 1989 a 2015," found at www.agricul tura.gov.br/internacional/indicadores-e-estatisticas/balanca-comercial, and WTO, Time Series on International Trade, found at http://stat.wto.org/StatisticalProgram/WSDBSta tProgramHome.aspx.

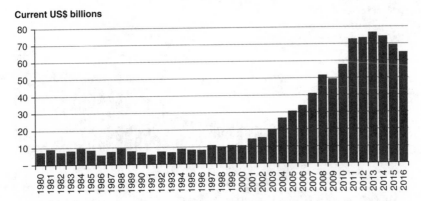

GRAPH 2.1: Balance of international agricultural trade of Brazil, 1980–2016
Source: WTO, Time Series on International Trade, and MAPA, Balança Comercial
do Agronegócio

years, Brazil had the largest positive agricultural trade balance in the
world.[36]

Without question the single product that best represents this new era in
Brazilian agriculture is soybeans. Although Brazil exported small quantities of soybeans from 1950 onward, these exports were of limited quantities and did not include soybean meal or soybean oils. In 1952 for
example it used only 60,000 hectares to produce 29,000 tons of beans.
It was only in 1972 that it began to export soybean meal and it was also in
that year that the bean exports suddenly expanded significantly. Growth
thereafter was explosive (see Graph 2.2). In the crop year 1976/77 some
6.9 million hectares were planted in soybeans, and output was 12 million
metric tons. By 2015 the major zones of production were well defined,
being concentrated in the Center-West, the Cerrado region and the
Southeastern area (see map 2.1).

By the crop year 2016/17 production of soybean is estimated to have
reached 113 million metric tons on some 33.8 million hectares.
Productivity was also systematically increasing in this period, so that
production outpaced land growth, and went from 1,748 kg per hectares
to an estimated 3,338 kg in the harvest of 2016/2017.[37]

[36] Thus already in 2010, Brazil was the world leader and as usual had double the income of
the next most important country. WTO, Time Series on International Trade, found at
http://stat.wto.org/StatisticalProgram/WsdbExport.aspx?Language=E.
[37] Conab, "SOJA – BRASIL, Série Histórica de Produção Safras 1976/77 a 2016/17," found
at http://www.conab.gov.br/conteudos.php?a=1252.

millions of tons

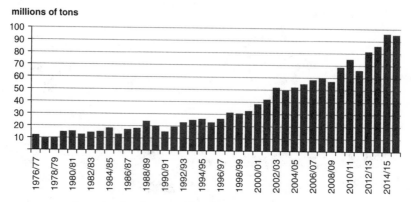

GRAPH 2.2: Growth of soybean production in Brazil,1976/77–2015/16
Source: Conab, "SOJA – BRASI ... 1976/77 a 2016/17"

It was only in 2000 that soybeans finally exceeded soybean meal in export volume, and thereafter it expanded at an ever more rapid pace, reaching 54 million tons of beans in 2015. In turn, soybean meal exports have remained relatively stagnant since that period, averaging between 13 and 14 million tons.[38] In 2015 60% of the beans produced were directly exported and 40% were used to create meal and oil. Brazil consumes 50% of the meal produced and 80% of the soybean oil. This explains why beans in 2015 represented 74% of exports, soybean meal 23% and soybean oil 3%.[39] Also countries like China, which consumed 75% of the soybeans exported by Brazil in 2015, tend to discriminate against processed agricultural products, wanting to do the processing in their own country.

All this growth changed Brazil's role in the international oilseeds market. By the 1980s national production was averaging 16 million tons of beans and at this point it was exporting approximately the same quantity of soybeans as Argentina, which had only recently begun production. By the 1990s production averaged 24 million tons and exports rose to over 5 million tons, and by the first decade of the twenty-first century Brazil surpassed Argentina and became a serious competitor to the United States as world exporter of this product. In the first decade of the new century, production was averaging almost 50 million tons and

[38] IPEADATA, "Exportações – farelo de soja – qde.," "Exportações – soja em grão – qde.," and "Área colhida – soja – Hectare," found at www.ipeadata.gov.br/.
[39] Bradesco/Depec, " Soja, Janiero 2017," in "Setor e Regional/Informações Setoriais," found at www.economiaemdia.com.br.

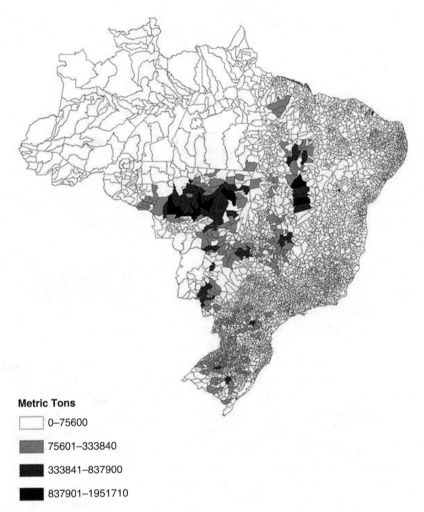

Metric Tons

☐ 0–75600

▨ 75601–333840

■ 333841–837900

■ 837901–1951710

MAP 2.1: Brazilian soybean production 2015 by *município*

exports 20 million tons.[40] By the harvest year 2000/2001 Brazil had passed Argentina and accounted for 22% of world production, but its 39.5 million tons of output was just under half of US production and was second to the US in exports. Five years later in 2005/06 its production was

---

[40] All these data on Brazilian, Argentine and US production and exports are from official statistics reproduced by the UN FAOSTAT and found at http://faostat.fao.org/beta/en/#data/QC.

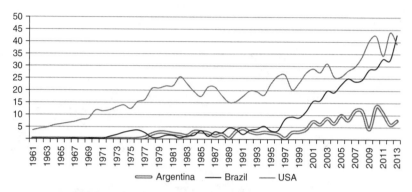

GRAPH 2.3: Volume of soybean exports by Argentina, Brazil and the USA, 1961–2014 (millions of metric tons)
Source: FAOSTAT

only 37% less than the US, but it now equaled the US in total exports. By 2016/2017 it finally reached the total production level of the USA, both now producing just over 100 million tons of soybeans, and in the 2012/13 harvest year it passed the US as the world's leading exporter and by 2016 accounted for 42% of all world exports (see Graph 2.3).[41]

Brazil also experienced a renaissance in sugarcane production and associated products such as ethanol. Although sugar had been the basic export of Brazil from the late sixteenth century, it was replaced by coffee in the early nineteenth century. Nevertheless it remained a fundamental agricultural product in many regions, and Brazil continued to both supply the internal market and engage in some modest exports into the twentieth century. It was then primarily produced in the Northeast. But in the mid-twentieth century, sugar production returned to São Paulo which quickly became the nation's largest producer, going from producing 7% of Brazil's total output in 1931, to a third of national production by the second half of the 1950s. By the late 1980s São Paulo accounted for half of national production and this was up to 60% by the first decades of the twenty-first century. In turn Brazil by mid-twentieth century had emerged as the world's largest producer of sugar by far, and now dominated world production, including the manufacturing of the latest refining technology. Whereas in 1930 it was producing less than 20 million tons of cane, by the 1990s it was growing an average of 296 million tons, which rose to an average of 408 million tons in the first decade of the twenty-first century, and by 2015 cane production reached 666 million tons. This cane when ground produced 33.5 million tons of refined sugar and 30.4 million cubic meters of ethanol. Depending on prices and demand, some 40 to 45% of Brazilian sugarcane goes toward ethanol production and the rest into refined sugar. The 39 million tons of refined sugar Brazil produced in 2016/2017 represented 23% of total world production, and since production exceeded national consumption, it was able to export 28.5 million tons. These sugar exports accounted for 48% of world exports of refined sugar, while Thailand, the second largest exporter, only accounted for 14% of these exports.[42] In terms of value, Brazilian sugar exports were worth US$5.9 billion in 2015, and ethanol exports added another US$880 million.[43] Aside from its dominance in exports, Brazil is also a leader in integrated sugarcane processing plants which can produce either sugar or alcohol. These mills can quickly produce a greater proportion of sugar or alcohol depending on their price and profitability.

In response to the first world petroleum crisis of 1973/1974 the government promoted a Pró-Álcool initiative in 1975 in order to reduce the nation's dependence on imported petroleum. It supported the construction of special refineries near the sugar plantations which produced anhydrous ethanol which was used as an additive to gasoline (which now was required to contain 24% of ethanol), which did not require any change in motor engines.[44] But as a response to the second international oil crisis the government proposed the construction of all-ethanol motors in Brazil and by 1984 some 94% of new cars burned only hydrous ethanol, but decline in world petroleum prices led to the abandonment of ethanol cars by the 1990s, though the government still required anhydrous ethanol in the gasoline mixture. But by the new century the government again became interested in promoting ethanol as a basic fuel, though this time with

---

[42] USDA, FAS, *Sugar: World Markets and Trade*, Nov. 2017.

[43] Ministério da Indústria, Comércio Exterior e Serviços (MDIC), table BCE014, "Exportação Brasileira, Principais Produtos – Ordem Decrescente Janeiro / Dezembro – 2015," found at www.mdic.gov.br/comercio-exterior/estatisticas-de-comercio-exterior/balanca-comercial-brasileira-acumulado-do-ano?layout=edit&id=1185; and Ministério da Agricultura, Pecuária e Abastecimento (MAPA), *Estatísticas e Dados Básicos de Economia Agrícola, Setembro 2016*, p. 37.

[44] This percentage is modified frequently, depending on the availability of ethanol in the market.

special flex motors that could use either ethanol or gasoline and with promotion of the conversion of centrals into integrated mills that could produce either sugar or alcohol. The first such flex motor cars were manufactured in 2002, and by 2009 over 90% of new cars had these engines. All these cars either consumed gasoline mixed with anhydrous ethanol or pure ethanol (hydrous ethanol).[45] These recent changes with flex motors have meant an increasing percentage of ethanol is now hydrous ethanol, which only overtook the production of additive ethanol in 2005 but now makes up over 60% of ethanol production.[46] Ethanol production has expanded so rapidly that Brazil was soon in a position to become the world's second largest exporter of ethanol fuel, selling 7 million gallons of exported fuel compared to the 14.8 million gallons exported by the United States.[47] But US biofuel production, using methanol produced from corn, is estimated by the UN to be relatively stagnant in the coming years, while Brazilian production will be expanding greatly. Thus the United Nations Food and Agriculture Organization (FAO) estimates that Brazilian production, now estimated at half of US ethanol production, will increase to three-quarters of US production by 2024, growing at 3.7% per annum compared to a US growth rate of 0.41%. Brazil is thus expected to go from generating a quarter to almost a third of world ethanol output by that year. Even more significantly its share of world exports will go from 39% today to an estimated 82% by 2024 as most producing countries consume higher ratios of their own production.[48]

Another traditional crop was oranges, which had been grown since the colonial period after their importation from Asia. By the 1970s Brazil was producing on average 114 million boxes of oranges at 40.8 kg per box. By the middle of the decade its output surpassed that of Spain, and Brazil became the second largest world producer after the United States. Then in the early 1980s its production passed that of the United States and was up to 267,000 boxes, which then rose to an average of 397

[45] Gerd Kohlhepp, "Análise da situação da produção de etanol e biodiesel no Brasil," *Estudos Avançados*, 24, no. 68 (2010): 226, 228.

[46] MAPA, *Estatísticas e Dados Básicos de Economia Agrícola, Setembro 2016*, 37.

[47] Renewable Fuels Association data found at www.ethanolrfa.org/resources/industry/statistics/#1454098996479-8715d404-e546.

[48] OECD–FAO, *Commodity Snapshots no. 3: Biofuels*, p. 141, table 3.A1.8, "Biofuel projections: Ethanol," found at www.fao.org/fileadmin/templates/est/COMM_MARKETS_MONITORING/Oilcrops/Documents/OECD_Reports/OECD_biofuels2015_2024.pdf.

million boxes in the 1990s and to 425 million boxes in the early years of the new century. As early as the 1920s Brazil began to export oranges, and the first orange juice factory was established in the country in 1959. By the middle of the 2010s Brazil had over 200,000 bearing trees located on some 600,000 hectares and was producing around 400 million boxes of oranges at 40.8 kg per box, of which 70% came from the state of São Paulo and the triangular area in the neighboring state of Minas Gerais. It exported some 5 million boxes of fresh oranges, mostly to the EU-28 countries.[49] Along with volume, productivity has increased steadily. Improved trees from protected nurseries have enabled Brazilian producers to go from a density of 250 trees per hectare in 1980 to 850 trees per hectare in 2010.[50]

But Brazil's primary export was not fresh oranges, but concentrated orange juice. This began to be exported in 1962, in the year of a massive freeze in Florida that opened up world markets for Brazilian orange juice.[51] Since Brazilians only consume fresh oranges, which absorbed about 30% of national orange production, Brazil was able to turn 70% of fruit production into orange juice, 98% of which could be exported. Given the amount it could produce and export, Brazil has become the dominant world player in the international market. Brazil makes 50% of the world's production of orange juice, but accounts for 85% of the international trade in this juice, since most other producers consume their own output. The state of São Paulo alone produces 53% of the world's orange juice, and Florida and São Paulo together account for 81% of world production.[52] Production was initially dominated by frozen concentrated orange juice, known as FCOJ. But in 2002 Brazil also began to export non-concentrated juice (NFC). This new product required major new investment in processing, storage and delivery overseas and is estimated to cost three times more to produce than an equivalent quantity of frozen concentrated juice.[53] But NFC is better accepted in international markets for its quality and taste, and by the

[49] USDA, FAS, *Brazil, Citrus Annual* (BR15012), December 15, 2015.
[50] Marcos Fava Neves and Vinícuis Gustavo Trombin, eds., *The Orange Juice Business: A Brazilian Perspective* (Wageningen: Wagenigen Academic Publishers, 2011), p. 13.
[51] Christian Lohbauer, "O contencioso do suco de laranja entre Brasil e Estados Unidos na OMC," *Política Externa*, 20 (Sept. 2011): 113.
[52] Marcos Fava Neves, ed., *O Retrato da Citricultura Brasileira* (São Paulo: Elaboração: Markestrat, Centro de Pesquisa e Projetos em Marketing e Estratégia, 2010), no pagination, tables 9 & 10 found at www.citrusbr.com/.
[53] Neves and Trombin, eds., *The Orange Juice Business*, pp. 50–51.

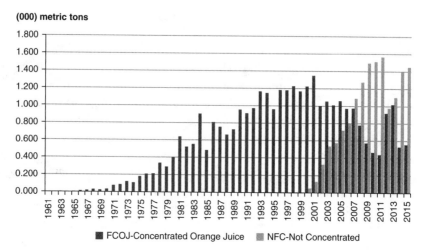

(000) metric tons

■ FCOJ-Concentrated Orange Juice   ▨ NFC-Not Concentrated

GRAPH 2.4: Brazilian exports of orange juice, 1961–2015
Source: FAOSTAT and MDIC table BCE010a for 2014–2015

end of the first decade of the twenty-first century NFC juice had become a significant export and now, with some variation by year, accounts for roughly half of the value of orange juice exports, even though it now makes up less than half of the volume of such exports (see Graph 2.4).[54] In 2015 exports of NFC represented only 28% of the volume of exports but made up 48% of the value of orange juice exports.[55] Moreover, unlike concentrate, which was more widely spread through world markets, NFC is still primarily consumed by Europe (approximately 70%, with North America consuming around 30%).[56]

Another traditional crop which has recently become a major export is corn, which had been produced in Brazil since the colonial period. It was only after 1960, however, that corn experienced an explosive growth

---

[54] Aline Zulian, Andréa Cristina Dörr and Sabrina Cantarelli Almeida, "Citricultura e agronegócio cooperativo no Brasil," Revista Eletrônica em Gestão, Educação e Tecnologia Ambiental,11, no. 11 (Jun. 2013): 2298–2299. Also see Leda Coltro, Anna Lúcia Mourad, Rojane M. Kletecke, Taíssa A. Mendonça and Sílvia P. M. Germer, "Assessing the environmental profile of orange production in Brazil," *International Journal of Life Cycle Assessment*, 14 no. 7 (Nov. 2009): 656.

[55] MDIC, table BCE009a "Exportação brasileira, produto por fator agregado Janeiro / Dezembro," for 2014–2015, found at www.mdic.gov.br/comercio-exterior/estatisticas-de-comercio-exterior/balanca-comercial-brasileira-acumulado-do-ano?layout=edit&id=1185.

[56] Neves and Trombin, eds., *The Orange Juice Business*, p. 29, table 6.

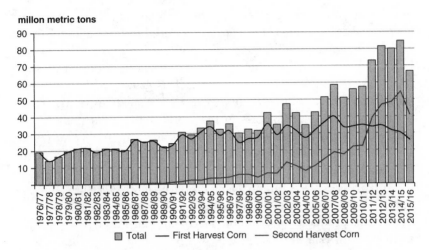

GRAPH 2.5: Total output of first and second harvest corn, 1976/77–2015/16
Source: Conab, Brasil Série Histórica de Produção, Safras 1976/77 a 2015/2016

which far surpassed domestic needs, especially as corn planting entered a
two harvest per annum cycle. This second crop corn production began to
be a serious activity starting in the mid-1990s as farmers planted a second
crop in the harvested fields without clearing the stalks or plowing. This
second harvest finally passed the total volume of first harvest production
in 2011/2012 (see Graph 2.5). The use of a two harvest cycle has enabled
Brazil to overcome its lower productivity per hectare in actual planting,
for example compared to the United States, and to rapidly increase its
volume of exports.

Brazil was a late entrant into international corn markets and remained
a modest importer until the late 1990s. While production increased over
time, almost all the crop was initially consumed in the country. The
dominant world producer and exporter of corn was the United States.
But quickly Brazil emerged as a competitor and by the harvest of 2016/17
Brazilian corn production was only a third less than US production, and it
was now the world's third largest world producer of corn after the United
States and China.[57] Also starting in the early part of the first decade of the
new century, Brazil was able to begin exporting some surplus corn. The
result was a slow and steady growth of its importance in world trade, and

[57] USDA, FAS, *World Agricultural Production*, February 2018, table "World Corn
Production."

Brazil went from being a minor exporter to becoming the second largest exporter after the United States when it replaced Argentina in this role in 2012/2013, going from less than 10% of world exports to well over 20% by the second decade of the century. By the harvest of 2016/2017 it accounted for 22% of world exports.[58] This growth of Brazilian corn exports, combined with the traditional levels of Argentine exports, led to a declining share of US exports in the world market. All this occurred despite the increase demand of the internal Brazilian market for corn as a feedstock for animals, now also being increasingly produced for the international market.

Moreover corn was rapidly being produced more efficiently, and output increased faster than the area dedicated to its production. Thus in 1976 Brazil produced 19.3 million tons of corn on 11.8 million hectares. By the harvest year of 2016/2017 it was producing 66.7 million tons of corn on 15.9 million acres. Thus corn output grew in this period at 3.2% per annum, compared to only 0.8% growth per annum in land dedicated to the crop. In that period productivity is estimated to have gone up from 1,632 kg per hectare to 4,189 kg per hectare.[59] Although grown everywhere in Brazil, major corn production by 2015 was concentrated in the Center-West, the Cerrado region and in the South and Southern states (see Map 2.2).

Along with such seasonal crops as soybeans, corn and sugar, Brazil has even become a significant producer of coarse grains (oats, barley, sorghum, rye and triticale – a mixture of rye and wheat).[60] Although occupying less than 2% of the lands dedicated to seasonal crops and accounting for less than 0.5% of the value of such crops, coarse grain land utilization has been growing at a rate of 3.8% per annum since 1990 and production has increased at 6.6% per annum, going from less than half a million tons in 1990 to 2.9 million tons for these five crops in 2015. Not all of these grains have grown at the same pace. Rye and barley have grown little in this period, whereas oats have gone from 178,000 tons to half a million tons at a growth rate of 4.3% per annum. Even more dramatic is the growth of sorghum, which grew from 236,000 tons in 1990 to 2.1 million in 2015, growth of 9.2% per annum, and is thus one of the fastest-

[58] Ibid., table "World Corn Trade."

[59] Conab, Safras: Séries históricas, "Milho 1ª e 2ª safra," found at www.conab.gov.br/conteudos.php?a=1252&.

[60] This is the OECD definition, see https://stats.oecd.org/glossary/detail.asp?ID=369. The USDA definition also includes corn in in these coarse grains, see USDA, FAS, *Grain: World Markets and Trade*, November 2016.

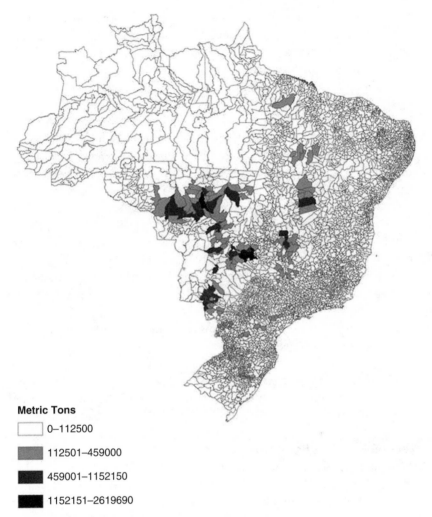

MAP 2.2: Brazilian corn production 2015 by *município*

growing crops in Brazil this period. In contrast, triticale, which only went into production in 2005, has suffered a systematic decline and looks to be a crop that will soon be abandoned in Brazil.[61]

Most of these grains go to national consumption and are sufficient to satisfy local markets. Brazil has been self-sufficient in rye since the 1960s,

---

[61] IBGE, SIDRA, *PAM*, "Tabela 1612 – Área plantada, área colhida, quantidade produzida, rendimento médio e valor da produção das lavouras temporárias," found at https://sidra .ibge.gov.br/tabela/1612.

and while it was still importing oats into the 1990s, it no longer imports that product.[62] But it imports more barley than it produces, consuming 500,000 tons in imports and producing just 186,000 tons in 2015.[63]

What is impressive is that even coffee, the classic export of Brazil throughout most of the nineteenth and twentieth century, still expanded in the post-1960 period, though its value no longer dominated even agricultural exports. As of 2016/2017 Brazil produced 56 million 60 kg sacks of coffee, and exported 35 million sacks, making it the largest year of coffee production and the second largest year of exports after 2015/2016 in Brazilian history. But this large export of coffee beans and soluble coffee, which was worth US$6.1 billion in 2015, only represented 3.2% of the value of all Brazilian exports in that year, and moreover was less than the US$6.2 billion obtained for exports of chicken meat, the US$6.7 billion of sugar and ethanol exports, and the extraordinary US$27.6 billion worth of soybeans and soybean meal exported in 2015.[64]

The two largest exporters of coffee in world markets today, Brazil and Vietnam, concentrate on producing different types of coffee. In 2016/2017 some 81% of the coffee produced in Brazil was Arabica beans, and only 29% was Robusta beans; the opposite was the case in Vietnam, where 96% of total of 27 million Vietnamese coffee beans were of the Robusta variety. The relative importance of Vietnam in world exports was due to the lower internal consumption of its 27 million bag 2015/2016 crop. The Vietnamese consumed 6% of the coffee they produced, whereas Brazil, the world's second largest consumer of coffee, absorbed 48% of that year's crop for internal use.[65] What is also significant about current Brazilian coffee production is that this great increase in total output and subsequent exports since the late 1980s has occurred as the total area planted in coffee trees has declined. Thus in 1961 Brazilian producers needed 4.4 million hectares to produce some 2.2 million tons of coffee, whereas by 2016 producers used less than half that amount of land, or just 1.9 million hectares, to produce 3 million tons of coffee, an historic volume (see Table 2.4).

---

[62] FOASTAT, Trade: Crops and livestock products, found at www.fao.org/faostat/en/#data/TP.

[63] USDA, FAS, *Grain: World Markets and Trade* (December 2016), table "World Barley Trade."

[64] MDIC, table BCE014 "Exportação Brasileira principais produtos – ordem decrescente Janeiro / Dezembro –2015, US$F.O.B. found at www.mdic.gov.br/comercio-exterior/estatisticas-de-comercio-exterior/balanca-comercial-brasileira-mensal?layout=edit&id=1184.

[65] USDA, FAS, *Coffee: World Markets and Trade*, December 2017.

TABLE 2.4: *Area planted in coffee and total production, 1961–2018*

Year	Area hectares	Production tons	Production by area (tons)	Year	Area hectares	Production tons	Production by area (tons)
1961	4,383,820	2,228,704	0.51	1990	2,908,960	1,464,856	0.50
1962	4,462,657	2,190,303	0.49	1991	2,763,440	1,520,382	0.55
1963	4,286,129	1,650,527	0.39	1992	2,500,320	1,294,373	0.52
1964	3,696,281	1,042,013	0.28	1993	2,259,330	1,278,759	0.57
1965	3,511,079	2,294,047	0.65	1994	2,097,650	1,307,289	0.62
1966	3,057,470	1,202,868	0.39	1995	1,869,980	930,135	0.50
1967	2,791,650	1,507,500	0.54	1996	1,920,250	1,369,196	0.71
1968	2,622,885	1,057,700	0.40	1997	1,988,190	1,228,513	0.62
1969	2,570,899	1,283,500	0.50	1998	2,070,410	1,689,366	0.82
1970	2,402,993	754,800	0.31	1999	2,222,925	1,651,852	0.73
1971	2,390,345	1,551,462	0.65	2000	2,267,968	1,903,562	0.84
1972	2,265,695	1,495,705	0.66	2001	2,336,031	1,819,569	0.78
1973	2,079,745	872,897	0.42	2002	2,370,910	2,649,610	1.12
1974	2,155,017	1,615,309	0.75	2003	2,395,501	1,987,074	0.83
1975	2,216,921	1,272,298	0.57	2004	2,368,040	2,465,710	1.04
1976	1,121,015	375,985	0.34	2005	2,325,920	2,140,169	0.92
1977	1,941,473	975,385	0.50	2006	2,312,157	2,573,368	1.11

(continued)

TABLE 2.4: *(continued)*

Year	Area hectares	Production tons	Production by area (tons)	Year	Area hectares	Production tons	Production by area (tons)
1978	2,183,673	1,267,661	0.58	2007	2,264,129	2,249,011	0.99
1979	2,406,239	1,332,772	0.55	2008	2,222,224	2,796,927	1.26
1980	2,433,604	1,061,195	0.44	2009	2,135,508	2,440,056	1.14
1981	2,617,836	2,032,210	0.78	2010	2,159,785	2,907,265	1.35
1982	1,895,486	957,931	0.51	2011	2,148,775	2,700,540	1.26
1983	2,346,007	1,671,588	0.71	2012	2,120,080	3,037,534	1.43
1984	2,505,435	1,420,281	0.57	2013	2,085,522	2,964,538	1.42
1985	2,533,762	1,910,646	0.75	2014	1,947,200	2,720,500	1.40
1986	2,591,461	1,041,406	0.40	2015	1,922,074	2,594,100	1.35
1987	2,875,641	2,202,708	0.77	2016	1,950,678	3,082,151	1.58
1988	2,951,493	1,348,014	0.46	2107	1,863,126	2,698,200	1.45
1989	3,041,387	1,532,335	0.50	2018 (est.)	1,916,145	3,266,484	1.70

Source: FAOSTAT for 1961–2013, Conab for 2014–2018

Another major feature of the agricultural economy was the growth of animal husbandry in this period, particularly cattle, pigs and chickens which began to be a serious export item from the 1980s onward as increasing production surpassed domestic needs and the industry underwent a profound transformation in terms of sanitary conditions and production. In all periods and all regions of Brazil these animals were raised, often on the same farms as commercial and food crops. Locally raised animals had been a part of Brazilian agriculture from the beginning of colonization as most of these species were brought originally by the Portuguese from the Old World and implanted in the Americas. Also a modern meat processing industry was established as early as the 1920s in Brazil, with plants producing fresh, frozen, chilled and canned beef, pork and other animal products for local consumption and export. Many of these so-called *frigoríficos* started with foreign capital, and by 1924 there were already four such factories in São Paulo alone, with the largest being the North American-owned Companhia Armour do Brasil in the city of São Paulo with 700 workers, followed by the Osasco-based Continental Products Company with 600 workers.[66]

Thus local agriculture had been satisfying internal demand for meat and hides from the earliest period, and had even begun to export processed meat early in the twentieth century. But it was only in the past thirty or forty years that modern breeding procedures were systematically introduced and new methods of housing and feeding animals were developed, and the result was both improved productivity and a major increase in the stock of animals without a major increase in land dedicated to pasture. There was also a major shift from natural pastures to planted ones especially as more natural grazing lands were incorporated into commercial crops. Finally there was a systematic increase in the stock of animals. Between 1920 and 2015 the number of cattle grew by a factor of 6, or by 2.2% per annum, those of pigs by 1.1% and chickens by a spectacular 4.8% per annum between 1940 and 2015 (see Graph 2.6). By 2015 the number of cattle had reached a stock of 215 million animals.

Already by 1980 Brazil had the fourth largest cattle herd in the world, with around 90 million cattle. But it was one of the lowest meat exporters in the world, due to serous sanitary problems of its animals. Brazil finally entered as a serious exporter of meat products only after it systematically moved to improve breeds, reduce diseases and modernize its production. This growth of herds and their improvement in health has changed the

---

[66] São Paulo, *Boletim de Indústria e Comércio* BDIC 15, no. 11 (Nov. 1924): 185.

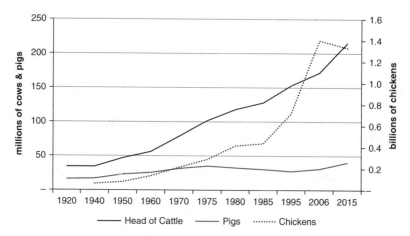

GRAPH 2.6: Growth of stock of animals, 1920–2015
Source: Gasques et.al., "Produtividade Total," table 1, p. 4, and IBGE, SIDRA, table 3939.

position of Brazil as an international exporter of processed beef. As late as 2000, Brazil was only the sixth largest exporter of cattle meat in the world. By 2001 it was the second largest exporter, and by 2004 it was the leading exporter.[67] Its local packing house firms have also become the leaders in the world. Three of the world's largest meatpackers are Brazilian companies, and the largest is JBS, now the world's leading slaughtering company.[68] In 2007 the packinghouse company Friboi bought out the US Swift and changed its name to JBS, becoming the world's largest meat-producing company. In 2009 it bought the second largest producer, Bertin, and increased its market share to 35%. In 2013 it bought Seara Brasil which gave it a major stake in production of chicken meat. The Brazilian meat-packers Minerva and Marfrig – the third and fourth largest in 2007 – also became international companies, and expanded. In 2009 Marfig purchased Margen and Mercosul and then in 2013 it bought Independência (which had been the fifth largest producer in 2007). By 2017 Marfig had become the second largest meat producer in Brazil and the third largest in the

[67] Rodrigo Moita and Lucille Golani, "O oligopsônio dos frigoríficos: uma análise empírica de poder de mercado," *RAC – Revista de Administração Contemporânea*, 18, no. 6 (Oct. 2014): 775.

[68] Fabiana Salgueiro Perobelli Urso, "A cadeia da carne bovina no brasil: uma análise de poder de mercado e teoria da informação" (PhD thesis, Fundação Getúlio Vargas, São Paulo, 2007), pp. 3–4.

world.[69] What is impressive about the export of Brazilian chickens is the role of religiously prepared meat. The first significant export of Brazilian chicken meat in 1975 went primarily to the Middle East, a region which to this day is a major consumer of halal chickens exported from Brazil.[70] By 2015 some 46% of the 3.9 million tons of chicken meat exported by Brazil was halal slaughtered animals, and accordingly the two leading importers of Brazilian chickens were Saudi Arabia and the Emirates.[71] But for all the initial and current successes, sanitation which is dependent on government inspections, has remained a major problem for the industry. In 2017 it was determined that weak inspection standards had led to significant exports of adulterated meats. This resulted in a temporary ban on Brazilian meat imports by JBS and other producers in several major importing countries.[72] Given the importance of Brazilian meat exports in world markets, most of the consuming nations have resumed importation, but with more stringent controls and continued demand that the Brazilian government improve its inspection system. As a result of this crisis and other activities, the owners of JBS have been imprisoned and the company has been forced to sell most of its non-meat activities to preserve the company and for the moment it remains the world's largest company in this area, with ever increasing sales.[73]

With this increased volume and productivity Brazil not only supplied the rapidly growing national population but also began to export animal products, and in fact has now emerged in the second decade of the twenty-first century as the world's leading producer and exporter of beef and veal, recently replacing India and Australia in this role in international commerce, and is now well ahead of Canada and the

---

[69] Moita and Golani, "O oligopsônio dos frigoríficos":775–776; and for the history of Marfig, see http://www.marfrig.com.br/en/marfrig-global-foods/business-unit/marfrig-beef, accessed February 13, 2017.

[70] Frida Liliana Cárdenas Díaz, "Competitividade e coordenação na avicultura de corte: análise de empresas (São Paulo – Brasil e Lima – Peru)" (MA thesis, Universidade Estadual Paulista "Julio de Mesquita Filho," Jaboticabal, 2007), pp. 34–35.

[71] Reported in www.aviculturaindustrial.com.br/imprensa/brasil-domina-as-exportacoes-de-frango-halal/20130426-085601-e600.

[72] See *Veja*, Mar. 17, 2017, " Carne Fraca: entenda o que pesa contra cada frigorífico," found at https://veja.abril.com.br/politica/carne-fraca-entenda-o-que-pesa-contra-cada-frigorifico/.

[73] On its sales and current strategy, see *Veja*, Feb. 10, 2017, "Irmãos Batista vendem quase metade do grupo para preservar a JBS," found at https://veja.abril.com.br/politica/carne-fraca-entenda-o-que-pesa-contra-cada-frigorifico/.

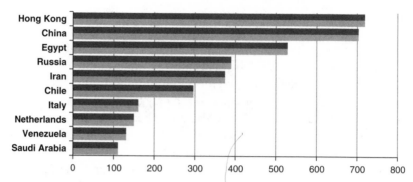

GRAPH 2.7: Value of frozen beef exports by major importing countries, 2016 (in US$ FOB billions)
Source: MDIC, table BCE020a "Exportação Brasileira Principais Produtos e Países – Ordem Decrescente Janeiro / Dezembro – 2015 / 2016"

United States. The number of cattle slaughtered went from 1.3 million in the 1960s to an average of 9 million according to the United Nations Food and Agriculture Organization (FAO) in the 2010s.[74] This slaughtering reflects a major growth in the stock of animals. In 1974, for example, Brazil had 92 million head of cattle and 203,000 Asian water buffalos. By 2016, the cattle numbered 218 million and the water buffalo 1.3 million.[75]

Brazil consumes 80% of what it produces, but was still able to export 1.9 million tons of beef in 2016, which makes it a very close second to India, currently the world's largest exporter of beef products.[76] As the volume of exports increased, the principal importing countries came from all regions of the world. In 2016 for example, the principal importers of Brazilian beef were China, Egypt and Russia (see Graph 2.7). In contrast to other agricultural exports, meat was also an important import for

---

[74] In this and all other animal slaughtering figures for Brazil, we have used the FAO data, which is estimated. The official data given by IBGE is consistently less than the official IBGE data, probably because, as IBGE notes "the data given [by IBGE] are based only on federal, state or municipally inspected establishments." See www.ibge.gov.br/home/esta tistica/indicadores/agropecuaria/producaoagropecuaria/abate-leite-couro-ovo s_201503_1.shtm.

[75] IBGE, SIDRA, *Pesquisa Pecuária Municipal* (hereafter *PPM*), table 3939 "Efetivo dos rebanhos, por tipo de rebanho," found at https://sidra.ibge.gov.br/pesquisa/ppm/tabelas.

[76] USDA, FAS, "Livestock and Poultry: World Markets and Trade," April 2017.

several Latin American countries, as well as Middle Eastern and even European ones.[77]

While Brazil now exports a number of beef products including casings, offal and salted beef, over 94% of the value of beef exports is processed meats and fresh animals. In the late 1990s these two sectors were exporting under 300,000 tons of meat per annum, by 2002 they were up to half a million tons and since 2004 their annual volume has remained well over a million tons. The value of these exports went from less than US$1 billion in the late 1970s to over US$5 billion by the second decade of the new century. In turn fresh beef started by accounting for half the value of meat exports and ended by reaching over 80% of the total value of such exports in the late 2010s.[78]

The growth in the production of poultry, above all of chickens, has been one of the most spectacular of the new export products, and poultry exports are currently more valuable than all meat exports. Slaughtered chicken meat went from annual production of under 300,000 tons in the 1960s to over 5 million tons by the second half of the first decade of the twenty-first century. It was only in the late 1970s that the volume of processed chicken meat passed the 1 million ton mark, finally reaching 12.5 million tons in 2014. As of 1974 the stock of chickens in Brazil was only 274 million animals, of which 41% were hens producing eggs, and by 2016 the stock of chickens in Brazil had reached 1.3 billion animals of which only 17% were hens.[79]

All this increasing production far exceeded local needs, and thus significant exports began by the late 1990s. In 1997 Brazil accounted for 12% of the world export market, and was the third largest exporter after the US and the European Union. But by 2016 Brazil had become the world leader in the production and export of broiler meats (mostly chickens – *frangos de corte*). It produces 15% of total world production, or 14 million tons, consumes 9.6 million tons and is expected to export 4.4 million tons in 2016/2017, which represents 38% of total world exports and is four times greater than its nearest competitor which are the

[77] MDIC, table BCE020A "Exportação Brasileira Principais Produtos e Países – Ordem Decrescente Janeiro / Dezembro – 2015/2016," found at www.mdic.gov.br/comercio-e xterior/estatisticas-de-comercio-exterior/series-historicas.

[78] MDIC, table "Grupos de Produtos: Exportação (Janeiro 1997 – Outubro 2016)," found at www.mdic.gov.br/comercio-exterior/estatisticas-de-comercio-exterior/series-historicas.

[79] IBGE, SIDRA, *PPM*, table 3939.

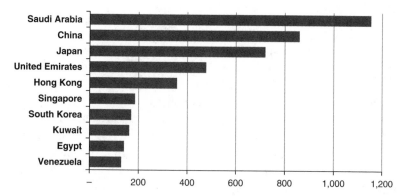

GRAPH 2.8: Value of exports of chicken fresh & frozen by major importing countries, 2016 (in US$ billions)
Source: MDIC, table BCE020a "Exportação Brasileira Principais Produtos e Países – Ordem Decrescente Janeiro / Dezembro – 2015/2016"

countries of the European Union.[80] It was the fifth most valuable export of Brazil, producing US$5.9 billion in exports in 2016, in contrast to the value of all beef exports, which reached just US$4.3 billion in that year.[81] In contrast to the mix of beef products in exports, from the beginning fresh chicken meat accounted for well over 90% of the volume and value of all chicken exports. The export of chicken meat went from just half a million tons in the late 1990s to over 3 million being exported by the late 2010s.

Whereas Brazilian meat exports were well distributed throughout the world, most of these chicken exports went to very specific regions of the world. Except for Venezuela most American and European countries were able to satisfy their own needs. In 2015, all the principal countries importing Brazilian chickens were Middle Eastern or Asian nations (see Graph 2.8).

Currently most of the industry of production of chickens for slaughter is an integrated market, with the factories entering into long-term contracts to buy the eggs and chickens from individual farmers, rather than buying them on the open market. This so-called vertical system had its origins in the United States where it developed in the middle of the twentieth century and was first adopted by the poultry industry in Santa

---

[80] USDA, FAS, "Livestock and Poultry: World Markets and Trade," October 2016.
[81] MDIC, table BCE020 "Exportação Brasileira Principais Produtos e Países – Ordem Decrescente Janeiro/Dezembro – 2015 US$ F.O.B."

Catarina by the giant meatpacker Sadia in 1960.[82] It has since become the norm in São Paulo as well.[83] In this system the processors offer animal feed and other inputs necessary to produce the broiler chickens which must be sold to the packinghouse.[84] Key to the development of the poultry industry in Brazil was the provision of cheap feedstock due to the boom in Brazilian soybean and corn production in the last quarter of the twentieth century. Soybean meal and corn were the primary food for the birds. This, combined with breeding of new strains of animals, permitted the industry to reduce the time of growing chickens for slaughter from 100 to 40 days and more than double the weight of the animals from 1.5 kg to 2.4 kg.[85]

Finally pork production grew significantly in the post-1960 period. The generation of pig meat went from an average of 9 million tons in the 1960s to an average of 35 million tons by the 2010s. By the beginning of the twentieth century Brazil was producing 2.6 million tons of pig meat and consuming almost 2 million tons, which left it a modest export of 590,000 tons, being well behind European Union and Canadian exports.[86] As in other meat products, this new level of production more than satisfied local markets and enabled Brazil to become a significant producer and exporter of pork, and by 2016 it had some 40 million pigs and by 2016 it was exporting over 900,000 tons of swine products and had become the world's third leading exporter after the EU and Canada.[87]

Non-meat-producing animals have varied patterns of growth in this period. Thus the number of milk cows has almost doubled in size in the forty-one-year period between 1974 and 2016, going from 10.8 million to

---

[82] Carlos Nayro Coelho and Marisa Borges, "O complexo Agro-industrial (CAI) da Avicultura," *Revista de Política Agrícola*, 8, no. 3 (1999): 5.

[83] Although this is an important support for growers, Martins argues that it has its negative aspects in that the relationship is asymmetrical as the packinghouses for chicken meat have become highly concentrated and just four of them dominate the market. See Sonia Santana Martins, "Cadeias produtivas do frango e do ovo: avanços tecnológicos e sua apropriação"(PhD thesis, Fundação Getúlio Vargas, São Paulo, 1996), pp. 11–12 .

[84] Antonio Carlos Lima Nogueira and Décio Zylbersztajn, "Coexistência de arranjos institucionais na avicultura de corte do estado de São Paulo" (Working Paper 03/22; USP–Faculdade de Economia, Administração e Contabilidade, 2003), accessed February 11, 2017, at. www.fundacaofia.com.br/PENSA/anexos/biblioteca/1932007111943_03-022.pdf.

[85] Coelho and Borges, "O complexo Agro-industrial (CAI) da Avicultura": 3.

[86] USDA, FAS, "Livestock and Poultry: World Markets and Trade" November 2006.

[87] USDA, FAS, "Livestock and Poultry: World Markets and Trade" October 2016; and IBGE, 'Tabela 1 – Efetivo dos rebanhos em 31.12 e variação anual, segundo as categorias – Brasil – 2014–2015."

19.7 million animals.[88] Egg-laying hens have also increased from 113 million to 219 million in this period and finally there has been a major growth of quails, which have gone from less than half a million to 22 million animals in this same period, and their egg production has become an important pastoral product.[89] But the herds of other animals have either changed only moderately in the period from 1975 to 2016 or have declined significantly. Pigs remain in the 30–35 million range, with some modest fluctuations. Goats have had some modest growth, but with fairly large variations by decades, and fluctuate between 9 and 10 million animals. While all sheep have remained relatively stable at around 18 million animals, wool-bearing sheep have actually declined from 12.3 million in 1974, to just 3.3 million animals in 2016,[90] which explains the long-term decline of wool production.

Other major products of the pastoral industry are milk, butter, eggs and cheese most of which were primarily produced for the local market. Although Brazilian production of milk is impressive by world standards and accounts for 75% of the value of all animal products (that is milk, eggs, honey, sheep's wool and silk worms), it is not a significant exporter of this product due to its low productivity by world standards. As of December 2016, Brazil had 17.4 million milk cows, the largest number in the western hemisphere, and the third largest herd of milk cows in the world, behind India and the European Union. Brazil thus accounted for 12% of the total world's milk cows. It currently produces 35 million metric tons of milk, up from just 5 million tons in 1961.[91] At the same time, productivity has doubled from 7,068 hectograms per animal in 1961.[92] But this is still below even South American producers like Argentina and Uruguay. Most of this milk is consumed in the country and while it has begun to export milk products, it is a net importer of milk products from other countries. The primary output of the industry is whole milk, although 2.2 million tons of skimmed milk was produced in 2013 along with 57,000 tons of condensed milk.[93] Brazil only began to export whole milk powder in 2013, and by 2016 was exporting some 41,000 tons of it, but at the same time it also imported 55,000 tons of this product in 2016 as well as importing another 35,000 tons of non-fat dry

---

[88] IBGE, SIDRA, *PPM*, table 94.   [89] Ibid., table 3939.   [90] Ibid., table 95.
[91] IBGE, "Tabela 74 – Produção de origem animal, por tipo de produto," found at https://sidra.ibge.gov.br/tabela/74; and FAOSTAT, Livestock Processed, found at www.fao.org/faostat/en/#data/QP.
[92] FAOSTAT, Livestock Processed.   [93] Ibid.

milk.[94] Brazil is also the hemisphere's second largest producer of butter, with some 92,000 tons produced in 2011, but in cheese production it was a relatively minor producer compared to several other Latin American countries. The 45,000 tons it made in 2011 was less than a third of Mexican production in that year and well behind the quantity of cheese produced in Colombia and Chile.[95]

As could be expected, since Brazil was the world's leading exporter of chickens, it also had some 219 million hens producing an estimated 3.8 billion dozens of eggs in 2016.[96] Overall Brazil is the world's seventh largest egg producer, just behind Mexico.[97] But it appears that eggs are not a significant export. Another egg product is quail eggs, which also are primarily consumed domestically. Their production has grown by 12.5% per annum between 1974 and 2016 and Brazil now produces 273 million dozens of eggs.[98] There are also several other animal products that have become important parts of the Brazilian agro-economy. In 2016 Brazil produced 40,000 tons of honey.[99] This placed it among the top five producers in the world. Significant exports of honey only began in this century, but already by the second decade of the century Brazil was exporting two-thirds of national output. By 2016 it was ninth largest exporter of honey in the world.[100]

While there has been a production explosion of numerous traditional and new agricultural crops and pastoral products since the 1990s, the opening up of Brazil's market to world competition has meant that some products were no longer competitive, or plagues and other natural disasters have slowed or even eliminated once quite important crops, leading farmers to shift to more profitable crops. Thus, for example, silkworm production was in a major spurt of growth from 1974, but peaked in 1993 and has been in severe decline ever since, dropping to 16% of the peak

[94] USDA, FAS, *Dairy: World Markets and Trade*, July 2016; and FAOSTAT, Livestock Primary, found at www.fao.org/faostat/en/#data/QL.

[95] FAO, *Statistical Yearbook 2014: Latin America and the Caribbean – Food and Agriculture*, p. 118, table 34.

[96] IBGE, SIDRA, *PPM*, table 74; and IBGE, "Tabela 1 – Efetivo dos rebanhos em 31.12 e variação anual, segundo as categorias – Brasil – 2014-2015," and "Tabela 2 – Quantidade e valor dos produtos de origem animal e variação anual – Brasil – 2014-2015," found at www.ibge.gov.br/home/estatistica/economia/ppm/2015/default_xls_brasil.shtm.

[97] FAO *Statistical Pocketbook 2015*, p. 30.   [98] IBGE, SIDRA, *PPM*, table 74.

[99] Ibid.

[100] ABEMEL – Associação Brasileira dos Exportadores de Mel, accessedNovember 2, 2018, at http://brazilletsbee.com.br/INTELIG%C3%8ANCIA%20COMERCIAL%20ABE MEL%20-%20DEZEMBRO.pdf.

production in 2016. Nevertheless it is the only commercial producer of silk in the Western world.[101] This is a pattern also seen in sisal hemp production, which went into such a severe decline that it no longer appears to be anything more than a quite marginal product even in its home in the Northern region. Cacao also shows some of this same pattern of boom and bust, though there has recently been some recovery of production. Thus despite its decline, cacao bean production is still a valuable crop (around 4–5% of total agricultural production), yet it has shown no increase in productivity and went into a long-term secular decline from 1990 to 2001 due to the impact of plant diseases. Even despite the recent growth, current output is still two-fifths below its 1990 production.[102]

But there are others traditional crops which have revived after a severe decline, or keep producing even with limited increase in productivity, and some which have achieved ever higher yields per hectare even though producing for just the internal market. Finally there are several which have gone through long periods of secular decline to re-emerge as major agricultural products. One example of a revival among the group of traditional crops is natural rubber, which of course was a boom product in the late nineteenth and early twentieth century and again for a short time during the Second World War. But it has experienced a major growth in the past twenty-five years, doubling the area of trees being exploited, increasing productivity per hectare and going from producing 24,000 tons of rubber latex in 1990 to collecting 316,000 tons in 2016.[103] Cotton is another significant crop which has recently had a revival. While Brazil was a major producer in the nineteenth and early twentieth century, production has varied considerably, with periods of steep decline followed by temporary boom periods. Recently, in the 1990s, there was a severe decline, again due to diseases. But in the new century productivity has increased to three times what it was in 1990, leading to a decline in total land devoted to its cultivation, with production going from 1.8 million tons to 3.4 million tons in 2016.[104] This growth has permitted Brazil to become a significant exporter of cotton, since it consumes only half its national production. Thus in the

[101] Conab. Indicadores da Agropecuária, Brasília, Ano XXV, n. 10, out. 2016, p. 7. Brazil exported 440 tons in 2015, with revenues of US$33 million.
[102] IBGE, SIDRA, *PAM*, table 1613.
[103] Data for these crops found in IBGE, SIDRA, *PAM*, table 1613 at https://sidra.ibge.gov .br/tabela/1613; and IBGE, SIDRA, *PAM*, table 1612.
[104] IBGE, SIDRA, *PAM*, table 1612.

crop year 2015/16, Brazil was the third leading exporter of cotton in the world.[105] Surprisingly, its yield per hectare is higher than that of the United States.[106]

A traditional internal consumption crop which has done extremely well in the recent period is bananas, which since 1990 have increased productivity from 1,128 kg per hectare in the former year to 14,380 kg per hectare in 2015. This has led to an average growth of the banana crop by a factor of 12 from 1990 to 2016 for a growth rate of 11% per annum, yet total land devoted to bananas has remained the same, at around half a million hectares during the entire period. Beans, a seasonal crop, have also seen an extraordinary increase in yield, from 477 kg per hectare to 1,079 kg per hectare in the same twenty-five-year period. At the same time the land devoted to the crop has declined by a million hectares, just as output increased by a million tons. But given the increasing value of some of the export crops, its share of the value of total agricultural production has declined from 6% to 2% in this same period. This same pattern is evident in other traditional crops devoted to the internal market. This is the case with rice. Rice has increased output at 2% per annum in this twenty-five-year period, its yield per hectare has increased by a factor of 3 in the same period, yet its current output of 12 million tons is worth only 4% of total agricultural output, which is half of what it was worth in 1990.[107]

Traditionally Brazil has been a significant exporter of tropical and non-tropical woods. In recent years, however, it has become an ever growing source of processed wood pulp and paper for the world economy. Brazil's vast forestry reserve has always been a source for exotic woods from the colonial period to the present day. Brazilian such woods were even used in the seventeenth and early eighteenth century in Stradivarius violins. But only since the 1980s and 1990s has there been a systematic attempt to create man-made forests for the production of wood and pulp products by modern manufacturing facilities. The resulting cellulose industry has grown so rapidly recently that Brazil is now the world's second largest exporter of wood pulp and the first in the world for the production of kraft papers (produced from

---

[105] USDA, FAS, *Cotton: World Markets and Trade Nov 2016* "Table 02 Cotton World Supply, Use, and Trade (Season Beginning August 1) (1000 Bales)."
[106] Ibid., "Table 04 Cotton Area, Yield, and Production."
[107] IBGE, SIDRA, *PAM*, table 1612.

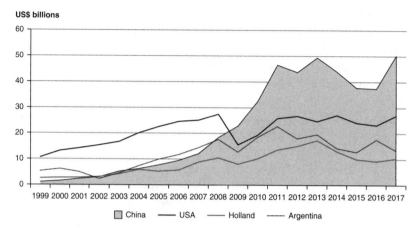

US$ billions

GRAPH 2.9: Value of Brazilian exports to the four leading importing countries, 1999–2017
Source: MDIC, table BCE020 for various years at http://www.mdic.gov.br/comer cio-exterior/estatisticas-de-comercio-exterior

bleached sulfate pulp).[108] Brazil accounts for 12% of world production of wood pulp for paper and paperboard in 2014, and ranks second in the world, just behind the USA. But as of 2013 it ranks first in exports of this product, accounting for 17% of world exports in this year. In paper and paperboard it accounts for 5% of world production capacity and is the world's fourth largest producer.[109] Brazil produces "short-fiber" cellulose pulp mostly from eucalyptus trees. This pulp is used to make such things as newsprint, diapers and banknotes. The "long-fiber" pulp comes primarily from pine trees and is used for high-grade paper and packaging. Whereas in other countries the pine tree is the primary source of cellulose, in Brazil the primary tree is the eucalyptus, which takes only seven years to produce.[110] Since the 1960s cellulose production has grown at 7.5% per annum, and paper and cardboard production at 6% per annum, both rates well above the rate of increase in world

[108] Fernanda Queiroz Sperotto, "A expansão do setor de celulose de mercado no Brasil: condicionantes e perspectivas," *Indicadores Econômicos FEE (Porto Alegre)*, 41, no. 4 (2014): 86.
[109] FAO, *Pulp, Paper and Paperboard Capacity Survey 2013–2018*, pp. 33, 64; and for the export ranking see FAO, *Forest Products 2009–2013*, p. A-5.
[110] "Pulp producers in Brazil: Money that grows on trees," *The Economist*, Mar. 26, 2016.

production.[111] Much of this growth has come in the more recent period, with paper and chemically bleached pulp accounting for most of this growth. Brazil today has 1.7 million hectares of trees planted for industrial purposes, of which 78% are eucalyptus trees and 19% are pines. Brazil was in fact a pioneer in the use of eucalyptus to produce cellulose. It imported the trees from Australia and after considerable research by local agronomists it adapted them to the local conditions for the efficient production of cellulose. Brazilian factories now produce 12.8 million tons of cellulose and export seven million tons, primarily to the EU countries. It also produces 9.1 million tons of paper, of which it exports 1.9 million tons, most of which goes to Latin America.[112] In 2017 cellulose exports were worth US$6.4 billion and ranked seventh in value among total Brazilian exports. The primary consumers of Brazilian cellulose exports were China, which took 40% of its exports, followed by the USA, the Netherlands and Italy – the four countries accounting for 77% of the total.[113]

The dynamic growth of a complex agricultural pastoral and forestry production, along with mineral exports, has led to major changes in the principal trading partners of Brazil. For almost a century the leading consumer of most Brazilian exports was the United States, largely due to its massive consumption of Brazilian coffee. But China has now emerged as the principal trading partner of Brazil. The Netherlands consistently took about 5–6% of the total exports, while the Argentine share was more varied and ranged between 7 and 11%, though slowly declining over time. But Chinese imports from Brazil rose quite dramatically from only 1% of Brazil's US$48 billion exports in 1999, to 13% of the US$153 billion worth of Brazilian exports by 2009, the year it replaced the US as Brazil's most important trading partner. The US share of Brazilian exports has now fallen to usually half of the value of Brazilian exports to China. By 2017 China accounted for 22% of all Brazilian exports compared to only 12% for the United States (see Graph 2.9). Moreover China was the

---

[111] Marcio Funchal, "Panorama mundial do setor de celulose, papel e papelão," *Painel Florestal*, July 4, 2014.

[112] Diniscor Agribusiness, "Industry of paper, cellulose and forest products," data found at http://diniscor.com.br/agronegocio/en/index.php/about-brazil/item/128-industry-of-paper-and-cellulose-and-forest-products.html.

[113] Data for 2017 is found in MDIC, *Balança comercial: Janeiro–dezembro 2017*, section III "Principais produtos e países," accessed at www.mdic.gov.br/index.php/comercio-exterior/estatisticas-de-comercio-exterior/balanca-comercial-brasileira-acumulado-do-ano?layout=edit&id=3056.

principal buyer of almost all the major export products. In that year it consumed 79% of Brazil's soybean exports, 54% of its mineral exports, and even 44% of its petroleum products.[114]

Between them, the EU-28, China, the USA and the Russian Federation account for over 50% of all Brazilian agricultural exports. The EU-28 was the dominant importing "nation" until 2013, when China became the principal recipient of Brazilian agricultural exports. Between them, China, the EU-28 countries, the USA and the Russian Federation together took about 70% of the value of all agro exports, with several states of the Middle East and Asia, along with the unique case of Venezuela, accounting for the rest, with each nation taking on average just 1 or 2% of the total Brazilian exports. Also there were considerable variations due to changes in tariffs, defense of local industries, outright prohibitions – usually of meats for sanitation or other reasons – and reduction in local national production – all could affect which countries consumed Brazilian agricultural exports and the level of their consumption.

When we refine the breakdown of Brazilian agricultural exports within individual countries, certain general patterns emerge. Although the American republics were major trading partners of Brazil, most of Brazil's agricultural exports went to Europe, the Middle East and Asian countries. American countries rather were major importers of minerals, airplanes and manufactured parts for vehicles and other Brazilian-made machinery, and, except for Venezuela, not significant importers of Brazil's agricultural products since they were all major agricultural producers themselves. This explains why only 11% of exports to the USA, and 9% of those to Chile were agricultural products. On the other hand, over half of China's imports from Brazil were made up of agricultural products, and many of the other Asian countries had a significant portion of their Brazilian imports made up of agricultural goods, usually over half of the total value of imports. In the exceptional case of Russia and Vietnam, agricultural imports made up over 85% of the total value of goods coming from Brazil.[115]

Given this history of agricultural production, Brazil itself imports relatively little in the way of agricultural products. Moreover agricultural imports have grown slowly over time, well below the rate of increase in exports. The prime import has been wheat from Argentina

---

[114] Data for 2017 is found in ibid.
[115] MDIC, table BCE018: "Exportação Brasileira Principais Países e Produtos," accessed at www.mdic.gov.br/component/content/article?layout=edit&id=1185.

and to a lesser extent from Uruguay. This has been the case since the nineteenth century and explains the consistently important share of imports coming from Argentina. Even to this day Argentina leads in imports, accounting for a fifth of the value, followed by the EU-28, the USA and now by China. For ecological reasons, the tropical and semi-tropical climate of Brazil makes it less viable to produce a temperate crop such as wheat, hence the traditional dependence of Brazil on neighboring Argentine imports.

The second largest food import in 2015 was non-toasted malt, processed from Barley, followed by Atlantic salmon. These two products along with wheat imports were valued at US$2.3 billion, or just 1.7% of the total value of all imports. Machines and fuels were the big import items.[116] In the current decade, the overall average of food imports in Brazil is between 2% and 3% of the total value of Brazilian commodity imports.[117]

After this recent and rapid growth of Brazilian agriculture, the question is what can be expected in the next decade. The Ministry of Agriculture recently offered a series of projections about the changing mix of products generated by national farms. They estimate (low estimate projections) that farmland devoted to the 15 major grains (which include cotton, peanuts, rice, oats, canola, rye, barley, beans, sunflower, castor bean, corn, soybeans, sorghum, wheat and triticale) will increase by 1.5% per annum between the crop years 2016/2017 and 2026/27. But production will increase even faster, by 2.6% per annum.[118] Only three of these major grains, corn, soybeans and wheat, will continue to expand their use of farm lands, whereas the other principal grains such as rice and beans will decline. It is estimated that the three expanding grains (corn, soybeans and wheat) currently use 91% of all lands devoted to these grain crops, and their share will increase to 96% in the next decade, with the amount of land devoted to rice and beans systematically declining.[119] Interestingly the Ministry of Agriculture projections assume that there will be relatively

[116] MDIC, "Importação Brasileira Principais Produtos, PPIMP 2014–2015," found at www.mdic.gov.br/comercio-exterior/estatisticas-de-comercio-exterior/base-de-dados-do-comercio-exterior-brasileiro-arquivos-para-download.

[117] FAOSTAT, Brazil, Country Indicators, "Value of food imports over total merchandise exports," found at http://www.fao.org/faostat/en/?#country/21.

[118] MAPA, *Projeções do Agronegócio – Brasil 2016/17 a 2026/27* (Brasilia, August, 2017), p. 17. Produtos considerados: algodão, amendoim, arroz, aveia, canola, centeio, cevada, feijão, girassol, mamona, milho, soja, sorgo, trigo e triticale.

[119] MAPA, *Projeções*, p. 18, table 3.

little change in productivity of soybeans per hectare, but that yield per hectare for rice will increase by an extraordinary 7.8% per annum and for cotton by 2.7% and for corn by 1.8% per annum.[120] In terms of animal production, it assumes that between 2016/17 and 2026/27, chicken production will grow at 2.9% per annum to 17.8 million tons, with pigs growing at 2.6% per annum to 4.9 million tons and bovine meat at just 1.9% per annum and 11.4 million tons by the end of the coming decade. While the growth of the national population means that meat consumption of all kinds will increase domestically, the ministry estimates that export growth will exceed national consumption and exports will grow by over 3.2% per annum for all three types of meat, resulting in 5.9 million tons of chicken meat exports, 1.3 million tons of pork meat and 2.4 million tons of *carne bovina*.[121]

Cellulose production, the fourth most important agricultural export, is also estimated to grow. In 2000 there was produced 71.7 million cubic meters of lumber, and in 2013 this had increased to 130.8 million cubic meters, with the non-frontier regions of the South and Southeast accounting for 81% of this production in that same year. In 2016/17 cellulose production was 20,000 tons, with exports of 13,900 tons. For 2026/27 it is estimated that total production will reach 26,300 tons, with an annual growth of 2.8%. It is projected that exports of 19,100 tons in that year, which will represent annual growth of 3.3% in the period. Exports will thus represent 73% of Brazilian production.[122]

But all this growth of domestic production does not translate into an increased share of exports for the world market. A recent ten-year projection of the US Department of Agriculture (USDA) estimates that by 2025/2026 Brazil will increase its role in export markets in only three products: soybeans, which by then will account for 48% of world exports; poultry, which will increase to 45% of world exports, from a current 42%; and cotton, to 17% of world exports from the current 12%. Only in soybeans and poultry is Brazil certain to remain the predominant producer, and probably in sugar, oranges and coffee as well – products not estimated by the USDA projections since the United States is not a serious competitor in these products. Because of increased consumption within Brazil, soybean oil is expected to decline to just 9% of the world market from its current 14%, and soybean meal

---

[120] Ibid., p. 19, table 4.   [121] Ibid., p. 65, table 17, and p. 70, table 19.
[122] Ibid., p. 73, table 20.

exports will grow more slowly than national consumption, so that Brazil would remain the same at approximately 24% of world trade. In contrast, the Brazilian Ministry of Agriculture (MAPA) and the Organization for Economic Cooperation and Development (OECD)–FAO estimates suggest that Brazil will produce 25% of total world soybean production, and USDA suggests that its exports will be almost double that ratio. Brazilian corn exports, which will be growing at an estimated 4.2% per annum, are nevertheless expected by USDA to remain at the same rate of one-fifth of world exports. By 2025, the OECD estimates that world corn production will only grow by 1.4%, whereas Brazilian output will increase by 2.4% per annum and will represent about 9% of total world production. Brazil, which now accounts for 20% of world raw sugar production, will increase that share to 22%.[123]

Thus increasing world production in other regions of the world will affect future Brazilian agricultural exports, just as increasing population growth and consumption at home will reduce the role of Brazil in some of these major export crops. Just how little of total production enters the world market has been calculated by the OECD which estimates that only 11% of the chickens and 12% of the corn produced in 2025 will be available for export by Brazil. In contrast, it estimates that one-third of sugar production, and 41% of all soybeans produced in that year will enter international trade.[124] Another set of estimated projections made by the MAPA suggest that by 2026/2027 some 30% of the corn produced, 58% of the soybeans, 87% of the sugar and a third of the chickens will be available for export.[125] Given changing climate and market conditions it is difficult to determine which of these estimates will be proven true. But all suggest that growth will continue and that Brazil will still be a very important world player in the international agricultural market through the next decade.

As this rapid survey has shown, Brazil has only recently entered the world market as a major agricultural producer and exporter in a wide

---

[123] USDA *Long-Term Projections, February 2016*, tables 26, 27, 32–38; share of world production comes from MAPA, *Projeções*, pp. 33 and 55, tables 8 and 15; and "OECD–FAO Agricultural Outlook 2016–2025, by commodity," accessed at http://stats.oecd.o rg/index.aspx?queryid=71240.

[124] OECD–FAO *Agricultural Outlook 2016–2025* (Paris, 2016), p. 44, figure 1.10.

[125] MAPA, *Projeções*: 65 table 17; 70 table 19. These numbers differ from the OECD projections, but given their origin is the government of Brazil, we think these more reliable.

range of products. Only sugar and coffee were traditional exports, and even sugar had known periods of relative decline from the late nineteenth century until most recently. As many commentators have noted, Brazil has been unique in the rapidity of its recent agricultural growth compared to the rest of the world. But its transition to a modern agricultural powerhouse is now assured and it will remain one of the world's most important agricultural nations for the foreseeable future. But it should be stressed that this national production came from a small selection of farms and from very specific districts, states and regions, with large parts of agricultural activity still subsistence-based and with large parts of the country only recently and partially incorporated into the commercial sector as modern agricultural production spread to more traditional areas of the country. Thus it is essential to examine this extraordinary revolution in agriculture at the regional, state and local level to fully appreciate and understand the patterns of change which have occurred.

3

Causes for the Modernization of Brazilian Agriculture

How did this dramatic growth of agriculture after 1960 occur, given the negative events which occurred in the 1980s and 1990s? This is basic question we will analyze in this chapter. There is little question that the collapse of government support in the 1980s and the opening of the national economy to world trade in the 1990s forced a profound and wrenching reorganization of the national economy. Of the two major areas of systematic government support in the previous decades, industry and agriculture, only agriculture survived the shock, prospered and in turn became competitive in the international market. This is a surprising result which has many causes, internally and internationally, but which is also explained by a series of policies, institutions and external events which had a profound effect on Brazilian agriculture from the late 1960s until the late 1990s. These factors included the introduction of state-subsidized agricultural credits on a massive scale, government price supports, the impact of the international oil crises, the growth of modern supermarkets, the entrance of foreign trading companies, the development of a national and foreign-based agricultural industrial system, the enormous growth of the Chinese market, and the impact of scientific research on Brazilian soils and plants carried out by Embrapa, the public enterprise of agricultural research created in 1973. It was also due to an extraordinarily entrepreneurial class of farmers who came to dominate national agriculture mostly under the leadership of southern and southeastern farmers who had to overcome a harsh economic and competitive environment, lack of government support and would do so by creating what has called their own "value chains." These were vertical and horizontal organizations organized by these farmers to collectively reduce costs, compensate for lack of agricultural extension programs, and enable farmers to quickly apply the latest technology to their fields and those of their cooperative or association members. This even led to value chains organized by new selective membership coops based on new cooperative models as well as the traditional ones, along with processors, trading companies and other corporations providing farmers with inputs and support in return for purchases of the resulting farm products.[1]

To understand the process of modernization of Brazilian agriculture, we can divide the period into two distinct phases. In the first phase, agriculture maintained a fundamental importance in the generation of exports and, at the same time, it supplied the local markets efficiently and cheaply not only with raw materials such as cotton, but also with food. The growing working class of the expanding cities spent a significant portion of their income on food. Thus the price of agricultural products had a direct influence on the cost of living indices, the real income of the workers and the eventual adjustment of salary. Keeping prices low by reducing costs, subsidizing farmers or controlling prices was the usual government practice. But at the same time agriculture was a consumer of raw materials, machinery and equipment. These were produced at high cost by the inefficient and heavily protected national industry, an industrial base created by import substitution policies adopted in Brazil from the 1940s and completed in the military period.

The problem for policymakers was how to sell domestically produced agricultural products cheaply if the agricultural sector could only modernize and increase productivity using high cost inputs produced from an inefficient and expensive national industry whose products they needed to modernize and increase their efficiency. The solution was the implementation of modern agricultural protection policies such as minimum prices and regulation of inventories, but particularly the creation of a large subsidized public or directed financial credit system that stimulated agricultural modernization by providing low-cost funds for the purchase of machinery and equipment and for the application of modern inputs in agriculture such as fertilizers, seeds and insecticides. This system benefited essentially the commercially oriented farmers who had the potential to modernize.[2]

---

[1] Fabio Chaddad, *The Economics and Organization of Brazilian Agriculture: Recent Evolution and Productivity Gains* (Amsterdam: Academic Press, 2016), pp. 14–15.
[2] See Antônio Márcio Buainain et al. "Sete teses sobre o mundo rural Brasileiro," in Antônio Márcio Buainain et al., *O Mundo Rural no Brasil do Século 21. A Formação de um Novo Padrão Agrário e Agrícola* (Brasília: Embrapa, 2014): 1159–1182.

It was this complex subsidy system which enabled agriculture to rapidly increase its productivity through the use of new national industrial inputs.[3] The system worked relatively well while there was economic stability. But with the state fiscal crisis and rampant inflation of the late 1980s and early 1990s, the system of abundant subsidized, public or directed credit at negative interest rates collapsed, and needed to be replaced by alternative forms of credit. There was also the need to better integrate agriculture with other parts of the production process, replacing the state price and commodity controls with private suppliers of inputs for agriculture (such as seeds, pesticides and fertilizers), processors of agricultural products (such as soy processors, millers and packinghouses) and distributors of agricultural products (such as supermarket chains and trading companies). On the other hand, the crisis stimulated an opening up of Brazilian agriculture to the world market, something few other sectors have practiced as intensively as agriculture. If agriculture lost its government subsidies, it nevertheless benefited from the opening of the economy, since it now could acquire its inputs in competitive markets and had open access to the international market for the placement of its production.

But when the generalized protection that defended national production ceased to exist, agriculture itself also faced international competition. Survival required increasing productivity which Brazil's entrepreneurial farmers were able to provide with new technology, new plants and more systematic application of fertilizers, insecticides and machinery. Much of this adaptability was due to the coming on line of years of government-sponsored research which provided Brazilian farmers with the seeds and technology to transform whole regions of Brazil into productive centers of modern agricultural production. This was the dynamic element which explains the revolution in Brazilian agriculture, which at the often high cost to less efficient producers, occurred in a phase of prolonged crisis of the Brazilian economy. It was only with great reluctance and under significant pressure from its international lending sources that Brazil opened up its economy. Beginning in the mid-1980s in Brazil as in the rest of Latin America, discussions became more common about market liberalization and the nature of government market intervention and the

---

[3] It was also essential in resolving short-term problems such as high fertilizer prices, coffee frosts, oil shocks and farmers' debt crises of the 1990s. Paulo F. C. de Araújo et al., "Política de crédito para a agricultura brasileira. Quarenta e cinco anos à procura do desenvolvimento," *Revista de Política Agrícola*, XVI, no. 4 (Oct./Nov./Dec. 2007): 29.

entire viability of the import substitution model. As a result of the crisis in the balance of payments and the need to reduce public expenditures, the government authorities were forced by their international lenders to reduce public sources of financing. In this reduction were included the multiplicity of subsidies directly linked to the agricultural sector, which included the monopolies of wheat and sugar. The liberalization of agricultural products and their inputs in the market was a major theme in this neo-liberal debate and it affected multiple public and private agents directly involved in the process. The government was under strong pressure from the IMF and the World Bank, to liberalize the national economy and expose it to international competition, as well as giving up all subsidies. External agreements and loans contracted with these entities imposed severe restrictions on government expenditures in all areas, but especially in agriculture.

By the late 1980s and throughout the 1990s most of the world was being swept away by a neo-liberal tide, which was fostered by all the international lending agencies. The opening of the Brazilian economy belatedly reflected this liberalization process. This movement was called the "Washington Consensus," and preached deregulation, fiscal balance and trade liberalization among other liberal measures.[4] In 1986, the Gatt Uruguay Round began, and when it was concluded in 1993 it included an important agreement on agriculture. The negotiations also resulted in the creation of the World Trade Organization (WTO). The agreement on agriculture focused on three main aspects: market access, export subsidies and domestic support for agriculture. In addition, it defined the objective of reducing tariffs on imported foods. This agreement effectively contributed to the liberation of trade and the entry of large multinational groups into underdeveloped countries.[5] During this period, a regional free market zone was created in 1991 through the Treaty of Asunción, which was the Common Market of the South, or Mercosur, which allowed for the free circulation of goods, services and productive factors among the signing nations of South America. In 1994, by the Ouro Preto Protocol, a Common External Tariff was defined for the Mercosur alliance.[6]

---

[4] John Williamson, "What Washington means by policy reform," *Peterson Institute for International Economics, Speeches & Papers* (Nov. 2002), 7–20.

[5] Gleydson Pinheiro Albano, "Globalização da agricultura: multinacionais no campo Brasileiro," *Terra Livre* (São Paulo) (Ano 27), I, no. 36 (Jan.–Jun. 2001): 126–151.

[6] For a discussion of the background to the creation of Mercosul and the evaluation of its results, see Luciana Aparecida Bastos, "Avaliação do desempenho comercial do Mercosul: 1004–2005" (PhD thesis, FFLCH-USP, São Paulo, 2008). On agricultural policies in

TABLE 3.1: *Estimates of the government subsidies to agriculture, 1986–1990* *(in million US$)*

	1986	1987	1988	1989
Wheat	2,249	2,104	91	108
Rural credit	54	742	261	455
Regulating stocks	473	381	1	22
Crop purchases (AGF)	162	1,108	159	80
Sugar and alcohol	675	1,028	1,256	269
Total	3,615	5,363	1,803	1,058

Source: José Graziano da Silva, *A Nova Dinâmica da Agricultura Brasileira*, 1996, p. 116
Note: million US$ in 1990

Amid governmental budget crises, international pressures, and, finally, the maturing of the rural sector in the 1980s, the opening of the agricultural market began. Once initiated, the process was not reversed and this opening up to the world market would be reinforced by the liberalization policies adopted by the Fernando Collor government (1990–1992). Agricultural subsidies were dramatically reduced. In 1987, the total subsidy was US$5.3 billion, and just two years later, total government support for agriculture had fallen to $1 billion.

To give a sense of these pre-1990 subsidies, we can examine the funding for 1987. In that year, US$2 billion went to support the growing of wheat; US$1.5 billion was earmarked for the government stock purchasing agency the AGFs (Aquisições do Governo Federal) and the purchase of regulatory stocks; the sugar and alcohol segment received US$1 billion; and rural credit got US$700 million (see Table 3.1). These values represented the actual subsidies, not the total resources mobilized for these policies, which involved much higher numbers. But after that date most of these government funds were no longer available.[7]

With the end of subsidies, there also came the end of tariff protection for the sector. In 1988, a major reduction in tariffs was adopted, reinforced in 1990, when all restrictions on imports of agricultural products were

Mercosul see Maria Auxiliadora de Carvalho and Roberto Leite da Silva, "Intensidade do Comércio Agrícola no Mercosul," paper presented at the 47th Sober Congress, accessed December 24, 2016, at www.sober.org.br/palestra/13/447.pdf.

[7] José Graziano da Silva, *A Nova Dinâmica da Agricultura Brasileira* (Campinas: Instituto de Economia da Unicamp, 1996).

eliminated. The following year, the reform was completed with the establishment of a deadline for tariff reduction and simplification. The average
tariff would drop from 32% to 14%; and the maximum rate, from 105% to
35%. When the system was fully implemented, most products began to be
taxed at only 10%. The extreme case was cotton, with zero tariffs due to the
government's intention to support the textile industry. The new tariff
structure also covered fertilizers and other agricultural inputs which could
be imported at zero tariffs. The machinery, equipment and tractor industry,
the least efficient segment of the new agricultural economy, was the most
protected and yet saw import tariffs drop to 20%. Between 1991 and 1992,
prior licenses for import and export of agricultural products were also
eliminated, as well as the taxes levied on exports of various agricultural
products. Even the sugar and alcohol segment, whose exports were regulated by a complex quota system, began to operate in the free market.

As occurred even in the United States, neo-liberal reforms did not
liquidate all government agricultural support programs. Thus price support continued despite the neo-liberal reforms, though with very important modifications. The Minimum Price Guarantee Policy (PGPM) and the
operation of regulatory stocks were reformed. Until the 1980s, most of the
cotton, rice, beans, maize and soybean crops were financed by the EGF
(Empréstimos do Governo Federal) and acquired by the AGF (see
Table 3.2). With the products purchased, the government formed the
regulatory stocks, made available when there was a need to intervene in
the market to control prices. At the outset, however, there were no clearly
defined rules to guide such interventions. Accumulation of stocks without
a clear sales policy for their input into the market created uncertainties in
the market. Only in 1988, with the fixing of prices for the liquidation of
stocks, was a clear rule defined to guide those interventions. For each
product, the moving average of the prices was calculated. When the
market price exceeded the average by 15%, the government would sell
its stockpiled agricultural crops. In 1993, in order to reduce EGF expenditures and transfer part of the inventory to the private sector, an EGF
settlement price for sale of these stocks was established. When the settlement price exceeded the market price, the producer had the right to sell the
product on the market and the government paid the difference between
the value obtained and the settlement price. Thus, the government avoided
the direct acquisition of the products, which in addition to requiring
a large amount of funding, also involved the administration of large
volumes of stocks. Aside from the tax and monetary benefits arising

TABLE 3.2: *AGF and EGF programs, 1975–1992*

A: Purchases as percentage of production for major crops				
	Cotton	Rice	Edible beans	Corn	Soybeans
1975	9.7	0	1.7	0.6	0
1985	6	17.3	22.8	15.2	12
1987	11	28.1	43.4	29.5	5
1988	1.5	18.8	4.8	6.6	0
1989	0.2	7.9	0	3.8	0
1990		1.1	0	2	0
1991		0	0.4	0	0
1992		0.8	0.2	1.1	0

B: Storage loans as percentage for major crops, Brazil				
	Cotton	Rice	Edible beans	Corn	Soybeans
1975	51	12	3	5.4	32.4
1985	13	21	5	7.9	17.2
1987	42	30	5	6.9	25
1988	38	31	7	15.6	18.7
1989	15	27	2	14.1	4.4
1990	4	4	3	2.2	3.9
1991	7	3	3	3.6	1.2
1992	3	38	17	19.6	9.5

Note: AGF (Government Stock Purchase Program); EGF (Government Storage Loan)
Source: World Bank, *Brazil: The Management of Agriculture*, 1994, p. 48

from the purchase restriction, there was a reduction in the costs of managing such inventories, which were generally managed inefficiently.

The government was also obliged to give some compensation for the abandonment of its support for agriculture. Because there was a shortage of credit in the economy and the producers could not honor their financial commitments, the government, after long negotiations and under strong political pressure, renegotiated the debts of the agricultural sector on conditions that were extremely favorable to the producers. This was due to the increasing power of rural producers, which included a large caucus (or "bancada ruralista") of pro-rural deputies in the national legislature. The political power of this rural world had passed from the older *latifundiários* to the modern rural producers, and although modern from the economic perspective, these newly empowered farmers were politically conservative.

The transformation in the Brazilian economy since the 1990s also was very much influenced by the *Real* Plan which finally brought Brazil's high inflation under control. After nearly half a century of economic instability and rising inflation, as well as several unsuccessful previous stability plans, the success of the *Real* Plan implemented in 1994 would create a new standard of stability that lasted for approximately twenty years. Along with control of inflation, the regimes of the mid to late 1990s also extended Fernando Collor's economic liberalization measures, including a comprehensive privatization program for state-owned enterprises. Ironically, the governments of Itamar Franco (1992–1994), a dedicated nationalist in favor of public monopolies, and Fernando Henrique Cardoso (1994–2002), a respected left-wing intellectual and one of the proponents of dependency theory, both promoted privatization and liberalization of the national economy.

The stability achieved with the *Real* Plan was based on three fundamental points: a currency anchor, the maintenance of an overvalued currency – the *real* – and the broad opening of the economy. Unlike the other previous plans, it was possible to use the exchange rate anchor because Brazil had renegotiated its external debt, allowing it free access to the international financial market, which offered Brazil abundant resources, with high liquidity and low interest rates. At the same time, in the domestic market real interest rates were extremely high, attracting foreign capital and thus generating an abundance of dollars that overvalued the national currency.

The deepening of the process of trade liberalization, another basic element of the *Real* Plan, also had a significant impact on the Brazilian economy, which had been one of the most closed in the world until the end of the 1980s. The rapid opening of the economy, its exposure to international competition, and the maintenance of an overvalued currency had a positive effect on price stability. Imported goods or Brazilian commodities with international prices had their prices controlled by the competition, which helped in the initial phase of the plan. The idea was to expose Brazil to international competition in order to have a modernizing impact on the economy, especially of national industry. To this end, all the government policies were designed to expose industry to the competition of foreign companies that entered Brazil in the process of globalization of production and international capital flows. This resulted in a marked increase in the degree of internationalization of national production and a sharp reduction of the vertical integration of Brazilian industry, along with increased productivity due to the greater use of foreign technology. The continuity of this policy was only possible thanks to the huge inflow of foreign capital into the country to finance the trade and the current account deficit.

As with all other inflation control plans, there was an explosion in demand, largely due to the immediate elimination of the inflationary tax, but also because of the reduction in prices of domestic and imported goods. Stabilization also stimulated the expansion of consumer and corporate credit. As a result, the level of activity accelerated and GDP grew 4.9% in 1993, and by 5.3% in 1994. The exchange rate, which started with parity between the *real* and the dollar, fell in March to 0.83 *reais* against the dollar. This was due to the strong inflow of foreign capital in the country, particularly short-term capital, which was attracted by the policy of appreciation of the *real* and the high interest rates in force in the country. That allowed foreign investors to obtain profits in the arbitration of the interest rates.

The price of all this expansion of demand and spending was a reversal in the trade balance. The trade surplus, which had remained above the $ 10 billion level between 1987 and 1994, turned negative in November of that year, reaching a monthly deficit of $1 billion between February and March of 1995. In this context of expansion and market opening and the growing dependence of Brazil on external resources, the Mexican crisis erupted in December 1994. In response to this crisis, the government adopted a series of drastic measures. It raised interest rates to over 60% per year, which represented a real interest rate of more than 40%. It restricted consumer credit and raised taxes on numerous imported products and instituted quotas for importing cars. In addition, it changed the exchange rate regime to promote the gradual devaluation of the *real*, which still remained overvalued. But the external scenario continued to be troubled by a succession of crises, such as the Asian (1997) and Russian crises (1998). Government efforts to deal with this succession of external crises were not enough to calm markets, since Brazil was considered very vulnerable in its economic fundamentals. The country had accumulated a high debt, whose servicing demanded US$15 billion a year, or the equivalent of one-third of its exports. In addition, in 1998 the current account deficit reached 4.3% of GDP. All international vulnerability indicators showed that the country was in critical condition. Reserves, which had reached a high of US$70 billion in 1998, declined rapidly and by October of that year they fell by 40%. Still, the *real* was worth US$1.18

and was still overvalued. The financial opening promoted by the government, which allowed relative mobility of cheap capital and the inflow of
dollars, in turn allowed capital flight and the massive drain of resources
from the country to the outside world in times of crisis.

With the worsening of the crisis, Brazil ended up receiving emergency
aid from the IMF and several developed countries. Because of the size of
Brazil and the size of its debt, it was feared that the deterioration of its
external conditions would cause the crisis to radiate to other emerging
countries. Thus there was a rapid signing of an agreement with the IMF
in December 1998, giving Brazil a credit of US$41.5 billion.
The agreement with the IMF involved commitments regarding government behavior in several important areas such as the reduction of the
public deficit, the need for the government to generate a positive balance
in the current account and the approval of various fiscal measures.
In addition, as a measure of adjustment to the crisis, the federal government launched the Fiscal Stabilization Plan, and presented a list of measures already implemented, such as constitutional and legal reforms, that
allowed the continuation of privatization of public companies. In 1998,
the country's growth was zero, unemployment grew and instability and
loss of reserves continued despite reforms and agreement with the IMF.
Now the international financial markets experienced the moment of the
"Brazilian crisis," with the government refusing to change its exchange
rate policy, which could have been done in a time of greater tranquility
and properly planned. However, in January 1999, in the midst of a major
external crisis, the government was forced to make such changes and
allow the free floating of the *real*. The country abandoned the currency
anchor and the *real* fell more than 60% against the dollar.

It was within this context of fiscal crisis; the opening of the economy;
the implementation of the *Real* Plan; intensification of the process of
liberalization; and successive external crises, that modernization of the
agrarian economy would occur. But given the successive internal and
external crises that marked the 1980s and 1990s, the subsequent transformations and modernization that occurred in Brazilian agriculture
could hardly be anticipated.

The most radical change occurred in the area of rural credit and financing of agricultural operations. These transformations began in the
mid-1980s. When the rural credit policy was implemented in the 1970s,
there were two main sources of credit. The official credit, based essentially
on the so-called movement account of the Banco do Brasil, which had the
issuing power of money to meet the needs of the National Treasury and its

main programs, including agricultural credit, in its various modalities. But when issuing public debt to sterilize the monetary issues generated by the movement account, the Treasury eventually assumed the burden of these credits granted by the movement account. These subsidies and burdens increased with increasing inflation since the rates paid by farmers were usually interest rates uncorrected by inflation. The need to control the public accounts led to the extinction of the movement account in 1986.[8] In addition, the private sector financed the agricultural sector with directed credit, the so-called liabilities (*exigibilidades*). These came from the banking sector. Part of the amount of demand deposits collected by Commercial Banks was applied to rural credit at highly subsidized rates. Although negative from the borrower's point of view, usually below inflation itself, they were positive from the point of view of the banking institution, which captured the zero financial cost, although there were normal operating costs for the institution and coverage for defaults on farm loans.

In the case of official credit, usually practiced by the Banco do Brasil, there was a great pulverization of operations in innumerable small loans. In the case of credit granted by commercial banks, credit was more concentrated to avoid the cost of processing lower-value transactions and with the need to guard against defaults. Although it operated with a positive spread between the funding rate and the application rate, the bank avoided loans to less financially secure farms, since defaults represented a direct cost of the operation in spite of using heavily subsidized rates.

A number of studies have shown that it was the most modern farmers in the market who were the main resource takers of these loans and such resources were less available to farmers not involved in commercial agriculture. Both the Banco do Brasil and private banks reduced credit operations in the 1980s. With the closing of the Movement Account of the Banco do Brasil in 1986 and the acceleration of inflation in the second half of the 1980s, there was a dramatic reduction in the volume of demand

---

[8] In the process of improving fiscal management of the government, the Union's three different public budgets (fiscal, monetary and state-owned enterprises) were unified in 1986, and there was also the extinction of the movement account, which had persisted even though it represented a monetary issue difficult to control. See Fernando de Holanda Barbosa, *O Sistema Financeiro Brasileiro*, accessed December 25, 2016, at www.fgv.br /professor/fholanda/Arquivo/Sistfin.pdf; Simone Yuri Ramos and Geraldo Bueno Martha Junior, *Evolução da Politica de Crédito Rural Brasileira* (Planaltina: Embrapa Cerrados, 2010), 17–19.

deposits. The funds available through the private banks for their *exigibilidades* program of loans to agriculture also declined. The size of the subsidy of rural credit between 1970 and 1986 was estimated to have been R$80.48 billion (at August 1995 prices) transferred to the agricultural sector, which represented 11.4% of agricultural GDP in the same period.[9] With the closing of the moving account and the drying up of funds for the *exigibilidades* program, agricultural credit disappeared, or was replaced with new credit arrangements at market prices and the result was a brutal reduction of available credit.[10]

According to Helfand and Rezende, the dramatic reduction in the supply of rural credit at the beginning of the 1990s was not an expression of a policy decision to reduce government involvement in the financing of agriculture. Rather, it was a side effect of macroeconomic decisions aimed at combating inflation. Regardless of the causes for this change of policy, the consequence was to put strong pressure on agriculture and the associated industrial and commercial sectors to develop alternative mechanisms for financing the production and marketing of agricultural products.[11]

This development of an alternative mechanism began in the early 1990s when there has been an increase in the flow of private international resources into agriculture. Also as the government adopted several measures to liberalize the country's external operations, the agricultural sector benefited disproportionately from the new situation of access to the international market because it had access to relatively low interest rates, and export-oriented farmers were less vulnerable to external borrowing denominated in dollars.[12] Also in 1986, in the same year that the Movement Account was terminated, the banks established a Rural Savings Account (Caderneta de Poupança Rural) whose resources were to be applied exclusively to agriculture.

These new directed Rural Savings Accounts were a traditional type of arrangement. There is a tradition in Brazil of applying parts of savings

[9] Carlos J. C. Bacha, Leonardo Danelon and Egmar Del Bel Filho, "Evolução da taxa de juros real do crédito rural no Brasil – período 1985 a 2003," *Teoria e Evidência Econômica* (Passo Fundo), 14, no. 26 (May 2006), 43–69; also see Carlos J. C. Bacha, *Economia e Política Agrícola no Brasil* (São Paulo: Atlas, 2004), p. 170.

[10] Sayad made an interesting critical analysis of the rural credit model as originally adopted and its problems. João Sayad, *Crédito Rural no Brasil* (São Paulo: IPE/USP, 1978).

[11] Steven M. Helfand and Gervázio Castro de Rezende, "Brazilian Agriculture in the 1990s: Impact of the Policy Reforms" (Discussion Paper 98; Brasília and Rio de Janeiro: Ipea, 2001), pp. 4–5.

[12] Ibid.

accounts to other directed activities. Usually this involves funding for the housing sector, which has always represented one of the main instruments for the capture of family savings, and which involves a large sector of the Brazilian population. The Rural Savings Account, following the same model, was widely accepted and quickly became an important fundraising instrument. Already in 1987 it represented more than a fifth of the resources allocated to agriculture, and with variations over time, it has provided a significant portion of the financing of agriculture until today. In the new Constitution approved in 1988, the Constitutional Financing Funds were created for the North, the Northeast and Central-West regions, and priority of financing was given to small rural and industrial producers of those areas.[13] From the mid-1980s, monetary adjustment rules on rural credit were gradually introduced. But the monetary correction was not always complete, and varied according to the regional characteristics or the producers.[14]

In 1991, the so-called Agricultural Law was enacted, which created the system of payment for equivalence in product in credit operations. This meant that the government put into practice a series of actions that prevented the small producer from being prejudiced by changes in the value of the currency or prices paid for crops when the farmer obtained a government loan. The law determined that in financing small agricultural producers, the government guaranteed that prices for basic foods should be kept in line with the financial costs of the producer in order to avoid the lag between the guaranteed price and the debt with the financial agent.[15] Since agricultural loan contracts had already been corrected for inflation, correcting the federal government's purchase guarantee prices by the same inflation index eliminated the risk of the disparity of indicators, which increased when inflation reached exceptional levels.[16] Agricultural products could also be used to pay for the loans, linking the

---

[13] See the excellent study of Paulo Fernando Cidade de Araújo, "Política de crédito rural: reflexões sobre a experiência brasileira" (Textos para Discussão CEPAL/IPEA, 37; Brasília: CEPAL/IPEA, 2001).

[14] Maura M. D. Santiago and Valquíria da Silva, "A política de crédito rural brasileira e o endividamento do setor agrícola. Antecedentes e desdobramentos recentes," *Agricultura*, São Paulo, 46 (1999): 47–69.

[15] Article 4 of Law 8.174, January 30, 1991.

[16] When inflation reached high levels, use of average prices could vary greatly. Thus the use of the same index for rural credit financing and the guarantee price of agricultural products eliminated this risk. João Sayad and Francisco Vidal Luna, "Política anti-inflacionaria y el Plan Cruzado," in *Neoliberalismo y Políticas Economicas Alternativas* (Quito: Corporacion de Estudios para el Desarrolo [CORDES], 1987): 189–204.

correction of the amounts lent to the evolution of the prices of the products financed.[17]

In the same year of 1991 the BNDES (Banco Nacional do Desenvolvimento Econômico e Social) intensified its activity in the agricultural area, using several lines of financing traditionally focused on the industrial sector to concentrate on agribusiness. Thus, gradually the Bank developed special lines of credit for the agricultural sector, essentially resources for investments in basic machinery and other productive inputs. In 1994, the Rural Producer's Certificate (CPR) was established. It could emit certificates in dollars, which was an instrument that represented the promise of future delivery of agricultural products, and could be issued by producers and cooperatives.[18] This was a fundamental instrument which permitted the integration of agriculture with the international market, since it allowed the direct sale of part of the production. The CPR could be traded freely, but for this purpose they had to be registered in the financial settlement system authorized by the Central Bank. In 2001, the law was supplemented, allowing the financial settlement of the certificate, in addition to the original law that allowed only liquidation in products. In 1998, a resolution created the so-called "63 caipira," authorizing the raising of external funds in dollars for the granting of loans in local currency for financing rural and agroindustrial activities.[19] That resulted in opening up the agribusiness market to foreign capital. It was another step toward the internationalization of agribusiness activities in Brazil, and as in other post-1990 instruments created in this period, it operated at market rates.

In 1996, the Family Agriculture Strengthening Program (Pronaf – *Programa Nacional de Fortalecimento da Agricultura Familiar*) was created to promote the sustainable development of the rural segment of family farmers, so as to increase their productive capacity, generate jobs and improve incomes.[20] In the same year, the government authorized the

---

[17] Araújo, "Política de crédito rural," pp. 29–30.

[18] Article 1 of Law 8929, August 22, 1994. The law created the Rural Product Certificate (CPR). Any product of agricultural origin can be the subject of CPR, the most common being those that have greater liquidity in the market. Lucas Gonçalves Ruiz, *Uma Visão Geral sobre a Cédula de Produto Rural (CPR)*, accessed December 27, 2016, at www.migalhas.com.br/dePeso/16,MI227850,11049-Uma+Visao+Geral+Sobre+a+Cedula+de+Produto+Rural+CPR.

[19] This was a traditional mechanism (Resolution 63) for banks in Brazil to borrow such funds on the international market and invest them in loans for local strategic sectors. Given that "caipira" is a popular term for rural persons, these special rural grants were given this name.

[20] Article 1 of Decree 1.946 of June 28, 1996.

use of funds from the substantial resources of unemployment Insurance (FAT – *Fundo de Amparo ao Trabalhador*) in the financing of Pronaf. The BNDES used these resources for industrial loans, and at this time it was expanded to allow the bank to make these funds available for rural loans for small and rural producers.[21] The support for these reforms came from the social and political movements related to the small rural producers and the agrarian reform MST (Movement of the Landless) movement which gained political force in this period

In 2004 several new financial instruments for the agricultural sector were created, giving it flexibility similar to that existing for other economic sectors, and expanding options for credit instruments, sales for future delivery, and financing based on product deposits. These are new instruments and they consolidated new alternative forms of agricultural financing, as the activity became more complex and value chains were formed that involve all stages of the agribusiness production process, from the farmer and his suppliers, to the industrial processor and the distributor of fresh and processed products.

Previously the state-supported credit, whether directly sponsored or through directed credit via its extensive system of subsidies, always had embedded in it negative interest rates. But in the mid-1980s and 1990s the government finally abandoned this policy and began making all interest rates positive in agriculture. Since then these government credits and subsidies have interest rates comparable to free market rates, or other public funds, which operated with positive interest rates, but below the interest being charged in the free market, which were traditionally quite high in Brazil. Several studies were done analyzing this phase of transition between negative and positive interest rates in rural credit. A study done in 2006 analyzes several previous studies and presents its own estimates.[22] It clearly shows that this transition to positive rates occurred in the late 1980s and early 1990s, and has continued since then. Since real interest

---

[21] Resolution no. 109 of July 1, 1996, of the Conselho Deliberativo do Fundo de Amparo ao Trabalhador. The resources could be used to finance small and mini rural producers individually or collectively.

[22] Carlos J. C. Bacha, Leonardo Danelon and Egmar Del Bel Filho, "Evolução da taxa de juros real do crédito rural no Brasil – período 1985 a 2003," *Teoria e Evidência Econômica* (Passo Fundo), 14, no. 26 (May 2006): 43–69. The author analyzes the rates practiced in relation to the IGP-DI (General Price Index – Internal Availability) and the INPC (National Consumer Price Index). In our chart we use the relationship with the INPC. On the other hand, in the graph we used one of the comparisons presented by the author, obtained in I. Goldin and G. C. de Rezende, *A Agricultura Brasileira na Década de 80: Crescimento Numa Economia em Crise* (Rio de Janeiro: Ipea, 1993).

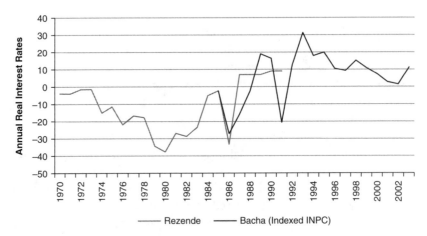

GRAPH 3.1: Real interest rates of rural credit, 1970–2003
Source: Bacha et al., "Evolução da taxa de juros (2006)": 69

rates in Brazil are very high, even for the average rural credit, which is relatively privileged compared to other economic sectors, agriculture has been burdened with interest rates of about 10% above inflation in several years (see Graph 3.1).

The relative availability of credit, the fluctuations in real interest rates, and price fluctuations for all crops, have generated frequent debt crises, and high delinquency rates in agriculture. These periodic crises of indebtedness place a relative risk potential on the loans made to agriculture. Thus in 1995, the Farmers Securitization Program was instituted, covering producers with debts of up to R$200,000, for a term of seven to ten years, with interest of 3% per year plus the minimum price variation. This was one of the several negotiations on debt of the rural producers in general, or for specific groups of producers, such as the sugar and ethanol producers, which have periodically occurred in Brazil to today. The positive interest rates that have become common since the end of the 1980s also reflect a different composition of the main sources of funds, alternatives that were created or modified after the exhaustion of the initial government agricultural financing model. These traditional sources became scarce with the retraction of demand deposits in the period of high inflation that preceded the *Real* Plan. Although scarce, the resources of the *exigibilidades*, today called compulsory resources, never disappeared. From the initiation of the *Real* Plan and the subsequent stabilization of the economy, there was a rapid recovery of on-demand deposits in commercial banks. These were still required to finance rural credit, but now with positive interest rates, although they are still below free market rates. The rural savings accounts have also gained importance as a credit source since the mid-1990s. Over the last twenty years, funds from both compulsory account transfers and rural savings accounts made up about two-thirds of the resources invested in financing agricultural activity in Brazil. At the same time foreign loans to agriculture were gradually reduced in importance. BNDES, whose resources are basically oriented toward structural investments, maintained a smaller but important position in the financing of rural activity, providing on average around 10% of all rural loans (see Table 3.3).

Although there was a significant recovery of rural credit after the *Real* Plan through various instruments, when we compare the total value of rural credit in relation to agricultural GDP, it did not recover the proportion it had reached in the 1970s when all that credit had negative interest rates. But this subsidized credit compensated for the income transferred from agriculture to others sectors in the economy through price controls, taxes and purchases of inputs and equipment in the highly protected domestic market. A study carried out in 1990 estimated that approximately 8.9% of agricultural GDP (average for the period 1975–1983) was transferred to other sectors. In compensation it was estimated that rural credit was on the order of 8% of agricultural GDP over the same period. It is important to emphasize that as this compensation came through rural credit, which was used to purchase modern inputs, such as fertilizers and machinery, it stimulated the modernization of Brazilian agriculture (see Graph 3.2).[23]

When we analyze the relationship between the prices received by producers and the prices paid by producers, the importance of the market liberalization process is clear. The index of the relationship fluctuated around 70 up to 1992, but then increased dramatically, reaching its peak of 111 just after the *Real* Plan in December 1994, thus indicating increasing gains for the producers. But in 1995, there was a strong decline in the ratio, which remained around 80 until 2005, when the available series ends (see Graph 3.3). But the liberalization of the market clearly was positive for farmers, since their costs dropped faster than the prices of the goods they sold. This index does not include the impact of increasing

---

[23] Araújo, "Política de crédito rural. Also see A. S. Brandão and J. L. Carvalho, "Economia política de las intervenciones de precios en Brasil," in A. O. Krueger, M. Schiff and A. Valdes, *Economia Política de las Intervenciones de Precios en America* (Washington, DC: Banco Mundial, 1990).

TABLE 3.3: *Source of rural credit, 2003–2013 (% participation)*

	1994/95	1995/96	1996/97	1997/98	1998/99	1999/2000	2000/01	2001/02	2002/03
Treasury resources	29%	12%	1%	2%	1%	0%	0%	2%	1%
Required resources	11%	13%	39%	39%	40%	45%	52%	51%	51%
Rural savings	31%	32%	6%	9%	16%	16%	12%	12%	14%
Free resources	16%	14%	7%	6%	5%	5%	4%	4%	5%
Constitutional funds	6%	13%	9%	8%	6%	6%	5%	6%	6%
FAT (1)	0%	5%	19%	17%	16%	15%	11%	10%	8%
BNDES/FINAME (2)	0%	0%	2%	4%	6%	7%	11%	13%	13%
Funcafé	0%	0%	1%	4%	5%	4%	2%	1%	2%
External resources	0%	0%	0%	1%	3%	1%	1%	0%	0%
Other sources	6%	11%	16%	9%	2%	1%	2%	2%	1%
Total	100%	100%	100%	100%	100%	100%	100%	100%	100%
Value (millions *reais*)	9,092	6,762	7,748	10,118	10,818	13,356	16,355	19,843	28,041

	2003/04	2004/05	2005/06	2006/07	2007/08	2008/09	2009/10	2010/11	2011/12	2012/13
Treasury resources	2%	5%	1%	1%	1%	0%	0%	0%	0%	0%
Required resources	39%	37%	40%	48%	58%	45%	39%	52%	36%	41%
Rural savings	22%	27%	24%	19%	17%	26%	29%	27%	38%	27%
Free resources	6%	5%	5%	4%	3%	6%	3%	2%	5%	3%
Constitutional funds	5%	7%	9%	8%	7%	9%	7%	8%	9%	9%
FAT (1)	8%	3%	9%	7%	2%	1%	1%	1%	1%	1%
BNDES/FINAME (2)	16%	13%	8%	7%	7%	8%	18%	7%	7%	11%
Funcafé	1%	2%	3%	4%	3%	3%	2%	2%	1%	1%
External resources	0%	0%	1%	1%	1%	1%	1%	1%	1%	1%
Other sources	0%	0%	1%	1%	1%	1%	0%	0%	0%	6%
Total	100%	100%	100%	100%	100%	100%	100%	100%	100%	100%
Value (millions *reais*)	35,233	44,137	44,146	46,816	61,046	69,148	88,867	87,252	96,971	124,407

Source: Banco Central – Anuário Estat.Crédito Rural: MAPA/SPA/DEAGRI; Política de Crédito Rural no Brasil, www.sober.org.br/palestra/2/138.pdf
Notes (1) FAT (*Fundo de Amparo ao Trabalhador*) is unemployment insurance.
  (2) FINAME is the credit agency of the Brazilian Development Bank which finances machines and equipment.

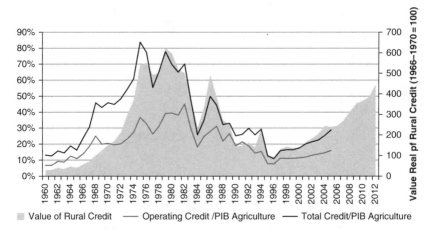

GRAPH 3.2: Rural credit in relation to GDP agriculture, 1960–2004
Source: Araújo et al., "Política de crédito" (2007), 30 and BCentral

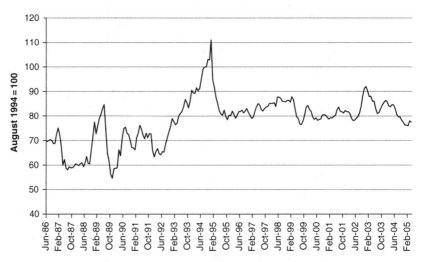

GRAPH 3.3: Relation between prices received and paid by producers, 1986–2005
Source: Conab (www.conab.gov.br) and Fundação Getúlio Vargas (www.fgv.br).

yields, which of course lowered the farmer's costs as well, since the same inputs produced ever higher volumes, as we will see below.

This new post-*Real* Plan rural credit system was less dependent on the public sector and had fewer fiscal resources and subsidies. The new system was still related to the government in terms of specific rates and sources, but these numerous financial instruments began to charge positive interest rates which were above inflation. As the system still had many specific sources of credit, the rates although positive were usually below the high free market interest rates charged in Brazil. The new system had numerous instruments which allowed for hedging and reduced the risks of an activity that requires a long productive process and that sells its products in highly competitive markets.

With the *Real* Plan there was greater economic stability, and the creation of a wide variety of alternative sources of credit especially from the first decade of the twenty-first century. There was also an international demand for agricultural commodities, with corresponding historically high prices. Nevertheless agriculture in Brazil has experienced some significant conjuncture crises in this period, for various reasons, some directly related to the sector, such as indebtedness and climatic conditions, and others derived from macroeconomic issues, such as the overvaluation of the *real* and the high interest rates practiced in Brazil. Among the various conjectural crises that occurred in Brazilian agriculture, one of the most difficult was the crisis of 2004/2005. According to Minister of Agriculture Roberto Rodrigues, there was a conjunction of dramatic factors which created this crisis. This included declining world prices, increased agricultural indebtedness, a reduction of planted area and an overvalued *real*. Rural producers stressed increased production costs, falling agricultural prices, loss of production due to climatic problems, lack of rural insurance, a currency lag, difficulties in extending bank financing, payment deadlines for the purchase of pesticides, fertilizers, machinery and other agricultural inputs from private suppliers, as well as the lack of logistics and infrastructure for the storage and disposal of their crops. Their biggest demand was for the renegotiation of bank indebtedness, which had been occurring periodically since market interest rates were implemented in agricultural credit operations.[24] From 2001 to 2013, agricultural GDP increased on average over 4% per annum. But in 2004 and 2005 agricultural GDP increased by only 2.6%.[25]

By the crop year 2013/2014, agriculture credit amounted to R$180 billion (corresponding to US$77 billion), which was an increase

[24] *Tratoraço. As razões da Crise. O Alerta do Campo*. Confederação da Agricultura e Pecuária do Brasil – CNA. Accessed January 29, 2018, at www.arrozeirosdealegrete .com.br/arroz/memorialdoarroz/movimentos/crise_no_campo_tratoraco.pdf.

[25] Ipeadata. PIB – agropecuária – var. real – ref. 2000 – (% a.a.) – Instituto Brasileiro de Geografia e Estatística, Sistema de Contas Nacionais Referência 2000 (IBGE/SCN 2000 Anual) – SCN_VAAGRO.

of 29% compared to the 2012/2013 harvest. So-called entrepreneurial or commercial agriculture accounted for 88% of the credit granted, and the government PRONAF program, which was directed to family farms, accounted for 12% of the credit in that year. Of the corporate credit, 73% was oriented to operating costs and commercialization and 27% to investments. In the segment of credit for commercial agriculture, 60% was carried out with controlled interest, and the rest loaned at free interest rates. The main sources of funds were mandatory resources (27%), rural savings (14%), BNDES (14%) and Banco do Brasil Agroindustrial (8%). Of the resources for investments, about two-thirds came from the various programs managed by BNDES (see Table 3.4).

Since the 1980s, there have also been new financing mechanisms created for agriculture from suppliers and distributors of inputs, such as companies selling seeds, fertilizers or pesticides; from national and international trading companies; from cereals producers; and from agro-industries and exporters. The system works in several ways. One way is through the advance of funds for the anticipated purchase of the crop by suppliers and distributors of inputs. This credit is not paid off until harvest time. In addition, there are barter exchange operations which involve the possibility of delivering crops after the harvest as a form of payment for the inputs purchased for the corresponding harvest at a pre-defined parity. According to a recent study, the share of bank credit is higher in the South of the country, while there is greater use of credit from suppliers of inputs and trading companies in the financing of production in the Center-West (see Graph 3.4).[26]

The traditional credit operates through commercial banks, including the Banco do Brasil, and Credit Cooperatives. The commercial credit is supplied by the trading companies who provide a type of barter by providing resources through the advancing of inputs. The suppliers and distributors of inputs grant a commercial credit for a period compatible with the duration of the corresponding harvest, or carry out barter exchange operations.[27]

The decline of the government financing model thus led to the development of commercial credit, which involved integrating the various parts of the agricultural sector into so-called agribusiness. The farmer had to become an entrepreneur to survive and grow in this new environment,

---

[26] Felipe Prince Silva, "O crédito rural no Brasil," *Animal Business Brasil*, 2, no. 6 (2012): 61–66.
[27] Ibid.

TABLE 3.4: *Rural financing – programs and application of resources – harvests 2012/2013 and 2013/2014*

Sources of funds and programs	Financing period		
	July 2012–June 2013	July 2013–June 2014	Participation
1. Operational & marketing costs	89,292.0	115,540.6	64%
1.1 Controlled interest rates	69,363.8	90,021.0	50%
1.2 Free interest rates	19,928.2	25,519.6	14%
2. Investments	31,075.5	41,768.6	23%
2.1 BNDES programs	17,720.2	24,972.3	14%
2.2 Other sources/programs	13,355.2	16,796.3	9%
3. Empresarial agriculture (1+2+3)	120,367.5	157,309.1	88%
4. Family agriculture (PRONAF)	18,634.7	22,283.4	12%
5. AGRICULTURE TOTAL (3+4)	139,002.2	179,592.5	100%
Percentage of family agriculture	13%	12%	

Source: RECOR/SICOR/BACEN, BNDES, BB, BNB, BASA, BANCOOB e SICREDI; elaboration: MAPA/SPA/DEAGRI, July 17, 2014

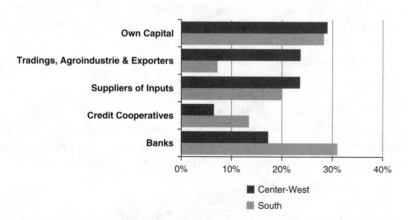

GRAPH 3.4: Composition of formal and informal credit in the regions South and Center-West (harvest, 2011)
Source: Agrosecurity, in Silva, "O crédito rural no Brasil" (2012)

where the producer can buy and sell his inputs and products in the free, open, global market but also has to compete in that market. It is the international market that now sets agricultural prices, which generates production dynamics, viability and profitability. If there are advantages, there are also risks.[28]

Aside from all the normal expenditures faced by agriculture, there is the so-called "Brazil Cost" – the extra costs involved in doing business in Brazil – which is quite high. Thus despite the relative abundance of credit, the financial cost in Brazil is higher than in the international market. There is also the volatility of the exchange rate, and the tendency for the overvaluation of the *real*. There are also unusual hidden taxes on exports, as well as the high costs of transport due to the poor quality of the national infrastructure. How then to explain the dynamism of the sector that transformed Brazil into one of the most important and competitive players in the international market for agricultural products?

First, it is important to emphasize this early phase of modernization, without which there would be no agribusiness in Brazil. It is productivity that explains the continued competitiveness of Brazilian agriculture despite the structural difficulties faced in all areas. But if it is productivity that allowed the country to play a significant role in the international agricultural market, it was also the international market that allowed for the continuous increase in productivity, since the international agricultural market was almost unlimited for a competitive producer. A process of continuous increase of competitiveness would have been impossible in a closed local market, no matter how broad. In that case the expansion of the supply would have caused a fall in agricultural prices, preventing sequential increases in production through higher agricultural productivity.[29]

The magnitude of the advances in agricultural productivity and the size that agribusiness acquired in Brazil are impressive. When we consider the area planted by Brazilian agriculture in the last forty years, we see that these croplands grew modestly from an average of 40 million hectares in the 1980s to 45 million in the first decade of the twentieth century, for an increase of 12%. As of 2010, these lands reached 50 million hectares and by the harvest of 2017/2018 it is estimated that 62 million hectares will be

---

[28] Buainain et al., "Sete teses sobre o mundo rural Brasileiro": 1176.

[29] Ruy Miller Paiva, Salomão Schattan and Claus F. Trench de Freitas, *Setor Agrícola do Brasil. Comportamento Econômico, Problemas e Possibilidades* (São Paulo: Secretaria da Agricultura, 1973), pp. 17–27.

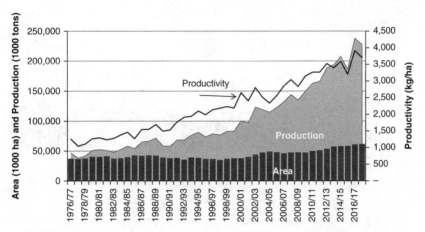

GRAPH 3.5: Area (ha), production and yield (kg/ha, 1976–2018)
Source: Conab – séries históricas (2017/2018 harvest is estimated): www
.conab.gov.br/conteudos.php?a=1252&t= www.conab.gov.br/conteudos.php?
a=1252&t=

planted in crops. In contrast to this relatively modest increase in planted
area, there was a massive growth in output, which went from approximately 50 million tons of crops to 238 million tons in the crop year 2016/
2017. This exceptional growth of harvests was basically due to growth in
productivity, which increased from approximately 1,400 kilograms per
hectare in the 1980s to about 3,500 in the first eight harvests of the 2010s,
a growth of 150% in this period (see Graph 3.5).

Although this increase in productivity occurred in all regions of Brazil,
there was no significant reduction in the historical disparity that exists
between the North-Northeast regions and the other areas of Brazil. In the
last eight harvests the average productivity of the North-Northeast zone
was approximately 2,100 kg per hectare, against 3,800 kg per hectare in
the Center-West and Southern regions. Nevertheless the difference has
slowly declined as the modernization of agriculture has become more
intense in the North-Northeast than in the Center-West and Southern
regions. Productivity doubled in the Center-West and Southern regions,
and multiplied by four in the North-Northeast regions in recent years.
In the harvest of 2016/2017, for example, the average of the North and
Northeast was 2,569 kg and the average of the Center-South regions was
4,197 kg. The reason, of course, is that these northern regions started
from very low levels of productivity and needed less input to raise their
productivity. Secondly and perhaps most importantly, important poles of

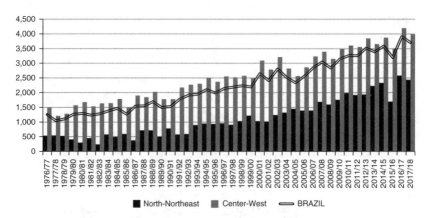

GRAPH 3.6: Productivity by regions (tons/ha), 1976–2018
Source: Conab – Séries históricas (2017/2018 harvest is estimated): http://www
.conab.gov.br/conteudos.php?a=1252&t=

commercial agriculture were created both in the Northeast, as in the Petrolina or the Barreiras region, and in the North with the development of commercial agriculture on the edges of the Amazon, with regions of high yield (Graph 3.6).

The confirmation of this general growth behavior in Brazilian agriculture can be demonstrated by the analysis of some of the most important products. Graph 4.8 shows the yields of corn, wheat and soybeans. It is evident that there was a greater increase in productivity of corn and wheat compared to soybeans. Corn is traditionally the most widely planted agricultural product in the Brazilian countryside. Produced in small, medium and large units, many farms were growing it for their own consumption. As production intensified, the share of modern commercial producers increased and thus productivity significantly increased. But while average productivity as a whole increased, there still was a great dispersion of productivity around the mean. The majority of farms in Brazil are still in fact subsistence or small farms producing only a small surplus for sale. This can be seen by comparing the average yield of grains in the various states of the Northeast, such as Ceará and Rio Grande do Norte, which are less than 600 kg/hectare, against the more than 4,000 kg/ hectare in the various states of the Center-West, Southeast and Southern regions of the country.[30]

---

[30] Conab – Companhia Nacional de Abastecimento. Acompanhamento da safra brasileira de grãos, V. 4 – SAFRA 2016/17- N. 8 – Oitavo levantamento, May 2017.

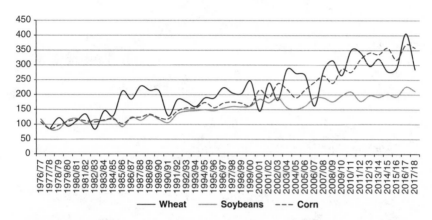

GRAPH 3.7: Productivity of wheat, corn and soybeans, 1976/2018 (tons/ha) (1976–1980=100)
Source: Conab tables found at www.conab.gov.br/conteudos.php?a=1252&t=

Wheat, as was noted earlier, had been a highly controlled and subsidized product until the 1980s. When the free wheat market was created, national production actually fell from about 6 million tons in the late 1980s to about 2 million in the early years of the next decade since Brazilian producers were not competitive. The recent gradual increase in wheat production, which eventually returned to the levels of the 1980s, shows that Brazilian farmers are now competitive with the production of such temperate countries as Argentina, which is more suitable for cultivation of this product. As for soybeans, their cultivation since their introduction has always been by commercially oriented farms which were more modern and thus from early on had high levels of productivity, which explains their lower productivity growth in comparison to wheat and maize which started at much lower levels of productivity growth (see Graph 3.7).

The historical production of rice, beans and cotton, three traditional products of Brazilian agriculture, has taken place in different types of farms. Beans have always been characterized by small farm production, often of subsistence level. Although Brazil is one of the largest bean producers in the world, it needs to complement its domestic consumption with sporadic imports, usually from neighboring countries. Productivity was traditionally very low, but it too has shown a significant increase in the post-1990 period. In contrast, rice was produced in special areas, such as the traditional irrigated rice in the Southern region of the country, and has always been more concentrated among commercial producers. But its production too has experienced significant productivity increases in the modern period.

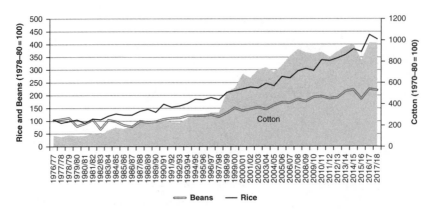

GRAPH 3.8: Productivity of cotton, rice and beans (tons/ha), 1976–2018 (1978–80=100)

Source: Conab tables found at www.conab.gov.br/conteudos.php?a=1252&t=

Relative to other crops of importance in the domestic market, such as maize and beans, cotton already had relatively higher levels of productivity. This explains why the evolution of its productivity was less pronounced than that of beans. Traditionally produced in the Northeast, it was practically abandoned there for a long period, due to a plague of boll weevils that reduced cotton production throughout Brazil in the 1980s and 1990s. Only in the last twenty years has there been a relative recovery of the area planted in cotton. This history can be seen in the cultivation statistics. In the 1976/1977 harvest, cotton was grown on 3.2 million hectares in the North-Northeast and 850,000 in the Center-West and Southern regions. In the 2017/2018 harvest, the planting of the North-Northeast occupied only 311,000 hectares and in the Center-South 739,000 hectares (see Graph 3.8).

Brazilian yields in major commercial crops are now close to those in the most advanced countries. Thus average soybean yield per hectare in 2014 in Brazil was above those in Argentina and 90% of those obtained in the United States. In the production of corn, the best yields from the Center-West state of Goiás are less advanced, although they are still up to 77% of the yield achieved in the United States and 89% of the yields per hectare for corn in Canada in that harvest year.[31]

Although indicators of production per area are a practical way to measure and compare agricultural productivity, the best way is through analyzing total factor productivity (or TFP), which measures the

---

[31] FAOSTAT accessed May 19, 2017, and Conab, "Milho Total (1ªe 2ª safra), BRASIL, Safras 1976/77 a 2015/16."

TABLE 3.5: *Sources for growth of Brazilian agriculture, 1975–2011 (annual rates of growth)*

Indicators	1975–2011	1975–1979	1980–1989	1990–1999	2000–2009	2000–2011
Index of production	3.77	4.37	3.38	3.01	5.18	4.85
Index of inputs	0.20	2.87	2.20	0.36	-0.51	-0.80
Total factor productivity	3.56	1.46	1.16	2.64	5.72	5.69
Productivity of labor	4.29	4.25	2.13	3.52	5.86	5.71
Productivity of land	3.77	3.15	2.91	3.25	5.61	5.32
Productivity of capital	3.05	2.77	2.87	1.89	4.62	4.35

Source: Gasques et al., "Produtividade da agricultura Brasileira" (2012): 89

relationship between the quantity of production and the quantity of inputs used, such as land, labor and capital. There are several studies that show that Brazil has had an exceptional performance in TFP comparable to the countries with the best agricultural performance.[32] In a 2012 study

[32] José Garcia Gasques et al., "Produtividade total dos fatores e transformações da agricultura Brasileira: análise dos dados dos censos agropecuários," in José Garcia Gasques, José Eustáquio, R. Vieira Filho and Zander Navarro, eds., *Agricultura Brasileira: Desempenho, Desafios e Perspectivas* (Brasília: Ipea, 2010): 19–44; José Garcia Gasques, Eliana Teles Bastos, Constanza Valdes and Mirian Rumenos P. Bacchi, "Produtividade da agricultura Brasileira e os efeitos de algumas políticas," *Revista de Política Agrícola*, XXI, no. 3 (Jul./Aug./Sept. 2012): 83–92; José Garcia Gasques et al., "Produtividade da agricultura: resultados para o Brasil e Estados Selecionados," *Revista de Política Agrícola*, XXIII, no. 3 (Jul./Aug./Sept. 2014): 87–98; Giovanna Miranda Mendes, "Produtividade total dos fatores e crescimento econômico na agropecuária brasileira: 1970–2006" (PhD thesis, Universidade Federal de Viçosa, 2010); Giovanna Miranda Mendes, Erly Cardoso Teixeira and Márcio Antônio Salvato, "Produtividade Total dos Fatores e Crescimento Econômico na Agropecuária Brasileira: 1970–2006," *Encontro da ANPEC*, accessed January 3, 2017, at www.anpec.org.br/en contro/ . . . /i11-a2721cea8a808e72157f9f97cfc7e14c.docx; Fernanda de Negri and Luiz Ricardo Cavalcanti, eds., *Produtividade no Brasil. Desempenho e Determinantes* (Brasília: ABDI, IPEA, 2014); Rogerio Edivaldo Freitas, "Produtividade agrícola no Brasil," in Negri and Cavalcanti, eds., *Produtividade no Brasil*: 373–410; Carlos Alberto da Silva and Léo da Rocha Ferreira, "Produtividade total dos fatores no crescimento da agricultura Brasileira," *Revista de Política Agrícola*, XXV, no. 3 (Jul./Aug./Sept. 2016): 4–15.

Gasques et al. estimated the productivity of labor, land and capital as well as the resulting TFP for the period 1975–2011. Land, labor and capital showed significant growth in the period 1975–2001, but the most growth was in labor at 4.29% per annum, followed by land at 3.77% per annum. Moreover all three factors intensified after 2000. In the case of land and labor, this is evident from the strong growth in agricultural production. According to the author, the productivity of the land grew in a systematic way throughout the years of the research. Some of this growth was due to the incorporation of new and more productive land and the adoption of new cultivation practices, but the greater effect resulted from investments in research, extension services and use of new technologies (see Table 3.5).

Total factor productivity between 1975 and 2011 grew at 3.56% per annum, an exceptional result for such a long period of time. This growth in TFP stems from continuous improvement in the quality of inputs allocated to production, and profound transformations in the technological and managerial input into Brazilian commercial agriculture. What is impressive is that in the last years of the study, the TPF increased, reaching the annual average of 5.6%. That is, production continues to grow at an accelerated pace although the amount of inputs remains practically stable. This intensification of productivity, especially during the last ten years, is even more relevant, since it is no longer based on extremely low original productivity indicators, such as those in the 1960s. Brazil can now be said to have sufficient productivity to be highly competitive in the world agriculture market (see Graph 3.9).

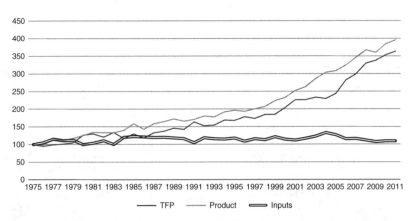

GRAPH 3.9: Index of product, inputs and TFP (1975=100)
Source: Gasques et al., "Produtividade da agricultura Brasileira" (2012)

In the same work, Gasques et al. also analyze the effects of public policies on productivity. They argue that credit is an essential factor for production and modernization. As the production process takes time, the availability of credit provides the liquidity necessary to acquire better-quality inputs and accelerates the adoption of better technologies. It also allows increasing scale of production by the incorporation of lands and equipment. Exports influence productivity because they require products to be improved, stimulate the expansion of the scale of production and require competitiveness made possible only by constant increases in productivity and the reduction of costs.[33]

Helfand and Levine, on analyzing agricultural productivity in the Center-West region, conclude that their results indicate that access to institutions and goods that are often provided by the public sector, such as market access via infrastructure creation and rural electrification, was among the most important determinants of differences in efficiency. Other important determinants included the use of inputs such as irrigation and fertilizers, and differences in the composition of output. These results identify the types of policies and production practices that could contribute to increased technical efficiency in this region. The authors also found a U-shaped relationship between farm size and technical efficiency. From farms of 1,000 to 2,000 ha, efficiency did fall as farm size increased, but beyond this size it started to rise again. The main reason for this is the preferential access by very large farms to institutions and services such as rural electricity, technical assistance and access to markets, which along with the more intensive use of technologies and inputs raised their productivity. These large farms may partially explain the dramatic growth in TFP in the Center-West relative to the rest of Brazil. But the authors believe that if farms under 2,000 hectares had equal access to productivity-enhancing factors, then these farms could still produce more efficiently than farms over 2,000 ha.[34]

Basic research is also essential in productivity growth, especially in a tropical country because it opens possibilities in terms of discoveries of new varieties, which are more resistant and productive; develops improved management techniques and new forms of planting; and brings

---

[33] José Garcia Gasques, Eliana Teles Bastos, Constanza Valdes and Mirian Rumenos P. Bacchi, "Produtividade da agricultura Brasileira e os efeitos de algumas políticas," *Revista de Política Agrícola*, XXI, no. 3 (Jul./Aug./Sept. 2012): 83–92.

[34] Steven M. Helfand and Edward S. Levine, "Farm size and the determinants of productive efficiency in the Brazilian Center-West," *Agricultural Economics*, 31 (2004): 248–249.

about improvement in the quality of inputs and in dealing with conditions often unique to the tropics. The effects of the research are not immediate, but cumulative, and also vary over time depending on the crop and soils. Along with the research, the results of the rural extension and guidance services provided by these research centers, public and private, or by processing or trading companies are also significant. In this regard, the role of Embrapa and other public and private entities was crucial since they provided farmers with the means and knowledge to both adopt technological changes and innovations in their production and to adapt them to the specific conditions of local climate and soils. According to the study of TFP results, the strongest effect on productivity is related to research spending. A 1% increase in research spending results in an increase of 0.35% in the TFP, followed in importance by credit and exports.[35]

Along with studies of TFP for the national level, there are also data for individual states for the period 1970–2006. In this period the cumulative TFP indicator resulted in a 2.27% increase per year. But there was great volatility in the state averages. If we compare the period 1970–2006 with the final period, 1995–2006, these disparities reflect the more recent modernization process, as well as the incorporation of new areas into the productive process. In this last period the states of Espirito Santo, Amapá, Maranhão and Bahia stand out. The states with consolidated agriculture, such as São Paulo, Paraná and Rio Grande do Sul, presented more modest results in this period (see Table 3.6).

Another broad study on agricultural productivity and the disparities between producers predicts that agricultural productivity can grow in the coming years from the same amount of inputs and technologies, through increased technical efficiency. Public and agricultural policies can contribute to this growth and promote the increase of TFP, especially in states with low efficiency.[36]

Brazil today is a leader in both world production and exports of various agricultural products. In the average of the years 2006–2009, the country was the fourth largest agricultural producer in terms of value, just below China, the United States and India. Furthermore, in general, Brazil's performance in agriculture has been very high, when compared with major world agricultural producers such as China, the United States, India, Australia, Canada and Argentina. Overall, Brazil's growth in actual

---

[35] Gasques et al., "Produtividade da agricultura Brasileira": 83–92.
[36] Mendes, "Produtividade Total dos Fatores," pp. 87–88.

TABLE 3.6: *Total factor productivity by state, 1970–2006*

	(Annual rates of growth)	
	2006–1970	2006–1995
Brasil	2.27	2.13
Acre	0.70	4.12
Amapá	2.32	8.59
Amazonas	−0.90	2.07
Pará	0.83	1.99
Rondônia	1.13	4.62
Roraíma	3.29	5.81
Tocantins		−3.58
Alagoas	3.43	6.19
Bahia	1.65	5.55
Ceará	3.86	4.63
Maranhão	2.50	6.37
Paraíba	2.47	1.39
Pernambuco	3.17	4.32
Piauí	2.57	3.30
Rio Grande do Norte	3.19	2.09
Sergipe	2.18	3.74
Espirito santo	3.06	9.49
Minas Gerais	1.72	2.77
Rio de Janeiro	1.64	1.32
São Paulo	1.71	1.09
Paraná	3.48	1.72
Rio Grande do Sul	1.43	1.03
Santa Catarina	3.53	2.96
Distrito Federal	3.02	1.07
Goiás	2.97	0.95
Mato Grosso	4.67	3.87
Mato Grosso Sul		0.32

Source: Gasques et al., "Produtividade Total dos Fatores e Transformações da Agricultura Brasileira" (2010)

production and value of production outstrips other countries, with the exception of China, which has also performed exceptionally well. From the 1980s the same occurs with the estimation of TFP. Among the major producing countries, Brazil and China have maintained an undeniable

TABLE 3.7: *Agricultural production by countries and groups of countries and value of production, and total factor productivity, 1961–2009 – annual change*

Countries and group of countries	Value of production	Agricultural output and productivity growth, annual change					Agricultural TFP, annual change				
		1961–70	1971–80	1981–90	1991–2000	2001–09	1961–70	1971–80	1981–90	1991–2000	2001–09
All developing countries		6.2	3.0	3.4	3.6	3.3	0.7	0.9	1.1	2.2	2.2
All developed countries		2.1	1.9	0.7	1.4	0.6	1.0	1.6	1.4	2.2	2.4
Transition economies		3.3	1.3	0.9	-3.5	2.0	0.6	-0.1	0.6	0.8	2.3
Brazil	127	3.6	3.9	3.4	3.7	4.5	0.2	0.5	3.0	2.6	4.0
USA	229	2.0	2.3	0.6	1.9	1.4	1.2	1.8	1.2	2.2	2.3
China	487	4.9	3.3	4.5	5.3	3.4	0.9	0.6	1.7	4.2	2.8
Argentina	41	1.8	3.0	0.5	3.2	2.7	0.2	3.1	-1.0	1.5	1.2
Australia	23	3.0	1.8	1.7	3.6	-0.8	0.6	1.7	1.3	2.9	0.6
India	205	1.7	2.8	3.4	2.5	3.3	0.5	1.0	1.3	1.2	2.1
Canada	28	2.8	2.3	1.3	2.5	2.0	1.4	-0.4	2.7	2.6	2.1

Source: Fuglie, "Productivity growth and technology capital" (2012)
Notes: Value of production: average period 2006–2009 (US$ – constant values of 2005)

leadership. In the period 2001–2009, for example, Brazil had an annual average growth of 4%, against 2.8% in China, 2.3% in the United States and 2.1% in Canada and India. Argentina and Australia presented significantly lower growth rates of TFP. China and India are not competitors of Brazil, and in fact they are its main markets. Brazilian competition is with the other major producers and exporters of meats and grains, such as the United States, Australia and Canada. In this sense, the Brazilian performance has been exceptional since the 1980s (see Table 3.7).[37]

The analysis of several studies on agricultural productivity and PFF shows the extraordinary performance of Brazilian agriculture, which occurred when the Brazilian economy as a whole did not have good results. Overall productivity in Brazil is low, even in comparison with similar countries, and has stagnated since the 1980s. This productivity stagnation can be attributed to several factors such as high business costs, high tax rates and import tariffs, inadequate infrastructure, low public and private investments in research and development, and low levels of education. The exceptional performance of Brazilian agriculture in terms of production and productivity has allowed Brazil to play an important role in the international market for agribusiness products. Today Brazil is the world's largest producer of coffee, orange juice and sugar; the world's largest exporter of beef and poultry; the world's leading producer of sugarcane; and the leader in sugar and ethanol exports. In addition, it is now the world's largest soybean producer. Although the agricultural sector has a reduced participation in the composition of the national GDP, on the order of 5%, what is called agribusiness includes a large share of the economy: not only agricultural production itself, but the processing of agricultural products; the distribution channels and the supply of basic machines, seeds, fertilizers and other products consumed

---

[37] Kleith O. Fuglie, "Productivity growth and technology capital in the global agricultural economy," in Keith O. Fuglie, Sun Ling Wang and V. Eldon Ball, eds., *Productivity Growth in Agriculture: An International Perspective* (Wallingford: CAB International, 2012), chap. 16. Accessed January 5, 2017, at http://agecon.unl.edu/9280a86c-342e-4c5a-afab-d350503401b8.pdf. Also see Keith O. Fuglie and Sun Ling Wang, "New evidence points to robust but uneven roductivity growth in global agriculture," *Amber Waves*, 10, no. 3 (Sept. 2012): 1–6. Accessed January 6, 2017, at http://baobab.uc3m.es/monet/monnet/IMG/pdf/globalag.pdf; Keith Fuglie and David Schimmelpfennig, "Introduction to the special issue on agricultural productivity growth: a closer look at large, developing countries," *Journal of Production Analysis*, 33 (2010): 169–172; Carlos Ludena, Thomas Hertel, Paulo Preckel, Kenneth Foster and Alejandro Nin Pratt, "Productivity Growth and Convergence in Crop, Ruminant and Non-Ruminant Production: Measurement and Forecasts," *GTAP Working Papers*. Paper 33(2006), accessed at http://docs.lib.purdue.edu/gtapwp/33.

by producers; and the support services including logistics, research, technical assistance, financial services and other similar activities. This larger entity known as Brazilian agribusiness has a major impact on the Brazilian economy, its products, its employment and its exports. Today it is one of the main dynamic elements in the Brazilian economy, is clearly a fundamental element for the future recovery of this economy and is estimated to represent 20% of the national GDP.

In the methodology adopted by CEPEA/USP/CNA (Centro de Estudos Avançados em Economia Aplicada, Universidade de São Paulo), of the total GDP value of this Brazilian agribusiness, the agricultural sector itself represents about 25%, the same percentage is contributed by the industry used to process agricultural products, and another 40% by the services allocated in the process of production, transformation and distribution of agricultural production. The inputs needed to grow and market the crops make up about 5% of agribusiness GDP. The decomposition of agribusiness into production sectors shows a preponderance of agriculture (with just over two-thirds), with the livestock sector accounting for about one-third (see Table 3.8).

When we analyze agricultural production from the perspective of the gross value of production, soybeans stand out as the most important product, with about 32% of the gross value of crops and 20% of the total gross value of crops and livestock. The others are, in order, sugar cane (14% of crops), corn in grain (11%), oranges (7%) and coffee (6%). Coffee, which represented the most dynamic and representative element of the Brazilian economy up to the 1950s, today stands at the same level of importance as bananas and tomatoes, both representing just 4%. In the animal production sector, the leadership is exercised by cattle and chickens, approximately one-third each, followed by milk production (15%), pigs and eggs (see Table 3.9).

The performance of agribusiness has been fundamental to resolve the balance of payments in Brazil. Agribusiness exports have been growing steadily since the beginning of the twenty-first century. Starting at about US$20 billion in 2000, these exports reached US$94 billion in 2011, representing a growth rate of 15% per year, and have since stabilized in amounts of around US$100 billion in the second decade of the century. The greatest importance of agribusiness performance in the external area is not only the amount of exports but its share in the total value exported by Brazil (46% in 2015). The most important result is due to the fact that agribusiness on average exports 80% more agricultural products than the nation imports. As the Brazilian trade balance, excluding agribusiness, is

TABLE 3.8: *Agricultural GDP and composition and participation in the Brazilian GDP, 1996–2017*

| | Agriculture (1) % of GDP | Agribusiness (2) % of GDP | Agribusiness | | | | | | Sector of agribusiness | |
| | | | Composition of agribusiness | | | | | | | |
			Inputs	Farming and animal production (3)	Industry	Services		Agriculture	Ranching
1996	5.5%	28.3%	2%	14%	37%	46%		75%	25%
1997	5.4%	25.8%	2%	15%	37%	46%		75%	25%
1998	5.5%	24.7%	3%	16%	36%	46%		76%	24%
1999	5.5%	24.7%	3%	16%	36%	45%		77%	23%
2000	5.6%	25.5%	3%	15%	36%	46%		77%	23%
2001	6.0%	25.7%	3%	17%	35%	45%		75%	25%
2002	6.6%	26.2%	4%	19%	33%	43%		77%	23%
2003	7.4%	27.0%	4%	22%	32%	42%		79%	21%
2004	6.9%	24.2%	5%	21%	33%	41%		78%	22%
2005	5.7%	21.4%	4%	18%	35%	42%		77%	23%
2006	5.5%	20.6%	4%	21%	34%	41%		81%	19%
2007	5.6%	20.1%	4%	21%	33%	42%		75%	25%
2008	5.9%	20.2%	5%	22%	31%	41%		72%	28%
2009	5.6%	19.1%	5%	20%	33%	43%		73%	27%
2010	5.3%	19.2%	4%	23%	31%	42%		73%	27%

(continued)

TABLE 3.8: *(continued)*

	Agriculture (1) % of GDP	Agribusiness (2) % of GDP	Composition of agribusiness				Sector of agribusiness	
			Inputs	Farming and animal production (3)	Industry	Services	Agriculture	Ranching
2011	5.5%	18.6%	5%	26%	30%	40%	75%	25%
2012	5.3%	17.2%	5%	24%	30%	40%	76%	24%
2013	5.7%	17.0%	5%	25%	30%	40%	72%	28%
2014	5.0%	16.9%	5%	25%	30%	41%	69%	31%
2015	5.0%	18.2%	5%	24%	30%	42%	68%	32%
2016		20.0%	5%	25%	29%	42%	70%	30%
2017 (prov.)			5%	26%	28%	41%	70%	30%

Source: CEPEA/USP/CNA; www.cepea.esalq.usp.br/br/pib-do-agronegocio-brasileiro.aspx

Notes: (1) Here includes all production of plants and animals.

(2) Agribusiness includes all processing of animals and plants as well as machines, seeds and other inputs.

(3) The Portuguese word *pecuário*, which we translate here as 'animal production,' usually includes all animals and not just cattle.

TABLE 3.9: *Gross value of production – farming and pastoral, 2015*

	R$ millions	% in farming	% in total talue
FARMING			
Soybeans	93,607	32%	20%
Sugarcane	42,363	14%	9%
Corn	32,125	11%	7%
Oranges	20,130	7%	4%
Coffee	18,322	6%	4%
Bananas	12,661	4%	3%
Tomatoes	11,167	4%	2%
Herbaceous cotton	10,658	4%	2%
Rice	9,535	3%	2%
Beans	7,595	3%	2%
Manioc	7,241	2%	2%
Tobacco	7,233	2%	2%
Potatoes	5,448	2%	1%
Wheat	3,978	1%	1%
Grapes	3,741	1%	1%
Apples	3,450	1%	1%
Onions	1,046	0%	0%
Cacao	881	0%	0%
Pepper	833	0%	0%
Peanuts	830	0%	0%
Cashews	114	0%	0%
TOTAL FARMING	292,956	100%	61%
ANIMAL PRODUCTION			
Cows	70,389	38%	15%
Chickens	63,044	34%	13%
Milk	27,524	15%	6%
Pigs	12,760	7%	3%
Eggs	10,876	6%	2%
TOTAL ANIMAL PRODUCTION	184,592	100%	39%
GVP TOTAL	477,548		100%

Source: SPA/MAPA

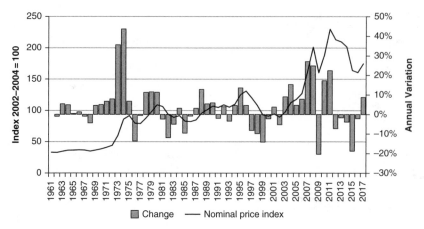

GRAPH 3.10: FAO price index, nominal, 1961–2017 (2002–2004=10)
Source: FAO. www.fao.org/worldfoodsituation/FoodPricesIndex/en/

highly negative, it is these agricultural exports that have allowed for the generation of exceptional positive trade balances in most of the years from 2004, or enabled Brazil to avoid greater imbalances in some problematic years, as in 2014. In that year, agribusiness generated a positive balance of US$83 billion, but despite this positive result, the balance of the trade was negative at US$4 billion, demonstrating the structural imbalance that exists in Brazilian foreign trade when agribusiness is excluded (see Table 3.10).

This exceptional performance of Brazilian agriculture also benefited from changes in the international commodity market, particularly the agricultural commodities market. After a long period of relative price stability, which lasted through the 1980s and 1990s, at the beginning of the twenty-first century agricultural commodity prices grew rapidly, largely influenced by China's strong growth and its increasing market penetration in commodities in general. The FAO Food Price Index, which is based on the average of the years 2002–2004, peaked at 230 in 2011.[38] This meant a growth of 130% in a decade. Since 2011 there has been a significant reduction in this index, reaching 169 in early 2018, a fall of 27% (see Graph 3.10). Despite this sharp decline, Brazilian agribusiness exports managed to remain relatively stable until 2014, showing a significant decline in 2015 and 2016 with a significant recovery in

---

[38] FAO Food Price Index, accessed August 1, 2017, at www.fao.org/worldfoodsituation/FoodPricesIndex/en/.

TABLE 3.10: *Value of total exports and of agricultural exports from Brazil,*
1977–2016

Years	Exports (US$ billions)			Imports (US$ billions)			Balance (US$ billions)	
	Total Brazil (a)	Agrib-usiness (b)	% b/a	Total Brazil (a)	Agrib-usiness (b)	% b/a	Total Brazil	Agribusiness
1989	34.4	13.9	40%	18.3	3.1	17%	16.1	10.8
1990	31.4	13.0	41%	20.7	3.2	15%	10.8	9.8
1991	31.6	12.4	39%	21.0	3.6	17%	10.6	8.8
1992	35.8	14.5	40%	20.6	3.0	14%	15.2	11.5
1993	38.6	15.9	41%	25.3	4.2	16%	13.3	11.8
1994	43.5	19.1	44%	33.1	5.7	17%	10.5	13.4
1995	46.5	20.9	45%	50.0	8.6	17%	-3.5	12.3
1996	47.7	21.1	44%	53.3	8.9	17%	-5.6	12.2
1997	53.0	23.4	44%	59.8	8.2	14%	-6.8	15.2
1998	51.1	21.6	42%	57.8	8.0	14%	-6.6	13.5
1999	48.0	20.5	43%	49.3	5.7	12%	-1.3	14.8
2000	55.1	20.6	37%	55.9	5.8	10%	-0.7	14.8
2001	58.3	23.9	41%	55.6	4.8	9%	2.7	19.1
2002	60.4	24.8	41%	47.2	4.5	9%	13.2	20.4
2003	73.2	30.7	42%	48.3	4.8	10%	24.9	25.9
2004	96.7	39.0	40%	62.8	4.8	8%	33.8	34.2
2005	118.6	43.6	37%	73.6	5.1	7%	45.0	38.5
2006	137.8	49.5	36%	91.4	6.7	7%	46.5	42.8
2007	160.7	58.4	36%	120.6	8.7	7%	40.0	49.7
2008	167.9	71.8	43%	173.2	11.8	7%	-5.3	60.0
2009	153.0	64.8	42%	127.7	9.9	8%	25.3	54.9
2010	201.9	76.4	38%	181.6	13.4	7%	20.3	63.1
2011	256.0	94.6	37%	226.3	17.1	8%	29.8	77.5
2012	242.6	95.8	39%	223.1	16.4	7%	19.4	79.4
2013	242.2	100.0	41%	239.6	17.1	7%	2.6	82.9
2014	225.1	100.0	44%	229.1	16.6	7%	-4.0	83.4
2015	191.1	88.2	46%	171.5	13.1	8%	19.7	75.2
2016	185.2	84.9	46%	137.5	13.6	10%	47.7	71.3

Source: To 2015: Agrostat Brasil based on data from SECEX/MDIC. Elaborated DAC/SRI/MAPA; 2016: Agrostat and MICES

2017. The penetration of Brazil into the international market was fundamental to enable a systematic growth in production, without the limita-
tions imposed by the size of the domestic market. But this was only
possible through the extraordinary increase in local agricultural productivity, without which Brazil would not become competitive in the international market, especially over the long run when it will have to face
periods of declining prices without departing from the market. The only
way to maintain the Brazilian position in the world market, occupying
leadership positions in many products, will be by the systematic increase
of productivity.[39]

It is important to emphasize that Brazil's transformation into a major
exporter of agricultural products occurred at the same time as it achieved
high levels of production and increased productivity even in traditional
food crops. This allowed Brazilian agriculture to adequately supply the
domestic market, which in turn led to a systematic fall in local food prices.
According to a recent study, between February 1976 and August 2006, the
value of a basic basket of foods declined at a significant 3.13% per annum.
The authors conclude that the major beneficiaries would have been the
poorest consumers and that without this fall in food prices the Cardoso
and Lula programs of income transfer would not have been successful.[40]

When we compare Brazilian agriculture and Brazilian industry, both of
which suffered the effects of a series of major national and international
fiscal crises, and their exposure to world market competition, we see that
both agriculture and industry have been forced to transform themselves in
order to survive international competition. But the results observed in
these two sectors of the economy are quite different. Industry has modernized itself, increased its productivity, but never reached international
standards of competitiveness that allowed it to actively participate in the
world market. Only in a few exceptional sectors, such as aeronautics,
represented by Embraer, has industry succeeded in the creation of value
chains that could compete internationally. Unfortunately Embraer is one
of the few industrial companies to achieve such integration, being able to
compete with the largest aeronautical companies in the world. But, in
general, Brazilian industry today, after more than twenty years of the

---

[39] Antonio Márcio Buainain et al., "Quais os riscos mais relevantes nas atividades
agropecuárias?" in Buainain et al., *O Mundo Rural no Brasil*: 135–208: 193.

[40] Eliseu R. A. Alves, Geraldo da S. e Souza and Daniela de P. Rocha e Renner Marra, "Fatos
marcantes da agricultura brasileira," in E. R. A. Alves, G. S. Souza and E. G. Gomes
(eds.), *Contribuição da Embrapa para o Desenvolvimento da Agricultura no Brasil*
(Brasília: Embrapa, 2013): 22.

process of opening of the Brazilian economy, is a low-competitive sector which has only a modest impact on Brazilian exports.

Undeniably industry suffered the perverse effects of both the so-called "Brazil Cost" of doing business and of economic policies which discouraged local production. Although there is no objective measure or definition of the "Brazil Cost," there are numerous studies that demonstrate the existence of factors that increase the cost of production in Brazil. A recent study by the Federation of Industries of the State of São Paulo points to the "Brazil Cost" as the main cause of the loss of competitiveness of the economy, particularly in manufacturing.[41] The study points out six factors which generate the cost differential in Brazilian production. These include the costs of working capital, of energy and raw materials, of infrastructure and logistics, the expenses of services and employees, the costs of non-tradeable services, and taxation (the actual tax and bureaucratic costs).

An example of the difficulties of the business environment faced by companies in Brazil is the complexity of paying taxes, which corresponds to 2.6% of total industrial prices. According to the World Bank in Brazil, 2,600 hours are spent annually to prepare, register and pay taxes, against 179 hours in developed countries, 255 in emerging countries, 227 in trade partners and 338 hours in China. If we add this differential tax burden, we obtain an increase of 15.5% in industrial prices compared to the partners and 16.1% in the developed countries.

The second item in importance of this "Brazil Cost" is represented by the financial cost. Brazil traditionally has one of the highest interest rates in the world, which starts with a high basic interest rate in the securities offered by the Central Bank, to which a high banking spread is added. Even after the stabilization achieved by the 1994 *Real* Plan, the Central Bank always maintained high real interest rates of around 5% in the last ten years (see Graph 3.11). But in addition to a high basic interest rate paid on federal public securities, a high bank spread is practiced in Brazil, remunerating bank costs, taxes, credit risk, etc. According to a report by the Central Bank of Brazil, average interest rate on financial system credit operations reached 32.0% per annum in March 2016. However, this rate varied widely among the various categories of credit. In credit operations with free resources, the average rate in March 2016 reached 51.0% per annum, while in the case of targeted loans, it was 10.9% per annum.

---

[41] Fiesp/Decomtec, *"Custo Brasil" e a Taxa de Câmbio na Competitividade da Indústria de Transformação Brasileira* (São Paulo, March 2013).

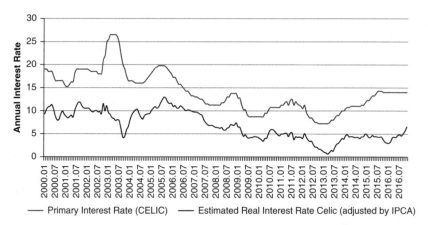

GRAPH 3.11: Primary interest rates and real interest rates, 2000–2016
Source: BCB and Ipeadata

In March 2016, inflation in twelve months reached 9.4% and the basic interest rate (Celic) was 14.25% per annum. The average free rate, at 51%, represented a spread of around 32% over the base rate and a real interest rate of 38% per annum. By aggregating the various factors that negatively influence domestic manufacturing costs, the study obtained

TABLE 3.11: *Differences in the "Brazil Cost" in relation to other world regions*

| | Differences in relation to other regions | | | |
	Commercial partners	Developed	Emergent	China
Fiscal charges	15.50%	16.10%	14.50%	14.10%
Short-term loans	4.50%	5.30%	3.20%	4.40%
Energy & primary materials	2.90%	0.10%	6.20%	7.70%
Logistic infrastructure	1.50%	1.60%	1.10%	1.20%
Extra costs of services & functions	0.70%	0.60%	0.90%	1.00%
Non-tradable services	0.20%	0%	2.40%	2.40%
Total	25.40%	22.60%	28.30%	30.90%

Source: FIESP/DECOMTEC, *"Custo Brasil" e a Taxa de Câmbio na Competitividade da Indústria de Transformação Brasileira* (2013).

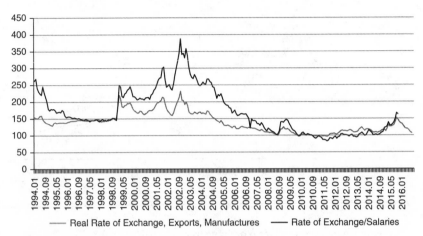

GRAPH 3.12: Effective rate of exchange in relation to change of salary, 1994–2016 (2010=100)
Source: Ipeadata

results ranging from 22.6% in relation to developed countries to 30.9% in relation to China, today Brazil's main trading partner (see Table 3.11).

In addition to the so-called Brazil cost, over the years the country has maintained an overvalued exchange rate for most of this time, reducing the competitiveness of local production. The effective exchange rate of manufactured exports in 1994 reached an average index of 146 and remained at this level for many years. From 2007 onward the *real* was also overvalued, with an average index below 110, prejudicing exports and stimulating imports. The wage exchange ratio followed a similar behavior, hampering the competitiveness of production in Brazil. Finally, countervailing government policies of market protection, tariff increases and direct subsidies in addition to discouraging the internal productivity of the industry, have even been questioned by international entities such as the WTO. There are several causes to explain the over-valuation of the exchange rate, but the maintenance of extremely high interest rates is undoubtedly one of them and perhaps the most important (see Graph 3.12).

The overvaluing of the national currency and the deterioration of the exchange–wage relationship hampered the competitiveness of national industry, which declined in importance in the national economy. Industry, which had consolidated the process of import substitution and completed its productive integration in the late 1980s, accounted then for approximately one-third of GDP; nowadays (2014) it accounts for only

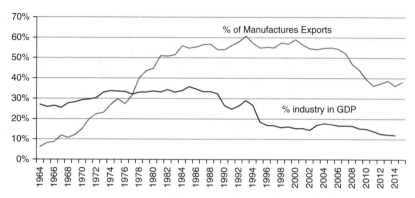

GRAPH 3.13: Industrial participation in the GDP and participation of manufactures in exports, 1964–2015 (%)
Source: Ipeadata and Ministério da Indústria e Comércio

12% of GDP. This is a trend which many scholars have suggested is the beginning of a process of premature deindustrialization, since it anticipates a path that mature countries have followed, but which does not correspond to the current economic and social development level of Brazil.[42] The loss of the importance of industry can also be attested by the significant reduction of the participation of manufactures in Brazilian exports. This percentage, which had remained around 55% since the beginning of the 1980s, has declined sharply in the last fifteen years, and has remained below 40% since 2010 (see Graph 3.13).

But it is not just external factors, such as the "Brazil Cost" and exchange rate behavior, that undermine the competitiveness of Brazilian industry. In general, the Brazilian economy, which includes industry, services and agriculture, has maintained an unfavorable performance when we analyze its productivity, as measured by TFP.[43] During the

---

[42] The debate on deindustrialization is wide-ranging and has received special attention from the academic world for several years. See José Luis Oreiro e Carmem A. Feijó, "Desindustrialização: conceituação, causas, efeitos e o caso brasileiro," *Revista de Economia Política*, 30, no. 2 (Apr./Jun. 2010): 219–232; and Regis Bonelli and Samuel de Abreu Pessoa, "Desindustrialização do Brasil: um Resumo da Evidência" (Texto para Discussão, no. 7; Rio de Janeiro: Fundação Getúlio Vargas/IBRE, 2010). We should note that by subtracting services from industrial production, the statistics eliminate part of the value added previously considered in industry and now incorporated in services, thus distorting the results of intertemporal comparisons.

[43] For the period 1982–2012 we use the series adjusted by Barbosa Filho and Pessoa (2014). The adjustment corresponded to the use of hourly data to calculate labor productivity, unlike earlier studies that used the employed population. The authors identify a tendency in the period to reduce the average hours worked by employed persons, which, if not

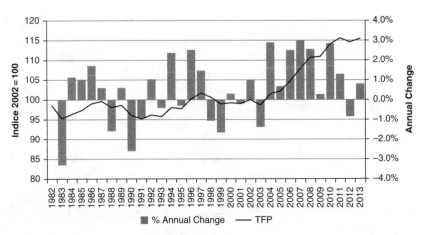

GRAPH 3.14: Total factor productivity of the Brazilian economy, 1982–2013 (2002=100)
Source: years 1982–2012: Barbosa Filho and Pessoa, "Pessoa ocupado e jornada de trabalho" (2014); year 2013: Barbosa Filho, *Nota sobre a produtividade no Brasil* (2014)

period 1982–2003, the Brazilian economy's TFP remained practically stable, with a relative growth in the period 2004–2010, stabilizing until 2013, the last year with available data. Even if we consider these initial years of the twenty-first century, which were more favorable in the TFP indicator of the economy as a whole, we still see a much lower performance of the economy as a whole than in agriculture in the period. Between 2000 and 2011 the agricultural TFP increased 78%. In the same period, the national economy grew by only 16% (see Graph 3.14).

If this occurs with industry, how can we explain the contrary strengthening of Brazilian agriculture in this same period? Agriculture faces external competition, and suffers the same effects of the Brazil Cost and the

taken into account, would distort the results. Fernando de Holanda Barbosa Filho and Samuel de Abreu Pessoa, "Pessoa ocupado e jornada de trabalho. Uma releitura da evolução da produtividade no Brasil," *Revista Brasileira de Economia*, 68, no. 2 (Apr./Jun. 2014): 149–169. For the year 2013 we utilized Fernando de Holanda Barbosa Filho, *Nota sobre a produtividade no Brasil*, FGV (Nota Técnica, 2014). Accessed January 8, 2017, at portalibre.fgv.br/lumis/portal/file/fileDownload.jsp?fileId. Also see Naercio Menezes Filho, Gabriela Campos and Bruno Komatsu, "Evolução da Produtividade no Brasil" (São Paulo, Insper, Policy Paper no. 12, August 2014), accessed at www.insper.edu .br/wp-content/uploads/.../Evolucao-Produtividade-Brasil.pdf; and Pedro Cavalcanti Ferreira, "Produtividade e Eficiência," Rio de Janeiro, FGV, 2013, accessed January 8, 2017, at www.insper.edu.br/wp-content/uploads/2013/06/2013_08_01_Insper_Produtivi dade_Pedro_Ferreira.pdf.

perverse effects of the exchange overvaluation, yet it was still able to become highly competitive, dramatically increasing its productivity and inserting itself deep into national and international value chains. Using modern financing, distribution and protection mechanisms against the inherent risks of the business, agribusiness also successfully integrates agriculture and industry in an organic way. This is also due to a small but dynamic sector of entrepreneurial farmers who have responded to all the new incentives both in their traditional areas and by opening up enormous new frontiers like the Cerrado to modern commercial farming. In their associations and cooperatives these farmers have strongly supported both public and private research, promoted agricultural research and developed new styles of commercial operations to expand their reach beyond the national borders.

But agriculture, despite its exceptional performance, still faces significant challenges. These include factors not directly under its control, such as the so-called cost of doing business in Brazil. Of these costs the deficient infrastructure is the most severe. Another factor outside its control is the periodic protection of national industry by the Brazilian government. This policy can hinder international trade, as reciprocity is the basic rule of such trade. Thus agricultural importing nations may be hostile to an economy that over-protects its national industry and prohibits their exports to Brazil. There are also other serious problems facing Brazilian agriculture, which we will address in the following chapters, such as the questions of sustainability and protection of the environment; the need for increasing productivity to maintain the position Brazilian agriculture has already achieved in the market, which involves moving all regions up to international productivity standards; and the persistence of a majority share of the rural population who are marginal to this highly competitive economy.

4

Inputs, Technology, Productivity and Sustainability

Although there were previous transformations, it was in the post-World War II period that effective public sector policies were implemented in favor of the modernization of Brazilian agriculture. This modernization was based on the promotion of the application of tractors and fertilizers to agriculture, first through importations and then through the development of national agribusinesses which could supply these crucial inputs. Moreover, like previous government initiatives going back to Vargas, these policies dedicated to transformations were timid until the 1960s.

It is also important to recognize that the history of the modernization of Brazilian agriculture occurred after the so-called "green revolution" of the mid-twentieth century.[1] This group of reforms promoted the modernization of agricultural production through technological packages of general application, which increased production and allowed for the expansion of agricultural production in different ecological environments. These technological packages replicated the technological processes successfully developed in the advanced countries as well as in underdeveloped and developing ones. This meant not only transporting methods from rich countries to poor countries but also adopting methods developed in temperate countries to tropical and subtropical countries.[2]

---

[1] Gordon Conway, *Produção de Alimentos no Século XXI: Biotecnologia e Meio Ambiente* (São Paulo: Estação Liberdade, 2003), pp. 69–74.
[2] Alan Kardec Veloso de Matos, "Revolução verde, biotecnologia e tecnologias alternativas," *Cadernos da Fucamp*, 10, no. 12 (2010): 1–7.

The first experience of this model occurred in Mexico during the 1940s.[3]

In the Brazilian case, the reproduction of such a model occurred from the 1960s. The credit policy then adopted was based on massive public subsidies, which led to the modernization of agriculture in the context of the intensification of industry through the import substitution process. This led to the consolidation of the petrochemical industry and its fertilizer sector, and the major expansion of local production of tractors and agricultural machinery. The government also supplied abundant and subsidized credit and guaranteed a minimum level of profit, but it required as well the implementation of modern production practices. Government and directed credit, a minimum price policy, regulation of producer stocks, and fixing prices provided the capital to expand the use of tractors, machine tools and agricultural inputs, particularly fertilizers. But not all farmers benefited or could take advantage of this price and credit support since they needed access to information and the education to take advantage of this information. The modernization of agriculture would thus lead to an increasing segmentation of the market between producers capable of using this credit and subsidies and producers without access to credit. With little education and only small parcels of land, many small farmers were unable to access these resources or use them profitably.

Fertilizers were produced in Brazil as early as 1940, with factories mixing the NPK using imported raw materials. But even at this early period they were already adapting the formulations to the specificities of Brazilian soils. Until 1960, local fertilizer production was limited to the exploration of a phosphate mine discovered in São Paulo in 1940, the product of some chemical plants of Petrobrás and a few simple super phosphate producers. In 1971 natural gas was used to produce ammonia and urea at the plant located in Camaçari, which was established by Nitrofertil, which later built another unit in the Northeast, thus consolidating nitrogen production in the country. At that time the First National Fertilizer and Agricultural Limestone Program (PNFCA) was created by the government with the objective of expanding and modernizing the fertilizer sector. PNFCA was part of the Second National Development Plan launched by the Geisel government (1974–1979), and its aim was to

---

[3] Beatriz Picardo Gonzáles, "La revolución Verde en México," *Agrária* (São Paulo), no. 4 (2006): 40–68; and John H. Perkins, *Geopolitics and the Green Revolution: Wheat, Genes and the Cold War* (New York: Oxford University Press, 1997), chap. 5.

make Brazil independent in this area by creating and protecting a series of industrial complexes for the domestic production of raw materials and fertilizers.[4] Between 1987 and 1995 the Second National Plan of Fertilizers was developed which completed the process of consolidation of the fertilizer industry in Brazil. At the end of this period these companies were privatized through the sale of minority interests in two companies and the control of three other companies, and eventually the private company Fertifos was established which now controls much of the sector.[5]

With national production established, fertilizer consumption increased significantly. Until 1965 the consumption of fertilizers (NPK) was extremely low in Brazil, amounting to 257,000 tons in that year. In 1970 this total increased to 990,000 tons, doubling successively in 1975 and 1980, and then stabilizing for the next fifteen years. The availability of subsidized credit allowed farmers to purchase these nationally produced fertilizers, even though they were offered at prices higher than those practiced in the international market. During the crisis of the 1980s, which continued until the consolidation of the *Real* Plan in the mid-1990s, the consumption of fertilizers remained practically stable. But recession, high inflation and the fiscal crisis dramatically reduced public credit and associated subsidies, and temporarily affected agriculture in terms of the expansion of planted area and the use of fertilizers.

With the opening of the economy, the privatization of the fertilizer sector and the stabilization of the economy, fertilizer use again expanded as the market became open and competitive, both in the placement of agricultural products and in the purchase of its inputs. Since the mid-1990s, agriculture has grown again and use of fertilizers has outpaced the expansion of cultivated area. Between 1995 and 2016 there was a 50% increase in cultivated area, whereas fertilizer consumption multiplied by three, doubling fertilizer consumption per unit of cultivated area (Table 4.1 and Graph 4.1). Currently, the highest fertilizer consumption occurs with crops of soybeans (43%), corn (16%), sugarcane (13%) and

---

[4] The investments in 1°. PNFCA were estimated to be US$2.5 billion, which received strong support from BNDES. Victor Pina Dias and Eduardo Fernandes. *Fertilizantes: Uma Visão Sintética* (Rio de Janeiro: BNDES, 2006). Accessed January 22, 2017, at www.bndes.gov .br/SiteBNDES/export/sites/default/bndes_pt/Galerias/Arquivos/conhecimento/bnset/se t2404.pdf.
[5] Victor Pina Dias and Eduardo Fernandes, *Fertilizantes: Uma Visão Sintética* (Rio de Janeiro: BNDES, 2006).

TABLE 4.1: *Apparent consumption of fertilizers (NPK), 1950–2016 (in tons)*

	Nitrogenated (N)	Phosphor (P)	Potassium (K)	Total (NPK)
1950	14	48	24	86
1955	24	71	30	125
1960	63	74	106	243
1965	71	87	100	257
1970	276	407	307	990
1975	506	913	558	1,977
1980	906	1,854	1,307	4,066
1985	828	1,238	1,062	3,127
1990	914	1,177	1,202	3,292
1995	1,216	1,583	1,764	4,564
2000	2,027	2,492	2,920	7,439
2001	1,731	2,592	2,882	7,205
2002	1,928	2,777	3,068	7,773
2003	2,483	3,653	3,994	10,130
2004	2,457	3,896	4,326	10,679
2005	2,428	3,350	3,465	9,243
2006	2,338	3,172	3,546	9,056
2007	3,079	4,316	4,457	11,852
2008	2,594	3,674	4,341	10,609
2009	2,536	2,940	2,517	7,993
2010	2,872	3,533	4,145	10,550
2011	3,643	4,297	4,933	12,872
2012	3,539	4,484	4,843	12,866
2013	3,935	4,876	4,975	13,786
2014	4,151	5,188	5,855	15,193
2015	3,647	4,661	5,383	13,691
2016	4,576	5,005	5,008	14,589

Source: International Plant Nutrition Institute. Accessed January 22, 2017, at http://brasil
.ipni.net/article/BRS313#evolucao

coffee (5%). Regionally, the Center-West dominates consumption (34%), followed by the South (27%) and the Southeast (24.5%).

Today the market is highly concentrated.[6] The Vale Fertilizantes, which bought Fertifos in 2010, controls almost 60% of productive capacity,

---

[6] On this sector see Yara Kulaif, "Perfil dos Fertilizantes," Ministério de Minas e Energia and Banco Mundial, Relatório Técnico no. 75, 2009. Accessed January 22, 2017, at www

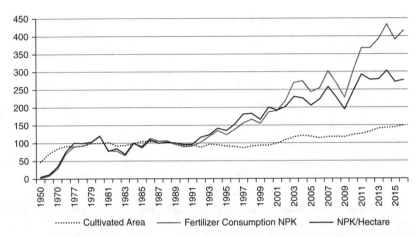

GRAPH 4.1: Area cultivated and use of fertilizers, 1950–2016 (1979–1981=100)
Source: IPNI (2017, 2018), Anda (2009) and Conab (2018) www.conab.gov.br
/conteudos.php?a=1252&t=&Pagina_objcmsconteudos=1#A_objcmsconteudos
http://brasil.ipni.net/article/BRS-3132#evolucao

followed by Anglo American Fosfatos with 12% and Petrobrás with 8%.[7]
Despite the strong growth of national fertilizer production and concentration in large companies, Brazil is still dependent on imports. For the compound NPK formed by nitrogen, phosphorus and potash,[8] Brazil, like most countries, needs to import all three elements which make up this product. Since the main source of hydrogen is natural gas, whose price is high in

.mme.gov.br/documents/1138775/1256652/P49_RT75_Perfil_dos_Fertilizantes_N-P-K
.pdf/f2785733-90d1-46d5-a09e-62f94ca302ad; Leticia M. da Costa and Martim F. de Oliveira e Silva, "A Indústria Química e o Setor de Fertilizantes," BNDES, accessed January 22, 2017, at www.bndes.gov.br/SiteBNDES/export/sites/default/bnde s_pt/Galerias/Arquivos/conhecimento/livro60anos_perspectivas_setoriais/Setorial60ano s_VOL2Quimica.pdf; and Dias and Fernandes. "Fertilizantes."

[7] Vale Fertilizantes was controlled by Vale S.A, formerly Companhia Vale do Rio Doce, which was privatized in 1997. Later, it consolidated the fertilizer sector and took a majority position in the sector through Vale Fertilizantes. At the end of 2016, the company was sold to the US firm "The Mosaic Company," one of the world's largest fertilizer companies.

[8] The main macronutrients for plants are nitrogen (N), phosphorus (P) and potassium (K). Nitrogen contributes to plant growth, amino acid and protein formation. Phosphorus is responsible for assisting in the chemical reactions of plants, interfering in the processes of photosynthesis, respiration, energy storage and transfer, cell division and cell growth. Potassium is important for plant water maintenance, fruit formation, resistance to cold and disease (Costa and Silva, pp. 27–30 "A Indústria Química"; Kulaif, "Perfil dos Fertilizantes," pp. 10–15).

Brazil, Brazil imported more than 90% of its consumption. The largest producers in the world are China, the United States and Russia. Phosphorus production, which comes from phosphate rock, is produced by China, the United States, India, Russia and Brazil. But although occupying fifth position in the world, with approximately 5% of phosphorus production, Brazil still depends heavily on imports, which account for about two-thirds of domestic consumption. Potassium, obtained from potassium chloride, is found in sedimentary layers. Canada, Russia, Belarus and Germany are the world's largest producers. Brazil relies almost completely on imports to supply this product for the domestic market.

As Brazil has become increasingly important in the world supply of agricultural products, it has also become one of the world's great consumers of fertilizer, but has not been able to increase its production of fertilizers proportionally to increasing domestic needs.[9] According to a BNDES study, the unavailability of basic raw materials, as well as logistical, tax and environmental issues, has created a bottleneck for new investments. National production of potassium, for example, a nutrient in great demand in the Brazilian agricultural sector, satisfies only a small portion of consumption. Brazil has only one exploitable potash mine. The others are economically unviable or pose great environmental risks. Brazil, which currently is the fourth largest consumer of fertilizers in the world (accounting for about 7% of world consumption), is thus dependent on imports from the largest world producers such as Russia, Canada, China and the USA.

Fertilizer costs account for about 20% of the total rural farmer's expenditure in agriculture, although there are large differences by product. The exchange ratio between fertilizer and agricultural products, which represents the amount of agricultural product needed to acquire a ton of fertilizer, allows us to see the economic evolution of this relation.[10] If we consider soybeans and corn, the two most representative products in the demand for fertilizers in Brazil, we see that in the case of corn approximately sixty bags are needed for the acquisition of one ton of fertilizer, while the relation with soybean is approximately twenty bags. But more important is the trend of this relationship. In the case of soybeans, this ratio remains relatively stable, while it is strongly increasing in the case of corn, particularly

---

[9] In 2016 Brazil imported 73% of its consumption of nitrogenous fertilizers, 34% of its consumption of phosphates and 67% of its consumption of potassium. Costa and Silva, "A indústria Química," pp. 41–47; International Plant Nutrition Institute, accessed at http://brasil.ipni.net/article/BRS-3132#evolucao; *Fertilizantes*. Bradesco – DEPEC, June 2017.

[10] Costa and Silva, "A Indústria Química," p. 46.

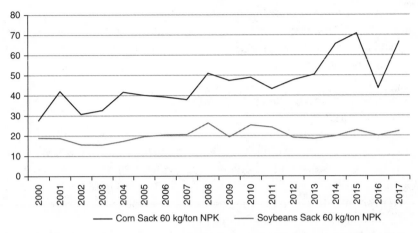

GRAPH 4.2: Relation of exchange between product per ton of fertilizer, 2000–2017
Source: Anda: www.anda.org.br/estatistica/Principais_Indicadores_2017.pdf

since 2007 (see Graph 4.2). This variability is related to technical parameters of the quantity of fertilizers per ton of production (which depends on the product and the physical conditions where the planting takes place), as well as the relative price between the type of fertilizer needed and the price of the final product. By world standards Brazil is an average consumer. There is, of course, also great variability in the consumption of fertilizers by country depending on the type of crop, soil, etc. Thus, Brazil, with an annual consumption of 175 kg per hectare of cultivated land consumes approximately the same amount as India, but on average consumes more than the United States, France, Spain, Italy, Australia, Canada and Argentina, but less than China, Germany, the United Kingdom, Chile and Colombia.[11]

The tractor industry was another segment of agribusiness that expanded significantly due to the stimulus provided by abundant and highly subsidized government credit. Already during the Juscelino Kubitschek administration in the 1950s, the tractor industry in Brazil was created in parallel to the auto industry.[12] In 1959 the Executive

[11] World Bank table "Fertilizer Consumption (kilograms per hectare of ariable land)," accessed January 3, 2017, at http://databank.worldbank.org/data/reports.aspx?source=2&series=AG.CON.FERT.ZS&country=#.
[12] See João Amato Neto, "A indústria de máquinas agrícolas no Brasil: origens e evolução," *Revista de Administração de.Empresas*, 25, no. 3 (Jul./Sept. 1985): 57–69; Carlos Eduardo de Freitas Vian and Adilson Martins Andrade Júnior, "Evolução Histórica da

Group of the Automobile Industry created the standards to be followed by the industries that settled in Brazil, and six tractor production plants were quickly established, five of them foreign. In 1961 these factories produced 1,679 wheeled tractors, but quickly reached the level of 10,000 tractors per annum in 1963. Production increased again from then until 1976, reaching a record production of 64,000 units, which would only be surpassed in 2008.

The crisis of the 1980s also affected the tractor industry, which dramatically reduced its output over the next twenty years. The crisis of the 1980s and the opening of competition with foreign producers forced a reorganization of national production. The manufacturers that managed to survive developed a sophisticated production technology, eliminating older models and establishing new production lines. In addition, during the crisis of this decade they turned to exporting to foreign markets, and, supported by special credit lines and bilateral trade agreements, local industry developed differentiation of models, the inclusion of new devices and optional accessories that met the demands of international clients.[13]

Since the beginning of the twenty-first century, following the recovery of domestic demand and the growth of tractor exports, there has been a resumption of previous levels of production, reaching a maximum of

Indústria de Máquinas Agrícolas no Mundo: Origens e Tendências," *48°. Congresso da Sober*, accessed January 23, 2017, at www.sober.org.br/palestra/15/1208.pdf; *O setor de máquinas agrícolas no Brasil: evolução nos últimos anos e perspectivas*, Celeres, 2014, accessed January 22, 2017, at www.celeres.com.br/o-setor-de-maquinas-agricolas-no-brasil-evolucao-nos-ultimos-anos-e-perspectivas/; Celso Luis Rodrigues Vegro, Célia Regina R.P. T. Ferreira and Flavio Condé de Carvalho, "Indústria brasileira de máquinas agrícolas: evolução e mercado, 1985–95," *Informações Econômicas*, 27, no.1 (Jan. 1997): 11–26; Bradesco/Depec, "Tratores e Máquinas Agrícolas," (Dec. 2016), accessed January 24, 2017, at www.economiaemdia.com.br/EconomiaEmDia/pdf/infset_tratores_e_maquinas_a gricolas.pdf; Julio Cavalheiro Kopf and Algemiro Luís Brum, "A cadeia produtiva de tratores brasileira à luz da teoria do comércio exterior: Aspectos Introdutórios," *Seminário Internacional sobre Desenvolvimento Regional*, Santa Cruz do Sul, RG, 2015, accessed January 24, 2017, at http://online.unisc.br/acadnet/anais/index.php/sidr/article/vie w/13429. On the mechanization of the Northeast see Kelly S. L. de Vasconcelos, J. Tiago, J. da Silva and Sonia R.S. Melo, "Mecanização da agricultura por tratores de rodas e máquinas agrícolas nos estados da Região Nordeste," *Revista em Agronegócio e Meio Ambiente* (Maringá), 6, no. 2 (May/Aug. 2013), 207–222.

[13] Julio Cavalheiro Kopf and Algemiro Luís Brum, "A cadeia produtiva de tratores brasileira à luz da teoria do comércio exterior: aspectos introdutórios," *Seminário Internacional sobre Desenvolvimento Regional*, Santa Cruz do Sul, RG, 2015. Accessed January 24, 2017, at http://online.unisc.br/acadnet/anais/index.php/sidr/article/view/13429.

TABLE 4.2: *Sales, production, importation and exportation of wheeled tractors and grain harvesters, 1961–2017*

Years	Wheeled tractors					Grain harvesters				
	Total sales	National sales	Imported sales	Production	Exports	Total sales	National sales	Imported sales	Production	Exports
1961–70	89,097	89,097		88,752	94	24,396	24,396		24,673	857
1971–80	443,136	443,136		471,627	28,173	45,899	45,899		50,997	5,383
1981–90	319,075	319,075		373,085	54,853	23,748	23,374	374	33,911	10,500
1991–2000	191,564	189,952	1,612	228,712	38,764	38,556	38,142	414	63,293	24,876
2001–10	334,434	329,571	4,863	494,803	164,040					
2001	28,203	28,090	113	34,781	5,814	4,098	4,054	44	5,196	1,202
2002	33,217	33,186	31	40,352	7,945	5,648	5,616	32	6,851	1,199
2003	29,476	29,405	71	46,435	16,589	5,440	5,434	6	9,195	3,232
2004	28,803	28,636	167	52,768	23,553	5,605	5,598	7	10,443	4,533
2005	17,729	17,543	186	40,871	23,968	1,534	1,533	1	4,229	3,001
2006	20,435	20,141	294	35,586	16,532	1,030	1,030		2,314	1,867
2007	31,300	30,691	609	50,719	20,068	2,377	2,347	30	5,148	2,783
2008	43,414	41,966	1,448	66,504	23,056	4,458	4,340	118	8,407	3,567
2009	45,437	44,206	1,231	55,024	12,344	3,817	3,683	134	4,503	1,231
2010	56,420	55,707	713	71,763	14,171	4,549	4,507	42	7,007	2,261
2011	52,296	50,966	1,330	63,427	12,620	5,343	5,306	37	7,630	2,390

(continued)

TABLE 4.2: (continued)

Years	Wheeled tractors					Grain harvesters				
	Total sales	National sales	Imported sales	Production	Exports	Total sales	National sales	Imported sales	Production	Exports
2012	55,819	53,893	1,926	64,456	12,167	6,278	6,187	91	7,485	1,238
2013	65,089	63,786	1,303	77,570	11,182	8,539	8,285	254	9,948	1,140
2014	55,612	55,230	382	64,783	9,418	6,448	6,433	15	7,623	1,026
2015	37,381	36,959	422	44,349	7,338	3,917	3,907	10	3,889	383
2016	35,956	35,874	82	43,360	6,277	4,498	4,491	7	4,869	431
2017	36,964	36,881	83	42,429	8,473	4,537	4,536	1	5,513	1,011

Source: Anfavea– www.anfavea.com.br/estatisticas-2017.html

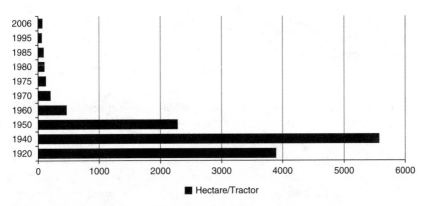

GRAPH 4.3: Average area of cultivation per tractor (ha), 1920–2006
Source: IBGE

77,000 tractors in 2013. The production of grain harvesters has remained at the level of 6,000–10,000 units per annum in this period, with exports of 1,000–2,000 units. Imports of this type of equipment are no longer significant (Table 4.2).

Four states, São Paulo, Rio Grande do Sul, Paraná and Mato Grosso, accounted for about 60% of the market for tractors in 2015. By region, the South represents 37%, the Southeast 32% and the Central West 16%. Three producers, John Deere, AGCO/Valtra and New Holland, which are among the world's largest producers of agricultural machinery, account for 80% of production in Brazil.

Although tractor use had grown dramatically since 1920 (see Graph 4.3), by world standards, Brazil in 2006 was still only a moderate user of tractors. By then it had 117 tractors per 100 km² of arable land. Other large land area countries were double that rate. Thus the US had 276 tractors for the same amount of arable land, and Canada used 162 tractors per 100 km², but Argentina had just 88 (as of 2002). The smaller countries of the European Union (for 2005) had an average of 708 tractors and Chile used 399 tractors in 2006.[14] If one were to use only the commercial farming areas of Brazil, the indices would be close to the other countries. It is worth stressing that any comparative average indicator per hectare for Brazil is somewhat misleading. Brazil has a highly segmented agriculture with a powerful but minority commercial sector,

---

[14] World Bank, "Agricultural machinery, tractors per 100 sq. km of arable land," at http://data.worldbank.org/indicator/AG.LND.TRAC.ZS, accessed January 3, 2017.

but also a majority of farms still practicing a traditional low capitalized and low productivity agriculture. In none of the other countries mentioned above is there a disparity in the structure of agricultural production, as in Brazil, in which two completely different productive segments coexist.

The introduction of fertilizers and agricultural equipment would be of great importance in the process of modernization of Brazilian agriculture, but the sector would not have reached its current competitiveness in the world agribusiness market without major technological transformations and the diffusion of modern farming ideas. In this sense, Embrapa and other public and private research institutes as well as the multinational agricultural companies, played a fundamental role. In the late 1960s and early 1970s, there was general agreement on the need to promote agricultural research and rural extension. In the 1950–70 period policymakers emphasised rural extension and neglected agricultural research. They thought that a vast array of technologies were already available for adoption by Brazil. But by the early 1970s they realized that this could not be done given the particular semi-tropical and tropical nature of Brazilian agriculture. Thus began a major effort in tropical agricultural research, and in turn science-based technologies fueled the extension service.[15] In this context, governmental agricultural credit was associated with public and private technical assistance. The idea was to strengthen human capital to better utilize the investments being made available for the acquisition of capital goods and modern inputs. Technical assistance was tied to rural credit and was compulsory until the 1990s, being paid for by the farmer. In the 2000s this association was only mandatory for a few credit lines, and since then farmers who are well integrated into markets have been predominantly using private technical assistance.[16]

Both rural extension and agricultural research have a long history in Brazil. According to a recent study, the process of information transfer between rural producers is traditionally characterized by a cooperative, free and interpersonal exchange of information. Producers get most of the information from a variety of sources: family, friends, neighboring producers, informal producer groups, community associations, unions and

---

[15] Geraldo B. Martha Jr., Elisio Contini and Eliseu Alves, "Embrapa: its origins and changes," in Werner Baer, ed., *The Regional Impact of National Policies. The Case of Brazil* (Cheltenham and Northampton, Mass.: Edward Elgar, 2012), 204–226.
[16] Ibid.

producer cooperatives. However, information is also acquired through rural extension services, both public and private. Thus, for generations, the diffusion of technologies was an important source of economic change. Although modern rural extension emerged as early as the nineteenth century, most countries began such services in the 1950s and 1960s. Also the agricultural extension cooperative system between government and agricultural universities established in the United States at the beginning of the twentieth century could not be reproduced in developing countries because even as late as the 1950s, their rural universities were fragile or nonexistent. For this reason, many rural extension services began their activities linked to the ministries of agriculture, but were little coordinated with agricultural research.[17]

The model adopted for rural extension followed the American standard, and was part of the technical cooperation agreements enacted between the US and Brazil in the 1940s and 1950s.[18] In 1948, in an agreement with an entity related to Nelson Rockefeller, the Association of Credit and Rural Assistance (ACAR-MG) was founded in Minas Gerais, which adopted the American idea of rural extension in Brazil. From its inception it conditioned supervised rural credit, with the need to accept extension services, and was organized in collaboration with Caixa

---

[17] Marcus Peixoto, "Mudanças e desafios da extensão rural no Brasil e no mundo," in Antonio Márcio Buainain et al., *O Mundo Rural no Brasil do Século 21. A Formação de um Novo Padrão Agrário e Agrícola* (Brasília: Embrapa, 2014): 891–924. Also see Marcus Peixoto, "Extensão Rural no Brasil. Uma Abordagem Histórica da Legislação" (Texto para Discussão no. 48; Brasília: Consultoria Legislativa do Senado Federal, 2008); Francisco Roberto Caporal, "Extensão Rural e os limites à prática dos extensionistas do Serviço Público" (MA thesis, Universidade de Santa Maria [RS], 1991); Odilio Sepulcri and Nilson de Paula, *A Emater e seu papel na Difusão de Tecnologia nos seus 50 anos*. Accessed January 28, 2017, at www.emater.pr.gov.br/arquivos/File/Biblioteca_Virtual/ Premio_Extensao_Rural/2_Premio_ER/02_A_Emater_papel_Dif_Tec.pdf; Sonia M. P. P. Bergamasco, "Extensão Rural: Passado e presente no discurso e na prática," pp. 353–364, Accessed January 28, 2017, at www.redeufscaragroecologica .ufscar.br/wp-content/uploads/2016/07/Extens%C3%A3o-rural-Passado-e-presente-no -discurso-e-na-pr%C3%A1tica-S%C3%B4nia.pdf; and for the history of the US cooperative system see https://nifa.usda.gov/cooperative-extension-history.

[18] In 1948 an agreement was signed between the State of Minas Gerais and the International American Association, led by Nelson Rockefeller, which resulted in the founding of the Association of Credit and Rural Assistance (ACAR), with the objective of establishing a technical and financial assistance program. Caporal, "Extensão Rural," and Claiton Marcio da Silva, "Nelson Rockefeller a a atuação da American International Association For Economic and Social Development: debates sobre missão e imperialismo no Brasil, 1946–1961," *História, Ciências, Saúde – Manginhos*, 20, no. 4 (Oct.–Dec. 2013): 1696–1711.

Econômica do Estado de Minas Gerais.[19] The public for this extension was preferably small farmers, individually or living in a given community. The extension program was essentially of a biological or physical character, like improved seeds, suitable planting information such as proper plowing techniques and how to use organic fertilizers. From the family point of view, the recommendations involved housing, formal education, clothing, health and food.[20] In the 1950s numerous similar entities were created in other Brazilian states, and in 1956 the national Brazilian Association of Credit and Rural Assistance (ABCAR) was created, involving existing state entities and numerous other public and financial entities. The model for the actions of the new entity, including orienting the rural credit policy, stopped concentrating on of the farm unit as a whole and began to focus more on productive activities.[21]

It was during the military government period that several systems of intervention were established. The Brazilian Rural Extension System (Siber) was created and ABCAR's structure was decentralized. These now covered more than 2,000 municipalities and were in turn absorbed by the Brazilian Technical Assistance and Rural Extension Company (Embrater), created in 1974. Its objective was to promote and coordinate programs of technical assistance and provide rural extension. The law creating Embrater stipulated that it should work closely with Embrapa, the new agricultural research company. In the same way, each state created its own rural extension company, tied to local agricultural research organizations. In 1980 the Sibrater was composed of twenty-two state companies of technical assistance and rural extension. Altogether, more than 10,000 technicians were added to the public system and approximately 7,000 more in the accredited private offices.[22]

---

[19] Supervised rural credit, created in 1948, aimed at serving a large mass of marginalized rural landowners, combining rural credit and education services. Cleonice Borges de Souza and David José Caume, "Crédito Rural e agricultura familiar no Brasil," *XLVI Congresso da Sober, 2008.* Accessed January 29, 2017, atwww.sober.org.br/palestra/9/882.pdf.

[20] Bergamasco, *Extensão Rural,* and Caporal, "Extensão Rural": chap. 3.

[21] Souza and Caume, "Crédito Rural e agricultura familiar": 3.

[22] The State of São Paulo maintained a parallel system of technical assistance and rural extension, implemented at the beginning of the twentieth century, by Law 678 of March, 1900, which created the Agronomic Service of the State. From its inception, the system aimed at improving production and increasing the supply of agricultural products. Later, several changes occurred in the formal structure of the assistance and extension service, but there was continuity of its actions, which would be carried out by the Coordination of Integral Technical Assistance (CATI), through the network of centers present in all municipalities.

But in 1990 during the process of economic liberalization and reduction of the state, Embrater and many other public companies were extinguished. In the absence of the coordinating activity that Embrater carried out, the system collapsed. A new organization called the Brazilian Association of State Entities for Technical Assistance and Rural Extension (ASBRAER) was created, but it did not become effective until many years later. Thus the extinction of Embrater led to the mergers or even extinctions of agricultural extension services in many of the states, and created a serious disconnect between research and education.[23]

In the early 2000s, the government again became more involved in technical assistance actions. In 2004 a law provided that the Ministry of Agrarian Development would become responsible for agricultural extension. In 2010, the General Law of Technical Assistance for Rural Extension (ATER) was approved, establishing the National Policy for Technical Assistance and Rural Extension for Family Agriculture of Agrarian Reform (PNATER) and the National Program for Technical Assistance and Rural Extension in Family Agriculture and Agrarian Reform (PRONATER), which directed public agencies of Technical Assistance and Rural Extension – ATER, reinforcing as well all the state extension entities.[24] The law defined ATER as a non-formal education service of a continuous nature in rural areas, which was to promote management, production, processing and marketing knowledge of agricultural and non-agricultural activities and services. But this technical assistance sponsored by the federal government was limited to family farming and specific groups of rural producers, as well as minority groups such as Indians.[25] Finally, in 2013 a federal agency was created to manage the program, the National Agency for Technical Assistance and Rural

---

[23] Peixoto, "Extensão Rural no Brasil," p. 26.

[24] Law 12.188, of January 11, 2010, established the National Policy for Technical Assistance and Rural Extension for Family Agriculture and Agrarian Reform – PNATER, whose formulation and supervision are the responsibility of the Ministry of Agrarian Development – MDA, which allocates financial resources to PNATER, and supports the official agencies of Technical Assistance and Rural Extension – ATER. It is also the main instrument of implementation of PNATER, the National Program of Technical Assistance and Rural Extension in Family Agriculture and Agrarian Reform – PRONATER.

[25] Law 11.326, of July 24, 2006, established the National Program of Family Agriculture and Rural Family Enterprises, for farmers who have less than four fiscal modules of land, predominantly use family labor and have a minimum percentage of income originated from the economic activities of their farms. In addition, its beneficiaries include foresters, fish farmers, extractivists, fishermen, indigenous peoples and members of *quilombolas*.

Extension (ANATER), which could accredit other public and private entities for the promotion of extension activities.[26]

Thus, the public system of technical assistance and rural extension in Brazil began to focus essentially on the small producer, a trend that occurred in other countries, leaving larger commercial producers to obtain such services from private sources. A number of studies, sponsored by the FAO and the World Bank, have pointed out that the technological modernization of agriculture, the specialization of producers and the expansion of the scale of production favored the emergence of a private market for agricultural information. In countries where specialization and increase in the scale of production in agriculture occurred, there was a trend toward a market for specialized agricultural information which is now provided by private entities such as agricultural suppliers and equipment makers, agroindustries, self-employed professionals and technical assistance companies. This type of information acquires a value that gives it a character of private good, which would stimulate the emergence of private services providing specialized agricultural information. However, producers who do not have commercial scale of production do not constitute an audience of interest for private extension, and still require free or subsidized services that provide more general information, being better served by the government, or by non-governmental organizations or association of producers. Thus several models or systems of rural extension can coexist, with quite different sources of financing, especially in countries where there is great heterogeneity of production profiles and producers.

Although in recent years budget resources have been increased to rural extension service providers in the states, the demand for rural extension services is greater than the supply for the 4.36 million family farmer establishments identified in the 2006 Agricultural Census. In contrast, the modern commercial sector, productive arrangements with machinery and equipment manufacturers, suppliers of inputs such as seeds and fertilizers, and private consulting firms, seem to successfully supply the informational and educational needs of these producers, as evidenced by

---

[26] Law 12.897 of December 18, 2013, authorized the executive power to create ANATER, in the form of Autonomous Social Service with the purpose of promoting the development of technical assistance and rural extension. It also declared that given its size and importance, Embrapa will play a fundamental role in the operationalization of ANATER. See documents accessed on January 29, 2017, at www.mda.gov.br/portalmda/sites/defa ult/files/user_img_193/Anater.pdf.

the widespread use of modern inputs in Brazil, including so-called genetically modified crops.

The area of agricultural research also has a long history in Brazil, with institutional stability since the creation of Embrapa, the Brazilian Agricultural Research Corporation, in 1972.[27] Until the 1950s, there was little public or private agricultural research in Brazil and little coordination among the few centers that existed. There were some modest research centers and extension services founded in the nineteenth and early twentieth century in both state and private centers, including in a few of the agricultural schools founded in Brazil at this time, which would eventually emerge as full-scale universities with modern teaching and research facilities in the late twentieth century, Given the competition with industry for capital, a scarce factor in Brazil, it was more convenient for agriculture to be based on abundant land and labor factors. This led to a low-capitalization, low-capital-intensity and low-productivity agriculture. Faced with the increasing demand for agricultural products caused by the growth in population, income and urbanization, the natural tendency was to open new agricultural areas and increase the number of workers. As long as there was an open and economically viable frontier, there would be an increase in production by the opening of new areas to production. But slowly this frontier disappeared in many regions of Brazil. In the states where the agricultural frontier was closing, such as São Paulo and Rio de Janeiro, there began to be established networks of research, technical assistance and agricultural science education. São Paulo, which led the process of industrialization in Brazil and represented the greatest value-producing state in agriculture, would be the state most focused on the modernization of agriculture. But in general, the responsibility for research and teaching of agrarian sciences remained at the federal level, and research initiatives initially did not have a positive impact on the productivity of land and labor factors.[28] State research institutes and centers were initially as

---

[27] According to Rodrigues and Alves, research in agrarian sciences has a long history in Brazil, dating back to the creation of the Agronomic Institute of Campinas in the second half of the nineteenth century. This was followed by centers in Rio Grande do Sul, Pernambuco and Minas Gerais. In the Ministry of Agriculture, Livestock and Supply (Map), following the example of São Paulo, several research institutes were created, which were later coordinated into the National Department of Agricultural Research (DNPEA). Roberto Rodrigues and Eliseu Alves. "O futuro da pesquisa agropecuária," *Revista de Política Agrícola*, XIV, no. 4 (Oct./Nov./Dec. 2005): 3–4.

[28] Eliseu Alves and Affonso Celso Pastore. "A política agrícola do Brasil e hipótese da inovação induzida," in Eliseu Alves, José Pastore and Affonso C. Pastore, *Coletânea de Trabalhos sobre a EMBRAPA* (Brasília: Embrapa, 1977): 9–19.

important as federal centers. These included such institutes as the Agronomic Institute of Campinas and such university centers as the Luiz de Queiroz School of Agronomy (ESALQ), the Lavras School of Agriculture and the Veterinary School of Viçosa, now all federal or state universities. In general this knowledge was often linked to academic teaching or research, but without a national infrastructure the diffusion of these scientific findings in the rural world was often limited. But this accumulated knowledge, as in the case of coffee, has been essential for Brazil's long-standing leadership of world coffee production, and would be fundamental for future advances in agricultural research and production in Brazil once such an infrastructure was created after the founding of Embrapa.[29]

As in other areas of activity, after the Vargas Revolution of 1930, there were strong transformations in the formal structure of the organs related to agriculture. The first attempt to centralize agricultural research took place in 1933, when a General Directorate of Scientific Research was created, but this institution had an ephemeral life. More successful was the creation in 1938 of the National Center of Education and Agronomic Research – CNEPA, which was established to coordinate agricultural research, teaching and experimentation.[30] In 1943 the CENPA was reorganized, creating the National Service of Agronomic Research (SNPA). The SNPA was composed of several older entities of research and agricultural education, such as the Institute of Ecology and Agricultural Experimentation, the Institute of Agricultural Chemistry, the National Institute of Oils, the Institute of Fermentation, the Agronomic Institute of the North, the Agronomic Institute of the Northeast, the Agronomic Institute of the South and the Agronomic Institute of the West. Under SNPA, each of the regional institutes and the federal government, directly or by agreement with the respective state governments, would create regional centers of education in the mold of the Rural University of the

---

[29] According to the Agronomic Institute of Campinas (IAC), the improvement of coffee genetics began in 1932, and these several coffee cultivars were used in all regions of Brazil and in several Latin American countries. In the National Register of Cultivars, there are sixty-seven registered by the IAC, of which sixty-six are of Arabica coffee and one of robust coffee. Two of these cultivars represent about 90% of the Arabica coffee grown in Brazil. See Embrapa information accessed February 1, 2018, at www.embrapa.br/busca-de-noticias/-/noticia/13774138/instituto-agronomico-iac-comemora-129-anos-de-relevantes-contribuicoes-para-desenvolvimento-da-agricultura.

[30] Cyro Mascarenhas Rodrigues, "A pesquisa agropecuária federal no período compreendido entre a República Velha e o Estado Novo," *Cadernos de Difusão de Tecnologia* (Brasília), 4, no. 2 (May/Aug. 1987): 129–153. CNEPA was created by Decree-Law no. 982 of December 23, 1938.

National Center of Education and Agronomic Research.[31] Despite the significant results obtained by the SNPA, the evolution of agricultural research was slow and disharmonious. In addition, important areas related to agriculture and livestock, especially zootechnical and veterinary research, were not integrated into the SNPA. Only in 1962 when the SNPA was replaced by the Department of Agricultural Research and Experimentation – DPEA, would this be corrected.[32]

Given the increasing price of land in São Paulo due to the closure of its frontier and the continued growth of its agriculture, it was the first state where a significant part of the growth in agriculture was due to productivity gains obtained through the use of biological, chemical and mechanization technologies.[33] The relative scarcity of land that occurred in Sao Paulo from 1940/1950 began to manifest itself in Brazil as a whole from 1960 and especially at the end of the decade. Good-quality and easily accessible land was already occupied and this generated pressure for increased productivity per hectare. Thus, data from the 1960s and 1970s indicate both gains in productivity throughout Brazil, except in the Northeast, and the steady reduction of labor in agriculture. In the pursuit of higher levels of productivity, the first attempt was to utilize existing technological knowledge by channeling it to producers through extension services and technical assistance. It was a period in which Brazil and other countries of the world invested more in rural extension than agricultural research.[34]

But the efforts did not have the intended results. First there was difficulty in transferring agricultural knowledge from other countries and the need to adapt them to the specific local conditions. In addition, "it was found that the internal stock of knowledge in Brazil was in many regions and for most of the products, poor and inadequate ... In short, the extension service itself became aware in the early 1970s that it could do little with its methods, given the country's technological poverty."[35] It became clear, as well, that only the federal government had the

---

[31] Decree-Law no. 6.155, of December 30, 1943.
[32] Rodrigues. "A pesquisa agropecuária federal," and Cyro Mascarenhas Rodrigues. "A pesquisa agropecuária no período do pós-guerra," *Cadernos de Difusão de Tecnologia*, 4, no. 3 (Sept./Dec. 1987): 205–254.
[33] Eliseu Alves and José Pastore, *Uma Nova Abordagem para a Pesquisa Agrícola no Brasil* (São Paulo: USP/IPE, 1975), pp. 55–84. According to the authors, the relative scarcity of land and labor that affected São Paulo were factors that promoted agricultural research while the rest of the country continued to use more and more traditional factors of production.
[34] Ibid., pp. 65–66   [35] Ibid., p. 66.

necessary resources to solve these problems. The creation of the DPEA in 1962 was the result of this process of rethinking agricultural research. But the greatest transformations would occur under the military regime from the late 1960s. After several reorganizations of the federal research program and its state affiliates, the National Department of Agricultural Research (DNPEA) was created in 1971.[36]

Then, in 1972, the Minister of Agriculture established a working group to define what were to be the main objectives and functions of agricultural research.[37] The working group created a model that served as a guide for the creation of Embrapa, which would bring a new and different configuration to the structure of agricultural research in Brazil and be of fundamental importance in the development of agribusiness in Brazil.[38] It recognized that an appreciable network of research and experimental institutions already existed, that these centers could be expanded and that there was already a structure available to disseminate the results of the research. It also noted the existence of a small group of highly qualified managers and professionals, but it said the

[36] According to Mengel, prior to the creation of Embrapa, agricultural research at the national level was conducted by an agency of the Ministry of Agriculture. It was variously named SNPA, DPEA, EPE and DNPEA. In 1962, the National Service of Agronomic Research – SNPA, through the Delegated Law no. 9 of October 11, 1962, was transformed into a Department of Agricultural Research and Experimentation – DPEA. In 1967, by Decree-Law no. 200 of February 25, the DPEA became known as the Office of Agricultural Research and Experimentation (EPEA). In 1971, through Decree no. 68,593, the National Department of Agricultural Research – DNPEA was created that replaced the EPEA. The last name of this research institution previous to Embrapa was DNPEA. Thus, when we allude to the old institution, we are referring to the structure of agricultural research started under the name SNPA and closed with the name DNPEA. Aléx Alexandre Mengel, "Modernização da agricultura e pesquisa no Brasil: a Empresa Brasileira de Pesquisa Agropecuária – Embrapa" (Phd thesis, Universidade Federal Rural do Rio de Janeiro, 2015), p. 12.

[37] In 1971 a working group was created, led by José Pastore, a professor at the University of São Paulo (USP), to investigate the reasons why agricultural productivity had not grown, despite investments in extension and rural credit. The group's response, after two years of research, was that the technology produced to date was not reaching the farmers. Embrapa was born as a response to this lack of integration between science and farming in Brazil. See E. R. A. Alves, G. S. Souza, and E. G. Gomes, eds., *Contribuição da Embrapa para o Desenvolvimento da Agricultura no Brasil* (Brasília: Embrapa, 2013), pp. 15–45, p. 22.

[38] The report was published as Embrapa Informação Tecnológica, *Sugestões para a Formulação de um Sistema Nacional de Pesquisa Agropecuária* (Memória Embrapa, Edição Especial do documento original de junho de 1972, reprinted Brasília, Embrapa, 2006). The document was known as the "Black Book" because of its black cardboard cover. J. Irineu Cabral, *Sol da Manhã: Memória da Embrapa* (Brasília: UNESCO, 2005), chap. 2.

lack of coordination of the current work prevented it from having an impact on agriculture and on research results affecting farming practices. Nor was there an adequate system to evaluate the results of this ongoing research.

The report presented a series of suggestions in the form of basic principles to be used in the restructuring of the sector. It emphasized that the need to adapt foreign technologies required educational reforms with training programs abroad and the development of postgraduate programs in Brazil, as well as using foreign technicians who could develop research with Brazilian teams. It also emphasized that research projects should be directly related to well defined programs by product or by region. This is perhaps one of the strongest ideas derived from the study, and represented the model which would be adopted by Embrapa when it was created. All research units were to be interdisciplinary and were to deal with regions, such as the Cerrado, or with a given product like corn. Thus it was not to be a research center divided by areas of knowledge, as was usually the norm in universities. It also stressed the need to tie extension work with research and to prepare an adequately trained group of field workers who could transfer these technological packages to the farmers. Finally, the document proposed an unusual institutional model of an autonomous government company, which would have the essential conditions for flexibility and efficiency, particularly in financial and human resources management.

This document served as the guidelines for the structure and aims of the Brazilian Agricultural Research Corporation (Embrapa, Empresa Brasileira de Pesquisa Agropecuária) when it was established in 1972.[39] The company was to promote research in agriculture and provide the federal executive with guidance on national policy issues related to agriculture. To perform its activities the company could sign agreements and contracts with public or private entities, national, foreign or international. Embrapa survives to this day, and has been of fundamental importance in the development of agricultural research in Brazil. Its unusual structure gave it great administrative autonomy, operational flexibility and allowed the implementation of a personnel policy of relative freedom of contracting and paying private market salaries.

---

[39] Law 5851 of December 7, 1972 authorized the executive power to establish a public company under the name of EMBRAPA (Brazilian Agricultural Research Corporation), linked to the Ministry of Agriculture, with legal personality of private law, equity and financial autonomy.

Some had wanted a smaller institution whose research agenda would be directed by the local research institutes and universities. This option was rejected because it soon became apparent that in a country of continental dimensions, the success of Embrapa would depend on its size and a critical mass of diversified researchers in all areas of the national territory. It was understood that Embrapa needed to have a scale as large as Brazil and that it needed to have its own research network so that it could be directly responsible for the results. This model would also allow for cooperation with universities, public and private research institutes from abroad, but on an equal footing. Finally the government was willing to put in significant resources to fund this new organization.[40]

Perhaps the most important factor explaining Embrapa's subsequent success has been its human resources policy and training program. Eliseu Alves, the first director of Embrapa and a Purdue University PhD, affirmed that "if you have to state a single reason for the success of Embrapa it was the so called 'postgraduate program.'"[41] This training program allowed Brazil to expand the supply of researchers with a global view of Brazilian development so that they could select their research projects within this model. Thus, Embrapa quickly hired and trained hundreds of researchers in educational institutions in Brazil and abroad, counting on its own resources and financial support from numerous national and international entities such as Finep, Bird, Bid and USAID.[42] In Brazil the predominant educational institutions in the first period between 1974 and 1979 were the local agricultural colleges and universities, which included the Superior School of Agronomy and Veterinary Sciences of Viçosa, the Superior School of Agronomy Luiz de Queiroz, the Federal University of Rio Grande do Sul and the Federal University of Minas Gerais. Those going abroad went almost exclusively to North American universities, at the instigation of the main leaders involved in the training program and

---

[40] Eliseu Alves, "Embrapa, a successful case of institutional innovation," *Revista Economia Política*, Year XIX – Special Edition on Mapa's 150th Anniversary, July 2010.

[41] Mengel, "Modernização da agricultura e pesquisa no Brasil," pp. 86–87.

[42] According to Mengel, the Brazilian government, through FINEP, was Embrapa's biggest incentive and partner in the graduate program, as well as being responsible for the resources invested by Embrapa itself in the payment of salaries when the researchers returned. The contribution of the International Bank for Research and Development (IBRD) and the Inter-American Development Bank (IDB), both nationally and internationally, was also very significant, as was training at the international level by the United States Agency for International Development (USAID). Ibid., p. 127.

due to the origin of external resources received.[43] This was a major training program. As a former director of Embrapa noted, when he arrived in June 1975, the entire Embrapa, in all its Brazilian centers, had only twenty-eight researches with PhDs, and by 1988 it had more than 1,000. Most of these PhDs were trained abroad and Embrapa by then also employed some 300 to 400 who graduated with master's degrees, most of whom were formed in Brazil.[44] By March 2016 Embrapa employed 2,444 researchers, of whom 330 had MAs, 1,829 had PhDs and another 285 had post-doctoral training.[45]

Despite some fluctuations, particularly in the second half of the 1990s and the beginning of the following decade, there was a steady increase in budget allocations to Embrapa by the federal government. In 2015, the budget totaled US$ 870 million. One of the criticisms made of Embrapa's budget is the large percentage in fixed costs, especially of salaries. In 1983, a decade after the creation of Embrapa, staff costs accounted for 53% of the budget, and capital expenditures accounted for 16%. In 2015, staff costs consumed 83% of the budget and capital expenditures accounted for only 2% (see Table 4.3). On the other hand, Embrapa estimated the value of its research at R26 billion, compared to expenditures of R$ 3 billion.[46]

Brazil currently spends a significant amount on agricultural research, when compared to others countries with a similar profile to Brazil, or even compared to total Brazilian science and technology expenditures as a whole. The percentage of agricultural research expenditures has remained around 2% of the GDP of the agricultural sector, a high

---

[43] Between 1974 and 1979, of the 484 researchers training abroad, 380 were in the United States, 29 in England and 23 in France. Cabral, *Sol da Manhã*, 142. As Fernando Campos noted, the source of financing resources (IDB, IBRD and USAID) was often crucial in the choice of universities. Mengel, "Modernização da Agricultura e Pesquisa no Brasil," p. 140.

[44] Testimony of Levon Yeganiantz, advisor to the first executive board, quoted in Mengel, "Modernização da agricultura e pesquisa no Brasil," p. 123.

[45] Embrapa Comunicações, *Embrapa em Números* (Brasília: Embrapa, 2016), p. 32.

[46] Embrapa, Balanço Social 2015, accessed February 25, 2017, at http://bs.sede.embrapa.br /2015/balsoc15.html. For an evaluation of the methodology adopted in such estimates see Elmar Rodrigues da Cruz, Victor Palma and Antonio F. D. Avila, *Taxas de Retorno dos Investimentos da EMBRAPA: Investimentos Totais e Capital Físico* (Brasília: EMBRAPA-DID, 1982); Antonio F. D. Avila et al., "Impactos econômicos, sociais e ambientais dos investimentos na Embrapa," *Revista de Política Agrícola*, XIV, no. 4 (Oct./Nov./Dec. 2005): 86–101; Regis Bonelli and Elisa de Paula Pessôa, "O papel do Estado na Pesquisa Agrícola no Brasil" (Texto para Discussão no. 576; Rio de Janeiro: IPEA, July 1998).

TABLE 4.3: *Budget and expenditures of Embrapa, 1975–2015*

Year	Personnel	Other expenses	Current expenditures	Capital expenditures	Total	Debt	TOTAL	Total budget – real prices (2000–2002=100)
1975	41%	55%	96%	4%	100%	0%	100%	27
1980	53%	31%	84%	16%	100%	0%	100%	42
1985	53%	37%	90%	10%	100%	0%	100%	55
1990	75%	20%	96%	4%	100%	0%	100%	71
1995	69%	17%	86%	9%	95%	5%	100%	82
2000	68%	23%	91%	3%	95%	5%	100%	91
2001	69%	21%	90%	3%	93%	7%	100%	101
2002	69%	20%	89%	3%	92%	8%	100%	99
2003	70%	19%	89%	3%	91%	9%	100%	95
2004			89%	9%	98%	2%	100%	87
2005			90%	9%	99%	1%	100%	91
2006			91%	8%	99%	1%	100%	100
2007			92%	8%	100%	0%	100%	98
2008			90%	10%	100%	0%	100%	95
2009			88%	12%	100%	0%	100%	94
2010	66%	20%	86%	14%	100%	0%	100%	103
2011	74%	18%	91%	8%	100%	0%	100%	103
2012	72%	17%	90%	10%	100%	0%	100%	102
2013	77%	16%	92%	8%	100%	0%	100%	95
2014	79%	16%	95%	5%	100%	0%	100%	102
2015	83%	16%	98%	2%	100%	0%	100%	115

Source: for 1975–2003: Alves & de Oliveira, "Orçamento da Embrapa" (2006): 73–85; for 2004–2014: accounts of Embrapa

percentage when compared to the 1% of GDP that Brazil spends on science and technology (see Table 4.4).[47] Brazil's research expenditures on science in general are at the lower end compared to advanced industrial countries. According to the World Bank, the leading countries, Israel and South Korea, each spent around 4% of GDP on research and development by the mid-2010s. The major Scandinavian countries spent in the 3–4% range and the US was at 2.7%. Brazil at 1.2% was just below Italy at 1.3% and well above the 0.8% average for all the Latin American and Caribbean nations in 2013.[48]

According to the Ministry of Science and Technology and Innovation, Brazilian agriculture is one of the most efficient and sustainable in the world. This is due, in large part, to the research and development work of such independent research centers as Embrapa, the State Agricultural Research Organizations (OEPAs) and some private national entities such as the Center of Sugar Technology (CTC) of the Cooperative Copersucar and the Fundação Mato Grosso. The country today has a produced a genuinely Brazilian tropical agriculture and livestock system and has overcome the barriers that limited the production of food, fiber and energy.[49] The agricultural sector incorporated a large area of degraded land from the Cerrado into national production, and today this previously abandoned zone accounts for almost 50% of national grain production. Brazil has also quadrupled the supply of beef and pork and expanded the supply of chicken by twenty-two times. These are some of the achievements that have taken the country from being a staple

---

[47] "Brazil's agricultural research system is by far the region's largest, in terms of both research capacity and spending. Almost half of all agricultural researchers are employed by the federal government agency, Embrapa, and a further quarter are employed by the state agricultural research organizations (OEPAS). During 2006–2013, agricultural R&D spending rose by 46 percent due to growth at Embrapa and in the higher education sector, particularly among federal universities. At 1.82 percent, spending as a share of AgGDP is the highest in Latin America. Brazil employs the largest number of PhD-qualified agricultural researchers in the region, and its share of researchers with PhD degrees, at 73 percent, is the highest by far." International Food Policy Research Institute (IFPRI), accessed February 23, 2017, at www.asti.cgiar.org/brazil.

[48] World Bank, "Research and development expenditure (% of GDP)," accessed July 3, 2017, at http://data.worldbank.org/indicator/GB.XPD.RSDV.GD.ZS.

[49] As Chaddad has noted, "Brazil was the first country to invest heavily in agricultural technologies and production systems adapted to tropical conditions." Fabio Ribas Chaddad, *The Economics and Organization of Brazilian Agriculture: Recent Evolution and Productivity Gains* (Amsterdam: Academic Press), p. 21.

TABLE 4.4: *Expenditures on agricultural research as a % of agricultural GDP, Brazil and selected countries, 1981–2013*

	Brazil US$ millions (1)	Research expenditures as % GDP agriculture				
		Brazil	Argentina	Chile	China	India
1981	1,217.8	1.1	1.6	1.7		
1982	1,461.1	1.6	0.8	1.8		
1983	1,194.3	1.1	0.8	1.7		
1984	1,129.3	1.0	0.8	1.5		
1985	1,260.3	1.0	1.5	1.3		
1986	1,314.5	1.0	1.3	1.6		
1987	1,466.4	1.2	1.3	1.8		
1988	1,381.2	1.1	1.2	1.5		
1989	1,543.7	1.3	1.0	1.6		
1990	1,543.8	1.7	1.4	1.2		
1991	1,781.7	1.9	1.5	0.9		
1992	1,536.5	1.6	1.4	0.9		
1993	1,745.2	1.8	2.0	1.0		
1994	1,717.1	1.3	2.0	1.2		
1995	1,624.2	2.1	1.8	1.1		
1996	1,815.5	2.4	1.5	2.0		0.2
1997	1,644.8	2.1	1.5	2.0		0.3
1998	1,587.8	2.0	1.5	1.6		0.3
1999	1,513.2	1.9	1.6	1.7		0.3
2000	1,552.9	1.9	1.4	1.4	0.4	0.3
2001	1,579.4	1.8	1.3	1.6	0.4	0.3
2002	1,518.3	1.5	0.5	1.5	0.5	0.4
2003	1,525.3	1.3	0.7	1.3	0.5	0.3
2004	1,577.1	1.4	0.9	1.3	0.4	0.4
2005	1,555.2	1.7	1.0	1.3	0.4	0.4
2006	1,624.8	1.8	1.2	1.5	0.5	0.3
2007	1,652.4	1.7	1.0	1.6	0.5	0.3
2008	1,847.9	1.7	1.2	1.8	0.5	0.3
2009	2,205.2	2.1	1.5	1.9	0.6	0.3
2010	2,179.3	2.1	1.0	1.8	0.6	0.3
2011	2,173.3	1.9	1.1	1.6	0.6	0.3
2012	2,326.7	2.0	1.3	1.8	0.6	0.3
2013	2,377.9	1.8	1.3	1.6	0.6	0.3

Source: ASTI: International Food Policy Research Institute (IFPRI); www.asti.cgiar.org/
Note: Spending, total (million constant 2011 US$) www.asti.cgiar.org/

food importer to being one of the world's largest producers and exporters.[50]

In this process Embrapa had a fundamental role.[51] Thus, for example, Embrapa was the leader in solving the problem of the low natural fertility and high acidity of the Cerrado soil, as well as discovering new varieties of seeds, that made the use of Cerrado land commercially viable. According to Alves, the conquest of the *cerrado* biome research has been considered one of the most important achievements of Brazilian agrarian sciences. In the Cerrado area, investment in technologies such as crop tropicalization, soil correction, nitrogen fixation in legumes, fertilization and crop management allowed Brazil to transform the very acidic and nutrient-poor Brazilian savannas into 139 million hectares of arable land. This area encompassing part of the states of Maranhão, Tocantins, Piauí and Bahia, known as Matopiba, has been nationally renowned for the rapid growth provided by the use of modern technologies and today it accounts for a large part of Brazil's grain and fiber production.[52]

Today Embrapa leads a national agricultural research network that, in a cooperative manner, carries out research in the different geographic areas and fields of scientific knowledge. In addition to the 46 Decentralized Research Units, the network consists of 18 State Agrarian Research Organizations (OEPAS), universities and research institutes at federal or state level, private companies and foundations. In addition to maintaining a collaborative network with important research institutions

---

[50] Ministério da Ciência e Tecnologia e Inovação, *Estratégia Nacional de Ciência, Tecnologia e Inovação, 2016–2019* (Brasília: Ministério da Ciência e Tecnologia e Inovação, 2016), p. 90.

[51] Although the overall evaluation of Embrapa's performance has been positive since its foundation, over time there have been criticisms of the management model. See Antonio Flávio Dias Avila, "Corporativismo na Embrapa: o fim de um modelo de gestão," *Cadernos de Ciência & Tecnologia*, 12, nos. 1/3 (1995): 83–94. More recently Embrapa has been criticized for being too big and bureaucratic and for losing out to large multinational companies when it came to supplying technologies in the main agribusiness chains. It has also failed to focus on providing technology to small farmers. See Zander Navarro, *Por favor, Embrapa: acorde!* Published in *Jornal o Estado de São Paulo*, on January 5, 2018, http://opiniao.estadao.com.br/noticias/geral,por-favor-embrapa-acorde,70002139015.

[52] Eliseu Alves and Geraldo da Silva e Souza, "A pesquisa agrícola numa agricultura integrada ao mercado internacional. O caso da Embrapa e do Cerrado," *Revista Política Agrícola*, XVI, no. 2 (Apr./May/Jun. 2007): 56–67, Embrapa Comunicações, *Embrapa em Números* (Brasília: Embrapa, 2016). On the challenges of exploring the savannas see Fábio Gelape Faleiro and Austeclinio Lopes de Farias Neto, *Savanas. Desafios e Estratégias para o Equilíbrio entre Sociedade, Agronegócio e Recursos Naturais* (Planaltina, DF: Embrapa, 2008).

abroad, it has virtual laboratories in several countries, such as the United States, France, Germany, the United Kingdom, Korea and China. It also maintains research and cooperation projects with Africa, Asia, Latin America and the Caribbean, involving forty countries.[53]

Embrapa also maintains the largest gene bank in Brazil and Latin America and one of the largest in the world, with 124,000 seed samples of 765 species of importance for agriculture and food. It invests in research on the conservation and sustainable use of locally adapted breeds of domestic animals and in the conservation of native strains of microorganisms, which can be used by the scientific community in research programs. The collections of microorganisms maintain species with potential for the biological control of pests and insects vectors of diseases.[54]

One of its main functions is to supply new seeds adapted to local conditions; these in turn have dramatically increased the production and yields in such traditional crops as rice, beans, corn, wheat and soybeans. It has produced 114 different breeds of rice, and these seeds are used to produce 22% of Brazilian rice, and 45% of the rice produced in dry lands. It also developed cultivars for rice irrigated in tropical and subtropical environments with emphasis on disease resistance and grain quality. Currently, Embrapa is one of the leaders in the bean market, since more than 40% of the area planted with beans in Brazil uses the sixty-five cultivars of beans created by Embrapa. The first Brazilian double hybrid of corn with high tolerance to acid soils, BR 201, was developed by Embrapa in the 1980s and enabled the cultivation of corn in extensive areas of the *cerrado*. Embrapa has registered eighty-one different corn cultivars, which are plants selected for desirable characteristics that can be maintained by propagation. In the harvest of 2015/2016 there were more than 477 different cultivars of corn to plant, of which 284 are genetically modified and the other 193 are conventionally bred.

The so-called "cultivance" soybean, the result of the partnership between Embrapa and a private company, is the first genetically modified plant developed entirely in Brazil and marked the beginning of a new era for biotechnology in the country. Embrapa, as the leading institution in the Brazilian conventional soybean market, participates along with Abrange and Aprosoja, among other partners, in the Soja Livre Program, making the conventional cultivars of the company available to producers. Today, more than thirty commercial cultivars of Embrapa are available and can be grown in almost all Brazilian regions.

---

[53] Embrapa Comunicações, *Embrapa em Números* (Brasília: Embrapa, 2016). [54] Ibid.

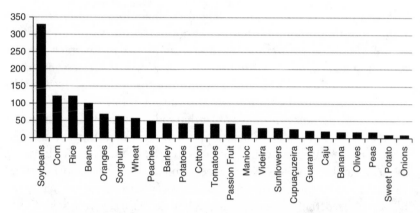

GRAPH 4.4: Number of cultivars registered by Embrapa (species with more than 10 cultivars)
Source: Embrapa Comunicações, *Embrapa em Números* (2017)

Wheat has also been strongly supported by Embrapa. In the last forty-two years, the company generated 117 wheat cultivars, which allowed it to hold more than 80% of the market in Central Brazil, where it has been introduced gradually, under both irrigation and regular farming. The contribution of Embrapa to the wheat cultivars market is also highlighted by the intense use of "Embrapa Genetics" seeds by other breeding companies. Of the total wheat cultivars used in 2012, about 60% came from Embrapa.

Even coffee has been the subject of major research. From 1999, the Brazilian Consortium for Coffee Research and Development (CBP & DCafé), which now has 103 teaching, research and extension institutions and more than 700 researchers, developed disease-resistant cultivars. Finally, four cultivars of transgenic cotton with glyphosate herbicide tolerance were made available by Embrapa to growers for planting in the 2014/2015 harvest. The new materials have greater flexibility in weed control, since they allow the use of the herbicide glyphosate at any stage of development of the cotton without damaging the crop. The development of highly productive cultivars for the Brazilian Cerrado was the milestone for the consolidation of cotton growing in the region. Embrapa has also bet on colored cotton as a differentiated product for the Northeast region (see Graph 4.4).[55]

[55] Ibid.

Livestock was also greatly benefited by Embrapa. Forages for cattle feed, for example, represent one of the research contributions to national livestock, since only five grass cultivars recommended by Embrapa account for almost 80% of the Brazilian forage seed business. With these materials, Brazil has also become the largest exporter of tropical forage seeds in the world. With its "pig light" research it contributed to the development of animals with a lower percentage of fat that today represent the standard of the national herd. Embrapa placed on the market in 2012 the third generation of the light pig, which accounts for 7% of the Brazilian breeding market. Similar advances were made in milk production and in broiler chicken meat production through programs supported by Embrapa. Brazil has dominated the animal cloning technique since 2001, when Vitória heifer was born, the first bovine clone of Latin America, of the simian breed. The method used by Embrapa was similar to that of the first cloned animal in the world, Dolly the sheep in 1997, but in the Brazilian case, the germinated cell of Vitória did not come from an adult animal, but from a heifer embryo. About 100 animals have already been copied in the laboratory using the technique adopted by Embrapa.[56]

Over the last forty years, Brazil has advanced technologies in soil management and conservation, integrated pest and disease management and biological nitrogen fixation. Among the several technologies to which Embrapa made a fundamental contribution was direct or non-till planting, in which cereals, legumes, oilseeds and cotton are produced without plowing. There are more than 33 million hectares of land under the no-till system in 2015, and more than 50% of the area dedicated to cereals uses this system (see Graph 4.5). This tropical technology avoids harrowing and plowing and represents enormous fuel economy. The reduction is of the order of 40% of CO_2 emissions. No-tillage also slows erosion and reduces the need for chemical fertilizer.[57]

---

[56] Ibid.

[57] On no-tillage planting see Paulino Motter and Herlon Goelzer de Almeida, eds., *Plantio Direto: A Tecnologia que Revolucionou a Agricultura Brasileira* (Foz de Iguaçu: Parque Itaipu, 2015); José Carlos Cruz et al., *Sistema de Plantio Direto de milho.* Accessed February 25, 2017, at www.agencia.cnptia.embrapa.br/gestor/milho/arvore/CONTA Go1_72_59200523355.html; Heliomar Baleeiro de Melo Júnior, Reginaldo de Camargo and Bueno Wendling, "Sistema de plantio direto na conservação do solo e água e recuperação de áreas degradadas. Goiânia," *Enciclopédia Biosfera*, 7, no. 12 (2011); Pedro Luiz de Freitas. *Histórico do Sistema de Plantio Direto*, accessed February 25, 2017, at www.linkedin.com/pulse/hist%C3%B3rico-do-sistema-plantio-direto-pedro-luiz-de-freitas; Vanderleia Trevisan da Rosa, "Tempo de implantação do sistema de plantio direto e propriedades físico-mecênicas de um

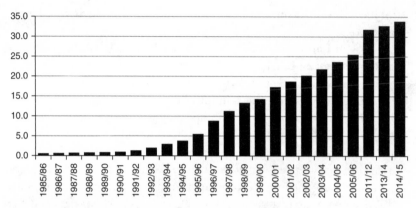

GRAPH 4.5: Cultivated fields using no-till planting in Brazil, 1985–2015 (millions of hectares)
Source: Embrapa Comunicações, *Embrapa em Números* (2017)

In the development of its research, Embrapa uses state-of-the-art technology, such as genomics, biotechnology, nanotechnology, geotechnology, precision agriculture and automation, and biofortification. In the case of genomics, Embrapa, in partnership with several research institutions and universities in Brazil and abroad, develops genomic sequencing research of plant and animal species of importance for agriculture and food. In 2004, Brazil pioneered the completion of the first stage of coffee sequencing, which resulted in the formation of the world's largest database for this culture. Today, more than 30,000 genes from the 200,000 sequences that make up the bank are already identified and used in research such as tolerance to weather stress and resistance to pests and diseases. In 2014 the complete sequencing of the eucalyptus genome was completed, a species of importance for the Brazilian economy used in its pulp, paper, steel and wood products industry. The study was developed by more than eighty scientists from thirty institutions in nine countries. In addition to the leadership of Embrapa, researchers from the Catholic University of Brasília, the University of Brasília, the Federal University of Viçosa, the Federal University of Rio de Janeiro

latossolo" (PhD thesis, Universidade Federal de Santa Maria, 2009); Elemar Antonino Cassol, José Eloir Denardin and Rainaldo Alberto Kochhann, "Sistema plantio direto: Evolução e implicações sobre conservação do solo e da água," in Carlos Alberto Ceretta, Leandro Souza da Silva and José Miguel Reichert, eds., *Tópicos em Ciência do Solo. Viçosa: Sociedade Brasileira de Ciência do Solo*, vol. 5 (2007): 333–369.

and the Federal University of Rio Grande do Sul also participated in the project.[58]

Although Embrapa is undeniably the leading entity in the process of transformation of Brazilian agriculture, there are other major public agricultural research centers, as well as the growing role of private entities in the supply of products and solutions for the modernization of Brazilian agriculture. In the public area, Embrapa plays the coordinating role of the national agricultural research network, composed of Embrapa and its forty-six decentralized units, as well as the eighteen State Research Organizations (OEPAs), universities and research institutes at the federal and state level, and private companies and foundations. The eighteen OEPAs contain 2,032 researchers, of whom 706 have masters and 918 doctors. Together they have 239 experimental stations and 209 laboratories. Although these other public research entities have a similar number of Embrapa employees, their annual budget is half of Embrapa's. Especially at the state level many of these centers have suffered from lack of funding.[59] Despite these constraints, they have actively participated in major research activities.[60]

The Agronomic Institute of Campinas (IAC), in São Paulo, is one of the most important and traditional of the entities gathered in the national research network coordinated by Embrapa. Created in 1887 by the imperial government, it became a state institution in 1892. Since its foundation it has played a fundamental role in consolidating the agricultural hegemony of São Paulo, particularly in the development of coffee culture. It is estimated that 90% of the 4.5 billion Brazilian coffee trees come from cultivars developed by the Institute, and some of these cultivars are the basis of coffee cultivation in other countries. The development by IAC in 1968 of cultivars of low size with high productivity modified systems of production and allowed the planting of coffee trees in new areas not only in São Paulo but also in the Triângulo Mineiro in Minas Gerais. The launching in 2000 of the cultivar Ouro Verde IAC H 5010-5 provided the Brazilian coffee grower with a new option for densified

---

[58] Embrapa Comunicações, *Embrapa em Números* (Brasília: Embrapa, 2016).

[59] Florindo Dalberto, "Pesquisa Estadual e Inovação no Agronegócio Brasileiro," *IX Encontro Nacional do Fortec*, Curitiba, maio de 2015; Adriano Batista Dias and Sérgio Kelner Silveira, *As OEPASs – Situação e Resgate*, accessed February 25, 2017, at http://aplicativos.fipe.org.br/enaber/pdf/161.pdf; Centro de Gestão e Estudos Estratégicos, *Estudo sobre o Papel das Organizações Estaduais de Pesquisa Agropecuária* (Brasília: CGEE, 2006).

[60] Dalberto, "Pesquisa Estadual," p. 12.

crops.[61] The IAC has also worked successfully on cotton produced in São Paulo. All the southern production of herbaceous cotton is based on the varieties created in the Agronomic Institute. Also through the IAC's research, the latex-producing rubber tree was introduced in São Paulo.[62] Almost as important has been the Mato Grosso Agricultural Research Foundation FMT (Fundação de Apoio à Pesquisa Agropecuária de Mato Grosso) established in 1993 with money provided by twenty-three major farmers of the region. It quickly signed an agreement with Embrapa and in 1996 brought to market nine soybean cultivars resistant to the cyst nematode and stem canker. Eventually over three-quarters of all soybean seeds produced in the state were cultivars developed by FMT–Embrapa. But conflicts over royalties led FMT to become independent and it has used its royalties to create new resistant cultivars in both soybean and cotton plantings.[63]

In the post-1950 period, Brazil has also undergone a modernization of its agricultural universities. The first agricultural school established in Brazil, the Imperial Agricultural School of Bahia, was created in 1877.[64] The second was the School of Agricultural and Veterinary Education created in Pelotas in 1883. Despite these two nineteenth-century initiatives, the dating of modern agricultural education is said to have begun with the creation of the Luiz de Queirós Practical School which was inaugurated in 1901 by private initiative and which today is part of the University of São Paulo.[65] In 1908 the Agricultural School of Lavras was

---

[61] Luiz Carlos Fazuoli et al., "Cultivares de café selecionados pelo Instituto Agronômico de Campinas," *Simpósio de Pesquisas dos Café do Brasil*, pp. 488–493. Accessed February 25, 2017, at http://www.sapc.embrapa.br/arquivos/consorcio/spcb_anais/simposio1/Genet27.pdf.

[62] Instituto Agronômico de Campinas – IAC, accessed February 25, 2017, at www.iac.sp.gov.br.

[63] Chaddad, *The Economics and Organization of Brazilian Agriculture*: 117–121.

[64] This school, after several transformations, today is part of the Federal University of the Recôncavo of Bahia. On the evolution of training in Agronomic Engineering, see Vanderli Fava Oliveira, et al., *Trajetoria e Estado da Arte da Formacao em Engenharia, Arquitetura e Agronomia* (vol. 1; Brasília: Instituto Nacional de Estudos e Pesquisas Educacionais Anisio Teixeira, Conselho Federal de Engenharia, Arquitetura e Agronomia,2010). Also see Rogério dos Santos Bueno Marques, "A construção do profissionalismo na agronomia: trabalho, ciência e poder" (MA thesis, Universidade Federal de Goiás, Goiânia, 2009).

[65] The school was planned and built by Luiz de Queiroz, and later passed on to the Government of the State of São Paulo. See Rodrigo Sarruge Molina and Mara Regina Martins Jacomeli, "Os ruralistas paulistas e seus projetos para a educação agrícola: a 'Luiz de Queiroz' (ESALQ/USP) em Piracicaba (1881 a 1903)," *Revista Brasileira de História da Educação*, 16, no. 4 (issue 43) (Oct./Dec. 2016): 190–215.

founded by American Presbyterian missionaries. From the beginning it concentrated on agriculture as its primary activity, and in the 1910s and 1920s it was recognized by the state of Minas Gerais as a legal entity within the state education system. It has its own experimental farms, organized agricultural extension and concentrated in the early years on research on corn. In the late 1930s the federal government recognized its titles and it became the Escolar Superior de Agricultura de Lavras. By the 1960s its ties to the Presbyterian Church lapsed and in 1994 it became the Federal University of Lavras (UFLA), one of the leading teaching and research centers in agriculture in Brazil.[66] Like the Lavras school, the agricultural school created by the government of Minas Gerais in Viçosa in 1920 was based on the US state land grant school model and also had North American teachers in its early years. It was called also called an "Escola Superior," granting advanced titles in agronomy, and it too became a federal institution known as the Federal University of Viçosa (UFV).[67] In 1961 the first postgraduate course was opened, a master's degree in Horticulture and Rural Economy, at the Federal University of Viçosa, in partnership with Purdue University. Other partnerships were founded between ESALQ/USP at Piracicaba and Ohio State University and UFRGS with the University of Wisconsin.[68] Also the creation of Embrapa

---

[66] On the history and evolution of this famous agricultural school see Ângelo Constâncio Rodrigues, "A Escola Superior de Agricultura de Lavras/ESAL e a Universidade Federal de Lavras/UFLA: a trajetória de uma transformação" (PhD thesis, Faculdade de Educação, Universidade Federal do Rio de Janeiro, 2013), chaps. 2 and 3; and for the early years see José Normando Gonçalves Meira, "Ciência e prática: ensino agrícola na educação presbiteriana em Minas Gerais (1908–1938)" (PhD thesis, PUC São Paulo, 2009); and Michelle Pereira da Silva Rossi, "'Dedicado à glória de Deus e ao progresso humano': a gênese protestane da Universidade Federal de Lavras – UFLA (Lavras, 1892–1938)" (PhD thesis, Universidade Federal de Uberlândia, 2010).

[67] For the early years of the school, see Fabrício Valentim da Silva, "Ensino Agricola, trabalho de modernização no campo: a origem da Escola Superior de Agricultura e Veterinária do Estado de Minas"(MA thesis, Universidade Federal de Uberlândia, 2007). Before the School of Viçosa, other agricultural education schools were set up in Rio Grande do Sul (now part of the Federal University of Rio Grande do Sul), in Rio de Janeiro (now Federal Rural University of Rio de Janeiro), in Pernambuco (Federal Rural University of Pernambuco), Paraná (now part of the Federal University of Paraná) and Ceará (currently part of the Federal University of Ceará).

[68] Cleimon Eduardo do Amaral Dias, "Abordagem histórica e perspectivas atuais do ensino superior agrícola no Brasil : uma investigação na UFRGS e na UC DAVIS" (PhD thesis, Universidade Federal de Rio Grando do Sul, 2001), p. 47.

led to a massive expansion in the training of professionals in post-graduate courses in Brazil and abroad.[69]

With these educational changes, Brazil by the twenty-first century had the resources to train its own agronomists in all the major areas of research and applied sciences.[70] In 1999 there were some seventy courses in Agronomy in Brazilian universities, with 6,000 students.[71] By 2007 there were 48,307 students enrolled in agricultural courses, 40,217 belonging to public institutions. Regionally the demand for agricultural education was initially concentrated in the South and Southeast regions (54%), but there has been strong demand in the new federal universities in the West-Central region.[72] Between 1998 and early 2017 some 8,000 MA theses and 3,000 doctoral dissertations had been written in this area in Brazilian universities.

Brazilian agriculture also has received significant technical support from the private sector, which intensified its activities in Brazil in the late 1990s after the approval of Law 8.974/95 which created the norms for the use of genetic engineering and use of genetically modified organisms; and Law 9.279/96, which regulated the rights and obligations relative to industrial property. Subsequently, in 1997, Law 9456 on Protection of Cultivars was approved. Finally, in 2005, the Biosafety Law was passed (Law No. 11105).[73] The regulation of intellectual property, including cultivars, especially favored private research activity.[74] Although these new laws were also beneficial for Embrapa, they stimulated even more private technology suppliers.

---

[69] Paulo Roberto da Silva, Francisco X. R. do Vale and Marcelo Cabral Jahnel, "Retrospecto e atualidade da engenharia agronômica," in Oliveira et al., *Trajetória e Estado da Arte da Formação em Engenharia, Arquitetura e Agronomia* (vol. 1): 45.

[70] Ibid.

[71] Dias, "Abordagem histórica e perspectivas atuais do ensino superior agrícola," p. 3.

[72] Oliveira et al., *Trajetória e Estado da Arte da Formação em Engenharia, Arquitetura e Agronomia*, pp. 133–135.

[73] Regulamenta II, IV and V of § 10 of art. 225 of the Federal Constitution established the National Biosafety Council – CNBS, and restructured the National Technical Committee on Biosafety (CTNBio. See Simone Yamamura, "Plantas transgênicas e propriedade intelectual: ciência, tecnologia e inovação no Brasil frente aos Marcos Regulatórios"(MA thesis, Unicamp, Campinas, 2006); Sérgio Paulino de Carvalho, Sergio Luiz Monteiro Salles Filho and Antonio Marcio Buainain, "A institucionalidade propriedade intelectual no Brasil: os impactos da política de articulação da Embrapa no mercado de cultivares no Brasil," *Cadernos de Estudos Avançados*, Rio de Janeiro, 2005.

[74] Alves and Souza, "A pesquisa agrícola numa agricultura integrada ao mercado internacional": 56–67.

The new legislation and the increased productivity results obtained with the introduction of genetically modified organisms (GMOs) have profoundly altered the domestic seed market, with the rapid introduction of such cultivars benefiting large multinationals controlling the international market in GMOs. Thus most of these genetically modified crops such as soybeans, corn and cotton have been produced by multinationals rather than Brazilian research centers. These companies have taken over a large share of the market for these products. Thus it was Monsanto that created the first genetically modified soybean seeds specifically for the Brazilian market.[75]

However, there are specific products of lesser interest to large multinational companies in which Brazilian researchers play a vital part. Along with coffee, this has also been the case with sugarcane. In this instance, research depends mainly on institutions related to the sector itself, such as the Sugarcane Technology Center (CTC), which developed a large share of the seeds used in Brazilian agriculture and in 2017 obtained approval for the first genetically modified sugarcane in the world.[76]

The Brazilian seed market, estimated at approximately R$10 billion, is the third largest industry in the world, exceeded only by the United States and China. In ten years it increased from 1.8 million tons of seeds in the harvest of 2005/2006 to 4 million tons of seeds in the harvest of 2015/2016.[77] In the harvest of 2013/2014 soybeans and corn seeds represented the two most significant products sold, each with a 37% share of the seed market, followed by forages (11%), and vegetables (6%), while wheat, rice, beans and cotton had a much lower percentage of such seed use.

There is a large difference in the use of registered seeds by crop. Thus corn, for example, heavily uses registered seeds, achieving a "utilization rate" of 90%. The same occurs with sorghum (93%) and barley (87%). Soybeans, however, have a much lower utilization rate, of the order of 64%. Cotton and rain-fed rice show even lower levels in the 50% range.

---

[75] Chaddad, *The Economics and Organization of Brazilian Agriculture*, p. 24

[76] Accessed February 3, 2018, at http://revistagloborural.globo.com/Noticias/Agricultura/ Cana/noticia/2017/06/primeira-cana-transgenica-e-aprovada-comercialmente-no-brasil .html.

[77] Fábio Galiotto; Folha de Londrina – Folha Rural, February 25, 2017; accessed February 28, 2017, at website of Abrates – Associação Brasileira de Tecnologia de Sementes: www.abrates.org.br/noticia/mercado-de-sementes-movimenta- r-10-bi-ao-ano-no-brasil; Mariana Barreto, "O Mercado de Sementes no Brasil,"*Associação Brasileira de Sementes e Mudas, 67°. Simpas*, Sinop-MT, November 24, 2015.

Noteworthy is the low level of utilization of seeds registered in bean plantings, with a utilization rate of only 19%. Soybeans, although with a lower utilization rate than maize, represent the cultivation with the highest demand for registered seeds, in the order of 1.2 million tons, which were used for the planting of 30 million hectares.

There are two types of seed usage, with farmers using either registered or unregistered seeds. If they are registered seed they can be produced by both private and public companies. Both types can be sold directly by patent owners or multipliers. These latter are companies that buy the rights of companies holding patents, public or private, multiply the seeds and sell them regionally. Even Embrapa operates in this system. There are different prices for the use of patented seed, since there is the cost of reproducing the seed, logistics and commercial costs. So all seeds have a price, and what can vary is the cost of royalties. Seeds generated in the public sector and seeds developed earlier have lower patent costs. On the other hand, there are the unrecorded seeds. These are the seeds produced by the farmer himself. Genetically modified seeds do not allow germination in a second crop, but the natural seeds can be generated by the producer himself. Thus farmers themselves are the primary source of unregistered seeds.

By 2015 more than 30,000 cultivars have been developed and registered. Of the main crops, there are 3,162 cultivars of corn,[78] and soybeans use 1,611 different cultivars. The great majority of these cultivators are in the public domain, and only a little more than 2,000 represent protected cultivars.[79] Brazilian legislation allows the patent registration of the cultivars, whose production can be done directly by the entity that developed the cultivar or by seed producers authorized by the patent holder. There is licensing and the corresponding royalty payment.

The production of these protected seeds absorbs a great quantity of agricultural lands. There are more than 3,700 seed producers, ranging from those that produce a few kilograms of seeds (mostly for vegetables and flowers) to those producing millions of bags. In general, the small seed producers use their own fields of production, and the large ones rent fields

---

[78] According to Peske, more than 200,000 hectares of seed are produced annually to supply farmers with this quantity of seeds, involving a complex system of cooperative farmers, isolation of production fields (200 meters minimum) and the irrigation systems (Central pivot). Silmar Teichert Peske, "O Mercado de Sementes no Brasil," *Seednews*. Reportagem de capa, maio/jun. 2016, ano XX. N. 3. Accessed February 28, 2017, at silmar@seednews.inf.br.

[79] Barreto, *O Mercado de Sementes*, p. 29.

to produce their seeds.[80] Soybean seed producers, for example, use close to 1 million hectares.

The arrival of biotechnology in agriculture through genetically modified cultivars began a new period of the Brazilian seed industry, significantly altering the market dynamics and relationship between breeders and seed producers. During the market restructuring movement, some of the largest agrochemicals companies also started to work in biotechnology and seeds, resulting in an unprecedented movement toward convergence among the key producers. The combination of research that combined knowledge in the areas of genetic engineering, seeds and agricultural chemicals allowed these companies to create a unique environment for innovation and development of new products.[81] By the end of 2016, there were seventy-four Genetically Modified Plants approved for commercialization, of which thirteen were for soybeans, forty-six for corns, thirteen for cotton, and one each for beans and eucalyptus. The market is now dominated by multinational companies, such as Monsanto with twenty-six GMOs, Syngenta and Dow both with eleven, Du Pont with twelve and Bayer with ten. In 2007 Embrapa launched *cultivante soybean*, developed in partnership with BASF, herbicide-tolerant, with adaptations to the various regions of Brazil. This product was the first vegetable GMO developed entirely in Brazil, and the result of more than ten years of joint research between the two companies.[82] In 2011, CTNBio approved the release of genetically modified beans developed by Embrapa for commercial cultivation in Brazil. The beans are resistant to the golden mosaic virus, the worst enemy of this agricultural crop in Brazil and South America, and the decision was a landmark for national science, since it was the first transgenic plant totally produced by Brazilian public research institutions.[83] Brazil is among the countries that most use genetically modified plants, along with the United States, Argentina, India and Canada. For the 2015/2016 crop it was estimated that 44.2 million hectares were planted with GMO seeds. This included 90.7% of the area cultivated with soybean, corn and cotton crops.

---

[80] Peske, "O Mercado de Sementes no Brasil," pp. 1–2.

[81] Associação Brasileira de Sementes e Mudas, *Anuário 2015*. Accessed February 28, 2017, at www.abrasem.com.br/wp-content/uploads/2013/09/Anuario_ABRASEM_2015_2 .pdf, p. 11.

[82] Embrapa. *Os benefícios da biotecnologia para a sua qualidade de vida*, accessed February 28, 2017, at www.embrapa.br/recursos-geneticos-e-biotecnologia/sal a-de-imprensa/se-liga-na-ciencia/a-biotecnologia-e-voce.

[83] Ibid.

The forecast is that 94% of all soybeans sown in Brazil, and approximately 85% of corn and 74% of the cotton will come from genetically modified materials.[84]

Along with the ongoing debate over GMCs in Brazil, a major theme that is much discussed is the issue of sustainability. The question of the sustainability of Brazilian agriculture is crucial not only for the country itself but for the world's sustainability in the future. Much of the Amazon rainforest, the world's largest, is in Brazil. Its future will play a key role in climate change, which today is a source of major concern about the future of humanity. In addition, Brazil occupies a prominent position in world food production, being one of the largest exporters of agricultural products. The country is considered an essential source of food supplies to meet the expected increase in world food needs in the next thirty years, when strong growth in demand will occur both due to population and income growth. Thus, understanding the sustainability of Brazilian agriculture, that is, the country's ability to maintain its main biomes, particularly the Amazon rainforest, is an essential element for understanding the future sustainability of the planet, particularly on the crucial issue of the greenhouse effect and climate change.

As a result of the United Nations Convention on Climate Change, held in 1992 (Eco-92), the Brazilian government adopted a series of measures to initiate the implementation of the decisions of the meeting, which were called Agenda 21, which was Brazil's version of the basic positions adopted. These proposals called for "sustainable development" through specific measures to reduce greenhouse gases in all areas of the world, and in all sectors of the economy in accordance with environmental protection, social justice and economic efficiency. Brazil was the first country to sign the document, and in 1994 the Inter-ministerial Commission for Sustainable Development (CIDES) was established to propose strategies, policies and national programs related to Agenda 21. It was decided that the Ministry of Science and Technology would be responsible for coordinating actions on climate change, and the Ministry of Environment would promote actions related to the Convention on Biological Diversity, also signed in 1992.[85] In 1997, the Kyoto Protocol was established, which set numerical targets for reducing greenhouse gases, initially leaving

---

[84] Associação Brasileira de Sementes e Mudas, *Anuário 2015*, p. 13.
[85] ABC – Observatório – Agricultura de Baixo Carbono. A evolução de um novo paradigma. Fundação Getúlio Vargas, Centro de Agronegócio da Escola de Economia de São Paulo. Accessed April 17, 2017, at www.observatorioabc.com.br.

developing countries free of obligations. In 1999 the federal government created the Inter-ministerial Commission on Global Climate Change (CIMGC), with the objective of coordinating the actions related to the convention. The Ministry of Science and Technology created the General Coordination of Global Climate Change in order to monitor the estimates of greenhouse gas emissions in Brazil and to define mitigation policies. In 2007, the Ministry of the Environment created the Secretariat for Climate Change and Environmental Quality and in 2008 the National Plan on Climate Change was approved, which voluntarily established numerical targets for the reduction of greenhouse gases, with the government committing itself to drastically reduce deforestation, above all in the Amazon. Finally, in 2009 the country made a new effort in this area, setting targets for reducing greenhouse gases for various sectors of the economy. It was agreed to reduce emissions by 36–38% compared to what would be expected in 2020 if mitigation measures were not taken. Also in that year the Agriculture Program of Low Carbon Emission (Plano ABC) was adopted. Through this voluntary plan Brazil agreed that it would no longer emit 1.2 billion tons of CO_2 and equivalents (CO_2eq).[86] In addition to targets for energy efficiency and other programs related to the industrial process, the Brazilian sustainability plans set specific targets for forest control, agricultural practices and the use of biofuels. The goals presented for land use were related to the control of two of the main Brazilian biomes, the Amazon and the Cerrado. Besides these massive land areas, Brazil also has other important biomes such as the Atlantic Forest, the Caatinga, the Pantanal and the Pampa. Although there were isolated initiatives on the part of several entities to oversee these other regions, until recently there has been a lack of monitoring of these biomes.

In 1988, the National Institute for Space Research (INPE) began monitoring the Amazon, developing a methodology that would later be used to monitor the other Brazilian biomes by the beginning of the twenty-first century. In 2008, with the support of the United Nations Development Program (UNDP), an agreement was signed between the Ministry of Environment and the Brazilian Institute of Environment and Renewable Natural Resources (IBAMA) to carry out the Deforestation Monitoring Program of Brazilian Biomes by Satellite, whose objective is the permanent monitoring of the coverage of the main Brazilian biomes, in order to quantify deforestation of native vegetation areas as a basis for actions to

[86] Ibid.

control and combat illegal deforestation in those biomes. This systematic surveillance has improved the supervision of these biomes with increased enforcement against predators by the IBAMA.[87]

The Amazon is currently the world's largest tropical forest, with about 5.4 million km^2. Approximately 80% of this forest is located in Brazil, and of the protected part of the rainforest, about 60% is Brazil territory. Due its size and characteristics, the Amazon represents a great depository of world biodiversity, being the host of approximately 20% of the known animal and plant species. It is also recognized as a repository of ecological needs not only for indigenous peoples and local communities, but also for the rest of the world. According to WWF-Brazil, of all the tropical forests in the world, the Amazon is the only one that is still preserved in terms of size and diversity.[88] Thus deforestation in the Amazon has a crucial impact on global warming. In addition, studies show that global warming could have dramatic consequences on the forest by reducing the period and volume of rainfall.[89]

The Cerrado, which is also included in the greenhouse gas emissions targets, has an area of approximately 203 million hectares. It is the second largest biome in South America, occupying about a quarter of the national territory. Its area reaches the states of Goiás, Tocantins, Mato Grosso, Mato Grosso do Sul, Minas Gerais, Bahia, Maranhão, Piauí, Rondônia, Paraná, São Paulo and the Federal District, as well as the enclaves in Amapá, Roraima and Amazonas. In the Cerrado are the headwaters of the three largest hydrographic basins of South America (Amazon/

---

[87] On this theme see http://siscom.ibama.gov.br/monitora_biomas/; Ministério do Meio Ambiente, *Estratégia do Programa Nacional de Monitoramento Ambiental dos Biomas Brasileiros*. Secretaria de Mudanças Climáticas e Qualidade Ambiental. Departamento de Políticas de Combate ao Desmatamento (Brasília: MMA, 2016).

[88] Accessed April 7, 2017, at http://www.wwf.org.br/wwf_brasil/organizacao/.

[89] Peter H. Raven, "Tropical floristic tomorrow," *Taxon*, 37, no. 3 (Aug., 1988): 549–560; Yadvinder Malhi, J. Timmons Roberts, Richard A. Betts, Timothy J. Killeen, Wenhong Li and Carlos A. Nobre, "Climate change, deforestation and the fate of the Amazon," *Science*, 319 (2008): 169–172, doi:10.1126/science.1146961. On the Amazon Forest see André de Arruda Lyra, "Estudo de vulnerabilidade do bioma Amazônia aos cenários de mudanças climáticas" (PhD thesis, Instituto Nacional de Pesquisas Espaciais, São José dos Campos, 2015). Governo do Estado da Amazônia, *A Floresta amazônica e seu Papel nas Mudanças Climáticas* (Manaus: Secretaria de Meio Ambiente e Desenvolvimento Sustentável, 2009); Maria Alice Dias Rolim Visentin, "A floresta Amazônica e as mudanças climáticas: proteção da biodiversidade," *Revista CEJ* (Brasília), XVII, no. 60 (May/Aug. 2013): 96–102; Carlos A. Nobre, Gilvan Sampaio and Luis Salazar, *Mudanças climáticas e a Amazônia*, accessed April 17, 2017, at http://mtc-m16b.sid.inpe.br/col/sid.inpe.br/mtc-m17@80/2007/09.24.12.18/doc/nobre_mudan%e7as.pdf.

Tocantins, São Francisco and Prata), which results in great availability of water resources. From the point of view of biological diversity, the Brazilian Cerrado is recognized as the richest savannah in the world, sheltering a flora with more than 11,000 species of native plants, of which 4,400 are indigenous to the region. In 2009, the Cerrado had vegetation on some 1 million km², equivalent to 51% of the area of the biome.[90]

The other biomes, although without specific programs of protection, are also crucially important in terms of greenhouse gases and global biodiversity. This is the case of the Atlantic Forest, where more than two-thirds of the Brazilian population live. It is the Brazilian biome with the lowest percentage of natural vegetation cover, but still has an important part in the country's biological diversity, with several endemic species and its water resources supplying a population that exceeds 120 million. Its original area is restricted to some already fragmented remnants, which unfortunately continue to be destroyed for extracting exotic species and flora. Only 22% of the original area of the biome remains of its 1,103,961 km².[91]

The Pantanal, another of the important Brazilian biomes, represents a periodic flood plain recognized nationally and internationally for its biodiversity as one of the world's most important wetlands. It was declared a Biosphere Reserve and Natural World Heritage Site by UNESCO and spreads into two states, Mato Grosso and Mato Grosso do Sul and across the border into Bolivia. It occupies an area of approximately 151,313 km², or about 2% of Brazil, and still preserves 83% of the biome.[92]

Located in the extreme south of Brazil and extending through Uruguay and Argentina, the Pampas represent one of the major Brazilian biomes, occupying about two-thirds of the area of the state of Rio Grande do Sul. It is a rural ecosystem with predominantly grass vegetation and some scattered shrubs. Close to the watercourses and on the plateau slopes, the vegetation becomes denser with trees. The Banhados, flooded areas near the coast, are also part of this biome. Although its landscape looks

[90] Accessed April 7, 2017, at http://siscom.ibama.gov.br/monitora_biomas/PMDBBS%20-%20CERRADO.html.

[91] Accessed April 7, 2017, at http://siscom.ibama.gov.br/monitora_biomas/PMDBBS%20-%20MATA%20ATLANTICA.html.

[92] Accessed April 7, 2017, at http://siscom.ibama.gov.br/monitora_biomas/PMDBBS%20-%20PANTANAL.html.

monotonous and uniform, it harbors a great biodiversity. In 2008, about 54% of its area had been deforested.[93]

Finally there is Caatinga, which is located in the semi-arid region of Brazil, home to a population of 20 million inhabitants and thus the most populous semi-arid region in the world. The Caatinga biome includes several plant formations; the term "Caatinga" designates a dominant vegetation that extends through almost all the States of the Northeast and part of Minas Gerais. This ecosystem is very important from the biological point of view because it presents unique fauna and flora. It is estimated that at least 932 species have already been recorded for the region, of which 380 are indigenous. Among Brazilian biomes, it is the least scientifically known and has been given low priority, despite being one of the most threatened due to the inadequate and unsustainable use of its soils. The Caatinga occupied an area of 844,453 km², with a native vegetation cover of 441,117 km², equivalent to 53% of its original area.[94]

The monitoring of these great Brazilian biomes began with the Amazon Rainforest because of its importance and national and international pressure for its preservation. Data available from the 1980s shows relatively stable but high deforestation, generally exceeding 20,000 km² per annum. These numbers began to fall from 2006 onwards, maintaining levels of around 6,000 km² as of 2009. Surprisingly, there was an increase in the last two years of 2015 and 2016, making it more difficult to meet Brazil's goal of maximum deforestation of 3.9 km² in 2020. There is a lot of speculation about the causes, but there is as yet no formal and official explanation (see Graph 4.6).[95]

---

[93] Accessed April 7, 2017, at http://siscom.ibama.gov.br/monitora_biomas/PMDBBS%20-%20PAMPA.html.

[94] Accessed April 7, 2017, at http://siscom.ibama.gov.br/monitora_biomas/PMDBBS%20-%20CAATINGA.html.

[95] The news startled national and international authorities and environmentalists. But despite the speculation, the causes that would have led to the increase are still unknown. Greenpeace, for example, speaks of weakening of command and control measures, and that the new Forest Code, by offering amnesty for past activity, created expectation of future leniency. www.greenpeace.org/brasil/pt/Noticias/Desmatamento-dispara-na-Amazonia-/.

INPE, responding to the first increase in 2015, said that "the increase in deforestation was attributed to several factors, including Brazil's unstable economy and currency, which makes the conversion of the forest to agriculture more attractive; drastic government cuts in funding programs to reduce deforestation; a renewed push for large-scale infrastructure projects in the Amazon; and relaxation of the Brazilian Forest Code, which regulates how much of the forest should be preserved in private properties." www.ccst.inpe.br/o-

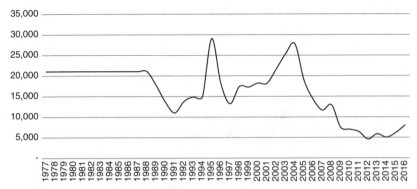

GRAPH 4.6: Annual deforestation of the Legal Amazon 1977–2016 (km²/year)
Source: www.obt.inpe.br/prodes/prodes_1988_2016 n.htm

The initially major reduction in deforestation in the Amazon was made possible by active monitoring. This led to a systematic reduction of the net emission of greenhouse gases by Brazilian forests, which in turn was most influenced by the fall in the deforestation of the Legal Amazon, which explains a large part of the fall in greenhouse gases which has occurred since 2004 (see Graph 4.7).[96] Decree 7,390, of December 9, 2010, which established targets for greenhouse gas emissions for 2020, determined that there would be a need to reduce by 80% annual deforestation rates in the Legal Amazon using as a base 1996–2005. The same decree stipulated that there should also be a reduction of 40% of the annual deforestation rates of the Cerrado Biome in relation to the average verified between 1999 and 2008. The two ambitious goals are considered reasonable by most experts, but clearly it will be necessary to return to the deforestation rates that were achieved before 2014.

desmatamento-na-amazonia-aumenta-no-brasil-mas-permanece-baixo-com-relacao-ao-passado/.

[96] According to the Ministério da Ciência e Tecnologia, Inovação e Comunicações, Brazil established the National Policy on Climate Change (PNMC) through Decree No. 12,187 / 2009, which defines the voluntary national commitment to adopt mitigation actions to reduce its greenhouse gas (GHG) emissions between 36.1% and 38.9% in relation to projected emissions by 2020. According to Decree No. 7,390 / 2010, which regulates the National Policy on Climate Change, the projection of greenhouse gas emissions for 2020 was estimated at 3,236 Gt CO_2eq. Thus, the reduction corresponding to the established percentages is between 1,168 Gt CO_2eq and 1,259 Gt CO_2eq, respectively, for the year in question. On the topic see Ministry of Science and Technology, Innovation and Communications, *Estimativas Anuais de Emissões de Gases de Efeito Estufa no Brasil* (3rd edn., Brasília: MCT, 2016).

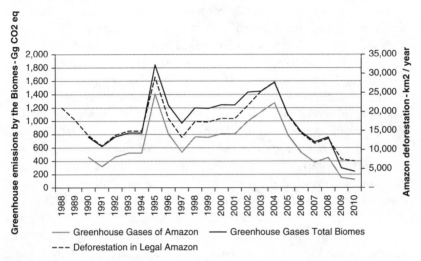

GRAPH 4.7: Greenhouse gas emissions from the biomes and Amazon deforestation, 1988–2010
Source: Ministério de Ciência, Tecnologia, Inovação e Comunicações (2016)

In addition to the direct effects of deforestation, activities related to agricultural activity have begun to be controlled and their effects measured on the emission of greenhouse gases. This has resulted in Brazilian plans to recover pastures, and to better integrate forests, crops and livestock; to use no-tillage plantings; and finally to develop biological nitrogen fixation. The greatest reduction should occur in pasture recovery. According to the Fundação Getúlio Vargas, the degradation of pasture leads to the progressive loss of soil productivity and its capacity to recover, leading to their inability to sustain the production and quality levels demanded by the animals, as well as to overcome the harmful effects of pests, diseases and invasive species. This process is the result of inadequate management, culminating in the deterioration of natural resources. The advancement of the degradation process, the loss of vegetation cover and the reduction in the organic matter of the soil also leads to the emission of CO_2 into the atmosphere. With the recovery of pastures, the process can be reversed and the soil can begin to accumulate carbon and significantly reduce the emission of CO_2. This process is slow and it is estimated that a 3–4% reduction in relation to the current trend can occur by 2020. Although the current government plan only targets 15 million hectares, there are in Brazil approximately 60 million degraded hectares.[97]

Brazil has also developed the so-called system of crop–livestock integration (ILP, or Integração Lavoura–Pecuária) and crop–livestock–forest integration (ILPF, or Integração Lavoura–Pecuária–Floresta) to deal with the negative impact of a monoculture system which in many of these biomes causes loss of organic matter and compromises soil quality. These integrated systems allow farms to produce grains, meat, milk and wood throughout the year in the same area of rural property through a system of rotation or succession. The result of this combination is increased income for the rural producer, reduced deforestation and reduced emissions of greenhouse gases. The increase in organic matter in the soil is one of the main benefits of the integrated system, since this improves the physical, chemical and biological conditions of the soil, promoting the fixation of carbon in the soil. The ILPF strategy is being adopted at different intensity levels in the Brazilian biomes, and is now estimated to be in use on some 1.6 million to 2 million hectares.[98] Preliminary research results developed at Embrapa in Mato Grosso

[97] ABC – Observatório – Agricultura de Baixo Carbono. A evolução de um novo paradigma. Fundação Getúlio Vargas, Centro de Agronegócio da Escola de Economia de São Paulo, pp. 10-17. Accessed April 17, 2017, at www.observatorioabc.com.br. In calculating the GHG balance, the emission of fertilizers applied to the soil and emissions from cattle, such as excreta, are taken into account. On the subject see the major study of Embrapa: Ademir H. Zimmer et al., *Degradação, Recuperação e Renovação de Pastagens* (Campo Grande,MS: Embrapa Gado de Corte, 2012). Accessed April 19, 2017, at www.embrapa.br/busca-de-publicacoes/-/publicacao/951322/degradacao-recuperacao-e-renovacao-de-pastagens.

[98] On this theme see Ramon Costa Alvarenga et al., "Sistema Integração Lavoura–Pecuária–Floresta: condicionamento do solo e intensificação da produção de lavouras," *Informe Agropecuário* (Belo Horizonte), 31, no. 257 (Jul./Aug. 2010); Luiz Carlos Balbino et al., "Agricultura sustentável por meio da integração Lavoura–Pecuária–Floresta (iLPF)," *Informe Agropecuário*, 31, no.257 (Jul./Aug. 2010); Luiz Carlos Balbino et al., "Evolução tecnológica e arranjos produtivos de sistemas de integração lavoura-pecuária-floresta no Brasil," Pesquisa Agropecuária Brasileira *(Brasília)*, 46, no. 10 (Oct. 2011); Maurel Behling, *ILPF – Integração Lavoura–Pecuária–Floresta. Experiências da Embrapa Agrossilvopastoril* (Sinop, MT: Embrapa), accessed February 25, 2017, at http://docplayer.com.br/17885191-Ilpf-integracao-lavoura-pecuaria-floresta-experiencias-da-embrapa-agrossilvopastoril.html; Tadário Kamel de Oliveira et al., *Experiências com Implantação de Unidades de Integração Lavoura–Pecuária–Floresta (iLPF) no Acre*. Rio Branco (Acre: Embrapa, 2012); Luiz Carlos Balbino, Alexandre de Oliveira Barcellos and Luís Fernando Stone, *Marco Referencial: Integração lavoura-pecuária-floresta* (Brasília: Embrapa, 2011); Ronaldo Trecenti, Maurício Carvalho de Oliveira, Gunter Hass and Marcos de Matos Ramos, *Integração Lavoura–Pecuária–Floresta: Cartilha do Produtor* (Brasília: Ministério da Agricultura, 2009).

demonstrated the efficiency of these ILPF systems in the reduction of greenhouse gases.[99]

So-called direct or non-tillage planting represents one of the most important technologies introduced in Brazilian agriculture, and is now used to produce cereals, legumes, oilseeds and cotton without plowing. There were more than 33 million hectares of land under the no-till system by 2015, more than 50% of the area devoted to cereals, thanks to the development of appropriate machinery and adequate inputs. This tropical technology avoids harrowing and plowing and represents tremendous fuel economy. The reduction in CO_2 emissions is of the order of 40%. No-tillage also allows erosion reduction and chemical fertilizer use. According to the study by Fundação Getúlio Vargas (FGV), this system of planting is quickly becoming the norm for all the grains produced in Brazil.[100]

The biological fixation of nitrogen in soils represents another technological innovation widely used in Brazil. Through this system the atmospheric N_2 gas is captured by microorganisms and converted into nitrogenous compounds available to the plants. This new environment increases crop productivity, reduces the use of industrialized inputs and contributes to the reduction of greenhouse gas emissions. Brazil maintains research and development programs with dozens of bacteria capable of supplying nitrogen to soybeans, rice, sugarcane, corn, wheat, beans, alfalfa, peanuts, etc. The inoculation of nitrogen-fixing bacteria in soybean seeds before sowing is a process that completely replaces the need for the use of nitrogen fertilizers in soybean crops. Estimates indicate that the non-use of nitrogen fertilizers in the 30 million hectares cultivated with soybeans in Brazil (crop 2013/2014) results in annual savings of around US$12 billion. Unlike the use of nitrogenous fertilizers, biological nitrogen fixation does not cause environmental pollution. The use of biological nitrogen fixation makes Brazil an example for the world in the adoption of low-carbon agriculture. The biological fixation of nitrogen is

---

[99] Accessed April 17, 2017, at www.embrapa.br/busca-de-noticias/-/noticia/2411761/est udo-comprova-mitigacao-de-gases-de-efeito-estufa-pela-ilpf; The research indicated that in conventional tillage area, there is a greater flow of N_2O emissions during the harvest, with intense peaks soon after fertilization. However, when analyzing an area with integration between agriculture and forest, it observed that the emissions of nitrous oxide tended to stay in balance.

[100] ABC – Observatório – Agricultura de Baixo Carbono, "A evolução de um novo paradigma." Fundação Getúlio Vargas, Centro de Agronegócio da Escola de Economia de São Paulo, pp. 19–23. Accessed April 17, 2017, at www.observatorioabc.com.br.

contemplated in the ABC Plan, with the proposed extension to 5.5 million hectares which would result in a reduction in the emission of CO_2 by 10 million tons by 2020.[101]

Although not directly linked to agriculture, bioenergy programs that Brazil has developed for many years have had undeniable success in reducing greenhouse gas emissions. According to data from the sugarcane sector, the use of ethanol produced through sugarcane reduces by 89% the emission of greenhouse gases such as carbon dioxide (CO_2), methane (CH_4) and nitrous oxide (NO_2).[102] Recent efforts have also been made to develop efficient processes for the use of bioenergy in the transport of cargo and passengers. Although still timid compared to the Pro-Alcool program based on ethanol usage, the use of biodiesel is advancing in Brazil, since a law passed in 2014 required an additional 6% of biodiesel be sold to the final consumer. This schedule was accelerated in 2016, setting a new timetable that starts with 8%, to be implemented in up to one year, then 9% in two years and finally 10% in up to three years. This represents an important measure in the gradual replacement of this fossil fuel.[103]

As of 2010, the government has created a systematic process for monitoring the goals established for the reduction of greenhouse gases in Brazil. When the data for 2014 were analyzed, it was evident that a few sectors caused the most pollution. Thus the energy sector emits 37% of the atmospheric gases, agriculture 33% and land and forest change 18%. These numbers vary over time, but between 2010 and 2014 the energy sector actually increased gas levels by 27%, while agriculture and ranching increased their emissions by only 4% and the restrictions now in place on the dismantling of national biomes have drastically reduced their emissions by a third (see Table 4.5). Brazilian energy production is relatively clean

[101] Ana Lucia Ferreira, *Fixação biológica de nitrogênio por reduzir as emissões de GEE na agricultura*. Accessed April 19, 2017, at www.embrapa.br/busca-de-noticias/-/noticia/ 8313328/fixacao-biologica-de-nitrogenio-pode-reduzir-as-emissoes-de-gee-na-agricultura; Ministério da Agricultura, *ABC Agricultura de Baixa Emissão de Carbono*. Accessed April 19, 2017, at www.agricultura.gov.br/assuntos/sustentabilidade/plano-abc; Embrapa, *Fixação Biológica de Nitrogênio*. Accessed April 19, 2017, at www .embrapa.br/tema-fixacao-biologica-de-nitrogenio/nota-tecnica.

[102] NovaCana.com quotes the IEA (International Energy Agency) as saying that compared to gasoline the use of ethanol produced through sugarcane reduces on average 89% of the emission of GHGs, such as carbon dioxide (CO_2), methane (CH_4) and nitrous oxide (NO_2). Accessed April 19, 2017, at www.novacana.com/etanol/beneficios/.

[103] Law13.033, September 24, 2014, and Law 13.263, March 25,2016.

TABLE 4.5: *Emissions of CO_2eq by sector, for the years 1990–2014*

Sectors	GgCO₂eq (1)						Change		
	1990	1995	2000	2005	2010	2014	2005–2010	2010–2014
Energy	185,808	223,727	284,273	312,747	371,086	469,832	18.7%	26.6%
Industrial processes	52,059	65,625	75,581	80,517	89,947	94,263	11.7%	4.8%
Farming & ranching	286,998	316,671	328,367	392,491	407,067	424,473	3.7%	4.3%
Change of land and forests (with removals) (2)	792,038	1,931,478	1,265,606	1,904,666	349,173	233,140	-81.7%	-33.2%
Treatment of residues	26,006	31,370	38,693	45,476	54,127	62,787	19.0%	16.0%
Total liquid emissions	1,342,909	2,568,872	1,992,520	2,735,898	1,271,399	1,284,496	-53.5%	1.0%
Change of land and forests (without removals) (2)	1,147,054	2,325,414	1,659,540	2,653,627	1,096,431	1,007,861	-58.7%	-8.1%
Total	1,697,925	2,962,807	2,386,454	3,484,859	2,018,658	2,059,217	-42.1%	2.0%

Source: Ministério da Ciência e Tecnologia, Inovação e Comunicações, *Estimativas Anuais de Emissões de Gases de Efeito Estufa no Brasil* (Brasília, 3rd edn., 2016), p. 10
Notes: (1) Gg=millions of tons.
(2) Removals refers to the positive effect of forests on the removal of greenhouse gases.

compared to most countries, since hydroelectricity accounts for 58% of total generation and renewable sources accounted for 75%.[104]

As can be seen from this survey, Brazil has taken sustainability issues seriously, both for ecological and economic reasons. Thus as commercial agriculture has dramatically expanded in recent years, leading sectors of the industry and major national research institutes have been concerned with these issues. Moreover the enormous growth of Brazilian agriculture since the 1960s has made these issues of paramount importance even for the continued growth of agricultural productivity. In turn, the state-sponsored creation of a modern agricultural educational and research system has been a fundemantal factor in generating the crucial productivity growth needed to sustain Brazil's position as a major world agricultural leader.

But in the area of sanitation, fundamentally dependent on state action, Brazil has been less successful. The creation of the World Trade Organization (WTO) in 1995 defined rules and standards for international trade which included the quality of food consumed. This had led many of the participating countries, including Brazil, to modernize services involving animal health. For Brazil, there have been significant advances in the control of the national animal herds and in the processing of their products. There has been real success in the control and eradication of such diseases as foot-and-mouth disease, classical swine fever and Newcastle disease. However, given the lack of its exports, the same improvement has not occurred with the milk sector, which currently represents the product with the greatest risk to national health. Moreover, although Brazil occupies an extraordinary position in the international meat market today, periodic weaknesses in the process of control and inspection of meat and other agricultural products remain an important problem.[105]

Sanitary control has been improved to meet the both internal requirements and those required by the international market. In this case, in

---

[104] In the area of energy, the shortage of electric power supply, also caused by delays in numerous planned works in the electricity sector, as well as the recent water shortages, required more intensive use of fossil fuel power generation systems, worsening, at least temporarily, the Brazilian energy matrix. The completion of these projects and the intensification of investments in renewable energy sources should reverse this process of deterioration of the Brazilian energy matrix.

[105] Recently, in 2017, there was a scandal regarding the sanitary control of meat produced in several Brazilian slaughterhouses. This provoked an immediate reaction in numerous importing countries. Accessed February 4, 2018, at https://economia.uol.com.br/noticias/reuters/2017/03/17/escandalo-da-carne-impacta-industria-no-brasil-e-ameaca-exportacoes.htm.

addition to the need for sanitary control against pathogens which affect human health, there is an attempt to control the impact of pesticides, the use of which is required in tropical agriculture, making Brazil one of the world's largest consumers of pesticides.[106]

Due to the importance, severity and complexity of the theme, which requires the farmers' technical competence and efficient public control, many experts believe that the health risk in agriculture is one of the greatest threats it faces, not only due to its potential impact, but also because of the lack of awareness of its importance and the precarious situation of the state system of sanitary control of agricultural crops and livestock. This is due to the operational fragility of the inspection process at all stages of the process.[107]

As this survey has show, Brazil has invested heavily in research and education and in many ways is a leader in modern technology and practice in commercial agriculture. This of course does not apply to the significant number of subsistence farmers who have only partially adopted the new methods or have been unable to have access to them. But in the commercial sector of Brazilian agriculture there is a progressive commitment to sustainability and resource support because it makes economic sense and makes a major difference in long-term agricultural activity. For all the entrepreneurial spirit of Brazil's farmers, it has been the tremendous investment in education and research, some of it supported by these same producers, which has made Brazil into one of the more advanced agricultural producers in the world.

---

[106] According to Pereira, in Brazil many pathogens have had an impact on agriculture and livestock. Examples are innumerable, both old and recent, such as: "rust" (a fungal disease) of coffee and soybeans; the "bicudo" insects (boll weevil) which destroyed cotton; outbreaks of foot-and-mouth disease (a virus-caused disease) in bovine animals; "cancer" and "greening" (bacterial diseases) of citrus orchards; or the arrival in 1989, of the fungal disease called "witch's broom" in Bahia's cocoa plantations, which devastated production, causing Brazil to lose the status of major producer and exporter of cocoa and to become an importer of this product. Luciano Gomes de Carvalho Pereira, *Controle Fitossanitário: agrotóxicos e outros métodos*, Brasília, Camara dos Deputados, Consultoria Legislativa, Estudo fevereiro 2013. On this theme also see Frederico Peres, Josino Costa Moreira and Gaetan Serge Dubois, "Agrotóxicos, saúde e ambiente. Uma Introdução ao tema," in Frederico Peres, Josino Costa Moreira and Gaetan Serge Dubois (orgs.), *É veneno ou remédio?: Agrotóxicos, saúde e ambiente* (Rio de Janeiro: Editora Fiocruz, 2003): 21–41.

[107] Antonio Márcio Buainain et al., "Quais os riscos mais relevantes nas atividades agropecuárias," in Buainain et al., *O Mundo Rural no Brasil do Século 21*: 175–208, 196–200.

5

Regional Pattern of Agriculture

Given the enormous continental size of Brazil, along with an extraordinary range of climates and soils, it was inevitable that there would be sharp differences in the population and economy by region. These differences are reflected in the regional grouping of the states that Brazil now uses to define the different areas of the country. These regions encompass enormous territory. Thus the Southern region, which is the smallest of the regions, is greater than France, Germany or Spain. The Southeast is almost the size of France and Germany combined; the Northeast and Center-West are each greater than France, Germany and Spain together. The North is larger than India. Moreover each region had its own historical evolution. The Northeast was the first region settled and developed in the sixteenth century. This was followed by the slow and steady evolution of the Southeastern region in the seventeenth and eighteenth centuries. The Southern region only came into full development in the eighteenth and nineteenth centuries, while the Center-West and North remained wilderness and under the control of unconquered indigenous people until the late nineteenth and early twentieth centuries.

Even early on, the regions concentrated on different crops. The large plantations were established along the coast of the Northeastern states and in the lowland coastal region of the Southeastern area. Here slave-produced sugar was the primary product. The discovery of gold in Minas Gerais opened up the economy and increased the population in the more interior parts of the Southeastern region in the eighteenth century, and the diamond boom opened up a small part of the Center-West in this same century. The growth of coffee, which passed sugar in its importance to

Brazilian exports in the 1830s, was concentrated almost exclusively in the Southeastern region. Cotton was a Northeastern product and grew substantially in the mid-nineteenth century, while natural rubber became an important and temporary export in the late nineteenth century and was concentrated in the North and Northeastern regions. In turn the promotion of European small farm settlements opened up the Southern region in the nineteenth and twentieth centuries, and produced commercial farming of multiple crops along with the traditional livestock and ranching economy of the region.

At the time of the first national census of 1872 most of the population was concentrated along the Atlantic coast, with little representation in the interior, which explains the low densities of less than 1 person per square kilometer in these interior regions. This in turn explains why their share of population was less than 3% of the total national population. In contrast, the coastal regions had the highest densities of persons to land and accounted for much larger shares of the national population. The composition of these coastal regions was influenced by the arrival before 1850 of some 3 million Africans, and a more modest stream of Portuguese migrants. The interior of the country still contained large numbers of unincorporated Indian tribes as well as a large percentage of mestizos of Europe–African and Indigenous mixture. The Northeast, buffered by periodic droughts and a decline of local agriculture, progressively lost population both to the South and West. Aside from obtaining these internal migrants, the South and Southeast also received most of the 5.1 million European and Asian immigrants who arrived in Brazil between 1872 and 1960.[1]

But change was rapid in the second half of the twentieth century. The total population grew very fast as fertility remained very high and mortality, and especially infant mortality, began to decline ever more rapidly by the mid-twentieth century. The peak decade of growth was the 1950s, when the population was increasing at 2.99% per annum. It grew at 2.89% per annum in the 1970s and 2.48% in the next decade – all high rates by world standards.[2] But in the 1980s, fertility began its long secular decline, and so the national population slowed its growth to less

---

[1] Maria Stella Ferreira Levy, "O papel da migração internacional na evolução da população brasileira (1872 a 1972)," *Revista de Saúde Pública*, Vol. 8 (Supl.) (1974), table 1, pp. 71–73.

[2] IBGE, *Sinopsis do Censo de 2010* (Rio de Janeiro, 2011), table 2.

MAP 5.1: Regions and states of Brazil

than 2% and in the first decades of the new century was heading for no-growth of the population by mid century.[3]

Along with the expansion of the national population, there was also a change in the share of this population among the regions (see Map 5.1). There were major movements of native-born populations from north to south and from the coast to the interior which shifted the relative demographic balance of the various regions. In the half century between the census of 1960 and that of 2010 both the North and the Center-West doubled their share of population, and together now accounted for 16% of the national population. The Northeast lost most, followed by the Southeast and South (see Table 5.1). The North and Center-West were

---

[3] The annual growth rate fell below 1% in 2010 and it is estimated that it will turn negative in 2045, after which the growth rate will be increasingly negative to 2060. IBGE, "Projeção da População do Brasil por sexo e idade: 2000–2060 [as of 2013]," accessed February 22, 2018, at www.ibge.gov.br/home/estatistica/populacao/projecao_da_populacao/2013/default.shtm.

TABLE 5.1: *Population resident in the regions of Brazil, 1960–2010*

	1960	1970	1980	1991	2000	2010
Brazil	70,992,343	94,508,583	121,150,573	146,917,459	169,590,693	190,755,799
North	2,930,005	4,188,313	6,767,249	10,257,266	12,893,561	15,864,454
Northeast	22,428,873	28,675,110	35419,156	42,470,225	47,693,253	53,081,950
Southeast	31,062,978	40,331,969	52,580,527	62,660,700	72,297,351	80,364,410
South	11,892,107	16,683,551	19,380,126	22,117,026	25,089,783	27,386,891
Center-West	2,678,380	4,629,640	7003,515	9,412,242	11,616,745	14,058,094

Source: IBGE, SIDRA, Sinopsis Censo 2010, table 1286

growing faster than the national average and each was still at or above 2% per annum growth in the new century.[4]

All of these changes affected the density of population in each of the regions. Whereas all regions had an increase in population and resulting increase in persons per km², with the nation as a whole reaching 22 persons per km² by 2010, the fastest growth (over 3% per annum) was on the frontier, encompassing the North and Center-West regions (see Table 5.2).

Internal migration was a constant in Brazil after the end of international migration in the 1920s. From the 1920s to the 1980s the primary movement was from the Northeast to the Southeast region. But at the end of the century a new powerful internal migration occurred to the Western frontier from all the coastal regions, including the South as well as the Northeast. This can be seen in the distribution of native-born residents by region compared with their birthplace by region. Clearly the Center-West held the most native-born immigrants whose birth was in another region, followed by the North region in the period 1991–2010. By this time the Southeast showed less of an inter-regional migration flow and the South had the fewest native-born migrants (see Table 5.3).

Not only was there migration across regions, there was also an even more massive movement of native-born to the growing urban centers in all regions. This resulted in a major change in the distribution of population between urban and rural residence, although with all these changes there were still marked major regional differences in the rates of change. In 1970 as in the decade before, only the Southeast with its major urban centers had a majority of its population listed as urban. The South and the Center-West looked little different from the North and Northeast. But by 2010 the nation as a whole was only 16% rural and even the North and Northwest were down to approximately a quarter of their respective populations that were still rural (see Table 5.4).

These regions not only differed in terms of population distribution, size and density, but also initially differed greatly in the health and well-being of their populations. The very marked regional differences in life expectancy in 1960 only slowly changed over time. In 1960 the difference in average life expectancy at birth was 7.5 years between the least healthy (Northeast) and the healthiest regions (South), but this gap did not really decline significantly until 2000. In this century these differences in life expectancy have continued to decline, and as of 2010 the Northeast was just 4.6 years behind the Southern rate (see Table 5.5).

[4] IBGE, *Sinopsis do Censo de 2010* (Rio de Janeiro, 2011), table 3.

TABLE 5.2: *Changing population per square kilometer by region, 1960–2010 (persons per km²)*

Year	North	Northeast	Southeast	South	Center-West
1960	0.76	14.43	33.6	20.64	1.67
1970	1.09	18.45	43.62	28.95	2.88
1980	1.76	22.79	56.87	33.63	4.36
1991	2.66	27.33	67.77	38.38	5.86
2000	3.35	30.69	78.2	43.54	7.23
2010	4.12	34.15	86.92	48.58	8.75

Source: IBGE, SIDRA, Censo 2010, table 1298

TABLE 5.3: *Percentage of native-born who resided in the region of their birth, by region of residence, 1991–2010*

Census	North	Northeast	Southeast	South	Center-West
1991	19%	2%	9%	6%	31%
2000	17%	2%	11%	6%	30%
2010	15%	3%	10%	6%	28%

Source: IBGE, SIDRA, table 617

TABLE 5.4: *Percentage of rural population by region, 1970–2010*

Region	1970	1980	1991	2000	2010
Brazil	44%	32%	24%	19%	16%
North	55%	48%	41%	30%	26%
Northeast	58%	50%	39%	31%	27%
Southeast	27%	17%	12%	10%	7%
South	56%	38%	26%	19%	15%
Center-West	52%	32%	19%	13%	11%

Source: IBGE, SIDRA, Censo Demográfico 2010, table 200

There were still significant differences by region in total fertility rates as late as 1970, though the differences between rural parts of the various regional populations were not as significant. Thus for example the regions

TABLE 5.5: *Life expectancy at birth by regions of Brazil, 1960–2010*

	1960	1970	1980	1991	2000	2010
Brazil	48.0	52.7	62.5	66.9	70.4	73.4
North	52.6	54.1	60.8	66.8	69.5	72.4
Northeast	40.0	43.3	58.3	62.9	67.1	70.8
Southeast	53.1	57.4	64.8	68.8	72.0	74.9
South	57.5	60.0	66.0	70.3	72.8	75.4
Center-West	52.9	57.6	62.9	68.4	71.7	74.5

Source: 1960–2000 is from IBGE, Tendencias Demográficas 1950–2000, table 2; 2010 is from DATASUS, at http://tabnet.datasus.gov.br/cgi/idb2011/a11tb.htm

with the highest and lowest rates (the Northeast and the Southeast) were 3.6 children different for the total population in 1970, whereas the rural difference was just 2.7 children. Although these fertility rates were high by world standards at mid century, the demographic transition, defined as a major fall in birth rates, finally occurred in Brazil in the 1960s and the 1970s and made its impact felt in the census of 1991, with fertility rates declining in both the total population in each region as well as in their rural populations (see Table 5.6).

The decline in fertility and the increase in life expectancy had a profound impact in all regions on the age distribution of the population, initially pushing down the average age of the population. But the pace varied by region, with the North having the slowest decline followed by the Northeast. The South was a special case, going from above the national average of the youth population (0–14 years) in 1970 to below the national average in 2010. The Center-West declined from above average in 1970 to the average in 2010. These initially large regional differences in age groups by region slowly changed, as Brazil experienced both an ever expanding fertility transition and a secular decline in mortality, though the spread between the North and the other regions remained the same from 1970 to 2010 (see Table 5.7).

Literacy is another area where regional differences still exist, but have declined over time. As in other indices, the Northeast still remains the least educated and the South and the Southeast the most educated regions of Brazil. In 1970 the difference was 30% fewer literates in the Northeast than in the South, and by 2010 the difference remained but had declined to 13% difference as overall the population had finally reached 90% literacy.

TABLE 5.6: *Total fertility rate by region for total and rural population, 1970–2010*

Region	Total				Rural				Urban			
	1970	1980	1991	2000	1970	1980	1991	2000	1970	1980	1991	2000
Brazil	5.8	4.4	2.9	2.4	7.7	6.4	4.4	3.5	4.6	3.6	2.5	2.2
North	8.2	6.5	4.2	3.2	9.6	8.0	5.5	4.6	6.8	5.2	3.4	2.7
Northeast	7.5	6.1	3.7	2.7	8.5	7.7	5.3	3.8	6.6	4.9	2.9	2.3
Southeast	4.6	3.5	2.4	2.1	7.1	5.5	3.5	2.9	3.9	3.2	2.2	2.0
South	5.4	3.6	2.5	2.2	6.8	4.6	3.1	2.8	4.1	3.2	2.4	2.1
Center-West	6.4	4.5	2.7	2.3	7.6	6.0	3.6	2.9	5.3	4.0	2.5	2.2

Source: IBGE, *Tendências Demográficas ... 2000,* table 7

TABLE 5.7: *Percentage of population 0–14 in total population by region,*
1970–2010

Census	Brazil	North	Northeast	Southeast	South	Center-West
1970	42%	47%	45%	39%	43%	45%
1980	38%	46%	43%	34%	36%	41%
1991	35%	43%	39%	31%	32%	35%
2000	30%	37%	33%	27%	28%	30%
2010	24%	31%	27%	22%	22%	24%

Source: IBGE, SIDRA, table 200

TABLE 5.8: *Rate of literacy of persons over 10 or 15 years of age by region,*
1970–2010 *

Region	1970	1980	1991	2000	2010
Brazil	67.1	74.6	79.9	86.4	91.0
North	65.0	69.4	75.4	83.7	89.4
Northeast	46.2	54.6	62.4	73.8	82.4
Southeast	77.0	83.2	87.7	91.9	94.9
South	76.3	83.8	88.2	92.3	95.3
Center-West	65.4	76.4	83.3	89.2	93.4

Source: IBGE, *Tendências Demográficas . . .* 2000, table 3; IBGE, SIDRA, Census 2010, table
1383
Note: * IBGE uses 15 years of age and above in all years to 2000, and 10 years and above in
2010

But when broken down by urban and rural residence, it is clear that
everywhere the proportion of illiterates is higher in rural areas than in
urban ones, and men are now more illiterate than women, though the
regional differences are still present as late as the census of 2010. It is
worth noting that the rural Southeast and the Center-West are quite
similar and it is the North and Northeast that have the highest illiteracy
rates and are also the poorest regions with the most very small farms (see
Table 5.8).

Finally, although there was little change in the color composition of the
differing regional populations, there was a slow decline everywhere of
people describing themselves as whites (*brancos*). Since their peak in

TABLE 5.9: *Color of the Brazilian population by region, 1960–2010*

Region	Branca (white)	Preta (black)	Amarela (Asian)	Parda (mulatto)	Indígena (Indian)*
1960					
North	23.0	3.5	0.2	73.1	
Northeast	38.2	10.7	0.0	51.1	
Southeast	70.7	9.7	1.2	18.3	
South	88.8	3.9	0.8	6.5	
Center-West	56.7	7.4	0.4	35.4	
Brazil	61.1	8.7	0.7	29.4	
1980					
North	20.8	3.2	0.2	75.0	
Northeast	26.8	6.7	0.1	65.8	
Southeast	66.3	7.0	1.0	25.3	
South	83.9	3.2	0.5	12.1	
Center-West	52.0	3.8	0.3	43.5	
Brazil	54.2	5.9	0.6	38.8	
2010					
North	23.2	6.5	1.1	67.2	1.9
Northeast	29.2	9.4	1.2	59.8	0.4
Southeast	54.9	7.8	1.1	36.0	0.1
South	78.3	4.0	0.7	16.7	0.3
Center-West	41.5	6.6	1.5	49.4	0.9
Brazil	47.5	7.5	1.1	43.4	0.4

Source: IBGE, *Tendências Demográficas ... 2000*, table 1; IBGE, SIDRA, Census 2010, table 2094
Note: * IBGE only gives Indigenous population by region since 1991

1960, whites have steadily declined from 61% of the total population to 48% in the last census of 2010. At the same time, ever more people over time have described themselves as mulattos (*pardos*) reaching 43% of the population in 2010 up from just 29% in 1960. This reflects changing ideas of identity throughout Brazil during this time since there has been no significant international migration to Brazil in this period. Even so the North and Northeast were still the most non-white regions, and by 2010 only the South and the Southeast still had a predominantly white population (see Table 5.9).

What is impressive about all the recent social changes is that they were occurring everywhere and were leading to the slow integration of all the regions into a more coherent common national pattern in the past half century and most especially after 2000. But in economic terms this integration has still not occurred and regional variations remain quite important. While all regions would experience economic growth and the expansion of commercial agriculture, the difference in wealth among the regions remains strong and is reflected in the size of their farms and the distribution of land ownership.

Thus in the distribution of land the older Northeastern region along with the North and Center-West all had more unequal distribution of farmlands than the other regions. The North was made up of very large cattle ranches with low productivity and thus had very high Gini coefficients of inequality. The Northeast also had these large relatively unproductive estates and an unusually high number of very small farms with little land. In this region almost half the farms were 5 hectares or less, but they only comprised 2% of the land. The same dominance of large estates was the norm in the Center-West, though small and medium farms were beginning to grow in this region and here most of the larger estates tended to be major commercial farms. Thus its Gini was the lowest of these three Northern and Western zones. In the South, the home of small commercial farms, 56% of the farms were 20 hectares or less, and these farms comprised 11% of the land, the highest such rate for any region in 1960. This same pattern can be seen in the land distribution numbers given in the agricultural census of 2006, the most recent one available. Here as well there is a sharp regional difference in land tenure in terms of median landholdings and average size. Clearly the North and the Center-West contain on average the largest farms. In both these regions the development of commercial farming and the decline of the largest unproductive estates had an impact on reducing their Gini considerably in this period. But the largest inequality is still shown by the Northeast even though its average farms are the smallest. Again the South and Southeast have the lowest inequality numbers and the same mean sized farms (see Table 5.10).

Using the standard categories now employed by the national census bureau we can see in more detail how these regions looked in 1970, the first year the new regional divisions were employed, and compare them with the last agricultural census of 2006. Just as in 1960 the North and Northeast stood out as regions with high ratios of farms of less than 10

TABLE 5.10: *Distribution of farmlands by region in 1960 and 2006*

	1960		
Region	Median category of land (ha)	Mean size farm (ha)	Gini
North	10,000–100,000	173	0.921
Northeast	200–500	45	0.841
Southeast	200–500	80	0.759
South	200–500	48	0.715
Center-West	2,000–5,000	376	0.837
BRAZIL	1,000–2,000	68	0.814

Source: *Censo agrario 1960*, vol. 1, table 14, pp. 22–24
Note: This reconstruction divided the Leste region into its component parts for the Northeast and Southeast.

	2006		
Region	Median category of land (ha)	Mean size farm (ha)	Gini
North	500–1000	125	0.798
Northeast	100–200	33	0.851
Southeast	200–500	61	0.793
South	200–500	42	0.752
Center-West	2500+	335	0.837
BRAZIL	500–1000	68	0.853

Source: IBGE, SIDRA, table 837

hectares which held less than 6% of all lands in 1970. By 2006 only the Northeast had over half of their farms – in this case two-thirds– in this category and they actually held a half a percentage less of total farmlands. The big change in this thirty-six-year period was the 10–199 hectares becoming the modal category and absorbing around a quarter of all lands – except in the South, where they contained a third of all lands, and the Center-West, where this category of farms had the lowest proportion of the total lands, and where the largest estates dominated. In 1970 only 4% of the farms in the Center-West were over 1,000 hectares, but they held two-thirds of the lands. By 2006 these large estates accounted for 7% of the establishments and an extraordinary 70% of the land (see Table 5.11).

The single most important factor for regional change in the post-1960 growth was the expansion of croplands in all the regions of Brazil. The North and Center-West regions experienced the most significant growth in these lands, and this led to the relative decline of the share of these croplands in other regions. Thus the North went from 2% of the nation's total croplands in 1970 to 5% of the total in 2015. The Center-West, the other major frontier region, went from 7% to 33% in the same period. The Northeast share declined by 14%, the Southeast by 9% and the South by 4%. A lot of this change was due to frontier land utilization by some of the newer or revitalized crops.

The dynamism of this growth in new agricultural lands put into production came primarily from the expansion of seasonal croplands. In general, except for the census year 1995, seasonal croplands expanded faster, especially in the Center-West, than did permanent croplands. In fact permanent croplands declined in three regions, were stagnant in the fourth and only grew in the Northern states (see Table 5.12). These changes overall meant that seasonal crops went from using 77% of all croplands in 1970 to absorbing 93% of them by 2016.

The growth of the seasonal crops had to do with a primary reorganization of Brazilian agriculture due to international market demands. Although traditional crops maintained or increased their production, there was an explosive growth of new and older seasonal crops, most of which were directed toward the international market in the post-1990 period. This was driven by the leading crops: soybeans, corn and sugar. There was also a new international market for Brazilian meat products, which in turn encouraged the regional expansion of the pastoral industries. There even emerged an industry of planted tree plantations – a new phenomenon in wood-rich Brazil – to provide basic products to the cellulose industry.

There was a shift in the total of croplands by region. Total volume of land in crops grew by 1.8% for all of Brazil, but in the Northeast croplands grew by only 0.2% per annum in this forty-six-year period. But they grew at 1.0% and 1.4% in the Southeast and South, an extraordinary 3.9% in the North and 5.3% in the Center-West. This latter region went from planting 2 million hectares in 1970 to planting 26 million hectares in 2016, and thus became the largest region in terms of agricultural lands cultivated, replacing the Southern region, which had been the leading zone until as late as the census of 2006.

Even though some crops were now produced nationally, the large range of climates and soils which define Brazilian agriculture still led to marked

TABLE 5.11: *Distribution of the farms by farm size by region in 1970 and 2006*

1970

Size of farm	North		Northeast		Southeast		South		Center-West	
	No. of farms	Land (ha)	No. of farms	Land (ha)	No. of farms	Land (ha)	No. of farms	Land (ha)	No. of farms	Land (ha)
<10 ha	37%	1%	68%	5%	33%	2%	42%	6%	24%	0%
10–100 ha	42%	12%	26%	24%	52%	24%	53%	38%	45%	7%
100–1,000 ha	19%	40%	6%	43%	14%	47%	4%	32%	27%	30%
>1,000 ha	1%	46%	0.4%	27%	1%	27%	0.4%	23%	4%	63%
Total	100%	100%	100%	100%	100%	100%	100%	100%	100%	100%
(*n*)	293,506	34,635,524	2,195,302	74,297,415	928,559	69,500,004	1,273,302	45,458,036	154,934	41,777,433

2006

Size of farm	North		Northeast		Southeast		South		Center-West	
	No. of farms	Land (ha)	No. of farms	Land (ha)	No. of farms	Land (ha)	No. of farms	Land (ha)	No. of farms	Land (ha)
<10 ha	28%	1%	66%	5%	44%	3%	41%	4%	17%	0%
10–100 ha	52%	17%	29%	26%	46%	24%	52%	33%	52%	6%
100–1000 ha	18%	34%	5%	38%	10%	43%	6%	40%	24%	24%
>1000 ha	2%	48%	0%	31%	1%	30%	0%	23%	7%	70%
Total	100%	100%	100%	100%	100%	100%	100%	100%	100%	100%
(*n*)	4,44,622	5,55,35,763	22,72,956	7,60,74,411	9,02,580	5,49,37,773	9,86,392	4,17,81,003	3,14,067	10,53,51,087

Source: IBGE, SIDRA, table 263

203

TABLE 5.12: *Changing volume of lands devoted to seasonal and permanent crops by region, 1970–2006 (in hectares)*

	1970	1975	1980	1985	1995	2006	2016	Annual % growth 1970/2016
Seasonal croplands								
North	484,645	956,354	1,207,566	1,942,621	1,974,329	2,374,735	3,075,863	4.1%
Northeast	6,344,971	7,073,060	9,339,591	10,082,458	10,906,502	11,674,184	9,218,024	0.8%
Southeast	7,439,430	7,835,136	8,549,203	9,788,079	8,775,128	9,346,721	12,380,361	1.1%
South	9,471,206	11,590,232	13,368,987	13,621,590	16,209,637	13,694,268	20,826,880	1.7%
Center-West	2,259,356	4,161,182	6,166,780	6,809,472	8,094,675	11,823,516	25,905,381	5.4%
TOTAL	25,999,608	31,615,964	38,632,127	42,244,220	45,960,271	48,913,424	71,406,509	2.8%
Permanent croplands								
North	132,366	239,015	536,079	738,106	475,942	545,213	499,577	2.9%
Northeast	3,977,911	3,960,172	4,852,359	4,253,368	2,371,927	2,570,287	2,259,652	–1.2%
Southeast	2,172,973	2,596,435	3,567,871	3,773,484	2,584,645	2,832,242	2,528,190	0.3%
South	1,557,247	1,401,227	1,202,459	901,889	356,095	447,575	376,027	–3.0%
Center-West	143,570	188,544	313,365	236,638	104,230	98,608	103,292	–0.7%
TOTAL	7,984,067	8,385,393	10,472,133	9,903,485	5,892,839	6,493,925	5,766,738	–0.7%

Source: IBGE, SIDRA, Agro, table 264 for data 1970–1985, and SIDRA, PAM, tables 1612 and 1613 for years 1995–2016.

regional variation in crops and animals produced. Historically crops tended to be concentrated in specific regions over long periods of time. Such concentrations meant that one region would dominate the commercial crops being produced. In the colonial period it was the Northeast which produced most of the important commercial crops. By the early nineteenth century the Southeast had replaced the Northeast as the dominant producer of these crops, which was supplemented by the Southern regional growth in the twentieth century. But the period of a domination of one region over all others has also changed in recent years. There has been migration of crops from one region to another either due to availability of new lands, the introduction of new farming techniques and/or new preparations of older crop soils, or the collapse of production in older ones due to plagues, droughts and other natural disasters. Once-dominant regions have lost their position, and once-marginal regions have become new centers for growth. Some crops are still almost exclusively grown in one region, but others have moved their center from one region to another, and several key crops are more evenly distributed across regions.

Thus sugarcane production has essentially moved out of the Northeast where it was mostly produced until well into the twentieth century, and is now concentrated in the Southeastern region. Another such example is cotton, which traditionally was concentrated in the Northeast, whose production is now dominated by the Center-West. While all regions produced corn, the new modern two-plantings harvest system means that the Center-West is quickly emerging as a major producer. Wheat on the other hand remains totally concentrated in the Southern zone (92% of the value of production of this crop in 2016) for ecological reasons. Cereals and food crops tend to be produced everywhere, while such new crops as soybeans which began in the South have now migrated to the Center-West as well. Finally, coffee is the one crop which remains firmly in the region in which it began in the nineteenth century, though it has shifted among the states of the region (see Table 5.13).

Animal husbandry has been widespread in Brazil, with all regions having significant stocks of animals, but slowly the Center-West has emerged as a leading zone in cattle. But the South remains the key center of small animal production, above all chicken and pigs, and for this reason originally contained most of the major meatpacking plants. Although all regions produced eggs and milk, the biggest producers are the Southeastern states (see Table 5.14).

This regional variation of production of crops and pastoral products resulted in marked differences in the gross agricultural wealth being

TABLE 5.13: *Share of value of crops by region, 2016/2017*

	Soybeans	Sugarcane	Corn	Coffee(1)	Bananas	Cotton
North	4%	1%	3%	3%	16%	0%
Northeast	5%	8%	9%	7%	35%	15%
Southeast	8%	65%	16%	87%	33%	2%
South	37%	7%	28%	2%	13%	0%
Center-West	46%	19%	45%	1%	3%	83%
Total	100%	100%	100%	100%	100%	100%
Value in million R$ (2)	116.4	52.4	41.2	23.3	15.4	13.6

Notes: (1) This includes all types of coffees
(2) These totals are summed from the regional totals
Source: www.agricultura.gov.br/ministerio/gestao-estrategica/valor-bruto-da-producao

TABLE 5.14: *Share of value of major pastoral products by region, 2016/17*

	Cattle	Chickens	Milk	Pigs	Eggs
North	19%	1%	5%	0%	3%
Northeast	10%	4%	5%	1%	16%
Southeast	22%	20%	41%	19%	49%
South	12%	59%	35%	65%	20%
Center-West	37%	15%	14%	15%	13%
Total	100%	100%	100%	100%	100%
Value in billion R$	70.7	51.4	26.3	12.8	12.3

Note: These totals are summed from the regional totals
Source: www.agricultura.gov.br/ministerio/gestao-estrategica/valor-bruto-da-producao

produced by the regions. The new Center-West region has only recently emerged as co-equally important as the traditional Southeastern and Southern regions. This growth of the Center-West in the past quarter century from a negligible producer to one of co-equal status with the two classic wealthiest regions has to do with the availability of large tracts of flat farmland and new techniques to enrich its soils, which had led to the rapid modernization of its farms that has enabled it to become important in a number of new and older commercial crops. In 1995 for example, the Center-West represented just 14% of the total value of Brazilian

TABLE 5.15: *Share of the value of crops and livestock and total gross value of production by region, 2016*

	Crops	Livestock & products	Total
North	4%	9%	6%
Northeast	10%	7%	9%
Southeast	28%	26%	27%
South	28%	34%	30%
Center-West	30%	24%	28%
Total	100%	100%	100%
Value in billion R$	334.9	173.6	508.4

Note: These totals are summed from the regional totals
Source: MAPA www.agricultura.gov.br/ministerio/gestao-estrategica/valor-bruto-da-producao

agricultural output and the Southeast was the leading region and accounted for 35% of the total. By 2016, the South has become the leading region in terms of the Gross Production Value of Agriculture, but was now followed in second place by the Center-West, with the Southeast being the third wealthiest agricultural producer. Of the other regions, the North has increased its share slightly from 1995, but the big loser was the Northeast which in 1995 accounted for 15% of the total agricultural production of the nation,[5] and has now declined to just 9% in 2016 (see Table 5.15).

While comparable data of the value of output is not easily available for earlier periods, there exists good historical data on the volume of agricultural output by crop by region from 1976 to 2015. In the production of grains (all seasonal crops) in the 1976/1977 harvest year, the leading region by far was the South, which generated 59% of the total crops harvested, with 19% produced by the Southeastern region, and with the North and Northeast regions together accounting for just 10% of output and the Center-West 12%. A decade later in the harvest year 1986/1987 there had been only minor change in grains production, with the two northern regions now reduced to 5% of total production, the Southeast remaining the same at 19% and the South still dominant and accounting for 53% of the total. But the Center-West increased its share to 22%.

[5] IBGE, *Censo agropecuário 1995*, Table 23 "Valor da Produção segundo as Grandes Regiões e as Unidades da Federação."

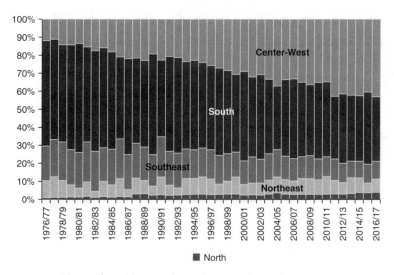

GRAPH 5.1: Share of total harvest by region, 1976–2016
Source: CONAB, Séries históricas, Brasil – Por Unidades da Federação, Grãos, Brasil UF

By 1996/1997 the Southern leadership was being eroded. It was now down to 47% of the total, and the Center-West had surpassed the Southeastern region to become the second largest grain producer, accounting for 26% of national production. A decade later the Center-West accounted for a third and the South was down to 44%, and by the last decade the estimated production figures for the 2016/2017 harvest showed the Center-West as leader with 43% of production, the South with 36%, the Southeast with 10% and the two northern regions with 11% each (see Graph 5.1).

The pastoral industry was also marked by major regional variations. As was evident in the agricultural census of 2006, there was a concentration of certain animals in particular regions. Clearly the smaller animals (pigs and chickens) tended to be ever more concentrated over time in the Southern region, while cattle (consisting of cattle and Asian buffalo cows had been concentrated in the Southeastern region, which more recently, however, has progressively lost its total share of such herds to the Center-West. There were also some major differences in the increase in flocks in this period. The total number of poultry (including all types of chickens, both egg-laying and those that are both egg producing and meat chickens) grew by a very significant

4.8% per annum between 1970 and 2006, and the number of cattle grew at 2.3%, but there was no growth in the total number of pigs, nor was there any significant change in their concentration within one region (see Table 5.16).

Of the seasonal crops planted, unquestionably the most important was soybeans. Soybeans were only introduced into Brazil in 1908 and only became a commercial crop of importance in the 1970s. Like several other commercial crops they were most rapidly and completely developed in the Southern region which initially dominated their production, accounting in 1990 for 58% of national output. It also had the highest yield of any region, producing 1,870 kg of beans per hectare. But already the Center-West had emerged as a significant producer and accounted for a third of production. Over the next several decades the ratio of soybean production in the Southern states as a share of national output declined, reaching just 37% in 2016 compared to 46% being produced in the Center-West. Also the North and Northeast steadily increased their share of production from 1% in 1990 to 9% in 2016. As average yield per hectare steady increased, reaching 3,309 kg per hectare, the differences between regions disappeared and, in contrast to many other crops, yields by region differed little, and most regions were close to the standard initially set by the Southern states (see Graph 5.2).

In contrast to soybeans, corn production yields varied considerably by region, suggesting that parts of national production were still being grown for local consumption by small traditional farms. The production of corn, mostly for animal feed, had experienced a major technological revolution and a basic change in its regional production in the second half of the twentieth century. Initially Brazil had only one planting per annum, but in the 1990s it began to experiment with a second seasonal planting, producing a second crop in the same fields as the first crop without plowing the fields. By the crop year 2011/2012 this second harvest finally passed the total volume of the first harvest crop and by 2016 the second planting accounted for 62% of total annual corn production.[6]

The second major change was the shift of corn production out of the South and Southeastern regions. Actual production of corn like soybeans in these areas did not decline, rather it was the expansion of production

---

[6] IBGE, PAM, table 839.

TABLE 5.16: *Distribution of principal animal groups by region, 1970–2006*

	1970	1975	1980	1985	1995	2006
			Poultry			
North	3%	4%	3%	4%	4%	3%
Northeast	17%	20%	16%	18%	14%	11%
Southeast	42%	41%	41%	34%	37%	31%
South	32%	31%	36%	39%	39%	47%
Center-West	6%	5%	4%	5%	6%	10%
Sum	100%	100%	100%	100%	100%	100%
Million	213.6	286.8	413.1	436.8	718.5	1,143.4
			Pigs			
	1970	1975	1980	1985	1995	2006
North	3%	4%	6%	8%	8%	5%
Northeast	23%	27%	22%	26%	23%	13%
Southeast	18%	18%	18%	18%	16%	17%
South	48%	43%	46%	39%	45%	54%
Center-West	8%	8%	8%	8%	8%	12%
Sum	100%	100%	100%	100%	100%	100%
Million head	31.5	35.2	32.6	30.4	27.8	31.2
			Cattle			
	1970	1975	1980	1985	1995	2006
North	2%	2%	4%	7%	12%	19%
Northeast	18%	18%	18%	17%	15%	15%
Southeast	34%	35%	29%	27.8%	23%	20%
South	24%	21%	21%	19%	17%	13%
Center-West	22%	24%	28%	28.1%	33%	34%
Sum	100%	100%	100%	100%	100%	100%
Million head	78.7	101.9	118.5	128.7	153.9	177.0

Source: IBGE, SIDRA, table 281 – Efetivo de animais em estabelecimentos agropecuários por espécie de efetivo – série histórica (1970/2006)

into new regions with high productivity which reduced their relative importance. In 1990 the South and Southeast produced 80% of the national corn crop, and even as late as 2003 the figure was 71%. But

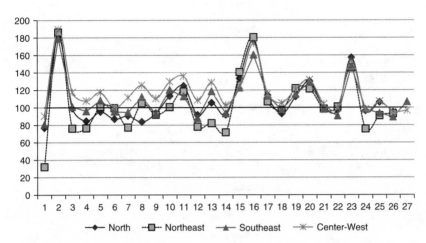

GRAPH 5.2: Three-year moving average of the comparative yield per hectare of soybeans by region, 1990–2016 (South=100)
Source: IBGE SIDRA, table 1612

change was rapid and by 2016 that percentage was down to 49%. In 1990 the states of the South region were the dominant producers, alone accounting for over half of the corn production, but by 2017 the Southern states produced only 16% of the national crop and the Center-West now replaced it as the lead region, accounting for 43% of the corn grown in that year. Moreover, the North and Northeastern regions were increasing their corn production by over 6% per annum in this period, double the rate in the older regions of the South and Southeast, and steadily increased their share of production from 6% to 12% in this same period. However, they still could not reach the yields that the South had obtained – with the North at half the yield and the Northeast a third of the yield obtained in the Southern region even in 2016. In contrast, the Center-West by 2003 was the fastest growing region at 10% per annum and was already close to yields per hectare of the South (2,489 kg per hectare) in 1990 and was at or above the yields obtained in the advanced Southern and Southeastern regions. Overall it is evident that from the mid-1990s, the three regions of the South, Southeast and Center-West all had approximately the same crop yield (see Graph 5.3).

By the end of the twentieth and beginning of the twenty-first century sugarcane production was again concentrated in the Southeastern region, with a secondary center in the Northeast. In 1990 the

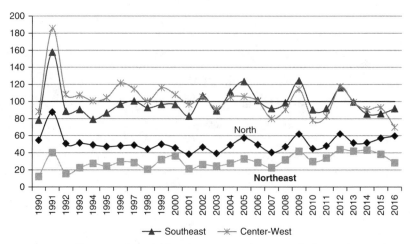

GRAPH 5.3: Comparative yields of corn per hectare of the major regions, 1990–2016 (South =100)
Source: IBGE SIDRA, table 1612

Southeast accounted for 62% of production and the Northeast for 27%. As sugarcane output in this period went from 263 million tons to 749 million tons, for an annual growth rate of 4% per annum, there also entered new players in its production. The Southeast region, and above all the state of São Paulo, maintained its leadership position, and accounted for 67% of the crop in 2016. But there was a major shift among the minor players. The traditional zone of the Northeast was down to just 7% of national production and had been replaced by the Center-West which now produced 19% of the national crop (see Graph 5.4). The Southeastern region was also home to the most advanced refining technology and its mills were the most productive in the nation and in the world producing a multiple of products from traditional refined sugar to ethanol.

While productivity increased considerably in this period, with the best regional yield going from 68,917 kg per hectare in 1990 to 76,961 kg in 2017, there was little difference in productivity by region. By the mid-2010s the Center-West was surpassing the Southeast in productivity, but even then the Northeast was still having yields only 15–20% below the Southeast. Nothing like the sharp variation among regions in terms of corn yield was found in sugar. Sugar, like soybeans, seem to have yielded roughly the same results for all regions in all

million metric tons

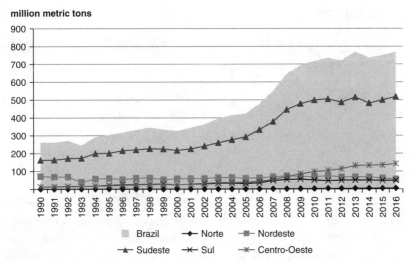

GRAPH 5.4: Production of sugarcane by region and nation, 1990–2016
Source: IBGE SIDRA, table 1612

periods.[7] The fact that the Northeast could maintain the same productivity of sugarcane was due to its traditional location along a narrow band of the coast (the Reconcavo) which had excellent soils and climate appropriate for sugar production.

Of the major commercial permanent crops, coffee was a staple in Brazilian production from the mid-nineteenth century onward, and was concentrated within the states of the Southeastern region. Although there was constant movement of production within states and even across state boundaries, the Southeast remained the center of production from the 1850s until 2016. From 1990 to 2016, the Southeast never lost its predominance, accounting for 73% of production in 1990 and 90% of production in 2016. Although there was considerable variation of yield by state and region, this had more to do with the age of trees than any differences in production practices by region. Moreover the total volume of production changed little during this period, being in the 250 million to

---

[7] The data for this and all subsequent temporary and permanent crops for the years 1990–2015 comes from the IBGE survey of municipal production in 2015 (Produção Agrícola Municipal 2015), found at IBGE, SIDRA, table 1612 – "Área plantada, área colhida, quantidade produzida, rendimento médio e valor da produção das lavouras temporárias," at www.sidra.ibge.gov.br/bda/tabela/listabl .asp?c=839&z=p&o=18.

300 million metric ton range, and the overall growth rate was –0.4% during this period.[8]

Production of oranges, another major permanent crop, was quite similar to coffee production. It mostly occurred in one region and there was very little change in the predominance of that region from 1990 to 2016. It also experienced wide annual fluctuations, but its growth was actually negative in this period. While production was in the 100 million metric tons range in the 1990s and in the first decade of the twenty-first century, in the recent decade the average production has dropped to just 18 million tons per annum. This drop has to do with the introduction of a new plague affecting the orange orchards of the Southeastern region. But in both boom times and more recently, the Southeast region was the primary producer, accounting for over 80% of the crop in most years. Nevertheless, like coffee, there appears to be a slow but modest growth of orange production in the Northeast and Southern regions.

Finally there was marked regional specialization of most fruits. Temperate fruits tended to be grown in the Southeast and Southern regions, and tropical fruits in the Northeastern region, and this concentration increased over time. Although passion fruit (*maracujá*) production declined over the period from 1988 to 2016, it was primarily produced in the Northeast, which went from producing 48% of the passion fruit in 1988 to 70% in 2016. Another Northeastern product was papaya (*mamão*) which in contrast grew dramatically in the recent period, going from just 73,000 tons total Brazilian production in 1974 to 1.4 million tons in 2016. While initially the Northeast and Southeast equally accounted for almost half the crop, by 2016 the Northeast produced 71% of the fruit, with the Southeast dropping to 24% of papaya production.

Apples, the classic temperate fruit, were grown exclusively in the Southeastern region. Their production grew at an impressive 5% per annum in the period from 1974 to 2016 and was almost exclusive to the South region, which accounted for 99% of production in 2016. Grapes were also initially confined to the two Southern regions, with the South being the primary producer, producing about three-quarters of the crop, followed by the Southern region. These two regions together took 96% of the crop. But as grape production increased, going from

[8] IBGE, SIDRA, table 1613 – "Área destinada à colheita, área colhida, quantidade produzida, rendimento médio e valor da produção das lavouras permanentes" at www.sidra .ibge.gov.br/bda/tabela/listabl.asp?c=1613&z=p&o=30.

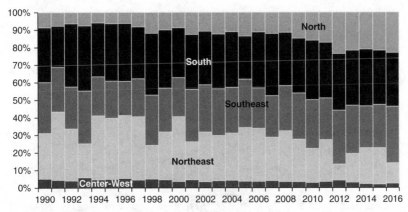

GRAPH 5.5: Share of bean production by region, 1990–2016
IBGE, SIDRA, table 1612

564,000 tons in 1974 to 984,000 tons in 2016, a new producer entered the market in a serious way. Northeastern production went from less than 1% in 1974 to 4% in 1990 and to a third of national output in 2016.[9]

Of the basic food crops, rice and beans tended to be grown in most regions. While beans continued to be produced everywhere, rice became far more concentrated in terms of market production. In 1974 for example, the South only accounted for 36% of the 6.7 million tons produced nationally in that year, but more recently the South has dominated rice production, going from producing half of the 7.4 million ton crop in 1990 to producing 82% of the 10.6 million ton crop in 2016. Although its own rate of increase in yield per hectare has grown at half the rate of the most of the other regions, the other regions had such low productivity that even in 2016 the Northeast, which had the next highest rice yield, obtained only half the South's rice per hectare.

In contrast, there is no one region predominating in bean production, though together the Southeastern and Southern region account for two-thirds of the crop. This was the rate in 1974 and again in 2016. The big change is the Center-West which went from producing 6% of the 2.2 million tons produced in 1974, to 23% of the 2.6 million metric tons produced in 2016. Although total volume of production has grown

---

[9] All fruit data comes from ibid.

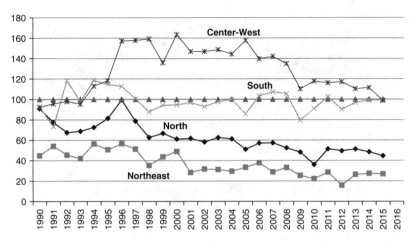

GRAPH 5.6: Comparative productivity of bean production per hectare by region, 1990–2016 (Southeast=100)
Source: IBGE, SIDRA, 1612

modestly in this period, yields have doubled (Graph 5.5), and this has resulted in an actual decline of lands dedicated to its production, which halved from 6 million hectares in 1988 to just 2.9 million hectares in 2016. But most of the growth in productivity has been confined to just three regions, the two southern ones and the Center-West. In contrast, bean yields per hectare have actually been declining in the North and Northeast compared to the Southeast (see Graph 5.6).

Productivity was of course influenced by mechanization and the application of fertilizers and insecticides. These factors differed significantly by region. For example, the South and the Southeast were consistently leaders in the mechanization process, with the Center-West quickly passing them in the latest agricultural census of 2006 as can be seen in the percentage of farms which had tractors. Interestingly, although their initial numbers were quite different, all regions saw a 4–6% per annum decline in the ratio of hectares per tractor, with the North and Northeast and Center-West reaching the 6% per annum figure (see Table 5.17).

The same pattern could be seen in the adoption of fertilizers. There is little question that the South and the Southeast regions were leaders in using fertilizers on their crops, both permanent and seasonal. The South used less on their permanent crops than the Southeast, but in contrast 92% of the lands and 82% of the farms used fertilizers on their crops.

TABLE 5.17: *Percentage of farms and ranches with tractors and hectares per tractor by region, 1970–2006*

	North	Northeast	Southeast	South	Center-West	Brazil
			% of farms with tractors			
1970	0.4%	0.3%	9%	5%	4%	3%
1975	0.5%	0.6%	15%	13%	11%	6%
1980	1.5%	1.6%	23%	21%	24%	11%
1985	2.2%	1.5%	24%	24%	32%	11%
1995	4.1%	2.4%	33%	33%	47%	17%
2006	5.6%	2.5%	28%	34%	40%	16%

			Hectares per tractor			Crop farms only
1970	20,570	10,204	842	704	7,902	1,773	205
1975	18,821	5,220	549	318	3,236	1,002	131
1980	6,602	2,325	363	204	1,789	669	106
1985	5,191	2,206	307	167	1,149	564	94
1995	3,154	1,411	229	132	946	440	63
2006	2,067	1,218	214	120	826	407	73

Source: IBGE, SIDRA, Agro tables 263 and 285; and Série Estatística Table CA 75

The other regions used far less of these inputs in either type of cropland. The only exception, as usual, was the Center-West, which used as little fertilizer on its permanent crops as the Northeast, but had 87% of their seasonal croplands fertilized in 2006 (see Table 5.18).

Only the South, Southeast and the Center-West use lime or other soil enhancers, and then the number of farms using it are quite low: 39% of the farms in the South, 31% in the Southeast and only 19% in the Center-West.[10] Also a surprisingly small ratio of farms and croplands were using insecticides in 2006. But the land covered by insecticides, at least for seasonal crops, accounted for 70% of all seasonal croplands. As could be expected, it was the South, Southeast and Center-West that were the main users of these chemicals, and seasonal croplands had higher ratios of usage than permanent croplands. Again the two outstanding zones are the

[10] IBGE, SIDRA, table 1245 "Número de estabelecimentos agropecuários por uso de calcário ...," at www.sidra.ibge.gov.br/bda/pesquisas/ca/#3.

TABLE 5.18: *Ratio of farms and of lands that use fertilizers by region by type of cropland, 2006*

	Brazil	North	Northeast	Southeast	South	Center-West
% farms						
Permament croplands	47%	12%	32%	65%	79%	33%
Seasonal croplands	41%	15%	20%	59%	82%	51%
% lands						
Permament croplands	51%	13%	33%	80%	66%	39%
Seasonal croplands	74%	31%	41%	80%	92%	87%

Source: IBGE, SIDRA, table 1247, found at www.sidra.ibge.gov.br/bda/pesquisas/ca/#3.

South, where two-thirds or more of the farms used insecticides, and the Center-West, where 82% of the seasonal crops consumed these products (see Table 5.19).

These changes also had an impact on the relative share of these regions in total agricultural exports. As these exports grew from US$23 billion in 1997 to US$87 billion in 2016, or at 6.6% per annum, the relative role of the Southeast and the South declined as the Center-West took an ever increasing share. Their combined share went from 83% of the total value of agricultural exports in the first year to just 64% in 2016, while the Center-West share grew from 7% to 26% in this same nineteen-year period for which we have the data. Interestingly, both the Northeast and the North grew sufficiently in this period to maintain their relative share in the value of exported agricultural products. The Northeast in this period remained approximately 8% of the total value and the North more or less maintained 4% of these exports (see Graph 5.10). Although all regions experienced positive growth, the rate of change was highest in the Center-West. There exports grew by an extraordinary 14.4% per annum, while for all the other regions the annual growth was between 5% and 8% per annum.

In most regions, agricultural exports predominated in the total mix of exports. Without question the Center-West and the South were the regions where agricultural products dominated exports. In the Center-

TABLE 5.19: *Ratio of farms and of lands that use insecticides by region by type of cropland, 2006*

	Brazil	North	Northeast	Southeast	South	Center-West
% farms						
Permanent croplands	31%	18%	19%	34%	66%	24%
Seasonal croplands	36%	14%	23%	30%	72%	33%
% lands						
Permanent croplands	39%	15%	23%	61%	53%	36%
Seasonal croplands	70%	28%	43%	69%	87%	82%

Source: IBGE, SIDRA, table 1247, found at www.sidra.ibge.gov.br/bda/pesquisas/ca/#3

West almost all of the principal exports were agricultural products, principally soybeans, followed in importance by corn, meat, wood pulp and paper, cotton and sugar. Second was the South which tended to have on average 72% of the value of its exports made up of agricultural products. These included soybeans, all types of meats, tobacco, sugar and corn. The North's exports were dominated by minerals, and only a fifth was made up of agricultural products. The Northeast also had significant mineral exports, and only half of its products were agricultural. In the Southeastern region, the industrial heartland of Brazil, in this period agricultural products averaged only 28% of the value of exports, with machinery, airplanes and other manufactured goods being an important part of the total regional exports (see Graph 5.7).[11]

There are some crops which clearly show signs of being an all regional export and others that are unique to one region in terms of production and export. The case of growing national production of all regions is

---

[11] To create this graph we have relied on two different sets of ministerial statistics: the Ministry of Foreign Trade (Ministério da Indústria, Comércio Exterior e Serviços) data found at www.mdic.gov.br/comercio-exterior/estatisticas-de-comercio-exterior/series-historicas; and the Ministry of Agriculture (Ministério da Agricultura, Pecuária e Abastecimento) MAPA, Agrostat, Exportação/Importação, Produto por Regão/UF/ Porto data at http://indicadores.agricultura.gov.br/agrostat/index.htm. The problem is that the two sources are not always in complete agreement. This is evident in the case of the Center-West region in which the agricultural export values in a few years are higher than the total exports given by the Ministry of Trade.

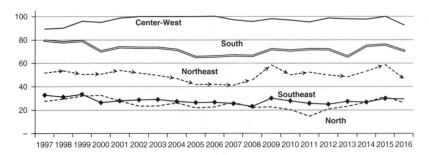

GRAPH 5.7: Percentage of agricultural exports within total regional exports, 1997–2016
Notes: The Ministry of Trade and Agricultural Ministry figures differ somewhat and have been corrected for the Center-West
Source: For total exports MDIC, and for agricultural exports MAPA Agrostat

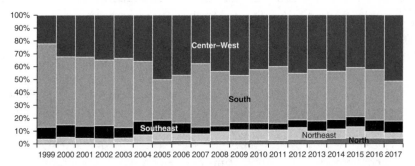

GRAPH 5.8: Participation of regions in the value of all soybean exports, 1999–2017
Source: MAPA. Agrostat/Series Historicas/Exportacao/Importacao/Regiao UF/Porto/Producto @ http://indicadores.agricultura.gov.br/index.htm

demonstrated by the exports of the soybean complex whose principal components are beans, soymeal and soy oil. Though the South began the soybean revolution, it was the Center-West which most recently came to dominate the export of these products. But all regions increased their share at the expense of the once dominant South region. Thus the North went from shipping just US$2.7 million in 1997 to exporting US$1 billion worth in 2016 and increased its share to 5% of all soybean exports. The Northeast went from US$168 million to US$1.2 billion in the same period (see Graph 5.8).

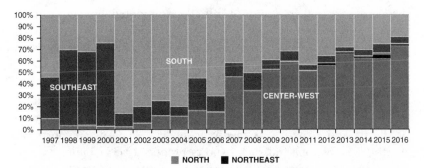

GRAPH 5.9: Participation of regions in the value of all cereals, flour and prepared products exported by region, 1997–2016
Source: MAPA, Agrostat, Exportação/Importação, Produto por região/Região/UF/Porto

Cereals, flour and associated products were exported from essentially three regions only: the South, the Southeast and the Center West. At the beginning of this period the Southern exports of such products dominated. But quickly the Center-West assumed leadership at the cost of both the South and Southeast. The export of such products from the other regions was negligible (see Graph 5.9).

A somewhat similar pattern occurred with the export of meats, which went from a value of US$1.6 billion to US$13 billion in this seventeen-year period. Initially the South still dominated exports – in 1997 accounting for 70% of the total value of such exports. Together with the Southeast states these two regions went from exporting 94% of the meats in terms of value to just 70% in 2016. The Northeast was an insignificant exporter of meats, but the rise of the Center-West and, to a smaller extent, the North region explains the progressive decline of the South and Southeast. By the second decade of the century the Center-West accounted for a quarter of the value of meat exports.

Leather exports, worth on average US$2.6 billion, followed the pattern of meat exports, with the overwhelming predominance of the South region eroding in the twenty-first century. Another minor animal export was honey. Though it reached a peak value of just US$103 million in 2016, Brazil then ranked fifth in world exports of honey, but has since declined in both value and volume of exports.[12]

---

[12] FAOSTAT, www.fao.org/faostat/en/#data/QL.

This was a product that was initially dominated by the Southeast (which exported over 90% of the product in the 1990s), but that dominance was reduced to 40%, with the Northeast and South now accounting for the rest.

In contrast to these more nationally exported crops, coffee was one product whose regional dominance never changed. On average between 1997 and 2016, 90% of coffee exported came from the states of the Southeast and growth was relatively modest. The 1997 exports were worth US$3 billion, and such exports produced US$4 billion in 2016. Almost as concentrated was the entire citrus juice industry. On average, 73% of the oranges and their juice was produced in the Southeast region, with only minor participation of the South and Center-West and with a long-term secular decline in Northeast production, which went from 28% of exports in 1979 to just 4% in 2016. This meant that its income from this product actually fell from US$508 million to US$412 million in this nineteen-year period. The total value of these exports went from US$1.8 billion to US$10.1 billion in 2016 with a peak year of US$16 billion in 2011.[13]

Regions in turn were made up of states not all of which produced the same products as the dominant regional leaders. This was the case of soybeans for example. They were produced within several regions but usually by only one or two states in the respective region, the exception being the Center-West. But the norm was more like two states in the South, or only three states in the Northeast or one state in the Southeast which could be considered important producers of this major cash crop (see Table 5.20).

A more dispersed pattern was evident in the value of cattle, the second most valuable product which was produced by agriculture in the second decade of the twenty-first century. All states had cattle, and in the Center-West and the Southeast and South almost all states were significant producers (see Table 5.21).

The third most valuable agricultural product in the second decade of the century was chickens, also a pastoral product. As with cattle, all states produced chickens. But it was only a few states in the Center-West, the South and the Southeast that predominated in national production (see Table 5.22).

---

[13] MAPA, Agrostat, Exportação/Importação, Produto por Regão/UF/Porto at http://indica dores.agricultura.gov.br/agrostat/index.htm.

TABLE 5.20: *Percentage importance of principal states/regions in the value of soybean production, 2007–2016*

State/region	2007	2008	2009	2010	2011	2012	2013	2014	2015	2016	10-year average
Mato Grosso/CW	24%	27%	29%	25%	27%	33%	27%	28%	26%	28%	28%
Paraná/S	21%	20%	16%	22%	21%	17%	20%	17%	18%	17%	18%
Rio Grande do Sul/S	17%	13%	14%	15%	16%	9%	16%	15%	16%	17%	15%
Goiás/CW	10%	10%	11%	9%	10%	12%	10%	10%	8%	10%	10%
Mato Grosso do Sul/CW	9%	8%	7%	7%	7%	7%	7%	7%	8%	8%	7%
Minas Gerais/SE	5%	4%	5%	5%	4%	5%	4%	4%	4%	5%	4%
Bahia/NE	4%	5%	4%	5%	5%	5%	3%	4%	5%	3%	4%
São Paulo/SE	2%	2%	2%	2%	2%	2%	2%	2%	2%	3%	2%
Maranhão/NE	2%	2%	2%	2%	2%	2%	2%	2%	2%	1%	2%
Santa Catarina/S	2%	2%	2%	2%	2%	2%	2%	2%	2%	2%	2%
Tocantins/N	1%	1%	1%	1%	2%	2%	2%	2%	2%	2%	2%
Piauí/NE	1%	1%	1%	1%	2%	2%	1%	2%	2%	1%	1%
Pará/N	0%	0%	0%	0%	0%	1%	1%	1%	1%	1%	1%
Rondônia/N	0%	1%	1%	1%	1%	1%	1%	1%	1%	1%	1%

Source: MAPA, Valor Bruto da Produção – Regional por UF – julho/2016, found at www.agricultura.gov.br/ministerio/gestao-estrategica/valor-bruto-da-producao

Notes: This table excludes states with less than 1% of the value of national production.
Regions: CW (Center-West); S (South); NE (Northeast); N (North); SE (Southeast).

TABLE 5.21: *Percentage importance of principal states/regions in the value of cattle production, 2007–2016*

Region/state	2007	2008	2009	2010	2011	2012	2013	2014	2015	2016	10-year average
Mato Grosso/CW	14%	13%	14%	14%	17%	16%	17%	16%	15%	14%	15%
São Paulo/SE	15%	15%	14%	13%	11%	11%	11%	11%	11%	11%	12%
Mato Grosso do Sul/CW	12%	12%	12%	12%	11%	13%	12%	12%	11%	11%	12%
Goiás/CW	9%	11%	9%	9%	10%	9%	10%	11%	10%	10%	10%
Minas Gerais/SE	8%	9%	8%	8%	7%	8%	8%	9%	9%	9%	8%
Pará/S	6%	5%	5%	7%	7%	7%	7%	7%	8%	8%	7%
Rondônia/N	5%	5%	6%	6%	6%	6%	6%	6%	5%	5%	6%
Rio Grande do Sul/S	5%	5%	5%	6%	6%	6%	5%	5%	5%	5%	5%
Paraná/S	4%	4%	4%	5%	4%	4%	4%	4%	4%	4%	4%
Bahia/NE	3%	3%	4%	4%	4%	4%	4%	4%	4%	4%	4%
Tocantins/N	3%	2%	3%	3%	3%	3%	3%	3%	3%	3%	3%
Maranhão/NE	2%	3%	2%	2%	2%	2%	2%	2%	3%	3%	2%
Santa Catarina/SE	1%	1%	1%	2%	1%	1%	1%	1%	1%	1%	1%
Acre/N	1%	1%	1%	1%	1%	1%	1%	1%	1%	1%	1%

Pernambuco/NE	1%	1%	1%	1%	1%	1%	1%	1%	1%	1%	1%
Espirito Santo/SE	1%	1%	1%	1%	1%	1%	1%	1%	1%	1%	1%
Ceará/NE	1%	1%	1%	1%	1%	1%	1%	1%	1%	1%	1%
Amazonas/N	0%	0%	0%	1%	1%	1%	1%	1%	1%	1%	1%
Alagoas/NE	1%	1%	1%	1%	1%	1%	1%	1%	0%	0%	1%
Rio de Janeiro/SE	0%	0%	0%	1%	0%	1%	1%	1%	0%	1%	1%

Source: MAPA, Valor Bruto da Produção – Regional por UF – julho/2016, found at www.agricultura.gov.br/ministerio/gestao-estrategica/valor-bruto-da-producao

Notes: This table excludes states with less than 1% of the value of national production

Regions: CW (Center-West); S (South); NE (Northeast); N (North); SE (Southeast).

TABLE 5.22: Percentage importance of principal states/regions in the value of chicken production, 2007–2016

State/region	2007	2008	2009	2010	2011	2012	2013	2014	2015	2016	10-year average
Paraná/S	23%	24%	25%	25%	25%	26%	28%	29%	30%	31%	27%
Santa Catarina/SE	20%	19%	19%	19%	20%	19%	18%	17%	16%	16%	18%
São Paulo/SE	18%	17%	15%	14%	15%	14%	12%	12%	11%	11%	14%
Rio Grande do Sul/S	15%	15%	14%	14%	13%	12%	13%	13%	12%	12%	13%
Minas Gerais/SE	7%	7%	7%	7%	7%	7%	7%	7%	7%	7%	7%
Goiás/CW	5%	5%	6%	6%	6%	6%	6%	6%	6%	7%	6%
Mato Grosso/CW	2%	3%	4%	4%	4%	5%	5%	4%	4%	4%	4%
Mato Grosso do Sul/CW	3%	3%	3%	3%	3%	3%	3%	3%	3%	3%	3%
Bahia/NE	1%	1%	1%	1%	1%	2%	2%	2%	2%	2%	2%
Pernambuco/NE	1%	1%	1%	1%	1%	1%	1%	1%	1%	1%	1%
Distrito Federal/CW						1%	0%	1%	1%	1%	1%
Pará/N	1%	1%	1%	1%	1%	1%	1%	1%	1%	1%	1%
Rio de Janeiro/SE	1%	1%	1%	1%	1%	1%	1%	1%	1%	1%	1%
Espírito Santo/SE	0%	0%	0%	1%	1%	0%	1%	1%	1%	1%	1%

Source: MAPA, Valor Bruto da Produção – Regional por UF – julho/2016, found at www.agricultura.gov.br/ministerio/gestao-estrategica/valor-bruto-da-producao

Notes: This table excludes states with less than 1% of the value of national production
Regions: CW (Center-West); S (South); NE (Northeast); N (North); SE (Southeast).

TABLE 5.23: *Percentage importance of principal states/regions in the value of sugarcane production, 2007–2016*

State/region	2007	2008	2009	2010	2011	2012	2013	2014	2015	2016	10-year average
São Paulo/SE	58%	56%	52%	49%	54%	56%	55%	54%	55%	54%	54%
Minas Gerais/SE	7%	7%	8%	8%	9%	10%	10%	10%	9%	9%	9%
Goiás/C-W	4%	6%	7%	6%	7%	8%	9%	9%	10%	10%	8%
Paraná/S	8%	8%	6%	6%	6%	7%	7%	7%	7%	7%	7%
Mato Grosso do Sul/C-W	3%	3%	4%	5%	5%	5%	6%	6%	6%	7%	5%
Alagoas/NE	5%	5%	4%	3%	4%	4%	4%	4%	4%	3%	4%
Pernambuco/NE	4%	3%	4%	4%	3%	2%	2%	2%	2%	2%	3%
Mato Grosso/CW	3%	3%	2%	2%	2%	2%	3%	3%	3%	3%	2%
Paraíba/NE	1%	1%	1%	1%	1%	1%	1%	1%	1%	1%	1%
Bahia/NE	1%	1%	1%	1%	1%	1%	1%	1%	1%	1%	1%
Rio de Janeiro/SE	1%	1%	1%	1%	1%	1%	1%	1%	1%	0%	1%
Espírito Santo/SE	1%	1%	1%	1%	1%	1%	1%	1%	0%	0%	1%
Rio Grande do Norte/NE	1%	1%	1%	1%	0%	1%	1%	1%	0%	0%	1%

Source: MAPA, Valor Bruto da Produção – Regional por UF – julho/2016, found at www.agricultura.gov.br/ministerio/gestao-estrategica/valor-bruto-da-producao

Notes: This table excludes states with less than 1% of the value of national production. Regions: CW (Center-West); S (South); NE (Northeast); N (North); SE (Southeast).

Finally the fourth most valuable product was sugarcane, which was concentrated in the Northeast and Southeast states, with the beginnings of a major participation of the Center-West zone (Table 5.23).

Corn was the next most important agricultural product in terms of value. Along with soybean, cows, chicken and sugarcane these products accounted for 63% of the value of all agricultural production in the ten-year period 2007–2016.[14] Like the others it was well represented in the states of the Center-West, the Southeast and the Northeast, but with only one significant state participation in the South and two in the North (see Table 5.24).

The role of these leading agricultural states is also reflected in their leadership in the socio-economic conditions of their residents. Thus the most productive states were those with the highest Human Development Index scores, which reflected life expectancy, education and per capita income (see Table 5.25).

As can be seen from this review of the production and value of agricultural products, it was the Center-West which experienced the most growth in this period, and this change was led by its crucial state of Mato Grosso. Already by 2000 Mato Grosso was the leading agricultural state in terms of the per capita value of agriculture.[15] By then it was almost 50% greater than the per capita agricultural value of São Paulo and over a third higher than Rio Grande do Sul and Paraná key agricultural states. Moreover its growth had been quite rapid. In 1970 it ranked only seventh in per capita value of agricultural production. Twenty-six years later it ranked second and was ahead of such traditional wealthy agricultural states as Paraná, Rio Grande de Sul and São Paulo. Just four years later it finally emerged as Brazil's leading agricultural state in per capita terms.

Not only was Mato Grosso the leading state in per capita agricultural sales by 2000, but by the crop year 2016/2017 it became a contender with São Paulo as the leading state in terms of total gross value of agricultural production. Whereas São Paulo had been the leading agricultural state from the late nineteenth century, since 2012 Mato Grosso has come close to equaling its output. Mato Grosso at 13.7% of the total value of Brazilian production has now been close to that of São Paulo in the past

---

[14] This is based on using a three-year average figure for the period 2012–2014. MAPA, Valor Bruto da Produção Completo, dated January 2015, and found at www.agricultura .gov.br/ministerio/gestao-estrategica/valor-bruto-da-producao.

[15] Clailton Ataídes de Freitas, Carlos José Caetano Bacha and Daniele Maria Fossatti, "Avaliação do desenvolvimento do setor agropecuário no Brasil: período de 1970 a 2000," *Economia e Sociedade* (Campinas), 16, no. 1 (abr. 2007): 115, table 1.

TABLE 5.24: *Percentage importance of principal states/regions in the value of corn production, 2007–2016*

State/region	2007	2008	2009	2010	2011	2012	2013	2014	2015	2016	10-year average
Paraná/S	23%	23%	19%	22%	22%	21%	17%	17%	15%	16%	19%
Mato Grosso/CW	9%	13%	13%	11%	14%	22%	25%	23%	25%	24%	19%
Minas Gerais/SE	13%	11%	11%	10%	11%	10%	9%	8%	7%	9%	10%
Goiás/CW	8%	9%	10%	8%	9%	11%	10%	11%	11%	8%	10%
Mato Grosso do Sul/CW	5%	5%	4%	6%	7%	9%	9%	10%	11%	10%	8%
Rio Grande do Sul/S	10%	9%	8%	10%	10%	4%	7%	7%	7%	7%	8%
São Paulo/SE	9%	8%	7%	7%	6%	6%	6%	5%	5%	6%	6%
Santa Catarina/SE	7%	7%	6%	7%	6%	4%	4%	3%	3%	4%	5%
Bahia/NE	4%	5%	6%	5%	4%	3%	4%	6%	7%	5%	5%
Maranhão/NE	1%	1%	1%	1%	1%	1%	2%	2%	2%	1%	1%
Pará/N	2%	1%	2%	2%	1%	1%	1%	1%	1%	1%	1%
Sergipe/NE	1%	1%	2%	2%	1%	0%	1%	1%	1%	1%	1%
Piauí/NE	0%	1%	1%	1%	1%	1%	1%	1%	1%	1%	1%
Rondônia/N	0%	0%	1%	1%	1%	1%	1%	1%	1%	1%	1%
Ceará/NE	1%	2%	1%	1%	2%	0%	0%	0%	0%	0%	1%
Distrito Federal/CW	1%	1%	1%	0%	0%	1%	1%	1%	1%	0%	1%
Tocantins/N	0%	1%	1%	1%	1%	1%	0%	1%	1%	1%	1%

Source: MAPA, Valor Bruto da Produção – Regional por UF – julho/2016, found at www.agricultura.gov.br/ministerio/gestao-estrategica/valor-bruto-da-producao

Notes: This table excludes states with less than 1% of the value of national production. Regions: CW (Center-West); S (South); NE (Northeast); N (North); SE (Southeast).

TABLE 5.25: *Human Development Index of Brazilian states, 1991–2010*

Brazil and states	1991	2000	2010
Brazil	0.493	0.612	0.727
São Paulo	0.578	0.702	0.783
Santa Catarina	0.543	0.674	0.774
Rio de Janeiro	0.573	0.664	0.761
Paraná	0.507	0.650	0.749
Rio Grande do Sul	0.542	0.664	0.746
Espírito Santo	0.505	0.640	0.740
Goiás	0.487	0.615	0.735
Minas Gerais	0.478	0.624	0.731
Mato Grosso do Sul	0.488	0.613	0.729
Mato Grosso	0.449	0.601	0.725
Amapá	0.472	0.577	0.708
Roraima	0.459	0.598	0.707
Tocantins	0.369	0.525	0.699
Rondônia	0.407	0.537	0.690
Rio Grande do Norte	0.428	0.552	0.684
Ceará	0.405	0.541	0.682
Amazonas	0.430	0.515	0.674
Pernambuco	0.440	0.544	0.673
Sergipe	0.408	0.518	0.665
Acre	0.402	0.517	0.663
Bahia	0.386	0.512	0.660
Paraíba	0.382	0.506	0.658
Pará	0.413	0.518	0.646
Piauí	0.362	0.484	0.646
Maranhão	0.357	0.476	0.639
Alagoas	0.370	0.471	0.631

Source: UNDP, Atllas do Desenvolvimento Humano no Brasil, at www.atlasbrasil.org.br/
2013/pt/.

five years, and is ahead of Paraná, Minas Gerais and Rio Grande do Sul, the traditional powerhouse states in terms of agricultural production. But then was followed by Goiás, another Center-West state, which accounted for 8.2% of the value of total production. In fact the three Center-West

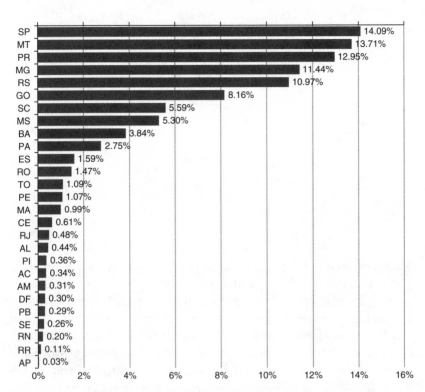

GRAPH 5.10: Share of gross value of agricultural production by state, 2016
Source: MAPA, "Valor Bruto da Produção Agropecuária, abril 2017"

region states produced 27% of the total value of agricultural output in Brazil in that year (see Graph 5.10).

In the following chapters, we will examine the role of several typical states in this recent agricultural revolution. These will include Mato Grosso and São Paulo, the leaders in many of the basic products being grown today. Finally we will examine Rio Grande do Sul, the leader in modern small-scale commercial agriculture and a major pastoral industry. By examining each state in detail it will be possible to obtain a more detailed analysis of some of the basic changes which have affected Brazilian agriculture since 1960.

6

The Case of Mato Grosso

Mato Grosso was the prime example of a poor semiabandoned frontier that was transformed into a modern center of agricultural production both by government and private initiative late in the twentieth century. It had been a zone of gold mining in the early colonial period, but significant settlements and mining primarily occurred in the eighteenth century, which led to both the establishment of the town of Cuiaba in 1720 and the creation of a separate government district (Capitania) in 1748. In 1856 navigation was opened on the Paraguay River which permitted agricultural exports from the region, and sugarcane plantations developed. Yerba mate and Polygala herbs and shrubs were also now exported and after the 1870s some natural rubber exports also left from Mato Grosso. But the primary agricultural activity aside from subsistence farming remained extensive ranching until late in the twentieth century.[1]

In the 1940s and 1950s the state government encouraged and supported both subsidized colonies and private immigrants with land sales. But even as late as 1970 a large part of the state contained vast tracts of undeveloped savannas and forested lands even after it had been divided into two in 1977 with the creation of the separate state of Mato Grosso do Sul. The construction of major highways in the region in the 1970s finally opened up most of the state for possible settlement. With these new roads connecting Mato Grosso to the rest of Brazil, the federal government as

---

[1] A summary of the economic development of this period is found in Antonio João Castrillon Fernández, "Do Cerrado à Amazônia, as estruturas sociais da economia da soja no Mato Grosso"(PhD thesis, Universidade Federal do Rio Grande do Sul, 2007), pp. 142–146.

well as private groups then sponsored migration of poor or disposed
farmers mostly from the Northeast region. But the most important migra-
tions were the spontaneous and self-supported ones which came in the
next two decades. Especially in the late 1980s and in the 1990s a steady
migration of well-funded farm families from the Southern region of Brazil,
above all from Paraná and Rio Grande do Sul, responded to the opening of
these new lands and brought with them modern agricultural techniques,
a knowledge of the market and a commitment to producer cooperatives.[2]
The majority of these migrants were married couples with children. Some
328,000 migrants arrived in the state in the 1970s, another 545,000 in the
1980s and another 420,000 in the 1990s, and of these 42% were from
the three Southern states in the 1970s, 40% in the 1980s and 27% in the
1990s, with Paraná always being the most important migrant state. If São
Paulo migrants are added to the Southern states, than half the migrants in
the first two decades came from these areas.[3] Although their original land
titles were often fraudulent, possession and production on these former
state lands usually led to legal titles to at least some of these plots. Also the
national government through its land reform program – which was essentially a colonization program which exploited government-owned lands
or expropriated lands which the government purchased – sponsored local
settlements in the state for poor migrants from various parts of Brazil,
some of whom were also organized into producer cooperatives. These
government colonists were mostly settled on smaller plots of 200 or less
hectares, while the southern "gaucho" migrants tended to purchase the
larger tracts. After often violent local conflicts between sponsored and
private migrants, almost all the core agricultural regions in the center and
north of the state were finally legalized in terms of land ownership. By the
late 1990s most of the principal regions of the state had been organized
into legal municipal districts and thus most land titles had finally been
legalized.[4] Early settlers cleared the lands and built the cities and roads,

---

[2] See José Marcos Pinto da Cunha, "Dinâmica migratória e o processo de ocupação do
Centro-Oeste brasileiro: o caso de Mato Grosso," *Revista Brasileira de Estudos de
População*, 23, no. 1 (2013): 87–107; and Cristiano Desconsi, *A marcha dos pequenos
proprietários rurais: trajetórias de migrantes do Sul do Brasil para o Mato Grosso* (Rio de
Janeiro: Editora E-papers, 2011), chap. 1; Iselda Corrêa Ribeiro, *Pioneiros Gaúchos:
A Colonização do Norte Matogrossense* (Porto Alegre: Tchê!, 1987).
[3] Cunha, "Dinâmica migratória e o processo de ocupação do Centro-Oeste brasileiro": 92,
96, tables 2 & 5.
[4] Matuzalem Bezerra Cavalcante, "Mudanças da estrutura fundiária de Mato Grosso
(1992–2007)" (MA thesis, Universidade Estadual "Julio de Mesquita," 2008), chap. 3;
and Wendy Jepson, Christian Brannstrom and Anthony Filippi, "Access regimes and

and more capitalized farming entrepreneurs would in turn come in and develop the modern agro-business of the state.[5]

Along with all these private efforts, there was a major impact of government investments through a host of institutions and projects. The idea of opening up the western frontier went back to the "March to the West" policy first formulated in the Vargas government of the 1930s, and was furthered by Kubistchek's policy of moving the national capital to Brasilia in the Center-West region. It was made effective by new road construction in the area in the 1950s and 1960s. A number of federal, state and international organizations invested heavily in colonization, modernization of agriculture, research and infrastructure in this region from the 1960s onward.[6] All of this was aided by the essentially level terrain of savannas, scrub forest and some regular forests of a large part of the biomass region known as the Cerrado, consisting of some 158 million hectares (approximately 2 million km², or a quarter of Brazilian territory) stretching south and east of the Amazon rainforest and incorporating all or parts of several regions (North, Northeast, Southeast and Center-West) of which Mato Grosso possessed the largest share. A part of the state also includes one of the world's largest wetlands, the Pantanal. But it was the Cerrado that was the key element in the agricultural revolution in the state.

The Cerrado consists mostly of level lands with grasslands, shrub forests, dry forests and open savannas which permitted large farming units to be created which could be processed by

---

regional land change in the Brazilian Cerrado, 1972–2002," *Annals of the Association of American Geographers*, 100, no. 1 (2010): 87–111.

[5] For a detailed history of these settlements in the Center-North and Eastern regions of the state see Lisa Rausch, "Convergent agrarian frontiers in the settlement of Mato Grosso, Brazil," *Historical Geography*, 42 (2014): 276–297; Ana Claudia Marques, "Pioneiros de Mato Grosso e Pernambuco: novos e velhos capítulos da colonização no Brasil," *Revista Brasileira de Ciências Sociais*, 28, no. 83 (Nov. 2013): 85–103; José Renato Schaefer, *As migrações rurais e implicações pastorais: um estudo das migrações campo-campo do sul do país em direção ao norte do Mato Grosso* (São Paulo: Edições Loyola, 1985).

[6] Among these were the joint public and private Brazilian–Japanese project called PRODECER which invested heavily in opening up soybean production for the entire so-called Cerrado region. Although Mato Grosso contains 21% of the Cerrado lands, the project mostly involved investment in other states, although they as well as others invested in the Lucas Rio Verde region, an important center of migrants from the Southern Region. In the 1960s the government also established SUDECO (Superintendência de Desenvolvimento do Centro-Oeste) to promote investment in the Center-West region, as well as the PRODOESTE (Programa de Desenvolvimento do Centro-Oeste). See Maria Erlan Inocêncio, "O PRODECER e as tramas do poder na territorialização do capital no Cerrado" (PhD thesis, Geografia, Universidade Federal de Goiás, 2010), chaps. 1 and 2.

machines.[7] But its acid soils deficient in minerals prevented any significant farming until government research developed the tools necessary to exploit these soils for modern farming in terms of soil enrichment and new seeds created for these soils, and this dated only from late in the twentieth century.[8] Thus subsistence farming and cattle ranching dominated the Cerrado economy for most of the past century and only a small portion of the land was deforested for use. All of this changed after the major input of agricultural credit, road building and the research of Embrapa in the second half of the century.[9] Today at least a third to half of the Cerrado is in cultivated pasture or farmlands (see Map 6.1).[10]

In 1960 the state of Mato Grosso had some 19,000 farms using 8 million hectares. By 1985 it had some 78,000 farms exploiting 38 million hectares. As late as 1970 there were only 600 tractors in the state; fifteen years later the number was 20,000. In 1970 there were 129,000 workers employed on the state's farms; by 1985 the number was 320,000.[11] Even the cattle herds had gone from 1.6 million head to 5.4 million in the same period. In 1980 soybean cultivation was introduced to the state for the first time. In that year some 7,000 hectares were planted in soybeans; just nine years later 1.7 million hectares were planted in soybeans and this represented 59% of all croplands in the state.[12]

---

[7] Carlos A. Klink and Ricardo B. Machado, "A conservação do Cerrado brasileiro," *Megadiversidade*, 1, no.1 (July 2005): 147–149; and Rodrigo Pedrosa Marouelli, "O desenvolvimento sustentável da agricultura no cerrado brasileiro"(MA thesis, Brasília, ISEA/FGV, 2003), p. 11.

[8] For a survey of some of these efforts see Wendy Jepson, Christian Brannstrom and Anthony Filippi, "Access regimes and regional land change in the Brazilian Cerrado, 1972–2002," *Annals of the Association of American Geographers*, 100, no. 1 (Jan. 2010): 91–94.

[9] On development of the Cerrado savannas see Charles Curt Mueller and Geraldo Bueno Martha Junior, "A agropecuária e o desenvolvimento socioeconomico recente do Cerrado," in Fábio Gelape Faleiro and Austeclinio Lopes de Farias Neto, eds., *Savanas. Desafios e Estratégias para o Equilíbrio entre Sociedade, Agronegócio e Recursos Naturais* (Planaltina, DF: Embrapa, 2008).

[10] On the various estimates of change in the Cerrado region see Mauro Augusto dos Santos, Alisson Flávio Barbieri, José Alberto Magno de Carvalho and Carla Jorge Machado, "O cerrado brasileiro: notas para estudo"(Texto para discussão; 387; Belo Horizonte: UFMG/Cedeplar, 2010), p. 7; and Christian Brannstrom, Wendy Jepson, Anthony M. Filippi, Daniel Redo, Zengwang Xu and Srinivasan Ganesh, "Land change in the Brazilian Savanna (Cerrado), 1986–2002: comparative analysis and implications for land-use policy," *Land Use Policy*, 25 (2008): 579–595.

[11] Maria Aparecida Anselmo Tarsitano, "Analise da Agricultura Matogrossense, 1970/85: modernização, desconcentração da terra e mão-de-obra" (PhD thesis, Fundação Getúlio Vargas, São Paulo, 1990), pp. 17, 42, 48 and 65.

[12] Cavalcante, "Mudanças da estrutura fundiária de Mato Grosso," p. 97.

MAP 6.1: The Cerrado region of Brazil

Quickly the state of Mato Grosso became the driving force behind the emergence of the Center-West region as one of the wealthiest zones in Brazil. Seasonal crops were the great source of this wealth, and the land devoted to these crops grew at 7.3% per annum for the state, compared to 5.3% for the region as a whole. This explains how Mato Grosso went from 7.3 million hectares of such land in 1990 to 25 million hectares in 2015, or from for a third of all seasonal lands to now accounting for over half of these croplands in the Center-West Region. In this same period, Mato Grosso increased its share from 5% to 20% of all such seasonal croplands in Brazil.[13] Both the state of Mato Grosso and the Center West region also had the nation's largest area of pasturelands, with the region

[13] IBGE, SIDRA, PAM, table 1612 found at https://sidra.ibge.gov.br/pesquisa/pam/tabelas.

accounting for 37% of the national total in the agricultural census of 2006. The nearest competitor was the Northeast, with only 19% of such lands. Within the region, it was also Mato Grosso which had the largest volume of such pastures, or 37% of the region's total, and alone contained for 14% of the national pasture lands.[14] In contrast, permanent croplands in the state were in decline, as local farmers shifted more and more into seasonal crops.[15]

Between 1985 and 2010 the state GDP grew at 6.9% per annum, while its agricultural sector grew at 7.8% per annum, both figures significantly above the national averages. It is currently the largest producer of soybeans, cotton and sunflowers in the nation, with all these crops produced at or above the national average yield per hectare. In 2010 state exports were valued at US$ 8.45 billion, which was 31% of the state's GDP, and these exports represented almost 6% of the value of national exports. It alone accounted for half of the Center-West region's purchases of tillers, wheeled and crawler tractors, combines and backhoe loaders.[16] In fact the state alone purchased one-fifth of all combines sold in the nation in 2014 and 2015.[17]

The state in 1960 contained some 1.3 million km² and had a population of only some 890,000 persons (of whom an estimated 330,000 were residing in what would be the post-division state) leading to a population density of 0.37 persons per square kilometer. Even after the division of the state into two parts in 1979, Mato Grosso still retained 903,198 km², which is more than twice the size of Germany and almost a third larger than France. Moreover, despite the spectacular growth of the population to 3.3 million persons as of 2015, it still had a population density of only 3.3 persons per km², the third lowest in Brazil, and especially low compared to a population density of 166 persons per km² for the state of São Paulo.[18] In 1960 the primary activity of this poor and backward region was cattle grazing and subsistence crops on what was then considered poor soil. Some 63% of the population resided in the rural area, a figure well above the 55%

[14] IBGE, SIDRA, Censo 2006, table 1031 found at https://sidra.ibge.gov.br/tabela/1031.
[15] IBGE, SIDRA, PAM, table 1613 found at https://sidra.ibge.gov.br/pesquisa/pam/tabelas.
[16] Pedro Abel Vieira Júnior, Eliana Valéria Covolan Figueiredo and Júlio César dos Reis, "Alcance e limites da agricultura para o desenvolvimento regional: o caso de Mato Grosso," in Antônio Márcio Buainain, ed., *O Mundo Rural no Brasil do Século 21: A Formação de um Novo Padrão Agrário e Agrícola* (Brasília: Embrapa, 2014): 1137–1139.
[17] *Anuário da Indústria Automobilística Brasileira 2016*, table 3.3 "Vendas internas no atacado por unidade da Federação – 2014/2015," p. 128.
[18] Official figures given by IBGE, at www.ibge.gov.br/estadosat/perfil.php?sigla=mt.

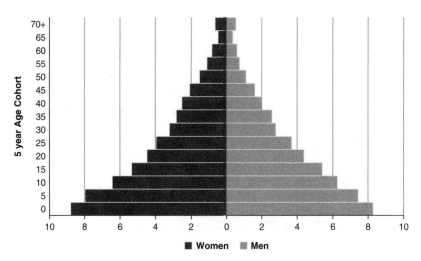

GRAPH 6.1: Age pyramid of Mato Grosso population, percentage in each age cohort by sex, 1960
Source: IBGE, VII Recenseamento Geral 1960, table 1, p. 2

rural for all of Brazil.[19] The capital Cuiabá was the largest city in the state and contained only 59,000 residents, and the state had only three towns with more than 20,000 persons.[20] The population was far more mixed than the Southern and Southeastern states, and was only 53% white, 40% mulatto (*pardo*), 6% black (*preto*) and 1% Asian. These rates differed from the national breakdown of color in 1960 and indicated that Mato Grosso was far more *pardo* than the national norm and far less white.[21] The literacy rate was surprisingly high, with 58% of the men and 53% of the women able to read and write.[22] But in other ways this population had

[19] IBGE, "Tabela 1,8 – População nos Censos Demográficos, segundo as Grandes Regiões, as Unidades da Federação e a situação do domicílio – 1960/2010," found at www,cens o2o1o,ibge,gov,br/sinopse/index,php?dados=8.

[20] The history of Cuiabá population growth from 1872, when it was 36,000, to 2010 is found in IBGE, "Tabela 1.6 – População nos Censos Demográficos, segundo os municípios das capitais – 1872/2010," found at www.censo2o1o.ibge.gov.br/sinopse/in dex.php?dados=6&uf=oo.
For the size of municipalities in Mato Grosso in 1960 see http://seriesestatisticas.ibge.gov .br/series.aspx?no=2&op=1&vcodigo=CD97&t=numero-municipios-censo-demografico-classes-tamanho.

[21] The national breakdown was 61% white, 30% *pardo*, 9% *preto* and 1% Asian. IBGE, *Censo Demográfico de 1960, Série Nacional, Brasil*, vol.1, table 5.

[22] IBGE, *Censo Demográfico de 1960, Série Regional*, "Mato Grosso," vol. 1, tomo XVII, tables 5, 10.

TABLE 6.1: *Size and share of rural population and sex ratio of Mato Grosso population by residence, 1970–2010*

Census year	Rural population	% total population	Sex ratio	
			Urban	Rural
1970	913,152	57%	97.6	118.6
1980	483,777	42%	101.5	120.8
1991	542,121	27%	101.5	124.9
2000	517,061	21%	101.3	125.0
2010	552,067	18%	100.4	124.0

Source: IBGE, SIDRA, table 200

a series of demographic indices of a poor population. The total fertility rate was 6.6 children for women 14 to 49 years of age, infant mortality was probably well over 120 deaths per thousand live births for males and 99 deaths per thousand live births for females and the resulting life expectancy was below the national average, which was 54 years for men and 57 years for women.[23] All this meant that this overwhelmingly rural population was a very young population, with an average age of 21 and with the pyramid age structure of a typical pre-modern population (see Graph 6.1). Although the growth of what would be the future state of Mato Grosso (without Mato Grosso do Sul after 1977) was a significant 1% per annum in the decade of the 1940s to 1950s, this growth was primarily due to local births exceeding local deaths.

But from the late 1960s migrants began arriving to the state from the rest of Brazil. The population of the future state of Mato Grosso doubled by 1970 to 601,000 and then to 1.1 million by 1980, and the population was now growing at over 6% per annum in these two decades, reaching a total of 3.3 million by the second decade of the twenty-first century.[24] Cuiabá the capital now stood at over half a million persons and there were now four cities in the state with over 100,000 residents. Now the state was predominately urban, especially as the mechanization of agriculture released large number of rural workers to migrate to the state's growing cities. By the census of 2010 only 18% of the population resided in rural

[23] The data on life expectancy and infant mortality comes from CEPAL, *Boletín Demográfico*, no. 74 (Santiago, July 2004), "Brasil: abridged life tables, 1960–1965."
[24] The data on population, density, fertility and growth rates is from IBGE and found at http://seriesestatisticas.ibge.gov.br/series.aspx?no=2&op=1&vcodigo=CD97&t=numero-municipios-censo-demografico-classes-tamanho.

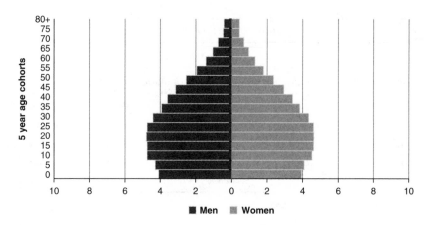

GRAPH 6.2: Age pyramid of Mato Grosso population, percentage in each age cohort by sex, 2010
IBGE www.censo2010.ibge.gov.br/sinopse/index.php?dados=12#topo_piramide

areas. But surprisingly there was no real decline in the numbers of persons living in the rural area, as happened in most of Brazil after 1991. On the other hand the state was typical of the rest of Brazil in having more women in the cities and more men in the rural areas (see Table 6.1).

What was unusual about the population in the last national census was the high ratio of immigrants who now resided in the state. Mato Grosso at the end of the twentieth century was a major zone of attraction because of its booming economy and cheap lands for migrants from all over Brazil. Whereas migrants from other states represented only 14% of the resident population in 1960,[25] by 2014 they represented 62% of the residents, with Paraná providing 20% of these migrants, followed by São Paulo, Rio Grande do Sul and Goiás.[26] Given the massive immigration, it was to be expected that the median age now rose to 29.7 years of age. This was also helped by a decline in fertility. By 1980 the total fertility rate had dropped to 4.7, and, with the drop as well in infant mortality, life expectancy began to increase at an impressive rate. The fertility rate then dropped to 2.08 children, or less than replacement levels,[27] infant mortality was now at 16.7 per thousand live births and life expectancy by the census of 2010 had climbed to 70 years for men and 76 years for women and for both sexes reached 74.5 years, an

[25] IBGE, *VII Recenseamento Geral –1960*, vol. 1, table 31, p. 77.
[26] Based on author's calculations from the PNAD 2013 and 2014.
[27] IBGE, *Síntese de Indicadores Sociais: Uma Análise das Condições de Vida da População Brasileira, 2015* (Rio de Janeiro, 2015), graph 1.4, p. 16

increase of almost twenty years since 1960.[28] All these changes in fertility, mortality and migration changed the age structure of the population of the state by 2010 so that it was now heavily concentrated in the working-age cohorts and with much fewer children – now a classic jar-shaped pyramid (see Graph 6.2).

The attraction for those migrants who came primarily from the wealthy regions of Brazil was the agricultural potential of the state. With abundant agricultural credit offered by the federal governments in the 1980s, and the development by Embrapa of crops adapted to the soil of this zone (which incorporated a large part of the Cerrado lands), commercial agriculture suddenly became a serious enterprise. This can be seen in the growth of crops in the region, which went from relatively small commercial production at mid century to extraordinary growth in output and in international exports by the agricultural census of 2006. Dominant of course were soybeans which were insignificant until 1985, but which really expanded in the late 1980s and by 2016 represented over a quarter of Brazilian production. The same can be said for cotton, of which Mato Grosso now produces almost two-thirds of national output, yet it became a significant crop only in the current century.[29] Equally from an insignificant producer of milk, Mato Grosso now produced just under a quarter of national production. Even sugarcane has become an ever more important crop since 1980 (see Table 6.2). But given problems of an adequate supply of water, this has required irrigation and even the beginnings of surface drip irrigation as an alternative.[30] The state by 2017 also had the largest number of cattle in the nation, over 29 million head, which represented 14% of the national herds.[31] Also of importance were dairy cows and milk production, plus a growing production of eggs, which although

---

[28] IBGE, "Tabela 1.31 – Tábua Abreviada de Mortalidade, por sexo, segundo os grupos quinquenais de idade – Mato Grosso – 2010," found at www.ibge.gov.br/home/estatistica/populacao/tabuas_abreviadas_mortalidade/2010/default.shtm. Also see http://atlas brasil.org.br/2013/consulta/ for the infant mortality and life expectancy of both sexes in 2010. In mortality and life expectancy Mato Grosso was close to the national norm, though its total fertility rate was considerably higher than the 1.89 child rate for the nation as a whole.

[29] For the evolution of cotton production in Brazil see Adriana Carvalho Pinto Vieira, Divina Aparecida Leonel Lunas and Junior Ruiz Garcia, "Ambiente institucional na dinâmica da cotonicultura brasileira," *Revista de Política Agrícola*, 25, no. 2 (2016): 53–66.

[30] For one such successful experiment see Antonio Marcos Iaia, "Irrigação por gotejamento em cana-de-açúcar no cerrado de Mato Grosso" (MA thesis, Universidade Federal de Paraná, 2014).

[31] IBGE, SIDRA, PMM, table 3939.

TABLE 6.2: *Growth of major agricultural products in Mato Grosso, 1970–2015*

	1970	1975	1980	1985	1996	2006	2016	Annual growth rate
Cotton (metric tons)	52,134	2,661	1,367	11,978	46,525	12,30,486	2,220,555	8.5%
Rice (metric tons)	379,660	355,691	1,000,971	608,945	588,731	3,25,013	501,045	0.6%
Sugarcane (metric tons)	74,393	71,058	308,020	1,086,341	7,450,702	1,33,83,587	19,209,764	12.8%
Corn (metric tons)	218,711	93,244	121,049	239,912	1,209,543	41,21,606	15,339,785	9.7%
Soybeans (metric tons)*			88,852	1,610,530	4,438,946	1,06,59,324	26,277,303	17.7%
Cows' milk (thousand liters)	150,269	39,138	91,572	122,917	375,426	5,17,305	662,720	3.3%

Source: IBGE, tables Agro34 and Agro73 found at http://seriesestatisticas.ibge.gov.br/lista_tema.aspx?op=0&no=1 and for 2015, IBGE, SIDRA, tables 1612 and 74

Notes: * For soybeans the growth rate is calculated from 1980

accounting for 1% of national production by that date made up a third of the value of the state's animal production, with milk accounting for two-thirds of the value by that date.[32]

This growth was unquestionably related to several government-sponsored developments. The most important was the opening up of most of the regions of the state in the 1980s through the construction of federal highways. Among the most important of these was a road built from Brasilia to the Mato Grosso city of Cáceres on the Bolivian border which finally connected the state to the Southern and Southeastern regions. Numerous roads, railroads and even water transport facilities were built slowly from the 1990s to the present day. Though still incomplete, this system finally allowed for the export of local products from most regions of the state to distant national and international markets.[33]

The cheapness of the land, its fertility and its level nature, the availability of transport, the sudden flooding of the rural economy with government-sponsored cheap credit starting in the 1970s and 1980s and the establishment of local and national agricultural research centers, all provided the incentive to growth. So cheap was the land relative to developed areas in other parts of Brazil that this frontier from the beginning was dominated by farms of over 1,000 hectares. In the traditional commercial agricultural states of São Paulo and Rio Grande do Sul, under 40% of the lands was held by farms of 1,000 hectares or above; in Mato Grosso the figure was 78% in the census of 2006. This is reflected in the Gini index of inequality which measured 0.875 in 1960 and was still at 0.852 in 2006.[34]

To get some comparative view of how unusual was the structure of landholding in Mato Grosso we can compare it with the other states we will be examining. Neither Rio Grande do Sul nor São Paulo, let alone Brazil as a whole, has such a large ratio of its lands in these immense holdings of over 1,000 hectares (see Table 6.3). Although the share of lands of these large estates in Mato Grosso have declined over time, they never approached the level of the other states. This did not mean the other

---

[32] IBGE, tables AGRO73 – Produção animal, and PP3 – Produção de origem animal – valor da produção, found at http://seriesestatisticas.ibge.gov.br/lista_tema.aspx?op=o&de=59&no=1.

[33] Vieira Júnior et al. "Alcance e limites da agricultura": 1130–1131.

[34] For pre-2006 years, the census provided only four categories of farm size; in the census of 2006 there were seventeen categories of size of farms. See IBGE, SIDRA, *Censo Agropecuário 2006 – Segunda apuração*, table 837, found at https://sidra.ibge.gov.br/tabela/837. In this and all calculations from IBGE, SIDRA, *Censo Agropecuário 2006 – Segunda apuração*, table 263, we have excluded all farms which were listed as having no lands.

TABLE 6.3: *Relative distribution of farmlands by farm size in selected states, 1970–2006*

Area	1970	1975	1980	1985	1996	2006
Mato Grosso						
<10 ha	0.5	0.6	0.3	0.3	0.1	0.1
10 to <100 ha	2.7	2.7	2.3	2.9	3.2	5.4
100 to <1,000 ha	11.6	10.3	11.8	13.3	14.5	17.0
1,000 ha or more	85.2	86.4	85.7	83.5	82.2	77.5
São Paulo						
<10 ha	3.3	2.4	2.4	2.4	1.8	2.2
10 to <100 ha	25.3	23.5	23.4	24.1	23.7	21.7
100 to <1,000 ha	43.5	44.3	45.5	45.7	47.1	40.5
1,000 ha or more	27.9	29.8	28.8	27.8	27.4	35.5
Rio Grande do Sul						
<10 ha	3.6	3.3	3.3	3.7	3.4	3.9
10 to <100 ha	32.3	31.5	30.3	30.5	29.5	29.8
100 to <1,000 ha	35.2	36.5	37.5	38.3	40.4	39.6
1,000 ha or more	28.9	28.8	28.9	27.5	26.7	26.8
Brazil						
<10 ha	3.1	2.8	2.5	2.7	2.2	2.4
10 to <100 ha	20.4	18.6	17.7	18.6	17.7	19.1
100 to <1,000 ha	37.0	35.8	34.8	35.1	34.9	34.2
1,000 ha or more	39.5	42.9	45.1	43.7	45.1	44.4

Source: IBGE, SIDRA, Censo Agropecuário, table 263 found at https://sidra.ibge.gov.br/Tabela/263.

states were extraordinarily equal compared to Mato Grosso, since in the case of São Paulo its Gini of land distribution was close to that of Mato Grosso. It just meant that the mean and median landholdings were much smaller in general than found in this typical Center-West state.

While land titles were often nonexistent or disputed as the Brazilian frontier was opened in the colonial and imperial periods, in the case of Mato Grosso this proved less of a problem since it was one of the last regions to be settled and because commercial agriculture followed closely upon the opening of the roads to this region. A legal land market thus predominated. According to the agricultural census of 2006, the overwhelming percentage of these farms of over 1,000 hectares were purchased (88%) or inherited (9%), and only 35 out of 8,694 such farms were taken by squatters who claimed ownership after long possession.[35] Moreover the state of Mato Grosso has one of the highest ratios of registered and measured lands in Brazil (some 77% are now titled).[36]

The agricultural labor force consisted of some 91,000 non-family workers fourteen years of age and older, 47% of whom worked in the production of seasonal crops and 45% in ranching. Half the farm laborers worked in units of less than 20 workers, though a significant 29% of them worked in farms employing 100 or more workers. Some 53% lived on the farms on which they worked, and 12% had training.[37] Taking all farm workers together, that is, including family members, the total labor force was 358,000, almost four-fifths of whom were males and 82% of whom were the owners of the farms. In this case, the production of seasonal crops involved only 24% of all persons working on farms, while ranching absorbed almost two-thirds of the workforce. In this respect, ranching clearly contained far more family farm operation than seasonal crop production.[38]

For Mato Grosso (and for Brazil) the leading agricultural product in terms of gross market value is soybeans, which have been growing in importance recently, going from 41% of the value of all ranching and farming production in the state in 2007 to an estimated 52% in 2017. One other significant factor in soybean farming in the state was the size of the producing units. In this, Mato Grosso differed significantly from soybean farms in Paraná or Rio Grande do Sul as early as the 1990s. Even as early as the agricultural census of 1995/1996 the median farm in Mato Grosso was over 5,000 hectares, whereas the median soybean farm in the Southern states was in the 100–500 hectare category.[39] The second most important state product is cattle and slaughtered meat, with the estimates being for the 2017 crop year

[35] IBGE, *Censo Agropecuário 2006*, table 3.25.1.7 – Forma da obtenção das terras do produtor proprietário, segundo as variáveis selecionadas – Mato Grosso – 2006 found at http://www.ibge.gov.br/home/estatistica/economia/agropecuaria/censoagro/2006_seg unda_apuracao/default_tab_uf_xls.shtm.

[36] For Brazil it was 49% of all lands for the same year of 2003. Cavalcante, "Mudanças da estrutura fundiária de Mato Grosso," p. 99.

[37] IBGE, *Censo Agropecuário 2006*, table 3.25.3.4 – Pessoal ocupado nos estabelecimentos em 31.12 sem laço de parentesco com o produtor, por idade e principais características em relação ao total do pessoal ocupado, segundo as variáveis selecionadas – Mato Grosso – 2006.

[38] IBGE, *Censo Agropecuário 2006*, table3.25.3.1 – Pessoal ocupado nos estabelecimentos em 31.12, por sexo, segundo as variáveis selecionadas – Mato Grosso – 2006.

[39] Fernández, "Do Cerrado à Amazonia," p. 133, table 23.

TABLE 6.4: *Ratio of gross production value of principal agriculture products in Mato Grosso, 2007–2017*

	2007	2008	2009	2010	2011	2012	2013	2014	2015	2016	2017
Soybeans	41%	43%	48%	39%	38%	45%	42%	42%	42%	45%	50%
Cattle	21%	16%	18%	19%	18%	14%	16%	17%	16%	15%	16%
Cotton	17%	19%	13%	20%	24%	16%	14%	17%	15%	17%	11%
Corn	9%	11%	8%	7%	9%	14%	16%	13%	16%	14%	10%
Chickens	3%	3%	4%	4%	4%	4%	4%	3%	3%	3%	3%
Sugarcane	3%	2%	2%	2%	2%	2%	2%	2%	2%	2%	3%
Milk	1%	1%	1%	2%	1%	1%	1%	1%	1%	1%	2%
Rice	2%	2%	2%	1%	1%	1%	1%	1%	1%	1%	1%
Pigs	1%	1%	2%	2%	1%	1%	1%	1%	1%	1%	1%
	98%	97%	97%	96%	98%	97%	97%	97%	97%	98%	95%

Source: MAPA, Valor Bruto da Produção – Regional por UF – julho/2016 found at www.agricultura.gov.br/ministerio/gestao-estrategica/valor-bruto-da-producao

18% of total gross value of production. Mato Grosso is in fact the most important cattle ranching state in the federal union, and ranching has been at this level of importance within the state for some time. It is estimated that cotton will increase by 14% in 2017 compared to the 2016 harvest, while the corn harvest is estimated to increase in value by 12% in 2017 (see Table 6.4).[40]

Support for the state's soybean production comes from a complex system of international and national entities which provide the credit to fuel the soybean economy after the relative decline of government credit support in the late 1980s. This credit has come from local cooperatives, the government and international trading companies. The major companies represented in the state are Bunge, ADM, Amaggi, Caramuru and Cargil, with their role being to arrange credit as middlemen between farmers, suppliers and/or being final sellers of the beans. Given the hardships of the early settlement and the crisis of the liberalization of the market in the 1990s and of diseases and low prices in the crisis year of 2005, the traditional cooperatives did not do too well in the state. Coopercana, the most important early sugar producer coop and most of the first-wave traditional cooperatives in Mato Grosso went bankrupt in the early 1990s. They were replaced by some 43 new-style "defensive coops," that is, coops designed just to save farmer costs by operating cooperatively but with no autonomous existence. By the 2010s these new-style coops had over 1,500 members controlling 2.4 million hectares and produced 20% of the soybean and corn and 90% of the cotton crop. These defensive coops have selective membership, in contrast to traditional open membership coops, and their aim is to reduce costs to producers and sometimes share sales, returning all profits to their members. They also required each member to pay for any special services they requested rather than all sharing costs. Thus, for example, the creation of storage facilities for those who did not have them on their farms was paid for by those using this facility, while those that did not need it paid nothing to the coop. Some coops concentrate on purchasing for their members all their needs, from seeds, fertilizers and insecticides to machines, while others just concentrate on purchasing fertilizers and insecticides since these latter two products are

---

[40] These 2017 estimates are given by the state agriculture ministry. See IMEA, *Boletim Semanal, Conjuntura Econômica*, 2 de junho de 2017/ n° 036, found at www.imea.com .br/imea-site/relatorios-mercado-detalhe?c=6&s=4.

controlled by monopoly producers. In this case, farmers themselves buy the seeds and machines, since the producers of these products are non-monopolistic, offer comparatively good prices and let the coop purchase the fertilizers and insecticides using its buying power to obtain better prices for them. Credit and purchases vary considerably both with private companies and coops. The final costs can either be paid for by pre-sale of crops, or actual ownership of the final crop by the input producers. Some of these defensive coops have subsequently turned themselves into more normal central coops. That is they began to add value to their members products. The most important of these central coops in Mato Grosso was Cooperfibra, the state's largest cooperative, which built a modern cotton-spinning factory in 2011.[41] It was the constitution of 1988, which eliminated government control over coops, that permitted these nontraditional coops to be created. But it should be noted that in almost all the other states with longer histories of agricultural production, traditional coops and the multi-coop central coops remained the dominant form of organization even after the liberalization of the 1990s.

After soybeans the next most important crops in terms of gross total value are cotton and then cattle followed by corn, chickens and sugarcane.[42] Together these six products accounted for an average of 95% of the total value of the state's agricultural and pastoral production in this ten-year period. Of these products, Mato Grosso was the leading state producer in Brazil of soybeans, cotton and corn (see Table 6.5).

Not only is Mato Grosso the primary state in Brazil for the production of soybeans, which is the single most important agricultural export of Brazil and often the principal export in general, but it is also the dominant producer of cotton. In both cases, Mato Grosso went from a relatively insignificant share of production to a leadership position by the end of the first decade of the new century.

Cotton production in the state is quite recent and uses a new variety of seasonally produced cotton. Traditional cotton was produced in the Northeast from the colonial period to the end of the nineteenth century, above all in Maranhão. But it migrated to other states of the Northeast in

---

[41] Chaddad, *The Economics and Organization of Brazilian Agriculture*: 139–140; Rosemeire Cristina dos Santos, "Custos de transação na comercialização antecipada de soja na região norte do estado de Mato Grosso" (MA thesis, Universidade de Brasilia, 2009), pp. 55–57.

[42] MAPA, Valor Bruto da Produção – Regional por UF – julho/2016, found at www.agricultura.gov.br/ministerio/gestao-estrategica/valor-bruto-da-producao.

TABLE 6.5: *Quantity of soybeans, cotton, corn and sugarcane produced and state's share of total Brazilian Production,* 1990–2016 (in tons)

Year	Soybeans	% of Brazil	Cotton	% of Brazil	Corn	% of Brazil	Sugarcane	% of Brazil
1990	3,064,715	15%	57,634	3%	618,973	3%	3,036,690	1%
1991	2,738,410	18%	73,458	4%	669,683	3%	3,110,876	1%
1992	3,642,743	19%	67,862	4%	763,907	3%	3,670,004	1%
1993	4,118,726	18%	85,641	8%	908,186	3%	4,284,369	2%
1994	5,319,793	21%	91,828	7%	1,163,551	4%	5,229,692	2%
1995	5,491,426	21%	87,458	6%	1,226,157	3%	6,944,989	2%
1996	5,032,921	22%	73,553	8%	1,514,658	5%	8,462,490	3%
1997	6,060,882	23%	78,376	10%	1,520,695	5%	9,988,027	3%
1998	7,228,052	23%	271,038	23%	948,659	3%	9,871,489	3%
1999	7,473,028	24%	630,406	43%	1,118,851	3%	10,288,549	3%
2000	8,774,470	27%	1,002,836	50%	1,429,672	4%	8,470,098	3%
2001	9,533,286	25%	1,525,376	58%	1,743,043	4%	11,117,894	3%
2002	11,684,885	28%	1,141,211	53%	2,311,368	6%	12,640,658	3%
2003	12,965,983	25%	1,065,779	48%	3,192,813	7%	14,667,046	4%
2004	14,517,912	29%	1,884,315	50%	3,408,968	8%	14,290,810	3%
2005	17,761,444	35%	1,682,839	46%	3,483,266	10%	12,595,990	3%
2006	15,594,221	30%	1,437,926	50%	4,228,423	10%	13,552,228	3%

(continued)

TABLE 6.5: *(continued)*

Year	Soybeans	% of Brazil	Cotton	% of Brazil	Corn	% of Brazil	Sugarcane	% of Brazil
2007	15,275,087	26%	2,204,457	54%	6,130,082	12%	15,000,313	3%
2008	17,802,976	30%	2,083,398	52%	7,799,413	13%	15,850,786	2%
2009	17,962,819	31%	1,415,921	49%	8,181,984	16%	16,209,589	2%
2010	18,787,783	27%	1,454,675	49%	8,164,273	15%	14,564,724	2%
2011	20,800,544	28%	2,539,617	50%	7,763,942	14%	14,050,998	2%
2012	21,841,292	33%	2,804,712	56%	15,646,716	22%	17,108,709	2%
2013	23,416,774	29%	1,867,422	55%	20,186,020	25%	19,681,574	3%
2014	26,495,884	31%	2,384,448	56%	18,071,316	23%	19,032,094	3%
2015	27,850,954	29%	2,373,581	58%	21,353,295	25%	20,077,293	3%
2016	26,277,303	27%	2,220,555	64%	15,339,785	24%	19,209,764	2%

Source: IBGE, SIDRA, PAM, table 1612

the twentieth century, as well as to São Paulo, mostly satisfying the national textile industry. Production in the Northeast was cotton produced from a tree (*arbórea*) which was a permanent crop, but in the South, cotton was a seasonally grown variety called *herbácea*. But a plague of insect infestations (of *bicudos* or boll weevils) destroyed a large area of Northeastern crop in the 1980s, and eventually production in São Paulo as well in the late 1990s, and for some time Brazil became a net importer of cotton.[43] But in the same decade Mato Grosso emerged as the second largest producer of cotton after São Paulo. It was unaffected by the insect plague and, after *paulista* production went into a very severe decline in 1996/1997, Mato Grosso not only became the leading producer in that year, but in just over a decade has increased production by a factor of ten. Also Bahia is now becoming the second most important state in the production of *herbácea* cotton. From these states production had increased so much in recent years that Brazil was able to satisfy national demands and still exports large volumes of cotton.[44] Equally, given the migration of the crop and its relative instability and problems of plague, cotton producers have been organizing at the state and national level since the 1990s, with the Mato Grosso cotton farmers being a powerful group which helped form the national association Abrapa (Associação Brasileira dos Produtores de Algodão) which represents all producers throughout Brazil. They have also promoted a state cotton research institute which works in conjunction with Embrapa to support basic research.[45]

Mato Grosso was always a major cattle ranching region, but since the 1970s it has become a major exporter of slaughtered meat exports, by 2004 it was the state with the largest cattle herds in the country and today it accounts for 14% of the stock of cattle in all of Brazil.[46] Because of this it was also the nation's greatest producer of animal meats, from a relatively small number of large meatpacking plants, and was also

[43] Vieira et al., "Ambiente institucional na dinâmica da cotonicultura brasileira": 60–64.
[44] See Rosana Sifuentes Machado, Benedito Dias Pereira, Meiresângela Miranda Muniz, Daniel Sneyder Campos Zambrano, and Heitor Tiago Gonçalves, "Otimização dos custos de transporte para exportação da pluma de algodão: contraste entre Mato Grosso e Bahia," paper given at the 53rd *SOBER, Sociedade Brasileira de Economia, Administração e Sociologia Rural*, 2015, section 2; and Adriana Carvalho Pinto Vieira, Divina Aparecida Leonel Lunas and Junior Ruiz Garcia "Ambiente institucional na dinâmica da cotonicultura brasileira," *Revista de Política Agrícola*, 25, no. 2 (Apr./May/Jun. 2016): 58–60.
[45] Vieira et al., "Ambiente institucional na dinâmica da cotonicultura brasileira": 59–60.
[46] IBGE, SIDRA, PPM, table 3939, found at https://sidra.ibge.gov.br/tabela/3939.

TABLE 6.6: *Number of meatpackers, animals and tonnage of cattle slaughtered of principal meat-producing States, all four periods of 2015*

State	Number of establishments*	Cattle	Metric tons of meat	% of meat produced
Mato Grosso	43	4,540,805	1,171,522,222	16%
Mato Grosso do Sul	42	3,408,741	851,616,228	11%
São Paulo	56	3,052,511	806,319,837	11%
Goiás	60	3,060,939	786,796,241	10%
Minas Gerais	95	2,840,812	665,014,233	9%
Pará	55	2,647,762	635,538,614	8%
Rondônia	20	1,904,823	461,751,161	6%
Rio Grande do Sul	229	1,821,798	395,347,119	5%
Paraná	96	1,246,820	300,324,566	4%
Bahia	31	1,218,785	295,551,658	4%
Tocantins	16	1,097,704	273,949,537	4%
Maranhão	50	839,121	200,062,216	3%
Santa Catarina	77	440,314	98,640,430	1%
All other states	338	2,530,867	551,001,295	7%
Brazil	1208	30,651,802	7,493,435,357	100%

Source: IBGE, SIDRA, table 1092
Notes: * The number of slaughterhouses varies by trimester in each state, so we have used an average for the four trimesters.

Brazil's largest internationally exporting state for beef products. In 2105 it produced 16% of the nation's slaughtered beef (see Table 6.6), and accounted for 15% of the total value of beef meat exports.

The state has also very recently become a major producer of poultry (*galináceos* or both meat and egg-laying chickens), but its 63.5 million chickens are just 5% of the total number of such poultry in Brazil and nowhere near the size of the chicken population of São Paulo, the leading state producer (with 198 million in 2016) and it ranks seventh in production. Even within the Center-West region it has fewer chickens than Goiás (see Table 6.7). With the addition of milk, eggs, leather hides and other products, the average of pastoral products in this period made up 23% of the total value of farm and ranch products in

TABLE 6.7: *Quantity of cattle and chickens produced by Mato Grosso and share of total Brazilian stock, 1980–2016 (animals)*

Year	Cattle	% of Brazil	Broiler chickens	% of Brazil
1980	5,249,317	4%	3,1,85,532	1%
1981	5,496,896	5%	2,9,35,177	1%
1982	5,967,282	5%	3,2,11,663	1%
1983	6,365,102	5%	3,3,40,712	1%
1984	6,787,575	5%	3,4,94,141	1%
1985	6,507,632	5%	3,6,72,827	1%
1986	6,859,161	5%	3,9,15,061	1%
1987	7,407,377	5%	4,2,14,373	1%
1988	7,850,069	6%	4,6,86,163	1%
1989	8,473,929	6%	6,2,27,761	1%
1990	9,041,258	6%	6,6,75,189	1%
1991	9,890,510	7%	7,1,08,625	1%
1992	10,138,376	7%	7,2,53,103	1%
1993	11,681,559	8%	9,5,02,768	1%
1994	12,653,943	8%	10,687,356	2%
1995	14,153,541	9%	11,408,968	2%
1996	15,573,094	10%	14,107,802	2%
1997	16,337,986	10%	14,234,821	2%
1998	16,751,508	10%	15,342,123	2%
1999	17,242,935	10%	15,509,681	2%
2000	18,924,532	11%	15,946,930	2%
2001	19,921,615	11%	15,917,039	2%
2002	22,183,695	12%	19,112,026	2%
2003	24,613,718	13%	19,790,394	2%
2004	25,918,998	13%	19,640,096	2%
2005	26,651,500	13%	21,115,447	2%
2006	26,064,332	13%	22,966,217	2%
2007	25,683,031	13%	27,850,977	2%
2008	26,018,216	13%	39,468,190	3%
2009	27,357,089	13%	47,094,310	4%
2010	28,757,438	14%	41,021,664	3%
2011	29,265,718	14%	46,305,618	4%
2012	28,740,802	14%	48,013,817	4%
2013	28,395,205	13%	39,037,025	3%

(continued)

TABLE 6.7: *(continued)*

Year	Cattle	% of Brazil	Broiler chickens	% of Brazil
2014	28,592,183	13%	46,327,158	4%
2015	29,364,042	14%	50,488,548	4%
2016	30,296,096	14%	63,572,414	5%

Source: IBGE, SIDRA, PAM, table 3939

the state from 2007 through 2016, compared to 77% which was made up of crops.[47]

Prior to the late twentieth-century development, ranching was a rather primitive affair with low-quality animals, natural feeding and extensive herding. The major exportable products were hides and dried meats, fresh meat being consumed locally. Moreover, until the 1980s, fresh meat only had a national market because of the lack of international standards of breeding and slaughtering. Thus along with the growth of the animal herds, there was also a revolution in breeding and care of animals. By the twenty-first century intensive ranching was replacing the extensive variety with planted pastured, vaccinated and better breeds of cattle and milk cows.[48] This involved the expansion of planted pastures which are usually first burned over and then planted with molassa, an African origin grass.[49] There are currently some 16 million hectares of planted pastures in the state (which in turn are 17% of such planted pasture lands in all Brazil), compared to 4 million natural pastures and another 1.6 million which are considered degraded pastures.[50] It also meant not only mechanization, but new breeding practices, animal vaccination, modern transport and adoption of international standards of production. These changes required technical help from state agencies, producer cooperatives and also from the newly arrived *figoríficos*, or meatpacking plants designed to export

[47] MAPA, Valor Bruto da Produção – Regional por UF – julho/2016.
[48] For a survey of all these modernization changes in the industry see Luís Otávio Bau Macedo, "Modernização da pecuária de corte bovina no brasil e a importância do crédito rural," *Informações Econômicas* (São Paulo), 36, no. 7 (July 2006): 86.
[49] Carlos A. Klink and Ricardo B. Machado, "Conservation of the Brazilian Cerrado," *Conservation Biology*, 19, no. 3 (Jun., 2005): 707–709.
[50] César Nunes de Castro, "A agropecuária na região Centro-Oeste: limitações ao desenvolvimento e desafios futuros" (Texto para Discussão no. 1923, IPEA, Rio de Janeiro, 2014), p. 13. It is worth noting that others estimate that only 25,000 hectares (250 km²) are degraded pasture. See Klink and Machado, "Conservation of the Brazilian Cerrado": 709.

state production. Some of these plants were created recently in the region or migrated, but several large ones came from the same Southern states as the cattlemen and farmers. The largest by far were the beef meatpackers, and the leader was the company then called Frigorífico Friboi (today JBS) which was founded in Goiás in 1953 and which acquired the US company Swift in 2009, thus becoming the largest meatpacker in the world. Many of the other major meatpackers come from the Santa Catarina. In 2005 Sadia which had been founded in Santa Catarina in 1944 established a major meatpacking plant in Lucas Rio Verde, a key center of soybean and corn production on the famous BR 163 highway, and another gaucho company, Perdigão, founded in Santa Catarina in 1934, also opened up a plant in 2005 in nearby Nova Mutum off the same highway.[51] In 2009 these two companies were joined into the Brazilian Food Company, the second largest meat exporter in Brazil and the world's tenth largest food company.[52] By 2006 there were 32 beef *frigoríficos* "subject to federal inspection" operating in the state, of which the most important groups were Sadia S/A, Grupo Friboi, Perdigão, Bertin (acquired by JBS in 2009), Marfrig, Margen and Agra which was a local Mato Grosso company founded in 2006.[53] In 2015, these Mato Grosso plants produced 18% of the beef, 4% of the chickens and 5% of the pigs slaughtered in Brazil in 2015. In this ranking Mato Grosso was the leading beef meat producer in Brazil, the fifth largest swine meat producer and seventh largest chicken meat producer.[54] Using the data on herds, we can estimate that in this same year, 16% of the cows grown in the state were slaughtered.

As they had in the Southern provinces from which many of these companies originated, they proceeded to organize a complex value chain providing support for the modernization of pig and chicken farming in the region in order to provide a steady supply of processed meats which could

[51] On the history of Perdigão see Armando João Dalla Costa, "A Perdigão, a passagem do poder e a profissionalização nas empresas familiares," paper presented at the *VI Congresso Brasileiro de História Econômica, 2005*. For the history of Sadia, see http://mundodasmarcas.blogspot.com/2006/06/sadia-saudvel-sadia.html.

[52] Lucille Golani and Rodrigo Moita, "O Oligopsônio dos Frigoríficos: Uma Análise Empírica de Poder de Mercado" (São Paulo, Insper Working Paper WPE: 228/2010), p. 5.

[53] M. de Cerqueira Vasconcellos, M. G. Pignatti and W. A. Pignatti, "Emprego e acidentes de trabalho na indústria frigorífica em áreas de expansão do agronegócio, Mato Grosso, Brasil," *Saúde e Sociedade*, 18, no. 4 (2009): 664. On the history of JBS see www.jbs.com .br/pt-br/historia; on Agra's history see www.agraagroindustrial.com.br/index.php? dest=institucional&dest2=historico&idioma=br.

[54] Data is from MAPA and was accessed at the website of the ABIEC, http://sigsif .agricultura.gov.br/sigsif_cons/!ap_abate_estaduais_cons? p_select=SIM&p_ano=2015&p_id_especie=9.

be exported internationally. These chicken and pork processing companies furnish farmers with basic inputs, including equipment, vaccines, animal feed and even the trucking of the animals to the meatpacking plants.[55] This did not occur with the beef producers, who were independent producers.

In 1990 the national census bureau decided to reorganize the collection of statistics and created new macroregions which better reflected differences in regions within state boundaries. Using these new designations gives us a better idea of which areas of the state are most productive. It turns out that there was very significant regional variation within the state, with one dominant zone – the North – and the two satellite zones of the Northeast and the Southeast making an arc around the poorest regions of the state which were the Southwest and above all the Center-South (see Map 6.2).

Within the state there were significant differences in production of these two key crops by macroregion. Of the five such regions, only three were significant producers of soybeans. The predominant one by 2016 was the North which accounted for 64% of the soybeans produced in the state, 70% of total corn, 92% of the rice, all the sunflower oil and even 21% of the sugarcane. The Northeast and the Southeast micro regions were the next major producers, but on a much smaller scale. The Northeast accounted for 18% of the soybeans grown in that year and 10% of the corn, and the Southeast produced 15% of the soybeans and 16% of the corn. The Southwest was only significant in the production of sugarcane, with 48% of the state's output. The Center-South produced insignificant amounts of all the other crops. Breaking this division further into municipalities, we can see the highly concentrated pattern within these mesoregions (see Map 6.3).[56]

But there had been some shifts in production over time. First of all volume increased. In 1990 the five regions generated 3 million tons of soybeans, which reached 27.8 million in 2015 for a growth rate of the state of 9.2% per annum in this twenty-five-year period. But the three largest producers expanded faster than the state average in this period. While state production grew at 9.2% per annum, the Northeast grew at 13.3% per annum, the North at 11% per annum and the Southeast at 10.9% (see Graph 6.3).

[55] Golani and Moita, "O Oligopsônio dos Frigoríficos," pp. 5–6.
[56] All the municipal maps are based on IBGE SIDRA, PAM, table 1612.

MAP 6.2: The five mesoregions of Mato Grosso

Corn generally followed the distribution pattern of soybeans. Here as well the North was the principal producer of the state, and the second most important producer was the Southeast (see Map 6.4). But here the Northeastern region, usually the third largest producer, was a bit more significant and was increasingly challenging the position of the Southeast. Corn production in the macroregion of the North from 1990 to 2016 was growing at an extraordinary 19% per annum, while the Southeast grew at 16% per annum, compared to a state average of 15%. The Center-South and the Southwest regions, which initially had been important producers, declined into insignificance by the end of the period, leaving just the North, Northwest and Southeast as the major centers of corn production (see Graph 6.4). By 2016 the two zones of the Center-South and the Southwest were no longer important centers of either soybean or corn production. The North with its 11 million tons of corn produced in

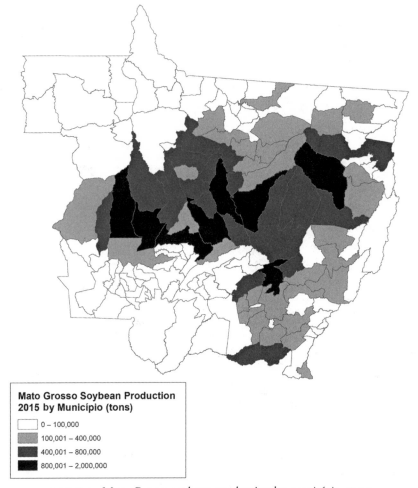

MAP 6.3: Mato Grosso soybean production by *município*, 2015

that year was clearly the dynamic heart of the three most important seasonal crops, followed by both the Southeast at 2.5 million tons and the Northeast by 1.6 million tons.

The fact that Mato Grosso now produced over half of Brazil's cotton is due to historical changes in cotton production within Brazil. Most of the Northeast region, its traditional center, went into severe decline due to plagues and production difficulties in the late twentieth century. This provided an opening for Mato Grosso, which in the late 1990s

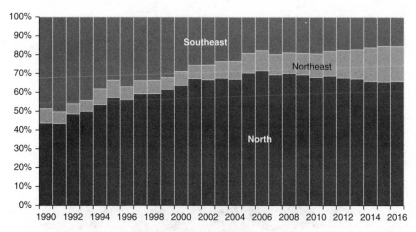

GRAPH 6.3: Share of soybean production by mesoregion, 1990–2016
Source: IBGE, SIDRA, PAM, table 1612

dramatically expanded its production and by the year 2000 became the primary national producer. Within the state of Mato Grosso, the North was the leading macroregion producer of the crop, accounting for over half the state's output, followed by the Southeast, but it was less spread out among the municipalities than corn and soybeans (see Map 6.5). The other three regions all began to produce in the 1990s, but slowly dropped out of production by the mid-2010s. Only the Northeast region grew its production in this period (see Graph 6.5).

In terms of cattle, the third most valuable agricultural product of the state, there was a more even distribution, though again the North was the single most important center of these animal herds, followed by the Northeast. But both the Southeast and the Center-South lost share of the state total herds over time (see Graph 6.6 and Map 6.6).

Like all other major commercial products, poultry (here meaning *galináceos* or both egg-laying hens and meat-producing chickens) is concentrated in the North, and, while all regions except the Southeast grew in number of poultry, the greater expansion of the North meant that their share was reduced over time (see Graph 6.7).

The existence of large open plains and the concentration in Mato Grosso of major commercial seasonal crops meant that the state was dominated by large farms. But there were significant differences between the macroregions (see Table 6.7). The Center-South and the Southwest, which were not significant producers of commercial crops, were clearly the poorest regions, with the largest number of small farmers with the most land, and the lowest

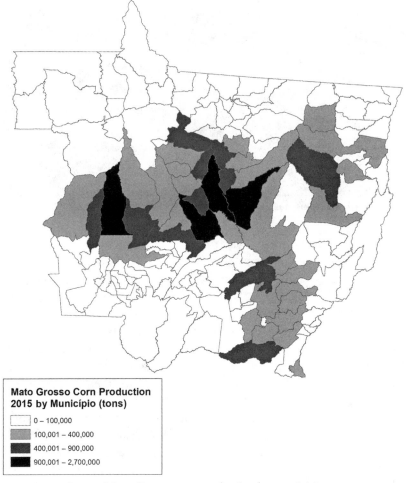

MAP 6.4: Mato Grosso corn production by *município*, 2015

ratio of farms over 1,000 hectares. Approximately three-quarters of their farm units were under 100 hectares, whereas the average for the other macroregions ranged from 55% to 69% of all farming units. While in all regions farms over 2,500 hectares occupied between 52% and 68% of all lands, in the Southeast they only controlled 45% of the land, which is clearly reflected in this region's lower Gini index of inequality (see Table 6.8).

Looking at just the farms growing seasonal crops, the same patterns emerge, with much higher Gini levels for the Southwest and Center-South. Despite this high Gini level, the Center-South had the fewest farms in the

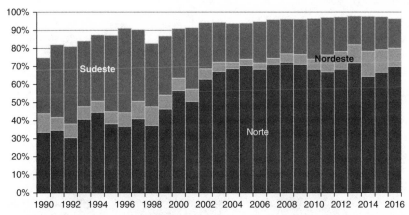

GRAPH 6.4: Share of corn production by mesoregions, 1990–2016 (in tons)
Source: IBGE, SIDRA, PAM, table 1612

>1,000 hectare category and they controlled the lowest percentage of the seasonal croplands (or 3%). The high Gini in these two regions appears due to the very significant number of farms under 50 hectares in both the Center-South (83% of the farms) and the Southwest (72%). In turn the much lower Gini of the Southeast was due to the high ratio of farms in this category (9%) but in this case they controlled a very significant 40% of all lands. In all the other macroregions, these small farmers controlled less than 2% of the lands (see Table 6.9).

The 88,000 ranches were more numerous than the 18,000 seasonal farmers by a factor of six, and had three and a half times more land than these farmers. Their distribution however was quite similar by region and by size of units, but with some subtle differences. The ranches over 1,000 hectares for all macroregions held a lower ratio of lands in the units of 1,000 hectares than did the seasonal crop farms. And in all regions but the North, there were fewer units among the ranchers in the <50 hectares category. But in their Gini rates they looked similar, with the Southeast having the most equal distribution and the Southwest and Center-South the most unequal (see Table 6.10).

Mato Grosso is also different not only in its large farming units, but even its workforce. All recent studies show that the majority of rural agricultural workers actually live in cities. Because of the high level of mechanization, a large share of the workforce can commute to their field work. At the same time some recent studies show that the region as a whole, and Mato Grosso in particular, had relatively low Gini rates of

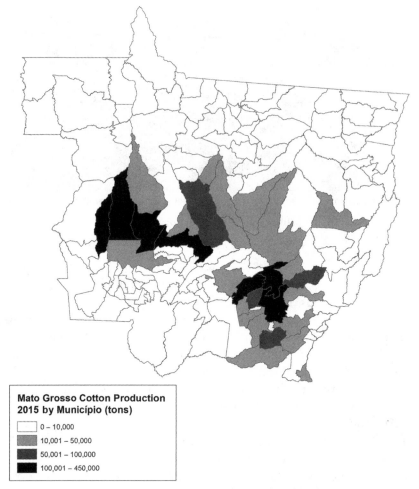

Mato Grosso Cotton Production
2015 by Município (tons)

☐ 0 – 10,000
▨ 10,001 – 50,000
▨ 50,001 – 100,000
■ 100,001 – 450,000

MAP 6.5: Mato Grosso cotton production by *município*, 2015

income distribution among such workers, compared to the national average (or 0.685 for the state compared to a national average of 0.702) and that it had a lower ratio of poor farmers (30%) compared to the national average (50%).[57]

---

[57] Angela M. C. Jorge Corrêa and Nelly Maria Sansígolo de Figueiredo, "Riqueza, desigualdade e pobreza: um perfil da região Centro-Oeste no início do século XXI," *Pesquisa e Debate*, 17, no. 1 (2006): table 5.

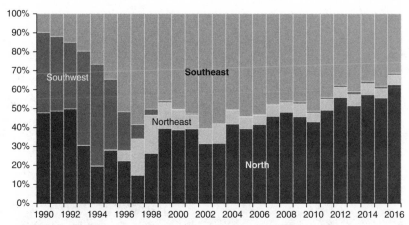

GRAPH 6.5: Relative participation of mesoregions in cotton production, 1995–2016
Source: IBGE, SIDRA, PAM, table 1612

Although large-scale farming would seem to indicate a totally capi-
talistic and individualist approach to farming, in reality the farmers and
cattlemen of Mato Grosso, just like the smaller farmers and ranchers of
the South from which many of them came, had experience with and
commitment to coordinated action. These farmers thus worked with
institutions as diverse as local producer cooperatives, state agricultural
agents, international trading companies and meatpackers to both insure
the quality of their products and obtain the technical knowhow needed
to produce exportable grade products. These institutions also help farmers with all their inputs and provide credit to buy them. Thus all
researchers have stressed the complex linkages which underlie the agricultural organization of the state. This has involved not only national
and international trading companies, meatpackers and various regional
and state associations of producers, but it has also fostered the growth of
agricultural producer cooperatives. In 2006 some 35% of the farms and
ranches and their owners or managers who owned 30% of all lands were
associated with either a cooperative, a class entity such as a union
(*sindicato*), association or movement of producers or neighbors and/or
both a class entity and a cooperative. Moreover as noted earlier, because
of the difficulties associated with frontier farming, the farmers of Mato
Grosso even created new types of cooperatives which were much more
limited and defensive than traditional ones. In the nation as a whole,
41% of the farms were in cooperatives and they owned 40% of the lands

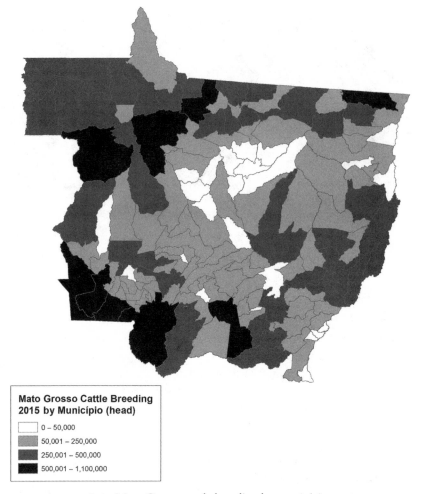

MAP 6.6: Mato Grosso cattle breeding by *município*, 2015

in cultivation, with the highest state being Rio Grande do Sul where 68% of the farms were in cooperatives and they controlled 72% of the land.[58] Given this southern tradition, many of these so-called "gauchos," the name applied to all these southern migrating farmers from whatever Southern state, tended to increasingly support producer coops.[59]

---

[58] IBGE, SIDRA, Censo Agrícola, Table 840.
[59] Nivea Muniz Vieira, "O trabalho em sua relação com a técnica e a reorganização espacial na cadeia carne/grãos da BR-163, MT" (MA thesis, PUC, Rio de Janeiro, 2009), p. 111;

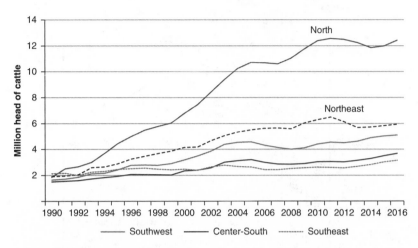

GRAPH 6.6: Percentage distribution of heads of cattle by mesoregions, 1990–2016
Source: IBGE, SIDRA, PPM, table 3939

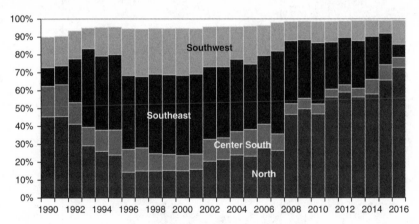

GRAPH 6.7: Percentage distribution of number of all poultry by mesoregions, 1990–2016
Source: IBGE, SIDRA, PPM, table 3939

As of 2011 there were 72 *agropecuário* cooperatives with some 12,000 members in the state. It was estimated that in 2012 some 13% of the corn

Also see *O Globo*, Section G1, August 25, 2012, found at http://g1.globo.com/mato-grosso/noticia/2012/08/cooperativismo-cresce-200-em-mato-grosso-puxado-por-agronegocio.html.

TABLE 6.8: *Land distribution all farming units by land area in the mesoregions of Mato Grosso in 2006*

ALL FARMS	North		Northeast		Southwest		Center-South		Southeast	
	Farms	Hectares	Farms	Hectares	Farms	Hectares	Farms	Hectares	Farms	Hectares
0.1-1 ha	779	319	53	20	151	56	231	76	286	109
1-5 ha	4,039	10,741	492	1,245	973	2,810	2,386	6,058	683	1,584
5-10 ha	1,963	14,413	461	3,537	672	5,271	1,284	8,782	536	3,587
10-20 ha	3,556	49,742	562	8,082	1,846	27,930	2,522	36,225	1,164	16,641
20-50 ha	11,893	382,223	3,089	120,050	5,820	180,447	4,189	126,991	3,236	89,632
50-100 ha	14,811	907,451	4,136	298,760	1,810	126,127	1,713	114,103	1,434	98,154
100-200 ha	6,401	770,636	2,288	314,438	1,250	170,925	1,019	135,080	1,044	143,419
200-500 ha	3,643	1,147,849	2,305	755,401	1,058	334,374	1,009	312,054	1,317	419,805
500-1,000 ha	2,134	1,505,046	904	640,603	537	384,026	589	404,738	959	664,295
1,000-2,500 ha	2,276	3,621,634	792	1,245,234	455	717,766	451	702,942	955	1,429,739
>2,500 ha	1,814	14,437,970	851	7,194,690	352	3,159,026	346	3,053,088	452	2,382,766
Total*	53,309	22,848,024	15,933	10,582,060	14,924	5,108,758	15,739	4,900,137	12,066	5,249,731
Gini	0.852		0.821		0.867		0.887		0.796	

Source: IBGE, SIDRA, Censo Agropecuário, table 837
Notes: * Farm units without lands are excluded

266

TABLE 6.9: *Distribution of farms growing seasonal crops by size of farm, macroregions, 2006*

Size	North		Northeast		Southwest		Center-South		Southeast	
	Farms	Hectares	Farms	Hectares	Farms	Hectares	Farms	Hectares	Farms	Hectares
0.1–1 ha	217	93	8	3	16	7	90	26	49	15
1–5 ha	1,112	2,359	155	310	166	383	589	1,496	110	246
5–10 ha	241	1,690	65	514	43	316	249	1,609	54	370
10–20 ha	485	6,656	43	583	99	1,411	486	6,910	91	1,331
20–50 ha	1,164	37,522	322	12,220	290	8,805	531	16,317	279	7,568
50–100 ha	1,853	115,620	236	16,007	62	4,230	181	11,869	83	5,611
100–200 ha	891	102,409	132	18,847	40	5,588	89	10,942	67	9,283
200–500 ha	570	186,611	168	55,730	48	14,478	48	13,387	146	49,052
500–1,000 ha	577	495,861	109	78,038	29	20,082	42	28,420	158	112,293
1,000–2,500 ha	729	1,146,579	98	143,225	30	46,452	16	23,069	245	376,030
>2,500 ha	580	4,524,512	112	1,022,819	31	458,426	16	180,183	173	997,132
Total*	8,419	6,529,912	1,448	1,348,296	854	560,178	2,337	294,228	1,455	1,558,931
Gini	0.835		0.836		0.921		0.900		0.730	

Source: Same as Table 6.7
Notes: * Farms with no lands excluded

TABLE 6.10: *Distribution of ranches by size of Unit, macroregions, 2006*

Size	North		Northeast		Southwest		Center-South		Southeast	
	Ranches	Land	Ranches	Land	Ranches	Land	Ranches	Land	Ranches	Land
0.1–1 ha	323	138	23	9	82	31	84	36	135	59
1–5 ha	1,964	5,632	273	791	676	2,083	1,425	3,644	421	998
5–10 ha	1,348	10,060	365	2,806	573	4,532	848	5,855	386	2,602
10–20 ha	2,577	36,222	483	6,992	1,638	24,936	1,766	25,445	958	13,719
20–50 ha	9,548	307,871	2,581	100,020	5,129	159,488	3,358	101,689	2,717	75,837
50–100 ha	11,467	704,190	3,698	267,466	1,692	118,079	1,443	96,169	1,280	87,690
100–200 ha	5,054	616,040	2,025	277,788	1,179	161,294	875	116,661	926	127,427
200–500 ha	2,892	906,036	2,050	671,378	989	312,982	915	284,600	1,120	354,403
500–1,000 ha	1,443	1,020,727	762	539,085	495	354,408	529	364,243	753	519,133
1,000–2,500 ha	1,390	2,224,655	658	1,042,556	411	650,736	424	662,128	665	982,048
>2,500 ha	1,124	8,876,125	716	5,997,096	298	2,502,992	320	2,822,619	263	1,299,576
Total*	39,130	14,707,696	13,634	8,905,987	13,162	4,291,561	11,987	4,483,089	9,624	3,463,492
Gini	0.840		0.816		0.855		0.878		0.781	

Source: Same as Table 6.7
Notes: *Farms with no lands excluded

and soybean farmers of the state were in coops and they accounted for 26% of the farmlands in these crops.[60]

It would seem that the frenetic pace of the early expansion has slowed, and the continuing modernization of agriculture in the state seems to be leading to a better awareness of sustainability of soils and environment. Unquestionably there have been significant advances in this area in Mato Grosso. Much is made of precision farming and its impact on reducing soil erosion and degradation. This is primarily used in corn farming with no tillage plantings over corn stalks (*plantio direto na palha*) in the second annual plantings. It can also mean individual field soil analysis and use of GPS to better distribute fertilizers, though in Brazil these as yet are a small part of precision farming. But as of the census of 2006 only some 2,000 farms of the state used precision planting, but they were quite large farms and absorbed 74% of the agricultural lands.[61] The smaller the farm the less likely it was to use precision planting. Thus 63% of the farms in seasonal crops which were over 2,500 hectares used the system, versus 7% of the 100–200 hectare farms and just 8% of those under 100 hectares.[62] Two-thirds of the state's farmers still did not practice any conservation methods as of 2006 (see Table 6.11). There also remain areas in the far north of the state which carry on traditional extensive grazing methods, and deforestation through illegal logging. It has been estimated that 41% of the wood products produced in the state between 2014 and 2017 came from illegal logging.[63] Even the intensive modern cattle industry as well as the new commercial agricultural sectors have been accused of dismantling too much of the northern forests as well as degrading Cerrado soils.[64]

It would also appear that fewer farmers used the basic fertilizers needed to maintain the soil. To obtain the best results, the Cerrado soils need fertilizers to increase their nutrients and also need to lime the soils with the application of limestone to reduce their acidity and increase plant

---

[60] www.ocbmt.coop.br/TNX/conteudo.php?sid=64&parent=63 and report in O Globo G1 found at http://g1.globo.com/mato-grosso/noticia/2012/08/cooperativismo-cresce-200-em-mato-grosso-puxado-por-agronegocio.html.

[61] IBGE, SIDRA, Censo Agrícola, Table 784.   [62] Ibid., table 792.

[63] Instituto Centro de Vida, "Ilegalidade prejudica setor madeireiro de Mato Grosso," found at www.icv.org.br/2018/02/15/ilegalidade-prejudica-setor-madeireiro-de-mato-grosso/; a report which is analyzed in *Folha*, February 15, 2018, p. B7.

[64] Sandra Cristina de Moura Bonjour, Adriano Marcos Rodrigues Figueiredo and José Manuel Carvalho Marta, "A pecuária de corte no estado de Mato Grosso," paper given at *XLVI SOBER, Sociedade Brasileira de Economia, Administração e Sociologia Rural*, 2008.

TABLE 6.11: *Distribution of farms in Mato Grosso by agricultural practices,*
2006

	Number of farms	
Planting on the level	13,230	11%
Use of terracing	2,524	2%
Rotation of crops	6,359	5%
Use of crops for pasture recovery	7,349	6%
Fallow or resting soil	2,884	2%
Burning	4,527	4%
Protection and/or conservation of slopes	10,010	8%
No agricultural practices	77,148	62%
TOTAL	124,031	100%

Source: Castro, "A agropecuária na região Centro-Oeste" (2014), p. 13, table 9

nutrients in the soil.[65] Yet in 2006 some 60% of the farms raising seasonal crops and 91% of the ranches in the state did not use any fertilizers.[66] It should be noted that fertilizers are costly in the state and represent a significant cost of production of soybeans, corn and cotton, both because most of the fertilizers are imported and because transportation costs from the coast are high.[67] But, as many authors have stressed, there is a large gap between the productivity of the large commercial producers and all other farmers, which in turn reduces the overall productivity growth of the state. It was estimated that the modern producers in 2006 had an average growth rate of 4.3% in total factor productivity. But the majority of farms had an annual total factor productivity of only 0.4%.[68]

Thus while progress has been made in bringing modern agriculture to a sizeable share of all lands, there are still too many small backward farms that do not practice modern farming and only partially are in the commercial market. Some of this is due to the haphazard and often poorly funded or properly prepared colonizing schemes which seeded the state with farmers lacking the education to practice modern farming,

---

[65] Castro, "A agropecuária na região Centro-Oeste," p. 22.

[66] IBGE, SIDRA, Censo Agrícola, table 3350.

[67] It is estimated that fertilizers represent around 38% of the cost of soybean production, 28% of cotton and a very high 41% of corn. João Bosco Lima Beraldo and Margarida Garcia de Figueiredo, "Formação do preço de fertilizantes em Mato Grosso," *Revista de Política Agrícola*, 25, no. 3 (2016): 17.

[68] Nicholas Rada, "Assessing Brazil's Cerrado agricultural miracle," *Food Policy*, 38 (2013): 153.

and partly to the generally low level of education of most of the region's farmers.

Finally Mato Grosso stands out as a special case of an almost exclusively raw materials producer and exporter, with only minimal processing of its products. Thus raw materials or minimally processed products in the total mix of exports went steady from 84% of the total value of all the state's international exports in 2000 to 98% of those exports by 2016.[69] Also without major transforming local industries needing imports, and with an ability to supply most of its food needs or manufactures inputs from national sources, it is not a major importer of foreign-made goods. It thus imports little in the way of food, raw materials or manufactured goods from abroad. This explains Brazilian agriculture's ability to generate a usually high positive balance in its international commerce. While both imports and exports have grown at 15% per annum in the period from 1997 to 2016, imports have averaged only 12% of the value of imports in this same period (see Graph 6.8). No other major exporting state has had such a high positive balance of trade. In fact, the biggest exporting state, São Paulo, had a negative balance of trade in most of these years and Rio Grande do Sul imported two-thirds as much as it exported. Despite the very high value of its international exports, the state exported on average only 20% of the gross value of its agricultural production (in the period 2007–2016), a relatively low ratio compared to Rio Grande do Sul which averaged 37% of the total gross value of its agricultural production.[70] This indicates that Mato Grosso corn and many of its other crops were also supplying the national market.

Though Mato Grosso in many ways is a late developing and a rather unique state with its high average farm size and large number of colonies, its special new-style coops, its state research program and the significant presence of multinational trading and seed and chemical companies are representative of most of the aspects of the new modernized Brazilian agriculture. Its commercial agriculture is modern and fully integrated into the world market. It has recently become Brazil's leading soybean and corn producing region and one which massively exports to the world

---

[69] MDIC,SEC, table FATEXP for MG accessed June 6, 2017, at www.mdic.gov.br/index .php/comercio-exterior/estatisticas-de-comercio-exterior/balanca-comercial-brasileira-unidades-da-federacao?layout=edit&id=2206.

[70] See MDIC, Valor Bruto da Produção – Regional por UF – December 2017 found at www .agricultura.gov.br/assuntos/politica-agricola/valor-bruto-da-producao-agropecuaria-vbp.

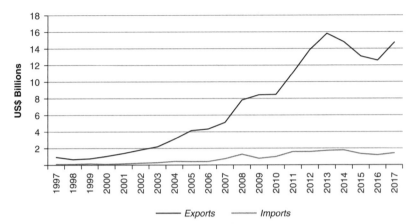

GRAPH 6.8: Commercial balance of the value of imports and exports of Mato Grosso, 1997–2017
Source: MDIC, Comércio Exterior, Séries históricas, "Estado Produtor e Estado Importador, accessed February 20, 2018, at www.mdic.gov.br/index.php/comercio-exterior/estatisticas-de-comercio-exterior/series-historicas

market while importing little from outside Brazil. It is also a major consumer of advanced agricultural inputs, and its commercial sector has adopted many of the most advanced farming techniques now being applied in tropical Brazilian agriculture. But like the rest of Brazil it also houses a large share of small-scale subsistence farmers who are barely integrated into this commercial sector and have little ability to participate in modern farming or in preserving soils and environments.

This pattern of an advanced sector residing within the same state as a subsistence and non-modern agriculture is common to Brazil, though in Mato Grosso this small farm subsistence sector is less important than in the rest of Brazil. At the same time, many of its largest farms have adopted no-till farming and second cropping in corn production and the state is now one of the key regions for experimental farming and livestock management. All this has meant that the extraordinary growth of production in the state in the past quarter century or so has been based on increasing yields and higher productivity rather than a never ending expansion into virgin lands. Thus the recent history of agriculture in this state marks a major transformation in the history of agriculture in Brazil.

7

Rio Grande do Sul

In many ways the southern province of Rio Grande do Sul is the opposite of Mato Grosso. It is a region with a long history of settlement going back to the early colonial period, it is a zone with a large population of European origin and it is home to some of the most advanced small commercial farms in the country and to a significant industrial sector. It is also in a more temperate climate, whereas most of the Center-West is tropical. This explains its ability to produce wheat, and apples, as well as most of the crops produced in other states. Unlike the Northeast and Northern states where small subsistence agricultural farms tend to be the norm, the majority of small farms are mostly in the modern commercial sector in all the states of the South, but especially in Rio Grande do Sul.

Rio Grande do Sul is also one of the classic southern states which early on created a vertically integrated production system of farm producers with either agroindustrial processors or central producer cooperatives. This unusual vertical integration has dominated three of the most important agricultural activities in the state, those of tobacco, pork and chicken production, and is also well developed among apple growers. It is the state with the most producer associations and cooperatives in Brazil.[1] Finally it and the other southern states were the home of some of the most important meatpacking and food processing plants, which eventually migrated to all parts of Brazil.

---

[1] Brazil as of 2012 had 1,548 agricultural coops with some 943,000 members. *Hortaliças em Revista* (Embrapa), Ano 1, no. 3 (May/June 2012), p. 5.

In 2017 the state ranked as the fourth wealthiest in Brazil in terms of the value of total agricultural production, and it is also fourth largest both in the value of all crops and all animals and pastoral products.[2] In terms of total exports, it was ranked third in 2015, due to its significant exports of manufactures – accounting for 9% of the value of all exports, compared to sixth place Mato Grosso at 7%. The leader, of course, was São Paulo, with 24% of the US$191 billion total exports.[3]

The region was first populated by Europeans in the early seventeenth century when Jesuit missionaries arrived to convert the Indians. The Jesuits seeded the region with cattle and in the early eighteenth century the Crown began effective colonization, granting land, building a road through the territory to the Rio de la Plata basin and finally establishing the first small towns along the coast.[4] The result was a thriving ranching industry which first exported hides and then turned to the production of charque, or dried meats, which was exported for slave food on the plantations to the north in the eighteenth and nineteenth centuries. It would also be the breeding ground for the mules which were the primary form of transport throughout colonial and Imperial Brazil until the arrival of railroads in the second half of the nineteenth century.[5]

After independence the imperial government subsidized agricultural colonies in the region, and German, Italian, Swiss and other European peasants were settled in small farms, the majority of which were concentrated in a 200 km range around the city of Porto Alegre. These were the so-called Old Colonies and by 1861 some 185,000 Europeans had been settled, mostly on the littoral and

---

[2] MAPA, Valor Bruto da Produção – Regional por UF – Dec/2017, found at www .agricultura.gov.br/ministerio/gestao-estrategica/valor-bruto-da-producao.

[3] MDIC, "Exportação Brasileira – Regiões e Estados, 2014–2015," found at www.mdic .gov.br/component/content/article?layout=edit&id=1184.

[4] For a history of early settlement see Fernando Cacciatore de García, _Fronteira Iluminada: História do Povoamento, Conquista e Limites do Rio Grande do Sul_ (Porto Alegre: Sulina, 2010).

[5] See Herbert S. Klein, "The supply of mules to Central Brazil: the Sorocaba market, 1825–1880," _Agricultural History_, 64, no. 4 (Autumn, 1990): 1–25; Paulo Afonso Zarth, _Do Arcaico ao Moderno: O Rio Grande do Sul Agrário do Século XIX_ (Ijuí: Unijuí, 2002), p. 234; and for the organization of the early nineteenth-century trade see Maria Petrone and Thereza Schorer, _O Barão de Iguape. Um Empresario de Época da Independência_ (Sao Paulo: Brasiliana, 1976), and Carlos Eduardo Suprinyak, _Tropas em Marcha: O Mercado de Animais de Carga no Centro-sul do Brasil Imperial_ (São Paulo: Annablume Editora, 2008).

along the major rivers.[6] From 1882 to 1914 another 155,000 immigrants entered the state, of whom 67,000 were Italians.[7] Then in the late 1910s and 1920s there was a new subsidized colonization which extended the farm frontier well into the western interior and brought Eastern European farmers to the state. There even arrived Dutch farmer immigrants in the middle of the twentieth century. All this interior settlement was aided by the expansion of the railroad system throughout the state from the 1870s to the 1890s.[8] Colonization continued into the twentieth century, with the remaining frontier of the state being settled by private initiative.[9]

Despite the growth of small farming colonies, the history of agricultural production in the state was marked by the dominance of the pastoral industry until the early twentieth century. The products of the state's ranches – which in the nineteenth century were jerked beef, hides and animal fats or lard (*banha*), still made up 57% of the value of all exports of the state in 1894. But by 1929 they fell to 44% of the value of all exports as rice became a significant export item.[10] In the 1880s barbed wire fencing was introduced to the ranches (*estâncias*) and this permitted the slow development of new breeds of cattle, and the simultaneous arrival of railroads and steamships permitted the expansion of jerked beef exports as well as hides. In the 1910s appeared the first meatpacking plants (*frigoríficos*) which led to the direct export of both frozen and fresh meat. In the next several decades modernization of the ranching industry occurred, with new breeds of cattle and with shorter growing times to

[6] Zarth, *Do Arcaico ao Moderno*, pp. 182–195. For the standard history of German agricultural colonies in the state see Jean Roche, *La colonisation allemande et le Rio Grande do Sul* (Paris: Institut des hautes études de l'Amérique latine, 1959).

[7] Franco Cenni, *Italianos no Brasil: "Andiamo in 'Merica"* (2nd edn.; São Paulo: Edusp, 2003), pp. 174–175. For a survey of the Italians in the southern region see Angelo Trento, *Do Outro Lado do Atlântico. Um Século de Imigração Italiana no Brasil* (São Paulo: Nobel, 1989), pp. 77–98.

[8] On the evolution of the railroad network in the state see Joseph L. Love, *Rio Grande do Sul and Brazilian Regionalism, 1882–1930* (Stanford, Calif.: Stanford University Press, 1971), p. 17; and Zarth, *Do Arcaico ao Moderno*, pp. 268–270.

[9] Benedito Silva Neto and Angélica de Oliveira, "Agricultura familiar, desenvolvimento rural e formação dos municípios do Estado do Rio Grande do Sul," *Estudos Sociedade e Agricultura*, 2 (Dec. 2013): 83–108.

[10] Jefferson Marçal da Rocha, "As raízes do declínio econômico da 'Metade Sul' do Rio Grande do Sul – uma análise da racionalidade econômica dos agentes produtivos da região," *Primeiras Jornadas de História Regional Comparada*. FEE, POA. 2000, tables on pp. 8, 15, found at http://cdn.fee.tche.br/jornadas/1/s12a5.pdf; and Marcelo Arend and Silvio A. F. Cário, "Origens e determinantes dos desequilíbrios no Rio Grande do Sul," *Ensaios FEE* (Porto Alegre), 26 (May 2005): 70.

produce animals for the market.[11] As the twentieth century progressed, state farmers began to produce a wide range of crops, from rice to wheat and corn, and expanded their animal production to include hogs and chickens and such ancillary products as milk and eggs. It would also be the first state to grow commercial quantities of soybeans.

Rio Grande do Sul is both the tenth largest state in Brazil with 269,000 sq kilometers and the tenth most densely populated one today at 40 persons per square kilometer. In 1960 its 5.4 million persons represented 8% of the national population and it was then the fourth most populous state in the nation, quite different from Mato Grosso with its 330,000 population in the same census year, which represented just 0.5% of the national population. By 2010 its population reached 10.7 million and it now ranks as the fifth most populous state. Moreover despite its being one of the classic states for European immigration, by 1960 the population of the state was 99% native-born. Although it would produce an important stream of emigrants to the Center-West, the state itself was not a significant destination for internal immigrants, and unlike Mato Grosso where 38% of the residents were born elsewhere, only 4% of the residents of Rio Grande do Sul in 2010 were born outside their state.[12] It was also 90% white, typical of the southern states but atypical for Brazil as a whole, where the census indicated that only 61% of the national population defined themselves as white in 1960.[13] Its literacy rate was also unusual by Brazilian standards. It was only in 1960 that the nation for the first time had both men and women being predominantly literate (for a combined national literacy rate of 54% of persons over five years of age). In contrast, Rio Grande do Sul already had a total literacy rate of 70% (with a literate rate of 71% for men and 69% for women) in that year.[14]

But with 53% of its population listed as being rural in 1960, it was close to the norm for all Brazil.[15] It was also close to the national rates in the distribution of men and women by local residence. The rural areas

---

[11] On the transformation of the cattle industry to 1960 see Luiz Fernando Mazzini Fontoura, "Agricultura da Associação a modernização," in Nelson Boeira and Tau Golin, eds., *História Geral do Rio Grande do Sul* (5 vols.; Passo Fundo: Méritos Editora, 2006/2009), IV, pp. 118–127; and Love, *Rio Grande do Sul*, pp. 16–17.

[12] IBGE, SIDRA, *Censo Demográfico 2010*, table 631, found at https://sidra.ibge.gov.br/t abela/631.

[13] *Censo Demográfico de 1960*, Série Nacional, vol. 1, table 5.

[14] For the national literacy rate see IBGE, *Brasil Século XX*, table pop_1965aeb-05.1.

[15] The national rate was 54% rural in 1960. IBGE, *Brasil Século XX*, pop_1965aeb-06.

contained more men than women and the urban areas more women than men. Thus the sex ratio in the city was 93 men per hundred women and in the rural areas the ratio was 106 men per hundred women.[16] Rio Grande do Sul was also one of the least urbanized states of the nation. In 2010 it still had only 45% of the total population living in cities of 20,000 or more persons, which was not that different from Mato Grosso which had 44% living in such towns and cities.[17] While its population density of 40 persons per km² was almost double the norm for all Brazil, it was the least densely populated of the states of the South region.[18] Because it was the premier zone of settlement for European immigrant agricultural colonies, it was also more Protestant than the rest of the country with 10% of the population adhering to that religion in 1960, versus 85% who declared themselves Roman Catholic. This was the lowest rate of Catholics in the country, the national population being 93% Catholic.[19] This unusual pattern had its origin in the decision of the imperial government to grant religious freedom to all arriving agricultural colonists, and thus Protestants were able to maintain themselves into the twentieth century, even having a Protestant from the state serving as president of the republic.

In age structure the state in 1960 was also more like the rest of Brazil. Its 5.3 million population were still largely a high fertility and high mortality population and its population under fifteen years of age was 42% compared to 43% nationally who were in this age group. Like the rest of Brazil after 1960 fertility rates dropped dramatically as did rates of mortality. The South and Southeastern states were in fact leaders of the fertility transition which began in this region before the arrival of oral contraceptives. But by 2000 all of Brazil had caught up with the South, and the structure of the population looked quite similar to both the national one and that of Mato Grosso. This was a classic post-transition model, with low birth and low death rates leading to a progressively older population. Whereas the population fourteen and under represented 42% of the state population in 1960, they now represented just 21% of the population in 2010.

---

[16] *Censo Demográfico de 1960*, Série Nacional, vol. 1, table 1.
[17] Ratios were calculated using IBGE, SIDRA, tables 1294 (for towns), and 1286 (for total population).
[18] IBGE, SIDRA, Censo 2010, table 1301, found at https://sidra.ibge.gov.br/tabela/1301.
[19] *Censo Demográfico de 1960*, Série Regional, vol. 1, tomo XVI, tables 1, 2 & 4 for all the demographic statistics on the state population.

TABLE 7.1: *Size and share of rural population and sex ratio of Rio Grande do Sul population by residence, 1970–2010*

Census year	Rural population	% total population	Sex ratio Urban	Sex ratio Rural
1960	2,975,780	55%	92.6	106.1
1970	3,110,602	47%	92.6	107.1
1980	2,523,825	32%	93.5	108.7
1991	2,142,128	23%	93.3	109.4
2000	1,869,174	18%	93.5	109.2
2010	1,593,087	15%	92.4	109.8

Source: IBGE, SIDRA, tables 200; and for 1960, IBGE, Censo Demográfico de 1960, Série Regional v.1 t.XVI, table 2

As was occurring throughout Brazil, the rural population of the state declined both in total and relative terms from census to census after reaching a peak in 1970. By 2010 the rural population had declined to 1.6 million persons or just 15% of the state's population. But at the same time there has been no basic change in the sex ratios of the urban and rural population, with women predominating in the cities and men in the rural areas since the 1960 census. As has been noted by many scholars, the urban domestic service market attracted a large number of women into urban occupations, while the industrial sector of the cities attracted a much lower ratio of men, leaving the rural areas more male than female, with more women migrating to the cities than men (see Table 7.1).

Unquestionably Rio Grande do Sul has one of the more equal divisions of lands for any region in Brazil. Despite a booming agriculture, a large pastoral industry and even with the introduction of soybean cultivation after 1970, the basic structure of land ownership in the rural area has changed little since the 1960s and that structure differs from Mato Grosso and most of the other states of Brazil. When we compare the farms and ranches by size of holdings in 1960 to that of the agricultural census of 2006, it becomes evident that there has been a change in the number of farms and the amount of total land used. But there has been little change in land distribution, as seen by the similar Gini numbers despite the major growth of commercial agriculture in the state in this period. The number of farms has increased 13% in this forty-six-year period, but despite the massive increase in output, the total land used for farming and ranching actually declined by 7%. At the same time the dominance of farms of less than 100 hectares continues. These smaller farms account in both years for an identical 93% of the farms and a third of the land. The significant change came at the farms and ranches over 1,000 hectares. These dropped from controlling 35% of the land area to just 27% in the same period (see Table 7.2).

Not only was the state unusual in its commercial small farming, but even in its agricultural labor force. Thus of the 1.4 million persons listed as working in agriculture in the census of 2006, an extraordinary 80% were related to the owner or administrator of the farm or ranch. This rate was well above the norm level both for Brazil as a whole and for the other sampled states (see Table 7.3).[20]

The distribution of these family member farm workers is what one would expect. That is that there is a high correlation between the size of holdings and the number of family workers. The larger the unit, the fewer such family workers, and the opposite occurs with non-family workers, though overall the majority of all farm workers were family members (see graph 7.1).

By the second decade of the twenty-first century the major agricultural products of the state in terms of value were a broad mix of agricultural crops, pastoral products and animals. The principal crops were soybeans, rice, tobacco, corn, temperate fruits and the root crops of manioc and potatoes. Milk, and to a lesser extent eggs, were among the principal pastoral products, and small and large slaughtered animals were significant sources of income (see Table 7.4).

Although the state currently ranks behind Mato Grosso in the value of its agricultural and pastoral production, as late as 2010 it was equal in the total value of these products to Mato Grosso – each producing approximately US$13 billion of agricultural and pastoral products – both being a third of the total gross value of these products for São Paulo. But six years later Mato Grosso was almost equal to São Paulo (US$21.8 billion to US$22.4 billion), and while the value of Rio Grande do Sul's agricultural production grew as well, it reached only US$17.4 million, or 22% below the gross value of São Paulo production.[21] But Rio Grande do Sul

---

[20] In Brazil the rate was 64% of farm workers, in the state of Mato Grosso it was 60% and in São Paulo 50%.

[21] We have used the conversion rate of US$3.15 to the *real* (as of February 1, 2017) to provide a proximate estimate of total agricultural value, which was given in *reais*.

TABLE 7.2: *Distribution of farms by size of land holding in Rio Grande do Sul, 1960 and 2006*

Size	1960 Farms	Area (ha)
0.1–1 ha	1,735	1,445
1–5 ha	39,253	117,633
5–10 ha	59,144	407,690
10–20 ha	110,162	1,502,791
20–50 ha	113,659	3,305,406
50–100 ha	28,644	1,909,114
100–200 ha	12,005	1,633,781
200–500 ha	8,744	2,689,645
500–1,000 ha	3,731	2,585,227
1,000–2,000 ha	1,945	2,669,927
>2,000 **	1,177	4,836,747
Total*	380,199	21,659,406
Gini	0.746	

Size	2006 Farms	Area (ha)
0.1–1 ha	11,219	4,077
1–5 ha	78,914	212,299
5–10 ha	81,449	563,003
10–20 ha	112,563	1,548,430
20–50 ha	94,667	2,767,630
50–100 ha	25,380	1,706,853
100–200 ha	12,600	1,704,205
200–500 ha	10,472	3,215,825
500–1,000 ha	4,508	3,067,245
1,000–2,500 ha	2,317	3,372,815
>2,500 ha**	526	2,164,332
Total*	434,615	20,326,714
Gini	0.765	

Source: for 1960: Censo Agrícola 1960 Serie Regional v. 2, t. 13, p. 1, table 2, p. 16; for 2006: IBGE, SIDRA, Censo Agropecuário, table 837
Notes: ** 1960 and 2006 use a different maximum number for largest farms but this has no significant effect on Gini

TABLE 7.3: *Distribution of farm labor by family membership and type of crop, Rio Grande do Sul, 2006*

Type of crop	Family	Non-family	Total
Permanent croplands	557,908	114,430	672,338
Seasonal croplands	51,123	32,234	83,357
Ranches	414,545	106,787	521,332
Total	1,092,498	278,226	1,370,724

Source: IBGE, SIDRA, Agro, table 805

TABLE 7.4: *Total gross value of major crops produced in Rio Grande do Sul, 2007–2016*

Product	2007	2008	2009	2010	2011	2012	2013	2014	2015	2016
Soybeans	23%	21%	22%	24%	25%	18%	28%	28%	31%	36%
Rice	12%	16%	17%	14%	12%	14%	14%	14%	13%	11%
Chickens	15%	15%	14%	14%	13%	14%	12%	12%	11%	11%
Tobacco	11%	10%	10%	7%	8%	10%	7%	7%	7%	5%
Milk	5%	6%	6%	7%	8%	10%	8%	8%	7%	7%
Cows	6%	6%	7%	8%	8%	8%	6%	7%	7%	7%
Corn	8%	8%	5%	6%	7%	4%	5%	5%	5%	5%
Pigs	5%	6%	4%	5%	5%	5%	5%	6%	5%	4%
Apples					4%	4%	4%	4%	3%	4%
Wheat	3%	4%	3%	3%	3%	4%	5%	2%	2%	3%
Grapes	5%	2%	6%	6%	1%	2%	2%	3%	3%	1%
Eggs	1%	1%	1%	2%	1%	2%	1%	2%	2%	2%
Potatoes	1%	1%	1%	2%	1%	1%	1%	1%	1%	1%
Manioc	1%	1%	1%	1%	1%	1%	1%	1%	1%	1%
Others	3%	2%	3%	3%	3%	3%	3%	3%	3%	2%
subtotal	100%	100%	100%	100%	100%	100%	100%	100%	100%	100%

Source: Valor Bruto da Produção-Regional por UF-Julho/2016, found at www.agricultura
.gov.br/ministerio/gestao-estrategica/valor-bruto-da-producao

compared to Mato Grosso has a much more diversified agricultural production, as can be seen in the relative share of their principal agricultural products – soybeans and their derivatives – within the total of agricultural production. In the case of Rio Grande do Sul, it is half as important as in

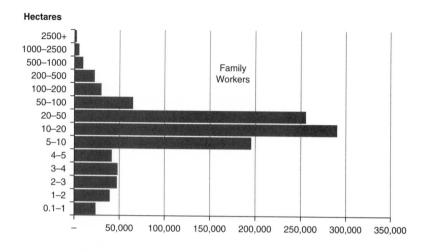

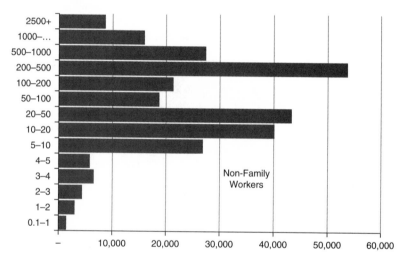

GRAPH 7.1: Distribution of type of worker by size of farm or ranch, 2006
Source: IBGE, SIDRA, Agro, table 805

Mato Grosso, even though the value of the crop in both states is relatively the same (see Table 7.5).

Of its agricultural crops, the state dominated the national production in tobacco, rice, grapes, and in the period up to 1990, in soybeans. But while soybeans were still the number one product of the state's agriculture in terms of value, in the past three decades Mato Grosso has become the leading producer, with Rio Grande do Sul second. Of the four leading

TABLE 7.5: *Value of principal agricultural products exported from Mato Grosso and Rio Grande do Sul in 2016*

Matto Grosso

Product	Value in US$	% of total value
Soybeans & derivatives	7,636,129,597	61%
Corn	2,407,526,297	19%
Beef & derivatives	993,089,211	8%
Cotton	854,207,230	7%
Chicken meat	210,143,604	2%
Woods	139,848,636	1%
Pork meat	88,554,837	1%
Subtotal		98%

Total value of all exports   12,5,88,619,662

Rio Grande do Sul

Product	Value in US$	% of total value
Soybeans & derivatives	5 24,9,628,287	32%
Tobacco	1,611,401,208	10%
Chicken meat	1,103,180,936	7%
Beef & derivatives	661,254,908	4%
Pork meat	420,636,116	3%
Rice	182,580,132	1%
subtotal		56%

Total value of all exports   16,578,206,410

Source: MDIC, "Exportação Brasileira, Principais Produtos, 2016"

283

agricultural or pastoral products of the state in terms of value in the second decade of the twenty-first century, only in rice, tobacco and grapes was the state the leading national producer. But it was also a significant producer of chickens of all types, and by 2016 accounted for 10% of all poultry raised in Brazil, or 9% of just meat chickens (see Table 7.6).

Most of these crops and pastoral products grown in the state have been produced over a long period of time, but there were several new products introduced in the recent period. Also most of the state's agricultural production has experienced significant and constant growth from the 1970s onward. Wheat had been grown in Rio Grande do Sul throughout the colonial period. In fact the state became a significant exporter in the late eighteenth and early nineteenth century due to the efforts of the Azorian colonists whom the Crown used to colonize the coastal region. But the fungus wheat rust destroyed most of the crop in the 1820s and wheat stopped being grown. In the mid-nineteenth century wheat production returned to the state with the arrival of non-Iberian European colonists.[22] In the mid-twentieth century wheat production was subsidized by the federal government and once again became an important state export product for national consumption. Whereas the state produced 106,000 tons of wheat on 120,000 hectares in 1920, by the 1950s it was producing around half a million tons on 500,000 or so hectares, By the 1970s local wheat farmers were using an average 1.6 million hectares to produce some 1.3 million tons of wheat. While yields have since improved significantly, the total volume of production has changed little since then, being on average just 1.4 million metric tons in the 1990–2016 period. But this volume of wheat was now produced on a much smaller land base, with the average lands devoted to wheat in the 1990–2016 period being only some 755,000 hectares.[23]

Like wheat, two other crops were also unique to Rio Grande do Sul and neighboring Santa Catarina. These were apples and grapes, both permanent crops. While grapes were a traditional product going back to colonial times, apples were only introduced into the state in the 1970s. Apples were

---

[22] Zarth, *Do Arcaico ao Moderno*, pp. 200–208; and Elza Maria Fonseca Falkembach, "Dinâmica social e cooperativismo: o caso da FECOTRIGO: 1958–72," in Maria Domingues Benetti, ed., *Desenvolvimento e Crise do Cooperativismo Empresarial do RS, 1957–84* (Porto Alegre: Fundação de Economia e Estatística, 1985): 108–109.

[23] For wheat output and land usage from 1970 to 1979 see Falkembach, "Dinâmica social e cooperativismo": table 1, p. 116; and for 1990–2016 see IBGE, SIDRA, PAM, table 1612.

TABLE 7.6: *Quantity of soybeans, rice, poultry*, tobacco and grapes produced in Rio Grande do Sul and state's share of total Brazilian production, 1990–2016 (in tons)*

Year	Production (tons)								Stock (units)	
	Soybeans	% of Brazil	Rice	% of Brazil	Tobacco	% of Brazil	Grapes	% of Brazil	Poultry*	% of Brazil
1990	6,313,476	32%	3,194,390	43%	204,615	46%	538,705	67%	78,665,321	14%
1991	2,220,502	15%	3,809,459	40%	186,568	45%	396,318	61%	103,318,336	17%
1992	5,648,752	29%	4,569,804	46%	280,330	49%	505,462	63%	109,475,430	17%
1993	6,067,494	27%	4,965,210	49%	318,690	49%	489,464	62%	120,525,320	18%
1994	5,442,728	22%	4,230,680	40%	229,524	44%	479,034	59%	123,507,243	18%
1995	5,847,985	23%	5,038,109	45%	223,159	49%	479,619	57%	132,829,214	18%
1996	4,235,532	18%	4,356,608	50%	206,918	43%	333,638	49%	103,939,335	14%
1997	4,755,000	18%	4,083,492	49%	274,451	46%	456,008	51%	110,229,659	14%
1998	6,462,515	21%	3,591,864	47%	235,519	47%	348,368	45%	108,468,644	14%
1999	4,467,110	14%	5,630,077	48%	306,393	49%	502,950	54%	112,067,698	14%
2000	4,783,895	15%	4,981,014	45%	294,873	51%	532,553	52%	113,613,050	13%
2001	6,951,830	18%	5,256,301	52%	298,193	52%	498,219	47%	117,659,492	13%
2002	5,610,518	13%	5,486,333	53%	339,832	51%	570,181	50%	123,232,042	14%
2003	9,579,297	18%	4,697,151	45%	322,078	49%	489,015	46%	127,469,034	14%
2004	5,541,714	11%	6,338,139	48%	482,968	52%	696,599	54%	12,8,823,60714	14%

(continued)

TABLE 7.6: (continued)

Year	Production (tons)								Stock (units)	
	Soybeans	% of Brazil	Rice	% of Brazil	Tobacco	% of Brazil	Grapes	% of Brazil	Poultry*	% of Brazil
2005	2,444,540	5%	6,103,289	46%	430,347	48%	611,868	50%	127,143,077	13%
2006	7,559,291	14%	6,784,236	59%	472,726	53%	623,878	50%	129,401,801	13%
2007	9,929,005	17%	6,340,136	57%	474,668	52%	704,176	51%	134,145,887	12%
2008	7,679,939	13%	7,336,443	61%	445,507	52%	776,964	55%	140,121,326	12%
2009	8,025,322	14%	7,977,888	63%	443,813	51%	737,363	54%	141,321,846	11%
2010	10,480,026	15%	6,875,077	61%	343,682	44%	694,518	51%	148,355,324	12%
2011	11,717,548	16%	8,940,432	66%	499,455	52%	830,286	56%	149,334,973	12%
2012	5,945,243	9%	7,692,223	67%	396,861	49%	840,251	55%	149,172,838	12%
2013	12,756,577	16%	8,099,357	69%	430,905	51%	807,693	56%	149,295,641	12%
2014	1,30,41,720	15%	8,241,840	68%	412,618	48%	812,517	56%	145,683,185	11%
2015	1,57,00,264	16%	8,679,489	71%	414,932	48%	876,215	59%	135,750,392	10%
2016	1,62,09,892	17%	7,493,431	71%	325,305	48%	413,735	42%	137,351,143	10%

Source: IBGE, SIDRA, PAM, tables 1612 and 1613 and PPM table 3939
Notes: * Poultry here defined as galináceos which are egg-laying and meat chickens

always consumed in Brazil, but until that period had been imported from Argentina and Chile. The introduction of the Fuji and Gala varieties both fitting with the climatic conditions and soils of the state become the dominant product in the orchards of Rio Grande do Sul, almost all of which were located in the mesoregion of the Northeast. Growers were of all sizes, from small and medium producers to large-scale orchards. The smaller producers tended to be vertically integrated with the packing houses that classified, refrigerated and packed the apples for market, and these packing houses were owned both by cooperatives and private companies. The larger estates were able to have their own packing houses. It takes five years for the apple tree to begin producing viable fruit, and the trees can still produce for twenty-five years, at which time the trees are replaced. Given the fact that picking apples is still a manual occupation, the local farmers employ a large volume of seasonal labor. So quickly did production expand that by the second decade of the twenty-first century producers were able to supply the national market as well as exporting some 15% of output.[24] Initially Santa Catarina was the leading state producer, and Rio Grande do Sul accounted for only 36% of the national crop in 1990, but by the 2010s it was producing half or more of the national crop in some years. But production has varied considerably by year due to weather conditions. Lands dedicated to apple orchards more than doubled from 7,000 to 16,000 hectares between 1990 and 2016, and output grew from less than 1 million tons to 2.6 million tons in 2000, then dropped dramatically to 300,000 tons in 2001 and has only reached 485,000 tons in 2016.[25] This quick rise and sharp decline was experienced in both states and was due to the unusually good climatic conditions in the late 1990s, which led to extraordinary levels of production, followed by poor weather conditions thereafter.[26]

The other major permanent crop was grapes. Although the Northeast and Southeast regions produce grapes, these are almost exclusively table grapes. The primary outputs of the Rio Grande do Sol grapes are wines and juices. The state accounts for 90% of the national production of wine and juices even though it produces only around 60% of the grapes in the nation. Although grapes are grown in the regions of the Northeast,

---

[24] Samara Rech, Silvio Antonio Ferraz Cario and Cleiciele Albuquerque Augusto, "Avaliação conjuntural da produção e comercialização da maçã em Santa Catarina e no Rio Grande do Sul: aspectos comparativos," *Indicadores Econômicos FEE*, Porto Alegre, 42, no. 1 (2014): 89–106.

[25] IBGE, SIDRA, PAM, 1613.

[26] Rech et al., "Avaliação conjuntural da produção e comercialização da maçã": 94.

Southeast and South, other state participation in national production is small. Thus the second largest grape-producing state is Pernambuco which accounts for only 16% of the national crop.[27]

Grapes have been produced in the region since as early as the Jesuit missions. Plantings were prohibited in the late colonial period, but in the 1830s some vineyards were installed in the coastal area of the state. German agricultural colonists after 1860 also planted the American originated grape variety known as Isabella.[28] But the big boom came with the arrival of the Italian agricultural colonists in the 1870s in the Serra Gaucho region (some 600–800 meters above sea level), with these migrants coming primarily from the Italian regions of Trento and Vêneto, both well-known wine growing regions. Already by the 1890s there was full-time specialization of some families in wine production, and by the middle decades of the twentieth century there were already wine producer associations and cooperatives operating in the state. The old colony areas, especially the Serra Gaúcha, were the major producers in the past and are so today, and they originally concentrated on the North American origin *Vitis labrusca* family which included Concord, Niagara and Isabella grape varieties.[29] But in the current century new zones have been developed in the state with modern vineyards installed, and this has occurred as well in the traditional Serra Gaúcha zone. Cabernet Sauvignon was first planted in the state as early as 1913 but did not become a major commercial crop until the 1980s. Equally the second most important of the new commercial grape varieties was the Chardonnay grape used in the production of white and especially sparkling wines (*espumantes*).[30] A state census of the industry in 2002 noted that there were 13,000 vineyards, involving 15,000 families in the state, with the average vineyard being 2 hectares. Some 80% of the wines

[27] IBGE, SIDRA, PAM, table 1613.

[28] On early winemaking in the colony and state see Kelly Lissandra Bruch, "Signos distintivos de origem: entre o velho e o novo mundo vitivinícola" (PhD thesis, Universidade Federal do Rio Grande do Sul, 2011), p. 118.

[29] Fernanda Quintanilha Azevedo, "Perfil vitivinícola, fenologia, qualidade e produção de uvas americanas e híbrida em Pelotas-RS" (MA thesis, Universidade Federal de Pelotas, 2010), pp. 15–18; and on the dominant grape types in Rio Grande do Sul, see Cláudia Marilei Gomes de Araújo, Patrícia K. W. Dalla Santa Spada, Daniel Silva dos Reis, Gilberto João Carnieli, Sandra Valduga Dutra and Regina Vanderlinde, "Influência climática em mostos e vinhos da safra 2015," *Revista Brasileira de Viticultura e Enologia*, 8 (2016): 67.

[30] Tiago Trindade Leite, "Tratamento pós-colheita em uvas e seus efeitos nos vinhos das variedades chardonnay e cabernet sauvignon" (MA thesis, Universidade Federal de Santa Maria, RS, 2009), pp. 24–25.

produced were table wines (*vinho comum*) and only 20% were fine wines, a ratio that varies by year. Of the total production, juices represented 8% of grape production and wine 80% (which includes sparkling wines) and the other 12% for various other grape products such as coolers. Tank trucks are used to move common table wines and juices to national markets, mostly to the Southern and Southeastern region, and only the fine wines are bottled. Of the 437 firms processing grapes, 21 are cooperatives. For the finer grapes there are only 118 producers bottling wines. Those dealing in table wines are also highly concentrated, with the ten largest farms accounting for just 42% of the production. But concentrated grape juice is made by only one company and in wines, coolers and non-concentrated grape juice the top ten firms have between 81% and 95% of production. By this date there were ninety-nine varieties of grape produced in the state, thirty-two of American origin and sixty-seven European ones, with 50% of production coming from Concord and Bordeaux grapes.[31]

The free trade crisis of the 1990s led to a new wave of cheap foreign wine imports, and this led growers to create a new associations of producers (*Aprovale*) to help them defend market share and define a new wine designated region and to promote the modernization of wine production. This new zone of white and rosé sparkling wines was created in 2002 and was recognized as a legitimate unique wine zone (*Denominação de Origem Vale dos Vinhedos*) by the European Union in 2007 and thus such wines became listed as the product of a fine wine district, distinct from the traditional table wine ones.[32] It is the sparkling white and rosé wines which have gained the most recognition in the national and international markets, and this local boom has brought in several famous multinational brands to engage in production, though the vineyards are still dominated by local families.[33]

[31] For an analysis of the Cadastro of 2002 see Marcelo Miele, "Análise do Cadastro Vinícola do Rio Grande do Sul para um processo inicial de caracterização do sistema agroindustrial vitivinícola gaúcho," *SOBER, Congresso Brasileiro de Economia e Sociologia Rural 2004*, vol. 42, found at http://www.sober.org.br/palestra/12/04O203.pdf.

[32] Maria Gabriela Vázquez Fernández, "Indicações geográficas e seus impactos no desenvolvimento dos pequenos produtores do Vale dos Vinhedos – RS" (MA thesis, Universidade de Brasília, 2012), chap. 2.

[33] Katia Zardo, "Vitivinicultura de precisão aplicada a produção e qualidade de uva pinot noir no Rio Grande do Sul" (MA thesis, Universidade Federal de Santa Maria, RS, 2009), p. 18.

TABLE 7.7: *Number of meatpackers, animals and tonnage of chickens slaughtered of principal meat-producing states, 2016*

State	Number of establishments*	Chickens	Metric tons of meat	% of Meat produced
Paraná	44	1,831,731,081	4,094,522,249	31%
Santa Catarina	31	870,682,440	2,120,803,300	16%
Rio Grande do Sul**	38	832,905,320	1,617,613,233	12%
São Paulo	32	618,732,177	1,531,214,664	12%
Minas Gerais	38	464,189,273	951,016,206	7%
Goiás	11	358,405,299	802,072,408	6%
Mato Grosso	6	242,748,277	561,464,518	4%
Mato Grosso do Sul	5	165,192,900	432,982,553	3%
Bahia	15	98,133,382	240,399,550	2%
All other states	220	377,596,460	882,870,549	7%
Totals**	382	5,860,316,609	13,234,959,230	100%

Source: IBGE, SIDRA, table 1094
Notes: *The number of slaughterhouses varies by trimester in each state, thus we have used an average for the four trimesters.

Another significant area of agribusiness in Rio Grande do Sul was the production of beef, chicken and pig meats. Though an important local product, beef slaughtered in Rio Grande do Sul accounted for only 6% of national output in 2016, ranking eighth among the states and producing just a third of the processed beef of Mato Grosso, the top state in tonnage of slaughtered beef.[34] This was not the case with chickens, the second most valuable animal product of the state. Rio Grande do Sul was the third most important producer in Brazil and alone accounted for 14% of the chickens slaughtered in 2016 (see Table 7.7).

Pig farming is a highly integrated market in Rio Grande do Sul organized into two major systems of vertical production. The first had the private *frigoríficos* writing long-term contracts with small-scale producers, and providing them with feed, medicines and technical help. The farmers are responsible for the costs of energy, water, labor and the removal of waste. These types of integrated production contracts written

[34] IBGE, SIDRA, table 1092.

between the meatpackers and the farmers were first developed by the Sadia company in Santa Catarina in the late 1940s, and soon became a norm throughout Brazil and now account for half the meat produced. A second integration pattern is with Central Cooperatives which slaughter pigs and prepare pork products, which usually work with individual producer coops which provide these same services.[35] Some 92% of these pig farms in the southern states were in these integrated contracts, or so-called value chains, with private producers or central coops in 2005, the highest ratio in Brazil. Most of these pig farms are quite small, being usually less than 20 hectares and mostly run by family labor or with just one or two salaried workers. These commercial farms typically produce pigs, are self-sufficient in corn and also have milk cows. Since pigs are primarily fed with corn and soybean meal, Brazil is an enviable position of not having to import these basic consumption items. Moreover corn is not a major human consumption item in Brazil, with the majority of the crop going for animal feed. Finally this is an industry dominated by national producers,[36] and is the second largest producer of pork meat in the country after the other South region state of Paraná. Here too the state had a very high number of slaughterhouses as it did in beef production. It was also the third largest producer of pig meat, the same role it played nationally with chickens, and it accounted for a significant 20% of national production (see Table 7.8).

In many ways the chicken industry in the Southern states is the same as the pork one, with the producers integrated through production contracts to the meatpackers, which consist of both private companies as well as major cooperatives. The three largest chicken meat producers in 2015 for example were BRF (amalgamated from the old Sadia and Perdigão brands), JBC and Aurora, the first two Brazilian based multinationals; the next three largest producers and exporters of chicken meat were cooperatives: Copacol, C.Vale, and União Brasileira de Avicultura.[37]

---

[35] For the origins of these contracts, see Fabiano José Coser, "Contrato de integração de suínos: formatos, conteúdos e deficiências da estrutura de governança predominante na suinocultura brasileira"(MA thesis, Universidade Federal de Brasília, 2010), pp. 33–34. On how they function see the study of Marcelo Miele and Paulo D. Waquil, "Cadeia produtiva da carne suína no Brasil," *Revista de Política Agrícola*, 16, no. 1 (2007): 80.

[36] Miele and. Waquil, "Cadeia produtiva da carne suína no Brasil": 77–81. BRF, which includes the old Sadia and Perdigão companies, ranks as the world's fifth largest producer of pigs in 2015. See www.wattagnet.com/articles/25011-infographic-worlds-top-10-pig-producers.

[37] ABPA, *Annual Report 2016*, p. 40 found at http://abpa-br.com.br/storage/files/abpa_re latorio_anual_2016_ingles_web_versao_para_site_abpa_bloqueado.pdf.

TABLE 7.8: _Number of meatpackers, animals and tonnage of pigs slaughtered of principal meat-producing states, 2016_

State	Number of establishments*	Pigs	Metric tons of meat	% of meat produced
Santa Catarina	92	10,728,698	968,830,981	26%
Paraná*	93	8,881,059	777,744,913	21%
Rio Grande do Sul	145	8,355,276	741,366,026	20%
Minas Gerais*	85	5,323,909	452,088,899	12%
Mato Grosso	10	2,352,603	206,460,317	6%
Goiás	24	1,830,677	165,359,743	4%
São Paulo	33	2,264,317	182,088,894	5%
Mato Grosso do Sul	12	1,505,455	136,892,746	4%
Distrito Federal	8	284,577	21,601,786	1%
Espírito Santo	7	251,192	21,630,828	1%
All other states	215	542,028	37,170,220	1%
Total*	722	42,319,791	3,711,235,353	100%

Source: IBGE, SIDRA, table 1093
Notes: *The number of slaughterhouses varies by trimester in each state, thus we have used an average for the four trimesters.

As we previously noted, these vertical integrated systems result in direct control of production by the meatpackers, who provide medicines, animal food and technical support for the producers, who are able to raise chickens of the proper weight within forty-five days.[38] Sometimes these industries even provide the animals to the farmers. This vertically integrated system is considered one of the most efficient in Brazil and it is estimated that 75% of national production is in these complex vertical contracts with the meatpackers.[39]

[38] Divanildo Triches, Renildes Fortunato Siman and Wilson Luis Caldart, "A cadeia produtiva da carne de frango da região da Serra Gaúcha: uma análise da estrutura de produção e mercado," _Congresso da Sociedade Brasileira de Economia e Sociologia Rural 2004_, vol. 43, p. 5

[39] Geraldino Carneiro de Araújo, Miriam Pinheiro Bueno, Veridiana Pinheiro Bueno, Renato Luis Sproesser and Ivonete Fernandes de Souza, "Cadeia produtiva da avicultura de corte: avaliação da apropriação de valor bruto nas transações econômicas dos agentes envolvidos," _Gestão & Regionalidade_, 24, no. 72 (2008): 7.

Overall there was a dramatic growth in most of the major agricultural and pastoral products in the state from 1970 to 2016. But in contrast to the other crops, cattle and pig herds, grapes and wheat production showed only a modest growth in the modern period (see Table 7.9).

What was most impressive is that in this state, as in most of Brazil, this increase in production occurred with little increase in land usage. Of the major grains which were produced in the state (rice, soybeans, corn and wheat), there was a doubling of output between 1988 and 2016 from 12 million tons to 31 million tons, but this occurred with only a very modest increase in land devoted to these crops, which went from 7 to 8 million hectares in the same period. This clearly reflected increased productivity in these crops.

Of all the major seasonal crops, soybeans were one of the more recent ones being planted in the state. Soybeans had been introduced into São Paulo in 1908 with the arrival of Japanese immigrants, but it was not until 1914 that soybeans were planted in Rio Grande do Sul. Until the late 1940s production was local and used mostly for animal feed. By the 1950s, however, significant commercial production had begun along with operation of the first plants to produce soybean oil. Already in the 1960s most of the major agricultural mesoregions of the state were producing soybeans, using the same machines and fertilizers that were applied to wheat. Soybeans only become a major commercial product in the mid-1970s, and it was Rio Grande do Sul which became the first state to massively produce soybeans for export. Whereas in 1970 soybean plantings occupied only 16% of the state's croplands, five years later it dominated state production and accounted for 40% of these croplands.[40] By 2016, it occupied 62% of the seasonal croplands.[41]

But if Rio Grande do Sul lost its leadership in soybean production, it maintained its position in rice growing. The state became a dominant producer of rice early in the twentieth century, and from the beginning this was a modern capitalist farming enterprise using irrigated lands and machines. Already by the 1920s rice had become a significant state export.[42] Though rice had been a major import into nineteenth century imperial Brazil, the new republic decided to create a protected market and

---

[40] Octavio Augusto C. Conceição, *A Expansão da Soja no Rio Grande do Sul 1950–75* (2nd edn., Porto Alegre: Fundação de Economia e Estatística, 1984), pp. 25–27; and table 4.1, p. 67.

[41] IBGE, SIDRA, PAM, table 1612.

[42] Marcelo Arend and Silvio A. F. Cário, "Origens e determinantes dos desequilíbrios no Rio Grande do Sul," *Ensaios FEE* (Porto Alegre), 26 (May 2005): 70.

TABLE 7.9: *Growth of major agricultural products in Rio Grande do Sul, 1970–2016*

Product	1970	1975	1980	1985	1996	2006	2016	Annual GR
Soybeans (metric tons)	1,295,149	4,419,465	5,103,538	5,710,859	4,253,171	7,465,655	16,209,892	7.1%
Rice (metric tons)	1,383,516	1,876,215	2,249,425	3,537,302	4,645,427	5,396,657	7,493,431	4.7%
Chickens (head)*	29,164,000	33,066,000	57,368,000	60,565,000	100,074,000	141,490,000	137,351,143	4.3%
Tobacco leaf (metric tons)	80,714	108,422	125,778	164,824	196,904	448,534	325,305	3.8%
Cow's milk (thousand liters)	778,479	943,461	1,325,945	1,280,804	1,885,640	2,455,611	3,249,626	3.9%
Cattle (head)	12,305,119	12,692,127	13,985,911	13,509,324	13,221,297	11,184,248	13,590,282	0.3%
Corn (metric tons)	2,230,302	2,155,592	2,435,320	2,428,297	2,885,333	5,234,311	4,729,948	2.1%
Pigs (head)	5,851,507	5,612,347	5,421,788	4,225,303	3,933,845	5,611,431	5,927,862	0.0%
Grapes (metric tons)	388,817	403,205	288,074	17,497	26,667	563,508	413,735	0.2%
Wheat (metric tons)	1,599,067	1,120,144	934,626	904,728	457,934	1,040,388	2,541,889	1.3%

Source: For 2015 and 2016, IBGE, SIDRA, 3939,72, and 1612; for all other years IBGE, Series historicals, Tables Agro34, Agro73 & Agro 120, found at http://seriesestatisticas.ibge.gov.br/lista_tema.aspx?op=0&no=1

Notes: * This includes all "Aves" (Birds), which is defined as all types of male and female chickens from egg-laying to those raised for meat consumption (broilers).

between 1898 and 1906 it raised the tariff on imported rice to 50%. Given Rio Grande do Sul's strategic location near the major littoral urban markets of consumption, and the available local resources, a thriving highly capitalized rice farming system emerged in the state by the 1920s.[43] Production grew quickly on modern farms, and by the end of the first decade of the twenty-first century it had become the predominant national producer. Although dry farming rice does occur in the Southeast and Central-West region, it cannot compete with the higher yield irrigated rice which is far more uniform and of better overall quality. In a state census of 2004/2005 it was estimated that there were over 9,000 farms in 133 municipalities of the state that were producing rice. Given the high consumption of rice nationally, the state exports only 8% of its production internationally.[44] Given the increasing productivity of rice, production increased from 3.8 million tons in 1988 to 7.5 million tons in 2016, yet the land used to produce this output only increased from 812,000 hectares to 1.1 million hectares. Yields have increased by 2.1% per annum from 1990 to 2016, rising from 4.5 tons per hectare to 6.8 tons per hectare, well above the national average of 5.7 tons.[45] In fact this is well above the 5.8 tons per hectare obtained in Vietnam, and identical to the 6.8 tons per hectare of mainland China, although below the US rate which was 8.5 tons.[46]

Tobacco has been produced in many of the regions of Brazil since the colonial period. The Northeast, from as early as the colonial period, was a center of cigar production, but it only became a more than local sector in Rio Grande do Sul when the state officially supported its production in the immigrant agricultural colonies in the late nineteenth century. In 1917 the British American Tobacco company entered the state and by 1918 had constructed the first processing plant in the town of Santa Cruz do Sul in the heart of the Rio Pardo region, the center of the state's tobacco farms. The company developed close relations with the local farmers and promoted modernization through the use of fertilizers, modern drying procedures and better leaf selection. In 1920 it introduced the seeds for Virginia tobacco plants, and thereafter Rio Grande do Sul become one of the three most important centers for Virginia tobacco production in the

[43] Paulo R. Beskow, "A formação da economia arrozeira do Rio Grande do Sul," *Ensaios FEE* (Porto Alegre), 4, no. 2 (1984): 55–84.
[44] Vanclei Zanin, "Panorama geral da orizicultura brasileira," *Indicadores Econômicos FEE*, Porto Alegre, 41, no. 2 (2013): 53, 60.
[45] IBGE, SIDRA, PAM, table 1612.
[46] FAOSTAT, Production, Crops, found at www.fao.org/faostat/en/#data.

world. In 1924 fertilizers were provided by the company to local tobacco farmers who used it for the first time. The company also supplied producers with capital and stoves (hot-air drying equipment). The region thus concentrated on production of Virginia leaf for cigarettes. Until the 1970s production was mostly for the national market, but crises in African producing countries opened up the international market, and several multinationals entered the state industry, among them Philip Morris and R. J. Reynolds who now coexist with British American Tobacco.[47] These production companies employed some 4,800 workers in 2012. They had long-term production contracts with the farmers. This included providing farmers with the latest in seeds of Virginia leaves, and extending credit, technical aid, fertilizers and even transport of leaf to the factories.[48] By 1985, it was estimated that 98% of the local tobacco farmers were using fertilizers and insecticides. The growers signed exclusive production contracts with the tobacco company, which provided for total sales to the processor, which determine the volume and quality of the leaf they produced. These commercial and modern tobacco farms were quite small. In 1985, for example, 62% of the farmlands producing tobacco were on farms of less than 20 hectares, and the figure was 94% for those under 50 hectares, with the average being 16 hectares.[49] The high returns for producing tobacco leaves more than compensate for the reduced cultivated area per producer.[50]

By the 1990s Brazil was exporting far more tobacco than it was consuming. Major foreign companies now are important participants in the local economy and are totally integrated with their producers. Their producers are quite small farmers, with the average size of units in the

---

[47] Rogério Leandro Lima da Silveira, "Complexo agroindustrial do fumo e território: a formação do espaço urbano e regional no Vale do Rio Pardo-RS" (PhD thesis, Universidade Federal de Santa Catarina, 2007), pp. 209–214, 239–240; and Olgário Paulo Vogt, "A produção de fumo em Santa Cruz do Sul, RS (1849–1993)" (MA thesis, Universidade Federal de Paraná, 1994), chap. 3.

[48] Áurea Corrêa de Miranda Breitbach, "A região de Santa Cruz do Sul e o fumo: panorama de uma 'especialização' nociva," *Indicadores Econômicos FEE*, Porto Alegre, 42, no. 1 (2014): 48–49.

[49] Silveira, "Complexo agroindustrial do fumo," pp. 255–256; and p. 275, table 14.

[50] One estimate suggests that the tobacco crop, which occupies on average 17% of the planted area of these tobacco farms, is responsible for 49% of household income. With the income obtained on 1 hectare of tobacco, for example, the producer would have to plant 7 to 8 hectares of corn, which would make small rural properties unfeasible. Report of Deputy Covatti Filho in the Chamber of Deputies, May 15, 2017. www.camara.gov.br/sileg/integras/1558650.pdf.

Southern region being just 17.5 hectares.[51] The three states of this Southern region produced 98% of the tobacco in Brazil in the crop year 2015/2016, with some 144,300 farms working on 271,070 hectares.[52] It was estimated in 2017 that Brazil was the world's second largest producer of tobacco and first in terms of international exports.[53]

As equally dominated by small farms as the tobacco growers are the highly competitive milk farmers in Rio Grande do Sul. Milk was produced in the region in the colonial period for local consumption, but the growth of significant local cities in the late nineteenth and early twentieth century led to the development of a more complex market. In 1936 the Associação dos Criadores de Gado Holandês do Rio Grande do Sul was founded, and the next year the state set up a pasteurizing plant in Porto Alegre. In 1970 the state created a mixed private and public company CORLAC (Companhia Rio-Grandense de Laticínios e Correlatos) to provide assistance to all the state's dairy farmers. Then a year later producers created the Cooperativa Central Gaúcha de Leite (CCGL) and within ten years it controlled half of the state's production. But the collapse of a large wheat cooperative in 1990 led to the temporary privatization of their holdings, since the milk cooperative lost funding with the collapse of the wheat cooperative.[54] In the 1990s Ultra-High Temperature processing (UHT) produced milk called *longa vida* in Portuguese which was introduced in the state and that enabled the industry to begin shipping milk long distances. The multinationals Parmalat and Nestlé entered the market in the 1990s, acquiring twenty-two and eight local plants respectively, and the CCGL returned in this period to again become a major producer.[55] In the late 1990s a survey of the state's milk industry found that the

---

[51] Vivien Diesel, Joaquim Assis, and Juliana Scheibler, "A dinâmica da integraçã o agricultor–agroindústria e o desenvolvimento territorial sustentável," *IV Coloquio sobre Tansformaciones Territoriales*, pp. 1–5,

[52] Data accessed October 1, 2017, at www.afubra.com.br/fumicultura-brasil.html.

[53] Report of Deputy Covatti Filho in the Chamber of Deputies, 15 May 2017. http://www .camara.gov.br/sileg/integras/1558650.pdf.

[54] On the collapse of this important wheat farmer coop, see Maria Domingues Benetti, "Endividamento e crise no cooperativismo empresarial do rio grande do sul: análise do caso FECOTRIGO/CENTRALSUL – 1975–83," *Ensaios FEE* (Porto Alegre), 6, no. 2 (1985): 23–55. Also see her book on the major wheat coops in the state, Maria Domingues Benetti, *Origem e formação do cooperativismo empresarial no Rio Grande do Sul uma análise do desenvolvimento da COTRIJUÍ, COTRISA e FECOTRIGO 1957/1980,1985* (3rd printing; Porto Alegre: Fundação da Economia e Estatistica, 1992).

[55] Guilherme Gadonski de Lima, Emerson Juliano Lucca and Dilson Trennepohl, "Expansão da cadeia produtiva do leite e seu potencial de impacto no desenvolvimento da região noroeste rio-grandense," *53rd Congresso da SOBER 2015* (João Pessoa).

average milk farm was only 20 hectares and had seven milk cows. It was estimated that there were 84,000 farms and half these farms produced only 30 liters a day and 89% produced less than 100 liters per day. The transport of milk was done by independent contractors and most of the milk was processed by only two major companies, one a coop and the other a private company which processes them for market. Although the state and the region have among the highest yields of milk, these yields are low by the standards of the neighboring countries, but this is compensated for by the processing plants, which are the most advanced among these countries.[56] By 2014 there were some 134,000 farms which produced milk, out of a total of 441,000 farms in Rio Grande do Sul. By 2014, it was still the case that 70% of the commercial milk farms produced less than 100 liters per day. Nevertheless productivity has increased greatly due to the widespread adaptation of artificial insemination, machines and artificial pastures. Between 1980 and 2016 total milk output increased by almost two-thirds, going from 1.2 to 3.2 billion liters. By 2016 Rio Grande was the second largest milk producing state in Brazil (see Table 7.10). In the period 1980 to 2016 it increased its dairy herds modestly from 1.28 million to 1.5 million dairy cows, but increased its output significantly.[57]

But for all the growth in output, the dairy industry is the least developed and least competitive major agricultural sector in Brazil. The average output per milk cow in Rio Grande do Sul is in the 2,000 liters per cow range, one of the highest in Brazil, yet this is half the production per dairy cow in Argentina and nowhere near that of the United States and other advanced agricultural producers which are in the 8,000 to 9,000 liters per cow range.[58] This low productivity means that Brazil cannot compete in quality with its Mercosul partners Argentina and Uruguay, and is why it produces only half as much milk from its herds compared to the United

---

[56] Cleber Carvalho de Castro, Antônio Domingos Padula, Juvir Luiz Mattuella, Laudemir André Müller and Aline Nuy Angst, "Estudo da cadeia láctea do Rio Grande do Sul: uma abordagem das relações entre os elos da produção, industrialização e distribuição," *Revista de Administração Contemporânea*, 2, no. 1 (Apr. 1998): 149, 156; and Rosangela Zoccal and Aloísio Teixeira Gomes, "Zoneamento da produção de leite no Brasil, "*XLIII Congresso da Sociedade Brasileira de Economia e Sociologia Rural* (Ribeirão Preto 2005), p. 17.

[57] IBGE, SIDRA, PPM, tables 74 & 94.

[58] Pascoal José Marion Filho, Jones de Oliveira Fagundes and Gabriela Schumacher, "A produção de leite no Rio Grande do Sul: produtividade, especialização e concentração (1990–2009)," *Revista de Economia e Agronegócio*, 9, no. 2 (2015): 242.

TABLE 7.10: *Units processing milk and quantity of milk produced by major producing states, 2016*

States	Number of processing plants	Total quantity of milk crude or chilled industrialized (thousand liters)	Percentage of milk produced by state
Minas Gerais	531	6,096,642	26%
Rio Grande do Sul	134	3,242,322	14%
Paraná	166	2,742,372	12%
São Paulo	161	2,556,274	11%
Goiás	150	2,309,472	10%
Santa Catarina	101	2,436,153	11%
Rondônia	71	699,591	3%
Mato Grosso	52	521,887	2%
Rio de Janeiro	100	557,985	2%
All other states	560	1,976,245	9%
Brazil	1,995	23,138,943	100%

Source: IBGE, SIDRA, table 1086

States in twice the number of dairy cows.[59] Much of this was due to the inability of the dominant cooperatives in this area to respond to liberalization of the market in the 1990s, which resulted in many of these coops being liquidated or selling their plants to private companies. But it is also due to the failure to liberalize the sector and open it up to full competition. Even for Mercosul producers, Brazil charges a 29% tariff and even then has recently added a quota system for Argentine imports and has placed various limits on imports from New Zeland and the European Union. Thus "Brazilian milk producers are shielded from imports and milk prices received at the farm gate are significantly higher than in more competitive countries." These two factors, continued tariff protection and prices above world prices, mean there are few incentives to improve productivity. Brazil still imports more than it exports in this sector and remains relatively uncompetitive on the international market. Milk is thus the one major industry whose market was not fully liberalized, which explains its

[59] USDA, Dairy: World Markets and Trade, December 2017, pp. 13–14. The US produced in 2017 97.8 million metric tons from 9.4 million dairy cows, and Brazil produced only 23.6 million metric tons from 17.6 million milk cows.

MAP 7.1: Seven mesoregions of Rio Grande do Sul

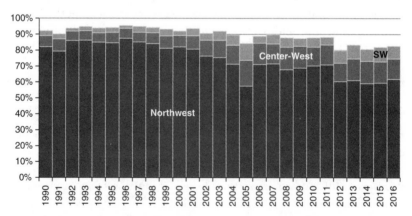

GRAPH 7.2: Ratio of soybean production by mesoregions, Rio Grande do Sul, 1990–2016
Source: IBGE, SIDRA, PAM, table 1612

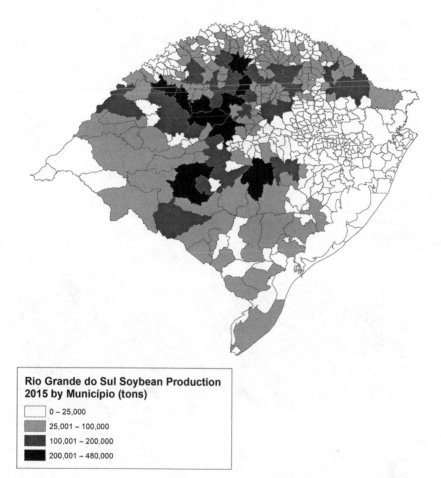

MAP 7.2: Rio Grande do Sul soybean production (tons) by *município* in 2015

relatively low productivity.[60] As in other agricultural sectors, there are technical conditions available for increasing productivity in the sector, and the costs of inputs are quite low given the competitive nature of Brazilian grain production. So in the future, milk could be produced at a level and quality that are competitive on the international market.

In examining the agricultural production of the state by mesoregions (see Map 7.1), we find sharp differences by crop produced or animals

[60] Chaddad, *The Economics and Organization of Brazilian Agriculture. Recent Evolution and Productivity Gains* (Amsterdam: Academic Press), p. 150.

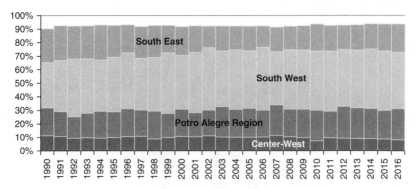

GRAPH 7.3: Ratio of rice production by mesoregions of Rio Grande do Sul,
1990–2016
Source: IBGE, SIDRA, PAM, table 1612

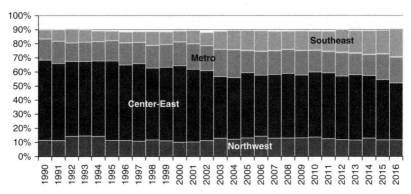

GRAPH 7.4: Ratio of tobacco production by macroregion of Rio Grande do Sul,
1990–2016
Source: IBGE, SIDRA, PAM, table 1612

raised. Interestingly enough, although there were soil and climate variations by mesoregions, all produced soybeans. The dominant region was
the Northwest, followed by the increasing importance of the Center-West
zone followed by the South-West region (see Graph 7.2). Even the metropolitan area of Porto Alegre in 2016 produced some 267,000 tons of
soybeans. But for all the soybean plantings throughout the state, the big
producers were highly concentrated by mesoregion and more particularly
by *município* in the state in 2015 (see Map 7.2).

Like soybeans, most regions produced some rice, although the
Northwest mesoregion produced no rice at all. But essentially production
involved four of the regions, all grouped in areas where soybeans had no

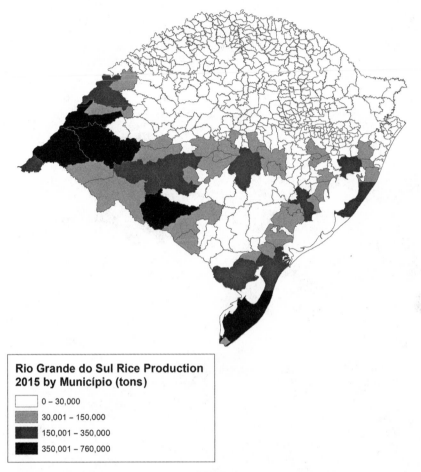

MAP 7.3: Rio Grande do Sul rice production (tons) by *município* in 2015

significant representation, with the metropolitan region of Porto Alegre, the Southwest and the Southeast accounting for 85% of production in 2016 (see Graph 7.3 and Map 7.3).

Within the state, tobacco was produced everywhere except in the Southwest, but its principal center was the Center-East mesoregion and its municipalities (see Graph 7.4 and Map 7.4).

Of the permanent crops, grapes were the most important for the economy of the state and were concentrated in the Northwest and Northeast mesoregions, with the former dominating. From 1990 to 2016 there was a steady increase in production at the rate of 2% per

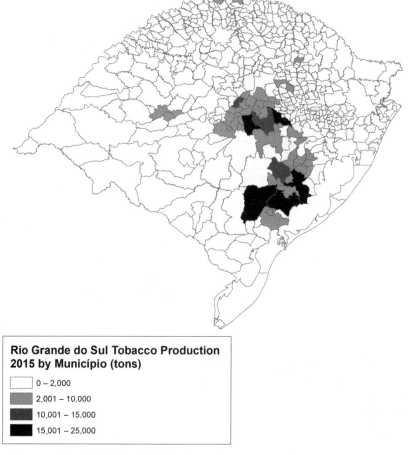

**Rio Grande do Sul Tobacco Production
2015 by Município (tons)**

☐ 0 – 2,000

▨ 2,001 – 10,000

▨ 10,001 – 15,000

■ 15,001 – 25,000

MAP 7.4: Rio Grande do Sul tobacco production (tons) by *município* in 2015

annum, but there was little change in geographic distribution of the crop, with the Northwest being the most prominent producer and accounting for 87% of grape production in 1990 and 86% in 2015 (see Map 7.5).

Among the pastoral products the most important economically was cattle, whose production was well distributed in all the mesoregions of the state, though with virtually no change in the size of the herds, which remained at 2 million head for this entire twenty-five-year period from 1990 to 2016 (see map 7.6)

The other important product of the pastoral sector was chickens, which were concentrated primarily in three districts: the two Northern

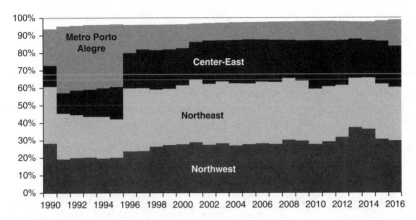

GRAPH 7.5: Distribution of poultry by the mesoregions of Rio Grande do Sul, 1990–2016
Source: IBGE, SIDRA, PAM, table 3939

mesoregions, the Center-East and the Porto Alegre Metropolitan region – altogether accounting for over 90% of the stock of birds in most years (see Graph 7.5). The other districts had only quite small stocks of the birds.

Though produced everywhere in the state, the most important region of milk production is the Northwest region, which is also the most important for Soybeans (see Graph 7.6).[61]

Because of differing crop mixes there were also important differences in size of holdings in these various mesoregions. But in general compared with Mato Grosso this is a region with one of the more equal land distributions in Brazil. The Northwest – the dominant soybean production region – and the Center-East had the lowest Gini (see Table 7.11).

In the crucial seasonal crops, here being soybeans, tobacco, rice and corn, the Gini indices are almost identical in their distribution by mesoregion, though in each case smaller than the entire farm and pastoral sector (see Table 7.12).

In general, the ranching sector, except for the Northwest, shows slightly higher Gini numbers than the seasonal croplands. The region with the largest number of large estancias is the Southwest, which in 2006 had 5% of the ranches with over 1,000 hectares and these large

---

[61] Tanice Andreatta, Ana Monteiro Costa, Rosani Marisa Spanevello, Patrícia da Rosa Leal and Adriano Lago, "Perspectivas e desafios da atividade leiteira no município de Jóia, Rio Grande do Sul: apontamentos a partir da visão dos produtores," *53rd Congresso da SOBER* (João Pessoa, 2015).

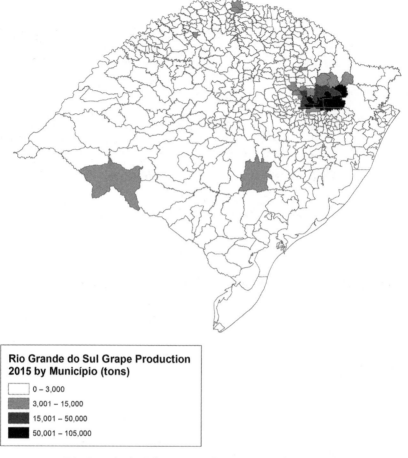

**Rio Grande do Sul Grape Production
2015 by Município (tons)**

☐ 0 – 3,000

▨ 3,001 – 15,000

▨ 15,001 – 50,000

■ 50,001 – 105,000

MAP 7.5: Rio Grande do Sul grape production (tons) by *município* in 2015

units held 48% of the total lands. The nearest competitor was the Center-West, where only 1% of the ranches were of this size and they contained just 27% of the land (See Table 7.13).

As this survey has shown, Rio Grande do Sul was the classic commercial small farming sector in Brazil, which has the highest ratio of producer coops of any state in the nation and a long history of organized response to the market. Some 68% of the farms were members of syndicates or producer coops and they accounted for 72% of the lands in the state. Many of these associations and cooperatives go back to the 1910s and 1920s. By 1930 there were seventy commercial, agricultural and pastoral

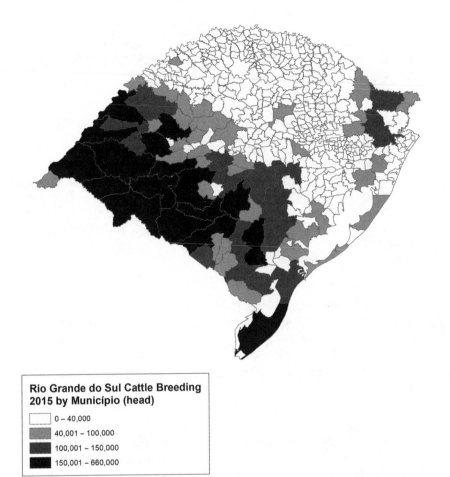

MAP 7.6: Rio Grande do Sul cattle production (head) by *município* in 2015

associations in the state.[62] But growth was even more dramatic in later years, and by the 1950s there were some 700 agricultural cooperatives in the state.[63] Not only did these cooperatives cut out middlemen and increase income of the farmers, but they played key roles in providing technical information and agricultural education for their members. But other key players have also enabled small farms to create integrated clusters of production of given products. These have included not only

[62] Love, *Rio Grande do Sul*, pp. 222–223.
[63] Falkembach, "Dinâmica social e cooperativismo," p.113.

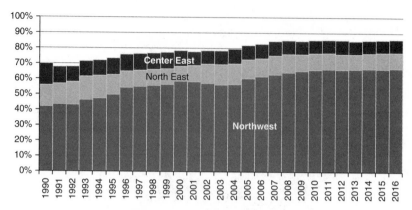

GRAPH 7.6: Ratio of milk production by mesoregion, Rio Grande do Sul, 1990–2016
Source: IBGE, SIDRA, PPM, table 74

the big cooperatives, but agro-industrial corporations such as the *frigoríficos*, and even the major supermarket chains.[64] Also important were government microcredit programs of support for small farmers, which had a major impact on the state's farms.[65] Thus the small farmers of the state had access to market information and the latest in technical information about farming. In many ways Rio Grande do Sul is thus the ideal model for showing how small farmers can be integrated into the market.

But of course this was because of a farm population that was educated and thus could absorb the technical information made available to the farmers by both state and the private sector. It is estimated that only 7% of the farm owners or managers in the state were illiterate, compared to 34% for Brazil as a whole. Interestingly enough the farm owners or managers who had a higher level of education (technical secondary, secondary, or university or technical college) represented only 11% of the state farmers or managers, which was close to the national average. The two states which were unusual in terms of highly educated farmers were São Paulo where 30% of farm owners or managers had such a level of education, and

[64] Renato S. Maluf, "Mercados agroalimentares e a agricultura familiar no Brasil: agregação de valor, cadeias integradas e circuitos regionais," *Ensaios FEE*, 25, no. 1 (2004): 307–308.
[65] Flávio Sacco dos Anjos et al. "Agricultura familiar e políticas públicas: impacto do PRONAF no Rio Grande do Sul," *Revista de Economia e Sociologia Rural*, 42, no. 3 (2004): 529–548.

TABLE 7.11: *Land distribution, all farming units by land area in the macroregions of Rio Grande do Sul in 2006*

ALL FARMS	Northwest		Northeast		Center-West		Center-East		Metro Area		Southwest		Southeast	
	Farms	Hectares	Farms	Hectares	Farms	Hectares	Farms	Hectares	Farms	Hectares	Farms	Hectares	Farms	Hectares
0.1–1 ha	4,585	1,684	553	226	1,261	405	1,686	601	2,169	786	352	127	613	248
1–5 ha	31,120	84,117	5,338	15,036	5,054	12,746	14,342	40,237	15,373	40,175	2,088	5,079	5,599	14,909
5–10 ha	36,483	252,645	6,600	46,375	4,255	28,934	14,178	98,776	12,402	84,406	1,646	11,244	5,885	40,623
10–20 ha	53,733	736,999	10,830	151,086	6,263	87,297	15,960	218,158	13,643	184,748	2,563	36,200	9,571	133,942
20–50 ha	40,273	1,176,642	10,243	304,050	7,561	228,662	9,771	276,717	9,330	266,901	5,290	156,130	12,199	358,528
50–100 ha	9,765	647,373	2,774	185,025	2,964	201,073	1,606	107,801	2,310	153,921	2,383	167,530	3,578	244,130
100–200 ha	3,857	512,604	1,350	182,202	1,608	218,063	705	94,633	1,076	143,735	1,951	271,697	2,053	281,271
200–500 ha	2,440	740,897	1,147	346,578	1,351	410,760	538	165,174	791	239,953	2,399	762,842	1,806	549,621
500–1,000 ha	784	515,201	400	271,793	540	370,543	189	128,632	290	195,204	1,523	1,054,837	782	531,035
1,000–2,500 ha	295	428,337	154	213,899	259	366,431	90	124,919	144	208,931	995	1,480,728	380	549,570
>2,500 ha	43	203,300	29	121,831	51	201,496	20	82,653	49	227,058	243	936,339	91	391,655
Total*	183,378	5,299,799	39,418	1,838,101	31,167	2,126,410	59,085	1,338,301	57,577	1,745,818	21,433	4,882,753	42,557	3,095,532
Gini	0.659		0.715		0.771		0.674		0.756		0.767		0.767	

Source: IBGE, SIDRA, Censo Agropecuário, table 837
Notes: * Farm units without lands are excluded

TABLE 7.12: *Land distribution, all seasonal crop farms by land area in the macroregions of Rio Grande do Sul in 2006*

ALL FARMS	Northwest		Northeast		Center-West		Center-East		Metro area		Southwest		Southeast	
	Farms	Hectares	Farms	Hectares	Farms	Hectares	Farms	Hectares	Farms	Hectares	Farms	Hectares	Farms	Hectares
0.1–1 ha	1,283	543	97	39	235	98	439	190	436	177	17	7	135	67
1–5 ha	16,617	46,675	1,359	3,894	2,462	6,593	8,906	25,987	5,616	15,138	332	863	2,311	6,358
5–10 ha	21,381	148,001	1,734	12,380	2,454	16,675	9,453	65,414	5,225	35,359	311	2,159	2,956	20,466
10–20 ha	30,877	423,045	2,928	41,013	3,531	49,110	10,198	138,723	5,910	79,844	552	7,778	4,929	68,694
20–50 ha	24,913	736,261	2,589	76,416	4,189	125,244	6,119	172,143	4,303	122,590	1,042	29,605	5,339	153,959
50–100 ha	6,969	465,591	680	44,747	1,408	94,872	905	60,178	926	61,095	438	30,605	867	57,023
100–200 ha	2,899	385,193	322	43,923	715	97,421	375	50,192	381	51,090	433	60,714	339	45,503
200–500 ha	1,842	560,537	264	79,499	632	192,866	277	83,913	291	86,571	624	198,465	265	80,646
500–1000 ha	612	403,102	106	71,829	253	175,052	88	60,320	135	91,696	445	304,393	128	87,056
1,000–2,500 ha	235	336,802	42	57,725	140	195,140	34	44,521	53	78,105	285	422,705	97	141,079
>2,500 ha	34	166,428	4	13,906	23	95,922	7	28,389	21	92,550	75	303,837	44	224,129
Total*	107,662	3,672,178	10,125	445,371	16,042	1,048,993	36,801	729,970	23,297	714,215	4,554	1,361,131	17,410	884,980
Gini	0.675		0.703		0.764		0.623		0.736		0.745		0.755	

Source: IBGE, SIDRA, Censo Agropecuário, table 837
Notes: * Farm units without lands are excluded

TABLE 7.13: *Land distribution, all ranches by land area in the macroregions of Rio Grande do Sul in 2006*

Size	Northwest		Northeast		Center-West		Center-East		Metro Area		Southwest		Southeast	
	Ranches	Hectares	Ranches	Hectares	Ranches	Hectares	Ranches	Hectares	Ranches	Hectares	Ranches	Hectares	Ranches	Hectares
0.1–1 ha	2,450	866	220	85	551	183	922	300	1,119	371	256	89	304	119
1–5 ha	11,997	31,329	1,692	4,552	2,021	4,956	4,049	10,640	5,280	13,248	1,466	3,563	2,309	6,095
5–10 ha	13,306	92,397	1,868	12,921	1,562	10,681	3,576	25,384	3,615	24,844	1,190	8,115	2,264	15,602
10–20 ha	20,822	286,296	3,277	45,908	2,403	33,604	4,560	62,794	4,188	57,186	1,872	26,538	3,789	53,552
20–50 ha	14,081	404,024	3,913	118,980	3,058	93,886	2,900	82,846	3,051	89,305	4,032	120,427	5,938	177,845
50–100 ha	2,573	167,350	1,450	98,870	1,461	99,827	548	37,505	1,020	68,678	1,881	132,596	2,479	171,170
100–200 ha	889	118,481	844	114,339	859	115,826	283	38,211	562	75,982	1,468	204,355	1,587	217,854
200–500 ha	553	167,315	759	230,101	697	211,727	234	73,045	406	122,638	1,739	553,113	1,413	429,675
500–1,000 ha	163	105,962	254	172,908	283	193,129	88	60,183	122	79,492	1,063	740,063	556	375,206
1,000–2,500 ha	57	87,222	82	113,764	118	170,291	51	73,213	66	91,725	696	1,038,438	238	341,463
>2,500 ha	9	36,871	17	71,722	28	105,574	6	24,823	12	52,521	166	624,280	32	98,395
Total*	66,900	1,498,113	14,376	984,150	13,041	1,039,684	17,217	488,944	19,441	675,990	15,829	3,451,577	20,909	1,886,976
Gini	0.608		0.729		0.767		0.732		0.773		0.764		0.734	

Source: IBGE, SIDRA, Censo Agropecuário, table 837
Notes: * Farm units without lands are excluded

Mato Grosso do Sul where a quarter of the owners and managers had such degrees.[66] This would suggest that a good basic level of education is necessary to produce such a managerial class, and that it was the large farms that tended to employ or were run by highly educated farm owners and managers.

Finally it is worth noting that the early colonization of the state and its elimination of a frontier by early in the twentieth century, combined with a dense and growing population and a thriving commercial agriculture, has led to a tight land market. At the same time, older methods of farming have caused major soil erosion in several parts of the state. For all these reasons good farming lands are expensive and not readily available. This explains the late twentieth-century migration of younger gaucho families to Mato Grosso seeking cheaper virgin lands to cultivate. The opening up of the roads to Mato Grosso in the 1970s and the federal government colonization program provided the incentive for these well educated and capitalized farmers from Rio Grande do Sul to migrate to this new frontier with extensive and cheap lands in which they could cultivate traditional crops such as corn and soybeans.

[66] IBGE, SIDRA, Agro, table 801.

8

São Paulo

As of the second decade of the twenty-first century São Paulo is still the preeminent agricultural state of Brazil. It was here that the coffee economy came to full development and it was coffee that dominated Brazilian exports until late in the twentieth century. It was the capital generated by coffee which fomented the economic and social development of the state. It was the coffee barons and immigrant capitalists who developed this state into Brazil's most important industrial and financial center by the second half of the twentieth century. To this day, the state is the leading agricultural, industrial and service center for the nation, and its capital city is not only the largest urban center in Brazil but is also the fourth largest metropolis in the world. Although coffee has declined in the past half century, São Paulo still dominates the production of permanent crops, such as coffee and oranges, and has expanded in seasonal crops as well. In this recent period it would also become the world's largest sugarcane producer and the leading maker of sugar and ethanol, with the creation of the most modern sugar refining industry in the world, as well as an important center of soybean production. Yet despite the continued importance of its agriculture, São Paulo has one of the lowest ratios of rural to urban population in the nation.

In the colonial period São Paulo was a marginal region with only a modest sugar industry, was dominated by subsistence agriculture and contained a small population living close to the coast. In the early decades of the nineteenth century its sugar economy slowly expanded and from the 1850s onward it began to produce coffee. But the production of these two crops was still relatively minor compared to the neighboring province of Rio de Janeiro, though the state developed a thriving plantation economy based on slave labor. The rapid expansion into the western frontier after the arrival of the railroads in the 1870s opened up the best interior lands, and by the end of the century São Paulo had come to dominate national coffee production. By 1889 it was producing 1.9 million bags of coffee, which represented 38% of the national total. By the late 1920s output was at 17 million bags and the state now accounted for 63% of national production.[1]

This booming economy permitted the state to bring in several million European and Asian immigrants to replace slave labor after emancipation in 1888. The resulting large free wage economy provided an incentive for the emergence of early industry. Growth thereafter was constant and by the second half of the twentieth century the state of São Paulo had become the leading industrial and agricultural producer in the nation, with a population double the size of any other state. This in turn made it attractive for internal migrants, and from the 1920s onward an increasing flow of migrants from the Northeast of Brazil entered the state, so that by the census of 1991 some 24% of the resident state population had been born outside the state.[2] By the census of 2010 the state contained 41 million persons, which represented 22% of the national population, and had a population density of 166 persons per km², the second most densely populated state in the nation.[3]

In 1960 its population of 12.9 million represented 18% of the national population.[4] Although São Paulo still had the largest foreign-born population of any state in Brazil, they made up just 6% of the state population.[5] It was also 83% white, compared to only 61% of the national population which was in this category in 1960.[6] Although the state's population at mid century were leaders in declining mortality and a slow-declining fertility, its population structure in 1960 differed little from the other regions of Brazil. Its high birth and death rates created the same pyramid structure of age distributions as found in all the other states and in the nation as a whole.

But here as well, fertility rates dropped dramatically as did rates of mortality after 1960. By 2010 the demographic transition had occurred in the state, with very low birth rates, which, combined with a significant

---

[1] For the economic history of the state see the two volumes of Francisco Vidal Luna and Herbert S. Klein, *Slavery and the Economy of São Paulo, 1750–1850* (Stanford, Calif.: Stanford University Press, 2003) and *The Economic and Demographic History of São Paulo 1850–1950* (Stanford, Calif.: Stanford University Press, 2017).

[2] IBGE, SIDRA, table 631, found at https://sidra.ibge.gov.br/tabela/631.

[3] IBGE, SIDRA, table 2094 and 1298.   [4] IBGE, SIDRA, table 1286.

[5] *Censo Demográfico de 1960*, Série Nacional, vol. 1, tomo xiii, table 6.   [6] Ibid., table 5.

TABLE 8.1: *São Paulo: size and share of rural population and sex ratio of population by residence, 1970–2010*

Census year	Rural population	% total population	Sex ratio Urban	Sex ratio Rural
1960	47,79,429	37%	97.0	111.2
1970	34,93,173	20%	98.3	112.9
1980	28,45,178	11%	98.5	112.5
1991	22,74,064	7%	96.7	112.1
2000	24,49,434	7%	95.1	109.8
2010	16,75,429	4%	93.9	119.0

Source: IBGE, SIDRA, table 200; and for 1960, IBGE, Censo Demográfico de 1960, Série Regional v.1 t.xiii, table 2

decline in infant and adult mortality rates, led to a modern age structure. The result was the classic jar-shaped post-transition model. Whereas the population fourteen and under represented 38% of the state population in 1960, they represented just 21% of the population in 2010.

But the state was already unusual by Brazilian standards in 1960 in that only 37% of the population was rural, well below the 53% rural national average in that year. Moreover this population consistently declined from 1960 onward and has currently reached one of the lowest rates in Brazil of only 4% rural in 2010, compared to the national average of 16%. However, the state was typical in its distribution of men and women in the rural and urban areas. Men persistently outnumber women in the rural area, and women are more numerous than men in the urban centers of the state in all census years (see Table 8.1).

São Paulo also had the highest rate of literacy of any state by 1950, when it finally passed Rio Grande do Sul as the most literate state in the nation.[7] Whereas in Brazil 43% of the population over the age of five was literate in that year, the figure for São Paulo was 59%. By 1950 the majority of both men (65%) and women (54%) in the state were literate, in contrast to the rest of the country which would not have a majority of women and men who were literate until the census of 1960. Of course the urban literacy rate was much higher than the rural one. In 1960 the urban

---

[7] The rate was 59.4% literates for the total population for São Paulo and 58.6% for Rio Grande do Sul. IBGE, *Recenseamento Geral de 1950*, Série Nacional, vol. 1 "Censo Demográfico" (Rio de Janeiro, 1956), p. 90, table 47.

population was 69% literate and the rural population was 44% literate
(rural men were 49% literate and rural women were 44% literate).[8] But
even this slowly changed over time, and by the census of 1991, 77% of the
rural population five years of age and older were literate, while the urban
literacy rate was 87%. For the country as a whole the rural literacy rate
was 54%.[9] By the agricultural census of 2006, only 6% of the farm
owners or managers were illiterate (compared to a national average of
30%). This high literacy rate and the rather technical nature of sugar
farming may explain the unusually high rates of farm owners and managers of the state who had a technical education. A surprising 30% of the
227,622 farm owners or managers in the state had higher level education
(technical secondary, secondary, or university or technical college) – compared to 10% of national farmers and managers. Of course the larger the
farm size, the higher the percentage of well-educated owners and managers. Thus over half of those who ran farms of 100 hectares or above in
São Paulo held these advanced degrees. But even around 20% of the
owners and managers of small farms (from a half hectare to 20 hectares)
were highly educated as well, while the ratio exceeded a third for farms
between 20 and 100 hectares.[10]

São Paulo remains the leader nationally in terms of the total value of
agricultural production, though second-ranking Mato Grosso is slowly
approaching the value of São Paulo's agricultural output. But there have
been profound changes in the recent agricultural development of the state.
Traditionally the leading coffee state in the nation, coffee is no longer
a dominant crop in the mix of the state's agricultural production, and its
traditional leadership in national coffee production has been eroded as
well.

It was also one of the earliest states to apply modern technology to crop
production, though as of 1960 only an estimated 22% of agricultural
lands were using modern agricultural inputs, and these were mostly for
food crops.[11] Already coffee was being replaced by a host of other products, but above all by sugarcane. In the past forty years São Paulo has

[8] *Censo Demográfico de 1960*, Série Nacional, vol. 1, tomo xiii, table 10.
[9] *Censo Demografico de 1991*, "População residente de 5 anos ou mais por situação
     (urbana e rural), segundo a alfabetização," found at www.ibge.gov.br/home/estatistica/
     populacao/censodem/tab203.shtm.
[10] IBGE, SIDRA, Agro, table 801.
[11] Geraldo Müller, *A Dinâmica da Agricultura Paulista* (São Paulo: SEADE, 1985), 56,
     table 19. These modern crops included sugar, cotton, potatoes, oranges, eggs and toma-
     toes, but did not include coffee. Ibid., 49.

emerged as a world leader in the production of sugarcane and the milling of sugar and ethanol. It is also the world's leading exporter of orange juice, and in several over products it is Brazil's premier producer. Despite the shock of the 1980s and 1990s caused by the loss of price supports, subsidized government credit and the end of protected markets, it has been able to recuperate and grow quite impressively after 2000.[12] The shock affected local agriculture, which (excluding agribusiness) declined in the late 1980s, accounting for only 3.5% of the state's GDP. But by 2002 it was back up to 7.8% and by 2015 it reached 12% of the state's GDP.[13]

But already in the 1970s and early 1980s São Paulo had revamped and modernized its sugar milling industry and brought it up to world standards.[14] Ethanol now became a major byproduct of sugarcane milling and, with major support from the government, Brazil became a world leader in production and consumption of this biofuel. Because of massive private and state investment, São Paulo has retained its dominant position as a producer of sugarcane and distiller of ethanol, and its complex production and distilling activity has continued to grow in the twenty-first century. Moreover, while the growth of sugarcane plantations in the Center-West region has reduced its share of total national production, the state still dominates the refining industry. Most of the major mills are in São Paulo, and in the harvest of 2015/2106 São Paulo was grinding about two-thirds of the sugar produced nationally, and had been at that percentage for the past five harvests as well.[15] It is also estimated that its 15 largest *usinas* account for 35% of ethanol production in 2010.[16]

In most years sugar and its derivative ethanol is the most valuable export for the state. In 2016 for example, it was São Paulo's leading

---

[12] César Roberto Leite da Silva and Sérgio Antonio dos Santos, "Política agrícola e eficiência econômica: o caso da agricultura paulista," *Pesquisa & Debate. Revista do Programa de Estudos Pós-Graduados em Economia Política*, 12, no. 2 (20) (2001): 66–82.

[13] José Sidnei Gonçalves, "Dinâmica da agropecuária paulista no contexto das transformações de sua agricultura," *Informações Econômicas, SP*, 35, no. 12 (Dec. 2005): 67.

[14] On the modernization of the *usinas* in this period see Marili Arruda Mariotoni, "O desenvolvimento tecnológico do setor sucroalcooleiro no estado de São Paulo (1975–1985)" (MA thesis, Universidade Estadual de Campinas, 2004).

[15] Unicadata|produção|histórico de produção e moagem|por safra, found at www .unicadata.com.br/historico-de-producao-e-moagem.php?idMn=32&tipoHistorico=4.

[16] Ricardo Castillo, "Região competitiva e circuito espacial produtivo: a expansão do setor sucro-alcooleiro (complexo cana-de-açúcar) no território brasileiro" (2009), pp. 1–7, found at www.observatoriogeograficoamericalatina.org.mx/egal12/Geografiasocioecon omica/Geografiaespacial/60.pdf.

export product, followed by airplanes. In that year São Paulo exported US\$ 5.1 billion worth of sugar, and if derivatives of sugarcane are added, the figure was US\$ 7.5 billion, or 17% of total state exports.[17] This total value of sugarcane product exports is close to the value of soybean exports from Mato Grosso. But it weighed far less in the context of overall São Paulo exports than did soybeans and their derivatives in Mato Grosso since the state exports were made up of manufactured goods, and was four times the total value of exports from Mato Grosso (see Table 8.2).

Although the state had once been a major center of producer cooperatives, there was a decline of these associations and centers in the crisis years of the 1990s. The 136 agricultural cooperatives operating in the state in 1992 had 164,000 farmers and was present in 242 municipalities, but the collapse of two key central associations (Cotia-CC and CC-Sul-Brasil) in this period led to a major reorganization and reduction of the system to 127 coops and half the numbers of members, but now more economically secure and some, like those in milk, becoming major industrial producers as well.[18] Though such milk coops were important both in São Paulo and Rio Grande do Sul, they are nowhere as dominant in milk production as in the United States. In the United States 83% of milk production comes from producer cooperatives, compared to between 20% and 40% in Brazil.[19] The state's farmers were about average for their membership in such cooperatives or producer syndicates by the time of the agricultural census of 2006, when some 29% of the farms with 48% of the farmlands were included in such institutions. This was well below the association rates in Rio Grande do Sul which had 68% of the farms and 72% of the lands in coops and syndicates, but above that of Mato Grosso, which had a higher ratio than São Paulo of farms in such associations, but these farms only accounted for 30% of the farmlands.[20].

In the last quarter of the twentieth century large sugar estates came to dominate state agriculture, replacing in importance the formerly

[17] MDIC, "Exportação Brasileira, São Paulo, Principais Productos, 2016," found at www.mdic.gov.br/comercio-exterior/estatisticas-de-comercio-exterior/balanca-comercial-brasileira-unidades-da-federacao.

[18] Sigismundo Bialoskorski Neto and Waldemar Ferreira Júnior, "Evolução e Organização das Cooperativas Agropecuárias Paulistas na Década de 90," Paper given at the XLII Congresso da Sociedade Brasileira de Economia e Sociologia Rural 2004.

[19] Fabio Ribas Chaddad, "Cooperativas no agronegócio do leite: mudanças organizacionais e estratégicas em resposta à globalização," *Organizações Rurais & Agroindustriais*, 9, no. 1 (2011): 70.

[20] IBGE, SIDRA, Agro, table 840.

TABLE 8.2: *Value of principal agricultural products exported from São Paulo and Mato Grosso in 2016*

	São Paulo			Matto Grosso	
Products	Value in US$	% of total value	Products	Value in US$	% of total value
Sugar, alcohol, ethanol, etc.	7,761,120,795	16.8%	Soybeans & derivatives	7,636,129,597	60.7%
Oranges & orange juices	1,950,515,245	4.2%	Corn	2,407,526,297	19.1%
Beef & Derivatives	1,669,063,612	3.6%	Beef & derivatives	993,089,211	7.9%
Soybeans & derivatives	1,181,555,989	2.6%	Cotton	854,207,230	6.8%
Coffee	671,666,609	1.5%	Chicken meat	210,143,604	1.7%
Chicken meat	327,422,942	0.7%	Woods	139,848,636	1.1%
Kraft paper	143,005,428	0.3%	Pork meat	88,554,837	0.7%
Mostly non-agricultural exports	32,501,638,365	70.3%	Mostly non-agricultural exports	259,120,250	2.1%
Total value of all exports	46,205,988,985	100.0%	Total value of all exports	12,588,619,662	100.0%

Source: MDIC, "Exportação Brasileira, Principais Produtos, 2016"

dominant coffee fazendas.[21] Although these new sugar estates are quite large, the structure of landholding in the state looks rather more like Rio Grande do Sul than Mato Grosso. Thus, despite a continuing expanding agriculture, the basic structure of land ownership in the rural area has changed little since the 1960s, when coffee was still a significant state crop. As in most of Brazil, in the period 1960 to 2006 there was a decline in both the number of farms (a decline of 29%) and in total lands (a decline of 12%). But there were also changes in the share of the smallest and largest properties. Farms of less than 100 hectares went from owning 28% of the agricultural lands to 23% of all rural lands, and units of over 1,000 hectares increased their share from 31% to 36% of all lands in the period from 1960 to 2006. Although high compared to the 27% share of such estates in Rio Grande do Sul, this was still below the national average of 44%, and considerably below the 78% share of these large farms in Mato Grosso (see Table 8.3).[22]

By the second decade of the twenty-first century the major agricultural products of the state in terms of value were a few basic crops, primarily sugarcane, animals, animal products, soybeans, oranges and orange juice, coffee and corn (see Table 8.4). Already by 1990 Minas Gerais had passed São Paulo production as the nation's biggest coffee producer, and it accounted for 33% of the crop in that year compared to just a quarter coming from São Paulo. By the second decade of the twenty-first century São Paulo was down to 10% of the national crop and Minas Gerais alone now accounted for 51% of national production. Whereas São Paulo planted over a half a million hectares in 1990, twenty-five years later it used just 200,000 hectares for coffee trees.[23] But despite the decline in production from the peak period of the 1980s, São Paulo still maintained its lead as the nation's orange and orange juice processor despite a negative pattern of growth.

Initially there was a very rapid growth in this other significant permanent crop which it produced. Oranges had been a traditional crop in São Paulo since colonial times. But they were locally consumed as whole fresh

[21] On the decline of coffee production in the state see Vera Lúcia F. dos Santos Francisco, Celso Luis Rodrigues Vegro, José Alberto Ângelo and Carlos Nabil Ghobril, "Estrutura produtiva da cafeicultura paulista," *Informações Econômicas, SP*, 39, no. 8 (Aug. 2009: 42–8. On the transition from sugar to coffee see Thiago Franco Oliveira de Carvalho, "Modernização agrícola e a região da alta mogiana paulista análise da expansão da produção de cana-de-açúcar em uma tradicional região cafeeira" (MA thesis, Universidade Estadual Paulista "Júlio de Mesquita Filho," Rio Claro, 2014).
[22] IBGE, SIDRA, Agro, table 839.   [23] IBGE, SIDRA, PAM, table 1613.

TABLE 8.3: *Distribution of farms by size of land holding in São Paulo,*
1960–2006

1960		
Size	Units	Area (ha)
0.1–1 ha	3,159	2,147
1–5 ha	82,842	2,99,772
5–10 ha	59,759	461,376
10–20 ha	53,332	775,224
20–50 ha	59,900	1,925,596
50–100 ha	25,789	1,854,565
100–200 ha	15,595	2,191,622
200–500 ha	10,985	3,397,470
500–1,000 ha	3,547	2,500,335
1,000–2,000 ha	1,584	2,164,387
>2,000 ha**	902	3,731,454
Total*	317,394	19,303,948
Gini	0.787	
2006		
0.1–1 ha	11,981	4,205
1–5 ha	40,782	126,919
5–10 ha	31,562	242,783
10–20 ha	46,547	689,651
20–50 ha	46,332	1,473,605
50–100 ha	20,688	1,467,925
100–200 ha	13,036	1,834,340
200–500 ha	9,583	2,965,789
500–1000 ha	2,846	1,975,819
1000–2500 ha	1,470	2,235,513
>2500**	623	3,938,399
Total*	225,450	16,954,948
Gini	0.799	

Source: For 1960: *Censo Agrícola 1960* Serie Regional v2,t.xiv, pt1, table 1; for 2006: IBGE,
SIDRA, Agro, table 837
Notes: ** The 1960 and 2006 censuses use a different maximum number for the largest
farms, but this has no significant effect on Gini

TABLE 8.4: *Growth of major agricultural products in São Paulo 1970–2016*

Product	1970*	1975	1980	1985	1996	2006	2016	Annual growth rate
Sugarcane (metric tons)	30,340,214	34,565,920	7,2257,080	12,5,000,840	153,768,067	231,977,247	442,282,329	6.0%
Broiler chickens [galinhas] (head)		73,670,496.0	104,640,587	99,411,227.0	134,924,522	180,148,271.0	197,562,326.0	2.4%
Oranges (metric tons)		21,175,000	42,400,000	58.670,619	87,734,705	14,367,011	12,847,146	-1.6%
Cattle (head)	9,110,633	11,381,957	11,867,074	11,260,601	12,797,505	12,790,383	11,031,408	0.4%
Corn (metric tons)	2,124,791	2,146,337	2,218,031	2,495,239	3,544,100	4,378,380	4,592,671	1.7%
Soybeans (metric tons)**					1,234,300	1,648,100	2,791,872	4.2%
Cows Milk (1,000 liters)		1,331,984	1,844,122	1,781,004	1,985,388	1,744,008	2,556,274	1.6%
Bananas (metric tons)					57,055	1,175,768	1,089,820	15.9%
Eggs (1,000 dozens)		332,987	516,610	600,440	729,866	826,925	1,020,540	2.8%
Coffee (metric tons)	466,757	849,728	793,870	1,048,578	382,800	259,820	340,114	-0.7%

Notes: * No data exists for broiler chickens for 1970. Growth rates are adjusted for different time spans.
** The soybean numbers in Agro 34 did not agree with the data in the PAM series in table 1612, so we have used only the second series. In cases with any conflict in the numbers we have used the more updated PAM series in tables 1613 and 1612.
Source: Crops to 2006 found at IBGE; tables Agro34 and Agro73 found at http://seriesestatisticas.ibge.gov.br/lista_tema.aspx?op=o&no=1; for crops for 2015, IBGE, SIDRA tables 1612, and 74; and for all years for animals and animal products, IBGE, SIDRA, tables 281, 3939

fruit. Oranges were first exported to Argentina after 1920 and to Europe after 1930, though most of the crop was consumed nationally.[24] Until 1957 Rio de Janeiro was the leading producer in the nation, but in that year São Paulo passed it in total production and has increased its share every decade thereafter.[25] By 1972 São Paulo was growing over half the national oranges and by 1983 this proportion passed 80%. Most of the oranges produced up to this period went for local consumption and until the late 1960s some 90% of oranges were consumed nationally. But in 1962 São Paulo began to process whole oranges into juice when it produced 203,000 tons of concentrated orange juice. In that year the first modern orange juice processor, the Companhia Mineira de Conservas, was established in the São Paulo municipality of Bebedouro.[26] This company eventually became part of Frutesp, a government company and was later bought out by Dreyfus. A year later a German company in alliance with a local German immigrant grower set up Citrosuco, which would become both the nation's and the world's largest producer of orange juice of all kinds by the end of the century. In 1967 Brazilians established Sucocítrico Cutrale which would become Brazil's second largest producer. The periodic crisis of freezes in Florida, especially those in the late 1970s and early 1980s, reduced US output of juice significantly and gave Brazil an opportunity to become a major international market participant. Once achieving this foothold, Brazil quickly outpaced US production. By 1975 Brazil controlled over half the world exports of orange juice, compared to the US share of only 17%, and even in total production of oranges it surpassed the USA as of the 1981/1982 harvest.[27]

The orange processors are distinct from the orchard owners. This value chain vertical system involves the processing companies providing credit to the farmers, the shipping of juices in special tank trucks and specially

---

[24] Sarah Silveira Diniz, Marcia Regina Gabardo da Câmara, Marcelo Ortega Massambani, João Amilcar Rodrigues Anhesini and Umberto Antonio Sesso Filho, "Analise espacial da produtividade da Laranja dos municípios do estado de São Paulo: 2002 a 2010," *50 Congresso da SOBER 2012*, p. 2.

[25] Luis Fernando Paulillo, ed., *Agroindústria e Citricultura no Brasil: Diferenças e Dominâncias* (Rio de Janeiro: Editora E-papers, 2006), p. 75.

[26] One of the fruit packing houses in Bebedouro is sometimes cited as being the first producer of juice as early as the 1950s, but the first modern plant is recognized as the Mineiro one in 1962.

[27] The standard survey of the modern history of the industry is Ronaldo Sued, *O desenvolvimento da agroindústria da laranja no Brasil: o impacto das geadas na Flórida e na política econômica governamental* (Rio de Janeiro: Fundação Getúlio Vargas, 1993), see especially chaps. 1 and 2.

equipped ocean vessels, and managing international sales and marketing.[28] Although considered to be highly efficient, this processing industry is highly concentrated. By the late 1980s four companies dominated the market. These were Citrosuco Paulista (with 28% of production in 1987) and Sucocítrico Cutrale (with 25% of orange juice). The two others were Cargill Agrícola S/A (15%) and the producer coop Coopercitrus Industrial Frutesp (7%). Even though there are currently 1,061 juice processing plants in São Paulo, these four firms control 94% of them.[29] Recently this concentration has increased and they have become multinationals. In 2012 Citrosuco bought out Citrovita, leaving just three large processors of juice, with Citrosuco now accounting for 40% of all juice exports.[30] In turn these major companies in the 1990s entered the US market by purchasing processing plants in Florida in order to get around US customs barriers. Cutrale bought Florida processing plants and became the primary supplier for the Minute Maid brand of Coca-Cola; in turn, Citrosuco took over major Florida plants and became the chief supplier of the Tropicana brand of Pepsi-Cola.[31]

These multinational companies with their international connections and highly capitalized plants and pipelines are in sharp contrast to the paulista sugar *usinas* which are typically the growers of the cane which they mill. This high level of industrial concentration has created a long-term tension between these few industrial processors and the large number of independent citrus growers. This tension has led to considerable judicial conflict, state action and local organization as growers try to balance their asymmetric relations with processors.[32]

---

[28] Marcos Fava Neves and Vinícius Gustavo Trombin, eds., *The Orange Juice Business: A Brazilian Perspective* (Wageningen: Springer Science & Business Media, 2012).

[29] Together the four big firms in 2010 owned 1,004 of them: Citrosuco (312), Cutrale (290); Deryfus (214) and Citrovita (188). Neves and Trombin, *The Orange Juice Business*, 19, 54.

[30] www.citrosuco.com.br/nossa-empresa.html.

[31] Chaddad, *The Economics and Organization of Brazilian Agriculture*, p. 106.

[32] Luiz Fernando Paulillo and Luiz Manoel de Moraes Camargo Almeida, "A coordenação agroindustrial citricola brasileira e os novos recursos de poder: dos politicos aos juridicos," *Organizações Rurais & Agroindustriais*, 11, no. 1 (2009): 11–27; Adelson Martins Figueiredo, Hildo Meireles de Souza Filho and Luiz Fernando de Oriani Paullilo, "Análise das margens e transmissão de preços no sistema agroindustrial do suco de laranja no Brasil," *Revista de Economia e Sociologia Rural*, 51, no. 2 (2013): 331–350; and Haroldo José Torres da Silva, "Estudo da viabilidade econômico-financeira da indústria de citros: impactos da criação de um conselho setorial" (PhD thesis, Escola Superior de Agricultura "Luiz de Queiroz," 2016).

TABLE 8.5: *Distribution of orange producers in São Paulo by number of trees,* 2009

Trees (×1,000)	Growers	% growers	% trees
<10	9,603	76.1%	13.4%
10–19	1,408	11.2%	8.0%
20–29	518	4.1%	5.3%
30–49	442	3.5%	7.0%
50–99	372	2.9%	10.8%
100–199	164	1.3%	9.0%
200–399	69	0.5%	7.4%
>400	51	0.4%	39.3%
Total	12,627	100.00%	100.00%

Source: Adapted from Table 14 in Neves & Trombin (2012), p. 63

The orange producers are far more fragmented and, despite their associations, the interaction between processors and growers is highly asymmetric. Growers are responsible for the production and delivery of the fruit to juice factories or packing houses, though they are given advance payments on their contracts with packers and factories.[33] In the crop year 2009/2010 the state had some 180.6 million orange trees, of which 9% were non-producing newly planted ones (up to two years of age), with production averaging around two boxes per tree.[34] Of these 12,627 farmers producing oranges, 76% of them had orange groves with less than 10,000 trees, but they accounted for only 13% of the total number of trees. In turn the 51 giant orchard owners, those with over 400,000 trees, were less than 1% of the farmers, but they had 39% of the trees (see Table 8.5).[35] This meant that despite the large ratio of small farmers, the distribution results in a Gini of 0.770, which was close to the norms in most crops farmed in São Paulo.

It is estimated that orange trees can produce fruit over a twenty-year period, but the norm is a bit higher in São Paulo than internationally. Since 2000 there has been a migration of producers within the state to the Southern regions. This migration was due to push and pull factors: the

[33] Neves and Trombin, eds., *The Orange Juice Business*, pp. 81, 85. [34] Ibid., p. 58.
[35] These figures include all of the state of São Paulo and a small adjacent section of the state of Minas Gerais which also produces oranges and is known as the Triângulo Mineiro district.

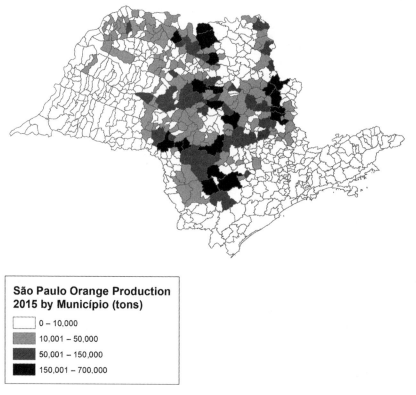

increasing cost of lands due to expansion of sugar in the older zones, better climatic conditions in the new areas, and also zones free from greening disease which had killed a significant number of trees. Three other tree diseases – citrus canker, citrus variegated chlorosis and citrus sudden death – in the first decade of the twenty-first century destroyed some 39 million trees in the traditional areas. In fact this was the third time that major plagues had affected orange production.[36] Exports stopped after a plague in 1937, and another one struck in 1957 and destroyed 300 million trees.[37] These plagues explains the fact that orange producers

---

[36] Diniz et al., "Análise espacial da produtividade da Laranja," pp. 3–4; Marcos Fava Neves and Vinícius Gustavo Trombin, "Mapping and quantification of the Brazilian citrus chain," *Fruit Processing* (Mar./Apr. 2012): 56.

[37] See IBGE, SIDRA, PAM, table 1613, and Neves and Trombin, eds., *The Orange Juice Business*, p. 55.

are the second greatest users of insecticides in Brazil after cotton growers, but they were only twelfth among crops in fertilizer usage.[38]

By 1990 São Paulo still accounted for 83% of the oranges grown in Brazil, which resulted in an output of 72 million tons of fruit gathered from 723,000 hectares of groves. Although production dropped to 12 million tons on just 413,000 hectares in the next quarter of a century, São Paulo was still the primary producing state and accounted for almost three-quarters of national production.[39] Recently production has increased and the estimate for the 2016/2017 crop year was for a production of 18 million tons of oranges. Brazil is the world's largest producer of oranges (accounting for 37% of world production in 2016/2017) and is the world's biggest exporter of orange juice (accounting for 62% of world's exports).[40] In turn, São Paulo producers accounted for 94% of all types of the nation's orange juice exports in the harvest of 2016/2017.[41] The leading orange-producing mesoregion in 2015 was Bauru which produced a fifth of the state's oranges, followed by Campinas, São José do Rio Preto, Ribeirão Preto, Itapetininga and Araraquara, which together accounted for 88%. This distribution can be seen in more detail in the orange production distribution by municipality (see Map 8.1).

Bananas were the third most important permanent crop produced in the state. São Paulo by 2015 was the second largest producer of bananas in Brazil and accounted for 15% of national production. But it was so close behind the leading producer, which was Bahia, that in some years in this century it has been the leading banana state in the nation. Moreover the productivity of banana production in São Paulo was double what it was in Bahia. Whereas Bahia and São Paulo were both producing 1.1 tons of bananas per hectare in 1990, by 2015 São Paulo was getting 20.1 tons per hectares from its banana trees while Bahia had only increased its yield to 14.1 tons per hectare.[42]

Despite their traditional importance, however, these permanent crops were absorbing an ever declining amount of land. While the state still had a significant amount of land in permanent crops compared to Rio Grande do Sul and Mato Grosso, their total volume of

---

[38] Neves and Trombin, "Mapping and quantification of the Brazilian citrus chain": 53.
[39] IBGE, SIDRA, PAM, table 1613.
[40] USDA, FAS, *Citrus: World Markets and Trade*, January 2017, pp. 7, 9.
[41] USDA, FAS, *Citrus Annual Brazil 2016*, GAIN Report Number: BR16020, 2/15/2016, p. 7.
[42] IBGE, SIDRA, PAM, table 1613.

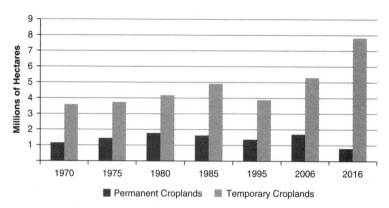

GRAPH 8.1: Growth of lands dedicated to permanent and temporary crops, São Paulo, 1970–2016
Source: IBGE, SIDRA, table 264; and for 2015 data tables 1612, 1613

land usage was in decline after the 1970 peak of 1.7 million hectares, going to half that rate (or just 803,000 hectares) in 2016 (see Graph 8.1). In the nation permanent crops had declined from 7.9 million hectares to 5.8 million in the same period. The big growth in the state, as in the rest of the nation, was in the expansion of seasonally planted (temporary) crops which in São Paulo went from using 3.6 million hectares in 1970 to using 7.8 million in 2016.[43] At the same time the size of these paulista farms differed significantly with the 18,000 farms listed as using seasonal crops averaging 59 hectares and the 17,000 farms in the census which were growing permanent crops averaging just 23 hectares.[44]

All this change in agricultural land usage by type of crops was due to the extraordinary expansion of sugarcane growing, which currently is the dominant product of the state in terms of value and land usage. But this was not the case historically. Throughout the second half of the nineteenth and most of the twentieth century the state imported the majority of its refined sugar from Pernambuco. The state did produce sugarcane, but in the 1920s plagues almost wiped out local plantings and only the importation of new plague-resistant plants from Java

---

[43] IBGE, SIDRA, table 264 for data from 1970 to 2006 and for 2015 data tables 1612, 1613.
[44] IBGE, SIDRA, table 1112.

(Indonesia) revived this industry by the end of the decade.[45] Next the crisis of sea transport which occurred as a result of World War II led to the relative decline of Pernambuco and increasingly São Paulo became self-sufficient in sugar.[46] Then in the 1950s São Paulo finally exceeded the sugar production of Pernambuco. Production costs were cheaper in São Paulo compared to Pernambuco, and the state even began exporting to the international market. This foreign market became far more open with the embargo carried out against Cuba by the United States in 1960. Brazil was given most of Cuba's quota of the sugar to be imported into the United States in 1962, first with the right to export 100,000 metric tons, a quota which the US increased in 1967 to 360,000 tons. In turn when Cuba created a new protected market in the socialist countries for cane sugar, their local beet sugar industries declined and their sugar consumption increased. Then when Cuban harvests failed, these markets were opened up to Brazilian exports. This boom primarily affected the sugar producers of São Paulo, rather than the older and relatively inefficient Northeastern plantations. By 1976 in fact, sugar became the single most valuable crop in São Paulo. In this boom period the size of sugar farms grew. Thus, for example in 1964 small producers accounted for 60% of cane brought to the mills but by 1970 these small farmers accounted for only 40% of the sugarcane. All of this growth put pressure on government control. The old Sugar and Alcohol Institute IAA (Instituto do Açúcar e do Alcool) founded by Vargas in 1933 in defense of small and medium producers had a quota system which required the mills to purchase 60% of their sugarcane from independent farmers. In the 1970s this quota system was temporarily abandoned, and under pressure from the new millers associations, the government slowly abandoned the quota system so that the mills progressively became producers as well. These mills were Brazilian-owned, often by immigrant entrepreneurs many of whom had gotten their start in coffee.[47]

---

[45] For a general survey of the developments of the paulista sugar industry to the 1970s see Mariotoni, "O desenvolvimento tecnológico do setor sucroalcooleiro no estado de São Paulo (1975–1985)," chap. 1.

[46] On the impact of the world war on cabotage shipping and its influence in shifting sugar production to the Southeast see Tamás Szmrecsányi and Eduardo Pestana Moreira, "O desenvolvimento da agroindústria canavieira do Brasil desde a Segunda Guerra Mundial," *Estudos Avançados*, 5, no. 11 (Apr. 1991): 57–79.

[47] Barbara Nunberg, "Structural change and state policy: the politics of sugar in Brazil since 1964," *Latin American Research Review*, 21, no. 2 (1986): 56–57.

Brazilian millers and growers responded to this opening of the international market by increasing sugar production through a whole series of technological and administrative reorganizations. First came the introduction of turbines to most of the mills, which by the harvest of 1960/1961 were averaging 100,000 to 200,000 sacks of sugar per harvest. Six years later, there were an increasing number of larger units among the ninety or so mills in production at that time, and these larger processors were generating on average 200,000–300,000 sacks of sugar, and there were even a few mills in this period that could produce over 1 million sacks per harvest.[48] A major event in this period was the founding in 1959 of the producers' cooperative, Copersucar (Cooperativa de Produtores de Cana-de-Açúcar, Açúcar e Álcool do Estado de São Paulo) by the amalgamation two local sugar producer cooperatives.[49] It began as a producers' association concentrating on marketing its members' sugar and alcohol. By the end of the decade, Copersucar represented 86% of the São Paulo millers and marketed over 90% of the state's sugar and alcohol production. It quickly evolved into a conglomerate providing everything from credit to owning distilleries, and was active in all aspects of the production process.[50] It also created a research branch which promotes technological change. It was Copersucar which is credited with increasing the productivity of the sugar mills by adopting the latest technology from other producing countries in a modernization program that began in 1973.[51] Thus the initial increase in yields was due to the modernization of the mills, and only later would yield increases come from new methods of planting and harvesting sugarcane. Finally the numerous local planters association in 1976 created a powerful growers association Orplana (Organização dos Produtores de Cana do Estado de São Paulo), which created another pressure group which sought changes in the traditional policies of the IAA in relation to production and milling of both sugar and alcohol. One result of all this pressure and the temporary sugar boom of the 1970s was that the IAA provided major government credit for the modernization and consolidation of the milling industry, which,

---

[48] Mariotoni, "O desenvolvimento tecnológico do setor sucroalcooleiro no estado de São Paulo," p. 31.

[49] Marcos Fava Neves, Allan W. Grayb and Brian A. Bourquard, "Copersucar: a world leader in sugar and ethanol," *International Food and Agribusiness Management Review*, 19, no. 2 (2016): 209.

[50] Nunberg, "Structural change and state policy": 63–64.

[51] On the role of Copersucar in modernizing the mills, see Mariotoni, "O desenvolvimento tecnológico do setor sucroalcooleiro no estado de São Paulo (1975–1985)."

combined with the technical changes promoted by Copersucar, succeeded in creating an efficient and productive system to replace the previous archaic organization. Many mills were closed and by the end of the 1970s small-scale mills (those producing less than 18,000 metric tons of sugar) were down to just 9% of all mills in all the country and by the end of the decade, output of the remaining mills doubled.[52]

Expansion was so rapid that the international market could not absorb all the sugar being exported from Brazil, and prices dropped significantly. This overproduction problem, a classic one for Brazil, led to calls for government support and intervention in the industry. Fortunately for the producers of the state, the world oil shock of 1973 occurred, which led the government to establish the Proálcool program in 1975 whose purpose was to promote sugar-produced ethanol as an alternative to gasoline. It did this by subsidizing increased plantings of sugarcane, encouraging the construction of ethanol distilleries at the side of the sugar mills (usinas) and forcing Petrobras, the government oil monopoly, to mix increasing quantities of ethanol in imported gasoline. Until this time alcohol production had been subservient to sugar in the output of the mills, but slowly this changed as demand for ethanol increased. The biggest impact of this program for producers was to create a whole new market for sugarcane.[53]

Although ethanol had been used in gasoline in Brazil since the 1930s and was important during World War II, this new program went even further and sought to encourage both private investment in distilling and create a guaranteed market for this biofuel. It also required Petrobras to purchase these new fuels and mix them with gasoline on a systematic basis – at this stage in concentrations under 20%, so engines did not need to be modified. But the Second World Oil Crisis of 1979 pushed the government to a new level of activity. Alcohol production goals were doubled, and the government encouraged the auto companies to create new ethanol engines. Biofuels were now increased to 25% in the admixture with gasoline, and massive credit enabled the construction of standalone alcohol distilleries or mills which could automatically switch between sugar and ethanol production, with the result that by 1980 alcohol production had doubled. That the long-term aims of the program succeeded is demonstrated by the figures for 2007, when there existed in the state 414

---

[52] Nunberg, "Structural change and state policy": 70–71, and table 7.
[53] Mariotoni, "O desenvolvimento tecnologico do setor sucroalcooleiro no estado de São Paulo," pp. 33–35.

mills processing cane, of which 248 were mixed *usinas* producing either sugar or ethanol, 151 autonomous distillers and 15 *usinas* producing just sugar.[54]

But in the late 1980s world petroleum prices were in a decline and the government abandoned its support for ethanol-only cars. In the late 1990s all prices were deregulated, and distillers were forced to control production because of the falling price of ethanol. World petroleum prices rose again after the terrorist attack on New York in 2001 and the subsequent Iraq War and the decline of Venezuelan oil production under Chavez, and the consequent increasing costs of Brazilian petroleum imports led to a new government program of ethanol support. Aside from promoting increased admixture of ethanol in gasoline and in diesel fuel, it also led to the introduction in 2003 of fuel flex motors for cars which could use any combination of ethanol or gas. This innovation created the modern open economy where ethanol could survive.[55] A reorganized state program in 2004 led to a major push to mix ethanol into previously excluded diesel engine cars. These now require 5% ethanol mixtures (compared to 25% in regular gasoline) and experimental activities have been undertaken to reduce the quantity of gasoline in these truck, farm machinery and electricity-producing engines.[56] All of these programs have proceeded in fits and starts, but by 2015 some 69% of the 36 million cars in Brazil were able to consume both products and the expectation is that in a decade all cars will be flex or run by natural gas or electricity.[57]

It was Copersucar which took most advantage of the first pro-alcohol program and by the 1980s it had over seventy *usinas* and five distilleries in

[54] Castillo, "Região competitiva e circuito espacial produtivo: a expansão do setor sucro-alcooleiro (complexo cana-de-açúcar) no território brasileiro," p. 3.

[55] Anil Hira and Luiz Guilherme de Oliveira, "No substitute for oil? How Brazil developed its ethanol industry," *Energy Policy*, 37 (2009): 2451–2454; and Antonio Carlos Augusto da Costa, Nei Pereira Junior and Donato Alexandre Gomes Aranda, "The situation of biofuels in Brazil: new generation technologies," *Renewable and Sustainable Energy Reviews*, 14 (2010): 3044.

[56] On these experiments, see Lauro Mattei, "Programa Nacional para Produção e Uso do Biodiesel no Brasil (PNPB): Trajetória, Situação Atual e Desafios," *BNB* [Banco Nordeste do Brasil], *Documentos Técnicos Científicos*, 41, no. 04 (2010): 731–740; and Fernando Ferrari Filho, "Análise de um motor do ciclo diesel operando no modo bicombustível: diesel / etanol"(MA thesis, PUC, Rio de Janeiro, 2011).

[57] UNICA, "Frota brasileira de autoveículos leves ... 2007–2015" accessed August 8, 2017, at www.unicadata.com.br/listagem.php?idMn=55. On the environmental impact of these pro-alcohol programs see José Goldemberg, Suani Teixeira Coelho and Patricia Guardabassi, "The sustainability of ethanol production from sugarcane," *Energy Policy*, 36 (2008): 2086–2097.

the Southern region and accounted for 61% of the alcohol produced in the state and 77% of the sugar. It had also created a research center in 1970 and by the 1980s this had gathered together a significant group of foreign engineers who promoted the introduction of the latest technological inventions. This group in turn was also closely associated with Dedini S.A. Basic Industries, the leading machinery manufacturer in the town of Piracicaba in the heart of the sugar zone. Dedini was founded in 1914 by an Italian engineer immigrant with experience in the Italian beet sugar industry. It then adopted the latest in French sugar milling technology and began producing small and medium-size milling plants. Starting with small mills and often reconditioned equipment, by the 1970s the company had accumulated enough experience to produce its first large mills ready for operation. Dedini today produces machinery for the production of sugar and ethanol (hydrated and anhydrous) and brandy. It can construct entire sugar refineries, cogeneration plants, plants for tanks, filtration systems and a host of other products for the industry. So advanced is its technology that it now licenses its designs for use in all types of industries.[58] But Dedini was not the only major supplier of machines. Another significant paulista producer of machines was Zanini Renk, a Brazilian company founded in 1976, which in 1983 created a joint company with the German manufacturer Renk AG. Since the 1970s these two major companies and several smaller ones have constructed approximately 200 independent distilleries and 200 co-generation mills capable of producing sugar or alcohol.[59] To maintain the state's major milling operations required a complex service and manufacturing sector which has been created by the big *usinas*. The majority of these services and the industries that build and provide replacement parts for the mills are found in the paulista regions of Piracicaba, Ribeirão Preto, Sertãozinho and Catanduva – a zone estimated to have some 500

---

[58] Mariotoni, "O desenvolvimento tecnólogico do setor sucroalcooleiro no estado de São Paulo," chap. 3; and Lara Bartocci Liboni, Luciana Oranges Cezarino, Michelle Castro Carrijo and Rudinei Toneto Junior, "The equipment supply industry to sugar mills, ethanol and energy in Brazil: an analysis based in leading companies and key-organizations of sector and of LPA of Sertãozinho," *Independent Journal of Management & Production*, 6, no. 4 (Oct.–Dec. 2015): 1070–1096.

[59] Lara Bartocci Liboni, Luciana Oranges Cezarino, Michelle Castro Carrijo and Rudinei Toneto Junior, "The equipment supply industry to sugar mills, ethanol and energy in Brazil: an analysis based in leading companies and key-organizations of sector and of LPA of Sertãozinho," *Independent Journal of Management & Production*, 6, no. 4 (Oct.–Dec. 2015): 1079–1080.

industrial and service companies, of which 90% are directly involved in the sugar-alcohol industry.[60]

Along with this technological revolution and systematic government support, there was also a major structural reorganization of production into vertically integrated sections. All the mills control their own cane lands or through long-term contracts have access to land of other owners. If the mills own the farms, this leads to a total vertical integration. A second arrangement is that the mill enters into a five-year contract or longer to rent the land of others and use it to produce cane. Finally there is a partnership or sharecropping arrangement called *parceria*, in which the farmer leaves the land prepared, and the mill plants and harvests the cane, and then divides the sugar output with the landowner. There are also variations on this with the *parceiro* growing the cane and the mill cutting, transporting and milling it. There are even spot producers who have no contract with the mills and sell on their own, though this is highly risky given the short life of cut cane.[61]

As production has grown, the mills which had been almost exclusively nationally owned have seen an increase in foreign ownership and the industry as a whole has become more complex. In the first decade of the twenty-first century major foreign companies and even foreign cooperatives entered the sugar and ethanol milling market of São Paulo. Bunge in 2006 acquired eight mills capable of turning out either sugar or ethanol. Dreyfus joined with a Brazilian company in 2009 to create Biosev with twelve mills. Royal Dutch Shell and a Brazilian company created Raizen with twenty-four mills and numerous other properties. Guarani with seven mills was bought by Tereos, a French beet sugar coop in conjunction with Petrobras, and finally Copersucar and Cargill created another milling and trading company called Alvean in 2014.[62] Copersucar itself with its forty-seven member mills also moved from being just a producer to

[60] Castillo, "Região competitiva e circuito espacial produtivo," pp. 1, 7.

[61] On the links created in this complex system, see Marco Antonio Conejero, Eduardo José Sia, Mairun Junqueira Alves Pinto, Ricardo Kouiti Santos Iguchi and Rafael Oliveira do Amaral, "Arranjos contratuais complexos na transação de cana à usina de açúcar e álcool: um estudo de caso no centro-sul do brasil," XXXII Encontro da ANPAS, 2008 (Rio de Janeiro), p. 5 accessed July 2, 2017, at www.anpad.org.br/adm in/pdf/GCT-D2072.pdf.

[62] Ben McKay, Sérgio Sauer, Ben Richardson and Roman Herre, "The politics of sugarcane flexing in Brazil and beyond," Transnational Institute (TNI) Agrarian Justice Program *Think Piece Series on Flex Crops & Commodities*, no. 4, September 2014, p. 6, table 2, "The Corporate Control of Brazilian Sugarcane," accessed July 2, 2017 at http://repub .eur.nl/pub/77677/Metis_202533.pdf.

becoming a transport company, and a trader reaching far into the world market. Finally the mills and cane farmers of the state also organized associations; the most important of these was ÚNICA (Associação das Usinas) founded in 1997 by 120 companies which are today responsible for more than 50% of ethanol output and 60% of the sugar produced in Brazil.[63]

By the end of this long process of investment and consolidation, multi-national companies controlled close to a third of the industry by 2011. But national players were still important and despite a series of crop failures, and changing government support policies, the industry has continued to advance in terms of modern agricultural practices. ÚNICA on its own has invested heavily in scientific research and worker education programs and has also pushed for all producers to adopt the latest sustainability practices.

Along with the growth of ÚNICA, Brazil's largest cooperative, Copersucar, has also been radically transformed into a new type of hybrid coop-corporation. In 2008 this newly reorganized entity called Copersucar SA concentrated all its capital on sugar and ethanol exports. Its União sugar brand was sold, Sara Lee bought its coffee processing plants and it spun off its successful Copersucar Technological Center (CTC) research center (founded in 1969 and the most advanced agricultural research center for sugar in the world) as an independent entity. It increased the number of its milling companies to forty-three, and by 2014 was producing 135 million tons of sugar and 4.9 billion liters of ethanol. By then it was producing alone 11% of world sugar exports and proposed to reach 30% of world total exports by the end of the decade. It also bought an American corn ethanol marketing company in 2012 and joined with Cargill to promote more international trading activities and built its own pipelines and port facilities.[64]

Along with new milling systems, new technology and new business structures, the sugar industry has revolutionized its production and cutting of cane in the past several decades. Burning of the *bagasse*, or remains of the plants, has declined and non-tillage planting has become the norm. As late as the harvest of 2006/2007, only 40% of the cane planted was cut

---

[63] Taís Mahalem do Amaral, Marcos Fava Neves and Márcia A. Dias de Moraes, "Cadeias produtivas do açúcar do estado de São Paulo e da França: comparação dos sistemas produtivos, organização, estratégias e ambiente institucional," *Agricultura São Paulo*, 50, no. 2 (2003): 70–71. Also see UNICA, "Histórico e Missão," accessed at www.unica .com.br/unica/?idioma=1.

[64] Chaddad, *The Economics and Organization of Brazilian Agriculture*, chap. 4.

by machines. This mechanization was part of an agreement made between the growers and the state of São Paulo, in which the growers committed themselves to mechanize the crop. In turn this mechanization reduced the number of workers cutting sugarcane from 260,000 to just half that number in the harvest of 2006/2007. Another major change has been the state prohibition of burning the cane stalks after harvest. In 2002 the state of São Paulo issued a decree proposing the slow decline of burning, to be replaced either by normal tilling over the stalks without plowing or by traditional plowing and this was eventually supported by ÚNICA. By the harvest of 2008/2009 the loading, transport and cultivation of sugarcane was 100% mechanized, and 40% of the cutting was done by machines. In fact there is a correlation between mechanization and the end of field burnings, with non-burned fields requiring cane cutting by machines.[65] By 2011 it was estimated that 60% of the mechanized and non-mechanized cane fields had moved to this new non-burning-of-*bagasse* system,[66] and by 2015 in the state of Sao Paulo some 85% of the cane was harvested by machines and only some 52,000 workers were employed in the industry.[67] The one area where there has been less development compared to other Brazilian crops is in the creation of new plants and seeds for sugarcane.

All of these developments resulted in the stimulation of sugar production throughout Brazil, but above all in São Paulo. Already by 1990 São Paulo produced 137 million tons of sugarcane (52% of the national total) and by 2015 it was up to 423 million tons, which was also well over half of national output. The amount of land planted in cane in 1990 was 1.8 million hectares and this increased to 5.6 million hectares twenty-six years later. Brazil is considered the lowest-cost producer of sugar in the world. The cost of producing a ton of sugar in São Paulo in 2007 was US$120 per ton, while in the US it was US$290 per ton.[68] It is also the

---

[65] Márcia Azanha Ferraz Dias de Moraes, "O mercado de trabalho da agroindústria canavieira: desafios e oportunidades," *Economia Aplicada* (Ribeirão Preto), 11, no. 4 (Oct./Dec. 2007): 607–611.

[66] Helena Ribeiro and Thomas Ribeiro de Aquino Ficarelli, "Queimadas nos canaviais e perspectivas dos cortadores de cana-de-açúcar em Macatuba, São Paulo," *Saúde Social* (São Paulo), 19, no. 1 (2010): 48–51.

[67] John Wilkinson, *O Setor Sucroalcooleiro Brasileiro na Atual Conjuntura Nacional e Internacional* (Rio de Janeiro: ActionAid, 2015), p. 11.

[68] Rosangela Aparecida Soares Fernandes and Cristiane Márcia dos Santos, "Competitividade das exportações sucroalcooleiras no Estado de São Paulo," *Anais do 4° ECAECO [Encontro Científico de Administração, Economia e Contabilidade] 2011*, vol. 1, no.1, p. 4; and and Beate Zimmermann and Jurgen Zeddies, "International

world's largest grower of sugarcane, and by the harvest of 2016/2017 São Paulo produced 366 million tons of cane, which it processed into 24.2 million metric tons of sugar and 13.5 billion liters of ethanol on 5.6 million hectares.[69] In this same harvest, São Paulo accounted for 77% of total national sugar exports.[70]

Along with growing sugarcane the state also became the nation's largest refiner of sugar and ethanol. Today it grinds over half of the sugar refined in Brazil, and produces over half of its ethanol from these same sugarcanes. In 1974 the state milled 39 million tons of sugarcane, whereas by 2016 it was cutting 442 million tons – for an annual growth rate of 5.9%.[71] Refined sugar output went from 4 million tons to almost 24 million tons by the harvest of 2016/2017, also for an annual growth rate of 4.9%. Total ethanol production also grew by 4.9% per annum, from 2.6 billion liters to 13 billion liters, in this same period from 1980/1981 to the harvest of 2016/2017.[72] Although growth of ethanol production in the Center-West region has reduced São Paulo's share of ethanol refining, it is still the leading state and accounts for 44% of this biofuel produced in Brazil.[73] Of the 1.3 billion liters of ethanol exported in 2016/2017, the refineries of São Paulo accounted for 97%.[74] In total Brazil produced 7 million gallons of biofuels in 2015, which accounted for 28% of the world's biofuels production from all sources.[75]

The fastest growing crops in the state in this period were sugarcane and its products, as well as bananas, followed by soybeans, eggs and corn.

Competitiveness of Sugar Production," Paper given at the 13th International Farm Management Congress, Wageningen, The Netherlands, July 7–12, 2002, p. 5 and found at http://econpapers.repec.org/paper/agsifmao2/.

[69] USDA, "2017 Sugar Annual Brazil" (Report BR17001, 4/28/2017). Unica estimates a slightly higher volume of total ethanol production for 2015/2016 at 14.5 billion liters. www .unicadata.com.br/historico-de-producao-e-moagem.php?idMn=31&tipoHistorico=2.

[70] UNICA, "Exportação anual de açúcar pelo brasil por estado de origem," accessed April 6, 2017, at www.unicadata.com.br/listagem.php?idMn=43.

[71] IBGE, SIDRA, table 1612.

[72] UNICA, Various production tables accessed April 6, 2017, for the period 1980/1981 to 2016/2017 by state at www.unicadata.com.br/historico-de-producao-e-moagem.php? idMn=32&tipoHistorico=4.

[73] Data from the harvest of 2016/2017 and that of 1980/1981 is found at UNICA, "Sugarcane, ethanol and sugar production," found at www.unicadata.com.br/.

[74] UNICA, "Exportação anual de etanol por estado brasileiro (mil litros) 2012/13 to 2015/ 16," accessed August 2, 2017, at www.unicadata.com.br/listagem.php?idMn=23.

[75] AFDC, "World Fuel Ethanol Production by Country or Region (Million Gallons)," accessed August 2, 2017, at www.afdc.energy.gov/uploads/data/data_source/10331/10 331_world_ethanol_production.xlsx.

Oranges, while still a major product in sales, have seen fairly wide swings in production from the 1980s to the present century, as did the broiler chickens. Of these crops and animal products the state was the dominant producer in Brazil of sugarcane, oranges, eggs (and of course it had the largest number of hens in Brazil), broiler chickens and peanuts. São Paulo egg production alone accounted for 26% of national production in 2015, with its output almost three times greater than the second leading state.[76] It had 21% of the broiler chickens in the country, and was the nation's leading producer. Its nearest rival, Paraná had only half the number of birds.[77] It produced 92% of the peanuts grown in 2015 and it was second in banana production, it was also an important, though not a leading, producer of soybeans and corn.[78]

In terms of the value of the state's agricultural production, sugar and pastoral products made up well over two-thirds of the gross value of agricultural production in the first and second decades of the twentieth century. Second were oranges and soybeans. All pastoral products alone, including meats, eggs and milk, now account for just under 30% of the total gross value of all crops, while sugar was 40% of the total. Coffee is now less important than oranges and soybeans and accounts for less than 5% of that value (see Table 8.6).

Although sugar, oranges, soybeans and corn have been absorbing ever more lands dedicated to these crops, São Paulo is still a major pastoral state. Ranching's share of agricultural lands declined from 11.4 million hectares in 1970 to 6.9 million hectares in 2006, but it still accounts for 41% of all lands in the state.[79] But this declining area had little effect on the total head of cattle being raised in the state. In 1970 the cattle numbered 9.1 million head and in 2006 there were 10.4 million, all of which demonstrated the increasing efficiency of the pastoral industry in the state.

In contrast to cattle, there was major growth in this period of the second most important animal produced in the state, chickens (both broiler and laying hens). As in the rest of the world, it is only since the middle of twentieth century that chicken meat has become a popular and important meat consumption item. A modern segmented production

---

[76] IBGE, SIDRA, PPM, table 74.   [77] IBGE, SIDRA, PPM, table 3939.

[78] For data on production of seasonal and permanent crops in 2015, IBGE, SIDRA, PAM, tables 1612 and 1613. For the analysis of peanut production in São Paulo see Renata Martins, "Produção de amendoim e expansão da cana-de-açúcar na Alta Paulista, 1996–2010," *Informações Econômicas, SP*, 41, no. 6 (Jun. 2011): 5–16.

[79] IBGE, SIDRA, Agro, table 264.

TABLE 8.6: *Total gross value of major crops produced in São Paulo, 2007–2016*

Product	2007	2008	2009	2010	2011	2012	2013	2014	2015	2016
Sugarcane	35%	30%	36%	35%	40%	46%	46%	42%	41%	40%
Cattle	11%	13%	13%	11%	9%	9%	10%	11%	12%	11%
Chickens	12%	12%	10%	9%	9%	9%	9%	8%	8%	8%
Oranges	16%	17%	15%	19%	19%	9%	5%	7%	6%	6%
Eggs	2%	3%	2%	2%	3%	4%	5%	5%	5%	5%
Soybeans	2%	3%	3%	2%	2%	3%	3%	3%	4%	5%
Cow's milk	4%	4%	4%	5%	4%	4%	5%	5%	4%	4%
Coffee	3%	3%	2%	3%	3%	4%	2%	3%	3%	4%
Corn	4%	5%	3%	3%	3%	3%	4%	3%	3%	4%
Bananas	1%	2%	1%	2%	2%	2%	2%	2%	2%	3%
Potatoes	2%	1%	2%	1%	1%	1%	1%	2%	2%	2%
Tomatoes	2%	2%	2%	2%	2%	2%	4%	5%	5%	2%
Others	5%	5%	5%	5%	4%	5%	5%	5%	5%	5%
sub total	100%	100%	100%	100%	100%	100%	100%	100%	100%	100%

Source: Valor Bruto da Produção-Regional por UF-Julho/2016 found at http://www.agricultura.gov.br/ministerio/gestao-estrategica/valor-bruto-da-producao.

organization, with new growing, feeding and breeding practices, has reduced chicken prices everywhere since the 1950s. In São Paulo, modern broiler production began in the 1940s in the Mogi das Cruzes region. In the next decade there was the beginning of new specialized *granjas* (chicken farms) using the latest sanitary procedures and in the 1960s came the importation of specific broiler breeds. At about this time, state producers adopted the vertical integrated system developed in Santa Catarina by Sadia in 1964, which involved the packinghouses writing long-term contracts with farmers and assisting them technically and with supplies and pullets.[80] As has occurred in the other major areas of meat production, there was an increasing concentration of production in an ever smaller number of producers. By the late 1980s there were over forty-five chicken slaughterhouses in the state, but just eight of them processed almost half of the chicken meat produced.[81] Between 1974 and 2015 São Paulo went from growing 29 million broiler chickens to 47 million, for an annual growth rate of 1.2%.[82] Currently the state is the fourth largest exporter internationally of chicken meat, behind the three Southern states and accounts for 6% of all such exports.[83]

But the state is currently Brazil's leading producer in the other chicken product, eggs. It accounts for 34% of national production, well ahead of any other state.[84] The modern system of industrialized production of eggs is estimated to have begun in Brazil in the 1950s and was promoted in the state by the major coop CAC (Cooperativa Agrícola de Cotia). From an artisanal production of chickens and eggs on a single farm, the eggs industry has now became part of the complex multi-farm system of production of broiler chickens (*galinhas de corte*) and laying hens (*poedeiras*, or *galinhas de postura*) from creating animals to producing eggs to processing chickens and eggs for sale.[85] Unlike the production of chicken

---

[80] Antonio Carlos Lima Nogueira and Decio Zylbersztajn, "Coexistência de arranjos institucionais na avicultura de corte do estado de São Paulo," USP–Faculdade de Economia, Administração e Contabilidade, Departasmento de Administração, working paper no. 03/022, 2003, p. 7; and Luiz Antonio Rossi de Freitas and Oscar Bertoglio, "A evolução da avicultura de corte brasileira após 1980," *Economia e Desenvolvimento*, 13 (Aug. 2001): 102.

[81] P. V. Marques, "Contribuição ao estudo da organização agroindustrial: o caso da indústria de frango de corte no estado de São Paulo," *Scientia Agricola*, 51, no. 1 (Jan./ Apr. 1994): 12, table 2.

[82] IBGE, SIDRA, tables 281, 3939.

[83] ABPA (Associação Brasileira de Proteína Animal), *Annual Report 2016*, p. 19.

[84] ABPA, Relatório Anual 2015, p. 184.

[85] Sérgio Kenji Kakimoto, "Fatores críticos da competitividade da cadeia produtiva do ovo no estado de São Paulo" (MA thesis, Universidade Federal de São Carlos, 2011), p. 46.

meat, for which there is a vibrant international market, eggs are almost exclusively consumed nationally.

The production of both the broiler and laying chickens is approximately the same and they are varieties of the standard species. Usually there are two levels of hatcheries (*incubatórios*) those producing the grandparents and parents of the layer or broiler chicks or pullets, and those which then produce the chicks themselves and produce either variety for sale to the farms when the pullets are one day old; those which will become layer hens are called *pintinhos de postura* and the meat ones *pintinhos de corte*. These take under a month to raise and are grown in large numbers so that they can be sold in large lots, especially important for the meat varieties. Before sale these one-day-old chicks are vaccinated. Broiler chickens are bought from the hatcheries by chicken farmers and then grown in large houses until they reach slaughter weight, which is usually in five to nine weeks, after which they are delivered to the packing-houses. In turn their slaughter is controlled by a few major companies. These companies have created a complex value chain vertical integration system providing basic inputs for the producers under long-term contracts.

In contrast to the broiler chicken industry with its vertical integration of hatcheries, farmers and packinghouses, the egg market is an independent system where producers sell their products to local consumers or wholesalers on the spot market. The relation between hatcheries, for which São Paulo is the leading state, the producers and the wholesalers is thus a simple purchase arrangement. In the late 1990s there were 80 to 100 wholesalers in the greater São Paulo market, of whom 30 to 40 supplied the half dozen major supermarket chains. This was a reasonably competitive market. But on the other hand, there has been a big concentration of primary producers, with one or two giant companies in each state providing most of the eggs.[86] It is estimated that the modal farm in the late 1990s was a unit with 20–50,000 egg-laying hens. But this was considered a small local producer among the 19,000 *granjas* producing eggs, whereas there were already eight major farms that had over half a million egg-laying animals which had 14% of all such animals in the state. The distribution of laying chickens among these farms produced a very high Gini of 0.825, showing how

---

[86] Sonia Santana Martins, "Cadeias produtivas do frango e do ovo: avanços tecnológicos e sua apropriação"(PhD thesis, Fundação Getulio Varas, São Paulo, 1996), chap. 2.

concentrated egg production had become by the end of the last century.[87] Typical of these large producers is the Granja Mizohata founded in 1957, which by 2005 had half a million hens producing 300,000 eggs per day.[88] These were the type of large farms that supplied inter-regional markets with unprocessed eggs. In 2005 it was estimated that the average egg farm in the state had 223,000 laying hens, comparable to those of Minas Gerais, but far greater than the average in Paraná which was just 79,000. The egg-producing farms are geographically concentrated in the state, with the two western mesoregions of Marília and Presidente Prudente accounting for half the eggs produced in 2015.[89]

Milk, another animal product of importance, was produced in Brazil from colonial times, but only at the beginning of the nineteenth century were specific breeds of milk cows introduced. The first was the Turino breed, of Portuguese origin. The first Brazilian dairy was opened in the city of Rio de Janeiro in the late nineteenth century, and a few years later a larger dairy was opened in the city of São Paulo. At the beginning of the next century the Holstein milk cows, originating in the Netherlands, were brought to Brazil.[90] For most of the second half of the twentieth century the government controlled the price of milk, the industry produced milk well below international yields and production was dominated by small dairy farms. The end of price controls in 1991 and the signing of the Mercosul treaties, along with progressive elimination of tariffs throughout the decade, led to falling prices, major importations of milk and milk products and thus forced a total reorganization of the national industry. Major importations of milk products from Argentina and Uruguay and the inefficiencies of Brazilian production made competition difficult. At the same time the stability of the national currency established with the *real* lead to increasing national consumption of milk. As late as 1998 two-thirds of milk was being produced by very small number of non-specialized producers. For such small farms it was a product which could

[87] Sonia Santana Martins, Ana Lúcia Lemos, Antônio de Pádua Deodato, Erica Salgado Politi and Nilce M. S. Queiroz, "Cadeia produtiva do ovo no estado de São Paulo," *Informações Econômicas. Governo do Estado de São Paulo. Instituto de Economia Agrícola.*, 30, no. 1 (Jan. 2000), based on data given in table 1, p. 11.

[88] Globo Rural, accessed November 2, 2017, at http://revistagloborural.globo.com/Revista/Common/0,,ERT216287-18283,00.html.

[89] IBGE, SIDRA, table 74.

[90] Joelma Cristina dos Santos, "Sistema agroindustrial do leite na região de Presidente Prudente – SP" (MA thesis, Universidade Estadual Paulista, Presidente Prudente, 2004), p. 51.

be sold on a daily basis and thus helped sustain the farm while their crops were maturing. But this lack of specialized production also had an impact on seasonal variation in production, with producers unable to satisfy markets all year long.[91]

The imbalances in the market thus led in the post-1990 period to a total reorganization of the entire chain of production of milk in Brazil, from the size and nature of the dairy herds to the production of finished milk. The most basic change was the purchasing of milk in bulk, which required the dairy farms to buy refrigeration tanks to hold milk to be then picked up by refrigerated tank trucks. Though this process was introduced into the US in 1939, its first occurrence in Brazil was in 1976 when the Cooperativa de Laticínios de São José dos Campos in the Valley of Paraíba used such refrigerated tank trucks to ship its products to the processing plant. By 2002 the government required producers to have refrigeration units and that all raw milk be moved by these refrigerated tank trucks.[92] This lowered the cost of production significantly. The next major innovation, also introduced in the 1990s, was the production in advanced factories of Longlife (UHT) milk which changed the whole geographical dynamics of the industry, permitting shipping of products to distant markets. By the first decade of the twenty-first century Longlife milk had replaced "C" milk as the dominant product consumed in Brazil.[93] There was also a systematic effort to increase production of milk herds, and better organization of the chain of production. This also led to a major introduction of multinationals and increasing concentration in the industry. Of the nine central milk cooperatives then in operation, the end of price supports forced out seven of them which sold their factories to Brazilian or multinational firms. The only two centrals that survived were Itambé of Minas Gerais and Leite Paulista of São Paulo and both eventually entered into partnership with private firms. Itambé was founded by the Cooperativa Central dos Produtores Rurais de Minas Gerais in 1950.[94] Currently it has 7,000

---

[91] Sérgio Rangel Figueira, "Transformações na cadeia produtiva do leite – uma análise a partir das cooperativas"(MA thesis, Universidade Estadual de Campinas, 1999), chap. 1.

[92] Flávia Lopes Dionizio, "Qualidade do leite e impacto econômico de diferentes tipos de coletas e condições de transporte da fazenda à indústria" (MA thesis, Universidade Federal de Minas Gerais, 2013), pp. 15–19.

[93] Paulo Roberto Scalco, "Identificação do poder de mercado no segmento de leite *in natura* e UHT" (PhD thesis, Universidade Federal de Viçosa, 2011), p. 27.

[94] Figueira, "Transformações na cadeia produtiva do leite," p. 2.

MAP 8.2: The mesoregions of São Paulo

dairy farms producing milk and owns numerous factories in Minas
Gerais and Goiás. In 2013 it allied with a private company (Vigor,
a subsidiary of JBS), which bought half of the company. The São Paulo
central coop was founded earlier in the year 1933 when several state
producer cooperatives created the central Cooperativa Central de
Laticínios do Estado de São Paulo, which has dominated the milk market
in the state with its brand of *Leite Paulista* until the present day.
In 2000, the coop sold part of the enterprise to the French multinational
Danone, but kept the production and sale of pasteurized milk, powdered
milk, UHT Longlife Milk, butter and cream.[95] But São Paulo also had
private dairy companies operating in the state from early in the twentieth
century. Thus Leite Vigor (1917), Nestlé (1921) and Leite União (1927)
were all operating before the Cooperativa Central de Laticínios do
Estado de São Paulo set up its own production unit.[96]

As late as 1940 most of the dairy farms were located in the Paraiba
Valley and Mogiana districts, largely due to their excellent connections to
the capital. But by the second half of the century there was a major

---

[95] Data accessed from Milkpoint on December 2, 2017, at www.milkpoint.com.br/cadeia-
   do-leite/giro-lacteo/cooperativa-central-de-laticiniossp-e-a-primeira-a-exportar-13192n
   .aspx.
[96] Santos, "Sistema agroindustrial do leite na região de Presidente Prudente," p. 53.

expansion throughout the state.[97] The introduction of the UHT Longlife ended the old "dairy basins" around the big cities, and dairy activity moved westward. Although the Valley of Paraíba has maintained a prominent role in state production, the leading zone since 1990 has been the region of São José do Rio Preto, with the Paraíba Valley second, followed by Campinas, Presidente Prudente and Ribeirão Preto.[98] The size of São Paulo's herd of milk cows has changed little since 1974. In that year it had 1.3 million dairy cows out of 10.8 million nationally. By 2016 the state listed only 1.2 million dairy cows, now out of 19.7 million nationally. It thus dropped nationally from second place to sixth place among state herds.[99]

The distribution of these herds and crops across the state is quite uneven, with some mesoregions dominating given crops and products and others not significant producers. As can be seen in Map 8.2, the state was divided into 15 mesoregional districts.

The distribution of these lands was biased toward larger holdings, and the Ginis tended to be quite high. But two regions stand out as less biased and with a higher percentage of smaller farms: São José de Campos and the Paraiba Valley, both with Ginis in the low 70s and both with farms of 10–100 hectares accounting for 30% of all agricultural lands – a higher proportion than any other region. In turn Ribeirão Preto and Bauru had only 15% of their lands held by farms of this size, but both had 83% of their lands in farms of over 100 hectares, while Ribeirão Preto had by far the highest percentage of lands in farms of 2,500 hectares and above (see Table 8.7).

Of these 15 districts, six accounted for 98% of sugarcane production, with the two Northern provinces of Ribeirão Preto and São José do Rio Preto and the Central province of Bauru the biggest producers, accounting in 2015 for over half of production (see Graph 8.2). The growth of production in each region was quite recent and dramatic. Thus for example Ribeirão Preto in 1974 planted only 168,000 hectares in sugarcane; by 2010 that had increased eight times to 1.2 million hectares planted in sugarcane.[100] Area mapping has shown that in the five years between the

---

[97] Evandro Cesar Clemente, "Formação, dinâmica e a reestruturação da cadeia produtiva do leite na região de Jales-SP" (MA thesis, Universidade Estadual Paulista, Presidente Prudente, 2006), pp. 26–28.

[98] IBGE, SIDRA, PMM, table 74.   [99] IBGE, SIDRA, table 94.

[100] Victor Hugo Junqueira, "O papel do Estado na expansão do setor sucroalcooleiro na região de Ribeirão Preto," *Revista NERA* (Presidente Prudente), 19, no. 31 (May–Aug. 2016): 56, table 1.

TABLE 8.7: *Distribution of lands in mesoregions of São Paulo in 2006*

Hectares	S. J. do Rio Preto		Ribeirão Preto		Araçatuba		Bauru		Araraquara	
	Farms	Lands	Farms	Lands	Farms	Lands	Farms	Lands	Farms	Lands
0.1–1	2.6%	0.0%	4.3%	0.0%	4.7%	0.0%	2.6%	0.0%	2%	0%
1–5	14.8%	0.8%	13.1%	0.3%	11.2%	0.4%	14.8%	0.4%	10%	0%
5–10	14.5%	1.9%	12.2%	0.8%	11.1%	0.9%	12.6%	0.8%	11%	1%
10–20	21.1%	5.1%	20.1%	2.4%	27.1%	4.3%	21.6%	2.9%	27%	4%
20–50	24.6%	12.9%	21.9%	5.9%	21.8%	7.7%	19.9%	5.6%	23%	7%
50–100	10.8%	12.5%	11.7%	7.0%	9.8%	7.7%	10.3%	6.4%	13%	8%
100–200	6.2%	14.0%	8.3%	9.8%	6.1%	9.6%	7.6%	9.4%	7%	9%
200–500	3.8%	18.9%	5.5%	14.1%	5.2%	17.8%	6.5%	18.0%	5%	15%
500–1,000	1.0%	11.5%	1.7%	9.8%	1.8%	13.7%	2.5%	15.1%	1%	8%
1,000–2,500	0.4%	10.1%	0.7%	9.1%	1.0%	15.9%	1.2%	16.0%	1%	15%
>2,500	0.1%	12.3%	0.5%	40.7%	0.4%	22.0%	0.5%	25.2%	1%	34%
Total*	100.0%	100.0%	100.0%	100.0%	100.0%	100.0%	100.0%	100.0%	100.0%	100.0%
(N)	37,679	23,02,772	20,256	24,24,738	13,769	12,45,057	18,190	20,82,033	5,998	6,47,621
Gini	0.727		0.826		0.791		0.804		0.799	

Hectares	Piracicaba		Campinas		Presidente Prudente		Marília		Assis	
	Farms	Lands	Farms	Lands	Farms	Lands	Farms	Lands	Farms	Lands
0.1-1	6.2%	0.0%	5.2%	0.0%	1.7%	0.0%	7.4%	0.0%	4.3%	0.0%
1-5	18.5%	0.8%	27.7%	1.6%	12.7%	0.6%	15.6%	0.5%	16.9%	0.6%
5-10	15.5%	1.7%	17.9%	2.7%	13.4%	1.3%	12.3%	1.0%	13.8%	1.3%
10-20	18.4%	3.8%	17.2%	4.9%	30.5%	6.2%	16.7%	2.7%	18.4%	3.2%
20-50	21.9%	9.8%	16.3%	10.3%	23.0%	9.0%	20.1%	7.1%	22.1%	8.5%
50-100	8.4%	8.3%	7.1%	9.9%	7.5%	6.9%	9.7%	7.6%	10.4%	8.7%
100-200	5.9%	11.6%	4.4%	12.3%	4.7%	8.6%	7.3%	11.3%	6.4%	10.7%
200-500	3.4%	14.8%	3.1%	18.7%	4.2%	16.9%	7.0%	24.5%	5.5%	20.2%
500-1,000	0.7%	7.2%	0.7%	9.7%	1.2%	11.0%	2.3%	17.3%	1.4%	11.2%
1,000-2,500	0.8%	20.8%	0.3%	9.2%	0.9%	17.5%	1.3%	19.9%	0.7%	12.5%
2,500+	0.3%	21.3%	0.2%	20.5%	0.3%	22.1%	0.2%	8.1%	0.3%	23.2%
Total*	100.0%	100.0%	100.0%	100.0%	100.0%	100.0%	100.0%	100.0%	100.0%	100.0%
(N)	7,458	5,32,168	18,536	9,28,160	26,496	20,37,543	7,069	6,46,959	1690	990180
Gini	0.805		0.799		0.784		0.777		0.791	

Hectares	Itapetininga Itapetininga		Macro Metro		Vale Paraiba		Litoral sul		Metro	
	Farms	Lands	Farms	Lands	Farms	Lands	Farms	Lands	Farms	Lands
0.1-1	7.4%	0.0%	14.9%	0.1%	10.6%	0.1%	4.5%	0.0%	15%	0%
1-5	21.6%	1.0%	32.4%	2.6%	17.6%	0.9%	23.2%	1.1%	42%	4%

(continued)

TABLE 8.7: *(continued)*

Hectares	Itapetininga Itapetininga		Macro Metro		Vale Paraiba		Litoral sul		Metro	
	Farms	Lands	Farms	Lands	Farms	Lands	Farms	Lands	Farms	Lands
5–10	15.1%	1.7%	15.9%	3.4%	12.6%	1.7%	14.3%	1.7%	18%	5%
10–20	17.9%	4.0%	13.8%	5.5%	16.2%	4.1%	17.7%	4.0%	12%	6%
20–50	18.7%	9.0%	12.8%	11.0%	19.8%	11.3%	21.6%	10.4%	8%	9%
50–100	8.5%	9.0%	4.8%	9.4%	10.9%	13.5%	8.7%	9.5%	3%	7%
100–200	4.9%	10.4%	2.7%	10.3%	7.1%	17.2%	4.9%	10.8%	1%	6%
200–500	3.8%	17.1%	2.0%	17.6%	3.7%	19.1%	3.3%	16.6%	1%	11%
500–1,000	1.3%	13.7%	0.5%	8.8%	0.9%	10.1%	1.2%	12.5%	0%	8%
1,000–2,500	0.6%	12.9%	0.2%	9.2%	0.4%	10.6%	0.5%	10.7%	0%	9%
2,500+	0.2%	21.3%	0.1%	22.1%	0.2%	11.3%	0.2%	22.8%	0%	36%
Total*	100.0%	100.0%	100.0%	100.0%	100.0%	100.0%	100.0%	100.0%	100.0%	100.0%
(N)	18,586	12,43,474	16,051	5,78,620	12,824	7,43,243	6,776	4,39,312	4072	113072
Gini	0.809		0.831		0.752		0.799		0.857	

Source: IBGE, SIDRA, Table 837

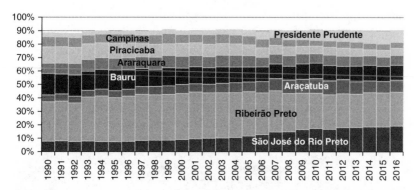

GRAPH 8.2: Distribution of sugarcane production by mesoregion of São Paulo, 1990–2016
Source: IBGE, SIDRA, table 1612

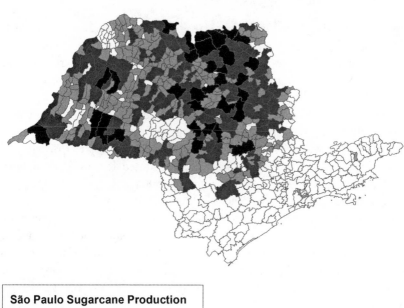

MAP 8.3: São Paulo sugarcane production in 2015 by *município*

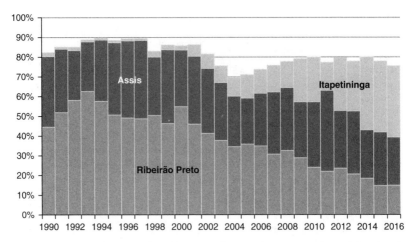

GRAPH 8.3: Distribution of soybean production by mesoregion of São Paulo, 1990–2016
Source: IBGE, SIDRA, PAM, table 1612

harvests of 2003/2004 and 2008/2009 the lands dedicated to sugar increased by an impressive 73% in the state, or from 2.6 million hectares to 4.4 million hectares.[101] Overall cane production in all regions has increased at a very rapid rate, but tended to be concentrated in a few well-defined zones of the western part of the state by 2015 (see Map 8.3).

The other major seasonal crops, soybeans and corn, were usually grown together, so their distribution is approximately the same by mesoregions of the state. The three Southern and Southwestern districts of Itapetininga, Assis and Ribeirão Preto accounted for 76% of soybean production in 2016 (see Graph 8.3 and Map 8.4).

Corn production, a key element in human and animal feed, was closely associated with the soybean crops and was often used as a rotating crop on the fields used for soybeans. Thus three of the leading soybean producing regions also accounted for 52% of the corn planted in 2016. Campinas was the outlier in that while it was not a major producer of soybeans, it was a significant producer of corn, accounting for 14% of the crop in 2016 (see Graph 8.4).

---

[101] Daniel Alves de Aguiar, Wagner Fernando da Silva, Bernardo Friedrich Theodor Rudorff, Luciana Miura Sugawara and Magog Araújo de Carvalho, "Expansão da cana-de-açúcar no Estado de São Paulo: safras 2003/2004 a 2008/2009," *Anais XIV Simpósio Brasileiro de Sensoriamento Remoto* (Natal, Apr. 2009), p. 12.

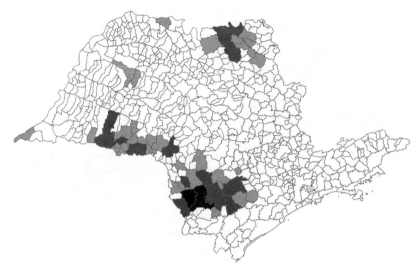

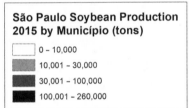

São Paulo Soybean Production 2015 by Município (tons)

- ☐ 0 – 10,000
- 10,001 – 30,000
- 30,001 – 100,000
- 100,001 – 260,000

MAP 8.4: São Paulo soybean production in 2015 by *município*

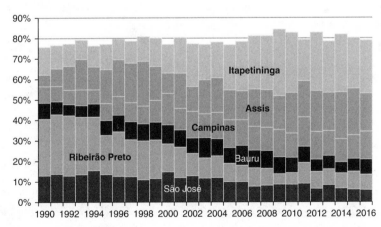

GRAPH 8.4: Distribution of corn production in the mesoregions of São Paulo, 1990–2016
Source: IBGE, SIDRA, 1612

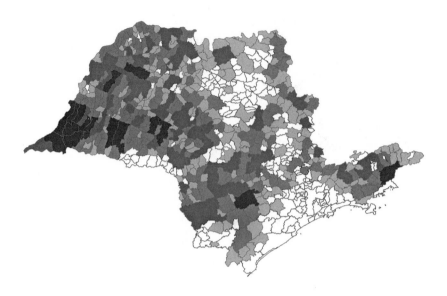

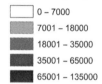

**2015 São Paulo Cattle Breeding
by Município (head)**

- [ ] 0 – 7000
- 7001 – 18000
- 18001 – 35000
- 35001 – 65000
- 65001 – 135000

MAP 8.5: São Paulo cattle production in 2015 by município

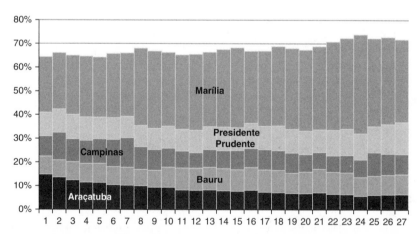

GRAPH 8.5: Distribution of egg production by mesoregions of São Paulo, 1990–2016
Source: IBGE, SIDRA, table 74

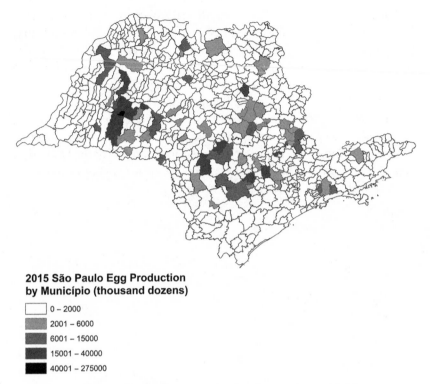

**2015 São Paulo Egg Production
by Município (thousand dozens)**

- ☐ 0 – 2000
- ▨ 2001 – 6000
- ▨ 6001 – 15000
- ▨ 15001 – 40000
- ■ 40001 – 275000

MAP 8.6: São Paulo egg production in 2015 by *município*

In contrast to almost all other agricultural activities, cattle could be found in all fifteen mesoregions of the state. Nevertheless the districts with the largest herds (each over 1 million cattle) were the four regions of Presidente Prudente, São José do Rio Preto, Bauru and Araçatuba. Together these regions in 2016 held almost half of the herds in São Paulo (see Map 8.5).

By 2016 Marilia was the principal producer of chicken eggs, followed by Presidente Prudente, and Bauru was also important in egg production. Along with the other western district of Campinas in the North they accounted for over half of egg production in the state in 2016. Broiler chicken production was even more concentrated in the Marília district (34% of the state's total) and to a lesser extent in Presidente Prudente (12%). With Bauru and Campinas these four municipalities accounted for close to two-thirds of the state's population of broiler chickens (see Graph 8.5 and Map. 8.6).

Thus the state of São Paulo, for all the growth of its urban centers, financial institutions, industrial parks and a world-class airplane industry, remains a vital part of Brazil's agricultural market, now just slightly ahead of Mato Grosso in total value of agricultural production. But in the period since 1960 there has been a radical shift in major agricultural activities. Sugarcane, sugar, biofuels, oranges and its derivatives, and chickens, eggs and milk have replaced the old coffee economy. The coffee which built the state is no longer a significant crop in that state. It is also worth noting that its road, rail and port complex still make São Paulo one of the key export areas for Brazil, with Santos being as important for soybeans and sugar exports as it was for coffee half a century ago.

9

The Agrarian Question

Over the last fifty-seven years, Brazilian agriculture has experienced a profound transformation. It went from a low-technology and mono-producing exporter to becoming a modern agricultural producer and a major world exporter of agricultural and pastoral products. It has now commercialized all stages of the productive chain of what has become a broad and fully developed agribusiness. This transformation involved a major expansion of the area occupied by commercial agriculture which has included the technological domination of the previously subsistence Cerrado region, now one of the main grain production centers in the world. At the same time as there was a systematic increase in land productivity, there was an ever stronger integration of production through complex value chains. In addition, instruments were created to manage, finance and reduce the inherent risk of this traditionally uncertain economic activity, with the implementation of futures markets and hedge mechanisms. The Brazilian farmer finally has become an entrepreneur, fully integrated into the international market, which is where the prices of the main products of Brazilian agribusiness are formed.

This summary of the main transformations, which were analyzed in the previous chapters, tells only part of the story about Brazilian agriculture in the recent period. Our analysis throughout this book has sought to explain how and why the transformations that occurred in traditional Brazilian agriculture led to a modern agricultural sector competitive on the international market. However, this transformation occurred only in a portion of the rural world. Unfortunately a majority of Brazilian farms and a large share of the rural population still live in conditions very similar to those existing in the middle of the twentieth century. It is this still traditional and largely subsistence farming sector which is the theme of this chapter.

The concentration of land ownership is a historical feature of Brazilian agriculture. Despite the major modernization of significant sectors of the rural economy, the distribution of rural properties has remained unchanged from the earliest censuses and cadastral surveys until today. In the countryside, land traditionally represented power and a reserve value. In general, the size of the property and efficient economic exploitation were not associated. Until the mid-twentieth century, unproductive latifundia and archaic labor relations prevailed and supported a backward and conservative power structure.

From 1950 until the military coup of 1964, the proposed solution to these problems in the rural area was agrarian reform. It was held that agrarian reform was the only way to modernize Brazilian agriculture. Many argued that the concentration of land, in addition to being politically conservative and socially damaging, would impede the modernization of agriculture. Several economists even claimed that pre-1960 agriculture was unable to provide an adequate, stable and cheap supply of food for the domestic market.

These debates of the 1950s and 1960s were part of a discussion about the paths to development in Latin America in general and Brazil in particular. The studies of CEPAL laid the theoretical foundations of development policies that gained support in Brazil, especially in the studies of Celso Furtado. It was held that unequal land distribution, the predominance of unproductive latifundia, as well as the existence of archaic labor relations, were the key elements blocking agrarian development. This structure limited the supply of food, with serious inflationary and distributional consequences. In addition, the rigid rural structure limited the expansion of the domestic market by excluding the rural poor from participation, and this expansion was itself essential for the process of industrialization and development of the country. For these reasons, it was held that changes in the land structure and labor relations in the countryside were the only means to expand food production.[1]

---

[1] Celso Furtado, *Formação Econômica do Brasil* (São Paulo: Companhia Editora Nacional, 1968) deals with the general question of underdevelopment of Brazil. On the agrarian question see Celso Furtado, *Um Projeto Para o Brasil* (Rio de Janeiro: Saga, 1969) and his *Análise do Modelo Brasileiro* (Rio de Janeiro: Civilização Brasileira, 1975). The regional question was treated in a study of Sudene, directed by Celso Furtado. GTDN, *Uma Política de Desenvolvimento para o Nordeste* (Rio de Janeiro: Imprensa Nacional, 1959). For a general vision of the ideas of Cepal, see Ricardo Bielschowsky, ed., *Cinquenta Anos de*

This line of thought was even enshrined in the Triennial Plan, directed by Celso Furtado and approved by the João Goulart government, where it was stated that the causes of the relative backwardness of Brazilian agriculture, its low productivity and the poverty of the rural populations originated in the country's agrarian structure, which was the most serious obstacle to the rational exploitation of land on a capitalist basis.[2] As part of its reform efforts, the Goulart Government in 1963 passed the important Rural Labor Statute, which brought to the rural workers labor rights which urban workers already possessed, such as the labor contract, the professional certificate, an eight-hour working day with weekly rest days and paid vacations.[3] This law represented an advance in workers' rights and destroyed the archaic labor relations then prevalent in Brazilian agriculture. It took many years for this law to be respected, and unfortunately it had a perverse side effect since it led to mass layoffs as farm owners ended the traditional *colonato* system on the coffee estates with their permanent workers resident on the farm, replacing it with a shift to part-time seasonal workers known as *boia-fria*.[4]

On the left there was also a debate between the *Cepalistas* and more traditional Marxists about the nature of rural society. Traditional Marxists held that the socialist revolution required Brazil to go through the various stages in terms of modes of production. As feudal features still subsisted in Brazilian agriculture, as seen in unproductive latifundia and archaic labor relations, the first stage in the revolutionary process would be agrarian reform.[5] The doctrinal position which argued for the feudal

Pensamento da CEPAL (Rio de Janeiro: Cofecon/Cepal, 2000), and for Brazilian ideas on this subject see Ricardo Bielschowsky, *Pensamento Econômico Brasileiro. O ciclo ideológico do desenvolvimento* (Rio de Janeiro: Contraponto, 2000).

[2] Presidência da Republica, *Plano Trienal de Desenvolvimento Econômico e Social, 1963–1965. Síntese* (December 1962).

[3] Law no. 4214, of 2 March 1963. By Law no. 5889, of 8 June 1973, the traditional labor laws (*Consolidação das Leis do Trabalho*) were extended to rural workers.

[4] Maria das Graças Prado Fleury, "Relações de emprego no campo: as diversas formas de contratação e a reestruturação produtiva" (MA thesis, Direito Agrário, Universidade Federal de Goiás, Goiânia, 2010); Angelo Priori et al., "Relações de Trabalho. Colonos, parceiros e camaradas," in *História do Paraná: Século XIX e XX* (Maringá: Eduem, 2012): 105–114; William S. Saint. "Mão-de-obra volante na agricultura brasileira: uma revisão da literatura," *Pesquisa e Planejamento Econômico*, 10, no. 2 (Aug. 1980): 503–526; David Goodman and Michael Redclift, "The 'Bóias-Frias': rural proletarianization and urban marginality in Brazil," *International Journal of Urban and Regional Research*, I, no. 2 (1977): 348–364.

[5] In this current of thought see the works of Alberto Passos Guimarães, *Quatro Séculos de Latifúndio* (Rio de Janeiro: Paz e Terra, 1977); Moisés Vinhas, *Problemas Agrário-*

nature of traditional agriculture was opposed by Caio Prado Jr, and others who understood that the field workers were wage earners and not peasants, although he recognized the concentrated nature of the agrarian structure. Brazilian agriculture he held could be fundamentally capitalist, structured in commercial enterprises, and could produce for the market. Although he defended the need for a social revolution, he held that any reform must be based on the understanding of the rural reality and not on theoretical models. Holding the belief that agriculture and labor relations in the countryside were capitalist, one of the strands of struggle should be to improve the lives of rural workers.[6] Thus Caio Prado was emphatic in praising the Rural Workers Statute, and although he pointed out flaws in the law, he said that the extension of social-labor legislation to the countryside and the legal protection of the rural worker would have an economic and social impact that few other acts have had on Brazil and it would promote one of the nation's greatest economic and social transformations.[7]

Other economists carried out studies which refuted the Marxist belief in the rigidity of Brazilian agricultural supply and sought to demonstrate that the domestic market was sufficiently supplied even under these traditional conditions and that Brazilian agricultural production responded adequately to price stimuli.[8] This current of thought proposed changes in agriculture through its modernization rather than through changes in land tenure. Future minister Delfim Netto would have a prominent position in this debate.[9] In addition to seeking to demonstrate that Brazilian agriculture was responding to price stimulus, that is, to demand pressure, these economists sought to demonstrate that agriculture in fact played an

Camponeses do Brasil (São Paulo: Civilização do Brasil, 1968); and Nelson Werneck Sodré, *Formação Histórica do Brasil* (São Paulo: Brasiliense, 1963).

[6] See Caio Prado Jr., *Formação do Brasil Contemporâneo: Colônia* (São Paulo, Brasiliense, 1973); and Caio Prado Jr., *Evolução Política do Brasil e Outros Estudos* (São Paulo, Brasiliense, 1972). He treated the agrarian question in various works, the most important of which was Caio Prado Jr., *A Revolução Brasileira* (São Paulo, Brasiliense, 1966). Ignácio Rangel also dealt with the agrarian question and provided an analysis based on the coexistence of two different and coexisting rural worlds. See his classic study Ignácio Rangel, *A Inflação Brasileira* (São Paulo: Bienal, 1963).

[7] Caio Pradro Jr., "O Estatuto do Trabalhador Rural," *Revista Brasiliense*, no. 47 (1963).

[8] Affonso Celso Pastore. *A Resposta da Produção Agrícola aos Preços no Brasil* (São Paulo: APEC, 1973).

[9] Antônio Delfim Netto, *Problemas econômicos da agricultura brasileira*, São Paulo, Faculdade de Ciências Econômicas e Administrativas da USP – Boletim. Antônio Delfim Netto, *Agricultura e desenvolvimento no Brasil*, São Paulo, Estudo Anpes, no. 5 (1969).

important functional role for national economic development, such as the ability to free labor for the expanding urban sector without harming agricultural production, creating a market for the industrial sector, and was in fact capable of generating exportable surpluses.[10] In their analysis of the performance of agriculture, these economists pointed out that the prices of agricultural products in the period 1949/1963 grew less than industrial prices. Moreover agricultural output grew at rates appropriate to the trajectory of industrial production. Although they recognized that agricultural exports were stagnant and without diversification, they held that the agrarian structure was not the cause.[11] In addition, several studies showed that in the existing structure of agricultural prices, exchange rates and industrial protection, agriculture actually transferred resources to other sectors of the economy.[12]

Using these analyses the military government sought to modernize Brazilian agriculture through three fundamental policies: massive subsidized agricultural credit; minimal price supports; and the creation and utilization of regulatory stocks. With this broad regulation of the market of agricultural products, inputs and even customs protection, the government sought to guarantee producer income and consumer price stability. Even products destined for the foreign market experienced major government intervention. Some sectors, such as sugar, alcohol and wheat, were fully controlled, including through the use of quotas. These policies, which made commercial agriculture viable and stimulated its modernization, were supplemented by major government support for research under

---

[10] Guilherme C. Delgado, "Expansão e modernização do setor agropecuário no pós-guerra: um estudo da reflexão agraria," *Estudos Avançados*, São Paulo, 15, no. 43 (2001): 157–172. On the debate see Alvaro Antonio Garcia, "Agricultura e desenvolvimento econômico no Brasil: debates nas décadas de 50 e 70," *Ensaios FEE*, Porto Alegre, 11, no. 1 (1990): 198–222. An interesting study of the period is by Ruy Miller Paiva, Salomão Schattan and Claus F. Trench de Freitas, *Setor Agrícola no Brasil. Comportamento Econômico, Problemas e Possibilidades* (São Paulo: Secretaria da Agricultura, 1973).

[11] Delgado. "Expansão e modernização do setor agropecuário no pós-guerra": 157–172; Ruy Miller Paiva, "V. Reflexões sobre as tendências da produção, da produtividade e dos preços do setor agrícola do Brasil" and "VI. Bases de uma política para a melhoria técnica da agricultura brasileira," in Caio Prado Jr. et al., eds., *A Agricultura Subdesenvolvida* (Petrópolis: Vozes, 1969): 167–261.

[12] According to Alves, agriculture was estimated to have transferred resources to industry in a proportion of 2.1% to 7.3% of the income of industry in the period 1955–57, and 11.5% to 19.1% in the period 1958–1960. Eliseu Roberto de Andrade Alves, *O Dilema da Politica Agrícola Brasileira – Produtividade ou Expansão da Área Agriculturável* (Brasília: Embrapa, 1984), 20. On this theme see Paiva, Schattan and Freitas, *Setor Agrícola no Brasil*.

the leadership of Embrapa, whose applied research proved crucial to the providing the crucial input of new knowledge for Brazilian agriculture to modernize.

The military governments put an end to the agrarian reform debate. Instead, with the goal of supplying abundant amounts of cheap food, they began to encourage the modernization of agriculture and stimulate the transfer of rural workers to urban industry. They also encouraged producers to enter international markets and proposed using new agricultural exports to generate the foreign exchange necessary for industrial growth. While putting pressure on landowners to use machinery, fertilizers and insecticides and providing them with abundant credit to do so, the military regime did not act against the concentration of land ownership nor did it challenge the power of conservative rural elites on whose support they depended. The military's solution to this debate was to follow the path of modernization, without changing the structure of land tenure or labor relations in the countryside. Opponents would call the path adopted a "conservative modernization."

Although totally suppressing the demand for a revolution in land tenure and also repressing the land reform peasant leaders,[13] the military regime as soon as it assumed power did approve a new Land Statute, which was more of a colonization scheme than a classic agrarian reform. It did include a set of measures that aimed at promoting better distribution of the land, through modifications in its possession and use, proposing that it be based on the principles of social justice and increased productivity, but with compensation for any lands seized. It was a way to reduce the pressure from land reform movements and at the same time favor the process of modernization of agriculture without changing the agrarian structure then in force.[14] But even this moderate decree generated strong conservative opposition in Congress and in parts of the Army.[15] Through this law, a process was initiated which involved colonization of either unproductive lands expropriated with the corresponding payment of the

---

[13] Regina Bruno. *Senhores da Terra, Senhores da Guerra: A Nova Face Política das Elites Agroindustriais no Brasil* (Rio de Janeiro: Forense/UFRJ, 1997), p. 99.

[14] José de Souza Martins. *A Militarização da Questão Agrária no Brasil* (Petrópolis: Vozes, 1985), p. 35; and Regina Bruno, *O Estatuto da Terra: entre a conciliação e o confronto*. Accessed March 18, 2017, at http://r1.ufrrj.br/esa/V2/ojs/index.php/esa/article/viewFile/80/76.

[15] Carmem Lúcia Gomes de Salis, "Estatuto da Terra: origem e (des) caminhos da proposta de reforma agrária nos governos militares" (PhD thesis, Assis, UNESP – Universidade Estadual Paulista, 2008).

indemnification or though using vacant public lands. Although it has undergone changes over the last fifty years, this would be the basic procedure adopted by all post-military governments, although the theme of radical agrarian reform remains an important one in certain political and social segments in Brazil, such as the Movement of Rural Workers without Lands (MST – Movimento dos Trabalhadores Rurais sem Terra).[16]

The actual colonization and settlement of poor farmers on expropriated non-producing lands was quite limited until 1994, totaling less than 60,000 families. The periods 1997–1999 (government of Fernando Henrique) and 2004–2006 (government of Lula) were the most active in terms of settlements. After 2007 there was a decline in settlement, but even despite this decline in his second term, it was the Lula period that saw the largest number of colonies established, benefiting 614,000 families, a bit above the 540,000 families served in the Fernando Henrique Cardoso administration. The settlements fell dramatically in President Dilma's first term, averaging less than half the number under the previous two presidents.

Since the beginnings of this new formal colonization program, some 9,000 settlements projects have been carried out. These projects involved a total area of 88 million hectares, which represents about a quarter of the total land area in agriculture in the country and 19% of all the farm families in the 2006 agricultural census. But the results are even more expressive when considered regionally. The first surprise is that in the North the total area of settlement projects that occurred until July 2006 exceeded the total area surveyed in 2006, and the total number of families, compared to the number of properties, is extremely high (86%). In the Northeast there is also a high percentage of settlements, both in land area

---

[16] The MST was created in 1979 with the occupation of lands in Rio Grande do Sul, became a more consolidated movement in the 1980s and was associated with the Catholic Church-sponsored Pastoral Land Commission (Comissão Pastoral da Terra). On this history see Bernardo Mançano Fernandes, *Formação do MST do Brasil* (Petrópolis: Vozes, 2000); Débora Franco Lerrer, "Trajetórias de militantes sulistas: nacionalizações de modernidade do MST" (PhD thesis, Universidade Federal Rural do Rio de Janeiro, 2008); José Carlos Lima de Souza, "O Movimento dos Trabalhadores Rurais sem Terra (MST). O moderno príncipe educativo brasileiro na história do tempo presente" (PhD thesis, Niterói, Universidade Federal Fluminense, 2008); "O MST e a questão agrária. Entrevista com João Stédile," *Estudos Avançados*, 11, no. 31 (1997): 69–97; José Flávio Bertero, "Sobre a Reforma agrária e o MST," *Lutas & Resistências* (Londrina), 1 (Sept. 2006): 163–183; and Xico Graziano, *O Carma da Terra no Brasil* (São Paulo: A Girafa, 2004).

and in families, and in the Center-West there is a large representation of these colonists in the farm population and the total number of properties in the 2006 census. Proportionally the settlements were less significant in the South and Southeast. The average area of these settlements also varies widely by region: being more than 100 hectares in the North, approximately 50 hectares in the Northeast and Center-West, 34 in the Southeast and 23 in the South, with the overall average being 91 hectares (see Table 9.1).

INCRA, the government colonizing agency, carried out a survey in 2010 assessing the quality of life, production and income of farmers in 1,164 reform settlements which involved some 804,000 families settled between 1985 and 2008. The population in these rural settlements was predominantly female (53%), which was not the norm in the rest of rural Brazil, 16% were illiterate, and less than 1% had completed high school. About 45% were under the age of twenty, and the estimated average family size was four persons, which meant that by 2010 the total population benefited would be on the order of 3.6 million people. Only 13% of the families had a sewage network or a septic tank. A quarter of the families did not have residential water sufficient to meet all the family's needs year-round, and only 44% of the families had regular access to electricity. Only 16% considered their local roads to be good – a crucial issue for these isolated settlements. The situation was also negative in the area of access to a hospital or health center, because 55% said that access was bad or impossible. Surprisingly almost half the families did not have access to the resources and programs of PRONAF. Of the group which had received government support and credits, 64% were in default on their loans. As for the credits provided by INCRA, 62% received funds for initial support, 26% for development and 63% for procurement of construction material.

The survey provided income information on the settlers of two states. In the case of Santa Catarina, most of the income came from milk, beans, cassava and corn, in that order. In the settlements of Ceará most of the income came from beans, milk and cheese. In terms of the number of producers in each activity, bean and maize and chicken farming were highlighted. In Ceará, 78% answered that the family income was up to three minimum wages. The situation in Santa Catarina was completely different. Only 44% obtained at least three minimum wages, which meant that 56% had family incomes higher than three minimum wages. These wealthier settlers also had a different source of income. In Santa Catarina, 76% obtained income from production, 12% from external work and

TABLE 9.1: *Agrarian reform – number of projects, families settled and area in hectares granted by region, from inception to July 2016*

Regions	Projects	Area (a)	Families settled	Averages			Census of 2006		Relation	
				Families/ project	Area/ project	Area/ family	Farms	Total area	(a)/(d)%	(b)/(c)%
North	2,096	60,992,320	409,230	195	29,099	149	475,775	54,787,297	111%	86%
Northeast	4,361	17,140,890	350,612	80	3,930	49	2,454,006	75,594,442	23%	14%
Center-West	1,264	8,009,125	136,790	108	6,336	59	317,478	103,797,329	8%	43%
Southeast	782	1,465,242	43,614	56	1,874	34	922,049	54,236,169	3%	5%
South	835	829,461	36,557	44	993	23	1,006,181	41,526,157	2%	4%
Total to July 2016	9,338	88,437,038	976,803	105	9,471	91	5,175,489	329,941,394	27%	19%
Total to 2015 (1)	7,523	69,462,791	833,017	111	9,233	83	5,175,489	329,941,394	21%	16%

Note (1): Settlements made until 2005, whose results are included in the agricultural census of 2006
Source: Ministério do Desenvolvimento Agrário, SIPRA; Censo Agropecuário, 2006

363

12% from benefits. In Ceará in contrast only 48% of total income came from farm production, income from state benefits was 44%, with external work accounting for just 8%.

More than half the colonist families claimed that the size of their farms was good, and a third rated it insufficient. In terms of housing, food, access to education and income generated, some 63% said it was better than expected, and only in access to health care was the response less than 50%. In the comparison between the situation before and after settlement, some items stand out. 47% had gas stoves before settling and 71% had them afterwards; 31% had televisions before arriving and 64% had them after settlement; 16% had vehicles before and 43% now. Even in the case of computers, before it was 0.63% and after settlement it reached 2.84%.[17]

Despite the massive colonization process that has occurred in the last twenty years, violent land conflicts persist in the countryside, including a major increase in such confrontations in 2016. In that year, there were 1,079 such land conflicts (which included expulsions, assets destroyed and persons attacked); there were also 194 illegal occupations or repossessions and 22 settlements. An extraordinary 686,000 people were involved in these events and a record number of murders occurred. The fragility of the land titling process, and the actions of landowners and their hired mercenaries generate continuous conflicts, particularly in the frontier regions. The existence of extensive rural labor legislation despite possible difficulties for its imposition, keeps reducing the number of labor conflicts including the existence of so-called slave workers, of which there were only 68 cases involving 751 persons in 2016. But government agencies and other state authorities have not been able to seriously reduce the bitter land conflicts which often end in violence and have been continuous since they were first recorded in 1985 by the very active Pastoral Land Commission (CPT) of the Catholic Church. To give some idea of these disputes, we have selected the most recent years of conflicts recorded by CPT (see Table 9.2).

[17] Ministério do Desenvolvimento Agrário – Instituto Nacional de Colonização e Reforma Agrária (Incra), *Reforma Agrária. Apresentação dos Primeiros Resultados* (Brasília: Incra, December 2010). Accessed March 26, 2017 at www.incra.gov.br/media/reforma_a graria/questao_agraria/pqra%20-%20apresentao.pdf. There is an interesting study of the settlements done by IPEA: see Brancolina Ferreira, ed., *Avaliação da Situação de Assentamentos da Reforma Agrária no Estado de São Paulo. Fatores de Sucesso e Insucesso* (Brasília: IPEA, 2013).

TABLE 9.2: *Rural conflicts, violence and confrontations in Brazil, 2007–2016*

	2007	2008	2009	2010	2011	2012	2013	2014	2015	2016
Conflicts over land										
Number of occurrences (1)	615	459	528	638	805	816	763	793	771	1,079
Occupations/repossessions	364	252	290	180	200	238	230	205	200	194
Camps	48	40	36	35	30	13	14	20	27	22
Total	1,027	751	854	853	1,035	1,067	1,007	1,018	998	1,295
Assassinations	25	27	25	30	29	34	29	36	47	58
Persons involved	612,000	354,225	415,290	351,935	458,675	460,565	435,075	600,240	603,290	686,735
Hectares	8,420,083	6,568,755	15,116,590	13,312,343	14,410,626	13,181,570	6,228,667	8,134,241	21,387,160	23,697,019
Labor conflicts										
Slave labor	265	280	240	204	230	168	41	131	80	68
Assassinations	1	1		1	1					
Persons involved	8,653	6,997	6,231	4,163	3,929	2,952	1,716	2,493	1,760	751
Exploitation	151	93	45	38	30	14	13	10	4	1
Assassinations				1	1			2	1	1
Persons Iinvolved	7,293	5,388	4,813	1,643	466	73	142	294	102	2

(*continued*)

365

TABLE 9.2: *(continued)*

	2007	2008	2009	2010	2011	2012	2013	2014	2015	2016
	Water conflicts									
Number of conflicts	87	46	45	87	68	79	93	127	135	172
Assassinations	2		1	2		2	2		2	2
Persons involved	163,735	135780	201,675	197,210	137,855	158,920	134,835	214,075	211,685	222,355

Source: Centro de Documentação Dom Tomás Balduíno – Comissão Pastoral da Terra – April 17, 2017
Notes (1): This total includes evictions and expulsions, threats of eviction and expulsions, destroyed goods and pistol whipping

Moreover, despite the very significant number of agrarian reform or colonized settlements in terms of the number of beneficiary families and areas involved, there had been little change nationally in the levels of concentration of land ownership in Brazil. As measured by the Gini Index, land distribution remains virtually unchanged since the first agricultural census in 1920. Since then its value has remained constant, in the mid-80s. Although the level of concentration has not changed, there has been a systematic reduction in the average size of properties. Between 1920 and 1960 there was a decline in the average size of farms, but since then average size has remained stable at between 60 and 70 hectares per property. There has also been a change in the smaller properties. Up to 1960, properties with up to 10 hectares represented about half the properties, and only about 3% of the area. The properties with up to 100 hectares represent about 90% of the farms but hold only one-fifth of the farm lands. At the opposite extreme, properties with more than 1,000 hectares, accounted for less than 1% of the farms but held approximately 45% of the agricultural areas surveyed in the various censuses conducted in the latter decades of the twentieth century. Despite the significant number of these settlements, the total number of properties since 1970 has remained around 5 million. This indicates that at the same time as the settlements occurred there was a proportional reduction of other small and medium sized properties (see Table 9.3).

There are, however significant regional differences. According to the 2006 census, about 50% of the rural properties are located in the Northeast, which has 17% of the agricultural lands counted in the census. The Southeast and South represent just under a fifth of the farms, with a percentage of about 15% in the total area. The highlight is the Center-West with only 6% of Brazil's rural properties, but about a third of the area. This is reflected in the differential in terms of average farm size: 64 hectares in Brazil, but 60 and 42 in the Southeast and South, respectively, and 332 in the Center-West. The Northeast has the smallest average farm size, with only 31 hectares. There is also a big difference when we consider the regional distribution by size of property. In the case of the Northeast, 63% of the properties had less than 10 hectares and accounted for only 5% of the agricultural lands. Properties with more than 1,000 hectares were less than 1% of all farms, but they controlled 31% of the agricultural lands. In the Center-West, only 16% of properties were less than 10 hectares and they held an insignificant portion of lands (0.2%). On the other hand, large estates, with more than 1,000 hectares represented 6% of all farms and controlled 70% of the farm lands. In the South and the

TABLE 9.3: *Number of properties and by size of holdings in hectares, census 1920–2006*

Year	Total	Gini index	Number of farms by area				
			Less than 10 ha	10–100 ha	Less than 100 ha	100–1,000 ha	More than 1,000 ha
1920	648,153	0.832	–	–	463,879	157,959	26,045
1940	1,904,589	0.833	654,557	975,441	1,629,995	243,818	27,822
1950	2,064,642	0.844	710,934	1,052,557	1,763,491	268,159	32,628
1960	3,337,769	0.842	1,495,020	1,491,415	2,986,435	314,831	32,480
1970	4,924,019	0.844	2,519,630	1,934,392	4,454,022	414,746	36,874
1975	4,993,252	0.855	2,601,860	1,898,949	4,500,809	446,170	41,468
1980	5,159,851	0.857	2,598,019	2,016,774	4,614,793	488,521	47,841
1985	5,801,809	0.857	3,064,822	2,160,340	5,225,162	517,431	50,411
1995	4,859,865	0.856	2,402,374	1,916,487	4,318,861	469,964	49,358
2006	5,175,636	0.872	2,477,151	1,971,600	4,448,751	424,288	47,578

Area of farms grouped by size categories in hectares

Year	Total	Average size	Less than 10 ha	10–100 ha	Less than 100 ha	100–1,000 ha	1,000+
1920	175,104,675	270	–	–	15,708,314	48,415,737	110,980,624
1940	197,720,247	104	1,993,439	33,112,160	36,005,599	66,184,999	95,529,649
1950	232,211,106	112	3,025,372	35,562,747	38,588,119	75,520,717	118,102,270
1960	249,862,142	75	5,592,381	47,566,290	53,158,671	86,029,455	110,314,016
1970	294,145,466	60	9,083,495	60,069,704	69,153,199	108,742,676	116,249,591
1975	323,896,082	65	8,982,646	60,171,637	69,154,283	115,923,043	138,818,756
1980	364,854,421	71	9,004,259	64,494,343	73,498,602	126,799,188	164,556,629
1985	374,924,929	65	9,986,637	69,565,161	79,551,798	131,432,667	163,940,463
1995	353,611,246	73	7,882,194	62,693,585	70,575,779	123,541,517	159,493,949
2006	333,680,037	64	7,798,777	62,893,979	70,692,756	112,844,186	150,143,096

Source: Basic data: IBGE – Censo Agropecuário – SIDRA; Gini: IBGE, Censo Agropecuário, 2006. Brasil, Grandes Regiões e Unidades da Federação, 2009, p. 109; Szmrecsányi, "O desenvolvimento da produção agropecuária (1930–1970)" (2007); Hoffmann and Ney, *Estrutura Fundiária e Propriedade Agrícola no Brasil* (2010).

Southeast the weight of the small units was around 40% in terms of number and 4% in terms of areas. The large ones, with more than 1,000 hectares, were less than 1% of all farms and controlled between 23% and 30% of the lands respectively (see Table 9.4).

When analyzing the value of production by size of farm and region, the concentration is evident. Although containing more than half of the agricultural establishments surveyed in 2006, the value of production in the North and Northeast accounted for just over one-fifth of the total value of national agricultural production. The Southeast with 18% of the farms generated 33% of the value of agricultural production in 2006. If we add the Center-West, the 23% of the farms found in these two regions accounted for more than half the value of agricultural production.

The average farm production differs dramatically by region, reaching R$123,000 in the Center-West and R$74,000 in the Southeast, compared to just R$14,000 in the Northeast and R$21,000 in the North. By size we also have a high concentration, because establishments of up to 10 hectares, representing almost half of the units, account for only 12% of the value of production. If we compute all units of up to 100 hectares, their weight among establishments reached 86%, against a participation in the value of production of only 40%. The opposite extreme can be observed among large producers, those with more than 1,000 hectares. These 38,000 establishments (1% of the units), generated almost a third of the value of production. In addition, the 16,000 establishments with more than 1,000 hectares in the Center-West (0.4% of the producers) generated 12% of the value of Brazilian agricultural production. All of this reinforces the idea of the high concentration of agricultural production in Brazil (Table 9.5).

On the other hand, small and medium-sized farms contain a large share of the rural population engaged in agriculture and equally are significant in the production of some of the main products grown and raised in Brazil. Half of the people employed in agriculture in 2006 were in properties with less than 10 hectares; if we consider properties with less than 100 hectares this percentage reached almost 90%. In addition, some products, such as tobacco, beans, manioc, arboreal cotton and bananas, have a high proportion of their production in small units of up to 10 hectares. The most representative products of the large properties are herbaceous cotton, rice, soybean and sorghum. Wheat, cacao and orange are primarily produced in farm units of between 100 and 1,000 hectares (Table 9.6).

As might be expected, there is a positive correlation between size of farm and educational level of the farm owner or manager. The low level of

TABLE 9.4: *Number of properties and by size of holdings in hectares by region, census 1920–2006*

Number of farms by area

Region	Total	Less than 10 ha	10–100 ha	Less than 100 ha	100–1,000 ha	More than 1,000 ha
Brazil	5,175,636	2,477,151	1,971,600	4,448,751	424,288	47,578
North	475,778	126,532	229,105	355,637	80,518	8,467
Northeast	2,454,060	1,498,395	650,865	2,149,260	115,484	8,212
Southeast	922,097	393,459	411,438	804,897	91,727	5,956
South	1,006,203	406,498	515,460	921,958	59,927	4,507
Center-West	317,498	52,267	164,732	216,999	76,632	20,436

Area of farms grouped by size categories in hectares

	Total	Average size	Less than 10 ha	10–100 ha	Less than 100 ha	100–1,000 ha	More than 1,000 ha
Brazil	333,680,037	64	7,798,777	62,893,979	70,692,756	112,844,186	150,143,096
North	55,535,764	117	361,729	9,338,721	9,700,450	19,016,345	26,818,968
Northeast	76,074,411	31	3,785,736	20,102,488	23,888,224	28,678,152	23,508,035
Southeast	54,937,773	60	1,568,990	13,450,983	15,019,973	23,629,860	16,287,940
South	41,781,003	42	1,839,140	13,657,121	15,496,261	16,594,702	9,690,040
Center-West	105,351,087	332	243,182	6,344,666	6,587,848	24,925,126	73,838,113

Source: IBGE – Censo Agropecuário – SIDRA.

TABLE 9.5: *Value of production and number of farms by size and region, agrarian census of 2006*

Number of farms

Region	Total	No land	0–2 ha	2–10 ha	10–100 ha	100–1,000 ha	>1,000 ha
North	356,333	24,530	47,463	51,082	167,480	59,566	6,212
Northeast	1,661,713	115,844	473,423	502,337	474,259	89,518	6,332
Southeast	650,169	10,192	61,087	190,759	308,795	74,448	4,888
South	818,097	11,827	46,219	252,246	452,002	51,855	3,948
Center-West	218,933	1,671	5,873	24,028	112,513	58,510	16,338
Brazil	3,705,245	164,064	634,065	1,020,452	1,515,049	333,897	37,718

Value of production in thousand *reais*

Region	Total	No land	0–2 ha	2–10 ha	10–100 ha	100–1,000 ha	>1,000 ha
North	7,759,807	181,058	274,848	488,383	2,619,369	2,061,372	2,134,777
Northeast	24,493,824	262,457	1,576,301	4,329,800	6,854,261	5,528,356	5,942,649
Southeast	47,947,658	156,432	734,595	3,590,863	13,187,955	16,454,084	13,823,729
South	38,081,152	178,833	617,638	4,901,495	16,665,519	10,583,156	5,134,511
Center-West	27,118,736	20,824	46,708	379,928	2,217,507	6,959,030	17,494,738
Brazil	145,401,177	799,603	3,250,092	13,690,469	41,544,610	41,585,997	44,530,405

	Average value of production in reais						
North	21,777	7,381	5,791	9,561	15,640	34,607	343,654
Northeast	14,740	2,266	3,330	8,619	14,453	61,757	938,511
Southeast	73,746	15,349	12,025	18,824	42,708	221,014	2,828,095
South	46,548	15,121	13,363	19,431	36,870	204,091	1,300,535
Center-West	123,868	12,462	7,953	15,812	19,709	118,937	1,070,800
Brazil	39,242	4,874	5,126	13,416	27,421	124,547	1,180,614

Source: IBGE – Censo Agropecuário – SIDRA

TABLE 9.6: *Production of principal agricultural products by size of property, agricultural census 2006*

	No land	0–10 ha	10–100 ha	100–1,000 ha	>1,000 ha	Total
Sesonal crops (metric tons)						
Herbaceous cotton	150	13,237	28,734	160,527	2,288,937	2,491,585
Peanuts in shell	330	29,846	28,715	34,867	24,683	118,441
Rice in shell	59,372	832,489	2,467,647	3,417,953	2,910,377	9,687,838
Beans	27,835	1,009,558	937,350	440,355	307,628	2,722,726
Dry leaf tobacco	11,797	442,855	642,234	10,674	1,475	1,109,035
Manioca (*aipim, macaxeira*)	157,668	4,109,796	5,685,034	1,870,189	89,940	11,912,627
Corn on the cob	113,560	5,532,384	14,911,502	11,392,848	9,477,317	41,427,611
Soybeans	2,347	703,345	6,628,958	15,793,874	23,067,318	46,195,842
Sorghum grain	236	17,516	80,066	301,119	390,013	788,950
Wheat in grain	59	34,586	585,479	1,165,247	447,704	2,233,075

(continued)

Permanent crops (metric tons)

Arboreal cotton		629	444	102		1,180
Bananas		1,253,230	2,105,168	697,966	111,954	4,168,318
Cocoa (almond)		24,142	90,154	78,974	5,902	199,172
Arabica coffee beans (green)		281,918	795,016	720,158	152,603	1,949,696
Oranges		753,883	3,064,019	5,391,645	2,966,045	12,175,593
Total workers employed in agriculture	632,303	5,993,568	5,014,642	1,014,735	146,158	12,801,406

Source: IBGE – Censo Agropecuário – SIDRA
Notes: No land farmers are renters

education of Brazilian farmers in general is remarkable: 81% were classified as illiterate or with an incomplete primary education, only 16% had a complete primary and middle school education and only 3% attended or completed a university degree. There is significant variation by region and, as expected, the Northeast had the worst educational levels. The best levels occurred in the Center-West, the Southeast and the South. The results show that the size of the farm explained the disparities. In Brazil as a whole, 86% of farmers with up to 10 hectares were illiterate or had not completed elementary school; for establishments between 100 and 1,000 hectares this percentage was reduced to 62% and 43% among owners and managers working on farms of 1,000 hectares or more. In this last group, 22% had a complete or incomplete university degree. In the South this percentage was 42% and in the Southeast 35%. But even in these two regions more than three-quarters of establishments with up to 10 hectares were controlled by illiterates or persons with less than a primary education. This low level of education undeniably limits the absorption capacity of modern technology that is gradually dominating commercial agriculture in Brazil (Table 9.7).

Differentiation in Brazilian agriculture can also be measured by the agricultural practices adopted. First of all, 42% of the establishments declared that they did not use any modern agricultural practice. Firing fields were practiced by 14%, mostly in the North and Northeast and were insignificant in the other regions. Level plowing was practiced by 29% of the establishments, without great variation by size or region. Crop rotation, was practiced by 12% of farms, with no difference by size, although the Southern region did this more frequently than any other region. In the case of the protection of the slopes, there was a significant difference based on size of farms, and here as well the South led in this practice. In general, the low level of use of modern agricultural practices was most pronounced among small and medium producers and, when analyzed by region, with significant differentiation between the North and the Northeast and the other regions (Table 9.8).

Only 22% of the farm units received some type of technical training and of these only 9% received technical guidance on a regular basis. Of farms up to 10 hectares, only 5% had such assistance. Almost a third of the farms of 10–100 hectares received occasional or regular support, with the government again being the most important supplier of such assistance. On the other hand, almost two-thirds of establishments with more than 1,000 hectares primarily received their technical guidance either from their own staff or from private planning companies, along

TABLE 9.7: *Farmers by level of education and size of farms by region,*
agricultural census of 2006

Level of education	Total	No land	0–10 ha	10–100 ha	100–1,000 ha	>1,000 ha
			BRAZIL			
Illiterate and basic level incomplete	81%	89%	86%	79%	62%	43%
Basic and intermediate complete	16%	10%	13%	18%	27%	35%
Higher education complete or not	3%	0%	1%	3%	11%	22%
			North			
Illiterate and basic level incomplete	86%	89%	88%	87%	80%	58%
Basic and intermediate complete	13%	11%	12%	12%	17%	31%
Higher education complete or not	1%	0%	1%	1%	2%	10%
			Northeast			
Illiterate and basic level incomplete	89%	91%	91%	88%	74%	55%
Basic and intermediate complete	10%	9%	9%	11%	20%	29%
Higher education complete or not	1%	0%	0%	1%	7%	16%
			Southeast			
Illiterate and basic level incomplete	70%	86%	78%	67%	48%	30%

(continued)

TABLE 9.7: *(continued)*

			Southeast			
Basic and intermediate complete	23%	13%	19%	25%	33%	35%
Higher education complete or not	6%	1%	3%	7%	19%	35%
			South			
Illiterate and basic level incomplete	75%	80%	79%	76%	47%	22%
Basic and intermediate complete	22%	19%	20%	21%	36%	36%
Higher education complete or not	3%	1%	2%	3%	17%	42%
			Center-West			
Illiterate and basic level incomplete	68%	81%	75%	74%	56%	40%
Basic and intermediate complete	26%	17%	22%	22%	33%	39%
Higher education complete or not	6%	1%	3%	3%	11%	21%

Source: IBGE – Censo Agropecuário – SIDRA

with some government assistance. Again the difficulty of access to guidance by small and medium-sized establishments is a fundamental weakness of the system, and the impact of public support for small producers is limited (see Table 9.9).

In spite of the strong initial military repression of all social movements, by the mid-1970s such social movements in the rural area were revived. In 1975 the National Conference of Bishops of Brazil (CNBB) created the Pastoral for Land Commission with the banner of "land for those who

TABLE 9.8: *Type of agriculture practiced by size of farm and region, agrarian census of 2006*

Type of agricultural practice	Farms by size of property					
	No land	0–2 ha	2–10 ha	10–100 ha	100–1,000 ha	>1,000 ha
Level planting	45,979	267,505	463,860	610,651	112,820	13,061
Use of terraces	3,853	19,190	47,924	94,308	23,770	5,060
Rotation of crops	10,663	80,699	187,239	309,602	46,354	6,526
Use of crops for reform and/or renewal and/or recovery of pastures	5,421	22,567	58,589	136,965	41,176	6,269
Fallow or soil rest	11,369	57,304	92,362	137,270	29,377	3,873
Burning	55,012	211,730	144,504	232,992	54,699	3,088
Protection and/or conservation of slopes	3,525	11,780	66,658	164,749	42,548	7,666
Nothing	138,407	458,673	588,761	776,237	191,964	22,843
Total (1)	255,019	1,049,000	1,428,151	1,971,600	424,288	47,578

Type of agricultural practice	North	Northeast	Southeast	South	Center-West	Brazil
Level planting	76,053	621,901	349,638	413,062	53,222	1,513,876

(continued)

379

TABLE 9.8: *(continued)*

Type of agricultural practice	No land	Farms by size of property					
		0–2 ha	2–10 ha	10–100 ha	100–1,000 ha	>1,000 ha
Use of terraces	2,782	39,165	40,286	99,409	12,463	194,105
Rotation of crops	18,495	177,815	85,594	337,387	21,792	641,083
Use of crops for reform and/or renewal and/or recovery of pastures	25,416	111,081	52,675	57,314	24,501	270,987
Fallow or soil rest	17,188	210,649	46,461	46,998	10,259	331,555
Burning	124,883	533,832	22,447	14,804	6,059	702,025
Protection and/or conservation of slopes	16,112	28,805	77,811	146,826	27,372	296,926
Nothing	241,996	1,026,469	423,801	281,640	202,979	2,176,885
Total (1)	475,778	2,454,060	922,097	1,006,203	317,498	5,175,636

Source: IBGE – Censo Agropecuário – SIDRA

Note (1) The sum is greater than the number of farms, since several farms practice more than one type of farming

TABLE 9.9: *Farms which receive technical training by type of training and size of farm, agricultural census 2006*

Technical education	Total	0–2 ha	2–10 ha	10–100 ha	100–1,000 ha	>1,000 ha
				Farms by size of farms		
Receive training	1,145,049	62,880	274,043	606,420	157,968	28,241
Government (federal, state or municipal)	491,607	37,560	130,307	266,979	44,215	3,790
Own or by the producer himself	250,263	12,915	40,697	106,828	68,304	18,235
Cooperatives	225,521	3,986	42,241	146,557	30,065	1,963
Integrated enterprises	153,860	4,982	51,510	85,966	7,780	1,460
Private planning companies	85,196	2,604	16,188	42,554	18,563	4,806
Non-governmental organizations (NGOs)	6,793	732	1,921	3,220	611	108
Other	30,376	1,763	7,176	14,526	5,566	1,011
Do not get training	4,030,587	986,120	1,154,108	1,365,180	266,320	19,337
Total	5,175,636	1,049,000	1,428,151	1,971,600	424,288	47,578

	Receive technical training occasionally					
Receive training	662,589	40,322	164,909	354,138	82,251	11,217
Government (federal, state or municipal)	330,143	24,698	89,421	179,317	28,746	2,202
Own or by the producer himself	147,810	9,861	27,979	67,461	33,589	6,411
Cooperatives	115,026	2,311	23,802	74,677	13,147	728
Integrated enterprises	55,194	1,761	18,301	30,411	3,278	587
Private planning companies	45,600	1,494	9,412	23,274	8,985	2,172
Non-governmental organizations (NGOs)	3,795	348	1,078	1,820	376	59
Other	18,797	1,107	4,526	9,189	3,241	546
Total	662,589	40,322	164,909	354,138	82,251	11,217
Receive technical training regularly						
Receive training	482,460	22,558	109,134	252,282	75,717	17,024
	161,464	12,862	40,886	87,662	15,469	1,588

(continued)

Government (federal, state or municipal)						
Own or by the producer himself	102,453	3,054	12,718	39,367	34,715	11,824
Cooperatives	110,495	1,675	18,439	71,880	16,918	1,235
Integrated enterprises	98,666	3,221	33,209	55,555	4,502	873
Private planning companies	39,596	1,110	6,776	19,280	9,578	2,634
Non-governmental organizations (NGOs)	2,998	384	843	1,400	235	49
Other	11,579	656	2,650	5,337	2,325	465
Total	482,460	22,558	109,134	252,282	75,717	17,024

Source: IBGE – Censo Agropecuário – SIDRA

work it," thus politically reinforcing the movement for land reform in Brazil. The intensification of these rural and urban social movements during the period of the democratic "opening" that extended from the late 1970s to early in the next decade, created increasing pressure for land reform. During this period there occurred several land seizures, which would become ever more effective with the so-called landless workers movement.[18] The MST – Landless Rural Workers Movement was created in 1984 in Cascavel, Paraná, and quickly received major support from the Bishops Land Pastoral Commission.[19] The National Confederation of Agricultural Workers – CONTAG would be another institution with great political force in the field. Formed before the military regime, CONTAG, unlike the MST, represents small farmers. In spite of the strong repression it suffered, CONTAG survived into the military era defending the interests of the small rural producers, but also now supported agrarian reform as well.[20] In 1995 CONTAG decided to join the CUT – Central Única dos Trabalhadores, thus joining the movements of urban and rural workers in a united front.

According to a study by the Ministry of Agrarian Development, from the end of the military regime until the promulgation of the 1988 Constitution was a period of construction of important organizations of rural workers and farmers. Commercial farmers organized themselves into the National Confederation of Agriculture (CNA), the Rural Democratic Union (UDR) and the Brazilian Agribusiness Association (ABAG). In turn family farmers joined the CONTAG, and the landless workers the MST, and Via Campesina, as well as the National Department of Rural Workers of the CUT (DNTR) which in turn would give rise to the Federation of Workers in Family Agriculture (FETRAF). In this new scenario new conflicts and new institutional arrangements

---

[18] In 1981, the Acampamento Natalino, in Rio Grande do Sul, would be the symbol of the landless movement, the manifestation of support received and repercussions generated in other parts of the country. *A História da Luta pela terra*. MST – Movimento dos Trabalhadores Rurais sem Terra. Accessed April 22, 2017, at www.mst.org.br/nossa-historia/inicio.

[19] At the 1985 congress the MST decided to be an autonomous non-party and non-government organization whose principal activity would be land occupations, and by May of that year they had seized twelve properties. Ibid.; and João Pedro Stedile and Bernardo Mançano Fernandes, *Brava Gente. A Trajetória do MST e a Luta Pela Terra no Brasil* (São Paulo: Editora Fundação Perseu Abramo, 2005).

[20] *Trajetória política da Contag – As Primeiras Lutas*. Accessed April 22, 2017, at http://enfoc.org.br/system/arquivos/documentos/43/Trajetria-poltica-da-contag–as-primeiras-lutas–revista-40-anos-da-contag.pdf.

were established. Until the early 1990s, agrarian reform revolved around the debate over what were unproductive lands which could be expropriated. The agrarian policy of the government of Fernando Henrique Cardoso in turn was based on the settlement of landless families on public lands and allowed expropriation only through legal constitutional means.[21]

In 1994, faced with the strong rural mobilizations, including that of the small rural producers who demanded access to rural credit, the government created the Program of Valorization of Small Rural Production (PROVAPE).[22] The decree which established the norms of rural credit provided by PROVAPE defined small rural producers whose gross income from agriculture was 80%, who did not employ permanent workers and had below a standard size of farms.[23] The defined interest rate of their credit was 4% per year. One criticism of the small producers was of their inability to survive in the face of agribusiness expansion, resulting in the disappearance of thousands of small rural producers. In 1996 these pro-small farm policies were strengthened with the creation of the National Program to Strengthen Family Agriculture (PRONAF). Its purpose was to promote the sustainable development of the rural segment made up of family farmers, so as to enable them to increase productive capacity, generate jobs and improve incomes.[24] In 2006, Law 11.326 defined that for legal purposes a family farmer and a rural family entrepreneur is considered to be one who practices activities in rural areas, while meeting the following requirements: does not hold, in any capacity, an area larger than four tax modules;[25] predominantly uses the labor force of the family itself in the economic activities of its establishment or enterprise; has

---

[21] Valter Bianchini. *Vinte Anos do PRONAF, 1995–2015. Avanços e Desafios* (Brasília: Ministério do Desenvolvimento Agrário, 2015), pp. 18–19.

[22] In 1993, the CUT South Rural Forum held a seminar in Chapecó, Santa Catarina, with the motto "Investment Credit – a struggle worth millions of lives." The seminar pointed out that credit would be the central banner of the trade union movement at that moment, which could trigger the conquest of other policies: technical assistance and rural extension, land credit, research, education and professional training, infrastructure and housing. This was to be the ideology behind the PRONAF. Bianchini. *Vinte Anos do PRONAF*, p. 23.

[23] Resolution 2101, of August 24, 1994.   [24] Law 1946, of June 28, 1996.

[25] The *módulo fiscal*, established by Law 6.746/1979, is an agrarian unit of measure that represents the minimum area required for rural properties to be economically viable. Its size varies from 5 to 110 hectares, according to the municipality. Elena C. Landau et al., *Variação Geográfica dos Tamanhos dos Módulos Fiscais no Brasil* (Sete Lagoas: Embrapa Milho e Sorgo, 2012).

family income predominantly originated from economic activities linked to the farm; and directed his or her establishment with their family labor. Under certain conditions, foresters, aquaculturists, fishermen and forest extractivists are also beneficiaries of the law, along with indigenous peoples and members of rural *quilombos* (runaway slave communities) and other traditional communities.[26] Decree 3508/2000 defined that the beneficiaries of settlements forming part of the National Agrarian Reform Program would also be considered family farmers, and thus beneficiaries of PRONAF.

The PRONAF program was based on a concept of family agriculture that used various definitions such as size of property, family labor and income from rural activities. There is much debate about the use of this PRONAF concept. Many authors believe that the group of farmers classified as family farmers would have characteristics of "peasants," but most scholars disagree with this classification defended by rural sociologists, and criticize the very use of the concept of family farming as a catchall for farmers with very distinct characteristics. They argue there needs to be a change of these policies to make the pattern of agrarian development more balanced and fair, opening new doors for the productive transformation of so-called family establishments, inserting them more solidly in markets and productive value chains, and increasing their income.[27] Credit-focused programs are held to be insufficient to deal with the problems of poor families, such as the low

---

[26] Article 3 of Law 1946.

[27] Various positions with respect to this theme can be found in Maria Thereza Macedo Pedroso, "Experiências internacionais com a agricultura familiar e o caso brasileiro: o desafio da nomeação e suas implicações práticas," in Antônio Márcio Buainain et al., eds., *O Mundo Rural no Brasil do Século 21. A Formação de um Novo Padrão Agrário e Agrícola* (Brasília: Embrapa, 2014): 761–792. Zander Navarro and Maria Thereza Macedo Pedroso, *Agricultura Familiar: É Preciso Mudar para Avançar* (Brasília: Embrapa Informações Tecnológicas, 2011); Zander Navarro. "A agricultura familiar no Brasil: entre a política e as transformações da vida econômica," in José Garcia Gasques, José Eustáquio Ribeiro Filho and Zander Navarro, *A Agricultura Brasileira: Desempenho, Desafios, Perspectivas* (Brasília: Ipea/Mapa, 2010), 185–209; José Eli da Veiga, "Agricultura familiar e sustentabilidade," *Cadernos de Ciência & Tecnologia*, Brasília, 13, no. 3 (1996): 383–404; Maria de Nazareth Baudel Wanderley, *Agricultura familiar e campesinato: rupturas e continuidade*; accessed March 26, 2017, at http://r1.ufrrj.br/esa/V2/ojs/index .php/esa/article/view/238/234; and Arilde Franco Alves, "As múltiplas funções da agricultura familiar camponesa: práticas sócio-culturais e ambientais de convivência com o semi-arido" (PhD thesis, Universidade Federal de Campina Grande, Campina Grande, 2009).

level of education of most small farmers, the lack of basic infrastructure in their regions and the limited access to technical assistance.[28]

But PRONAF has had some success. It has been able to aggregate all government programs aimed at small producers, smallholders and undoubtedly the poorest portion of Brazilian farmers. It has also achieved a significant increase in resources. Between 2003/2004 and 2014/2015, there was a real growth of 9% per year in resources, and by this latter date PRONAF accounted for approximately 12% of the total credit granted in the rural credit system (Table 9.10).[29] For the 2016/2017 crop, R$26 billion was made available for the program. Interest rates are highly favorable as they range from 2.5% to 5.5%, well below the other interest rates of the economy, and contemplate the transfer of subsidies to such producers. In addition to credit, the program provides rural insurance and some rural extension services. But beyond credit, perhaps the most important government support for small farmers came when the National School Feeding Program (PNAE) was created in 2009, which required that at least 30% of the food purchased for by the National Education Development Fund (FNDE) must compulsorily be used in the purchase of foodstuffs from family farms.[30]

The 2006 census introduced the classification of family and non-family farming, allowing a broad characterization of this segment of the rural world. Whatever the validity of this definition of family farms, the fact that government programs are targeted to this group means that they now are a distinct element in the agricultural world. In the agricultural census

---

[28] Buainain states that the analysis of the crop plan of 2013–2014 shows the fragmentation of the programs, making it difficult to evaluate their effectiveness. There were sixteen programs, divided into Operational Costs, Investment, Rural Microcredit, Agroecology, Women, Agribusiness, Semiarid, Youth, Forest, Marketing, etc. In addition the group of beneficiaries has expanded, with non-agricultural activities, such as fishermen, shellfish, now included. Antônio Marcio Buainain, "O tripé da política agrícola brasileira: crédito rural, seguro e PRONAF: in Antônio Márcio Buainain et al., *O Mundo Rural no Brasil do Século 21*: 826–864.

[29] See Input *Evolução do Crédito Rural no Brasil entre 2003 e 2016*. Accessed March 26, 2017, at www.inputbrasil.org/wp-content/uploads/2016/08/Evolucao_do_Credito_Rur al_CPI.pdf.

[30] Law no. 11.947, of June 16, 2009. On this theme see FNDE, *Aquisição de Produtos da Agricultura Familiar para a Alimentação Escolar*, accessed March 23, 2017, at www.fnde .gov.br; Elisa Braga Saraiva, et al., "Panorama da Compra de Alimentos da Agricultura Familiar para o Programa Nacional de Alimentação Escolar," accessed March 23, 2017, at www.scielo.br/pdf/csc/v18n4/04.pdf; Eduardo Sá, "Merenda escolar: uma revolução para para os agricultores familiares.ANA – Articulação Nacional de Agroecologia," accessed March 23, 2017, at www.agroecologia.org.br/2016/08/17/merenda-escolar-uma-revolucao-para-os-agricultores-familiares/.

TABLE 9.10: *Value of rural credit by family and commercial farms, 2003/ 2004–2014/2015 (in millions of reais)*

| Year | Family farms | | | Commercial farms | |
	Value	% Change	% Total	Value	Total
2003/2004	8,695		11%	70,325	79,020
2004/2005	10,983	26%	12%	79,642	90,125
2005/2006	12,300	12%	14%	74,029	86,328
2006/2007	13,191	7%	15%	77,391	90,582
2007/2008	13,074	−1%	11%	106,761	119,835
2008/2009	14,779	13%	13%	99,999	114,777
2009/2010	16,760	13%	12%	126,536	143,296
2010/2011	16,046	−4%	11%	131,732	147,778
2011/2012	16,759	4%	12%	122,219	138,978
2012/2013	23,107	38%	13%	149,290	172,397
2013/2014	26,001	13%	12%	183,552	209,552
2014/2015	24,477	−6%	14%	152,918	177,395

Source: Input. Mapeamento. Evolução do crédito rural no Brasil entre 2003–2016,
Note: Values are up to August 2015 www.inputbrasil.org/wp-content/uploads/2016/08/Ev olucao_do_Credito_Rural_CPI.pdf

of 2006, 3.9 million family farmers and 736,000 non-family farmers were counted.[31] Family farmers represent 84% of total rural producers, but their production is equivalent to only a third of the total value of production in 2006. There is much regional difference in these aggregate outcomes. The Northeast has the largest number of family farmers, with almost 2 million classified in this category, representing half of the family farmers surveyed in 2006; these family producers constitute the extraordinary percentage of 89% of the total number of farmers in the Northeast that year. The South comes in second place, with 792,000 family farmers, representing one-fifth of the region's total farmers. In terms of the value of family agriculture production, the South occupies the lead, accounting for about 40% of the total value of family agriculture production in 2006. The Northeast and Southeast follow in total production (see Table 9.11).

[31] Carlos Guanziroli et al. present an in-depth study of family farming based on the 1996 census, using the methodology developed in the FAO/INCRA Convention, which previously used data from the 1985 census. Guanziroli et al., *Agricultura Familiar e Reforma Agrária no Século XXI* (Rio de Janeiro: Editora Garamond, 2001).

TABLE 9.11: *Family and non-family farms by value of production, agricultural census of 2006 (in reais)*

Region	Total			Family farms			Non-family farms		
	Farms	Value of production	Average	Farms	Value of production	Average	Farms	Value of production	Average
North	412,935	9,141,737,000	22,138	357,447	5,077,655,000	14,205	55,488	4,064,082,000	73,243
Northeast	2,225,605	29,218,651,000	13,128	1,978,236	13,403,163,000	6,775	247,369	15,815,488,000	63,935
Southeast	797,846	52,879,410,000	66,278	599,688	11,775,027,000	19,635	198,158	41,104,382,000	207,432
South	938,446	43,926,142,000	46,807	792,535	21,103,471,000	26,628	145,911	22,822,671,000	156,415
Center-West	264,043	28,820,355,000	109,150	174,776	3,134,801,000	17,936	89,267	25,685,554,000	287,739
Brazil	4,638,875	163,986,294,000	35,350	3,902,682	54,494,117,000	13,963	736,193	109,492,177,000	148,728

Source: IBGE – Censo Agropecuário – SIDRA

In relation to land area, we can see the same imbalance identified in the case of the value of production. Although family farms accounted for 84% of total producers, their share of farming land was limited to 25%. The Northeast was the region with the largest area belonging to family farmers (35%), although it had the smallest average farm size, with only 13 hectares per establishment. The opposite extreme occurred in the Center-West, with a smaller area belonging to family farmers and at the same time the highest average area per establishment (43 hectares). In the comparison between family and non-family farmers, family farmers had an average of 18 hectares per establishment in Brazil, while for non-family farmers the average was 313 hectares. The Center-West as could be expected had the largest average size for non-family farmers (955 hectares), with the North being the second highest (617 hectares). In the Southeast, the average family and non-family reached 18 hectares and 190 hectares respectively (Table 9.12).

Although the average number of staff employed by non-family establishments is higher than family establishments (6.0 workers to 3.6 workers), the large number of family farm households means that they contain three-quarters of those employed in rural areas. And among the 12.3 million people employed in family units, half were in family establishments located in the Northeast. The South accounted for 18% and Southeast for 15%. The average number of persons employed per household varied from 4.1 in the Northeast to 2.7 in the Center-West.

In the non-family units, the Southeast and Northeast had the highest number of persons employed (see Table 9.13). Proportionally we find more members of non-family agriculture with activity outside the home, compared to households with family farming. In the case of non-relatives, half had members performing activities outside the home. In families, this percentage was just under 30%. There was no large regional variation in this indicator (Table 9.14).

Of the 4.6 million farmers only 919,000 took some form of loan. In the case of family farmers, this number reached 736,000, corresponding to 20% of the establishments in this category. The Southern regions had the highest proportion (40%) of small farmers who obtained these loans. The vast majority of these loans for family farmers were in the form of investment and for costs of inputs. Marketing loans were infrequent. In the case of non-family farms, the percentage of those who made some kind of loans was similar to the levels observed among family farmers (19%). Among the non-family farms, the higher credit penetration was also in the Southern region. By modality, the loans given for operating

TABLE 9.12: *Family and non-family farms by size and region, agrarian census of 2006 (in hectares)*

Region	Total			Family farms			Non-family farms		
	Farms	Area	Average size	Farms	Area	Average size	Farms	Area	Average Size
North	475,778	55,535,764	117	412,666	16,611,277	40	63,112	38,924,487	617
Northeast	2,454,060	76,074,411	31	2,187,131	28,315,052	13	266,929	47,759,359	179
Southeast	922,097	54,937,773	60	699,755	12,771,299	18	222,342	42,166,474	190
South	1,006,203	41,781,003	42	849,693	13,054,511	15	156,510	28,726,492	184
Center-West	317,498	105,351,087	332	217,022	9,350,556	43	100,476	96,000,530	955
Brazil	5,175,636	333,680,038	64	4,366,267	80,102,695	18	809,369	253,577,342	313

Source: IBGE – Censo Agropecuário – SIDRA

TABLE 9.13: *Family and non-family farms by numbers of persons employed by region, agricultural census of 2006*

Region	Total			Family farms			Non-family farms		
	Farms	Workers	Average	Farms	Workers	Average	Farms	Workers	Average
North	400,767	1,655,649	4.1	342,306	1,383,640	4.0	58,461	272,009	4.7
Northeast	1,769,362	7,699,138	4.4	1,556,168	6,365,251	4.1	213,194	1,333,887	6.3
Southeast	809,965	3,283,049	4.1	607,416	1,798,935	3.0	202,549	1,484,114	7.3
South	862,059	2,920,445	3.4	726,931	2,244,347	3.1	135,128	676,098	5.0
Center-West	293,725	1,009,924	3.4	200,126	530,937	2.7	93,599	478,987	5.1
Brazil	4,135,878	16,568,205	4.0	3,432,947	12,323,110	3.6	702,931	4,245,095	6.0

Source: IBGE – Censo Agropecuário – SIDRA

TABLE 9.14: *Farm families and non-family farms with outside work by household and region, agricultural census 2006*

Region	Total of farns		Family farms			Non-family farms	
	Total	Outside work	Total	Outside work		Total	Outside work
North	412,935	114,120	357,447	90,469		55,488	23,651
Northeast	2,225,605	692,599	1,978,236	556,492		247,369	136,107
Southeast	797,846	303,967	599,688	204,289		198,158	99,678
South	938,446	266,000	792,535	198,719		145,911	67,281
Center-West	264,043	102,730	174,776	62,693		89,267	40,037
Brazil	4,638,875	1,479,416	3,902,682	1,112,662		736,193	366,754

Source: IBGE – Censo Agropecuário – SIDRA

393

costs were significantly more important in number of users than the credit for investments, while marketing credit was insignificant (see Table 9.15).

There were also significant differences in the gross value of production of family farms by region and type of activity. Family farms producing permanent crops had a higher average value of production than those growing temporary crops. Family farms producing livestock averaged less than half of the value of production derived from agricultural crops. Since each establishment could declare more than one activity and the value presented in Table 9.16 corresponds to the value of each declared crop or animals created.

Unquestionably these family farmers were the majority of establishments in the rural area. They constitute the great majority of the farms, they concentrate a significant part of the manpower occupied in agriculture and were important in several crops. However, proportionally, the value of agricultural production of these small producers and family farmers is less representative. But this type of aggregate analysis hides important information about differing yields per farm. Depending on the distribution of income, even among small producers or family producers, the average obtained from the aggregated values can distort the results. Thus, in the last few years numerous studies have emerged using microdata from the 2006 census which allow for a more accurate assessment of the distribution of gross and net yields and identify the set of producers with negative net income.[32]

---

[32] On this theme see Eliseu Alves, Geraldo da Silva and Souza e Daniela de Paula Rocha, "Lucratividade da agricultura," *Revista de Política Agrícola*, XXI, no. 2 (Apr./May/Jun. 2012): 45–63; Antonio Márcio Buainain and Junior Ruiz Garcia, "Os pequenos Produtores rurais mais pobres ainda tem alguma chance como agricultores?" in Silvia Kanadani Campos and Zander Navarro, *A Pequena Produção Rural e as Tendências do Desenvolvimento Agrário Brasileiro: Ganhar Tempo é Possível?* (Brasília: CGEE, 2013): 29–70; Eliseu Alves and Daniela de Paula Rocha, "Ganhar tempo é possível?" in José Garcia Gasques, José Eustáquio Ribeiro Filho and Zander Navarro (orgs.), *A Agricultura Brasileira: Desempenho, Desafios e Perspectivas* (Brasília: IPEA, 2010): chap. 11, 275–290; Navarro and Campos, "A 'pequena produção' no Brasil," in Campos and Navarro, *A Pequena Produção Rural*: 13–28; José Eustáquio Ribeiro Vieira Filho, "Distribuição produtiva e tecnológica dos estabelecimentos agropecuários de menor porte e gestão familiar," in Campos and Navarro *A Pequena Produção Rural*: 177–199; Antonio Márcio Buainain and Junior Ruiz Garcia, "Contextos locais ou regionais: importância para a viabilidade econômica dos pequenos produtores," in Campos and Navarro *A Pequena Produção Rural*: 133–176; Steven M. Helfand, Vanessa da Fonseca Pereira and Wagner Lopes Soares, "Pequenos e médios produtores na agricultura brasileira: situação atual e perspectivas," in Buainain et al., *O Mundo Rural no Brasil do Século 21*: 533–558; Ajax Reynaldo Bello Moreira, Steven M. Helfand and Adriano Marcos Rodrigues Figueiredo, "Explicando as diferenças de pobreza entre produtores agrícolas no brasil," *48°. Congresso Sober*, July 2010, accessed April 4, 2007, at www.sober.org.br/palestra/15/156.pdf.

TABLE 9.15: *Family and non-family farmers who obtained credit for investments, operating costs and marketing of products, agricultural census of 2006*

Region	Total farmers			Number of family farmers who took loans				Number of non-family farmers who took loans			
	Total	Family	Non-family	Total	Investments	Operating costs	Marketing	Total	Investments	Operating costs	Marketing
North	412,935	357,447	55,488	36,237	19,651	12,188	435	6,155	3,103	2,618	92
Northeast	2,225,605	1,978,236	247,369	294,993	192,602	65,515	5,673	30,406	18,938	8,672	696
Southeast	797,846	599,688	198,158	102,641	49,464	43,897	965	37,337	13,421	23,476	836
South	938,446	792,535	145,911	317,990	69,313	269,502	1,014	49,262	11,210	41,191	436
Center-West	264,043	174,776	89,267	28,483	12,837	14,624	197	15,612	4,889	10,947	210
Brazil	4,638,875	3,902,682	736,193	780,344	343,867	405,726	8,284	138,772	51,561	86,904	2,270

Source: IBGE – Censo Agropecuário – SIDRA

TABLE 9.16: *Family farms by origin of the value of production and region, agricultural census of 2006 (1)*

	Farmers	Animal production (3)	Crops (2)				
			Permanent	Sesonal	Others	Total crops	Agro-industries
Number of family farms							
North	357,447	595,740	95,479	185,094	405,119	685,692	23,868
Northeast	1,978,236	3,150,775	320,273	1,526,932	2,191,795	4,039,000	104,565
Southeast	599,688	1,105,775	176,520	293,064	744,649	1,214,233	18,363
South	792,535	1,996,847	77,631	625,964	1,318,149	2,021,744	23,404
Center-West	174,776	436,277	9,601	60,029	156,291	225,921	2,983
Brazil	3,902,682	7,285,414	679,504	2,691,083	4,816,003	8,186,590	173,183
Total value of family farm production – R$1,000							
North	5,077,655	2,547,893	753,725	2,315,478	4,161,775	7,230,978	73,030
Northeast	13,403,163	5,306,766	4,146,826	5,432,068	11,594,223	21,173,117	135,381
Southeast	11,775,027	6,061,004	3,927,025	3,056,369	10,337,798	17,321,192	57,021
South	21,103,471	13,843,007	1,676,086	10,765,160	15,808,602	28,249,848	22,746
Center-West	3,134,801	3,196,729	99,138	1,199,162	1,730,554	3,028,854	6,867
Brazil	54,494,117	30,955,400	10,602,800	22,768,237	43,632,949	77,003,986	295,046

Average value of the production of family farms – R$

North	14,205	4,277	7,894	12,510	10,273	10,546	3,060
Northeast	6,775	1,684	12,948	3,558	5,290	5,242	1,295
Southeast	19,635	5,481	22,247	10,429	13,883	14,265	3,105
South	26,628	6,932	21,590	17,198	11,993	13,973	972
Center-West	17,936	7,327	10,326	19,976	11,073	13,407	2,302
Brazil	13,963	4,249	15,604	8,461	9,060	9,406	1,704

Source: IBGE – Censo Agropecuário – SIDRA

Notes: (1) The same farm can have several types of production. (2) Includes horticulture, orchards, forest and plant extractions, etc. (3) Includes animals of all sizes, and fowl.

One of the most complete datasets available on this theme comes from the study of Alves, Souza and Rocha carried out in 2012.[33] This study which examined all farming units based on their income shows the high concentration of gross income in a small percentage of farms, which was already evident when we examined the value of production, and property size by region. Their study shows that gross monthly income of up to two minimum wages accounted for two-thirds of the establishments, but these poorer units produced only 3.3% of the gross value of production in 2006. On the other hand, the farms that had an average production of 861 minimum monthly salaries, just 27,000 establishments, accounted for more than half of the gross value of production, . Based on these results, the authors conclude that 53,345 establishments would be enough to produce the entire production of Brazilian agriculture in any year.[34] This estimation makes sense, since in the 2006 census, 500,000 establishments (or 11% of all farms) generated 87% of the total value of production of that year. This demonstrates the elevated concentration of income in the agrarian sector (Table 9.17).

Alves and Rocha (2010) in another study have further divided the establishments with gross production value of up to two minimum wages (see Table 9.18). There are 3.7 million such farm units, with some 11 million rural workers.[35] The results are dramatic. A total of 579,000 did not declare self-consumption or any sales of production. On the other hand, more than 2 million establishments, which represent practically half of the registered farms, declared monthly gross income to be half a minimum wage. These had an annual production, which included self-consumption, of only 643.84 *reais*, that is, average annual income of just over two minimum wages. Considering three people per establishment, this annual rent represents R$18 per month per person, to be compared with the monthly minimum wage of R$300 in that year. The authors explained these results as due to the low technological standard adopted by these farmers and their very low educational level, and they see no possibility of further investments in agriculture resolving this poverty. They suggest that the income of these poor farmers can only be supplemented by income distributive programs, such as Bolsa Familia, rural retirement programs, and the Bolsa Escola (School Grant). Part of the problem is being solved by gradual migration of these poor farmers to urban areas, and the growing portion of the rural population earning

---

[33] Alves, Souza and Rocha, "Lucratividade da agricultura": 45–63.   [34] Ibid.: 48.

[35] The authors estimate three persons per establishment. Alves and Rocha, "Ganhar tempo é possível?": 276.

TABLE 9.17: *Distribution of the annual gross value of production, by classes of minimum monthly salaries, agricultural census of 2006*

Minimum monthly salary	Farms (1)	%	Gross value production	%	GVP/farm (value)	GVP/farm in minimum monthly salaries
0–2	2,904,769	66.0%	5,518,045,129	3.3%	1,900	0.52
2–10	995,750	22.6%	16,688,283,807	10.1%	16,760	4.66
10–200	472,702	10.7%	58,689,461,376	35.5%	124,157	34.49
>200	27,306	0.6%	84,727,015,692	51.2%	3,102,872	861.91
Total	4,400,527	100.0%	165,522,806,004	100.0%	37,614	10.45

Source: Alves, Souza and Rocha, "Lucratividade da agricultura" (2012): 48
Notes: IBGE Censo 2006, data updated to 2010. Minimum Monthly Salary = R$300.00. IBGE (2012).
(1) Only farms which declared GVP are considered.

TABLE 9.18: *Annual gross value of production of poor farms of less than two monthly minimum salaries, 2006*

Class of monthly minimum salaries	Number	Percentage	Average by class (R$/farm)
No information	579,024	15%	–
0–1/2	2,014,567	53%	643.64
1/2–1	611,755	16%	2,574.84
1–2	570,480	15%	5,142.65
Total	3,775,826	100%	1,537.57

Source: Alves and Rocha, "Ganhar tempo é possível?" (2010)
Note: Based on agrarian census of 2006

income from work outside these inherently inefficient farms in other agricultural units or the urban area.[36]

The analysis of the distribution of agricultural establishments by income can be enriched with the introduction of the variable region. There was significant difference between the North and the Northeast and the other regions of the country. Some 88% of the establishments located in the Northeast region and 76% in the Northern region had gross income lower than two monthly minimum wages. In the Center-West and the Southeast this percentage was reduced to two-thirds and in the South it was below 50%. If we take establishments with more than ten monthly minimum wages, the disparity is repeated, since 3–4% of the establishments in the North and Northeast of this group were in this group, against 13% in the Southeast and 17% in the Southern region. In all regions, the value of production represented by establishments with up to two minimum wages was reduced, usually less than 5%, except in the Northeast, where the percentage increased to 11%.

The same exception occurred when we consider establishments with an income greater than ten minimum monthly salaries. The value of their production represented over 80% of the value of production in the South, Southeast and Center-West, but they were about ten percentage points lower in the North and Northeast.

---

[36] According to the authors, their income needs to be complemented by Bolsa Família, the rural retirement program, Bolsa Escola, and rural and urban transport to facilitate the education of children and of urban employment of family members. Labor laws need to be simplified to permit part-time employment in agriculture, and stimulating agribusiness that has great potential to generate temporary jobs. This will give the urban centers time to acquire capacity to house part of this population. Ibid.

TABLE 9.19 *Distribution of gross value of production by value of monthly minimum salary, by region, agricultural census 2006*

Regions	Number	% by region	% in Brazil	% production/ region	Average value of production
Annual gross value of production = 0–2 minimum monthly salary					
BRAZIL	3,775,826		73.0	4.0	0.43
North	360,190	75.7	9.5	11.1	0.53
Northeast	2,149,279	87.6	56.9	9.6	0.35
Center-West	216,215	68.1	5.7	1.8	0.46
Southeast	572,859	62.1	15.2	2.0	0.46
South	477,283	47.4	12.6	2.6	0.63
Annual gross value of production = 2–10 minimum monthly salary					
BRAZIL	975,974	18.9	18.9	11.1	4.53
North	92,799	0.2	1.8	21.8	4.01
Northeast	228,076	9.3	4.4	12.2	4.22
Center-West	71,287	22.5	1.4	5.6	4.30
Southeast	226,625	24.6	4.4	7.8	4.60
South	357,187	35.5	6.9	15.1	4.88
Annual gross value of production = 10+ minimum monthly salary					
BRAZIL	423,689	8.2	8.2	84.9	80.04
North	22,786	4.8	0.4	67.1	50.32
Northeast	76,651	3.1	1.5	78.2	80.49
Center-West	2,976	9.4	0.6	92.7	170.35
Southeast	122,565	13.3	2.4	90.2	98.01
South	171,711	17.1	3.32	82.28	55.19

Source: Alves and Rocha, "Ganhar tempo é possível?" (2010)

In the case of the average value per establishment, which reflected size and productivity, there was a significant difference between the various regions. The Center-West average (170 monthly minimum salaries) was practically double the average observed in the other regions of Brazil (see Table 9.19).

The basic findings of these microdata and census materials show the existence of a large segment of Brazilian farms with low productivity, low value of production and income less than the minimum necessary for family survival and a population with little technical knowledge. Alves, Souza and Rocha affirm that "the technology created by Brazilian and foreign research has spread, but in an asymmetrical way, leaving millions of establishments marginalized, especially those with the lowest income monthly minimum wages – therein lies the Brazilian problem of technology diffusion."[37]

The relationship between gross income and liquid income per capita is similar to all the other indices. It shows that 2.5 million establishments had net income less than zero, that is, negative income.[38] Of these establishments with incomes lower than zero, 77% obtained gross income less than or equal to two monthly minimum wages. These establishments produced only 8% of the gross income generated by the agricultural activity in the year of the agricultural census of 2006. Of a total of 2.9 million producers with a gross income of less than two monthly minimum wages, two-thirds had negative net income. If we consider the establishments with gross income exceeding 200 minimum wages, only 19% declare net negative income. That is, there was negative net income in all classes of minimum wage farm units, though of declining importance as gross income increased (see Table 9.20).

These data and other studies raise important questions about the future of small farms. They suggest that the potential of agricultural income alone being able to take agricultural producers out of poverty cannot be achieved by increasing land, or productivity alone would solve the problem of rural poverty. In the Northeast, for example, about two-thirds of the establishments have less than 10 hectares. At the level of productivity observed for establishments in the fifth productivity decile, an increase in size from 5–10 hectares to 20–50 hectares would not reduce the incidence of poverty below 70%. On the other hand, even if the establishments with 5–10 hectares could be as productive as those with the ninth productivity decile, 60% would still be classified as poor.[39]

---

[37] Alves, Souza and Rocha, "Lucratividade da agricultura": 48.   [38] Ibid.: 51–53.

[39] Ajax Reynaldo Bello Moreira, Steven M. Helfand, and Adriano Marcos Rodrigues Figueiredo, "Explicando as diferenças de pobreza entre produtores agrícolas no brasil," *48°. Congresso SOBER*, July 2010, accessed April 1, 2007, at www.sober.org .br/palestra/15/156.pdf.

TABLE 9.20: *Net and gross income of farms in terms of minimum monthly salary, agricultural census of 2006*

Class of minimum salary	Greater than or equal to 0		Less than 0		Net income % of farms		Gross income % of farms	
	Farms	%	Farms	%	≥0	<0	≥0	<0
0–2	1,010,785	52%	1,893,984	77%	35%	65%	2%	8%
2–10	585,792	30%	408,958	17%	59%	41%	8%	18%
10–200	332,060	17%	140,633	6%	70%	30%	33%	44%
>200	22,239	1%	5,067	0%	81%	19%	57%	30%
Total	1,951,885	100%	2,448,642	100%	44%	56%	100%	100%

Source: Alves, Souza and Rocha, "Lucratividade da agriculture" (2012): 52

Another study concluded that these small poorly operating farms could only survive with government income transfers and part-time or alternative labor arrangements in urban centers.[40] Several of the studies cited in this chapter conclude that Brazil seems to be undergoing a bifurcated development, with an advanced part with rapid growth in agricultural production based on high productivity rates, and a socially negative sector that seems unable to advance. Government policies directed to this sector often had little impact due to lack of knowledge of local conditions.[41] There are also numerous impediments, from lack of education and an inability to use the new technology, to poor infrastructure, lack of adequate credit and an inability to productively use what is available, that make it difficult for poor farmers to break out of their poverty and adopt modern techniques. Despite this, there is the possibility to move some of them into the productive sector. Although poor rural producers are homogeneous in terms of low production, this group is heterogeneous in terms of the potential to raise productivity, production and agricultural income. That is, it is a group of producers and establishments that have different potentials. To identify these potential producers it is necessary to study them in detail and for government policies to distinguish the factors that have the potential to move some of these poor farmers into the modern sector, rather than treat them as a homogeneous group of family farmers.[42] But the solution for many will be the classic ones. For a large portion of these poor farmers, a reasonably high overall national economic growth that increases urban employment opportunities will lead to a rapid rural exodus with a continuing loss of rural population that has been typical of all rural regions in the last fifty years.[43]

---

[40] Silvia Kanadani Campos and Zander Navarro, eds., *A Pequena Produção Rural e as Tendências do Desenvolvimento Agrário Brasileiro: Ganhar Tempo é Possível* (Brasília: CGEE, 2013).

[41] Zander Navarro and Silvia Kanadani Campos, "A pequena produção rural no Brasil," in ibid.: chap. 1,13–27.

[42] Ibid.: 39–40.

[43] Navarro and Campos, "A pequena produção rural no Brasil": 16. An alternative view was presented by Carlos Guanziroli for whom the competitiveness of family production in agriculture is given by the relation between the net value per unit of labor and its reduced opportunity cost, to place the sectors of family producers with a low level of capitalization in conditions to start projects – such measures do not require large investments in land and labor-saving equipment. According to the authors, with a minimum of credit support and technical assistance, the most important requirement for success is the organization of producers that reduces transaction costs and creates an environment of trust that allows new ways of social insertion. Guanziroli, *Agricultura Familiar e Reforma Agrária*, p. 40.

Conclusion

There are several crucial moments to understand the process of transformation of Brazilian agriculture, which has gone from a traditional activity of low productivity, based on abundant land and cheap labor, to the current situation in which Brazil represents one of the most important players in the international market for agricultural products. The first was in its role as a handmaiden to industrialization, which was a theme throughout Latin America in the post-World War II period. From the middle of the last century agriculture has been identified as fundamental to the development process, a process designed to create an industrial base through an intense and induced process of import substitution. The viability of the import substitution model required capital and machine imports, and a subservient role for agriculture which was to supply cheap food for the growing urban population, and agricultural raw materials for industry and for export to pay for imports. In this import substitution model, agriculture was supposed to transfer resources to other sectors of the economy by buying products from a poorly productive, inefficient, protected industry with a small scale of production, and by selling its products cheaply. This induced industrialization needed an abundant and cheap labor supply, and it was agriculture which was to fulfill this need.

As the urban centers of Brazil expanded rapidly in this period, civil construction itself was a major contender for labor with the nascent industry. In turn many of these new light industries were primarily food and textile industries and needed to be supplied with raw materials produced by national agriculture. It was expected that Brazilian agriculture would be able to release the labor necessary for the import substitution process, without affecting the supply of the agricultural products necessary for these various national and international markets.

In addition, agriculture was the basis of Brazilian exports, supplying the foreign exchange necessary for the precarious balance of external accounts. It was expected to help pay for the growing demand for equipment and raw materials required by import substitution processes. The process of import substitution initially faced serious problems in the balance of payments because of its capital and machine import needs in the initial intensive phase of construction and before any exports could occur to pay for these imports. This was particularly acute when, as in the case of Brazil, it was desired to establish heavy capital goods industries producing basic inputs or durable consumer goods.

In this model it was assumed at the time that agriculture could only meet these demands through agrarian reform, which would liberate productive forces that were held in check by an archaic land tenure system and seemingly feudal labor relations. Many Latin American nations attempted such a reform in this period. But in the case of Brazil, authoritarian military governments or democratic regimes dependent on the rural elite were the initiators of the intense import substitution program, and for political reasons it was decided that this process of agrarian modernization could only succeed with the political support of the rural landowners, or at least without their opposition. This meant that the perverse agrarian structure that historically characterizes Brazil should be preserved, without radical changes in the concentrated structure of land tenure. For this reason, since its inception this process of transformation of the Brazilian rural world has been classified as a conservative modernization.

There is little question that the transformations that took place in agriculture, beginning modestly in the 1930s and 1940s, but intensified after the 1960s, were made possible by direct government action, through the modernization of agricultural support instruments such as subsidized and massive credit, rural extension, agricultural research, minimum price support policies, the regulation of agricultural stocks and measures to protect local production. In addition, numerous institutions were created to guide the structure of production, distribution and marketing of individual products. At the same time that these modern instruments of public management of agriculture were created in the 1960s and 1970s involving policies of price support, a broad and sophisticated system of public or compulsory credit for agriculture was made available. These abundant agricultural loans were heavily subsidized with below market interest rates and were used to finance investments, cover operating costs and support the commercialization of the crop. They enabled and stimulated farmers to purchase modern machinery, equipment, and such crucial inputs as fertilizers and insecticides. They also were only granted to those who modernized their production, and left aside those who could not enter into the world of modern commercial agriculture because they lacked the education, sufficient property, available infrastructure or technical assistance to participate, or were unwilling to use their lands for production.

This abundant and cheap credit also stimulated the construction of industries related to agriculture. But this new agricultural machinery and inputs industry was still not very efficient and depended on strong tariff protection. Thus it provided relatively less efficient products at a much higher cost than international markets. Subsidized credit compensated for this extra cost due to farmers' limited access to the international machinery and input markets. The subsidized credit also compensated for the eventual loss of profitability in the export of agricultural products due to the overvaluation of the national currency, a practice usual in Brazil, and the traditional control of prices for the main food consumption crops, particularly those that had greater weight on the cost of living index. The management of a comprehensive system of cross subsidies, management of regulatory stocks, setting of production quotas, control over imports and support for the export of agricultural products, along with this abundant credit, compensated farmers for these higher costs and potential loses on export revenues, or at least in the sales to the internal market. Agricultural credit in this scheme elaborated from the 1960s to the 1980s required major public resources and the administration of a large system of compulsory banking credit from bank deposits drawn from the public without remuneration despite high and growing inflation. From the late 1980s, the fundamentals of this model were dramatically altered due to the depletion of government funds and the reduction of the compulsory resources allocated by the banks, since demand deposits were drastically reduced due to the acceleration of inflation.

Subsequently the neoliberal reforms which reached Brazil in the decade of the 1990s created a rapid opening and integration of the Brazilian economy into the world market. What could have been the deathblow to the process of productive modernization of Brazilian agriculture was, on the contrary, a process of acceleration of this modernization. The subsidies were terminated, but price tagging, production quotas, difficulties in exporting, and the need to buy local inputs, were also extinguished.

The prices of agricultural commodities became directly related to international prices adjusted to the logistical costs, which in Brazil were and are traditionally high. In addition, agriculture gained free access to the international market where it acquired machinery and equipment, as well as the inputs needed for production at international prices. Thus input costs were greatly reduced.

But the key question which needed to be resolved was how to change the existing financial model, which was based on significant subsidies from public resources and the compulsory financing offered by the banking network. The resulting solution, created by market forces, and supported by the government, was a complex system made up of many different private sources, from regular bank loans, to cooperatives, supermarket chains, and international trading companies providing loans which even included a substantial introduction of barter arrangements. New vertical integration chains, also known as value chains, were established in many sectors of agriculture which allowed processors to supply the basic inputs needed by farmers. These multiple resources rather quickly filled the gap left by declining government resources, and by the twenty-first century the government itself returned to again providing major fiscal support. All this led to the creation of new and modern financing and risk mitigation systems made possible by the opening up of the economy. At the same time, costs declined for commercial farms though their access to the external market, all of which led to accelerated increases in productivity. This increased productivity in turn made it possible for Brazilian farms to both supply the local market, despite the new international competition, and also to win international markets, quickly becoming the leading seller in world markets of soybeans, corn, meats, sugar and orange juice as well as maintaining its traditional coffee dominance.

A response to all this credit and modernization was a dramatic increase in agricultural productivity. Older soils were rejuvenated with modern technology, average farm sizes declined and by the end of the last century production was increasing faster than land put into production. The traditional link between virgin lands and expanding production was finally broken and increased production was now based on increasing yields in traditional farming regions. Latifundia were replaced by modern large farms using machinery and the latest in modern seeds, fertilizers and insecticides.

This was possible only because in parallel with the creation of the sophisticated system of management of agricultural policy, Brazil for the first time was able to establish a significant public agricultural research program. Initially it was thought that it would be possible to develop Brazilian agriculture using existing technical knowledge, simply by bringing that knowledge to farmers through a broad extension program. But Brazil's tropical conditions were unique and required new solutions or the careful adoption of existing knowledge to local tropical conditions. Thus the government creation of Embrapa with its own units scattered throughout the country, and organized in the form of products or regions, was fundamental for increasing national productivity through modern scientific research specifically related to Brazilian conditions. In turn Embrapa's success was due to its human resources and training programs. It was able to form, in Brazil and abroad, thousands of professionals from various fields related to agriculture, many of whom become part of their staff.

The third factor explaining the success of Brazilian agriculture was the emergence of modern farmer entrepreneurs who were able to respond to the opening of the globalized world market, utilizing credit efficiently from both internal and international sources, using capital markets, hedging instruments and risk mitigation, and capable of successfully integrating into highly sophisticated production chains. Here the unusual role of well-educated and experienced Southern and Southeastern farmers was crucial. It was the famous gaucho migration to the Center-West which opened up this previously backward region to modern commercial agriculture. This migration in turn was made possible by massive government road construction in the middle decades of the twentieth century which opened up new marginal regions and incorporated large parts of western Brazil into the national economy. Finally the modern farmers have created numerous producer cooperatives, farmer associations and lobbies which have come to exercise major economic and political power, with representation in Congress, where they fiercely defend their interests.

Although Brazilian agriculture today accounts for about 5% of GDP, so-called agribusiness has reached an expressive dimension in the Brazilian economy. It is estimated that it represents between 20 and 25% of the national product. This industry not only includes agricultural production, but also incorporates the processing industry; a highly advanced services sector associated with agricultural production; the production of modern inputs which includes important branches of the chemical industry and products of modern biotechnology; and banking and financial services. This also includes transportation, which is perhaps one of the worst performing sectors of the agricultural complex, given the current deficiencies in this area and the magnitude of the investments needed for a continental country like Brazil.

Along with the modernization of these sectors and the increasing productivity of national agriculture, there are also the so-called "Brazil Costs," which burden national production. These include inefficient and excessive government bureaucracy, the irrational system of taxation, the high financial costs and exchange rate volatility, and the logistic inefficiency. Despite being heavily burdened by these extra costs, Brazilian agriculture is able to place its products on the international market at competitive prices. This is only possible because of the exceptional productivity of the commercial portion of Brazilian agriculture, which can compensate for the additional costs incurred for producing in Brazil.

Today it is recognized in Brazil that, in addition to competitiveness, the survival of Brazilian agriculture must be sustainable. This is an increasing value in the market and a factor of production differentiation. In a highly competitive market, Brazilian agricultural producers are showing an increasing concern for the environment, and also for cultural and social values related to "sustainability," which is a general concept, to some extent abstract, but a requirement for countries who want to play a prominent role in the international market for agricultural products, commodities or higher added value products. Also it is fundamental to recognize that today Brazil can increase its participation in the growing international market without requiring additional virgin lands. As we have noted, increasing production has occurred with an essentially stable supply of land, and will do so in the future. Moreover given the new Forestry Code, and the existing availability of already deforested lands, which can be highly productive by the modern techniques adopted today, future Amazonian deforestation will only occur if Brazil is not capable enforcing its current laws, not because it needs those lands for agricultural expansion.

Current estimates of the future growth of the world market suggest that there will be a large growth in demand for agricultural products over the next twenty to thirty years, particularly in China, India and Africa, not so much due to population growth, but mainly because of the increased income of large parts of those populations with access to the market. In all studies, Brazil is singled out as one of the main sources of future supply for this additional world demand. Brazil is also seen as an example of the competitive development of tropical agriculture, including the sustainability aspect, which is more complex than temperate agriculture since it involves more moisture, more insects and more plagues. But the country has managed to master these challenges and has thus become one of the most advanced in tropical agriculture in the world. Everyday sustainability becomes more important for any country that wishes to occupy a prominent position in the international market of agricultural products. The same is true of product quality, which involves all aspects of the production process, and is especially crucial in livestock production.

But the question of sustainability is not limited to the land factor. In practicing modern agriculture, Brazil has been adopting a so-called low carbon economy. In this regard there has been major adoption of no-tillage planting, biological nitrogen fixation and forest–animal-husbandry–crop integration. The intense use of biotechnology, particularly biologically modified seeds, also contributes to the reduction of harmful pesticides to the environment. In addition, Brazilian agriculture has been responsible for sustaining ethanol production and consumption for more than forty years. Yet there are some failures, which correspond to a weakened federal government not able to fully control logging and mining in the Amazon, with subsequent increases in deforestation. Brazil has the world's second largest extension of forests, with over 500 million hectares of natural forests. It is also the country with the largest tropical rainforest in the world. This is of value for humanity, which Brazil has the obligation to preserve.

The modern commercial agriculture sector does not define the entire rural world in Brazil. Rural poverty persists despite the settlement of over 1 million poor households on 90 million hectares of public lands. The concentration of landholdings is practically the same as that seen in the first censuses realized in the first half of twentieth century. This means that there has been an actual decline of small producers, probably in a larger proportion than the settlements of poor colonists made in the period. Moreover the demand for agrarian reform continues, and there continue to be deaths due to land conflicts in the frontier zones of occupation and in indigenous areas. Although relatively restricted, this is a serious problem, not acceptable in a modern country such as Brazil, which wishes to be identified as a sustainable country in the broadest sense of the term.

In essence the modernization of Brazilian agriculture affected only a minority of rural properties. The majority of the rural population is poor by whatever criteria are used and can be sustained only through government social welfare programs of income transfers. The census shows that an expressive share of the properties cannot obtain at least a monthly minimum wage as total family income, and many have negative net income. Moreover recent studies show that although part of this poor farm universe could be added to modern commercial agriculture, the vast majority of poor farmers do not have characteristics that enable them to survive only through farming. Many of these small rural producers have additional income outside rural property and / or live from social income transfer programs such as family grants and rural pensions, which enables them to survive. The alternative would be a massive rural exodus, further worsening the living conditions of urban centers.

Rural poverty is based not just on the size of the properties, although there is clearly a correlation between size of property and poverty, but is a more complex issue which involves characteristics of the lands owned, infrastructure, market access, and personal attributes of owners, particularly education. Also there is a strong regional element to this poverty, with most of it concentrated in the North and Northeast. Yet even here, some areas of the North and Northeast have been integrated into commercial agriculture, with great success both from the point of view of production and individual income, as well as the regional wealth generated by the new economic activity that is emerging in some specific poles. The revolution that occurred in the Cerrado in the last thirty years is still expanding to other areas in the south and north of the Amazon and in the western zone of the Northeast, generating jobs, wealth and stimulating the implementation of the economic infrastructure necessary for its full integration into the productive complex of agribusiness. Although labor relations in commercial agriculture have improved greatly in recent years, there are still problems. Although such employed rural workers now enjoy social benefits equivalent to those enjoyed by urban workers, they sometimes do not benefit from existing legal rights.

Maintaining the Brazilian position in the world commodity market requires a continuous increase in total productivity. Part of this increase in productivity is due to the increasing sophistication of production which occurs in Brazil and abroad. Another part, and perhaps the most important, may come from the gradual absorption into the commercial sector of already deforested areas currently exploited with low productivity. The high variance in yield in similar crops between regions needs to be reduced and all regions need to be more completely integrated into modern commercial agriculture. The knowledge of how to reach international levels of productivity already exist, but needs to reach a greater proportion of farmers, even those already integrated in commercial agriculture, and a significant share of small producers with low economic returns also need to be integrated into this modern agricultural market economy.

Finally, although Embrapa, other Brazilian research institutes and the federal universities have become important centers for research and innovation, the Brazilian market, like the world market, depends on a few multinational agricultural suppliers who develop their research based on their own strategic interests. Brazil currently is highly dependent on external suppliers of fertilizers and biologically modified seeds produced by a declining number of multinational foreign suppliers. The external dependence on such foreign companies represents risks that will need to be evaluated and administered if Brazil is to maintain its ongoing productivity. Equally agribusiness productivity in Brazil is affected by the logistics within Brazil, which are still precarious and one of the main obstacles to reducing the costs of Brazilian products abroad.

Bibliography

PRIMARY SOURCES

Banco Central do Brasil, *Anuário estatístico do crédito rural (Até 2012)* found at www.bcb.gov.br/?RELRURAL.

CEMA, *Economic Committee Tractor Market Report Calendar year 2014*, found at cema-agri.org/sites/default/files/publications/2015–02%20Agrievolution %20Tractor%20Market%20Report.pdf.

Censo Agrícola de 1905, available in digital format from the Núcleo de Estudos de População (NEPO), of the Universidade de Campinas.

Centro de Gestão e Estudos Estratégicos, *Estudo Sobre o Papel das Organizações Estaduais de Pesquisa Agropecuária (OEPAs)* (Brasilia: Ministério de Ciência e Tecnologia, 2006).

CEPAL, *Boletín Demográfico*, no 74 (July 2004).

Conab (Companhia Nacional de Abastecimento), *Acompanhamiento da safra brasileira, grãos*, various years, found at www.conab.gov.br/OlalaCMS/upl oads/arquivos/18_02_08_17_09_36_fevereiro_2018.pdf.

"Brasil: Oferta e demanda de produtos selecionados," found at www.agricul tura.gov.br/vegetal/estatisticas.

"Indicadores da Agropecuária," various years.

Série Histórica de Produção Safras 1976/77 a 2016/17," found at www.conab .gov.br/conteudos.php?a=1252.

Direção Geral de Estatíticas, *Recenseamento Geral do Brasil 1920* (Rio de Janeiro 1920).

Embrapa, *Balanço Social 2015*, accessed February 25, 2017, at http://bs.sede.em brapa.br/2015/balsoc15.html.

Fixação Biológica de Nitrogênio. Accessed April 19, 2017, at www.embrapa .br/tema-fixacao-biologica-de-nitrogenio/nota-tecnica.

Os benefícios da biotecnologia para a sua qualidade de vida. Accessed February 28, 2017, at www.embrapa.br/recursos-geneticos-e-biotecnologia/sala-de-i mprensa/se-liga-na-ciencia/a-biotecnologia-e-voce.

Embrapa Comunicações, *Embrapa em Números* (Brasília: Embrapa, 2016).

Embrapa Informação Tecnológica, *Sugestões para a Formulação de um Sistema Nacional de Pesquisa Agropecuária* (Memória Embrapa, Edição Especial do documento original de junho de 1972, reprinted Brasília, Embrapa, 2006).

EMIS, *Machinery and Equipment Sector Brazil*, January 2014, found at www.e mis.com/sites/default/files/EMIS%20Insight%20-%20Brazil%20Machinery %20and%20Equipment%20Sector.pdf.

Fundo Nacional de Desenvolvimento da Educação (FNDE), *Aquisição de Produtos da Agricultura Familiar para a Alimentação Escolar*, accessed March 23, 2017, at www.fnde.gov.br.

Governo do Estado da Amazônia, *A Floresta Amazônica e seu Papel nas Mudanças Climáticas* (Manaus: Secretaria de Meio Ambiente e Desenvolvimento Sustentável, 2009).

INPE/CCST (Instituto Nacional de Pesquisas Espaciais, Centro de Ciência do Sistema Terrestre), accessed February 21, 2018, at www.ccst.inpe.br/o-des matamento-na-amazonia-aumenta-no-brasil-mas-permanece-baixo-com-rel acao-ao-passado/.

Instituto Agronômico de Campinas – IAC, accessed February 25, 2017, at www .iac.sp.gov.br.

Instituto Brasileiro de Geografia e Estatística (IBGE), *Anuário Estatístico do Brasil* (Rio de Janeiro), various years.

Censo Agropecuário 1995 (Rio de Janeiro: IBGE, 1998).

Censo Agropecuário 2006, Brasil, Grandes Regiões e Unidades da Federação Segunda apuração (Rio de Janeiro, IBGE, 2012).

Censo Agropecuário 2006, Resultados Preliminares (Rio de Janeiro: IBGE, 2006).

Estatísticas do século XX, available at www,ibge.gov.br.

Indicadores IBGE: Estatística da Produção Agrícola (September 2016).

Pesquisa Nacional por Amostra de Domicílios (PNAD), various years.

PNAD, Síntese de Indicadores 2014 (Rio de Janeiro: IBGE, 2014), found at www.ibge.gov.br/home/estatistica/populacao/trabalhoerendimento/pna d2014/sintese_defaultxls.shtm.

Recenseamento Geral de 1950. Série Nacional & Série Regional, various volumes.

Sinopsis do Censo de 2010 (Rio de Janeiro, 2011), table 2.

Síntese de Indicadores Sociais: Uma Análise das Condições de Vida da População Brasileira, 2015 (Rio de Janeiro, 2015).

VII Recenseamento Geral – 1960. Série Nacional and Serie Regional, various volumes.

Instituto Centro de Vida, "Ilegalidade prejudica setor madeireiro de Mato Grosso," found at www.icv.org.br/2018/02/15/ilegalidade-prejudica-setor-madeireiro-de-mato-grosso/; a report which is analyzed in *Folha*, February 15, 2018, p. B7.

International Food Policy Research Institute (IFPRI), accessed February 23, 2017, at www.asti.cgiar.org/brazil.

IPEADATA, the PIB and other serial data sources found at www.ipeadata.gov.br/.

Ministério da Agricultura, Indústria e Comércio, *Indústria Assucareira no Brazil* (Rio de Janeiro: Directoria Geral de Estatística, 1919).

Ministério da Agricultura, Pecuária e Abastecimento (MAPA), *ABC Agricultura de Baixa Emissão de Carbono.* Accessed April 19, 2017, at www.agricultura .gov.br/assuntos/sustentabilidade/plano-abc.

"Balança comercial do agronegócio – síntese . . ." found at www.agricultura .gov.br/internacional/indicadores-e-estatisticas/balanca-comercial.

Estatísticas e Dados Básicos de Economia Agrícola, Setembro 2016, p. 37.

Agrostat, Estatisticas de Comercio Exterior do Agronegócio Brasileiro, at Agrostat, Exportação/Importação, Produto por Região/UF/Porto, *Projeções do Agronegócio – Brasil 2016/17 a 2026/27* (Brasilia, August, 2017), found at http://indicadores.agricultura.gov.br/agrostat/index.htm.

Agrostat, Estatisticas de Comercio Exterior do Agronegócio Brasileiro, found at Agrostat, Exportação/Importação, Produto por Região/UF/Porto, at *Projeções do Agronegócio – Brasil 2016/17 a 2026/27* (Brasilia, August, 2017),

Agrostat, Estatisticas de Comercio Exterior do Agronegócio Brasileiro, found at Agrostat, Exportação/Importação, Produto por Região/UF/Porto, at "Balança Comercial Brasileira e Balança Comercial do Agronegócio: 1989 a 2015," found at www.agricultura.gov.br/internacional/indicadores-e-estatisticas/bal anca-comercial.

Agrostat, Estatisticas de Comercio Exterior do Agronegócio Brasileiro, found at Agrostat, Exportação/Importação, Produto por Região/UF/Porto, at Valor Bruto da Produção – Regional por UF, found at www.agricultura.gov.br/mi nisterio/gestao-estrategica/valor-bruto-da-producao.

Ministério da Ciência e Tecnologia e Inovação, *Estratégia Nacional de Ciência, Tecnologia e Inovação, 2016–2019* (Brasília: Ministério da Ciência e Tecnologia e Inovação, 2016).

"O MST e a questão agrária. Entrevista com João Stédile," *Estudos Avançados*, 11, no. 31 (1997): 69–97.

Ministério da Comércio Exterior e Serviços (MDIC). "Balança comercial brasileira: Estados," found at www.mdic.gov.br/index.php/comercio-exter ior/estatisticas-de-comercio-exterior/balanca-comercial-brasileira-unidades-da-federacao.

"Estatísticas de Comércio Exterior," found at www.mdic.gov.br/index.php/c omercio-exterior/estatisticas-de-comercio-exterior.

"Séries Históricas," found at www.mdic.gov.br/index.php/comercio-exterior/ estatisticas-de-comercio-exterior/series-historicas.

"Balança comercial brasileira: Acumulado do ano," found at www.mdic.gov .br/index.php/comercio-exterior/estatisticas-de-comercio-exterior/balanca-c omercial-brasileira-acumulado-do-ano/balanca-comercial-brasileira-acumu lado-do-ano.

Ministério de Meio Ambiente. Secretaria de Mudanças Climáticas e Qualidade Ambiental. Departamento de Políticas de Combate ao Desmatamento, *Estratégia do Programa Nacional de Monitoramento Ambiental dos Biomas Brasileiros.* (Brasília: MMA, 2016). Accessed April 7, 2017, at http://siscom.ibama.gov.br/monitora_biomas/PMDBBS%20-%20CERRAD O.html.

Estimativas Anuais de Emissões de Gases de Efeito Estufa no Brasil, found at http://redd.mma.gov.br/pt/noticias-principais/760-lancada-a-3-edicao-das-e stimativas-anuais-de-emissoes-do-brasil.

Ministério do Desenvolvimento Agrário – Instituto Nacional de Colonização e Reforma Agrária (Incra). *Reforma Agrária. Apresentação dos Primeiros Resultados* (Brasília: Incra, December 2010). Accessed March 26, 2017, at www.incra.gov.br/media/reforma_agraria/questao_agraria/pqra%20-%20a presentao.pdf.

OECD–FAO Agricultural Outlook 2016–2025 (Paris, 2016), accessed at http://s tats.oecd.org/index.aspx?queryid=71240.

Agricultural Outlook, *Commodity Snapshots no. 3: Biofuels,* found at www .fao.org/fileadmin/templates/est/COMM_MARKETS_MONITORING/Oilc rops/Documents/OECD_Reports/OECD_biofuels2015_2024.pdf.

Presidência da Republica. *Plano Trienal de Desenvolvimento Econômico e Social, 1963–1965. Síntese.* December 1962.

Renewable Fuels Association (RFA), data found at www.ethanolrfa.org/resour ces/industry/statistics/#1454098996479-8715d404-e546.

Report of Deputy Covatti Filho in the Chamber of Deputies, May 15, 2017, at www.camara.gov.br/sileg/integras/1558650.pdf.

São Paulo, *Boletim de Indústria e Comércio,* 15, no. 11 (Nov. 1924).

UNICA, "Exportação anual de açúcar pelo brasil por estado de origem," accessed April 6, 2017, at www.unicadata.com.br/listagem.php?idMn=43 & =23.

"Frota brasileira de autoveículos leves … 2007–2015," accessed August 7, 2017, at www.unicadata.com.br/listagem.php?idMn=55.

"Sugarcane, ethanol and sugar production," found at www.unicadata.com.br/.

UNICADATA|produção|histórico de produção e moagem|por safra, found at www.unicadata.com.br/historico-de-producao-e-moagem.php? idMn=32&tipoHistorico=4.

United Nations, Food and Agricultural Organization (UN, FAO), "Food Price Index," accessed at www.fao.org/worldfoodsituation/FoodPricesIndex/en/.

Forest Products 2009–2013 (Rome: FAO, 2017).

Pulp, Paper and Paperboard Capacity Survey *2013–2018* (Rome: FAO, 2014).

Statistical Pocketbook *2015* (Rome: FAO, 2015).

Statistical Yearbook 2014: Latin America and the Caribbean, Food and Agriculture (Santiago: FAO & CEPAL, 2014).

UN, FAOSTAT, found at www.fao.org/faostat/en/#home.

United States Department of Agriculture (USDA), *Long-term Projections,* February 2016.

USDA, FAS (Foreign Agricultural Service), "2017 Sugar Annual Brazil" (Report BR17001, April 28, 2017).

Brazil, Citrus Annual, various months and years.

Citrus: World Markets and Trade, various months and years.

Coffee:World Markets and Trade, various months and years.

Cotton: World Markets and Trade, various months and years.

Dairy: World Markets and Trade, various months and years.

Grain: World Markets and Trade, various months and years.
Livestock and Poultry: World Markets and Trade, various months and years.
Oilseeds: World Markets and Trade, various months and years.
Sugar: World Markets and Trade, various months and years.
World Agricultural Production, various months and years.
United States Department of Commerce, International Trade Administration, *Industry & Analysis, 2015: Top Markets Report Agricultural Equipment: A Market Assessment Tool for U.S. Exporters*. July 2015.
VDMA Agricultural Machinery Report 2015, found at http://lt.vdma.org/docu ments/105903/8575467/VDMA%20Economic%20Report%202015%20p ublic%20version.pdf/a25a564f-614e-4e67-95f2-6f16b7604f9b.
World Bank, "Agricultural machinery, tractors per 100 sq. km of arable land," found at http://data.worldbank.org/indicator/AG.LND.TRAC.ZS.
"Fertilizer Consumption (kilograms per hectare of ariable land)," found at http://databank.worldbank.org/data/reports.aspx?source=2&series=AG.C ON.FERT.ZS&country=#.
"Research and development expenditure (% of GDP)," accessed March 7, 2017 at http://data.worldbank.org/indicator/GB.XPD.RSDV.GD.ZS.
World Development Indicators, World Cereal Production, found at http://data .worldbank.org/indicator/AG.PRD.CREL.MT.
World Trade Organization [WTO], Time Series on International Trade, accessed February 10, 2018, at http://stat.wto.org/StatisticalProgram/WsdbExport.as px?Language=E.
WWF-Brazil. Accessed April 7, 2017, at www.wwf.org.br/wwf_brasil/organiza cao/.

SECONDARY SOURCES

A História da Luta pela terra. MST – Movimento dos Trabalhadores Rurais sem Terra. Accessed April 22, 2017, at www.mst.org.br/nossa-historia/inicio.
ABC Observatório. *Agricultura de Baixo Carbono. A evolução de um novo paradigma*. Fundação Getúlio Vargas, Centro de Agronegócio da Escola de Economia de São Paulo. Accessed April 17, 2017, at www.observatorioabc .com.br.
ABEMEL – Associação Brasileira dos Exportadores de Mel. Accessed February 11, 2018, at http://brazilletsbee.com.br/INTELIG%C3%8ANCIA%20CO MERCIAL%20ABEME %20-%20DEZEMBRO.pdf.
ABPA (Associação Brasileira de Proteína Animal). *Annual Report* 2015, found at http://abpa-br.com.br/files/publicacoes/c59411a243d6dab1da8e605 be58348ac.pdf.
Annual Report 2016, found at http://abpabr.com.br/storage/files/abpa_relator io_anual_2016_ingles_web_versao_para_site_abpa_bloqueado.pdf.
AFDC (Alternative Fuels Data Center), "World Fuel Ethanol Production by Country or Region (Million Gallons)," accessed February 8, 2017. at www .afdc.energy.gov/uploads/data/data_source/10331/10331_world_ethanol_ production.xlsx.

AFUBRA (Associação dos Plantadores de Fumo em Folha no Rio Grande do Sul). Data accessed October 1, 2017, at www.afubra.com.br/fumicultura-brasil .html.

Aguiar, Daniel Alves de, Wagner Fernando da Silva, Bernardo Friedrich Theodor Rudorff, Luciana Miura Sugawara and Magog Araújo de Carvalho. "Expansão da cana-de-açúcar no Estado de São Paulo: safras 2003/2004 a 2008/2009," *Anais XIV Simpósio Brasileiro de Sensoriamento Remoto* (Natal, April 2009).

Albano, Gleydson Pinheiro. "Globalização da agricultura: multinacionais no Campo Brasileiro," *Terra Livre* (São Paulo), (Ano 27), I, no. 36 (Jan.–Jun. 2001): 126–151.

Alvarenga, Ramon Costa et al. "Sistema Integração Lavoura-Pecuária-Floresta: condicionamento do solo e intensificação da produção de lavouras," *Informe Agropecuário* (Belo Horizonte), 31, no. 257 (Jul./Aug. 2010): 59–67.

Alves, Arilde Franco. "As múltiplas funções da agricultura familiar camponesa: práticas sócio-culturais e ambientais de convivência com o semi-arido" (PhD thesis, Universidade Federal de Campina Grande, Campina Grande, 2009).

Alves, Eliseu. *Dilema da Política Agrícola Brasileira: Produtividade ou Expansão da Área Agricultável* (Brasília: Embrapa, 1983).

"Embrapa, a successful case of institutional innovation." *Revista Economia Política*, Year XIX – Special Edition of Mapa's 150th Anniversary, July 2010. *O Dilema da Politica Agrícola Brasileira – Produtividade ou Expansão da Área Agriculturável* (Brasília: Embrapa, 1984).

Alves, Eliseu, and Affonso Celso Pastore. "A política agrícola do Brasil e hipótese da inovação induzida," in Eliseu Alves, José Pastore and Affonso C. Pastore, *Coletânea de Trabalhos sobre a EMBRAPA* (Brasília: Embrapa, 1977): 9–19.

Alves, Eliseu and Antônio Jorge de Oliveira. "Orçamento da Embrapa," *Revista de Economia Agrícola*, XIV, no. 4 (Oct./Nov./Dec. 2005): 73–85.

Alves, Eliseu, and Daniela de Paula Rocha. "Ganhar tempo é possível?" in José Garcia Gasques, José Eustáquio Ribeiro Filho and Zander Navarro (orgs.), *A Agricultura Brasileira: Desempenho, Desafios e Perspectivas* (Brasília: IPEA, 2010): 275–290.

Alves, Eliseu, and Geraldo da Silva e Souza. "A pesquisa agrícola numa agricultura integrada ao mercado internacional. O caso da Embrapa e do Cerrado," *Revista Política Agrícola*, XVI, no.2 (Apr./May/Jun. 2007): 56–67.

Alves, Eliseu, and José Pastore. *Uma Nova Abordagem para a Pesquisa Agrícola no Brasil* (São Paulo: USP/IPE, 1975).

Alves, Eliseu, G. S. Souza, and E. G. Gomes. "Fatos marcantes da agricultura Brasileira," in E. R. de A. Alves, G. da S. e Souza, and E. G. Gomes, eds., *Contribuição da Embrapa para o Desenvolvimento da Agricultura no Brasil* (Brasília: Embrapa, 2013): 15–45.

Alves, Eliseu, Geraldo da S. e Souza,Daniela de P. Rocha and Renner Marra. "Fatos marcantes da agricultura brasileira," in Alves, E. R. A., G. S. Souza and E. G. Gomes, eds., *Contribuição da Embrapa para o Desenvolvimento da Agricultura no Brasil.* (Brasília, Embrapa, 2013): 13–45.

Alves, Eliseu, Geraldo da Silva e Souza and Daniela de Paula Rocha. "Lucratividade da agricultura," *Revista de Política Agrícola*, XXI, no. 2 (Apr./May/Jun. 2012), 45–63.

Amaral, Taís Mahalem do, Marcos Fava Neves and Márcia A. Dias de Moraes. "Cadeias produtivas do açúcar do estado de São Paulo e da França: comparação dos sistemas produtivos, organização, estratégias e ambiente institucional," *Agricultura São Paulo*, 50, no. 2 (2003): 65–80.

Amato Neto, João. "A indústria de máquinas agrícolas no Brasil: origens e evolução," *Revista de Administração dos.Empresas*, 25, no. 3 (Jul./Sept. 1985):57–69.

Andreatta, Tanice, Ana Monteiro Costa, Rosani Marisa Spanevello, Patrícia da Rosa Leal and Adriano Lago. "Perspectivas e desafios da atividade leiteira no município de jóia, rio grande do sul: apontamentos a partir da visão dos produtores," *53rd Congresso da SOBER* (João Pessoa, 2015).

Anfavea – Associação Nacional dos. Fabricantes de Veículos Automotores. Accessed May 17, 2017, at www.anfavea.com.br/estatisticas.html.

Anjos, Flávio Sacco dos et al. "Agricultura familiar e políticas públicas: impacto do PRONAF no Rio Grande do Sul," *Revista de Economia e Sociologia Rural*, 42, no.3 (2004): 529–548.

Anuário da Indústria Automobilística Brasileira. 2016. Accessed February 21, 2018, at www.automotivebusiness.com.br/abinteligencia/pdf/Anfavea_anua rio2016.pdf.

Araújo, Antônio Carlos de, Lúcia Maria Ramos Silva and Rosalina Ramos Midlej. "Valor da produção de cacau e análise dos fatores responsáveis pela sua variação no estado da Bahia," *43 Congresso da Sociedade Brasileira de Economia, Administração e Sociologia Rural – SOBER*, 2005.

Araújo, Cláudia Marilei Gomes de, Patrícia K. W. Dalla Santa Spada, Daniel Silva dos Reis, Gilberto João Carnieli, Sandra Valduga Dutra, and Regina Vanderlinde. "Influência climática em mostos e vinhos da safra 2015," *Revista Brasileira de Viticultura e Enologia*, 8 (2016): 67.

Araújo, Geraldino Carneiro de, Miriam Pinheiro Bueno, Veridiana Pinheiro Bueno, Renato Luis Sproesser and Ivonete Fernandes de Souza. "Cadeia produtiva da avicultura de corte: avaliação da apropriação de valor bruto nas transações econômicas dos agentes envolvidos," *Gestão & Regionalidade*, 24, no.72 (2008), 16 pp.

Araújo, Paulo Fernando Cidade de. "Política de crédito rural: reflexões sobre a experiência brasileira" (Textos para Discussão CEPAL/IPEA, 37; Brasília: CEPAL/IPEA, 2001).

Araújo, Paulo Fernando Cidade de, Alexandre Lahóz Mendonça de Barros, José Roberto Mendonça de Barros and Ricardo Shirota. "Política de crédito para a agricultura brasileira. Quarenta e cinco anos à procura do desenvolvimento," *Revista de Política Agrícola*, XVI, no. 4 (Oct./Nov./ Dec. 2007): 27–51.

Arend, Marcelo and Silvio A. F. Cário. "Origens e determinantes dos desequilíbrios no Rio Grande do Sul," *Ensaios FEE* (Porto Alegre), 26 (May 2005).

Associação brasileira de sementes e mudas, *Anuário 2015*. Accessed February 28, 2017, at www.abrasem.com.br/wpcontent/uploads/2013/09/Anuario_ABR ASEM_2015_2.pdf.

Avila, Antonio Flávio Dias. "Corporativismo na Embrapa: o fim de um Modelo de Gestão." *Cadernos de Ciência & Tecnologia*, 12, nos. 1/3 (1995):83–94.

Avila, Antonio Flávio Dias, Marília Magalhães Castelo, Graciela Luzia Vedovoto, Luis José Maria Irias and Geraldo Stachetti Rodriguest. "Impactos econômicos, sociais e ambientais dos investimentos na Embrapa," *Revista de Política Agrícola*, XIV, no. 4 (Oct./Nov./Dec. 2005): 86–101.

Azevedo, Fernanda Quintanilha. "Perfil vitivinícola, fenologia, qualidade e produção de uvas americanas e híbrida em Pelotas-RS" (MA thesis, Universidade Federal de Pelotas, 2010).

Bacha, Carlos J. C. *Economia e Política Agrícola no Brasil* (São Paulo: Atlas, 2004).

Bacha, Carlos J. C., Leonardo Danelon and Egmar Del Bel Filho. "Evolução da taxa de juros real do crédito rural no Brasil – período 1985 a 2003," *Teoria e Evidência Econômica* (Passo Fundo) 14, no. 26 (May 2006): 43–69.

Bacha, Edmar L. and Robert Greenhill. *150 Anos de café* (2nd edn. rev.; Rio de Janeiro: Marcellino Martins & E. Johnston Exportadores, 1993).

Balbino, Luiz Carlos, Luiz Adriano Maia Cordeiro, P. de Oliveira, J. Kluthcouski, P. R. Galerani and L. Vilela. "Agricultura sustentável por meio da integração lavoura-pecuária-floresta (iLPF)," *Informações agronômicas*, 138 (2012): 1–18.

Balbino, Luiz Carlos, Luiz Adriano Maia Cordeiro, Vanderley Porfírio-da-Silva, Anibal de Moraes, Gladys Beatriz Martínez, Ramon Costa Alvarenga, Armindo Neivo Kichel et al. "Evolução tecnológica e arranjos produtivos de sistemas de integração lavoura-pecuária-floresta no Brasil," *Pesquisa Agropecuária Brasileira*, 46, no. 10 (2011): i–xii.

Balbino, Luiz Carlos, Alexandre de Oliveira Barcellos and Luís Fernando Stone. *Marco Referencial: integração lavoura-pecuária-floresta* (Brasília: Embrapa, 2011).

Barbosa Filho, Fernando de Holanda. *Nota sobre a produtividade no Brasil*, Fundação Getúlio Vargas (FGV) (Nota Técnica, 2014). Accessed January 8, 2007, at portalibre.fgv.br/lumis/portal/file/fileDownload.jsp?fileId.

O Sistema Financeiro Brasileiro. Accessed December 25, 2016, at www.fgv.br/ professor/fholanda/Arquivo/Sistfin.pdf.

Barbosa Filho, Fernando de Holanda and Samuel de Abreu Pessoa. "Pessoa ocupado e jornada de trabalho. Uma releitura da evolução da produtividade no Brasil," *Revista Brasileira de Economia*, 68, no.2 (Apr./ Jun. 2014):149–169.

Barreto, Mariana. "O Mercado de Sementes no Brasil,"*Associação Brasileira de Sementes e Mudas, 67°. Simpas*, Sinop-MT, November 24, 2015.

Barros, José Roberto Mendonça de. "Prolegômenos. O passado no presente: a visão do economista,"in Antônio Márcio Buainain et al., *O Mundo Rural no Brasil do Século 21. A Formação de um Novo Padrão Agrário e Agrícola* (Brasília: Embrapa, 2014): 15–22.

Bastos, Luciana Aparecida. "Avaliação do desempenho comercial do Mercosul: 1004–2005" (PhD thesis, FFLCH-USP, História, São Paulo, 2008).

Batista Filho, Malaquias and Anete Rissin. "A transição nutricional no Brasil: tendências regionais e temporais," *Cadernos de Saúde Pública*, 19, Supl. 1 (2003): 181–191.

Behling, Maurel. *ILPF – Integração Lavoura-Pecuária-Floresta. Experiências da Embrapa Agrossilvopastoril.* Sinop (MT), Embrapa, accessed February 25, 2017, at http://docplayer.com.br/17885191-Ilpf-integracao-lavoura-pecuaria-floresta-experiencias-da-embrapa-agrossilvopastoril.html.

Benetti, Maria Domingues. "Endividamento e crise no cooperativismo empresarial do Rio Grande do Sul: análise do caso FECOTRIGO/CENTRALSUL – 1975–83," *Ensaios FEE* (Porto Alegre), 6, no. 2 (1985): 23–55.

"Origem e formação do cooperativismo empresarial no Rio Grande do Sul uma análise do desenvolvimento da COTRIJUÍ, COTRISA e FECOTRIGO 1957/1980,1985," 3rd printing; Porto Alegre: Fundação da Economia e Estatistica, 1992.

Beraldo, João Bosco Lima and Margarida Garcia de Figueiredo. "Formação do preço de fertilizantes em Mato Grosso," *Revista de Política Agrícola*, 25, no. 3 (2016): 17.

Bertero, José Flávio. "Sobre a Reforma agrária e o MST," *Lutas & Resistências* (Londrina), 1 (Sept. 2006): 163–183.

Beskow, Paulo R. "A formação da economia arrozeira do Rio Grande do Sul," *Ensaios FEE* (Porto Alegre), 4, no. 2 (1984):55–84.

Bialoskorski Neto, Sigismundo and Waldemar Ferreira Júnior. "Evolução e Organização das Cooperativas Agropecuárias Paulistas na Década de 90," Paper given at the *XLII Congresso da Sociedade Brasileira de Economia e Sociologia Rural* 2004.

Bianchini, Valter.*Vinte Anos do PRONAF, 1995–2015. Avanços e Desafios* (Brasília: Ministério do Desenvolvimento Agrário, 2015).

Bielschowsky, Ricardo, ed., *Cinquenta Anos de Pensamento da CEPAL* (Rio de Janeiro: Cofecon/Cepal, 2000).

Pensamento Econômico Brasileiro. *O ciclo ideológico do desenvolvimento* (Rio de Janeiro: Contraponto, 2000).

Bonelli, Regis and Elisa de Paula Pessôa. "O papel do Estado na Pesquisa Agrícola no Brasil" (Texto para Discussão no. 576; Rio de Janeiro: IPEA, July 1998).

and Samuel de Abreu Pessoa. "Desindustrialização do Brasil: um Resumo da Evidência" (Texto para Discussão, no. 7; Rio de Janeiro: Fundação Getúlio Vargas/IBRE, 2010).

Bonjour, Sandra Cristina de Moura, Adriano Marcos Rodrigues Figueiredo and José Manuel Carvalho Marta. "A pecuária de corte no estado de Mato Grosso," Paper given at *XLVI SOBER, Sociedade Brasileira de Economia, Administração e Sociologia Rural*, 2008.

Bradesco/Depec (Departamento de Pesquisas e Estudos Econômicos). "Fertilizantes," June 2017.

"Soja, Janeiro 2017," in "Sector e Regional/Informações Setoriais," found at www.economiaemdia.com.br.

"Tratores e Máquinas Agrícolas" (December 2016), found at www.econo miaemdia.com.br/EconomiaEmDia/pdf/infset_tratores_e_maquinas_agrico las.pdf.

"Tratores e Máquinas Agrícolas, Janeiro de 2017," in "Sector e Regional/ Informações Setoriais," found at www.economiaemdia.com.br.

Brandão, A. S. and J. L. Carvalho. "Economia politica de las intervenciones de precios en Brasil, in A. O. Krueger, M. Schiff and A. Valdes, *Economia Política de las Intervenciones de Precios en America* (Washington, DC: Banco Mundial, 1990): 81–144.

Brannstrom, Christian, Wendy Jepson, Anthony M. Filippi, Daniel Redo, Zengwang Xu and Srinivasan Ganesh. "Land change in the Brazilian Savanna (Cerrado), 1986–2002: comparative analysis and implications for land-use policy," *Land Use Policy*, 25 (2008): 579–595.

Breitbach, Áurea Corrêa de Miranda. "A região de Santa Cruz do Sul e o fumo: panorama de uma 'especialização' nociva," *Indicadores Econômicos FEE*, Porto Alegre, 42 no. 1 (2014): 43–62.

Bruch, Kelly Lissandra. "Signos distintivos de origem: entre o velho e o novo mundo vitivinícola" (PhD thesis, Universidade Federal do Rio Grande do Sul, 2011).

Bruno, Regina. *O Estatuto da Terra: entre a conciliação e o confronto*. Accessed March 18, 2017, at http://r1.ufrrj.br/esa/V2/ojs/index.php/esa/article/viewFi le/80/76.

Senhores da Terra, Senhores da Guerra: A Nova Face Política das Elites Agroindustriais no Brasil (Rio de Janeiro: Forense/UFRJ, 1997).

Buainain, Antonio Márcio. "O tripé da política agrícola brasileira: crédito rural, seguro e Pronaf," in Antônio Márcio Buainain et al., *O Mundo Rural no Brasil do Século 21. A Formação de um Novo Padrão Agrário e Agrícola* (Brasília: Embrapa, 2014): 826–864.

Buainain, Antonio Márcio and Junior Ruiz Garcia. "Contextos locais ou regionais: importância para a viabilidade econômica dos pequenos produtores," in Silvia Kanadani Campos and Zander Navarro, *A Pequena Produção Rural e as Tendências do Desenvolvimento Agrário Brasileiro: Ganhar Tempo é Possível?* (Brasília: CGEE, 2013): 133–176.

"Os pequenos Produtores rurais mais pobres ainda tem alguma chance como agricultores?" in Silvia Kanadani Campos and Zander Navarro, *A Pequena Produção Rural e as Tendências do Desenvolvimento Agrário Brasileiro: Ganhar Tempo é Possível?* (Brasília: CGEE, 2013): 29–70.

Buainain, Antonio Márcio et al. "Quais os riscos mais relevantes nas atividades agropecuárias?" in Antônio Márcio Buainain et al., *O Mundo Rural no Brasil do Século 21. A Formação de um Novo Padrão Agrário e Agrícola* (Brasília: Embrapa, 2014): 135–208.

"Sete teses sobre o mundo rural brasileiro," in Antônio Márcio Buainain et al., *O Mundo Rural no Brasil do Século 21. A Formação de um Novo Padrão Agrário e Agrícola* (Brasília: Embrapa, 2014): 1159–1182.

Cabral, J. Irineu, *Sol da Manhã: Memória da Embrapa* (Brasília: UNESCO, 2005).

Campos, Silvia Kanadani and Zander Navarro. *A Pequena Produção Rural e as Tendências do Desenvolvimento Agrário Brasileiro: Ganhar Tempo é Possível* (Brasília: CGEE, 2013).

Canabrava, Alice P. "A grande Lavoura," in Sérgio Buarque de Holanda, ed., *História da Civilização Brasileira* (São Paulo: Difusão Europeia do Livro, 1971), II, no. 4): 85–140.

O Algodão no Brasil, 1861–1875 (São Paulo: T. A. Queiróz Editor, 1984).

Caporal, Francisco Roberto. "Extensão Rural e os limites à prática dos extensionistas do Serviço Público" (MA thesis, Universidade de Santa Maria [RS], 1991).

Carli, Gileno de. *O Açúcar na Formação Econômica do Brasil* (Rio de Janeiro: Annuário Açucareiro, 1937).

Carvalho, Maria Auxiliadora de and Roberto Leite da Silva. "Intensidade do Comércio Agrícola no Mercosul," Trabalho apresentado na 47°. *Congresso da Sober*, accessed December 24, 2016, at www.sober.org.br/palestra/13/447.pdf, .

Carvalho, Sérgio Paulino de, Sérgio Luiz Monteiro Salles Filho and Antonio Marcio Buainain. "A institucionalidade propriedade intelectual no Brasil: os impactos da política de articulação da Embrapa no mercado de cultivares no Brasil," *Cadernos de Estudos Avançados*, 2, no. 1 (2005): 35–46.

Carvalho, Thiago Franco Oliveira de. "Modernização agrícola e a região da alta mogiana paulista análise da expansão da produção de cana-deaçúcar em uma tradicional região cafeeira" (MA thesis, Universidade Estadual Paulista "Júlio de Mesquita Filho," Rio Claro, 2014).

Cassol, Elemar Antonino, José Eloir Denardin and Rainaldo Alberto Kochhann, "Sistema plantio direto: evolução e implicações sobre conservação do solo e da água," in Carlos Alberto Ceretta, Leandro Souza da Silva and José Miguel Reichert, eds., *Tópicos em Ciência do Solo. Viçosa: Sociedade Brasileira de Ciência do Solo, vol.* 5 (2007): 333–369.

Castillo, Ricardo Abid. "Região competitiva e circuito espacial produtivo: a expansão do setor sucro-alcooleiro (complexo cana-de-açúcar) no território brasileiro," *Centro*, 289, no. 373, 416 (2009): n.p.

Castro, César Nunes de. "A agropecuária na região Centro-Oeste: limitações ao desenvolvimento e desafios futuros" (Texto para Discussão no. 1923, IPEA, Rio de Janeiro, 2014).

Castro, Cleber Carvalho de, Antônio Domingos Padula, Juvir Luiz Mattuella, Laudemir André Müller and Aline Nuy Angst. "Estudo da cadeia láctea do Rio Grande do Sul: uma abordagem das relações entre os elos da produção, industrialização e distribuição," *Revista de Administração Contemporânea*, 2, no. 1 (April 1998): 143–164.

Castro, Josué de. *Geografia da Fome: o Dilema Brasileiro – Pão ou Aço.* 10th edn. rev. (Rio de Janeiro: Edições Antares, 1984).

Cavalcante, Matuzalem Bezerra. "Mudanças da estrutura fundiária de Mato Grosso (1992–2007)" (MA thesis; Universidade Estadual "Julio de Mesquita," 2008).

Cenni, Franco. *Italianos no Brasil: "Andiamo in 'Merica,"* 2nd edn. (São Paulo: Edusp, 2003).

Chaddad, Fabio Ribas. "Cooperativas no agronegócio do leite: mudanças organizacionais e estratégicas em resposta à globalização," *Organizações Rurais & Agroindustriais*, 9, no. 1 (2011): 69–78.

The Economics and Organization of Brazilian Agriculture. Recent Evolution and Productivity Gains (Amsterdam: Academic Press, 2016).

Clemente, Evandro Cesar. "Formação, dinâmica e a reestruturação da cadeia produtiva do leite na região de Jales-SP" (MA thesis, Universidade Estadual Paulista, Presidente Prudente, 2006).

Coelho, Alexandre Bragança. "A cultura do Algodão e a questão da integração entre preços internos e externos" (MA thesis, Universidade de São Paulo, 2002).

Coelho, Carlos Nayro. "70 anos de política agrícola no Brasil (1931–2001)," *Revista de Política Agrícola*, X (Número Especial) (Jul./Aug./Sept. 2001): 3–58.

Coelho, Carlos Nayro and Marisa Borges. "O complexo Agro-industrial (CAI) da Avicultura," *Revista de Política Agrícola*, 8, no .3 (1999): 1–36.

Coelho, Suani Teixeira and Patricia Guardabassi. "The sustainability of ethanol production from sugarcane," *Energy Policy*, 36 (2008):2086–2097.

Cole, Célio Alberto. "A cadeia produtiva do trigo no Brasil: contribuição para geração de emprego e renda" (MA thesis, Porto Alegre: Iepe/UFRGS, 1998).

Coltro, Leda, Anna Lúcia Mourad, Rojane M. Kletecke, Taíssa A. Mendonça and Sílvia P. M. Germer. "Assessing the environmental profile of orange production in Brazil," *The International Journal of Life Cycle Assessment*, 14, no 7 (November 2009): 656–664.

Conceição, Octavio Augusto C. *A Expansão da Soja no Rio Grande do Sul 1950–75*, 2nd edn. (Porto Alegre: Fundação de Economia e Estatística, 1984).

Conejero, Marco Antonio, Eduardo José ʼSia, Mairun Junqueira Alves Pinto, Ricardo Kouiti Santos Iguchi and Rafael Oliveira do Amaral. "Arranjos contratuais complexos na transação de cana à usina de açucar e alcool: um estudo de caso no centro-sul do brasil," *XXXII Encontro da ANPAS*, 2008 (Rio de Janeiro).

Conway, Gordon. *Produção de Alimentos no Século XXI: Biotecnologia e Meio Ambiente* (São Paulo: Estação Liberdade, 2003).

Corrêa, Angela M. C. Jorge and Nelly Maria Sansígolo de Figueiredo. "Riqueza, desigualdade e pobreza: um perfil da região Centro-Oeste no início do século XXI," *Pesquisa e Debate*, 17, no. 1 (2006): 45–65.

Coser, Fabiano José. "Contrato de integração de suínos: formatos, conteúdos e deficiências da estrutura de governança predominante na suinocultura brasileira"(MA thesis, Universidade Federal de Brasilia, 2010).

Costa, Antonio Carlos Augusto da, Nei Pereira Junior and Donato Alexandre Gomes Aranda. "The situation of biofuels in Brazil: new generation technologies," *Renewable and Sustainable Energy Reviews* 14 (2010): 3041–3049.

Costa, Armando João Dalla. "A Perdigão, a passagem do poder e a profissionalização nas empresas familiares," Paper presented at the VI *Congresso Brasileiro de História Econômica*, 2005.

Costa, Leticia M. da and Martim F. de Oliveira e Silva. "A indústria Química e o Setor de Fertilizantes," 15 BNDES, accessed January 22, 2017 at www.bn des.gov.br/SiteBNDES/export/sites/default/bndes_pt/Galerias/Arquivos/co nhecimento/livro6oanos_perspectivas_setoriais/Setorial6oanos_VOL2Qui mica.pdf.

Cruz, Elmar Rodrigues da, Victor Palma and Antonio F. D. Avila. *Taxas de Retorno dos Investimentos da EMBRAPA: Investimentos Totais e Capital Físico* (Brasília: EMBRAPA-DID, 1982).

Cruz, José Carlos et al. *Sistema de Plantio Direto de milho.* Accessed February 25, 2017, atwww.agencia.cnptia.embrapa.br/gestor/milho/arvore/CONTA G01_72_59200523355.html.

Cunha, José Marcos Pinto da. "Dinâmica migratória e o processo de ocupação do Centro-Oeste brasileiro: o caso de Mato Grosso," *Revista Brasileira de Estudos de População*, 23, no. 1 (2013): 87–107.

Dalberto, Florindo. "Pesquisa Estadual e Inovação no Agronegócio Brasileiro," *IX Encontro Nacional do Fortec*, Curitiba, May 2015.

Deer, Noel. *The History of Sugar* (London: Chapman and Hall Ltd., 1949).

Delgado, Guilherme C. "Expansão e modernização do setor agropecuário no pós-guerra: um estudo da reflexão agrária." *Estudos Avançados*, São Paulo, 15 no. 43 (2001): 157–172.

Desconsi, Cristiano. *A marcha dos pequenos proprietários rurais: trajetórias de migrantes do Sul do Brasil para o Mato Grosso.* Rio de Janeiro: Editora E-papers, 2011.

Dias, Adriano Batista and Sérgio Kelner Silveira. *As OEPASs – Situação e Resgate.* Accessed February 25, 2017, at http://aplicativos.fipe.org.br/enaber/pdf/161 .pdf.

Dias, Cleimon Eduardo do Amaral. "Abordagem histórica e perspectivas atuais do ensino superior agrícola no Brasil: uma investigação na UFRGS e na UC DAVIS" (PhD thesis, Universidade Federal de Rio Grande do Sul, 2001).

Dias, Guilherme Leite da Silva and Cicely Moutinho Amaral. "Mudanças estruturais na agricultura brasileira, 1980–1998," in Renato Baumann, ed., *Década de Transição* (Rio de Janeiro: Campus/Cepal, 2000).

Dias, Victor Pina and Eduardo Fernandes. *Fertilizantes: Uma Visão Sintética* (Rio de Janeiro: BNDES, 2006). Accessed January 22, 2017, at www.bndes.gov .br/SiteBNDES/export/sites/default/bndes_pt/Galerias/Arquivos/conheci mento/bnset/set2404.pdf.

Díaz, Frida Cárdenas. "Competitividade e coordenação na avicultura de corte: análise de empresas (São Paulo – Brasil e Lima- Peru)" (MA thesis, Universidade Estadual Paulista "Julio de Mesquita Filho," Jaboticabal, 2007).

DIEESE. "O mercado de trabalho assalariado rural brasileiro," *Estudos e Pesquisas*, no. 74 (October 2014): 2–33.

Diesel, Vivien, Joaquim Assis and Juliana Scheibler. "A dinâmica da integração agricultor–agroindústria e o desenvolvimento territorial sustentável," *IV Coloquio sobre Tansformaciones Territoriales.*

Diniscor Agribusiness. "Industry of paper, cellulose and forest products," found at http://diniscor.com.br/agronegocio/en/index.php/about-brazil/item/128-i ndustry-of-paper-and-cellulose-and-forest-products.html.

Diniz, Sarah Silveira, Marcia Regina Gabardo da Câmara, Marcelo Ortega Massambani, João Amilcar Rodrigues Anhesini, Umberto Antonio Sesso Filho. "Análise espacial da produtividade da Laranja dos municípios do estado de São Paulo: 2002 a 2010," *50 Congresso da SOBER 2012*.

Dionizio, Flávia Lopes. "Qualidade do leite e impacto econômico de diferentes tipos de coletas e condições de transporte da fazenda à indústria" (MA thesis, Universidade Federal de Minas Gerais, 2013).

Eisenberg, Peter. *The Sugar Industry in Pernambuco: Modernization without Change, 1840–1910* (Berkeley: University of California Press, 1974).

Faleiro, Fábio Gelape and Austeclinio Lopes de Farias Neto. *Savanas. Desafios e Estratégias para o Equilíbrio entre Sociedade, Agronegócio e Recursos Naturais* (Planaltina, DF: Embrapa, 2008).

Falkembach, Elza Maria Fonseca. "Dinâmica social e cooperativismo: o caso da FECOTRIGO: 1958–72," in Maria Domingues Benetti, ed., *Desenvolvimento e Crise do Cooperativismo Empresarial do RS, 1957–84* (Porto Alegre: Fundação de Economia e Estatística, 1985): 113–228.

Favaret Filho, Paulo. "Evolução do Crédito Rural e Tributação sobre alimentos na década de 1990: implicações sobre as cadeias de aves, suínos e leite," *BNDES Setorial* (Rio de Janeiro), no. 16: 31–55.

Fazuoli, Luiz Carlos, Herculano Penna Medina Filho, Oliveiro Guerreiro Filho, Wallace Gonçalves Maria Bernadete Silvarolla and Paulo Boller Gallo. "Cultivares de café selecionados pelo Instituto Agronômico de Campinas," *Genética, Simpósio de Pesquisas dos Café do Brasil*: 488–493. Accessed February 25, 2017, at www.sapc.embrapa.br/arquivos/consorcio/spcb_a nais/simposio1/Genet27.pdf.

Fernandes, Bernardo Mançano. *Formação do MST do Brasil*. Petrópolis: Vozes, 2000.

Fernandes, Rosangela Aparecida Soares and Cristiane Márcia dos Santos. "Competitividade das exportações sucroalcooleiras no Estado de São Paulo," *Anais do 4° ECAECO [Encontro Científico de Administração, Economia e Contabilidade]*, 2011 vol. 1, no. 1: 50–57.

Fernandes Filho, J. F. "A política brasileira de fomento à produção de trigo, 1930–1990," *Anais do XXXIII Congresso Brasileiro de Economia Rural* (1995), vol .1, 443–474.

Fernández, Antonio João Castrillon. "Do Cerrado à Amazônia, as estruturas sociais da economia da soja no Mato Grosso"(PhD thesis; Universidade Federal do Rio Grande do Sul, 2007).

Fernández, Maria Gabriela Vázquez. "Indicações geográficas e seus impactos no desenvolvimento dos pequenos produtores do Vale dos Vinhedos – RS"(MA theis, Universidade de Brasília, 2012).

Ferrari Filho, Fernando. "Análise de um motor do ciclo diesel operando no modo bicombustível: diesel / etanol"(MA thesis, PUC, Rio de Janeiro, 2011).

Ferreira, Ana Lucia. *Fixação biológica de nitrogênio por reduzir as emissões de GEE na agricultura*. Accessed April 19, 2017, at www.embrapa.br/busca-de-noticias/-/noticia/8313328/fixacao-biologica-de-nitrogenio-pode-reduzir-as-emissoes-de-gee-na-agricultura.

Ferreira, Brancolina, ed., *Avaliação da Situação de Assentamentos da Reforma Agrária no Estado de São Paulo. Fatores de Sucesso e Insucesso* (Brasília: Ipea, 2013).

Ferreira, Pedro Cavalcanti. "Produtividade e Eficiência," Rio de Janeiro, FGV, 2013. Accessed August 1, 2017, at www.insper.edu.br/wp-content/uploads/2013/06/2013_08_01_Insper_Produtividade_Pedro_Ferreira.pdf.

FIESP/DECOMTEC, *Custo Brasil" e a Taxa de Câmbio na Competitividade da Indústria de Transformação Brasileira* (São Paulo, March 2013).

Figueira, Sérgio Rangel. "Transformações na cadeia produtiva do leite – uma análise a partir das cooperativas"(MA thesis, Universidade Estadual de Campinas, 1999).

Figueiredo, Adelson Martins, Hildo Meireles de Souza Filho and Luiz Fernando de Oriani Paullilo. "Análise das margens e transmissão de preços no sistema agroindustrial do suco de laranja no Brasil," *Revista de Economia e Sociologia Rural*, 51, no. 2 (2013): 331–350.

Fishlow, A. "Origens e consequências da substituição de importações no Brasil, in F. R. Versiani and J. R. M. de Barros, eds., *Formação Econômica do Brasil: A Experiência Brasileira* (São Paulo: Saraiva, 1977): 7–41.

Fleury, Maria das Graças Prado. "Relações de emprego no campo: as diversas formas de contratação e a reestruturação produtiva" (MA thesis, Direito Agrário, Universidade Federal de Goiás, Goiânia, 2010).

Fontes, Eliana M. G., F. de S. Ramalho, E. Barroso Underwood, P. A. V. Simon, M. F. Sujii, E. R. Pires, C. S. S. Beltrão, N. Lucena, W. A. Freire. "The cotton agricultural context in Brazil,"in Angelika Hilbeck, David A. Andow, and Eliana M.G. Fontes, eds., *Environmental Risk Assessment of Genetically Modified Organisms: Methodologies for Assessing Bt Cotton in Brazil* (Wallingford: CAB International, 2006): 21–66.

Fontoura, Luiz Fernando Mazzini. "Agricultura da Associação a modernização," in Nelson Boeira, and Tau Golin, eds., *História Geral do Rio Grande do Sul* (5 vols.; Passo Fundo: Méritos Editora, 2006/2009). IV: 118–127.

Francisco, Vera Lúcia F. dos Santos, Celso Luis Rodrigues Vegro, José Alberto Ângelo and Carlos Nabil Ghobril. "Estrutura produtiva da cafeicultura paulista," *Informações Econômicas, SP*, 39, no. 8 (Aug. 2009): 42–48.

Frank, Zephyr and Aldo Musacchio. Overview of the Rubber Market, 1870–1930; at http://eh.net/encyclopedia/article/frank.international.rubber.market.

Freitas, Clailton Ataídes de, Carlos José Caetano Bacha and Daniele Maria Fossatti. "Avaliação do desenvolvimento do setor agropecuário no Brasil: período de 1970 a 2000," *Economia e Sociedade* (Campinas), 16, no. 1 (Apr. 2007): 111–124.

Freitas, Luiz Antonio Rossi de and Oscar Bertoglio. "A evolução da avicultura de corte brasileira após 1980," *Economia e Desenvolvimento*, 13 (Aug. 2001): 100–135.

Freitas, Pedro Luiz de. *Histórico do Sistema de Plantio Direto.* Accessed February 25, 2017, at www.linkedin.com/pulse/hist%C3%B3rico-do-sistema-plantio-direto-pedro-luiz-de-freitas.

Freitas, Rogerio Edivaldo. "Produtividade Agrícola no Brasil," in Negri and Cavalcanti, eds. *Produtividade no Brasil*, 373–410.

Fuglie, Keith O. "Productivity growth and technology capital in the global agricultural economy," in Keith O. Fuglie, Sun Ling Wang and V. Eldon Ball, eds., *Productivity Growth in Agriculture: An International Perspective* (Wallingford: CAB International, 2012), chap. 16. Accessed January 5, 2017, at http://agecon.unl.edu/9280a86c-342e-4c5a-afab-d35 0503401b8.pdf.

Fuglie, Keith and David Schimmelpfennig. "Introduction to the Special Issue on Agricultural Productivity Growth: a closer look at large, developing countries," *Journal of Production Analysis*, 33 (2010): 169–172.

Fuglie, Keith O. and Sun Ling Wang. "New evidence points to robust but uneven productivity growth in global agriculture," *Amber Waves*, 10, no. 3 (September 2012): 1–6.

Funchal, Marcio. "Panorama mundial do setor de celulose, papel e papelão," *Painel Florestal*, April 7, 2014.

Furtado, Celso. *Análise do Modelo Brasileiro* (Rio de Janeiro: Civilização Brasileira, 1975).

Formação Econômica do Brasil (São Paulo: Companhia Editora Nacional, 1968).

GTDN. *Uma Política de Desenvolvimento para o Nordeste* (Rio de Janeiro: Imprensa Nacional, 1959).

Um Projeto para o Brasil (Rio de Janeiro: Saga, 1969).

Garcia, Alvaro Antonio. "Agricutura e desenvolvimento econômico no Brasil: debates nas décadas de 50 e 70," *Ensaios FEE*, Porto Alegre, 11, no. 1 (1990): 198–222.

Garcia, Fernando Cacciatore de. *Fronteira iluminada: história do povoamento, conquista e limites do Rio Grande do Sul* (Porto Alegre: Sulina, 2010).

Garcia, Junior Ruiz. "Ambiente institucional na dinâmica da cotonicultura brasileira," *Revista de Política Agrícola*, 25 no. 2 (Apr./May/Jun. 2016): 58–60.

Gasques, José Garcia, Eliana Teles Bastos, Miriam Rumenos Piedade Bacchi and Constanza Valdes. "Produtividade Total dos Fatores e Transformações da Agricultura Brasileira: análise dos dados dos Censos Agropecuários," *48th Congreso, SOBER Sociedade Brasileira de Economia, Administracao e Sociologia Rural*, Campo Grande MS, 2010.

Gasques, José Garcia, Eliana Teles Bastos, Constanza Valdes and Mirian Rumenos P. Bacchi. "Produtividade da agricultura Brasileira e os efeitos de algumas políticas," *Revista de Política Agrícola*. XXI, no. 3 (Jul./Aug./Sept. 2012): 83–92.

"Produtividade da agricultura: resultados para o Brasil e Estados Selecionados," *Revista de Política Agrícola*, XXIII, no. 3 (Jul./Aug./Sept. 2014): 87–98.

Gasques, José Eustáquio R.Vieira Filho, and Zander Navarro, eds., *Agricultura Brasileira: Desempenho, Desafios e Perspectivas* (Brasília, Ipea, 2010): 19–44.

Golani, Lucille and Rodrigo Moita. *O oligopsônio dos frigoríficos: uma análise empírica de poder de mercado*, Insper Instituto de Ensino e Pesquisa, Insper Working Paper no. 222, 2010.

Goldsmith, Raymond W. *Brasil 1850–1984. Desenvolvimento Financeiro Sob um Século de Inflação* (São Paulo: Editora Harper & Row do Brasil Ltda), 1986.

Gonçalves, José Sidnei. "Dinâmica da agropecuária paulista no contexto das transformações de sua agricultura," *Informações Econômicas, SP*, 35, no. 12, (Dec. 2005): 65–98.

Gonzáles, Beatriz Picardo. "La revolución Verde en México," *Agrária* (São Paulo), no. 4 (2006): 40–68.

Goodman, David and Michael Redclift. "The "Bóias-Frias": rural proletarianization and urban marginality in Brazil," *International Journal of Urban and Regional Research*, I, no. 2 (1977): 348–364.

Grandin, Greg, *Fordlandia. The Rise and Fall of Henry Ford's Forgotten Jungle City* (New York: Metropolitan Books, 2009).

Graziano, Xico, *O Carma da Terra no Brasil* (São Paulo: A Girafa, 2004).

Guanziroli, Carlos E. *Agricultura Familiar e Reforma Agrária no Século XXI* (Rio de Janeiro: Editora Garamond, 2001).

Helfand, Steven M. and Gervázio Castro de Rezende. "Brazilian Agriculture in the 1990s: Impact of the Policy Reforms" (Discussion Paper 98; Brasília and Rio de Janeiro: Ipea, 2001).

Helfand, Steven M. and Edward S. Levine. "Farm size and the determinants of productive efficiency in the Brazilian Center-West," *Agricultural Economics*, 31 (2004): 241–249.

Helfand, Steven M., Vanessa da Fonseca Pereira and Wagner Lopes Soares. "Pequenos e médios produtores na agricultura brasileira: situação atual e perspectivas,"in Antônio Buainain, Márcio et al., eds., *O Mundo Rural no Brasil do Século 21, A Formação de um Novo Padrão Agrário e Agrícola* (Brasília, DF: Embrapa, 2014): 533–558.

Hira, Anil and Luiz Guilherme de Oliveira. "No substitute for oil? How Brazil developed its ethanol industry," *Energy Policy*, 37 (2009): 2451–2454.

Hoffmann, Rodolfo. "Evolução da distribuição da posse de terra no Brasil no período 1960–80," *Reforma Agrária*, 12, no. 6 (Nov.–Dec. 1982): 17–34.

Hoffmann, Rodolfo and Marlon Gomes Ney. *Estrutura Fundiária e Propriedade Agrícola no Brasil, Grandes Regiões e Unidades da Federação* (Brasília: Ministério do Desenvolvimento Agrário, 2010).

Hortaliças em Revista (Embrapa), Ano 1, no. 3 (May/Jun. 2012), www.agricul tura.gov.br/assuntos/politica-agricola/valor-bruto-da-producao-agrope cuaria-vbp.

Iaia, Antonio Marcos. "Irrigação por gotejamento em cana-de-açúcar no cerrado de Mato Grosso" (MA thesis, Universidade Federal de Paraná, 2014).

IMEA. *Boletin Semanal, Conjuntura Econômica*, June 2,2017/no. 036 found at www.imea.com.br/imea-site/relatorios-mercado-detalhe?c=6&s=4.

Inocêncio, Maria Erlan. "O PRODECER e as tramas do poder na territorialização do capital no Cerrado" (PhD thesis; Geografia, Universidade Federal de Goiás, 2010).

Input *Evolução do Crédito Rural no Brasil entre 2003 e 2016.* Accessed March 26, 2017, at www.inputbrasil.org/wp-content/uploads/2016/08/Evolucao_do_C redito_Rural_CPI.pdf.

International Plant Nutrition Institute. "Evolução do consumo aparente de N, P, K e Total de NPK no Brasil," found at http://brasil.ipni.net/article/BRS-3132#evolucao.

International Plant Nutrition Institute, found at http://brasil.ipni.net/article/BRS-3132#evolucao.

Jepson, Wendy, Christian Brannstrom and Anthony Filippi. "Access regimes and regional land change in the Brazilian Cerrado, 1972–2002," *Annals of the Association of American Geographers*, 100, no. 1 (January 2010): 87–111.

Junqueira, Victor Hugo. "O papel do Estado na expansão do setor sucroalcooleiro na região de Ribeirão Preto," *Revista NERA* (Presidente Prudente), 19, no. 31 (May–Aug. 2016): 51–71.

Kakimoto, Sérgio Kenji. "Fatores críticos da competitividade da cadeia produtiva do ovo no estado de São Paulo" (MA thesis, Universidade Federal de São Carlos, 2011).

Klein, Herbert S. "The supply of mules to Central Brazil: the Sorocaba market, 1825–1880," *Agricultural History*, 64, no. 4 (Autumn, 1990): 1–25.

Klink, Carlos A. and Ricardo B. Machado. "Conservation of the Brazilian Cerrado," *Conservation Biology*, 19, no. 3 (Jun., 2005): 707–713.

Kohlhepp, Gerd. "Análise da situação da produção de etanol e biodiesel no Brasil," *Estudos Avançados*, 24, no. 68 (2010): 223–253.

Kopf, Julio Cavalheiro and Algemiro Luís Brum. *A cadeia produtiva de tratores brasileira à luz da teoria do comércio exterior: Aspectos Introdutórios.* Globalização em Tempos de Regionalização – Repercussões no Território Santa Cruz do Sul, RS, Brasil, 9 a 11 de setembro de 2015. Accessed June 12, 2017: http://online.unisc.br/acadnet/anais/index.php/sidr/article/view/13429.

Kulaif, Yara. "Perfil dos Fertilizantes," Ministério de Minas e Energia and Banco Mundial, Relatório Técnico no. 75, 2009. Accessed January 22, 2017, at www.mme.gov.br/documents/1138775/1256652/P49_RT75_Perfil_dos_Fer tilizantes_N-P-K.pdf/f2785733-90d1-46d5-a09e-62f94ca302ad.

Landau, Elena C. et al. *Variação Geográfica dos Tamanhos dos Módulos Fiscais no Brasil* (Sete Lagoas: Embrapa Milho e Sorgo, 2012).

Leite, Tiago Trindade. "Tratamento pós-colheita em uvas e seus efeitos nos vinhos das variedades chardonnay e cabernet sauvignon" (MA thesis, Universidade Federal de Santa Maria, RS, 2009).

Lerrer, Débora Franco. "Trajetórias de militantes Sulistas: nacionalizações de modernidade do MST" (PhD thesis, Universidade Federal Rural do Rio de Janeiro, 2008).

Lessa, Carlos. *Quinze Anos de Política Econômica* (São Paulo, Brasiliense/Unicamp, 1975).

Levy, Maria and Stella Ferreira. "O papel da migração internacional na evolução da população brasileira (1872 a 1972)," *Revista de Saúde Publica*, Vol. 8 (Supl.) (1974): 49–90.

Liboni, Lara Bartocci, Luciana Oranges Cezarino, Michelle Castro Carrijo, Rudinei Toneto Junior. "The equipment supply industry to sugar mills, ethanol and energy in Brazil: an analysis based in leading companies and key-organizations of sector and of LPA of Sertãozinho," *Independent Journal Of Management & Production*, 6, no. 4 (October–December 2015): 1070–1096.

Lima, Guilherme Gadonski de, Emerson Juliano Lucca and Dilson Trennepohl. "Expansão da cadeia produtiva do leite e seu potencial de impacto no desenvolvimento da região noroeste rio-grandense," 53rd Congresso da SOBER 2015 (João Pessoa).

Lima, Ruy Cirne. *Pequena História Territorial do Brasil. Sesmarias e Terras Devolutas* (São Paulo: Secretaria do Estado da Cultura, 1990).

Lohloauer, Christian. "O contencioso do suco de laranja entre Brasil e Estados Unidos na OMC" (2011): 113–123, accessed at www.ieei-unesp.com.br/por tal/wp-content/uploads/2011/10/Politica-Externa-20-02-Christian-Lohbaue r.pdf.

Lopes, José Cláudio Bittencourt. "O Proálcool: uma avaliação" (MA thesis, Universidade Federal de Viçosa, 1992).

Love, Joseph L. *Rio Grande do Sul and Brazilian Regionalism, 1882–1930* (Stanford, Calif.: Stanford University Press, 1971).

Ludena, Carlos, Thomas Hertel, Paulo Preckel, Kenneth Foster and Alejandro Nin Pratt. "Productivity Growth and Convergence in Crop, Ruminant and Non-Ruminant Production: Measurement and Forecasts" *GTAP Working Papers*. Paper 33(2006), accessed at http://docs.lib.purdue.edu/gtapwp/33.

Luna, Francisco Vidal and Herbert S. Klein. *The Economic and Demographic History of São Paulo 1850–1950* (Stanford, Calif.: Stanford University Press, 2018).

Slavery and the Economy of São Paulo, 1750–1850 (Stanford, Calif.: Stanford University Press, 2003).

Luna, Francisco Vidal, Herbert S. Klein and William Summerhill. "Paulista agriculture in 1905," *Agricultural History*, 90, no. 1 (Winter 2016): 22–50.

Lyra, André de Arruda. "Estudo de vulnerabilidade do bioma amazônia aos cenários de mudanças climáticas" (PhD thesis, Instituto Nacional de Pesquisas Espaciais, São José dos Campos, 2015).

Macedo, Luís Otávio Bau, "Modernização da pecuária de corte bovina no brasil e a importância do crédito rural," *Informações Econômicas* (São Paulo), 36, no. 7 (Jul. 2006): 83–95.

Malhi, Yadvinder, J. Timmons Roberts, Richard A. Betts, Timothy J. Killeen, Wenhong Li, Carlos A. Nobre, "Climate change, deforestation and the fate of the Amazon, *Science*," 319 (2008), 169–172, doi:10.1126/science.1146961.

Maluf, Renato S. "Mercados agroalimentares e a agricultura familiar no Brasil: agregação de valor, cadeias integradas e circuitos regionais," *Ensaios FEE*, 25, no. 1 (2004): 299–322.

Marion Filho, Pascoal José, Jones de Oliveira Fagundes and Gabriela Schumacher, "A produção de leite no Rio Grande do Sul: produtividade, especialização e concentração (1990–2009)," *Revista de Economia e Agronegócio*, 9, no. 2 (2015): pp. 333–352.

Mariotoni, Marili Arruda. "O desenvolvimento tecnológico do setor sucroalcooleiro no estado de São Paulo (1975–1985)" (MA thesis, Universidade Estadual de Campinas, 2004).

Marouelli, Rodrigo Pedrosa. "O desenvolvimento sustentável da agricultura no cerrado brasileiro"(MA thesis, Brasília, ISEA/FGV,2003).

Marques, Claudia Marques. "Pioneiros de Mato Grosso e Pernambuco, novos e velhos capítulos da colonização no Brasil," *Revista Brasileira de Ciências Sociais*, 28, no. 83 (Nov. 2013): 85–103.

Marques, P. V. "Contribuição ao estudo da organização agroindustrial: o caso da indústria de frango de corte no estado de São Paulo," *Scientia Agricola*, 51, no. 1 (Jan./Apr. 1994): 8–16.

Marques, Rogério dos Santos Bueno. "A construção do profissionalismo na agronomia: trabalho, ciência e poder" (MA thesis, Universidade Federal de Goiás, Goiânia, 2009).

Martha Junior, Geraldo B., Elisio Contini and Eliseu Alves. "Embrapa: its origins and changes," in Werner Baer, ed., *The Regional Impact of National Policies. The Case of Brazil* (Cheltenham and Northampton, Mass.: Edward Elgar, 2012): 204–226.

Martinelli, Luiz A., Rosamond Naylor, Peter M. Vitousek and Paulo Moutinho. "Agriculture in Brazil: impacts, costs, and opportunities for a sustainable future," *Current Opinion in Environmental Sustainability*, 2, nos. 4–5 (2010): 431–438.

Martins, José de Souza. *A militarização da Questão Agrária no Brasil*. Petrópolis: Vozes, 1985.

Martins, Renata. "Produção de amendoim e expansão da cana-de-açúcar na Alta Paulista, 1996–2010," *Informações Econômicas, SP*, 41, no. 6 (Jun. 2011): 5–16.

Martins, Sonia Santana. "Cadeias produtivas do frango e do ovo: avanços tecnológicos e sua apropriação"(PhD thesis, Fundação Getúlio Vargas, São Paulo, 1996).

Martins, Sonia Santana, Ana Lúcia Lemos, Antônio de Pádua Deodato, Erica Salgado Politi and Nilce M. S. Queiroz. "Cadeia produtiva do ovo no estado de São Paulo," *Informações Econômicas. Governo do Estado de São Paulo. Instituto de Economia Agrícola*, 30, no. 1 (2000).

Matos, Alan Kardec Veloso de. "Revolução verde, biotecnologia e tecnologias alternativas," *Cadernos da Fucamp*, 10, no. 12 (2010): 1–7.

Mattei, Lauro. "Programa Nacional para Produção e Uso do Biodiesel no Brasil (PNPB): Trajetória, Situação Atual e Desafios," *BNB [Banco Nordeste do Brasil], Documentos Técnicos Científicos*, 41, no. 4 (2010): 731–740.

McKay, Ben, Sérgio Sauer, Ben Richardson and Roman Herre. "The politics of sugarcane flexing in Brazil and beyond," Transnational Institute (TNI) Agrarian Justice Program *Think Piece Series On Flex Crops & Commodities*, No. 4, September 2014, "The Corporate Control of Brazilian

Sugarcane," accessed July 2, 2017, at http://repub.eur.nl/pub/77677/Meti s_202533.pdf.

Meira, José Normando Gonçalves. "Ciência e prática: ensino agrícola na educação presbiteriana em Minas Gerais (1908–1938)" (PhD thesis, PUC São Paulo, 2009).

Melo, Fernando B. Homem de. "*Agricultura de exportação e o problema da produção de alimentos*" (São Paulo: FEA-USP, Texto para Discussão 30, 1979).

"Composição da produção no processo de expansão da fronteira agrícola brasileira," *Revista de Economia Política*, 5, no. 1 (Jan.–Mar. 1985), 86–111.

O Problema Alimentar no Brasil (Rio de Janeiro: Paz e Terra, 1983).

Melo, Fernando B. Homem de and Eduardo Giannetti. *Proálcool, Energia e Transportes* (São Paulo: Fipe/ Pioneira, 1981).

Melo Júnior, Heliomar Baleeiro de, Reginaldo de Camargo and Bueno Wendling. "Sistema de plantio direto na conservação do solo e água e recuperação de áreas degradadas. Goiânia," *Enciclopédia Biosfera*, 7, no. 12 (2011): 1–17.

Melz, Laércio Juarez, and Hildo Meirelles de Souza Filho. "Avaliação da competitividade da produção de carne de frango em Mato Grosso," *Revista Brasileira de Gestão e Desenvolvimento Regional*, 7, no. 2 (2011): 25–57.

Mendes, Giovanna Miranda. "Produtividade total dos fatores e crescimento econômico na agropecuária brasileira: 1970–2006" (PhD thesis, Universidade Federal de Viçosa, 2010).

Mendes, Giovanna Miranda, Erly Cardoso Teixeira and Márcio Antônio Salvato. "Produtividade Total dos Fatores e Crescimento Econômico na Agropecuária Brasileira: 1970–2006," *Encontro da ANPEC* (2010), accessed at www.anp ec.org.br/encontro/ ... /i11-a2721cea8a808e72157f9f97cfc7e14c.docx.

Menezes Filho, Naércio, Gabriela Campos and Bruno Komatsu. "Evolução da Produtividade no Brasil" (São Paulo, Insper, Policy Paper no. 12, Aug. 2014). Accessed at www.insper.edu.br/wp-content/uploads/ ... /Evolucao-Produtividade-Brasil.pdf.

Mengel, Aléx Alexandre. "Modernização da agricultura e pesquisa no Brasil: a Empresa Brasileira de Pesquisa Agropecuária – Embrapa" (PhD thesis, Universidade Federal Rural do Rio de Janeiro, 2015).

Merrick, Thomas and Douglas H. Graham. "População e desenvolvimento no Brasil: uma perspectiva histórica," in Paulo Nauhaus, ed., *Economia Brasileira: Uma Visão Histórica* (Rio de Janeiro: Editora Campus, 1980): 45–88.

Population and Economic Development in Brazil, 1800 to the Present (Baltimore: Johns Hopkins University Press, 1979).

Miele, Mercelo. "Análise do Cadastro Vinícola do Rio Grande do Sul para um processo inicial de caracterização do sistema agroindustrial vitivinícola gaúcho," *SOBER, Congresso Brasileiro de Economia e Sociologia Rural* 2004. Vol. 42, found at www.sober.org.br/palestra/12/04O203.pdf.

Miele, Marcelo and Paulo D. Waquil. "Cadeia produtiva da carne suína no Brasil," *Revista de Política Agrícola*, 16, no. 1 (2007):75–87.

Moita, Rodrigo and Lucille Golani. "O Oligopsônio dos Frigoríficos: uma análise empírica de poder de mercado," *RAC-Revista de Administração Contemporânea*, 18, no. 6 (Oct. 2014): 772–771.

Molina, Rodrigo Sarruge and Mara Regina Martins Jacomeli. "Os ruralistas paulistas e seus projetos para a educação agrícola: a 'Luiz de Queiroz' (ESALQ/USP) em Piracicaba (1881 a 1903)," *Revista Brasileira de História da Educação*, 16, no. 4 (issue 43) (Oct./Dec. 2016): 190–215.

Monteiro, Carlos Augusto and Wolney Lisboa Conde. "Tendência secular da desnutrição e da obesidade na infância na cidade de São Paulo (1974–1996)," *Revista de Saúde Pública* 34, no. 6 (2000): 52–61.

Monteiro, Carlos Augusto, Lenise Mondini and Renata B. L. Costa. "Mudanças na composição e adequação nutricional da dieta familiar nas áreas metropolitanas do Brasil (1988–1996)," *Revista de Saúde Pública*, 34, no. 3 (June 2000): 251–58.

Moraes, Márcia Azanha Ferraz Dias de. " O mercado de trabalho da agroindústria canavieira: desafios e oportunidades," *Economia Aplicada* (Ribeirão Preto), 11, no. 4 (Oct./Dec. 2007): 607–611.

Moreira, Ajax Reynaldo Bello, Steven M. Helfand and Adriano Marcos Rodrigues Figueiredo. "Explicando as diferenças de pobreza entre produtores agrícolas no brasil," *48º*. *Congresso Sober*, July 2010, accessed April 1, 2007, at www .sober.org.br/palestra/15/156.pdf.

Motter, Paulino and Herlon Goelzer de Almeida, eds., *Plantio direto: a tecnologia que revolucionou a agricultura brasileira* (Foz de Iguaçu: Parque Itaipu, 2015).

Mueller, Charles and George Martine. "Modernização agropecuária, emprego agrícola e êxodo rural no Brasil – a década de 1980," *Revista de Economia Política*, 17, no.3 (Jul.–Sept. 1997): 85–104.

Mueller, Charles Curt and Geraldo Bueno Martha Junior. "A Agropecuaria e o desenvolvimento socioeconomico recente do Cerrado," in Fábio Gelape Faleiro and Austeclinio Lopes de Farias Neto, eds., *Savanas. Desafios e Estratégias para o Equilíbrio entre Sociedade, Agronegócio e Recursos Naturais* (Planaltina, DF: Embrapa, 2008).

Müller, Geraldo. *A Dinâmica da Agricultura Paulista* (São Paulo: SEADE, 1985).

Navarro, Zander. "A agricultura familiar no Brasil: entre a política e as transformações da vida econômica," in José Garcia Gasques, José Eustáquio Ribeiro Filho and Zander Navarro, *A agricultura braileira: desempenho, desafios, perspectivas* (Brasília: Ipea/ Mapa, 2010): 185–209.

Por favor, Embrapa: acorde! Published in *Jornal o Estado de São Paulo*, on January 5, 2018, http://opiniao.estadao.com.br/noticias/geral,por-favor-em brapa-acorde,70002139015.

Navarro, Zander and Silvia Kanadani Campos. "A 'pequena produção rural' no Brasil," in Silvia Kanadani Campos and Zander Navarro, eds., *A Pequena Produção Rural e as Tendências do Desenvolvimento Agrário Brasileiro: Ganhar Tempo é possível?* (Brasília: CGEE, 2013): 13–27.

Navarro, Zander and Maria Thereza Macedo Pedroso. *Agricultura Familiar: É Preciso Mudar para Avançar* (Brasília: Embrapa Informações Tecnológicas, 2011).

Negri, Fernanda de and Luiz Ricardo Cavalcanti, eds., *Produtividade no Brasil. Desempenho e Determinantes* (Brasília: ABDI, IPEA, 2014).

Neto, Benedito Silva and Angélica de Oliveira. "Agricultura familiar, desenvolvimento rural e formação dos municípios do Estado do Rio Grande do Sul," *Estudos Sociedade e Agricultura* 2 (Dec. 2013): 83–108.

Netto, Antônio Delfim. *Agricultura e desenvolvimento no Brasil* São Paulo, Estudo Anpes, no. 5, 1969.

O Problema do Café no Brasil (São Paulo: IPE-USP, 1981).

Problemas econômicos da agricultura brasileira. São Paulo, Faculdade de Ciências Econômicas e Administrativas da USP – Boletim no. 40.

Neves, Marcos Fava, ed., *O retrato da citricultura brasileira* (São Paulo: Elaboração: Markestrat, Centro de Pesquisa e Projetos em Marketing e Estratégia, 2010), no pagination, tables 9 & 10 found at www.citrusbr.com/.

Neves, Marcos Fava and Vinícius Gustavo Trombin. "Mapping and quantification of the Brazilian citrus chain," *Fruit Processing* (March/April 2012): 50–59.

eds., *The Orange Juice Business, A Brazilian Perspective* (Wageningen: Wagenigen Academic Publishers, 2011).

Neves, Marcos Fava, Allan W. Grayb and Brian A. Bourquard. "Copersucar: a world leader in sugar and ethanol," *International Food and Agribusiness Management Review*, 19, no. 2 (2016): 207–240.

Nicol, Robert N. V. C. "A agricultura e a Industrialização no Brasil (1850/1930)" (PhD thesis, Economics, Universidade de São Paulo, FFLCH-USP, 1974).

Nobre, Carlos A., Gilvan Sampaio and Luis Salazer. *Mudanças climáticas e a Amazônia*. Accessed April 17, 2017, at http://mtc-m16b.sid.inpe.br/col/sid.i npe.br/mtc-m17@80/2007/09.24.12.18/doc/nobre_mudan%e7as.pdf.

Nogueira, Antonio Carlos Lima and Décio Zylbersztajn. "Coexistência de arranjos institucionais na avicultura de corte do estado de São Paulo" (Working Paper 03/22; USP–Faculdade de Economia, Administração e Contabilidade, 2003). Accessed November 2, 2017, at www.fundacaofia.co m.br/PENSA/anexos/biblioteca/1932007111943_03–022.pdf.

Nova Cana. Accessed April 19, 2017, at https://www.novacana.com/etanol/bene ficios/.

Nunberg, Barbara. "Structural change and state policy: the politics of sugar in Brazil since 1964," *Latin American Research Review*, 21, no. 2 (1986): 53–92.

O setor de máquinas agrícolas no Brasil: evolução nos últimos anos e perspectivas, Celeres, 2014, accessed January 22, 2017, at www.celeres.com.br/o-setor-de-maquinas-agricolas-no-brasil-evolucao-nos-ultimos-anos-e-perspectivas/.

Oliveira, Tadário Kamel de et al. *Experiências com Implantação de Unidades de Integração Lavoura-Pecuária-Floresta (iLPF) no Acre* (Rio Branco, Acre: Embrapa, 2012).

Oliveira, Vanderli Fava et al. (eds.), *Trajetória e Estado da Arte da Formação em Engenharia, Arquitetura e Agronomia* (vol. 1; Brasília: Instituto Nacional de Estudos e Pesquisas Educacionais Anísio Teixeira, Conselho Federal de Engenharia, Arquitetura e Agronomia, 2010).

Oreiro, José Luis e Carmem A. Feijó. "Desindustrialização: conceituação, causas, efeitos e o caso brasileiro," *Revista de Economia Política*, 30, no. 2 (Apr./Jun. 2010): 219–232.

Paiva, Ruy Miller, Salomão Schattan and Claus F. Trench de Freitas. *Setor Agrícola do Brasil. Comportamento Econômico, Problemas e Possibilidades* (São Paulo: Secretaria da Agricultura, 1973).

Parsons, James J. "Spread of African pasture grasses to the American Tropics," *Journal of Range Management*, 25, no. 1 (Jan., 1972): 12–17.

Pastore, Affonso Celso, Guilherme L. Silva Dias and Manoel C. Castro. "Condicionantes da produtividade da pesquisa agrícola no Brasil," *Estudos Econômicos*, 6, no. 3 (1976): 147–181.

A Resposta da Produção Agrícola aos Preços no Brasil (São Paulo, APEC, 1973).

Paulillo, Luis Fernando, ed., *Agroindústria e citricultura no Brasil: diferenças e dominâncias* (Rio de Janeiro: Editora E-papers, 2006.

Paulillo, Luis Fernando and Luiz Manoel de Moraes Camargo Almeida. "A coordenação agroindustrial citricola brasileira e os novos recursos de poder: dos politicos aos juridicos," *Organizações Rurais & Agroindustriais*, 11, no. 1 (2009): 11–27.

Pedroso, Maria Thereza Macedo. "Experiências internacionais com a agricultura familiar e o caso brasileiro: o desafio da nomeação e suas implicações práticas," in Antônio Márcio Buainain et al., eds., *O Mundo Rural no Brasil do Século 21. A Formação de um Novo Padrão Agrário e Agrícola.* (Brasília: Embrapa, 2014): 761–792.

Peixoto, Marcus. "Extensão Rural no Brasil. Uma Abordagem Histórica da Legislação" (Texto para Discussão no. 48; Brasília: Consultoria Legislativa do Senado Federal, 2008).

"Mudanças e desafios da extensão rural no Brasil e no mundo," in Buainain et al., *O mundo rural no Brasil*: 891–924.

Pereira, Luciano Gomes de Carvalho. *Controle Fitossanitário: agrotóxicos e outros métodos.* Brasília, Camara dos Deputados, Consultoria Legislativa, Estudo February 2013.

Peres, Frederico, Josino Costa Moreira and Gaetan Serge Dubois. "Agrotóxicos, saúde e ambiente. Uma Introdução ao tema," in Frederico Peres, Josino Costa Moreira and Gaetan Serge Dubois (orgs.), *É veneno ou remédio?: Agrotóxicos, saúde e ambiente* (Rio de Janeiro: Editora Fiocruz, 2003): 21–41.

Perkins, John H., *Geopolitics and the Green Revolution: Wheat, Genes and the Cold War* (New York: Oxford University Press, 1997).

Peske, Silmar Teichert. "O Mercado de Sementes no Brasil," *Seednews*. Reportagem de capa, May/jun. 2016, ano XX. N. 3. Accessed February 28, 2017, at silmar@seednews.inf.br.

Petrone, Maria Thereza Schorer. O Barão de Iguape. Um empresario de epoca da independência Sao Paulo: Brasiliana, 1976.

Prado Júnior, Caio. *A Revolução Brasileira* (São Paulo: Brasiliense, 1966).

"O Estatuto do Trabalhador Rural," *Revista Brasiliense*, no. 47 (1963) 1–9.

Evolução Política do Brasil e Outros Estudos (São Paulo: Brasiliense, 1972).

Formação do Brasil Contemporâneo: Colônia (São Paulo: Brasiliense, 1973).

Prado, Maria Lígia and Maria Helena Rolim Capelato. "A borracha na economia brasileira na primeira república," in Boris Fausto, ed., *História Geral da Civilização Brasileira*, III, no. 1: 285–307.

Priori, Angelo et al. "Relações de Trabalho. Colonos, parceiros e camaradas," in *História do Paraná: Século XIX e XX* (Maringá: Eduem, 2012): 105–114.

Queiroz, Maria Isaura Pereira de. *O Mandonismo Local na Vida Política Brasileira* (São Paulo: Alfa-Omega, 1976).

Quimarães, Alberto Passos. *Quatro Séculos de Latifúndio* (Rio de Janeiro: Paz e Terra, 1977).

Rada, Nicholas. "Assessing Brazil's Cerrado agricultural miracle," *Food Policy* 38 (2013): 146–155.

Ramos, Simone Yuri and Geraldo Bueno Martha Junior. *Evolução da Politica de Crédito Rural Brasileira* (Planaltina: Embrapa Cerrados, 2010).

Rangel, Ignácio. *A Inflação Brasileira* (São Paulo: Bienal, 1963).

Rausch, Lisa. "Convergent agrarian frontiers in the settlement of Mato Grosso, Brazil," *Historical Geography*, 42 (2014): 276–297.

Raven, Peter H. "Tropical floristic tomorrow," *Taxon*, 37, no. 3 (Aug., 1988), 549–560.

Rech, Samara, Silvio Antonio Ferraz Cario and Cleiciele Albuquerque Augusto. "Avaliação conjuntural da produção e comercialização da maçã em Santa Catarina e no Rio Grande do Sul: aspectos comparativos," *Indicadores Econômicos FEE*, Porto Alegre, 42, no. 1 (2014): 89–106.

Reydon, Bastiaan Philip. "Governança de terras e a questão agrária no Brasil," in Antônio Márcio Buainain, et al., eds., *O mundo rural no Brasil do século 21: a formação de um novo padrão agrário e agrícola* (Brasilia: Embrapa, 2014): 725–760.

Ribeiro, Helena and Thomas Ribeiro de Aquino Ficarelli. "Queimadas nos Canaviais e Perspectivas dos Cortadores de Cana-de-açúcar em Macatuba, São Paulo," *Saúde Social* (São Paulo), 19, no. 1 (2010): 48–51.

Ribeiro, Iselda Corrêa. *Pioneiros gaúchos: a colonização do norte matogrossense* (Porto Alegre: Tchê!, 1987).

Rocha, Jean. *La colonisation allemande et le Rio Grande do Sul* (Paris: Institut des hautes études de l'Amérique latine, 1959).

Rocha, Jefferson Marçal da. "As raízes do declínio econômico da 'Metade Sul' do Rio Grande do Sul – uma análise da racionalidade econômica dos agentes produtivos da região," *Primeiras Jornadas de História Regional Comparada*. FEE, POA. 2000, found at http://cdn.fee.tche.br/jornadas/1/s12a5.pdf.

Rodrigues, Ângelo Constâncio. "A Escola Superior de Agricultura de Lavras/ ESAL e a Universidade Federal de Lavras/UFLA: a trajetória de uma transformação," (PhD thesis: Faculdade de Educação, Universidade Federal do Rio de Janeiro, Rio de Janeiro, 2013).

Rodrigues, Cyro Mascarenhas. "A pesquisa agropecuária federal no período compreendido entre a República Velha e o Estado Novo," *Cadernos de Difusão de Tecnologia* (Brasília), 4, no. 2 (May/Aug. 1987): 129–153.

"A pesquisa agropecuária no período do pós-guerra," *Cadernos de Difusão de Tecnologia*, 4, no. 3 (Sept./Dec. 1987): 205–254.

Rodrigues, Roberto and Eliseu Alves. "O futuro da pesquisa agropecuária." *Revista de Política Agrícola*, XIV, no. 4 (Oct./Nov./Dec. 2005): 3–4.

Rosa, Vanderleia Trevisan da. "Tempo de implantação do sistema de plantio direto e propriedades físico-mecênicas de um latossolo" (PhD thesis, Universidade Federal de Santa Maria, 2009).

Rosana Sifuentes Machado, Benedito Dias Pereira, Meiresângela Miranda Muniz, Daniel Sneyder Campos Zambrano and Heitor Tiago Gonçalves. "Otimização dos custos de transporte para exportação da pluma de algodão: contraste entre Mato Grosso e Bahia," Paper given at the 53rd *SOBER, Sociedade Brasileira de Economia, Administração e Sociologia Rural*, 2015. Accessed February 19, 2018, at https://portalseer.ufba.br/inde x.php/revnexeco/article/view/14227.

Rossi, Michelle Pereira da Silva. "'Dedicado à glória de Deus e ao progresso humano': a gênese protestante da Universidade Federal de Lavras – UFLA (Lavras, 1892–1938)"(PhD thesis, Universidade Federal de Uberlândia, 2010).

Ruiz, Lucas Gonçalves. *Uma Visão Geral sobre a Cédula de Produto Rural (CPR)*. Accessed December 27, 2016, at www.migalhas.com.br/dePeso/16,M I227850,11049-Uma+Visao+Geral+Sobre+a+Cedula+de+Produto+Rural +CPR.

Ruy Miller Paiva. "V. Reflexões sobre as tendências da produção, da produtividade e dos preços do setor agrícola do Brasil." e "VI. Bases de uma política para a melhoria técnica da agricultura brasileira," in Caio Prado Jr. et al., eds., *A Agricultura Subdesenvolvida* (Petrópolis: Vozes, 1969): 167–261.

Sá, Eduardo. "Merenda escolar: uma revolução para os agricultores familiares. ANA – Articulação Nacional de Agroecologia," accessed March 23, 2017, at www.agroecologia.org.br/2016/08/17/merenda-escolar-uma-revolucao-par a-os-agricultores-familiares/.

Saint, William S. "Mão-de-obra volante na agricultura brasileira: uma revisão da literatura," *Pesquisa e Planejamento Econômico*, 10, no. 2 (Aug. 1980): 503–526.

Salis, Carmem Lúcia Gomes de. "Estatuto da Terra: Origem e (Des) Caminhos da Proposta de Reforma Agrária nos Governos Militares" (PhD thesis, Assis, UNESP – Universidade Estadual Paulista, 2008).

Santiago, Maura M. D. and Valquíria da Silva. "A política de crédito rural brasileira e o endividamento do setor agrícola. Antecedentes e desdobramentos recentes," *Agricultura, São Paulo*, 46 (1999): 47–69.

Santos, Joelma Cristina dos. "Sistema agroindustrial do leite na região de Presidente Prudente – SP"(MA thesis, Universidade Estadual Paulista, Presidente Prudentes, 2004).

Santos, Mauro Augusto dos, Alisson Flávio Barbieri, José Alberto Magno de Carvalho and Carla Jorge Machado. "O cerrado brasileiro: notas para estudo" (Texto para discussão; 387; Belo Horizonte: UFMG/Cedeplar, 2010).

Santos, Rosemeire Cristina dos. "Custos de transação na comercialização antecipada de soja na região norte do estado de Mato Grosso"(MA thesis, Universidade de Brasília, 2009).

Saraiva, Elisa Braga et al. "Panorama da Compra de Alimentos da Agricultura Familiar para o Programa Nacional de Alimentação Escolar," accessed March 23, 2017, at www.scielo.br/pdf/csc/v18n4/04.pdf.

Sayad, João. *Crédito Rural no Brasil* (São Paulo: IPE/USP,1978).

Sayad, João and Francisco Vidal Luna. "Política Anti-inflacionaria y el Plan Cruzado," in *Neoliberalismo y Políticas Economicas Alternativas* (Quito: Corporacion de Estudios para el Desarrolo [CORDES], 1987): 189–204.

Scalco, Paulo Roberto. "Identificação do poder de mercado no segmento de leite *in natura* e UHT" (PhD thesis, Universidade Federal de Viçosa, 2011).

Schaefer, José Renato. *As Migrações Rurais e Implicações Pastorais: Um Estudo das Migrações Campo-campo do sul do País em Direção ao Norte do Mato Grosso* (São Paulo: Edições Loyola, 1985).

Sepulcri, Odilio and Nilson de Paula. *A Emater e seu papel na Difusão de Tecnologia nos seus 50 anos*. Accessed January 28, 2017, atwww.emater.p r.gov.br/arquivos/File/Biblioteca_Virtual/Premio_Extensao_Rural/2_Premi o_ER/02_A_Emater_papel_Dif_Tec.pdf.

Silva, Carlos Alberto da and Léo da Rocha Ferreira. "Produtividade total dos fatores no crescimento da agricultura brasileira," *Revista de Política Agrícola*, XXV, no. 3 (Jul./Aug./Sept. 2016): 4–15.

Silva, César Roberto Leite da and Sérgio Antonio dos Santos. "Política agrícola e eficiência econômica: o caso da agricultura paulista," *Pesquisa & Debate. Revista do Programa de Estudos Pós-Graduados em Economia Política*, 12, no. 2 (2001): 66–82.

Silva, Claiton Marcio da. "Nelson Rockefeller a a atuação da American International Association For Economic and Social Development: debates sobre missão e imperialismo no Brasil, 946–1961," *História, Ciências, Saúde – Manginhos*, 20, no. 4 (Oct.–Dec., 2013): 1696–1711.

Silva, Fabrício Valentim da. "Ensino Agricola, trabalho de modernização no campo: a origem da Escola Superior de Agricultura e Veterinária do Estado de Minas"(MA thesis, Universidade Federal de Uberlândia, 2007).

Silva, Felipe Prince. "O crédito rural no Brasil," *Animal Business Brasil*, 2, no. 6 (2012): 61–66.

Silva, Haroldo José Torres da. "Estudo da viabilidade econômico-financeira da indústria de citros: impactos da criação de um conselho setorial" (PhD thesis, Escola Superior de Agricultura "Luiz de Queiroz," 2016).

Silva, Iliane Jesuina da. "Estado e agricultura no primeiro governo Vargas (1930–1945)" (PhD thesis, Campinas, Universidade Estadual de Campinas, 2010).

Silva, José Graziano da. *A Nova Dinâmica da Agricultura Brasileira* (Campinas: Instituto de Economia da Unicamp, 1996).

Silva, Paulo Roberto da, Francisco X. R. do Vale and Marcelo Cabral Jahnel. "Retrospecto e atualidade da engenharia agronômica," in Vanderli Fava Oliveira et al. (eds.), *Trajetória e Estado da Arte da Formação em Engenharia, Arquitetura e Agronomia* (vol. 1; Brasília: Instituto Nacional de Estudos e Pesquisas Educacionais Anísio Teixeira, Conselho Federal de Engenharia, Arquitetura e Agronomia, 2010).

Silveira, Rogério Leandro Lima da. "Complexo agroindustrial do fumo e território: a formação do espaço urbano e regional no Vale do Rio Pardo-RS" (PhD thesis, Universidade Federal de Santa Catarina, 2007).

Sochaczewski, António Claudio. *O Desenvolvimento Econômico e Financeiro do Brasil, 1952–1968* (São Paulo: Trajetória Cultural, 1993).

Sodré, Nelson Werneck. *Formação Histórica do Brasil* (São Paulo: Brasiliense, 1963).

Sola, Lourdes, ed., *O Estado e a transição: política e economia na Nova República* (São Paulo: Vértice, 1988).

Sonia M. P. P., Bergamasco. "Extensão Rural: Passado e presente no discurso e na prática," pp. 353–364, accessed January 28, 2017, at www.redeufscaragroe cologica.ufscar.br/wp-content/uploads/2016/07/Extens%C3%A30-rural-Pa ssado-e-presente-no-discurso-e-na-pr%C3%A1tica-S%C3%B4nia.pdf.

Souza, Cleonice Borges de and David José Caume. "Crédito Rural e agricultura familiar no Brasil." *XLVI Congresso da Sober*, 2008. Accessed January 29, 2017, at www.sober.org.br/palestra/9/882.pdf.

Souza, Francisco H. Dübbern de, "Evolución de la industria de semillas de pastos tropicales en Brasil." *X Seminario de Pastos y Forajes* (2006), accessed March 13, 2018, and found at http://avpa.ula.ve/congresos/seminario_pasto_X/Co nferencias/A14-Francisco%20Souza.pdf.

Souza, José Carlos Lima de. "O Movimento dos Trabalhadores Rurais sem Terra (MST). O Moderno Príncipe Educativo brasileiro na história do tempo presente" (PhD thesis, Niterói, Universidade Federal Fluminense, 2008).

Sperotto, Fernanda Queiroz. "A expansão do setor de celulose de mercado no Brasil: condicionantes e perspectivas" *Indicadores Econômicos FEE (Porto Alegre)*, 41, no. 4 (2014): 85–100.

Stedile, João Pedro and Bernardo Mançano Fernandes. *Brava Gente. A trajetória do MST e a luta pela terra no Brasil* (São Paulo: Editora Fundação Perseu Abramo, 2005).

Sued, Ronaldo. *O desenvolvimento da agroindústria da laranja no Brasil: o impacto das geadas na Flórida e na política econômica governamental* (Rio de Janeiro: Fundação Getúlio Vargas, 1993).

Summerhill, William R. *Order against Progress: Government, Foreign Investment, and Railroads in Brazil, 1854–1913* (Stanford, Calif.: Stanford University Press, 2003).

Sumner, Daniel A. "American farms keep frowing: aize, productivity, and policy," *Journal of Economic Perspectives*, 28, no. 1 (Winter 2014): 147–166.

Suprinyak, Carlos Eduardo. *Tropas em Marcha: O Mercado de Animais de Carga no Centro-sul do Brasil Imperial* (São Paulo: Annablume Editora, 2008).

Szmrecsányi, Tamás. "O desenvolvimento da produção agropecuária (1930–1970)," in Boris Fausto, ed., *História da Civilização Brasileira. III. O Brasil Republicano*, vol. 4, "Economia e Cultura (1930–1964)" (Rio de Janeiro: Beltrand Brasil, 1995): 107–207.

Szmrecsányi, Tamás and Eduardo Pestana Moreira. "O desenvolvimento da agroindústria canavieira do Brasil desde a Segunda Guerra Mundial," *Estudos Avançados*, .5, no. 11 (Apr. 1991): 57–79.

Tarsinato, Maria Aparecida Anselmo. "Analise da Agricultura Matogrossense, 1970/85: modernização, desconcentração da terra e mão-de-obra" (PhD thesis, Fundação Getúlio Vargas, São Paulo, 1990).

Tavares, Maria da Conceição. "Auge e Declínio do processo de substituição de importações no Brasil," in *Maria da Conceição Tavares. Da Substituição de Importações ao Capitalismo Financeiro* (Rio de Janeiro: Zahar, 1973).

Tomasini, Roque Silvestre Annes and Ivo Ambrosi. "Aspectos econômicos da cultura do trigo," *Cadernos de Ciência e Tecnologia*, 15, no. 2 (May–Aug. 1998), 59–84.

Trajetória politica da Contag – As Primeiras Lutas. AccessedApril 22, 2017, at http://enfoc.org.br/system/arquivos/documentos/43/Trajetria-poltica-da-con tag–as-primeiras-lutas–revista-40-anos-da-contag.pdf.

Tratoraço. As razões da Crise. O Alerta do Campo. Confederação da Agricultura e Pecuária do Brasil – CNA. Accessed January 29, 2018, at www.arrozeiros dealegrete.com.br/arroz/memorialdoarroz/movimentos/crise_no_campo_tra toraco.pdf.

Trecenti, Ronaldo, Maurício Carvalho de Oliveira, Gunter Hass and Marcos de Matos Ramos. *Integração lavoura-pecuária-floresta: cartilha do produtor* (Brasília: Ministério da Agricultura, 2009).

Trento, Angelo. *Do Outro Lado do Atlântico. Um Século de Imigração Italiana no Brasil* (Sao Paulo: Nobel, 1989).

Triches, Divanildo, Renildes Fortunato Siman and Wilson Luis Caldart. "A cadeia produtiva da carne de frango da região da Serra Gaúcha: uma análise da estrutura de produção e mercado," *Congresso da Sociedade Brasileira de Economia e Sociologia Rural* 2004, Vol. 43.

Urso, Fabiana Salgueiro Perobelli. "A cadeia da carne bovina no Brasil: uma análise de poder de mercado e teoria da informação"(PhD thesis, Fundação Getúlio Vargas, São Paulo, 2007).

Vasconcellos, M. de Cerqueira, M. G. Pignatti and W. A. Pignati. "Emprego e acidentes de trabalho na indústria frigorífica em áreas de expansão do agronegócio, Mato Grosso, Brasil," *Saúde e Sociedade*, 18, no. 4 (2009): 662–672.

Vasconcelos, Kelly S. L. de, J. Tiago, J. da Silva and Sonia R. S. Melo. "Mecanização da Agricultura por Tratores de rodas e máquinas agrícolas nos estados da Região Nordeste," *Revista em Agronegócio e Meio Ambiente* (Maringá), 6, no. 2 (May/Aug. 2013): 207–222.

Vegro, Celso Luis Rodrigues, Célia Regina R.P. T. Ferreira and Flavio Condé de Carvalho. "Indústria brasileira de Máquinas Agrícolas: evolução e mercado, 1985–95," *Informações Econômicas*, 27, no. 1 (Jan. 1997): 11–26.

Veiga, José Eli da. "Agricultura familiar e sustentabilidade," *Cadernos de Ciência & Tecnologia*, Brasília, 13, no. 3 (1996): 383–404.

Veja. Feb. 10, 2017 "Irmãos Batista vendem quase metade do grupo para preservar a JBS," found at https://veja.abril.com.br/politica/carne-fraca-ente nda-o-que-pesa-contra-cada-frigorifico/.

Mar. 17, 2017 " Carne Fraca: entenda o que pesa contra cada frigorífico," found at https://veja.abril.com.br/politica/carne-fraca-entenda-o-que-pesa-c ontra-cada-frigorifico/.

Vian, Carlos Eduardo de Freitas and Adilson Martins Andrade Júnior. "Evolução Histórica da Indústria de Máquinas Agrícolas no Mundo: Origens e Tendências," *48°. Congresso da Sober*, Accessed January 23, 2017, at www.sober.org.br/palestra/15/1208.pdf.

Vianna, Sérgio Besserman. "Duas tentativas de estabilização: 1951–1954," in Marcelo de Paiva Abreu, ed., *A Ordem do Progresso* (Rio de Janeiro: Editora Campus, 1992).

Vieira, Adriana Carvalho Pinto, Divina Aparecida Leonel Lunas, and Junior Ruiz Garcia. "Ambiente institucional na dinâmica da cotonicultura brasileira," *Revista de Política Agrícola*, 25, no. 2 (2016): 53–66.

Vieira Filho and José Eustáquio Ribeiro. "Distribuição produtiva e tecnológica os estabelecimentos agropecuários de menor porte e gestão familiar," in Campos and Navarro, *A Pequena Produção Rural* : 177–199.

Vieira Júnior, Pedro Abel Vieira, Eliana Valéria Covolan Figueiredo and Júlio César dos Reis. "Alcance e limites da agricultura para o desenvolvimento regional: o caso de Mato Grosso," in Antônio Márcio Buainain, ed., *O Mundo Rural no Brasil do Século 21: Aformação de um Novo Padrão Agrário e Agrícola* (Brasília: Embrapa, 2014): 1125–1155.

Vieira, Nivea Muniz. "O trabalho em sua relação com a técnica e a reorganização espacial na cadeia carne/grãos da BR-163, MT" (MA thesis, PUC, Rio de Janeiro, 2009).

Vinhas, Moisés. *Problemas Agrário-camponeses do Brasil* (São Paulo: Civilização do Brasil, 1968).

Visentin, Maria Alice Dias Rolim. "A floresta Amazônica e as mudanças climáticas: proteção da biodiversidade," *Revista CEJ* (Brasília), XVII, no. 60 (May/Aug. 2013): 96–102.

Vogt, Olgário Paulo. "A produção de fumo em Santa Cruz do Sul, RS (1849–1993)" (MA thesis, Universidade Federal de Paraná, 1994).

Vollrath, Dietrich. "Land distribution and international agricultural productivity," *American Journal of Agricultural Economics*, 89, no. 1 (February 2007): 202–216.

Wanderley, Maria de Nazareth Baudel. *Agricultura familiar e campesinato: rupturas e continuidade.* Accessed March 26, 2017, at http://r1.ufrrj.br/esa/V2/ojs/index.php/esa/article/view/238/234.

Weinstein, Barbara. *The Amazon Rubber Boom, 1850–1920* (Stanford, Calif.: Stanford University Press, 1983).

West, Sherlie H. and W. D. Pitman. "Seed production technology of tropical forages," in W. D. Pitman and Antonio Sotomayor-Rios, eds., *Tropical Forage Plants: Development and Use* (Boca Raton, Fla.: CRC Press, 2000): chap. 9.

Wilkinson, John. *O Setor Sucroalcooleiro Brasileiro na Atual Conjuntura Nacional e Internacional* (Rio de Janeiro: ActionAid, 2015).

"What Washington Means by Policy Reform," *Peterson Institute for International Economics, Speeches & Papers* (Nov. 2002), 7–20.

Yamamura, Simone. "Plantas transgênicas e propriedade intelectual: ciência, tecnologia e inovação no Brasil frente aos Marcos Regulatórios" (MA thesis, Unicamp, Campinas, 2006).

Zanin, Vanclei. "Panorama geral da orizicultura brasileira," *Indicadores Econômicos FEE*, Porto Alegre, 41, no. 2 (2013): 53–60.

Zardo, Katia. "Vitivinicultura de precisão aplicada a produção e qualidade de uva pinot noir no Rio Grande do Sul' (MA thesis, Universidade Federal de Santa Maria, RS, 2009), p. 18.

Zarth, Paulo Afonso. *Do arcaico ao moderno: o Rio Grande do Sul Agrário do século XIX*. Ijuí: Unijuí, 2002.

Zimmer, Ademir H. et al. *Degradação, recuperação e renovação de pastagens* (Campo Grande, MS: Embrapa Gado de Corte, 2012). Accessed April 19, 2017, at www.embrapa.br/busca-de-publicacoes/-/publicacao/951322/degra dacao-recuperacao-e-renovacao-de-pastagens.

Zimmermann, Beate and Jurgen Zeddies. " International Competitiveness of Sugar Production," Paper given at the 13th International Farm Management Congress, Wageningen, The Netherlands, July 7–12, 2002, found at http://econpapers.repec.org/paper/agsifma02/.

Zoccal, Rosangela and Aloísio Teixeira Gomes. "Zoneamento da produção de leite no Brasil," *XLIII Congresso da Sociedade Brasileira de Economia e Sociologia Rural* (Ribeirão Preto, 2005).

Zulian, Aline, Andréa Cristina Dörr and Sabrina Cantarelli Almeida. "Citricultura e Agronegócio Cooperativo n Brasil," *Revista Eletrônica em Gestão, Educação e Tecnologia Ambiental*, 11, no. 11 (Jun. 2013): 2298–2299.

Index

"63 caipira" Resolution, 104

abolition of slavery, 8, 18
Abrapa (Associação Brasileira dos
    Produtores de Algodão), 251
Africa, 410
African slave labor, 5
Agenda 21, 177
agrarian reform, 3, 38, 356, 360, 406
Agrarian Research Organizations (OEPAS),
    165, 170
agrarian structure, 37, 358, 406
agribusiness, 104, 112
    balance of payments, 126
    dimension of, 409
    financing system of, 46
    internationalization of, 104
    production process, 105
agricultural
    census of 1960, 31
    census of 2006, 154, 200, 208, 216, 241,
        244, 278
    credit, 40, 407
    equipment, 52
    imports, 86
    policies, 40
agricultural exports
    breakdown of, 86
    share of regions, 218
    value of, 49
agricultural frontier
    expansion of, 46
    policies, 40

production, 126
production in the 1960s, 29
production per inhabitant, 48
protection policies, 92
revolution, 3, 50
subsidies, 42
subsidized credit, 407
trade balance, 59, 99
Agricultural Law, 103
agricultural modernization, 40
    military support, 38
    modern farming technologies, 53
    process of, 2, 92, 406
agricultural policy
    system of management, 408
agricultural production, 126
    gross value of, 228
    sugarcane, 125
agricultural productivity
    advances in, 114
    effects of public policies, 121
    factors of productivity stagnation, 125
    mechanization, fertilizers, insecticides, 216
agricultural support instruments
    modernization of, 406
agriculture
    private international resources, 102
Agriculture Program of Low Carbon
    Emission (Plano ABC), 178
Agronomic Institute of Campinas, 46, 156
alcohol, 40, 43, 95
alcohol production, 331
alternative colonization models, 3

445

Alves, Eliseu, 160
Amado, Jorge, 16
Amazon, 4, 15, 116, 178, 179, 412
Amazon rainforest, 177, 181, 234
Amazonian deforestation, 410
animal husbandry, 205
    growth of, 73
apples, 214, 273, 284, 287
Aprovale–RS, 289
Argentina, ix, 51, 57, 60, 62, 68, 80, 85, 86,
    117, 118, 124, 164, 176, 287, 298, 323
Associação dos Criadores de Gado
    Holandês do Rio Grande do Sul, 297
Association of Credit and Rural Assistance
    (ACAR-MG), 151
Atlantic Forest, 178, 180
Australia, 4, 75, 85
automobile industry, 15
    implantation of, 28

balance of payments
    crisis in, 94
Banco do Brasil, 100, 101
    Movement Account, 102
bandeirantes, 5
beans, 42, 53, 56, 117, 215
Bid
bioenergy programs, 186
Biological Fixation of Nitrogen in soils, 185
biomes, 177, 178, 180, 186
Biosafety Law, 173
biotechnology in agriculture
Bird
BNDES (Banco Nacional do
    Desenvolvimento Econômico e Social),
    43, 104, 107, 112, 144
boia-fria (seasonal workers), 357
Brasília
    construction of, 28
Brazil
    international exporter of processed beef,
    74
    as a world agricultural powerhouse, rise
    of, 1
Brazil by region
    average farm production, 370
    average farm size, 367
    average of food imports, 87
    citrus juice industry, 222
    color compositions, 198
    leather exports, 13, 221

meat exports, 221
modern agricultural practice, 376
pastoral industry regional variations, 208
population, 191
production of crops and pastoral
    products, 205
productivity, 212
regional populations, 198
specialization of most fruits, 214
use of fertilizers, 216
value of output, 207
variation of production of crops and
    pastoral products, 205
Brazil Cost, 114, 133, 134, 135, 136, 137
    factors of, 133, 410
    infrastructural and tax costs, 57
Brazilian Agribusiness Association (ABAG),
    384
Brazilian agriculture
    consumer of fertilizers and insecticides, 1
    cycles of growth, 50
    growth of productivity, 57
    introduction of new commercial crops, 55
    modernization, 2, 55, 139, 407, 411
    sustainability of, 177
Brazilian Association of Credit and Rural
    Assistance (ABCAR), 152
Brazilian Association of State Entities for
    Technical Assistance and Rural
    Extension (ASBRAER), 153
Brazilian Coffee Institute (IBC), 40
Brazilian Consortium for Coffee Research
    and Development (CBP & DCafé), 167
Brazilian economy
    integration into the world market, 407
    opening to world trade, 91
Brazilian industry, 132
Brazilian Institute of Environment and
    Renewable Natural Resources
    (IBAMA), 178
Brazilian meatpackers, 74
Brazilian Ministry of Agriculture (MAPA)
    estimated projections, 89
Brazilian problem of technology diffusion,
    402
Brazilian Rural Extension System (Siber), 152
Brazilian seed market, 174
Brazilian Technical Assistance and Rural
    Extension Company (Embrater), 152
Brazilian trade balance, 126
    flows, 26

Caatinga, 178, 181
cacao, 16, 55
Caixa Econômica do Estado de Minas
Gerais, 152
Canada, 4, 49, 52, 118, 176
Cardoso, Fernando Henrique
agrarian policy, 385
Carteira de Crédito Agrícola e Industrial
(CREAI of the Banco do Brasil), 19
cattle industry, 16
cellulose industry, 83, 202
processed wood pulp and paper, 83
Center of Sugar Technology (CTC), 163
Center-West, 30, 35, 39, 46, 59, 68, 112,
113, 115, 116, 118, 121, 142, 190, 192,
193, 194, 196, 198, 200, 201, 202, 205,
206, 209, 211, 212, 215, 216, 217, 219,
234
Central Bank
central mills, 13
CEPAL, 356
CEPEA/USP/CAN (Centro de Estudos
Avançados em Economia Aplicada,
Universidade de São Paulo), 126
Cerrado, 25, 28, 39, 46, 51, 138, 163, 178,
179, 234, 269, 412
opening up to, 28
chicken industry, 291
broiler chickens (*galinhas de corte*), 340
hatcheries (*incubatórios*), 341
hens (*poedeiras*, or *galinhas de postura*),
340
layer hens (*pintinhos de postura*)
chicken meat
exports of, 70
Chile, 287
China, 4, 49, 52, 60, 67, 85, 122, 144, 295,
410
cocoa, 31, 55
coffee, 1, 6, 21, 27, 29, 35, 49, 53, 88, 190,
205, 213, 222
arrival of, 6
expansion of, 7
international market, 11
overproduction, 29
production, 9, 70
regulatory stocks, 38, 96
Coffee Institute of São Paulo, 11
coffee market, 10
Collor, Fernando
economic liberalization measures, 98

colonato system, 357
"colonel" landowners, 21
commercial agricultural production
small and medium sized farms, 54
commercial agriculture in Brazil, 1
Commission for Sustainable Development
(CIDES), 177
Common Market of the South (Mercosur),
94
Compulsory Resources, 106
conservative agricultural revolution, 2
conservative modernization, 406
Constitutional Financing Funds, 103
cooperatives, 2, 92, 138, 150, 247, 263,
273, 306, 318, 408
Copersucar (Cooperativa de Produtores de
Cana-de-Açúcar, Açúcar e Álcool do
Estado de São Paulo), 330, 332, 334,
335
CORLAC (Companhia Rio-Grandense de
Laticínios e Correlatos), 297
corn, 16, 41, 53, 56, 116, 202, 205, 228, 279
corn production, 209
international markets, 67
seeds, 174
use of two havest cycle, 67
coronels (*coronéis*), 16
cotton, 1, 14, 26, 29, 31, 39, 53, 118, 191,
205, 241
production, 248, 258
revival of, 82
textiles, 22
counties (*munícipios*), 7
credit for agriculture, 406
crises
1929, 11
1990s, 42, 146
2004/2005, 111
oil crisis, 289
croplands
expansion of, 202
crop-livestock integration (ILP, or
Integração Lavoura-Pecuária, 184
crop-livestock-forest integration (ILPF, or
Integração Lavoura-Pecuária-Floresta),
184
Cuba, 14
CUT – Central Única dos Trabalhadores, 384

deforestation, 178, 179, 182
direct effects of, 183

deforestation (cont.)
  impact on global warming, 179
Deforestation Monitoring Program of
  Brazilian Biomes, 178
Department of Agricultural Research and
  Experimentation – DPEA, 157
direct or non-tillage planting, 185

EGF (Empréstimos do Governo Federal), 96
eggs industry, 340
Embraer, 132
Embrapa – the Brazilian Agricultural
  Research Corporation, 46, 91, 122,
  150, 155, 165, 235, 241, 360, 409, 413
  animal cloning technique, 158, 168
  creation of, 3
  cultivance soybean, 166
  gene bank, 166
  livestock, 168
  non-till planting, 168
  research program, 41
  transgenic cotton, 167
engenhos, 14
Estrada de Ferro D. Pedro II, 9
ethanol, 42, 62, 106, 313, 317, 331
  exports, 125
  government program support, 332
  production, 45, 64, 337, 411
European and Asian immigrants, 314
European immigrant agricultural colonies
European Union, 4, 77, 80
exchange market
  mechanism of control, 27
  overvaluation, 138
  policy, 100
  rate, 10, 26, 28, 40, 46, 98, 99, 114, 410
  volatility, 410
export crops
  productivity of, 46
export of beef and poultry, 125

Family Agriculture Strengthening Program
  (Pronaf – Programa Nacional de
  Fortalecimento da Agricultura
  Familiar), 104
family and non-family farming, 387, 404
FAO Food Price Index, 64, 76, 130, 154
farm workers, 50, 279
farmers
  associations, 409
  entrepreneurs, 91, 93, 138

level of education, 376
Farmers Securitization Program, 106
FAT-Fundo de Amparo ao Trabalhador,
  105
Federal Government Acquisitions (AGF), 38
Federal Government Loans (EGF), 38
Federal University of Lavras (UFLA), 172
Federal University of Minas Gerais, 160
Federal University of Rio Grande do Sul,
  160
Federal University of Viçosa (UFV), 172
Federation of Industries of the State of São
  Paulo, 133
Federation of the Workers of Family
  Agriculture (FETRAF), 384
fertility, 191, 195, 196, 277, 314
fertilizer, 1, 24
  consumption, 51
  costs, 144
  Second National Plan, 140
fertilizer sector
  privatization of, 141
First National Fertilizer and Agricultural
  Limestone Program (PNFCA), 140
fiscal crisis
  context of, 100
  Stabilization Plan, 100
Florida, 65
Ford, Henry, 15
Forestry Code, 410
Franco, Itamar, 98
free wage labor, 7
frigoríficos, 73, 308
  integrated production contracts, 290
Fundação Getúlio Vargas, 183
Furtado, Celso, 356
  Triennial Plan, 357

Gatt Uruguay Round, 94
gauchos (southern migrating farmers), 264
  migration, 409
GDP, 19, 20, 21, 22, 36, 42, 45, 99, 102,
  107, 125, 126, 136, 161, 237, 317, 409
Geisel, General Ernesto
  Second National Development Plan, 140
General Coordination of Global Climate
  Change, 178
General Law of Technical Assistance for
  Rural Extension (ATER), 153
Goiás, 6, 118
Goulart, João, 357

government policies in the 1960s
change in, 2
government social welfare programs of
income transfers, 411
granjas (chicken farms), 340
grapes, 282, 284, 287, 288
green revolution, 139
greenhouse gases
effect, 177
emissions, 177, 178, 179
process for the reduction of, 186

halal slaughtered animals, 75
harvests (*safras*), 23
Human Development Index scores, 228

IBGE, 4
IMF, 42, 44, 94, 100
agreement with, 100
Imperial Agricultural School of
Bahia, 171
import substitution
model, 94
policies, 92
process of, 135, 140, 405, 406
income distributive programs, 398
INCRA, 362
India, 49, 52, 75, 80, 122, 176, 410
Indian slave labor, 5
industrial economy, 18
opening to world markets, 3
premature deindustrialization, 136
industrial growth
censuses of 1920 and 1950, 20
inflation, 42, 43, 102
acceleration of, 407
control of, 98
insecticides, 1
Institute for the Permanent Defense of
Coffee, 11
interest rates, 133
Inter-ministerial Commission on
Global Climate Change (CIMGC),
178
internal migration, 194, 314
International Coffee Organization (ICO),
29
international commodity market
changes in, 130
international oilseeds market, 60
international trading companies, 2, 408

Japan–Brazil Cooperation Program for the
Development of Cerrados (Prodocer),
39
Japanese Agency for International
Cooperation (JCA), 39

Kubitschek, Juscelino
administration, 145
construction of Brasilia, 234
development plan, 28
Kyoto protocol, 177

labor legislation, 21
labor relations, 37, 356, 406, 412
land conflicts, 364, 411
land ownership, 26
concentration of, 356, 367
distribution of, 54, 200
legalization of title, 55
structure of, 320
land reform, 2, 37, 384
latifundia, 2, 32, 37, 50, 356
Lavras School of Agriculture, 156
Law 9456 on Protection of Cultivars, 173
liabilities (*exigibilidades*) program, 101
life expectancy, 194, 196
literacy, 196, 315
livestock, 35, 126, 191
Luiz de Queirós Practical School, 171
Luiz de Queiroz School of Agronomy
(ESALQ), 156
Lula period, 361

Mato Grosso
balance of trade, 271
cattle and slaughtered meat, 245
cotton production, 258
farm laborers, 245
frigoríficos (meatpacking plants), 275
macroregions, 256, 259, 261
migration to, 232
modernization of animal herds, 53
opening up of the roads to, 312
pastoral products, 279
pastoral vertical system, 256
population, 237, 240
size of producing units, 245
soyabean cultivation, 235
structure of landholding, 243
sustainability of soils and environment,
269

Mato Grosso (cont.)
  union (*sindicato*), 263
Mato Grosso Agricultural Research
  Foundation FMT (Fundação de Apoio
  à Pesquisa Agropecuária de Mato
  Grosso), 171
Mato Grosso do Sul, 232
meat processing industry, 73
Mercosul treaties, 342
mestizos (*caboclos*), 5
Mexican crisis, 99
Mexico, 140
migratory movement, 42
military government period, 152, 359
military regime, 384
  agricultural policy, 37
  end of, 384
  Land Statute, 360
milk production, 318
Minas Gerais, 6, 7, 25
  oranges production, 65
Minimum Price Guarantee Policy (PGPM),
  96
mining activity, 6
moratorium on external debt, 42
mortality rates, 28
Movement of Rural Workers without Lands
  (MST – Movimento dos Trabalhadores
  Rurais sem Terra), 105, 361, 384
mulattos (*pardos*), 199
multinational agricultural suppliers, 413
município, 4

National Agency for Technical Assistance
  and Rural Extension (ANATER), 154
National Agrarian Reform Program, 386
National agricultural machinery program
  creation of, 3
National Center of Education and
  Agronomic Research – CNEPA, 156
National Confederation of Agricultural
  Workers – CONTAG, 384
National Conference of Bishops of Brazil
  (CNBB), 378
National Department of Agricultural
  Research (DNPEA), 158
National Education Development Fund
  (FNDE)), 387
National Institute for Space Research
  (INPE), 178

National Plan on Climate Change – 2008,
  178
National Policy for Technical Assistance
  and Rural Extension for Family
  Agriculture of Agrarian Reform
  (PNATER), 153
national production of wine and juices, 287
National Program for Technical Assistance
  and Rural Extension in Family
  Agriculture and Agrarian Reform
  (PRONATER), 153
National Program to Strengthen Family
  Agriculture – or PRONAF, 385
National Rural Credit System (SNCR), 38
National School Feeding Program (PNAE),
  387
National Service of Agronomic Research
  (SNPA), 156
national sugarcane processing technology,
  45
natural rubber, 15, 82, 191
neo-liberal reforms 1990s, 407
Netto, Delfim, 358
next decade, expectation for, 87
North, 190, 191, 192, 194, 196, 198, 199,
  200, 202, 209, 211
North and Northeast, 4
Northeast, 22, 24, 29, 30, 32, 35, 55, 62,
  103, 115, 116, 118, 140, 146, 156, 157,
  167, 181, 190, 191, 192, 193, 194, 196,
  199, 200, 202, 205, 209, 211, 212, 214,
  215, 216, 266

OECD-FAO, 89
Old Republic, 7, 12, 14
orange juice, 1, 41, 125, 317, 327
  producers, 325
oranges, 64, 88, 320
Orplana (Organização dos Produtores de
  Cana do Estado de São Paulo), 330
Ouro Preto Protocol, 94

Pampa, 178, 180
Pantanal, 178, 180, 234
Paraiba Valley, 7, 8
Paraná, 23, 29, 122, 149, 228
parceria, 334
pastoral industries, 202
Pastoral Land Commission (CPT) of the
  Catholic Church, 364

pasture lands, 53
permanent croplands, 202, 237
permanent crops, 25, 31, 53, 327
  production of, 313
pesticides, controlling the impact of, 189
Petrobras, 140, 331
petrochemical industry and its fertilizer
    sector
  consolidation of, 140
Polocentro, 39
pork production, 79
poultry industry
  development of, 79
  growth in the production of, 77
  vertical system, 78
Prado Jr., Caio, 358
Pro-Alcool program, 186
Prodocer, 39
Program of Valorization of Small Rural
    Production (PROVAPE), 385
promulgation of the 1988 Constitution, 384
PRONAF program, 105, 112, 362, 386, 387
protection of the environment, 138
public deficit, 44

quilombos (runaway slave communities),
    386

railroads, 6, 9
rainforest, 4, 179
real, 99, 100, 114, 135
Real Plan, 98, 100, 106, 107, 133, 141
  fundamental points, 98
  rural credit system, 110
Reconcavo, 213
republic
  emergence of, 7
rice, 16, 17, 23, 24, 29, 35, 39, 42, 53, 56,
    83, 117, 215, 256, 275, 279, 282, 293
Rio de Janeiro, 5, 7, 9, 25
Rio Grande do Sul, 3, 24, 25, 35, 149, 180,
    228, 273
  age structure, 277
  agricultural machine production, 52
  dairy industry, 298
  European immigrant agricultural
    colonies, 277
  expansion of the railroad system, 275
  labor force, 279
  land ownership, structure of, 278
  level of education, 312

literacy rate, 276
meatpacking and food processing plants,
    273
mesoregions agricultural production of,
    301
milk, 297
pastoral industry, 80
pastoral products, 222
production of beef, chicken and pig
    meats, 290
ranches (estâncias), 275
rates of mortality, 277
soybeans, 293
system of vertical integration production,
    273
tobacco, 282
value of total agricultural production, 274
wheat production, 284
Rockefeller, Nelson, 151
Rodrigues, Roberto, 111
Rousseff, Dilma
rural
rural credit
  interest rates, 105
  supply of, 42
  system, 39
Rural Democratic Union (UDR), 384
rural exodus, 37
  extension, 122, 150
  labor legislation, 364
  model of, 151
  results of, 122
Rural Labor Statute, 357
  population, 37, 42, 138, 411
  poverty, 411, 412
Rural Producer's Certificate (CPR), 104
rural producers
  power of, 97
Rural Savings Account (Caderneta de
    Poupança Rural), 102, 107
rural workers' labor rights, 357
Rural Workers Statute, 358
Russia, 144
Russian Federation, 49, 52, 86

Santa Catarina, 78, 362
São Paulo, 3, 5, 7, 9, 21, 25, 149, 228
  concentrated orange juice, 323
  granjas (chicken farms), 341
  mesoregions, 345
  milk production, 457

São Paulo (cont.)
milk production,, 343
milling industry, 330
modern sugar refining industry, 313
oranges, 65
pastoral products, 338
population, 314
price of milk, and the industry, 342
rates of mortality, 314
rural population, 278
sugar-alcohol industry, 334
total value of agricultural production, 316
Única (Associação das Usinas), 335, 336
value of sugarcane product exports, 318
value of the state's agricultural production, 338
São Paulo Railway, 9
School of Agricultural and Veterinary Education, 171
seasonal croplands, 202
seasonal crops, 25, 31, 53, 236, 260, 313
growth of, 202
Second National Plan of Fertilizers, 141
Secretariat for Climate Change and Environmental Quality, 178
settlement of Brazil, 5
settlement projects, 361, 367
settlers of two states, 362
sharecroppers (*com parcerias*), 35
silkworm production, 81
size of farm and region
value of production, 370
slave labor, 7, 8, 314
small farms
future of, 402
South, 191, 192, 194, 196, 199, 200, 201, 202, 205, 207, 210
Southeast, 117, 190, 191, 192, 194, 196, 199, 202, 206, 209, 210, 211, 212, 213, 214, 215
soybean meal, 59
soybean producer, 125
soybeans, 1, 41, 46, 49, 53, 59, 88, 117, 126, 202, 205, 209, 222, 241, 279, 282
soybeans and soybean meal exports, 70
State Agricultural Research Organizations (OEPAs), 163
subsistence agriculture, 3
sugar, 12, 31, 40, 88, 95, 106, 190, 202

Sugar and Alcohol Institute IAA (Instituto do Açucar e do Alcool – IAA), 40, 329
sugar and ethanol exports, 70
sugar industry
new business structures, 335
sugar milling industry, 13
sugar overporduction, 331
sugar plantation economy, 5
sugarcane, 45, 53
integrated processing plants, 63
mechanization, 336
production of, 317
Sugarcane Technology Center (CTC), 174
sunflowers, 53
Superior School of Agronomy and Veterinary Sciences of Viçosa, 160
Superior School of Agronomy Luiz de Queiros, 160
sustainability, 138, 177, 188, 410
low carbon economy, 411
system of public and private finance, 2

Taubaté Agreement, 11
Technical Assistance and Rural Extension – ATER, 153
Technological Center (CTC) research center, 335
Thailand, 63
tobacco, 279
Total Factor Productivity, 120, 123, 136
tractor industry, 145
tractors and agricultural machinery
local production of, 140
trade liberalization
process of, 98
trading companies, 112
traditional land tenure system
process of modernization of, 2
Treaty of Asunción, 94

United Nations Convention on Climate Change
Eco-92, 177
United Nations Development Program (UNDP), 178
United States, 1, 4, 29, 49, 54, 60, 64, 67, 85, 118, 122, 144, 151, 176, 298, 329
Civil War, 13, 14

Department of Agriculture (USDA), 89
University of São Paulo, 171
urban population, 21, 42
Uruguay, 80, 87
usinas (sugar factories), 14, 40, 317, 333

value of agricultural production between
    1938 and 1947, 23
value of beef exports, 77
value of crops and animal products, 57
value of orange juice exports, 66
Vargas, Getúlio, 19, 21, 139, 156, 329
    March to the West policy, 234
    second period of, 27
vertical integration, 334
vertical system oranges, 323
Veterinary School of Viçosa, 156
Vietnam, 295

virgin lands, 1, 8, 9, 312, 408
    decline of, 6
    expansion to, 272

wage labor force, 18
Washington Consensus, 94
wheat, 44, 53, 56, 117, 205, 273, 284
    quota system, 40
wine production
    modernization of, 289
wood, 31
World Bank, 44, 94, 133, 154
World Trade Organization (WTO), 94
    creation of, 188
World War II, 12, 13, 19, 329, 331, 405
WWF-Brazil, 179

zona da mata, 7